COMPUTER ARCHITECTURE
AND ORGANIZATION

McGraw-Hill Computer Science Series

Ahuja: *Design and Analysis of Computer Communication Networks*
Barbacci and Siewiorek: *The Design and Analysis of Instruction Set Processors*
Ceri and Pelagatti: *Distributed Databases: Principles and Systems*
Collins: *Intermediate Pascal Programming: A Case Study Approach*
Debry: *Communicating with Display Terminals*
Donovan: *Systems Programming*
Filman and Friedman: *Coordinated Computing: Tools and Techniques for Distributed Software*
Givone: *Introduction to Switching Circuit Theory*
Goodman and Hedetniemi: *Introduction to the Design and Analysis of Algorithms*
Hayes: *Computer Architecture and Organization*
Hutchison and Just: *Programming Using the C Language*
Katzan: *Microprogramming Primer*
Keller: *A First Course in Computer Programming Using Pascal*
Kohavi: *Switching and Finite Automata Theory*
Korth and Silberschatz: *Database System Concepts*
Liu: *Elements of Discrete Mathematics*
Liu: *Introduction to Combinatorial Mathematics*
MacEwen: *Introduction to Computer Systems: Using the PDP-11 and Pascal*
Madnick and Donovan: *Operating Systems*
Manna: *Mathematical Theory of Computation*
Milenkovic: *Operating Systems: Concepts and Design*
Newman and Sproull: *Principles of Interactive Computer Graphics*
Payne: *Introduction to Simulation: Programming Techniques and Methods of Analysis*
Revesz: *Introduction to Formal Languages*
Rice: *Matrix Computations and Mathematical Software*
Salton and McGill: *Introduction to Modern Information Retrieval*
Shooman: *Software Engineering: Design, Reliability, and Management*
Tremblay and Bunt: *An Introduction to Computer Science: An Algorithmic Approach*
Tremblay and Bunt: *An Introduction to Computer Science: An Algorithmic Approach, Short Edition*
Tremblay and Manohar: *Discrete Mathematical Structures with Applications to Computer Science*
Tremblay and Sorenson: *Introduction to Data Structures with Applications*
Tremblay and Sorenson: *The Theory and Practice of Compiler Writing*
Tucker: *Programming Languages*
Wiederhold: *Database Design*
Wiederhold: *File Organization for Database Design*
Wulf, Levin, and Harbison: *Hydra/C.mmp: An Experimental Computer System*

McGraw-Hill Series in Computer Organization and Architecture

Bell and Newell: *Computer Structures: Readings and Examples*
Cavanagh: *Digital Computer Arithmetic: Design and Implementation*
Gear: *Computer Organization and Programming: With an Emphasis on Personal Computers*
Hamacher, Vranesic, and Zaky: *Computer Organization*
Hayes: *Computer Architecture and Organization*
Hayes: *Digital System Design and Microprocessors*
Hwang and Briggs: *Computer Architecture and Parallel Processing*
Lawrence and Mauch: *Real-Time Microcomputer System Design*
Siewiorek, Bell, and Newell: *Computer Structures: Principles & Examples*
Stone: *Introduction to Computer Organization and Data Structures*
Stone and Siewiorek: *Introduction to Computer Organization and Data Structures: PDP-11 Edition*

McGraw-Hill Series in Supercomputing and Artificial Intelligence

Consulting Editor

Kai Hwang, *University of Southern California*

Hwang/Briggs: *Computer Architecture and Parallel Processing*
Quinn: *Designing Efficient Algorithms for Parallel Computers*

McGraw-Hill Series in Artificial Intelligence

Allen: *Anatomy of LISP*
Davis and Lenat: *Knowledge-Based Systems in Artificial Intelligence*
Nilsson: *Problem-Solving Methods in Artificial Intelligence*
Rich: *Artificial Intelligence*

COMPUTER ARCHITECTURE
AND ORGANIZATION

Second Edition

John P. Hayes
University of Michigan

McGraw-Hill Book Company

New York   St. Louis   San Francisco   Auckland   Bogotá   Caracas   Colorado Springs
Hamburg   Lisbon   London   Madrid   Mexico   Milan   Montreal   New Delhi
Oklahoma City   Panama   Paris   San Juan   São Paulo   Singapore   Sydney   Tokyo   Toronto

COMPUTER ARCHITECTURE AND ORGANIZATION

INTERNATIONAL EDITION

Copyright © 1988

1st Printing 1988

Library of Congress Cataloging-in-Publication Data

Hayes, John P. (John Patrick), 1944–
    Computer architecture and organization

    Includes bibliographies and index.
    1. Computer architecture. 2. Electronic digital
computers—Design and construction. I. Title.
QA76.9A73H39   1988   004.2'2   87-22593
ISBN 0-07-027366-9

This book was set in Times Roman by York Production Services, Inc.
The editor was David M. Shapiro;
the production supervisor was Denise L. Puryear.
Project supervision was done by York Production Services.

When ordering this title use ISBN 0-07-100479-3

Printed and bound in Singapore by Kim Hup Lee Printing Co Pte Ltd

Engineering

ABOUT THE AUTHOR

John P. Hayes is Professor of Electrical Engineering and Computer Science at the University of Michigan, Ann Arbor and the Director of the Advanced Computer Architecture Laboratory, which he helped establish in 1985. Dr. Hayes teaches and conducts research in the areas of computer architecture, parallel processing, digital system testing, and VLSI design. He is the author of the text *Digital System Design and Microprocessors* (McGraw-Hill, 1984) and over ninety technical papers. He has also served as editor of Computer Architecture and Systems for the *Communications of the ACM*.

Dr. Hayes received his undergraduate education at the National University of Ireland, Dublin, and his M.S. and Ph.D. degrees in electrical engineering from the University of Illinois. He is a member of the Association for Computing Machinery and a Fellow of the Institute of Electrical and Electronics Engineers.

TO MY FATHER
Patrick J. Hayes
(1910–1968)

IN
MEMORIAM

CONTENTS

PREFACE

Computer architecture is concerned with the structure and behavior of digital computers. It has developed into a discipline for the design and evaluation of computers largely in response to the proliferation of these machines over the last couple of decades. This proliferation has, in turn, been driven by advances in computer technology, both hardware and software. In particular, the development of very large scale integration (VLSI) has had a profound influence in lowering the cost and improving the performance of all types of computers. Recent developments such as VLSI-based personal computers and relatively low-cost supercomputers have allowed computers to be used in many new applications. Consequently, the concepts of computer architecture and organization have become increasingly relevant to a large number of scientists, engineers, and other professionals.

Computer Architecture and Organization, second edition, is intended primarily as a text for computer science and electrical engineering courses at the advanced undergraduate or beginning graduate levels. While its emphasis is on computer hardware and systems, the relevant aspects of software are also treated. A basic knowledge of computer programming and familiarity with the workings of a simple computer are assumed. There are no special mathematical prerequisites beyond elementary calculus and probability theory, which are occasionally used. The book aims at providing a comprehensive and self-contained view of computer architecture. The underlying design principles are stressed, as well as their impact on computer performance, and a uniform terminology and notation has been used throughout. Over two hundred problems are included to provide the reader with meaningful exercises in computer analysis and design. An Instructor's Manual containing solutions to all the problems can be obtained by course instructors directly from the publisher.

The book is divided into seven chapters. Chapter 1 traces the evolution of computers from a historical viewpoint and introduces much of the terminology and notation used later. Chapter 2 deals with computer design methodology and examines the three major computer design levels—the gate, register, and processor levels—in detail. The basic concepts of computer performance evaluation are introduced in this chapter. The next two chapters are concerned with the design of the central processing unit (CPU), which is at the heart of every computer. Chapter 3 covers the data-processing or execution unit of a CPU and addresses the topics of information formats, instruction set design, and assembly-language programming. The principles of arithmetic-logic unit (ALU) design for both fixed-point and floating-point operations are examined in detail. The design of the program control or instruction unit of a CPU is considered in Chapter 4. Hardwired control is covered briefly, and a thorough discussion of microprogramming is presented. Chapter 5 is concerned with memory design. The major memory technologies and their characteristics are surveyed, along with virtual memory organization, caches, and associative memories. Chapter 6 addresses overall system organization including inter- and intrasystem communication, input-output (IO) systems, and operating system design. Examined in detail here are bus structures, computer networks, IO design methods, and the control of concurrent processes. The final chapter (Chapter 7) considers the increasingly important issue of using parallel processing to achieve very high performance and reliability. This chapter covers the design and programming of pipeline architectures which form the basis of traditional vector supercomputers, and multiprocessor architectures which provide an alternative approach to very high-speed computing. Many actual computer systems are used as examples in the book, including von Neumann's influential IAS computer, the IBM System/360-370 series and its modern successors, the DEC VAX minicomputer series, the Motorola 68020 32-bit microprocessor, the Cray vector supercomputers, the NCUBE/ten hypercube multiprocessor, the Ethernet local-area network architecture, and the UNIX operating system.

The book has been used for a number of years in both senior-level (final-year) undergraduate and introductory graduate courses at many universities around the world. It contains more than sufficient material for a typical one-semester (15-week) course, allowing the instructor some leeway in choosing the topics to emphasize. Much of the background material in Chapter 1 and the first part of Chapter 2 can be left as a reading assignment or omitted, if the students are suitably prepared. The more advanced material in Chapters 6 and 7 can be covered briefly or skipped if desired, without loss of continuity. Also left to the instructor's discretion are some of the more specialized topics in the earlier chapters such as Section 2.4.4 on "Queueing Models," Section 4.3.2 on "Control Memory Optimization," and Section 5.3.3 on "Associative Memories." A detailed representative course outline can be found in the Instructor's Manual.

The second edition has been designed to expand and update the book's contents and to respond to the suggestions of users of the first edition. The principal change is an additional seventh chapter on "Parallel Processing," which examines this important topic in depth. More emphasis has been given to software issues in the second edition, with new sections on assembly language programming (Section 3.2.3), operating systems (Section 6.3), and coverage of parallel and vector programming in Chapter 7. Most of the numbered examples that serve as case studies have been replaced, and more such examples have been added. The number of problems at the end of each chapter has been more than doubled, and their solutions can be found in the second edition of the Instructor's Manual.

The specific changes made in the second edition are as follows. The historical material in Chapter 1 has been streamlined, and the material on recent developments has been completely rewritten under the title "The VLSI Era" (the new Section 1.4). The summary material on combinational and sequential logic circuit design appearing in Chapter 2 of the first edition has been expanded into a new Section 2.2 "The Gate Level," giving this topic a complete and self-contained treatment. The main register-level design example of Section 2.3 has been thoroughly revised, and the subsection on simulation has been deleted from Section 2.4. Topics newly added to Chapter 3 are reduced instruction set computers (RISCs), assembly-language programming, the IEEE Floating-Point Standard, and arithmetic (co-) processors. The old Section 3.3 covering computer arithmetic has been enlarged and split into two sections, while the old Section 3.4 on "Parallel Processing" has been superseded by Chapter 7. New material on microcode compaction has been added to Section 4.3.2, and the discussion of nanoprogramming (Section 4.4.3) has been expanded. Section 5.1 on "Memory Technology" has been completely revised to reflect current technology trends, and new real-world examples have been added to the remainder of Chapter 5 covering such topics as virtual memory address mapping and cache design. The material on bus control in Section 6.1 "Communication" now has the Multibus (IEEE 796 Standard Bus) as its main example, and the discussion of computer networks has been extended to cover communication protocols and local-area networks (LANs). The old Section 6.3 on "Multiple CPU Systems," which are now covered in Chapter 7, has been replaced by a new Section 6.3 on "Operating Systems." This section explores the main functions of an operating system and its role in managing concurrently executing processes. Chapter 7 is new to the second edition and covers all aspects of parallel processing, many of which were mentioned only briefly or not at all in the first edition.

I would like to express my thanks for the many useful comments and suggestions provided by colleagues who reviewed this text during the course of its development, especially to Ming-Yang Chein, Northwestern University; Michael Faiman, University of Illinois at Urbana; Richard Reid, Michigan State University; Rob Rutenbar, Carnegie-Mellon University; Sharad Seth, University of Nebraska at Lincoln; and Frank Wagner, University of Cincinnati.

The material for this book has been developed primarily for a senior/graduate-level course on computer architecture and organization which I have taught over the years, initially at the University of Southern California and later at the University of Michigan. I am grateful to my colleagues and students at these schools for their helpful comments and suggestions. As always, I owe a special thanks to my wife Terrie for her never-failing support and love.

J.P.H.

COMPUTER ARCHITECTURE
AND ORGANIZATION

CHAPTER ONE

THE EVOLUTION OF COMPUTERS

This chapter traces the historical development of digital computers. It provides a broad overview of computer architecture and introduces most of the concepts that are examined in depth in later chapters. Detailed descriptions of a number of representative computers are presented.

1.1 THE NATURE OF COMPUTERS

Throughout most of history human beings have relied mainly on their brains to perform calculations; in other words, they were the computer. A variety of computational aids such as the abacus and the slide rule were invented; they simplified but did not replace manual computation. As the size and complexity of the calculations being carried out increased, two serious limitations of manual computation became apparent.

1. The speed at which a human computer can work is limited. A typical elementary operation such as addition or multiplication takes several seconds or minutes. Problems requiring billions of such operations are now routinely tackled and quickly solved using computing machines. Such problems could never be solved manually in a reasonable period of time or at reasonable cost.
2. Human beings are notoriously prone to error, so that complex calculations performed by hand are generally unreliable unless the most elaborate precautions are taken to eliminate errors. Since machines are not affected by the usual sources of human error (distractions, carelessness, fatigue, etc.), they can provide results that are, within very broad limits, free of error.

The following example was frequently cited by Charles Babbage (1792-1871) to justify the construction of his first computing machine, the Difference Engine

[22]. In 1794 a project was begun by the French government under the direction of Baron Gaspard de Prony (1755-1839) to compute entirely by hand an enormous set of mathematical tables. Among the tables constructed were the logarithms of the natural numbers from 1 to 200,000 calculated to 19 decimal places. Comparable tables were constructed for the natural sines and tangents, their logarithms, and the logarithms of the ratios of the sines and tangents to their arcs. The entire project took about 2 years to complete and employed from 70 to 100 people. The mathematical abilities of most of the people involved were limited to addition and subtraction. A small group of skilled mathematicians provided them with their instructions. To minimize errors, each number was calculated twice by two independent human calculators and the results were compared. The final set of tables occupied 17 large folio volumes (which were never published, however). The table of logarithms of the natural numbers alone was estimated to contain about 8 million digits.

1.1.1 Computers and Computation

Elements of a computer. It can be useful as a starting point to analyze the processes involved in a manual calculation using pencil and paper. The primary purpose of the paper is *information storage*. The information stored on paper may include a list of instructions—i.e., an *algorithm* or *program*—to be followed in carrying out the calculation, as well as the *data* (numbers) to be used. During the calculation, intermediate results and, ultimately, the final results, are recorded on the paper. The computational processes needed take place in the brain, which can be called the *processor*. Two major functions performed by the brain can be distinguished: a control function, which interprets the instructions and ensures that they are performed in the correct sequence; and an execution function, which carries out specific calculations such as addition, subtraction, multiplication, and division. In the execution function, the human brain is aided nowadays by the ubiquitous electronic pocket calculator. Figure 1.1a illustrates this view of human computation.

The major components of a computing machine are similar; these are illustrated in Fig. 1.1b. The *memory unit* corresponds to the paper used by the human calculator; its purpose is to store both instructions and data. The *program control unit* interprets and sequences instructions. The *arithmetic-logic unit* executes instructions. It is so called in recognition of the fact that instructions either involve numerical operations (arithmetic) or nonnumerical operations, such as program branching and symbolic processing. A convenient, if not very expressive, term for the latter is logical operations. The program control and arithmetic-logic units together form the *central processing unit* (CPU), which corresponds roughly to the brain in human computations. A significant difference between the human and the machine lies in the way in which they represent information, i.e., instructions and data. Humans employ natural languages with a wide range of symbols and usually represent numbers in decimal (base 10) form. In modern computing machines, however, information is stored and processed in binary form, i.e., using two sym-

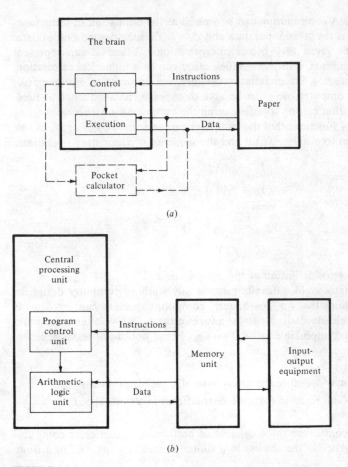

FIGURE 1.1
The main components of (*a*) human computation and (*b*) machine computation.

bols conventionally denoted by 0 and 1, and called *bits* (*b*inary dig*its*). To provide for communication between the machine and its human users, a means of converting information from machine language to human language is thus needed. This is a major function of the box labeled *input-output (IO) equipment* in Fig. 1.1*b*.

Consequently, every computer, whether human or artificial, must have the following components.

1. A processor capable of interpreting and executing programs
2. A memory for storing programs and data
3. A means of transferring information between the memory and the processor, and between the computer and the outside world

An abstract model. A *computation* can be viewed as the evaluation of some function $f(X)$, where X is the given input data and $Z = f(X)$ is the desired output data. X, Z, and f can be given very broad interpretations. X and Z can represent numbers, word statements, information files, etc. f can be a numerical calculation, the proof of a theorem, a file updating procedure, etc. In order to evaluate $f(X)$ using a particular computer, we must be able to express f as a sequence of functions $f_1, f_2, \ldots, f_n$ that can be specified using the computer's *instruction set*, i.e., the set of elementary functions that the computer can perform. $f_1, f_2, \ldots, f_n$ can be viewed as a program to evaluate $f(X)$, and the sequence of elementary operations

$$Y_1 = f_1(X)$$
$$Y_2 = f_2(Y_1)$$
$$\cdots \cdots \cdots \cdots \cdots$$
$$Y_{n-1} = f_{n-1}(Y_{n-2})$$
$$Z = f_n(Y_{n-1})$$

can be taken as a formal definition of the computation.

A question that should naturally precede any study of computer design is: Are there computations that no "reasonable" computing machine can perform? If there are, then it is clearly desirable to be aware of them, lest we attempt to build machines to carry out impossible tasks. Two very broad notions of reasonableness are generally accepted.

1. The machine should not store the answers to all possible problems.

2. It should process information (execute instructions) at a finite speed.

Such a machine is considered to be capable of performing a particular computation only if it can generate the answer in a finite number of steps, i.e., in a finite amount of time.

An abstract model of a computer that satisfies the foregoing criteria of reasonableness was introduced by the English mathematician Alan M. Turing (1912–1954) in 1936 [30]. This model is now called a *Turing machine*. Figure 1.2 shows the components of a Turing machine. As noted in the preceding section, two essential elements of any computer are a memory and a processor. The memory of a Turing machine is a tape M of unbounded length divided lengthwise into squares. Each square may be blank or contain one of a finite set of symbols. The processor is a digital machine with a finite number of internal configurations or *states*. It has a read-write head capable of reading the contents of any one square on the tape, changing the contents of that square, and moving the tape one square to the left or right of its current position.

A Turing machine can be viewed as having a finite set of instructions with the following format:

$$s_h \quad t_i \quad o_j \quad s_k$$

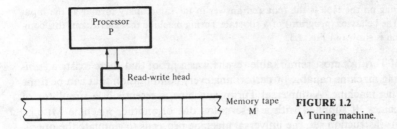

FIGURE 1.2
A Turing machine.

meaning if the control processor P is in state s_h and the symbol t_i is currently under the read-write head, then perform the operation o_j and change the state of P to s_k. The operation o_j can be any one of the following four.

1. $o_j = t_j$, meaning write the symbol t_j on the tape (this replaces the previous symbol t_i)
2. $o_j = R$, meaning position the read-write head over the square to the right of the current square, i.e., move the tape to the left
3. $o_j = L$, meaning position the read-write head over the square to the left of the current square, i.e., move the tape to the right
4. $o_j = H$, meaning halt the computation

The instruction set thus defines the possible state transitions of P.

A computation $Z = f(X)$ is performed by a Turing machine in the following way. First the input data X is placed in suitably coded form on an otherwise blank tape. Then the Turing machine is started, causing the sequence of operations $f_1, f_2, \ldots, f_n$ to be performed. At the conclusion of the nth operation, the machine should halt, and the tape should contain the result Z.

Example 1.1 A Turing machine that can add two natural numbers. Any natural number n can be represented in unary form by a sequence of n 1s. The tape symbol alphabet need only consist of the two symbols, 1 and b, where b denotes a blank. The two numbers n_1 and n_2 to be added are initially written on the tape in the following format:

$$b \underbrace{1\,1\cdots 1}_{n_1} b \underbrace{1\,1\cdots 1}_{n_2} b$$

and the read-write head is positioned over the blank to the left of the leftmost 1. The machine computes $n_1 + n_2$ by the simple expedient of replacing the blank that separates n_1 and n_2 by the symbol 1, and then deleting the leftmost 1. The resulting pattern

$$b\,b\underbrace{1\,1\cdots 1\,1\,1\cdots 1}_{n_1 + n_2}b$$

appearing on the tape is the required answer in the same unary format as the input data. The behavior (program) of a six-state Turing machine that carries out this computation is shown in Fig. 1.3.

One of Turing's most remarkable results was a proof that there exists a *"universal"* Turing machine capable of performing every computation that can be done by any Turing machine. A universal Turing machine is essentially a simulator of Turing machines. If supplied with a description dM of another machine M, e.g., a listing of its instruction set, the universal machine proceeds to simulate the operations performed by M. It has also been shown that a universal Turing machine need only have t tape symbols and an s-state processor where $ts < 30$. Such a machine has a very small instruction set, but it is nevertheless believed to be capable of executing all the computations that can be performed by the most powerful "reasonable" computer. (This claim, often referred to as Church's thesis after the American mathematician Alonzo Church, cannot be rigorously proven because the notion of a reasonable computer is intuitive.)

1.1.2 Limitations of Computers

Unsolvable problems. Since Turing machines appear to be capable of performing all possible computations, we can define the concept of a computable function in terms of Turing machines. A function f is (*effectively*) *computable* if $f(X)$ can be evaluated for any specified X in a finite number of steps by a Turing machine. Surprisingly, there are reasonable functions that are not computable in this sense, a fact first demonstrated by Kurt Gödel (1906–1978) in his celebrated 1931 paper [13].

Let (M, X) denote a Turing machine M with input tape X, that is, X is the initial information on its tape. We will say that (M, X) halts if M, when started with input tape X, halts after a finite number of steps. Let $f_H(M, X)$ be a function defined for all Turing machines and input tapes as follows:

$$f_H(M, X) = 1 \qquad \text{if } (M, X) \text{ halts}$$
$$f_H(M, X) = 0 \qquad \text{if } (M, X) \text{ never halts}$$

Instruction				Comments
s_0	b	R	s_0	
s_0	1	R	s_1	Move read-write head to right across n_1
s_1	1	R	s_1	
s_1	b	1	s_2	Replace blank between n_1 and n_2 by 1
s_2	1	L	s_3	Move read-write head to left
s_3	1	L	s_3	
s_3	b	R	s_4	End of 1s reached; backspace
s_4	1	b	s_5	Delete leftmost 1
s_5	b	H	s_0	$n_1 + n_2$ now on tape

FIGURE 1.3
A Turing machine program to add two unary numbers.

It can be shown that the function f_H is not computable [21]. This implies that the problem of devising a general method to determine if (M,X) halts, where (M,X) is any Turing machine and input tape pair, is *unsolvable* (also called *undecidable*). This particular problem is known as the Turing machine halting problem. A large number of related problems are also known to be unsolvable.

The existence of unsolvable problems has some important implications. A common and often costly error made by inexperienced computer programmers is to write programs that contain infinite loops and therefore fail to halt under certain input conditions. It would be useful to have a universal debugging program or machine that could determine whether any given program halts. The unsolvability of the Turing machine halting problem immediately implies that no such debugging tool can be designed. It is important to note that this assertion is only true when applied to the class of *all* possible programs. For any specific program or set of programs, it may be possible to devise a solution to the halting problem. Hence the limitations imposed by the existence of unsolvable problems can be ignored in most practical design situations.

Intractable problems. The Turing machine model of digital computers discussed in the preceding section has at least one unrealistic, if not unreasonable, aspect: the number of tape states is unbounded. Real computers have a finite amount of memory and are therefore *finite-state machines*. This means that there are certain computations which can be performed by Turing machines but cannot, in principle, be performed by finite-state machines. For example, a finite-state machine cannot multiply two arbitrarily large binary numbers, but a Turing machine can. The number of states of a typical computer is extremely large, so the finiteness limitation has no significant practical impact. For example, the main memory of a large computer can contain 10^7 or more binary storage cells. The number of possible states is therefore $2^{10^7} \approx 10^{3,000,000}$. The binary numbers that cannot be multiplied by this machine would have to contain about 10^7 bits!

Many computational problems can, in principle, be solved to an acceptable degree of accuracy by real finite-state computers. There is, however, a large class of "difficult" problems, some of great practical importance, that are solvable by real machines but require such an excessively large amount of memory space or computation time that no reasonable computer, no matter how fast, can ever be expected to solve them.

Suppose that an algorithm A is to be executed by a computer. Two questions can be raised concerning the difficulty of the algorithm.

1. How much memory space is needed to execute it?
2. How much time is needed to execute it?

The answers to these questions are termed the *space complexity* and the *time complexity* of A, respectively [1]. These quantities are generally difficult to measure, and they depend on the particular input data to which A is applied. The limitations imposed by time seem to be much more restrictive than those imposed by memory space. We will therefore confine our discussion to time complexity. An algorithm is said to have *time complexity* $O(f(n))$ if the number of steps it needs to process data of "size" n is at most $cf(n)$, where $f(n)$ is some function of n and c is a constant. The *size* of the input data is typically defined as the number of independent input parameters. The time complexity of the algorithm provides an approximate indication of the time required to execute it on some computer, e.g., a Turing machine.

It is common to regard a problem as *tractable* if and only if there is an algorithm to solve it that has time complexity $O(p(n))$, where $p(n)$ is a polynomial function of the input size n. A problem, all of whose algorithms have time complexity $O(k^n)$, that is, which have an execution time that grows exponentially with n, is intractable. There are many important problems for which no algorithm of time complexity $O(p(n))$ is known. These are therefore considered to be intractable.

Example 1.2 Finding the minimum sum-of-products form of an n-variable Boolean function $f(x_1, x_2, \ldots, x_n)$. This is a classic problem in the logical design of computers, which is discussed further in Chap. 2 [29]. Most algorithms for solving it involve the following two steps:

Step 1. Compute all the prime implicants of f. (A prime implicant is a simple product-like Boolean function, which can be used to define f.)

Step 2. Select a minimal set of prime implicants whose logical sum is f.

The maximum number of prime implicants of an n-variable function lies between 2^{n-1} and 3^{n-1}. Thus step 1 can easily require more than 2^n operations to generate the prime implicants (and also a memory space that is of the order of 2^n if all the prime implicants are to be stored). Step 2 requires selection of one of the 2^p possible subsets of the p prime implicants of f. Clearly, in the worst case, this algorithm has a complexity that is exponential in the input size n.

The fact that a problem is intractable generally means that it can be solved exactly in a reasonable amount of time only when the input size is below some maximum value m. The value of m depends on the speed (number of operations per second) of the computer used to solve the problem. It might be expected that computer speeds could be increased to make m any desired value. We now present some arguments which indicate that this is most unlikely.

Speed limitations. The speed at which computers operate, as measured by the number of basic operations performed per second, has undergone rapid and continual improvement. This has been mainly due to improvements in the technology of computing circuits and memory devices. Figure 1.4 shows the influence of the major technologies introduced since 1930 on computer speed. It can be concluded that computer speed has increased linearly by a factor of about 100 per decade since 1930. Let us suppose that computer speeds continue to increase at a steady linear rate.

Consider four algorithms A_1, A_2, A_3, and A_4 with time complexity $O(n)$, $O(n^2)$, $O(n^{100})$, and $O(2^n)$, respectively. Suppose that all four are run on a comput-

Technology	Date	Number of operations per second
Mechanical	1930	1
Electromechanical	1940	10
Vacuum tube	1945	10^3
Discrete semiconductor	1960	10^6
Integrated semiconductor	1970	10^8
Integrated semiconductor	1980	10^{10}

FIGURE 1.4
The influence of technology on computing speed.

er M having a speed of s operations per second. Let m_i denote the input size of the largest problem that can be solved by algorithm A_i in a fixed time period t seconds. Let m_i' denote the input size of the largest problem that can be solved by A_i in t seconds on a new computer M' with a computing speed of $100s$ operations per second. Figure 1.5 shows the values of m_i' for the four algorithms. In the case of the intractable algorithm A_4, the increase in the size of the problem that can be handled on moving from M to M' is insignificant. This is also true of A_3, even though it does not fall within the strict definition of intractable given above. In order to increase the maximum problem sizes that can be processed by A_3 and A_4 in the given time period by a factor of 100, i.e., from m_i to $100m_i$, we would need computers with speeds of $10^{200}s$ and $10^{30m_4}s$, respectively. It is reasonable to suppose that problems of these magnitudes can never be solved using the given algorithms.

Because so many important problems are intractable, inexact or nonalgorithmic methods have been devised to solve them. Two major techniques can be identified.

1. The intractable problem Q is replaced by a tractable problem Q' whose solution approximates that of Q.
2. A relatively small set of possible solutions to Q is examined using reasonable, intuitive, but often poorly understood selection criteria. The "best" of these

Algorithm	Time complexity	Maximum problem input size	
		Computer M	Computer M'
A_1	$O(n)$	m_1	$100m_1$
A_2	$O(n^2)$	m_2	$10m_2$
A_3	$O(n^{100})$	m_3	$1.047m_3$
A_4	$O(2^n)$	m_4	$m_4 + 6.644$

FIGURE 1.5
Effect of computer speedup by a factor of 100 on maximum problem input size for four algorithms.

potential solutions is taken as the solution to Q. Methods such as this, which are designed to produce acceptable, if not optimal, answers using a reasonable amount of computation time, are sometimes called *heuristic procedures*.

It is widely believed that the rate of increase in computer speed due to technology improvements is diminishing, which suggests that significant increases in speed can come only from improved algorithms or heuristics, although the intractable problems may not permit such improvement. An important way of increasing the overall operating speed of a computer is to introduce *parallel processing*. Most conventional computers perform their basic operations in strict sequence; only one operation may take place at any time. This is termed *sequential (serial) processing*. The parallel processing approach attempts to replace a computation requiring n sequential steps by n independent subcomputations that can be carried out simultaneously, i.e., in parallel. This often results in a substantial reduction in overall computation time. Not all problems are amenable to this technique, since many algorithms are inherently sequential in nature; step $i + 1$ cannot begin until step i computes its results.

In conclusion, it might be asked: What are the ultimate physical limitations on computing speed? Using arguments based on quantum mechanics, H.J. Bremermann has conjectured that no computer, either living or artificial, can process more than 2×10^{47} bits of information per gram of its mass per second [8]. If true, a computer the size of the earth (6×10^{27} g) operating continuously for a period equal to the estimated age of the earth (10^{10} years) could then process fewer than 10^{93} bits! This is far fewer than the number of possible states $10^{3,000,000}$ of the computer with 10^7 storage cells cited earlier. It is also less than the number of possible sequences of moves in chess, which has been estimated at 10^{120}.

1.2 THE FIRST COMPUTERS

Special-purpose machines capable of performing the four elementary arithmetic operations (addition, subtraction, multiplication, and division) can be traced back at least as early as the seventeenth century. These were mechanical devices constructed from mechanisms such as gears, levers, and pulleys. The ideas underlying the general-purpose programmable computer were developed by Babbage in the mid-nineteenth century, but could not be adequately implemented using mechanical technology. The modern computer era began around 1940, when electronic devices, in which the motion of electrons replaces mechanical motion, became the building blocks for the construction of general-purpose computing machines.

1.2.1 The Mechanical Era

The earliest mechanical calculator seems to have been designed and built in 1623 by Wilhelm Schickhard (1592–1635), who was a professor at the University of Tübingen. Schickhard's machine was little known in his day. Far more influential was the machine built by the great French philosopher and scientist Blaise Pascal (1623–1662) in 1642. This was essentially a mechanical counter for performing addition and subtraction "automatically." It contained two sets of six dials, or "counter wheels," for representing decimal numbers. (Two additional dials were used for calculations involving nondecimal currency; for simplicity, we ignore them.) Each dial had the 10 decimal numerals engraved on it, separated by equal intervals. The position of the dial indicated the decimal value being stored. One set of dials $W = w_5w_4w_3w_2w_1w_0$ acted as a six-digit accumulator register; the other set $W' = w_5'w_4'w_3'w_2'w_1'w_0'$ was used to enter a number to be added to (or subtracted from) the accumulator. W and W' were connected by gears so that when w_i' was rotated k units, w_i also rotated k units to indicate the number $w_i \pm k$. Pascal's main technical innovation was a ratchet device for automatically transferring a carry from w_i to w_{i+1} whenever w_i passed from 9 to 0. Negative numbers were handled by a complements representation, so that the same mechanical motion could perform both subtraction and addition.

Around 1671 the German philosopher and mathematician Gottfried Leibniz (1646–1716) constructed a mechanical calculator that could perform multiplication and division automatically. It consisted of two parts: an adding-subtracting machine that, in Leibniz's words "coincides completely with the calculating box of Pascal" [28]. Two additional sets of wheels were provided to represent a multiplier and a multiplicand. Multiplication was implemented by means of chains and pulleys. (A clear account of the machine by Leibniz can be found in Ref. 28.) Leibniz's machine was the forerunner of many machines that are now called four-function calculators. They remained academic curiosities until the nineteenth century, when the commercial production of mechanical calculators was begun.

Babbage's computers. One of the most remarkable figures in the history of computing machines is the Englishman Charles Babbage [22]. He designed two computers: the Difference Engine (begun in 1823) and the Analytical Engine (conceived in 1834), both of which represented fundamental advances. For a variety of reasons, neither machine was ever completed.

The objective of the Difference Engine was automatic computation of mathematical tables. Babbage was greatly impressed by the number of errors in tables that were computed manually. His machine was intended to calculate the entries of a table automatically and transfer them via steel punches to an engraver's plate, from which the tables could be printed. The only arithmetic operation performed was addition. However, using only addition, a large number of useful functions can be calculated by a technique called the *method of finite differences*.

Let

$$f(x) = \sum_{j=0}^{n} a_j x^j$$

be an nth-degree polynomial with constant coefficients, which is defined for some sequence $x_1, x_2, x_3, \ldots$ of values of x separated by equal intervals Δx. Let $y_j = f(x_j)$. The ith *difference* of y_j, denoted $\Delta^i y_j$, is defined recursively as follows:

$$\Delta^0 y_j = y_j$$

$$\Delta^i y_j = \Delta^{i-1} y_{j+1} - \Delta^{i-1} y_j \qquad \text{for } i \geq 1 \tag{1.1}$$

It can easily be shown that $\Delta^n y_j = $ constant and $\Delta^i y_j = 0$ for $i > n$. Suppose that the values of the first $n + 1$ nonzero differences of y_j are known. Then we can calculate the corresponding differences for y_{j+1} from Eq. (1.1); thus:

$$\Delta^i y_{j+1} = \Delta^i y_j = \Delta^{i+1} y_j \tag{1.2}$$

In this way, starting from y_0, we can compute successive values of y_j. It will be observed that the only operation in Eq. (1.2) is addition. Any continuous function can be approximated as closely as desired by a polynomial; the method of finite differences can hence be used to evaluate such functions.

Example 1.3   Computation of sin x over the range $0.0 \le x \le 0.5$ at intervals of 0.1 rad by the method of finite differences. The sine function can be expressed as a power series:

$$\sin x = x - \frac{x^3}{3!} + \frac{x^5}{5!} - \frac{x^7}{7!} + \cdots$$

We can therefore employ the polynomial

$$y = x - \frac{x^3}{3!}$$

to approximate $\sin x$ for small values of x. Four differences (including $\Delta^0 y = y$) must be computed using the following equations:

$$y_{j+1} = y_j + \Delta^1 y_j$$
$$\Delta^1 y_{j+1} = \Delta^1 y_j + \Delta^2 y_j$$
$$\Delta^2 y_{j+1} = \Delta^2 y_j + \Delta^3 y_j$$
$$\Delta^3 y_{j+1} = \Delta^3 y_j$$

In order to start the computation we need the initial values y_0, $\Delta^1 y_0$, $\Delta^2 y_0$, and $\Delta^3 y_0$. These values can be found by computing y_0, y_1, y_2, and y_3 directly from the defining polynomial $x - x^3/3!$ and using the following relations implied by Eq. (1.1).

$$y_0 = 0.0$$
$$\Delta^1 y_0 = y_1 - y_0$$
$$\Delta^2 y_0 = y_2 - 2y_1 + y_0$$
$$\Delta^3 y_0 = y_3 - 3y_2 + 3y_1 - y_0$$

Figure 1.6 contains a table for computing y to five decimal places using the method of finite differences.

Figure 1.7 shows the logical structure of a Difference Engine. It contains a set of mechanical registers (counter wheels) to store the differences $\Delta^0 y_i$, $\Delta^1 y_i$, . . . , $\Delta^n y_i$. Each pair of adjacent registers is connected by an adding mechanism similar in principle to Pascal's to implement Eq. (1.2). Once initial values are assigned to each register, the Difference Engine can, if driven by a suitable motor (presumably a steam engine), automatically "crank out" successive values of y.

x_j	$y_j \approx \sin x_j$	$\Delta^1 y_j$	$\Delta^2 y_j$	$\Delta^3 y_j$
0.0	0.00000	0.09983	−0.00100	−0.00100
0.1	0.09983	0.09883	−0.00200	−0.00100
0.2	0.19866	0.09683	−0.00300	−0.00100
0.3	0.29549	0.09383	−0.00400	−0.00100
0.4	0.38932	0.08983	−0.00500	−0.00100
0.5	0.47915	0.08483	−0.00600	−0.00100

FIGURE 1.6
Computation of $\sin x$ by the method of finite differences.

Babbage proposed to build a Difference Engine that would accommodate sixth-degree polynomials and 20-digit numbers. The project was begun in 1823 and abandoned in 1842, despite a grant of £17,000 from the British government. One reason for Babbage's failure to complete his engine was the inadequacy of the mechanical technology then available. A second reason was Babbage's loss of interest in the Difference Engine when he conceived of a much more powerful and ambitious machine he called the Analytical Engine. Several modest difference engines were successfully completed, notably that of the Swede Georg Scheutz (1785–1873), which was built during the period 1837 to 1853. The Scheutz machine could handle third-degree polynomials and 15-digit numbers.

Unlike the Difference Engine, the Analytical Engine was intended to perform any mathematical operation automatically. Figure 1.8 shows the general structure

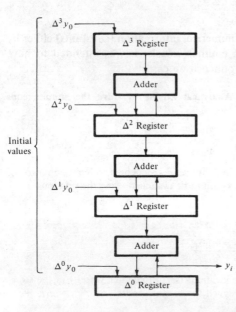

FIGURE 1.7
Structure of Babbage's Difference Engine.

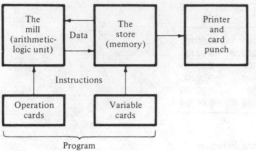

FIGURE 1.8
Structure of Babbage's Analytical Engine.

of the final design proposed by Babbage. It consists of two main parts: *the store*, a memory unit comprising sets of counter wheels, and *the mill*, which corresponds to a modern arithmetic-logic unit. The mill was to be capable of performing the four basic arithmetic operations. In order to control the sequence of operations of the machine, Babbage proposed to use punched cards of the type developed earlier for the Jacquard loom. The cards, which constituted a computer program, were divided into two groups.

1. *Operation cards*, used to control the operation of the mill. Each operation card selected one of the four possible operations ($+$, $-$, $\times$, $\div$) to be performed at each step in the program.
2. *Variable cards*, intended to select the memory locations to be used by a particular operation, i.e., the source of the input operands and the destination of the results.

Provision was also made for supplying numerical information (constants) either by punched cards or by manually setting counter wheels. It was intended to have output data either printed on paper or punched on cards.

Example 1.4   A program for the Analytical Engine to solve the simultaneous equations

$$a_{11}x_1 + a_{12}x_2 = b_1$$

$$a_{21}x_1 + a_{22}x_2 = b_2$$

This hypothetical program was devised by L. F. Menebrea, a contemporary of Babbage's [22]. The variables x_1 and x_2 are to be evaluated using the relations

$$x_1 = \frac{a_{22}b_1 - a_{12}b_2}{a_{11}a_{22} - a_{12}a_{21}}$$

$$x_2 = \frac{a_{11}b_2 - a_{21}b_1}{a_{11}a_{22} - a_{12}a_{21}}$$

Let W_0, W_1, . . . denote the number locations (sets of counter wheels) in the store. The constants of the problem are assigned to the store as follows: $W_0 = a_{11}$, $W_1 =$

a_{12}, $W_2 = b_1$, $W_3 = a_{21}$, $W_4 = a_{22}$, $W_5 = b_2$. Figure 1.9 shows the sequence of operation and variable cards needed to calculate x_1. A similar sequence can be used to calculate x_2.

One of Babbage's most significant contributions was a mechanism for enabling a program to alter the sequence of its operations automatically. In modern terms, he conceived of conditional branch instructions. They were to be implemented by testing the sign of a number; one course of action was to be taken if the sign were positive; another, if negative. He also proposed a mechanism for both advancing and reversing the control cards to permit branching to any desired instruction.

The design of the Analytical Engine embodied all the features essential to a general-purpose automatic computing machine. Again Babbage proposed to build it on a grand scale. The store was to have a capacity of 1000 50-digit decimal numbers. He estimated that the addition of two numbers would take a second, and multiplication, a minute. It is very unlikely that a mechanical computer of this size could ever be successfully built. Babbage spent much of the latter half of his life refining the design of the Analytical Engine. Only a small part of the machine was actually constructed.

Later developments. A number of improvements in the design of four-function mechanical calculators were made in the nineteenth century which led to their widespread use. The first to achieve commercial success was the Arithmomètre designed in France by Charles X. Thomas (1785–1870) about 1820. The Comptometer, designed by the American inventor D. E. Felt (1862–1930) in 1885, was one of the earliest calculators to use depressible keys for entering data and commands; and it also printed its results on paper. A later innovation was the use of electric motors to drive the mechanical components and thus increase the speed of operation.

Operation cards	Program		Comments
	Variable cards		
	Source	Destination	
×	W_2, W_4	W_8	$W_8 \leftarrow a_{22}b_1$
×	W_1, W_5	W_9	$W_9 \leftarrow a_{12}b_2$
×	W_0, W_4	W_{10}	$W_{10} \leftarrow a_{11}a_{22}$
×	W_1, W_3	W_{11}	$W_{11} \leftarrow a_{12}a_{21}$
−	W_8, W_9	W_{12}	$W_{12} \leftarrow a_{22}b_1 - a_{12}b_2$
−	W_{10}, W_{11}	W_{13}	$W_{13} \leftarrow a_{11}a_{22} - a_{12}a_{21}$
÷	W_{12}, W_{13}	W_{14}	$W_{14} \leftarrow W_{12} \div W_{13}$

FIGURE 1.9
Part of a program for the Analytical Engine.

Another important development in the late nineteenth century was the commercial application of punched-card equipment for sorting and tabulating large amounts of data. The inventor of the punched-card tabulating machine was the American Herman Hollerith (1860–1929). The first major application of Hollerith's system was to process the data collected in the 1890 United States census. Hollerith's punched cards, like those of Babbage, were based on the cards used in the Jacquard loom. The various characteristics of the population were indicated by holes punched in specific locations on the cards. These holes were then sensed by an electrical mechanism and counted (tabulated) mechanically. In 1896 Hollerith formed the Tabulating Machine Company to manufacture his equipment. In 1911 his company merged with several others to form the Computing-Tabulating-Recording Company, which was renamed the International Business Machines Corp. (IBM) in 1924.

No significant attempts to build general-purpose digital computers were made after Babbage's death until the 1930s when, independently, such computers were constructed in several countries. In Germany in 1938, Konrad Zuse built a mechanical computer, the Z1, apparently unaware of Babbage's work. The Z1, unlike previous mechanical computers, used binary instead of decimal arithmetic. A subsequent machine, the Z3, completed in 1941, is believed to have been the first operational general-purpose program-controlled computer. The arithmetic unit of the Z3 was constructed from relays (electromechanical binary switches) and employed floating-point number representation. Zuse's work was interrupted by the Second World War and had very little influence on the subsequent development of computers. A much larger electronic computer called Colossus was completed in England in 1943 and intended for code breaking; however, its existence remained an official state secret until the 1970s. A number of special-purpose relay computers were also built around this time in the United States, notably at AT&T Bell Laboratories [25].

Howard Aiken (1900–1973), a physicist at Harvard University, proposed the design of a general-purpose electromechanical computer in 1937. Unlike Zuse, Aiken was apparently aware of the work of Babbage and earlier pioneers. An arrangement was made to have IBM construct the machine according to Aiken's basic design. Work was begun on the computer, originally called the Automatic Sequence Controlled Calculator and later the Harvard Mark I, in 1939, and it became operational in 1944. Like Babbage's machines, the Harvard Mark I employed decimal counter wheels for its working memory. It had a storage capacity of seventy-two 23-digit decimal numbers. The machine was controlled (programmed) by means of a punched paper tape which combined the functions of Babbage's operation cards and variable cards. Each instruction had the format

$$A_1 \quad A_2 \quad OP$$

where OP was an operation to be performed, e.g., multiplication, A_1 and A_2 were the registers storing the input operands to be used, and A_2 was also the destination of the result.

Figure 1.10 summarizes the major steps in the development of mechanical computers.

Date	Inventor: machine	Capability	Technical innovations
1642	Pascal	Addition, subtraction	Automatic carry transfer; complements number representation
1671	Leibniz	Addition, subtraction multiplication, division	"Stepped reckoner" mechanism for multiplication and division
1827	Babbage: Difference Engine	Polynomial evaluation by method of finite differences	Automatic multistep operation
1834	Babbage: Analytical Engine (never completed)	General-purpose computation	Automatic sequence control mechanism (program)
1941 1944	Zuse: Z3 Aiken: Harvard Mark I	General-purpose computation	The first operational general-purpose computers

FIGURE 1.10
Milestones in the development of mechanical computers.

1.2.2 The Electronic Era

Mechanical computers suffer from two serious drawbacks:

1. Computing speed is limited by the inertia of the moving parts.
2. The transmission of information by mechanical means (gears, levers, etc.) is cumbersome and unreliable.

For electronic computers, on the other hand, the "moving parts" are electrons. Information can be transmitted by electric currents at speeds approaching the speed of light (300,000 km/s). The triode vacuum tube invented by Lee de Forest (1873–1961) in 1906 permits the switching of electrical signals at speeds far exceeding those of any mechanical device. Vacuum tubes can also be used to construct very fast binary storage devices.

Electronic computers. The first attempt to construct an electronic computer using vacuum tubes appears to have been made by John V. Atanasoff in the late 1930s at Iowa State University. This was a special-purpose machine for solving simultaneous linear equations. The first widely known general-purpose electronic computer was the ENIAC (*E*lectronic *N*umerical *I*ntegrator *a*nd *C*alculator) built at the University of Pennsylvania under the direction of John W. Mauchly (1907–1980) and J. Presper Eckert. Like Babbage's Difference Engine, part of the motivation for the ENIAC was the need to construct tables automatically—in this case, ballistics tables for the U.S. Army Ordnance Department, which funded the project. Work on the ENIAC began in 1943 and it was completed in 1946. It was an enormous machine weighing 30 tons and containing over 18,000 vacuum tubes. It was also substantially faster than any previous computer. Thus, while the Harvard

Mark I required about 3 s to perform a 10-digit multiplication, the ENIAC required only 3 ms.

The ENIAC had a working memory comprising 20 electronic accumulators, each of which could accommodate a signed 10-digit decimal number. A decimal digit was stored in a ring counter consisting of 10 vacuum-tube flip-flops (single-bit storage devices) connected in a closed loop. Digit i was stored by setting flip-flop i to the 1 state and the remaining nine flip-flops to the 0 state. Thus the ring counter was the electronic equivalent of the mechanical counter wheel. The ENIAC was basically a decimal rather than a binary computer. The accumulators in the ENIAC combined the functions of storage and addition and subtraction as do counter wheels. Additional units were included for multiplication, division, and extraction of square roots.

Figure 1.11 shows the architecture of the ENIAC. It was programmed manually by setting switches and plugging and unplugging cables. Thus, for example, to add the contents of accumulator A_1 to accumulator A_2, a data path from A_1 to A_2 had to be established manually. A "master programmer" unit (which was also set manually) could be used to cause multistep or iterative operations to take place automatically. Data was entered via a "constant transmitter" (usually a punched-card reader). Special memories, called "function tables," were used for storing tables of constants. Results could be punched on cards or printed on an electric typewriter.

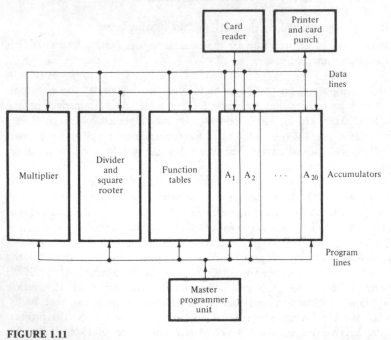

FIGURE 1.11
Structure of the ENIAC.

Stored-program computers. In the Analytical Engine and its modern successors the Harvard Mark I and the ENIAC, programs and data were stored in separate memories. Entering or altering programs was an extremely tedious task. The idea of storing programs and data in the same high-speed memory unit, the *stored-program concept,* is usually attributed to the ENIAC designers, most notably the Hungarian-born mathematician John von Neumann (1903–1957), who was a consultant on the ENIAC project. It was first published in a 1945 proposal by von Neumann for a new computer, the EDVAC (*E*lectronic *D*iscrete *V*ariable *C*omputer). Besides facilitating the programming process, the stored-program concept makes it possible for a program to modify its own instructions, a property which has some undesirable features and is now rarely used.

As well as being a stored-program computer, the EDVAC differed from its predecessors in several important respects. It had a much larger store, provided by a mercury-delay-line main memory with a capacity of 1024 or 1K words (numbers or instructions); and a secondary, slower, magnetic-wire memory with a capacity of about 20K words. Unlike earlier machines, binary rather than decimal number representation was used. Because access to the main delay-line memory was serial (bit by bit) rather than parallel (word by word) the EDVAC used serial binary arithmetic-logic circuits.

Before a program could be executed by EDVAC, all instructions and data were placed in its main memory. Arithmetic instructions had the following format:

$$A_1 \quad A_2 \quad A_3 \quad A_4 \quad OP$$

meaning perform the operation OP (addition, subtraction, multiplication, or division) on the contents of the main-memory locations with addresses A_1 and A_2 and place the results in memory location A_3. The fourth address A_4 specified the location of the next instruction to be executed. Conditional branch instructions had the format

$$A_1 \quad A_2 \quad A_3 \quad A_4 \quad C$$

meaning if the number in A_1 is not less than the number in A_2, take the next instruction from A_3; otherwise take the next instruction from A_4. Finally, a pair of input-output instructions were provided for transferring information between the main and secondary memories. In these instructions, the second address field was split into two components, an operation modifier m, indicating the direction of the data transfer, and a number n, which represented the address of the particular secondary storage wire to be used. The instruction format was

$$A_1 \quad m, n \quad A_3 \quad A_4 \quad W$$

meaning

1. If $m = 1$, transfer to wire n the sequence of words stored in locations A_1, $A_1 + 1$, $A_1 + 2$, . . . , A_3.
2. If $m = 2$, transfer from wire n a sequence of words to main-memory locations A_1, $A_1 + 1$, $A_1 + 2$, . . . , A_3.

Again A_4 was the address of the next instruction to be used. The input-output equipment of the EDVAC consisted of a typewriter-like device, which transferred information directly to magnetic wires, and a printer, which reversed this process. The EDVAC became operational in 1951.

In 1946, von Neumann and his colleagues began the design of a new stored-program computer, now referred to as the IAS computer, at the Institute for Advanced Studies in Princeton. This machine employed a random-access cathode-ray-tube main memory, which permitted an entire word to be accessed in one operation. Unlike the EDVAC, parallel binary circuits were employed. Each instruction contained only one memory address and had the format

$$OP \quad A$$

The central processing unit (CPU) contained several high-speed (vacuum-tube) registers used as implicit storage locations for operands and results. Although its input-output facilities were limited, the IAS machine was quite modern in its conception. It can be regarded as the prototype of all subsequent general-purpose computers. Several reports describing its design were published and had a far-reaching influence on the development of computers. Because of its importance, the IAS machine is described in detail in Sec. 1.2.3.

The first generation. Figure 1.12 shows the architecture typical of general-purpose computers in the late 1940s and early 1950s. It is common to refer to machines of this period as *first-generation computers*, which exhibits a somewhat short-sighted view of computer history. The control of the computer was centralized in a single CPU; all operations in the system, e.g., the transfer of a single word of information between an IO device and main memory, required direct intervention by the CPU. This is suggested in Fig. 1.12 by broken arrows which represent control lines.

In the late 1940s and early 1950s, the number of computers being built grew very rapidly. Besides those already mentioned, notable early machines include the Whirlwind I constructed at Massachusetts Institute of Technology (MIT) and a series of machines culminating with the ATLAS computer that were designed at Manchester University. Whirlwind I was the first computer to have a ferrite-core main memory, while the Manchester machines introduced the concepts of one-level storage (now called virtual memory) and B registers (now called index registers).

In 1947 Eckert and Mauchly formed a company, the Eckert-Mauchly Computer Corporation, to manufacture computers commercially. Their first successful machine was the UNIVAC (*Universal Automatic Computer*), delivered in 1951. It employed a mercury delay-line main memory of the type used in EDVAC and had a magnetic-tape secondary memory. IBM, which had built the Harvard Mark I and was then the major manufacturer of punched-card processing equipment, delivered its first electronic stored-program computer, the 701, in 1953. The 701 employed an electrostatic (cathode-ray-tube) main memory, and magnetic-drum and -tape secondary memories. The 701 was the first of the long 700 series of IBM machines.

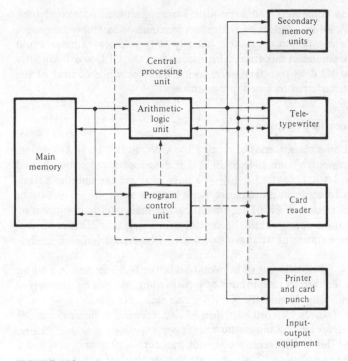

FIGURE 1.12
Architecture of a first-generation computer.

The earliest computer programs were written in the binary code, or *machine language*, used to represent the instructions in memory. Thus the binary string

$$0011 \quad 1011 \quad 0000 \quad 0000 \quad 0111$$

might represent the instruction add the contents of memory location 7 to the accumulator. Machine-language instructions are tedious to write and difficult to recognize. A substantial improvement is obtained by allowing operations and addresses to be specified in symbolic mnemonic form. The above instruction might then be written as

$$ADD \quad X1$$

This type of programming, which came into use in the early 1950s, was called *symbolic programming*; it is now called *assembly-language* programming. Assembly language is obviously much easier to use than machine language. It does, however, require a special system program, called an *assembler*, to translate a user's program from assembly language to machine language before the user's program is to be executed.

First-generation computers had very little system software compared with modern machines. Programs had to be written in machine or assembly languages which varied from computer to computer. Usually only one programmer could have access to the computer at any time. This meant that the CPU was frequently idle, e.g., while slow IO data transfers were taking place or while control of the machine was being transferred to a new programmer.

1.2.3 A First-Generation Computer

This section is based on a classic series of reports by A. W. Burks, H. H. Goldstine, and J. von Neumann written from 1946 to 1948 that described the logic design and programming of the IAS computer [9, 14]. We have changed the authors' terminology and notation to conform more closely with current usage. The structure of the IAS computer is shown in Fig. 1.13, including the main registers, processing circuits, and information paths within the central processing unit. This computer can be taken as representative of what are now called first-generation computers.

Information formats. The basic unit of information in the IAS machine is a 40-bit *word*, which may be defined as the amount of information that can be transferred between the main memory M and the CPU in one step. The memory M has a capacity of $2^{12} = 4096$ words. A word stored in M can represent either instructions or data. The basic data item is a binary number having the format shown in Fig. 1.14. The leftmost bit (bit 0) represents the sign of the number (0 for positive and 1 for negative), while the remaining 39 bits indicate the number's size in a particular 0/1 encoding called twos-complement code. The numbers are assumed to have an implicit binary point corresponding to the decimal point in ordinary decimal notation. It may be placed in any fixed position within the number word format; hence these numbers are called *fixed-point*. If the implicit binary point is assumed to lie between bits 0 and 1, then all numbers are treated as fractions. Some examples of the IAS representation of fractions follow:

$$+0.5 = 01000000\ 00000000\ 00000000\ 00000000\ 00000000$$
$$+0.1 = 00001100\ 11001100\ 11001100\ 11001100\ 11001100$$
$$\text{Zero} = 00000000\ 00000000\ 00000000\ 00000000\ 00000000$$
$$-0.1 = 11110011\ 00110011\ 00110011\ 00110011\ 00110100$$

Because fractions are restricted to lie between -1 and $+1$, all numbers used in calculations that lie outside this range must be adjusted by some suitable scaling factor. Fixed-point numbers are also sometimes interpreted as integers, in which case the implicit binary point lies immediately to the right of the rightmost bit in the number word.

IAS instructions are 20 bits long, so that two instructions can be stored in each 40-bit memory location. As indicated in Fig. 1.14, an instruction consists of two parts: an 8-bit *opcode* (operation code) that defines the operation to be performed (add, subtract, etc.) and a 12-bit *address* part that can identify any of the 2^{12} memory locations that may be used to store an operand of the instruction. Note

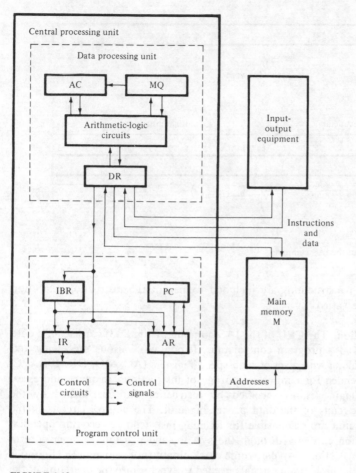

FIGURE 1.13
Structure of a first-generation computer: IAS.

that while each EDVAC instruction contained four memory addresses, the IAS instruction allows only one. This results in a substantial reduction in word length. Two aspects of the IAS organization make this possible.

1. Fixed registers in the CPU are used to store operands and results. The IAS instructions automatically make use of these registers as required. In other words, CPU register addresses are implicitly specified by the opcode.
2. The instructions of a program are stored in main memory in approximately the sequence in which they are to be executed. Hence the address of the next instruction pair is usually the address of the current instruction pair plus one. The need for a next instruction address in the instruction format is eliminated.

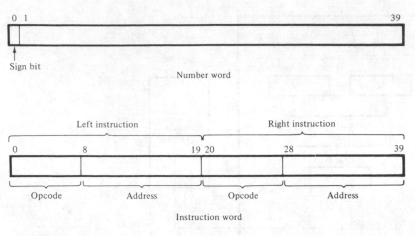

FIGURE 1.14
Information formats of the IAS computer.

Special branch instructions are included to permit the instruction execution sequence to be varied.

System organization. The CPU of the IAS computer (Fig. 1.13) consists of a data processing unit and a program control unit. It contains various processing and control circuits, along with a set of high-speed registers (AC, MQ, DR, IBR, PC, IR, and AR) intended for temporary storage of instructions, memory addresses, and data. The main actions specified by instructions are performed by the arithmetic-logic circuits of the data processing unit. The control circuits in the program control unit are responsible for fetching instructions, decoding opcodes, routing information correctly through the system, and providing proper control signals for all CPU actions. An electronic clock circuit (not shown in the figure) is used to generate the basic timing signals needed to synchronize the operation of the different parts of the system.

The main memory M is used for storing programs and data. A word transfer can take place between the 40-bit *data register* DR of the CPU and any location M(X) with address X in M. The address X to be used is stored in a 12-bit *address register* AR. The DR may be used to store an operand during the execution of an instruction. Two additional registers for the temporary storage of operands and results are included: the *accumulator* AC and the *multiplier-quotient* register MQ. Two instructions are fetched simultaneously from M and transferred to the program control unit. The instruction that is not to be executed immediately is placed in an *instruction buffer register* IBR. The opcode of the other instruction is placed in the *instruction register* IR where it is decoded. The address field of the current instruction is transferred to the memory address register AR. Another address register called the *instruction address register* or the *program counter* PC is used to store the address of the next instruction to be executed.

Instruction set. Following Burks et al., we use a formal notation, called a description language, or *register transfer language*, as a shorthand way of describing instructions and the primitive actions or *microoperations* within the computer. The description language approximates an assembly language used to prepare programs for the computer. The use of computer description languages can be traced to Babbage [22]. The one introduced here and used throughout this book is representative and largely self-explanatory. Storage locations (in the CPU or M) are referred to by acronym. The transfer of information is denoted by an arrow; thus $A \leftarrow B$ means copy the contents of storage location B to storage location A without altering the contents of B. Elements of storage arrays are indicated by subscripts or by appending a list of indices in parentheses to the array name. Thus M is considered to be a 4096×40 array so that $M(X, 0:19)$ denotes bits 0 through 19 of word X in M.

Figure 1.15 illustrates the use of our descriptive notation in a simple IAS program that adds two numbers. The numbers to be added are stored in memory locations 100 and 101. The sum is stored in location 102. Note the central role played by the accumulator AC in this program.

The set of instructions defined for the IAS computer in [9], which excludes IO instructions, are given in Fig. 1.16. We have divided them into five groups: data transfer, unconditional branch, conditional branch, arithmetic, and address modify instructions. They make explicit use of only the AC and MQ registers, which are referred to as the *programmable registers*. The data-transfer instructions cause data to be transferred unchanged (except possibly in sign) among CPU registers and main-memory locations. There are two unconditional branch instructions (also called "jump" or "go to" instructions), which cause the next instruction to be taken from either the left or the right half of $M(X)$. The conditional branch instructions permit a jump to take place if and only if the accumulator contains a nonnegative number. These instructions allow the results of a computation to alter the instruction execution sequence, and are of great importance. The arithmetic instructions provide the basic data processing commands of the computer. The last two, which we call address modify instructions, permit addresses to be computed in the arithmetic-logic unit and then inserted into instructions stored in main memory. Address modification allows a program to alter its own instructions, an important feature of early stored-program machines.

Instruction	Comments
$AC \leftarrow M(100)$	Transfer contents of memory location 100 to the accumulator
$AC \leftarrow AC + M(101)$	Add the contents of memory location 101 to the contents of the accumulator and place the result in the accumulator
$M(102) \leftarrow AC$	Store the contents of the accumulator in memory location 102

FIGURE 1.15
An IAS program to add two numbers.

Instruction type	Shorthand notation	Description
Data transfer	AC ← MQ	Transfer contents of register MQ to the accumulator AC
	MQ ← M(X)	Transfer contents of memory location X to MQ
	M(X) ← AC	Transfer contents of accumulator to memory location X
	AC ← M(X)	Transfer M(X) to the accumulator
	AC ← −M(X)	Transfer −M(X) to the accumulator
	AC ← |M(X)|	Transfer absolute value of M(X) to the accumulator
	AC ← −|M(X)|	Transfer −|M(X)| to the accumulator
Unconditional branch	**go to** M(X, 0:19)	Take next instruction from left half of M(X)
	go to M(X, 20:39)	Take next instruction from right half of M(X)
Conditional branch	**if** AC ≥ 0 **then go to** M(X, 0:19)	If number in the accumulator is nonnegative, take next instruction from left half of M(X)
	if AC ≥ 0 **then go to** M(X, 20:39)	If number in the accumulator is nonnegative, take next instruction from right half of M(X)
Arithmetic	AC ← AC + M(X)	Add M(X) to AC; put the result in AC
	AC ← AC + |M(X)|	Add |M(X)| to AC; put the result in AC
	AC ← AC − M(X)	Subtract M(X) from AC; put the result in AC
	AC ← AC − |M(X)|	Subtract |M(X)| from AC; put the result in AC
	AC.MQ ← MQ × M(X)	Multiply M(X) by MQ; put most significant bits of result in AC, put least significant bits in MQ
	MQ.AC ← AC ÷ M(X)	Divide AC by M(X); put the quotient in MQ and the remainder in AC
	AC ← AC × 2	Multiply accumulator by 2, i.e., shift left one bit position
	AC ← AC ÷ 2	Divide accumulator by 2, i.e., shift right one bit position
Address modify	M(X, 8:19) ← AC(28:39)	Replace left address field at M(X) by 12 rightmost bits of AC
	M(X,28:39) ← AC(28:39)	Replace right address field at M(X) by 12 rightmost bits of AC

FIGURE 1.16
Instruction set of the IAS computer.

Method of operation. Instructions are fetched and executed in two separate consecutive steps called the *fetch cycle* and the *execution cycle*. Together they form the *instruction cycle*. Figure 1.17 shows the principal actions carried out in each cycle. The fetch cycle is common to all instructions. Since two instructions are obtained simultaneously from M, the next instruction may be in the instruction buffer register. If not, the previously incremented contents of the program counter are transferred to the address register and a READ request is sent to M. The required data at memory location X is then transferred to the data register DR. The opcode of the required instruction (which is in either the left or right half of the fetched word) is sent to the instruction register and decoded. The address part of the instruction goes to the address register, while the second instruction may be transferred to the instruction buffer register IBR. The program counter PC is incremented whenever the next instruction is not in IBR.

The computer now enters the execution cycle, and its subsequent actions depend on the particular instruction being executed. Figure 1.17 shows the execution cycles of four representative instructions. Note that each instruction is executed by a sequence of microoperations. A microoperation typically involves a single register transfer operation of the form $S \leftarrow f(S_1, S_2, \ldots, S_k)$, where $S_1, S_2, \ldots, S_k$ are the storage locations of the operands, f is a logical or arithmetic operation, and S is where the result is stored. Thus the ADD instruction $AC \leftarrow AC + M(X)$ is implemented by two microoperations, as shown in Fig. 1.17. First the contents of the memory location $M(AR)$ specified by the address register AR are transferred to the data register DR. Then the contents of the data register and the

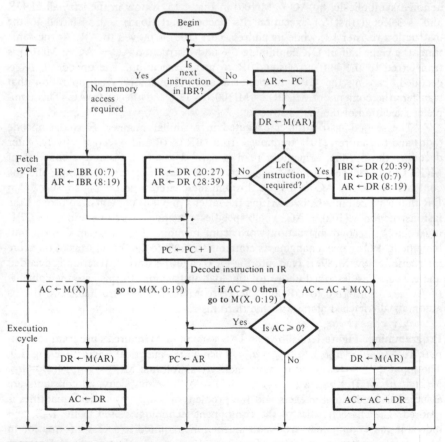

FIGURE 1.17
Partial flowchart of IAS computer operation.

accumulator are added and the result is placed in the accumulator AC. Certain instructions are implemented by a much larger number of microoperations. For example, a multiplication algorithm requiring 39 addition and shift microoperations is used. The intrinsic capabilities of the arithmetic-logic circuits are limited to addition, subtraction, and simple operations such as shifting and complementing.

Consider the execution of the simple addition algorithm described in Fig. 1.15. The symbolic program given in the figure is assumed to have been translated to the binary (machine) format of Fig. 1.14. Since IAS can store two machine instructions in each location of memory M, two consecutive locations, say, M(88) and M(89), are needed to store this three-instruction program. PC is first loaded with the starting address of the program, which in this case is the 12-bit binary equivalent of the number 88. This address is then transferred (copied) from PC to the address register AR, and a memory read operation is executed bringing the word at M(AR) = M(88) into the CPU and putting it in DR. The load instruction, denoted symbolically by AC ← M(100) in Fig. 1.15, is now in the left half of DR and is selected first for execution. Its opcode part (load) is transferred to the instruction register IR, while its address part (100) is moved to AR. At the same time, the right half of DR containing the add instruction AC ← AC + M(101) is transferred to the buffer register IBR to await execution. The opcode in IR is decoded, causing the CPU to perform another memory read operation that transfers the contents of M(AR) = M(100) to DR and thence to AC. This completes execution of the first instruction.

The second instruction is executed in a similar manner. First the opcode (add) and the address (101) are moved from IBR to IR and AR, respectively. After decoding the opcode, a memory read is carried out to transfer the contents of M(101) to DR. The arithmetic-logic circuits are set to perform addition, and the contents of DR and AC are passed through these circuits producing a result AC + DR that is placed in AC, overwriting the latter's previous contents. To process the last instruction M(102) ← AC, which specifies a memory store operation, the CPU must fetch a second instruction word from memory. The program control unit increments PC by one, changing its contents from 88 to 89, the address of the store instruction. Now M(89) is read into the CPU, and the store instruction is decoded and executed as described above for the load instruction. In this case the contents of AC are transferred to DR and thence to M(102). The extra half-word that is automatically fetched along with the third instruction is ignored.

Programming. Figure 1.18 shows an IAS version of Menabrea's program to compute $x_1 = (a_{22}b_1 - a_{22}b_2)/(a_{11}a_{22} - a_{12}a_{21})$ using the Analytical Engine; see Fig. 1.9. The input data are assigned to main memory as follows: $M(0) = a_{11}$, $M(1) = a_{12}$, $M(2) = b_1$, $M(3) = a_{21}$, $M(4) = a_{22}$, $M(5) = b_2$. For simplicity, all constants are assumed to be decimal integers and the problem of scaling numerical quantities is ignored. The characteristics of the component technologies used in the IAS, and indeed in most computers, are such that the time required to access information in M is much greater (by a factor of perhaps 10) than the time required to access information in CPU registers. Hence it is desirable to use the CPU's programmable

Instruction	Comments
$MQ \leftarrow M(1)$	Transfer a_{12} to MQ
$AC.MQ \leftarrow MQ \times M(3)$	Compute $a_{12}a_{21}$
$M(11) \leftarrow AC$	Transfer $a_{12}a_{21}$ to $M(11)$
$MQ \leftarrow M(0)$	Transfer a_{11} to MQ
$AC.MQ \leftarrow MQ \times M(4)$	Compute $a_{11}a_{22}$
$AC \leftarrow AC - M(11)$	Compute $a_{11}a_{22} - a_{12}a_{21}$
$M(13) \leftarrow AC$	Transfer $a_{11}a_{22} - a_{12}a_{21}$ to $M(13)$
$MQ \leftarrow M(1)$	Transfer a_{12} to MQ
$AC.MQ \leftarrow MQ \times M(5)$	Compute $a_{12}b_2$
$M(9) \leftarrow AC$	Transfer $a_{12}b_2$ to $M(9)$
$MQ \leftarrow M(4)$	Transfer a_{22} to MQ
$AC.MQ \leftarrow MQ \times M(2)$	Compute $a_{22}b_1$
$AC \leftarrow AC - M(9)$	Compute $a_{22}b_1 - a_{12}b_2$
$MQ.AC \leftarrow AC \div M(13)$	Compute x_1
$M(14) \leftarrow AC$	Transfer remainder of x_1 to $M(14)$
$AC \leftarrow MQ$	Transfer quotient of x_1 to AC
$M(15) \leftarrow AC$	Transfer quotient of x_1 to $M(15)$

FIGURE 1.18
An IAS version of Menabrea's program.

registers (AC and MQ) for storage of intermediate results as often as possible. The steps of Menabrea's program have been reordered with this objective in view. It should be noted that the IAS program is the longer of the two, since it is a *one-address* machine, permitting only one main-memory address per instruction. The Analytical Engine program permits three addresses per instruction. We turn now to a more complex IAS programming problem.

Example 1.5   An IAS program to perform vector addition. Let A = A(1), A(2), . . . , A(1000) and B = B(1), B(2), . . . , B(1000) be two vectors (one-dimensional arrays) comprising 1000 numbers each that must be added in pairs. The result C is computed by 1000 additions of the form C(I) = A(I) + B(I), where I = 1, 2, . . . , 1000. Using the IAS instruction set, each addition can be implemented by three instructions thus:

$$AC \leftarrow A(I)$$
$$AC \leftarrow AC + B(I)$$
$$C(I) \leftarrow AC$$

Clearly, a straight-line program with 1000 copies of these three instructions, each with a different value of the index I, would perform the desired vector addition. Such a program, besides being extremely inconvenient to write, would not fit in M with the 3000 words needed to store A, B, C. Some type of loop or iterative program structure is thus needed.

Figure 1.19 shows such a program. The data A, B, and C are stored sequentially, beginning in locations 1001, 2001, and 3001, respectively. The symbol to the left of each instruction in Fig. 1.19 is its location in M; thus 2L (2R) denotes the left (right) half of M(2). M(0) is used to store a count N and is initially set to 999. N is

Location	Instruction or data	Comments
0	999	Count N
1	1	Constant
2	1000	Constant
3L	AC ← M(2000)	Transfer A(I) to AC
3R	AC ← AC + M(3000)	Compute A(I) + B(I)
4L	M(4000) ← AC	Transfer sum to C(I)
4R	AC ← M(0)	Load count N
5L	AC ← AC − M(1)	Decrement N by 1
5R	**if** AC ≥ 0 **then go to** M(6, 20:39)	Test N
6L	**go to** M(6, 0:19)	Halt
6R	M(0) ← AC	Update N
7L	AC ← AC + M(1)	Increment AC by 1
7R	AC ← AC + M(2)	
8L	M(3, 8:19) ← AC(28:39)	Modify address in 3L
8R	AC ← AC + M(2)	
9L	M(3, 28:39) ← AC(28:39)	Modify address in 3R
9R	AC ← AC + M(2)	
10L	M(4, 8:19) ← AC(28:39)	Modify address in 4L
10R	**go to** M(3, 0:19)	

FIGURE 1.19
An IAS program for vector addition.

systematically decremented by one; when it reaches −1, the program halts. The address modify instructions in locations 8L, 9L, and 10L are used to decrement the address fields of the three instructions in locations 3L, 3R, and 4L, respectively. Thus the program is continuously modifying itself during execution. Figure 1.19 shows the program before execution commences. At the end of the computation, the first three instructions will have changed to the following:

$$3L \quad AC \leftarrow M(1001)$$
$$3R \quad AC \leftarrow AC + M(2001)$$
$$4L \quad M(3001) \leftarrow AC$$

Critique. In the years that have elapsed since the IAS computer was designed, many refinements in computer organization have appeared. Thus, with hindsight, some of the shortcomings of its design can be pointed out.

1. The address modification scheme (indexing) used in Example 1.5 was awkward and inefficient. To restart a program, the original unmodified program must be reloaded into main memory. By providing special addressable CPU registers, called index registers, the indexing operation can be made simpler and faster, and the need to modify instructions stored in main memory can be eliminated.

2. No facilities were provided for structuring programs, e.g., instructions to link program modules such as subroutines (procedures) that implement frequently used program steps.

3. Floating-point arithmetic, which provides automatic scaling of numbers was not implemented mainly due to the cost of the hardware needed. Special subroutines had to be written for this purpose.

4. The storing of two instructions in each word added to the complexity of the program control unit and the instruction set. This feature was dropped from most later computers. However, it had the advantage of reducing the time spent fetching instructions from main memory by a factor of about $\frac{1}{2}$.

5. The instruction set was heavily oriented toward numerical computation, so that programming logical and nonnumerical problems was difficult.

6. Input-output instructions were considered of minor importance. In fact no mention of them is made in Ref. 9 beyond the observation that they are needed. IAS was implemented with two basic IO instruction types INPUT and OUTPUT [12]. INPUT(X, N) caused N words to be transferred from a punched-card reader to the CPU and thence to N consecutive main-memory locations starting at address X. OUTPUT(X, N) transferred N consecutive words from the main-memory region with starting address X to an output device, again via the CPU. A similar pair of IO instructions transferred blocks of information between main memory and a magnetic-drum unit used for secondary storage. Since the IO devices in IAS were electromechanical, they operated at much slower speeds than the electronic CPU and main memory. Hence the CPU was largely idle while executing an IO instruction. This rather inefficient way of controlling IO operations was frequently responsible for poor overall system performance.

1.3 THE LATER GENERATIONS

The first-generation machines established many of the basic features of electronic computers, so much so that the term "von Neumann computer" has become synonymous with any computer of conventional design independent of its date of introduction. Later innovations in computer hardware technology and, to a lesser degree, program design methodology (software technology) have been used in a somewhat loose way to define several additional generations of computers. The second and third generations, which further defined the basic architecture of modern computers, are reviewed in this section.

1.3.1 The Second Generation

The so-called second-generation computers can be taken to be those produced during the second decade of the electronic computer era (approximately 1955 to 1964). They are mainly characterized by the change from vacuum tube to transistor technology; however, several other important developments also occurred, which are summarized below.

1. The transistor, which had been invented in 1948 at AT&T Bell Laboratories, gradually replaced vacuum tubes in the design of switching circuits.

2. Cathode-ray-tube memories and delay-line memories were replaced by ferrite cores and magnetic drums as the technologies used in main memories.

3. The use of index registers and floating-point arithmetic hardware became widespread.

4. Machine-independent "high-level" programming languages such as ALGOL, COBOL, and FORTRAN were introduced to simplify programming.

5. Special processors (IO processors) were introduced to supervise input-output operations, thus freeing the CPU from many time-consuming housekeeping functions.

6. Computer manufacturers began to provide system software such as compilers, subroutine libraries, and batch monitors.

The earliest transistor computer appears to have been an experimental machine, the TX-0, built at the Lincoln Laboratory of MIT, which was operational in 1953. Many of the improvements associated with second-generaiton computers actually first appeared in vacuum tube or hybrid machines. The IBM 704, a vacuum-tube computer produced in 1955, had index registers and floating-point hardware. It was also the first commercial machine with a "control program," which was a rudimentary operating system. Later models of the 704 and its successor, the 709, had *input-output processors* (then called "data synchronizers" and later "channels"), which were special-purpose processors used exclusively to control input-output operations. In early machines such as the IAS computer, all IO operations were controlled directly by the CPU; this is now termed *programmed IO*. The IBM 7090 and 7094 were essentially transistorized versions of the 709 and were very successful commercially.

With the second generation it became necessary to talk about computer *systems*, since the number of memory units, processors, IO devices, and other system components could vary between different installations, even though the same basic computer was used.

> **Example 1.6 A second-generation computer.** Figure 1.20 shows the structure (slightly simplified) of the IBM 7094 system, which is a representative large-scale scientific machine of the second generation [4, 17]. The CPU differs from that of the IAS computer mainly in the addition of a set of index registers, and arithmetic circuits that can handle both floating-point and fixed-point operations. All input-output operations are controlled by a set of IO processors which have direct access to the main memory M. A control unit is used to switch the memory between the CPU and the various IOPs. In the following description of the 7094, only those aspects that are significantly different from the IAS machine are discussed.
>
> Figure 1.21 shows the basic information formats of the 7094. A 36-bit word is used, which may represent a fixed-point number, a floating-point number, or an instruction. The format for fixed-point numbers is the same as the IAS computer's except for the word length. The floating-point number format is composed of a pair of fixed-point numbers, a mantissa M and an exponent E, and has the value $M \times 2^E$. M is taken to be a fraction, while E is an integer ranging in value from -128 to $+128$.

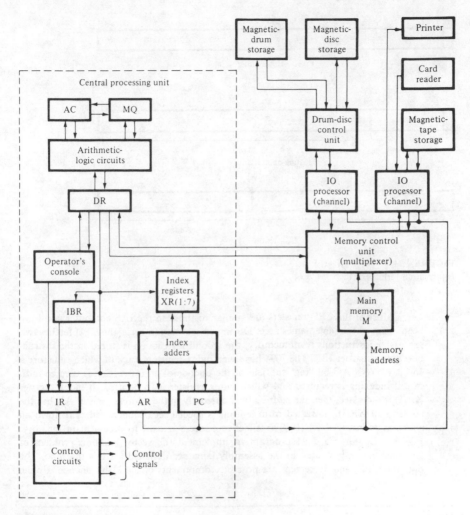

FIGURE 1.20
Structure of a second-generation computer: the IBM 7094.

Thus floating-point numbers can have magnitudes from 2^{-128} to 2^{+127}, or 2.9×10^{-39} to 1.7×10^{38} approximately. In contrast, the 7094's fixed-point format interpreted as a fraction can only represent numbers with nonzero magnitudes lying in the range 2^{-35} or 2.9×10^{-11} to one. Bit 0 determines the sign of the floating-point number; again 0 is used for positive numbers and 1 for negative. The 7094's instruction word also follows the style of the IAS machine, with an opcode and a single memory address. The longer format used here makes it possible to have more instruction types and a larger memory address space. With 15 address bits, a main memory containing up to $2^{15} = 32K$ storage locations can be employed.

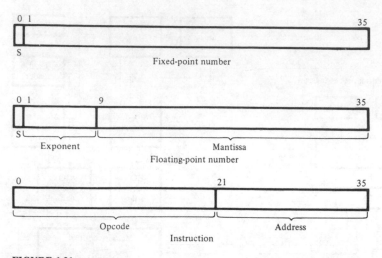

FIGURE 1.21
Information formats of the IBM 7094.

Most of the CPU registers are similar to those in the IAS computer and have been assigned the same names here. During an instruction cycle, the CPU fetches two successive instructions from memory; the second instruction is stored in the instruction buffer register IBR. The 7094 has seven index registers, each of which can store a 15-bit address. A 3-bit "tag" subfield of the opcode of an instruction is used to indicate if indexing is required and which index register is to be used. If index register XR(I) is indicated, then the address field currently in the address register AR has the contents of XR(I) subtracted from it using a special set of index adders to form an *effective address* AR-XR(I). The effective address is used to access main memory. Figure 1.22 shows a 7094 program to implement the vector addition problem of Example 1.5. It is written in the assembly language designed for this machine. The operation, tag, and decrement are possible components of the 21-bit opcode. Unlike

Location	Operation	Address, tag, decrement	Comments
	AXT	0, 2	Load zero into index register XR(2)
START	CLA	2000, 2	Clear accumulator and add M(2000-XR(2)) to it
	ADD	3000, 2	Add M(3000-XR(2)) to accumulator
	STO	4000, 2	Store accumulator contents in M(4000-XR(2))
	TXI	TEST, 2, 1	Increment XR(2) by 1 then go to instruction TEST
TEST	TXL	START, 2, 999	If XR(2) $\leq$ 999, go to START
	HPR		Halt

FIGURE 1.22
An IBM 7094 assembly-language program for vector addition.

the IAS vector-addition program of Fig. 1.19, this program does not alter its own instructions, since the address modification operations are carried out in the CPU and not in main memory.

The instruction repertoire of the 7094 has more than 200 types of instructions. They can be classified as follows:

1. Data-transfer instructions for transferring a word of information between the CPU and memory or between two CPU registers.
2. Fixed-point and floating-point arithmetic instructions.
3. Logical (nonnumerical) instructions.
4. Instructions for modifying index registers.
5. Conditional and unconditional branching, and related control instructions.
6. Input-output operations for transferring data between IO devices and main memory. (Some of these are executed by the CPU, but most are executed by the IOPs.)

An important feature of second-generation machines is the provision of special branch instructions to facilitate the transfer of control between different programs, e.g., calling subroutines. In the 7094 an instruction TSX (*t*ransfer and *s*et inde*x*) is available for this purpose. Suppose execution of a subroutine that begins in location SUB is desired. Then the instruction

LINK   TSX   SUB, 4

causes its own address (LINK) to be placed in the designated index register XR(4), and the next instruction is taken from the memory location SUB. In order to return control to the calling program, the subroutine must terminate with an instruction such as

TRA   1, 4

meaning: go (*tra*nsfer) to the address $1 + XR(4)$, which contains the next instruction after LINK in the main program.

Input-output processing. IO processors, such as those of the 7094, supervise the flow of information between main storage and IO devices. They do so by executing special *IO programs*, which are composed of IO instructions and are stored in main memory. An IOP begins execution of an IO program only when an initiation instruction is sent to the IOP by the CPU. This instruction typically contains the address of the first instruction in the IO program to be executed. The IOP can then execute the program without reference to the CPU. The CPU can, however, monitor IO operations by means of instructions that obtain status information from the IOPs. An IOP may also be able to communicate with the CPU to indicate unusual conditions, such as the end of an IO operation, by means of special control signals called *interrupts*. Interrupt facilities, introduced in some second-generation machines, enable the CPU to respond rapidly to changes in IO activity and greatly improve its overall efficiency.

The structure of an IOP based on that of the IBM 7094 computer system is presented in Fig. 1.23. Data is transferred between the IOP and main memory a word (36 bits) at a time, but transfer between the IOP and IO devices, e.g., magnetic tapes, is by character (6 bits). The IOP therefore has circuits for assembling characters into words and disassembling words into characters. The main data register DR stores one word and is connected to the memory data bus. Its role is that of a buffer register. A 5-bit instruction register IR stores the opcode part of the current IO instruction, while the address register AR holds a 15-bit memory address. The number of words to be transferred during data-transfer operations is stored in a data count register DC. A program counter register PC stores the address of the next IO instruction to be executed by the IOP. Finally, the status of the current IO operation is maintained in a status register SR in the IOP. This register may be used to store abnormal or error condition information and can be examined by the CPU.

An IO operation typically proceeds in the following way:

1. The CPU initiates the operation when it encounters an IO instruction while executing some program. This instruction specifies that IO device *d* connected

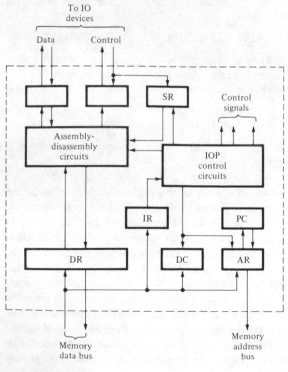

FIGURE 1.23
Structure of an input-output processor.

to IOP c is to be selected for an input (read) or output (write) operation. It (or a subsequent instruction) also specifies the address a in main memory of the first instruction in the IO program to be executed by the designated IOP.

2. The CPU transfers the IO device name d and the IO program starting address a to IOP c.

3. IOP c then proceeds to execute the IO program in question. When the IO operation terminates, either normally or abnormally, the status register SR is set accordingly, and an interrupt signal may be sent to the CPU.

The IOP instruction set is considerably simpler than that of the CPU. For example, it has limited arithmetic capabilities. IOP instructions fall into three groups.

1. *IO device-control instructions.* These are transmitted from the IOP to the active IO device and are peculiar to the device in question. Some examples are rewind magnetic tape, skip a line on a printer, and position a magnetic-disk unit's read-write head.

2. *Data-transfer instructions.* These have the form: transfer n words between the active IO device and main storage. Each such instruction contains the data count n, which is stored in the IOP data count register DC, and the initial address of the main-memory-data area to be used, which is placed in the address register AR. The IOP then proceeds to carry out the data transfer. Each time a word is transmitted through the IOP, DC is decremented by 1 and AR is incremented by 1. When DC reaches zero, i.e., all n words have been transferred, the IOP can proceed to the next instruction whose address is in its program counter PC.

3. *IOP control instructions.* These are mainly conditional and unconditional branch instructions not unlike those executed by the CPU.

IOPs and the CPU share a common access path to main memory, usually via a memory control unit and a set of shared communication lines called the *system bus.* Since IO operations are typically very slow compared with CPU speeds, most of the memory-access requests can be expected to come from the CPU. When a memory access is requested by an IOP, it may cause a CPU request to be delayed for one or more memory cycles until the system bus becomes available.

Programming languages. While assembly languages are much easier to use than machine languages, they are quite different from a typical user's problem specification language. Furthermore, different computers have different assembly languages; hence an assembly language program for one machine cannot be used on a different machine. An important development of the mid-1950s was the introduction of automatic programming languages, now called *high-level* languages, which permit a program to be written in a form closer to the user's problem specification than to the machine instruction set [26]. Such languages are intended to be usable on many different computers. They require programs, called *compilers*, to translate the high-level language into the machine language of the particular computer being used.

The first widely used high-level language was FORTRAN (*For*mula *Trans*lation), developed by an IBM group under the direction of John Backus from 1954 to 1957. FORTRAN permits the specification of algebraic operations in a form approximating normal algebraic notation. Thus the vector addition programs of Figs. 1.19 and 1.22 can be replaced by the following two-line FORTRAN program:

$$DO\ 10\ I = 1,\ 1000$$

$$10\quad C(I) = A(I) + B(I)$$

High-level languages were also developed for business applications. These are characterized by instructions that resemble statements in English and operate primarily on alphanumeric information files. One of the earliest such languages was COBOL (*Co*mmon *B*usiness *O*riented *L*anguage), which was specified in 1959 by the CODASYL (*C*onference *o*n *D*ata *S*ystems *L*anguages) committee, a group representing users and manufacturers, and sponsored by the U.S. Department of Defense. FORTRAN and COBOL have continued to be among the most widely used high-level programming languages.

Addressing methods. A source of controversy during the early days of computers was the number of memory addresses to include in each machine language instruction. The IAS and 7094 computers were one-address machines, while the EDVAC had four addresses per instruction. Two-address and three-address machines were also common. As noted earlier, fewer addresses means a reduction in the memory space occupied by an individual instruction. However, this is balanced by the fact that more instructions are required. Thus the FORTRAN addition statement

$$C = A + B$$

can be implemented very naturally by a single instruction in a three-address machine. In a one-address machine, three instructions are required, as in the IAS program of Fig. 1.15.

A number of companies developed machines that permit so-called zero-address instructions. These make use of a special memory organization, called a *stack*. Two of the earliest stack-oriented computers were the English Electric KDF-9 and the Burroughs B5000, both of which were first delivered in 1963. The B5000 was the first of a continuing line of stack computers from Burroughs (now a division of Unisys Corp.). The arithmetic registers of the B5000 are organized as a last-in first-out (LIFO) or pushdown stack. The top two words of the stack are fast CPU registers, while the rest of the stack is in main memory. All instructions take their operands from the top of the stack and place their results in the stack; hence in most cases, no address has to be specified. Thus the instruction

ADD

causes the top two numbers stored in the stack to be removed from the stack and added; the resulting sum is placed in the top of the stack. Two instructions characteristic of stack processing are PUSH X and POP X, which cause the contents of memory location X to be transferred to the stack or from the stack, respectively. Stack instructions simplify the programming of certain types of arithmetic operations by reducing the need for operand address specification. They also facilitate the transfer of control between programs, particularly when recursion is involved (a recursive program can call itself). Successive return addresses can be pushed into the stack and later removed (popped) from the stack in the correct (LIFO) sequence.

Large systems. In the early days, all programs or jobs were run separately, and the computer had to be halted and prepared manually for each new program to be executed. With the improvements in IO equipment and programming that came with second-generation machines, it became feasible to prepare a batch of jobs in advance, store them on magnetic tape, and then have the computer process them in one continuous sequence, placing the results on another magnetic tape. This mode of IO operation management is termed *batch processing*. It also became common to employ a small auxiliary computer to process the input and output tapes off-line, allowing the main computer to devote all its attention to user program execution. Batch processing requires the use of a supervisory program termed a *monitor*, which is permanently resident in main memory. A batch monitor is an example of a system program designed to provide a set of common services to all users of a computer, i.e., it is a rudimentary operating system. Later operating systems were designed to enable a single CPU to process a set of independent programs concurrently, a technique called *multiprogramming*. This is accomplished by the CPU temporarily suspending execution of its current program, beginning execution of another program, and then returning to the first program later. Where possible, a suspended program is transferred to an IOP, which performs any needed IO operations. Consequently, multiprogramming attempts to keep a CPU and one or more IOPs busy by overlapping CPU and IO operations. Multiprogramming systems that process many user programs concurrently in an interactive manner are called *timesharing* systems.

Because of their small size, transistors made it possible to build extremely powerful computers, popularly termed *supercomputers*. Such computers are of special value in areas like weather forecasting and artificial intelligence, where important problems exist that require a vast number of computational steps for their solution. Examples of early supercomputers are the UNIVAC LARC (*Liver-more Atomic Research Computer*) and the IBM 7030 (also called the Stretch computer). These machines introduced some important techniques for increasing effective computation speed by performing several CPU operations simultaneously or in parallel. Unlike the concurrency provided by IOPs, which only perform secondary housekeeping functions in parallel with CPU operations, supercomputers speed up the main CPU computations directly, which is referred to as *parallel processing.* Two major parallel processing techniques developed during the 1950s for the LARC, the 7030, and other computers, were the following:

1. Overlapping the fetching and execution of individual instructions within a single program. This is implemented by special hardware facilities such as pipeline processors and multiple arithmetic-logic units.
2. Overlapping the execution of different programs. This can be achieved by designing systems called *multiprocessors* that have more than one CPU. Like multiprogramming, multiprocessing requires a relatively complex supervisory program.

Both the LARC and the Stretch were commercial failures; nevertheless, they had considerable influence on the design of the next generation of computers.

1.3.2 The Third Generation

1965 may be considered as marking the beginning of the third computer generation, but the distinction between the second and third generations is not very clearcut. The following developments are frequently singled out:

1. Integrated circuits (ICs) began to replace the discrete transistor circuits used in second-generation machines, resulting in a substantial reduction in physical size and cost.
2. Semiconductor (IC) memories began to augment, and ultimately replace, ferrite cores in main-memory designs. The two main types are read-only memories (ROMs) and read-and-write memories, which are usually referred to as random-access memories (RAMs).
3. A technique called microprogramming came into widespread use to simplify the design of CPUs and increase their flexibility.
4. A variety of techniques for concurrent or parallel processing were introduced such as pipelining and multiprocessing. These had the objective of increasing the effective speed at which programs could be executed.
5. Efficient methods for automatic sharing of the facilities or resources of a computer system, e.g., its processors and memory space, were developed and incorporated into operating systems.

The number of different third-generation computers is very great. Probably the most influential computer introduced in the mid-1960s was IBM's System/360 series [5]. This is a family of computers (distinguished by model numbers) intended to cover a wide range of computing performance. The various models are largely compatible in that a program written for one model should be capable of being executed by any other model in the series; only the execution time and, perhaps, the memory space requirements should be affected. The System/360 was announced by IBM in 1964 and first delivered in 1965. Many of its features have become standard in the computer industry. The architecture of this family of machines is discussed in detail in Sec. 1.3.3.

The design of large powerful computers that began with the LARC and the Stretch was continued. Control Data Corporation (CDC) produced a series of large machines beginning with the CDC 6600 in 1964 and continuing with the 7600 delivered in 1969, and the subsequent CYBER series. These machines are characterized by the inclusion of many IOPs (called peripheral processors) with a high degree of autonomy. In addition, each CPU is subdivided into a number of independent processing units which can be operated simultaneously. A CPU organization called pipelining was used to achieve very fast processing in several computers such as the CDC STAR-100 (*St*ring *Ar*ray computer) and the Texas Instruments ASC (*A*dvanced *S*cientific *C*omputer). Another notable supercomputer was ILLIAC IV (*Illi*nois *A*utomatic *C*omputer), designed in the late 1960s at the University of Illinois. ILLIAC IV had 64 separate CPU-like processing elements all supervised by a common control unit and all capable of operating simultaneously.

A contrasting development of this period was the mass production of small low-cost computers called *minicomputers*. The origins of minicomputers can be traced to the LINC (*L*aboratory *I*nstrument *C*omputer) developed at MIT in 1963. The LINC greatly influenced the design of the PDP (*P*rogrammed *D*ata *P*rocessor) series of small computers produced by Digital Equipment Corporation (DEC), which did much to establish the minicomputer market. The first commercial minicomputer was the DEC PDP-5 produced in 1963. It was superceded in 1965 by the very successful PDP-8 series. Minicomputers are characterized by short word lengths (8 to 32 bits), limited hardware and software facilities, and small physical size. Their low cost, however, makes them suitable for a wide variety of applications such as industrial control, where a *dedicated* computer, i.e., a computer which is permanently assigned to one application, is needed. In recent years, improvements in device technology have resulted in minicomputers which are comparable in performance to large second-generation machines and which greatly exceed the performance of most first-generation machines.

Microprogramming. Microprogramming is a technique for implementing the control function of a processor in a systematic and flexible manner. The concept was first enunciated by Maurice V. Wilkes in 1951 [33]. It was implemented in several first- and second-generation machines. However, it was not until the mid-1960s, with its appearance in some models of the IBM System/360 series, that the use of microprogramming became widespread.

Microprogramming may be considered as an alternative to *hardwired* control. A hardwired control unit for a processor is typically a sequential circuit with the general structure shown in Fig. 1.24. A microprogrammed processor control circuit has the structure shown in Fig. 1.25. Each instruction of the processor being controlled causes a sequence of microinstructions, called a *microprogram*, to be fetched from a special ROM or RAM, called a *control memory*. The microinstructions specify the sequence of microoperations or register transfer operations needed to interpret and execute the main instruction. Each instruction fetch from

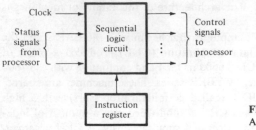

FIGURE 1.24
A hardwired control unit.

main memory thus initiates a sequence of microinstruction fetches from control memory.

Microprogramming provides a simpler and more systematic way of designing control circuits and greatly increases the flexibility of a computer. The instruction set of a microprogrammed machine can be changed merely by replacing the contents of the control memory. This makes it possible for a microprogrammed computer to execute directly programs written in the machine language of a different computer, a process called *emulation*. Microprogrammed control units tend to be more costly and slower than hardwired units, but these drawbacks are generally outweighed by the greater flexibility provided by microprogramming. Because of the close interaction of software and hardware in microprogrammed systems, microprograms are sometimes referred to as *firmware*.

Parallel processing. The increased level of parallel processing characteristic of the third generation was achieved in part by the use of multiple processors with a high degree of autonomy and flexible intrasystem communication facilities. This is illus-

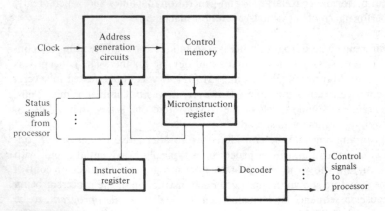

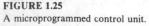

FIGURE 1.25
A microprogrammed control unit.

trated in Fig. 1.26, which shows a possible configuration of the Burroughs B5000 and its successor the B5500. The main memory is partitioned into eight independently accessible modules $M_1:M_8$. These are connected via the memory exchange to two CPUs and four IOPs. The memory exchange, which is a crossbar switching network, permits simultaneous access by the six processors to main memory provided that they each access different modules. A similar interconnection network, the IO exchange, connects the IOPs to up to 32 input-output devices. This organization permits many operations to take place simultaneously.

Parallelism can also be introduced on a lower level by overlapping the fetching and/or the execution of individual instructions by a single CPU. Two distinct methods of achieving this have evolved.

1. More than one unit can be provided to carry out a particular operation, e.g., addition. By employing n independent adders, n additions can be performed simultaneously. This type of structure permits array operations (cf. Example 1.5) to be performed very rapidly.
2. A processing unit can be designed in the form of a pipeline, which allows the execution of a sequence of microoperations to be overlapped.

Figure 1.27 shows how a floating-point adder can be implemented in pipeline form. The addition operation is broken into four independent sequential steps,

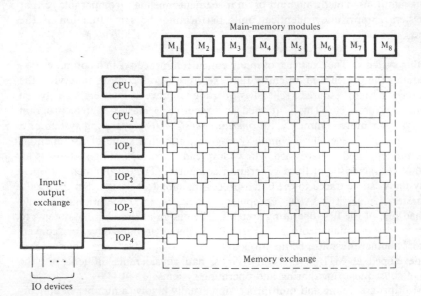

FIGURE 1.26
Organization of a multiprocessor: the Burroughs B5000.

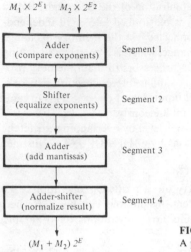

$$M_1 \times 2^{E_1} \quad M_2 \times 2^{E_2}$$

Adder (compare exponents)	Segment 1
Shifter (equalize exponents)	Segment 2
Adder (add mantissas)	Segment 3
Adder-shifter (normalize result)	Segment 4

$$(M_1 + M_2) \, 2^E$$

FIGURE 1.27
A pipelined floating-point adder.

each of which is carried out in a separate subunit, or *segment*, of the pipeline. The intermediate results produced by each segment are transferred to the next segment. The segments are isolated so that at any time each segment can be executing a different add instruction. The pipeline can therefore overlap the execution of four separate additions. The throughput of an n-segment pipeline is comparable to that of a system comprising n identical units performing the same function as the pipeline.

Operating systems. The existence of many concurrent processes in a computer system requires the presence of an entity that exercises overall control, supervises the allocation of system resources, schedules operations, prevents interference between different programs, etc. This is termed an executive, a master control program (Burroughs), or more commonly, an *operating system*. The operating system of a large computer is generally a complex program, although some of its functions may be implemented in hardware. The widespread use of operating systems is an important characteristic of third-generation computers. The development of operating systems can be traced to the batch-processing monitors designed in the 1950s. Manchester University's Atlas computer, which became operational around 1961, had one of the first operating systems. The design of timesharing systems to allow many users simultaneous access to a computer in an interactive, or "conversational," manner must also be mentioned. CTSS (Compatible *T*ime-*S*haring *S*ystem), developed at MIT in the early 1960s, had considerable influence on the design of subsequent timesharing and operating systems.

Multiprogramming and multiprocessing usually involve a number of concurrently executing programs sharing the same main memory. Because main-memory capacity is limited by cost considerations, it is generally impossible to store all executing programs and their data sets in main memory simultaneously. Thus it becomes necessary to allocate memory space dynamically among different competing programs and move or "swap" information back and forth between main and secondary memory as required. A major function of an operating system is to perform these memory management operations automatically.

Programming is greatly simplified if the computer can be viewed as having a single addressable memory of essentially unlimited size to which each programmer has unrestricted access. This is the *virtual-memory* concept, which is considered an attribute of third-generation computers, even though it originated with the one-level-store concept implemented in the Manchester University machines of the late 1940s. To understand virtual-memory systems, we must distinguish between the set of (symbolic) memory addresses specified by a program, called the *logical address space L*, and the set of actual addresses used in main memory, called the *physical address space P*. The L may be larger than the P—hence the term virtual. During execution of the program, each logical address in L is translated into a physical address in P. Thus an address mapping mechanism is needed which implements a function $f: L \rightarrow P$. If it is determined that the specified item is not in main memory, execution of the program is suspended while the relevant item is transferred from secondary to main memory.

It is convenient when implementing a virtual memory system to divide main memory into fixed-sized contiguous areas, called *page frames*, and to divide programs into pieces of the same size, called *pages*. In a paging system, all swapping and reallocation of stored information is by pages. Figure 1.28 contains a flowchart of a typical *demand paging algorithm*. A page swap takes place only when the page containing a word required by the CPU is not currently stored in main memory. When this condition, called a *page fault*, occurs, the execution of the program in question is suspended until the required page is brought into main memory. In a multiprogramming environment, the CPU can switch to another program while the page swap takes place. Since page swapping is basically an IO operation, it can proceed independently under control of an IOP.

A simple mechanism for dynamically allocating memory space is a *base register*. This is a CPU register, which is controlled by the operating system. Every memory address generated by a program then has the contents of a base register, called a base address, added to it. The operating system can change all addresses in a program during execution by the simple expedient of changing the contents of the program's base register. In a memory management system using paging, it is convenient to store page addresses in the base registers, in which case they may be called *page registers*.

Parallel processing by the CPU implies a need to be able to transfer several words simultaneously between the CPU and main memory. This can be satisfied by providing multiple memory modules that can be accessed independently, and by including buffer storage registers in the CPU. Both these features exist in rudimentary form in the IBM 7094. The development of semiconductor IC RAM technology made it feasible to provide relatively large high-speed buffer memories to act as an intermediate store between the CPU and main memory. These memories are now called *caches* and are used for storing both instructions and data.

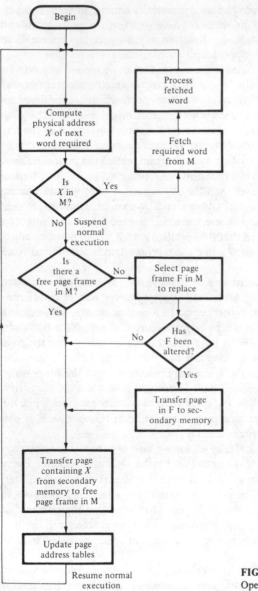

FIGURE 1.28
Operation of a demand paging system.

1.3.3 A Third-Generation Computer Family

In this section we examine the large and important class of third-generation computers that began with the announcement of the System/360 by IBM in 1964 [5]. The System/370 introduced by IBM in 1970 retains the basic System/360 architecture, but has a number of performance improvements or "enhancements."

IBM has continued to add new computers to this family from time to time using various system names, for instance, the 4300 and 3090 subseries, which were introduced in 1979 and 1985, respectively. The design of all these machines, which we will refer to collectively as the *S/360-370 series,* has been extraordinarily influential, and has become a de facto standard for large computers produced by many manufacturers. For example, Amdahl Corp.'s computers, beginning with the Amdahl 470 series introduced in 1976, can be considered as members of the S/360-370 series in that they are designed to execute the same instruction set, be controlled by the same operating systems, and accept the same peripheral devices as the corresponding IBM machines. The Ryad computer series produced by the Soviet bloc countries in Eastern Europe is also S/360-370–compatible in the above sense.

With the advent of the System/360, the distinction between a computer's architecture and its implementation became apparent. As defined by the System/360 designers [5], the *architecture* of a computer is its structure and behavior as seen by an assembly-language programmer, and includes the following: information formats; addressing modes; instruction set; and the general organization of the CPU registers, main memory, and IO system. The *implementation,* on the other hand, refers to the logical and physical design techniques used to realize the architecture in any specific instance. The term (computer) *organization* is sometimes employed to mean the logical aspects of the implementation. Thus all the members of the S/360-370 series share a common architecture, but they have many different implementations. For example, some S/360-370 CPUs employ fast hardwired control units, whereas others use a slower but more flexible microprogrammed approach to implementing the common instruction set. As semiconductor technology has developed over the years, the types of integrated circuits employed in these processors have changed considerably in complexity and speed.

The major design goals of System/360 have been well documented [3, 6].

1. The members of the series were to be equally suited for business and scientific data-processing tasks. The required generality was achieved in part by including many data types and providing both binary and decimal (i.e., binary coded decimal) arithmetic instructions.
2. The different models were to be program-compatible, so that users starting with a small model could move with ease to larger models as their computing needs increased. All models were required to be able to execute a common instruction set, despite differences in logical and physical implementation.
3. The design was intended to be open-ended in the sense that new or additional units such as processors or I/O devices could be easily attached to the system. This objective greatly influenced the design of the IO subsystem, which included several types of IOPs ("channels") and a standard IO interface connecting IOPs to IO devices.
4. The system was to be capable of supporting both multiprogramming and multiprocessing. To this end, a very large and complex operating system OS/360 was designed.

Figure 1.29 shows some original design parameters for two early System/360 models, the small Model 30 and the large Model 70. These parameters indicate the wide performance range desired.

System structure. Figure 1.30 illustrates the general structure of a typical S/360-370 series computer. It bears a strong resemblance to that of the IBM 7094; cf. Fig. 1.20. Two types of IOPs are used: multiplexer channels and selector channels. Multiplexer channels can interleave (multiplex) data transmission between main memory and several IO devices, whereas only one IO device connected to a selector channel can transmit or receive information at a given time. Selector channels are intended for use with very high speed IO devices, e.g., magnetic disk units, while multiplexer channels are intended for controlling a number of low-speed devices, e.g., printers, card readers, and card punches. Each IOP is connected to a bus, called the I/O interface, which is composed of a standard set of data and control lines. The IO interface bus is shared by all devices attached to a given IOP. An IO device, or a group of IO devices of the same type, is supervised locally by a control unit which is peculiar to the type of IO device in question. An S/360-370 IOP is generally similar to the channel used in the IBM 7094 computer, which was discussed in detail in Sec. 1.3.1.

Data formats. The basic unit of storage employed is the *byte,* or 8 bits; a byte is capable of representing up to 256 different symbols. Every byte location in main memory can be accessed directly. The term "word" is used for a group of 4 bytes. Numerical data can be represented in four ways: unpacked or "zoned" decimal, packed decimal, fixed-point binary, and floating-point binary, as illustrated in Fig. 1.31.

The decimal formats are so called because each digit of a decimal number is represented separately by a 4-bit field, and corresponds to a power of 10. The following standard coding scheme known as *binary-coded decimal (BCD)* is used to represent the 10 decimal digits by means of 0s and 1s.

Subsystem	Design parameter	Model 30	Model 70
Main memory	Memory cycle time	2 μs	1 μs
	Memory bus width	8 bits	64 bits
	Number of interleaved modules	1	2
	Maximum data-transfer rate	4×10^6 bits/s	128×10^6 bits/s
CPU	Nominal delay per gate	30 ns	6 ns
	CPU cycle time	1 μs	0.2 μs
	Working register technology	Ferrite core	Semiconductor
	CPU internal bus width	8 bits	64 bits
	Relative computing speed	1	50

FIGURE 1.29
Design parameters of two early models in the IBM System/360 series.

Decimal digit	BCD form
0	0000
1	0001
2	0010
3	0011
4	0100
5	0101
6	0110
7	0111
8	1000
9	1001

In the S/360-370's unpacked (zoned) decimal format, each byte of a number stores only one BCD digit, which occupies the right halfbyte position. This format is typically employed only when communicating with IO devices that expect a single digit in each byte. The left halfbyte (the zone) has no numerical significance, except in the low-order (rightmost) byte where it is used to store the number's sign; see Fig. 1.31. The packed decimal format makes more efficient use of the available storage space by placing two BCD digits in each byte; this format is typically used when large amounts of decimal data must be stored in the computer's internal

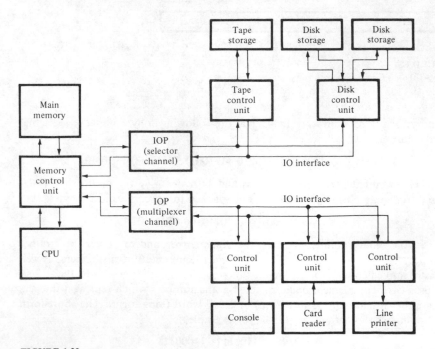

FIGURE 1.30
Structure of an S/360-370 series computer.

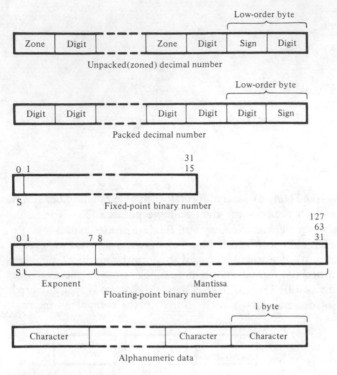

FIGURE 1.31
S/360-370 data formats.

memory. Thus the number -12345 has the following 5-byte unpacked decimal representation:

$$-12345 = 11110001 \ 11110010 \ 11110011 \ 11110100 \ 11010101$$

with 1111 occupying the zone positions and 1101 denoting the minus sign. (1100 is used to denote plus.) The corresponding packed form requires just 3 bytes:

$$-12345 = 00010010 \ 00110100 \ 01011101$$

In the binary number formats, the digits correspond to powers of 2 rather than powers of 10. This allows a more compact representation of numbers, as well as faster implementation of arithmetic functions. Like earlier machines, the S/360-370 uses twos-complement code for fixed-point numbers which represent integers using either a half word (short form) or a full word (long form). The short-form fixed-point representation of -12345, for example, is

$$-12345 = 11001111 \ 11000111$$

The S/360-370's floating-point format consists of a mantissa, which is a fraction that is usually, but not always, normalized by eliminating leading zeros, and a

7-bit exponent, which represents a power of 16. Bit 0 is the sign of the mantissa. Floating-point numbers may be one, two, or four words long. Alphanumeric data is represented by a variable sequence of bytes, where each byte represents a character in some code such as EBCDIC (*E*xtended *B*inary *C*oded *D*ecimal *I*nterchange *C*ode).

CPU organization. The CPU structure common to many S/360-370 models is depicted in Fig. 1.32. The arithmetic-logic unit is divided logically into three subunits with the following functions.

1. Fixed-point operations, including binary integer arithmetic and effective address computation
2. Floating-point operations
3. Variable-length operations, including decimal arithmetic and character string operations

Two sets of independent addressable registers are used for data and address storage. The 16 general registers can be used to store operands and results and can also be used as index registers. Four floating-point registers are used in floating-point

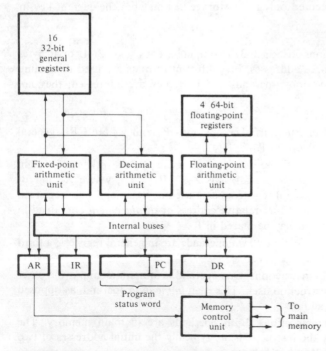

FIGURE 1.32
CPU structure of S/360-370 series computers.

arithmetic. The general and floating-point registers augment the accumulator and multiplier-quotient registers of earlier computers. The data register DR, the address register AR, and the instruction register IR are standard. A *program status word* PSW (actually two 32-bit words), stored in a special register, indicates program status, interruptions ("interrupts") that the CPU may respond to, and the address of the next instruction to be executed. The CPU responds to an interrupt request by storing the current PSW in main memory and fetching a new PSW. This PSW specifies the program to be executed to process the interrupt, e.g., an error-handling routine from the operating system. After the interrupt program has been executed, the CPU can retrieve the old PSW from main memory and resume execution of the interrupted program.

The CPU is at any time in one of several control states. When it is executing a routine from the operating system, i.e., the operating system has explicit control of the CPU, it is said to be in the *supervisor state*. Certain instructions can be executed by the CPU in this state only. The CPU is normally in the *user* or *problem state* when executing user programs. The state of the CPU at any time is specified by its PSW.

The PSW register also contains a key used for memory protection. Main memory is divided into blocks of 2K bytes, each of which is assigned a storage key. The storage key specifies the type of access allowed (read only, read and write, neither read nor write). An operation that involves accessing information in a particular 2K-block B is executed only if B's storage key matches the current key in the PSW register.

Instruction set. Instructions in S/360-370 computers consist of 2, 4, or 6 bytes and can contain up to three addresses. Five different formats are used depending on the locations of the various operands and how they are addressed; they are illustrated in Fig. 1.33.

1. RR (register-register) instructions. The operands R_1 and R_2 are CPU general registers. The result is placed in R_1.
2. RX (register-index) instructions. One operand is in R_1, the other is in main memory. The effective memory address is $X_2 + B_2 + D_2$, where X_2 and B_2 denote the contents of general registers being used as index and base registers, respectively, and D_2 is the 12-bit relative address or *displacement* contained in the instruction. The result may be placed in R_1.
3. RS (register-storage) instructions. Two operands are in general registers; a third is in main memory.
4. SI (storage-immediate) instructions. One operand is in main memory, the other is in bits 8:15 of the instruction itself. This is an *immediate* operand, as opposed to the usual operand address.
5. SS (storage-storage) instructions. Both operands are in main memory. The addresses specified by the instructions are typically the initial addresses of two operand fields, whose length is L bytes.

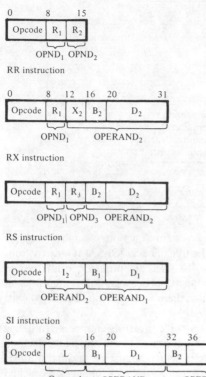

FIGURE 1.33
Basic S/360-370 instruction formats.

The CPU instruction set of the S/360-370 family includes all the major types encountered earlier: data transfer, arithmetic, logical (Boolean), branch, and IO instructions [18]. Close to 200 distinct opcode types were defined for System/360; this relatively large number reflects the profusion of different data types and addressing modes that are available. An indication of this is given by Fig. 1.34, which lists most of the instructions available for performing addition. Subsequent enhancements to the series have introduced new instruction types; for example, the System/370 architecture defined in 1970 contains 40 new instruction types including yet another add instruction AXR (add normalized extended). Among the S/360-370 instructions not discussed previously are an SS instruction called MOVE, which can transfer a block of information of specified length from one part of main memory to another. Certain program-control instructions are called *privileged* because they can be executed by the CPU only when it is in the supervisor

Opcode mnemonic	Instruction type	Operand type
A	RX	Long fixed-point
AR	RR	Long fixed-point
AH	RX	Short fixed-point
AP	SS	Packed decimal
AD	RX	Long floating-point (normalized)
ADR	RR	Long floating-point (normalized)
AE	RX	Short floating-point (normalized)
AW	RX	Long floating-point (unnormalized)
AU	RX	Short floating-point (unnormalized)

FIGURE 1.34
Some S/360-370 addition instructions.

state. They are intended for such operating system functions as modifying the PSW, altering storage protection keys, and the like. The S/360-370 IO instructions are similar to those of the 7094; they allow the CPU to initiate, terminate, and monitor the execution of an IO program by an IO processor. A large number of IO instructions (called *commands* to distinguish them from CPU instructions) exist which are executed by the IOPs.

There are several S/360-370 instructions for converting numbers from one format to another. These include PACK, which converts an unpacked decimal number to the packed format; UNPK (unpack), which changes a decimal number from packed to unpacked; CVB (convert to binary), which changes a packed decimal number to fixed-point binary form; and CVD (convert to decimal), which changes a fixed-point binary number to packed decimal form. The availability of both decimal or binary formats gives the programmer the flexibility to simplify or speed up certain programming tasks. Suppose, for example, that unpacked decimal data must be read from an input device, undergo some arithmetic processing denoted by OP, and the results must be transferred to an output device in packed decimal form. Generally speaking, this task may be implemented using only decimal arithmetic as follows.

Input the required unpacked decimal data.

Convert to packed form using PACK.

Execute the appropriate (packed) decimal version of OP.

Output the decimal results.

This approach has the advantage of allowing all the program steps to be expressed in a short and fairly natural decimal form. Alternatively, the following program structure can be used.

Input the required unpacked decimal data.

Convert to packed form using PACK.

Convert to binary form using CVB.

Execute the appropriate binary version of OP.

Convert the results to (packed) decimal form using CVD.

Output the decimal results.

In this case, the program is complicated by the need to convert the IO data to and from binary form. However the internal arithmetic operations represented by OP can usually be executed faster in their binary versions than in decimal. If the time saved exceeds the data conversion time, then it is preferable to use binary arithmetic for OP. This situation is typical of scientific computation. If, as is often the case in commercial data processing, there is little arithmetic but large amounts of decimal IO operations to be done, then the first, decimal, version of the program is preferable.

Operating system. One of IBM's original design goals was to develop a common system control program or operating system for all S/360-370 computers. This was intended to provide largely automatic management of the available computer resources and allow multiple users to share these resources efficiently. In fact, a family of operating systems, which we collectively term *OS/360-370*, has evolved since 1964; its members vary in the types of S/360-370 computers they control (small, large, timesharing, multiprogramming, etc.), and the control functions they provide. DOS (*D*isk *O*perating *S*ystem), for instance, was designed for smaller System/360 computers equipped with disk units as secondary memory. Another OS/360-370 operating system called MVS (*M*ultiple *V*irtual *S*torage) was introduced in the mid-1970s for use in large S/360-370 installations, including those with multiple CPUs. It can provide virtual memory and IO support for a large number of independent users with widely varying system requirements.

The main functions provided by a typical OS/360-370 operating system are memory, processor (CPU), and IO management. The physical and virtual memory spaces are partitioned into blocks of pages that can be assigned to different jobs. Demand paging (see Fig. 1.28) is used to swap pages between main and secondary memory. As discussed earlier, when a page fault occurs, the desired new page is transferred to main memory, replacing an old page. The page that is replaced is the one that has not been used (referenced) for the longest time; this is termed the *LRU (least recently used)* replacement algorithm and is widely used in operating system design. User programs are selected for processing by a part of the CPU called the *job scheduler*. Based on information provided by the user which specifies the (system) programs to be executed, the memory space needed, the IO devices needed, the anticipated execution time, etc., OS/360-370 assigns the jobs to various priority classes such as *CPU bound* (requiring relatively little IO processing), *IO bound* (requiring more IO processing than CPU processing), balanced (similar CPU and IO processing requirements), or express (highest priority for execution). The job scheduler then, based on their execution priority and the current utilization of the required system resources, selects jobs for execution from the pool of available jobs in a way that attempts to maximize the system's overall job execution rate or *throughput*. Other parts of the operating system control the assignment of jobs to specific CPUs and IO devices. A substantial part of OS/360-370 is also devoted to the management of data files stored in the secondary memory subsystem.

The user communicates with the operating system via *job control* statements accompanying the user's program. These statements are written in a special "job control" language called JCL, which can be viewed as a command language for OS/360-370. For example, the JCL statements for compiling a FORTRAN program via a compiler named FORTRANC have the following general form:

```
//JOB1      JOB     USER=DOE, TIMELIMIT=5
//          EXEC    FORTRANC
//OUTPUT    DD      UNIT=DISK7, SPACE=(CYL,(10)), . . .
//INPUT     DD      *
    {FORTRAN source program goes here}
/*
```

The JCL statements are identified by the // prefix. The first, JOB, statement specifies the user's name DOE and the job name JOB1. The JOB statement may also be used to place a limit on the job's total CPU execution time, and indirectly on its execution cost. The operating system automatically terminates the job when the specified time limit of 5 s is exceeded. The EXEC statement names the program to be executed, in this case the compiler FORTRANC, which would be stored in a system program library. The DD (*data definition*) statements define the IO data sets to be used by the program named in the EXEC statement, including their location, size, and format. In the present example, the output data (the object program created by the compilation) is to be stored in the disk unit named DISK7 in an area of size 10 "cylinders." (Certain other formatting information must also be supplied here.) The second DD statement defines the input data set, namely, the source program to be compiled. The asterisk indicates that the program in question follows immediately in standard 80-column punched-card format.

As the foregoing example indicates, the characteristics of the particular operating system being used are bound into a user's program in a way that makes the program unusable under other operating systems without modifications that may be quite extensive. Since many similar but not fully compatible versions of OS/360-370 exist, a computer center might be required to make temporary changes of operating system periodically to meet all its users' needs. To avoid the many operational difficulties resulting from frequent operating system switches, IBM developed a special form of operating system for S/360-370 machines called VM (*Virtual Machine*). VM multiplexes the system resources between the users in such a way that each user appears to have undivided access to all the machine's resources. In other words, the user appears to have a separate copy of the entire machine; this copy is termed a *virtual machine*. Each virtual machine is logically isolated from all others; consequently it can be controlled by its own separate operating system. This leads to the system organization depicted in Fig. 1.35, where

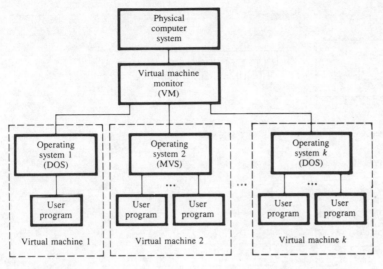

FIGURE 1.35
Role of the virtual machine monitor VM.

several different operating systems are being used concurrently. System programs like VM that create a virtual machine interface are called *virtual machine monitors*.

1.4 THE VLSI ERA

Since the 1960s the dominant technology for manufacturing computer components has been the integrated circuit (IC) [7]. This technology has evolved steadily from ICs containing just a few transistors to those containing hundreds of thousands of transistors; the latter case is termed *very large-scale integration*, or VLSI. The impact of VLSI technology on computer design has been profound. It has made it possible to fabricate an entire CPU, main memory, or similar device with a single IC that can be mass produced at very low cost. This has resulted in new classes of machines such as inexpensive personal computers, and high-performance parallel processors that contain thousands of CPUs. The term *fourth generation* is occasionally applied to VLSI-based computer architecture.

1.4.1 Integrated Circuits

An *integrated circuit (IC)* incorporates a complete transistor circuit into a tiny rectangle or "chip" of semiconductor material, typically silicon. The IC chip is then mounted in a suitable package that protects it and provides electrical connection points (pins or leads) to allow several ICs to be connected to one another, to IO devices, and to power supplies. Figure 1.36 depicts two representative IC package types. In the *dual in-line package* (DIP) of Fig. 1.36*a*, the pins

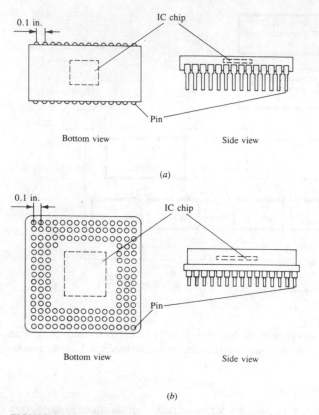

FIGURE 1.36
Integrated circuit packages: (*a*) 28-pin dual in-line package (DIP); (*b*) 144-pin pin-grid-array (PGA) package.

are organized in two parallel rows with 0.1 in. (2.54 mm) spacing between adjacent pins in each row. For very complex chips requiring a hundred or more pins, a *pin-grid array* (PGA) package such as that illustrated in Fig. 1.36*b* may be used. Here the pins are also 0.1 in. apart, but substantially less surface area is needed to accommodate a given number of pins.

A complete computer system can be constructed by mounting a set of ICs (and other required components such as discrete electronic devices) on carriers or substrates that provide both mechanical support for the components and a means for interconnecting them. A typical IC carrier is a circuit board made of fiberglass or a similar insulating material. The interconnections can be formed either by discrete wires or by conductors that are printed—again a manufacturing technique that facilitates low-cost mass production—in one or more layers on the circuit board. In the latter case, the substrate is called a *printed-circuit board* (PCB). Finally, a set of circuit boards can be mounted in a metal enclosure or cabinet that contains power supplies, cooling fans to dissipate the heat generated by the ICs as they operate, and possibly some IO equipment. Complex packaging technologies have also been developed to allow even more ICs to be packed into a given volume. For example, the *thermal conduction modules* developed by IBM and used for some recent S/360-370 series computers accommodate 100 or more IC chips on a tilelike ceramic substrate about 90 mm on the side and 5 mm thick. Within this substrate are 33 layers of conductors, while an array of 1800 pins intended for external connections covers the bottom of the substrate. The entire package is enclosed in a metal housing that is cooled via chilled water.

IC types. Within IC technology, many subtechnologies exist that are distinguished by the manufacturing processes employed and the physical behavior of the resulting circuits. Two of the more important of these technologies are *bipolar* and *MOS*. They both use transistors as the basic switching elements; they differ, however, in the polarities of the charges associated with the primary carriers of electric current within the IC chips. Bipolar circuits use both negative carriers (electrons) and positive carriers (holes). MOS circuits use field-effect transistors in which there is only one type of charge carrier: positive in the case of *P*-type MOS and negative in the case of *N*-type MOS. The term MOS (*metal oxide semiconductor*) describes the materials from which MOS circuits are typically formed; the term unipolar might be more appropriate, but it is not used. An important MOS subtechnology called *CMOS* (*complementary* MOS) combines *N*- and *P*-type MOS transistors in the same IC in a very efficient manner. MOS ICs are generally smaller and consume less power than the corresponding bipolar circuits. On the other hand, bipolar ICs generally have faster switching speeds. Although most ICs are presently manufactured from silicon, increasing attention is being given to other semiconducting materials such as gallium arsenide. Gallium arsenide ICs are more difficult to process than silicon ICs, but they are inherently faster by a factor of about 5.

Integrated circuits may be roughly classified on the basis of their *density*, which is defined either as the number of transistors included in a chip, or else as the number logic gates per chip, where a typical logic gate is composed of about five transistors. The earliest ICs—the first commercial IC appeared in 1961—contained from 1 to about 10 gates; these are now said to employ *small-scale integration* (SSI). *Medium-scale integration* (MSI) implies a density of 10 to 100 gates per chip, while the term *large-scale integration* (LSI) covers ICs containing hundreds or thousands of gates. The term *very large-scale integration* (VLSI) is employed for the densest ICs, such as the 1M-bit (2^{10}-bit) memory chips first marketed in 1986, each of which contains more than 1 million MOS transistors. The economically achievable IC density has increased steadily over the years as a result of improvements in IC manufacturing techniques; see Fig. 1.37. Especially noteworthy has been the continued reduction in the physical dimensions of the transistors and their on-chip interconnections, which, of course, allows a chip of fixed area to accommodate larger and larger circuits. A typical VLSI IC chip has an area of about 1 cm^2, and internal connections that are about 1 μm wide. Because IC

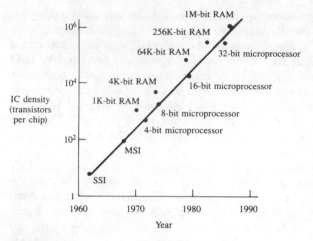

FIGURE 1.37
Evolution of the density of commercial ICs.

manufacture is almost entirely automated (in many respects it resembles a printing process), the cost of making a complex IC is small provided a high production volume is maintained. Furthermore, this cost is not greatly affected by IC density. ICs are presently manufactured in huge quantities in all density ranges from SSI to VLSI. The characteristics of many of these ICs (functions performed, pin configurations, electrical requirements, nomenclature, etc.) e.g., the 7400 series of SSI/MSI bipolar ICs originally defined by Texas Instruments Inc., have become standardized.

LSI circuits began to be produced in large quantities around 1970 for computer main memories and pocket calculators. For the first time it became possible to fabricate a CPU or even an entire computer (excluding IO devices, which cannot be miniaturized) on a single IC chip. A CPU or similar programmable processor on a single IC or, occasionally, several ICs, is called a *microprocessor*. A one-chip computer, or a computer assembled from a few LSI/VLSI circuits including a microprocessor, memory, and IO interface circuits, is called a *microcomputer*. (Note that the prefix *micro* in the terms microprocessor and microcomputer refers to physical size only; it has nothing to do with whether or not microprogrammed control is used.) Because of the low manufacturing costs noted above, microprocessors and microcomputers are very inexpensive. This enables them to be sold to high-volume users at prices comparable to those of the discrete transistors used in second-generation machines, e.g., a few dollars per component. Low cost and small size also make microcomputers suitable for many applications where computers were not previously used, e.g., toys and domestic appliances.

VLSI design. IC technology has not only introduced a new class of mass-produced or off-the-shelf computer components in the form of standard microprocessors and microcomputers, it has also made it possible for designers to produce nonstandard or "custom" computer components quickly and at relatively low cost. This has resulted from the introduction of computer-aided design (CAD) techniques for IC design that can easily be coupled to the already highly automated IC fabrication technology. The influential VLSI design methodology due to Carver Mead and Lynn Conway [20] enables custom MOS ICs to be produced as follows:

1. The proposed design is "drawn" or laid out in terms of cells whose complexity can vary from a single transistor to a complex processor. Simplified design rules concerning transistor dimensions, interconnection spacing, etc., make this design process accessible to computer designers with only a modest knowledge of IC technology. Computer programs have been developed that convert the graphical input into a computer file in some standard format. Typically the CRT screen of a computer, termed a CAD workstation, serves as the designer's drawing board.
2. A variety of CAD programs have been developed to assist in the design process by, for instance, allowing trial layouts to be easily modified, and allowing cells from a precomputed cell library to be incorporated into the current design. Programs called simulators are used to verify the correctness of a proposed design whose complexity may make it very difficult to check manually.
3. The computer file describing the proposed circuit is processed automatically to create the optical templates or *masks*, which are the printing plates from which the ICs are manufactured. Even if only a few copies of a particular IC are required, some economies of scale can be achieved by combining a group of different designs on the same set of masks as a "multiproject chip."

1.4.2 Microprocessors and Microcomputers

Microprocessors. The first commercial microprocessor was Intel Corp.'s 4004, which appeared in 1971. This was the CPU member of a set of four *P*-MOS LSI ICs called the MCS-4 (*Micro*computer *Set* Four), which was originally designed for use in a calculator but was marketed as a "programmable controller for logic replacement" [15]. The 4004 is referred to as a 4-bit microprocessor since it processes only 4 bits of data at a time, i.e., the CPU word size is 4 bits. This very short word size is due mainly to the limitations imposed by the maximum IC density then achievable. The MSC-4 series was soon followed by a large number of microprocessor families produced by various manufacturers; most of these employ the faster *N*-MOS and CMOS technologies. As IC densities increased with the rapid development of IC manufacturing technology, the power and the performance of the microprocessors also increased. This is reflected in the increase in the CPU word size to 4, 8, 16, and, by the mid-1980s, 32 bits; see Fig. 1.37. The smaller (4- and 8-bit) microprocessors have relatively simple instruction sets, e.g., no floating-point instructions, but they are nevertheless suitable as controllers (the "logic replacements" cited above) for a very wide range of applications such as automobile engines and microwave ovens. The larger (16- and 32-bit) and more recent microprocessor families have gradually acquired most of the features of large computers (IOPs, operating systems, and the like). Many of the distinctions made in the past between large (mainframe), mini-, and microcomputer systems are much less valid today. For example, by the mid-1980s it became possible to implement the basic S/360-370 "mainframe" architecture by a single-chip microprocessor, the Micro/370 [10].

As the microprocessor industry has matured, several families of microprocessors have evolved into de facto industrial standards with multiple manufacturers and numerous "support" chips including RAMs, ROMs, IO controllers, etc. One such family traces its origins to the 8080, an 8-bit microprocessor introduced by Intel in 1973. Among the widely used 8-bit microprocessors derived from, and largely compatible with, the 8080 are the Intel 8085, Zilog Corp.'s Z80, and National Semiconductor Corp.'s NSC800, the latter having been introduced in 1980. Figure 1.38 shows the internal structure of the one-chip Intel 8085 microprocessor [16]; the 8080 differs primarily in its bus structure and power requirements. The CPU and memory word size is 8 bits, while the memory address size is 16 bits, enabling the 8085 to address up to 2^{16} or 64K 8-bit words (bytes) of main

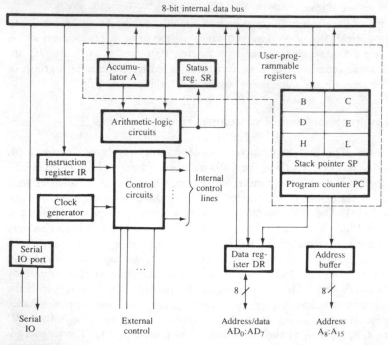

FIGURE 1.38
Structure of the Intel 8085 microprocessor.

memory. Because of the pin limitations imposed by the 8085's 40-pin DIP package, the pins for transmitting addresses and data between the CPU and main memory are shared or multiplexed; first a 16-bit address word is transmitted to memory via pins $AD_0:AD_7$ and $A_8:A_{15}$; then the corresponding data is sent via pins $AD_0:AD_7$. The address/data lines AD and A are used to attach IO devices as well as main memory to the 8085; there is also, however, a separate serial (2-line) connection port for IO devices.

The 8085 has over 70 instruction types, which include all the basic data-transfer, data processing, and program control instructions. Input-output operations are controlled by two instructions called IN and OUT, which cause a byte of information to be transferred between the accumulator A and the addressed IO device via the $AD_0:AD_7$ lines; this is a basic form of programmed IO. The main arithmetic instructions are addition and subtraction of 8-bit fixed-point (binary and decimal) numbers. Addition and subtraction of longer numbers, fixed-point multiplication and division, and all floating-point operations must be implemented by software routines. Note, however, that for many microprocessor applications these more complex operations are rarely needed. The 8085 has six 8-bit registers designated B, C, D, E, H, and L, which, in addition to the accumulator A, can be used as addressable general-purpose or scratch-pad registers for temporary storage of data in the CPU. The 5 bits forming the 8085's status (flag) register SR are set or reset to indicate certain conditions resulting from instruction execution such as an all-zero result, a negative result, or overflow from an arithmetic operation.

The register pairs B.C, D.E, and H.L, where $R_1.R_2$ denotes the concatenation of R_1 and R_2, can be treated as 16-bit registers for storing memory addresses. The 16-bit program counter PC maintains the address of the next instruction byte required from main memory in the usual manner. An important address register found in the 8085 and, indeed, most modern computers, is the *stack pointer* SP. This is designed to address (point to) the next available location at the top of a user-defined pushdown stack area in main memory. Pushdown stacks were mentioned previously (Sec. 1.3.1) as an alternative to general-purpose CPU registers employed by certain "stack" computers. In this case, the stack is intended only to facilitate the transfer of control between two programs. For example, to call (transfer control to) a subroutine named SUB1, the 8085 instruction

CALL SUB1

is used. CALL causes the current contents of PC to be transferred (pushed) into the top of the stack region under the control of SP. Then the address SUB1 is placed in PC causing the subroutine in question to begin execution. The contents of SP are automatically adjusted to account for the new address in the stack. Program control is returned to the first program by including the instruction RET (return) in the subroutine code. Execution of RET causes the CPU to retrieve (pop) the last address stored in the stack top and transfer it to PC, thereby returning control to the original calling program; again SP is adjusted automatically to point to the new stack top. Note that if a sequence of n (nested) calls are made, the last-in first-out access method of the stack ensures that the return addresses are retrieved in the proper order by executing n return instructions.

Another important 8-bit microprocessor is the 6800 introduced by Motorola Inc. in 1974. Like the 8080, the 6800 gave rise to a large family of microprocessors and support ICs with varying degrees of hardware and software compatibility. As microprocessors moved into the 16/32-bit range in the 1980s, new families appeared that retained only a modest resemblance to their 8-bit predecessors. The Intel 8085 microprocessor was succeeded by the 16-bit 8086 and 80286 series, and subsequently by the 32-bit 80386. The corresponding successor of the Motorola 6800 was the 68000 series. Early members of this family, including the 68000 microprocessor chip can be regarded as 16-bit implementations of a 32-bit architecture. We now examine one microprocessor in that series, the 68020, which is a full-fledged 32-bit machine that provides a good illustration of commercial VLSI technology circa 1985.

Example 1.7 The Motorola 68020 32-bit microprocessor [19,24]. The 68020 is a high-performance one-chip microprocessor intended to function as the CPU of a general-purpose computer controlled by a multiuser operating system. Physically it consists of a high-density CMOS integrated circuit composed of almost 200,000 transistors, which is housed in a 114-pin PGA package. The functional organization of the 68020 is that of a third-generation mainframe computer, and is shown in Fig. 1.39. The data processing or execution unit contains 16 general-purpose 32-bit data and address registers, and the arithmetic circuits needed to execute a full set of fixed-point (but not floating-point) instructions. Instruction interpretation and other control functions are implemented by a microprogrammed control unit. As the length of the data registers indicates, the 68020 is designed to handle 32-bit words (termed "long" words in 68000-series literature) efficiently, but instructions are also provided to handle operands of 1, 8, 16 and 64 bits. Memory addresses are 32 bits long, permitting a total of 2^{32} different addresses to be used. As in most modern computers since the System/360, main memory is organized as an array of individually addressable bytes. Thus the maximum memory size of a 68000-series computer is 2^{32} bytes, also referred to as 4 gigabytes (4G bytes). Like their 8-bit predecessor, the 6800, 68000-series processors share the available address space between main memory devices (ROMs and RAMs) and IO devices. Consequently, the same data-transfer (MOVE) instructions used for CPU-memory transfers are also used for IO operations. This design technique, which eliminates the need for a special class of IO instructions is called *memory-mapped IO*, and is contrasted with the more common *IO-mapped IO* found in such machines as the S/360-370 and 8085.

The 68020 has about 70 distinct instruction types, including some not in the original 68000 microprocessor; these are summarized in Fig. 1.40. A given instruction such as MOVE can be defined with several different types of operands, and the operands can be addressed in a variety of different ways. For example, the assembly-language instruction

MOVE.L D1, A6

causes the entire contents (a long word denoted by the opcode suffix .L) of data register D1 to be copied to address register A6. If .L is replaced by .B, then the resulting instruction

MOVE.B D1, A6

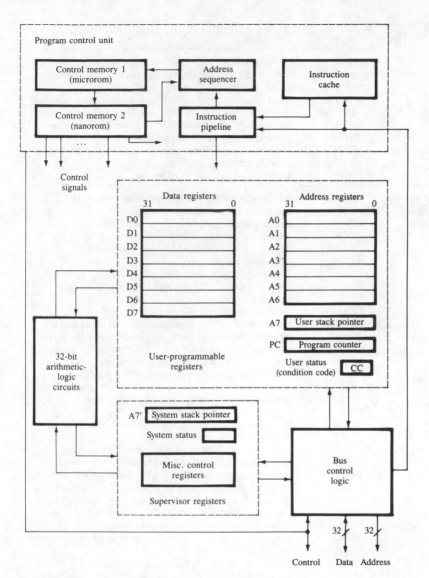

FIGURE 1.39
Structure of the Motorola 68020 microprocessor.

causes only the byte stored in the low-order position (bits 0:7) of D1 to be copied to the corresponding part of A6. In addition to the *direct addressing* mode illustrated by this example, the 68020 has a number of other addressing modes which give the programmer considerable flexibility in accessing data. Figure 1.41 gives an example of a 68020 assembly-language code that illustrates several of the available addressing methods. This program adds two 1000-number vectors A and B to produce a third

Instruction type	Opcode	Description
Data transfer	EXG	Exchange (swap) contents of two registers
	MOVE	Move (copy) data unchanged from source to destination
	MOVEA	Move data to address register
	MOVEC	Move data to or from control register (privileged instruction)
	MOVEM	Move multiple data to or from specified list of registers
	MOVEP	Move data between register and alternate bytes of memory
	MOVEQ	Move "quick" (8-bit) immediate data to register
	MOVES	Move data using address space specified by a control register (privileged instruction)
	SWAP	Swap left and right halves of register
Data processing	ABCD	Add decimal (BCD) numbers with carry (extend) flag
	ADD	Add binary (twos-complement) numbers
	ADDA	Add to address register (unsigned binary addition)
	ADDI	Add immediate binary operand
	ADDQ	Add "quick" (3-bit) immediate binary operand
	ADDX	Add binary with carry (extension) flag
	ANDx	Bitwise logical AND ($x = $ I denotes immediate operand)
	ASx	Arithmetic left ($x = $ L) or right ($x = $ R) shift with sign extension
	CLR	Clear operand by resetting all bits to 0
	DIVx	Divide signed ($x = $ S) or unsigned ($x = $ U) binary numbers
	EORx	Bitwise logical EXCLUSIVE OR ($x = $ I denotes immediate operand)
	EXT	Extend the sign bit of subword to fill register
	LSx	Logical (simple) left ($x = $ L) or right ($x = $ R) shift
	MULx	Multiply signed ($x = $ S) or unsigned ($x = $ U) binary numbers
	NBCD	Negate decimal number (subtract with carry from zero)
	NEG	Negate binary number (subtract from zero)
	NEGX	Negate binary number (subtract with carry from zero)
	NOT	Bitwise logical complement
	ORx	Bitwise logical OR ($x = $ I denotes immediate operand)
	PACK*	Convert number from unpacked to packed BCD format
	ROx	Rotate (circular shift) left ($x = $ L) or right ($x = $ R)
	ROXx	Rotate left ($x = $ L) or right ($x = $ R) including the X (extend) flag
	SBCD	Subtract decimal (BCD) numbers
	SUB	Subtract binary (twos-complement) numbers
	SUBA	Subtract from address register (unsigned binary subtraction)
	SUBI	Subtract immediate binary operand
	SUBQ	Subtract "quick" (3-bit) immediate binary operand
	SUBX	Subtract binary with borrow (extend) flag
	UNPK*	Convert number from packed to unpacked BCD format
Program control	Bcc	Branch relative to PC if specified condition code cc is set
	Bxxx	Test, modify, and/or transfer (depending on xxx) a specified bit, and set Z flag to indicate old bit value
	BFxxx*	Test, modify, and/or transfer (depending on xxx) a specified bit field, and set flags to indicate old bit–field value

FIGURE 1.40
Instruction set of the 68020.

Instruction type	Opcode	Description
	BKPT*	Execute a breakpoint trap (used for debugging)
	BRA	Branch unconditionally relative to PC
	BSR	Call (branch to) subroutine at address relative to PC; save PC state (return address) in stack
	CALLM*	Call subroutine (program module) saving specified control (module state) information in stack
	CASx*	Compare specified operands and update register
	CHKx	Check register against specified values serving as address bounds, and trap if bounds are exceeded
	CMPx	Compare two operand values and set flags based on result; x indicates operand type
	DBcc	Loop instruction: Test condition cc and perform no operation if condition is met; otherwise decrement specified register and branch to specified address
	ILLEGAL*	Perform trap operation corresponding to an illegal opcode
	JMP	Branch unconditionally to specified (nonrelative) address
	JSR	Call (jump to) subroutine at specified (nonrelative) address; save PC state (return address) in stack
	LEA	Compute effective address and load into address register
	LINK	Allocate local data and parameter region in the stack
	NOP	No operation but instruction execution continues
	PEA	Compute effective address and push into stack
	RTD	Return from subroutine and deallocate stack parameter region
	RTE	Return from exception (privileged instruction)
	RTM*	Return and restore control (module state) information
	RTR	Return and restore condition codes
	RTS	Return from subroutine
	Scc	Set operand to 1s (0s) if condition code cc is true (false)
	STOP	Load status register and halt (privileged instruction)
	TRAP	Begin exception processing at specified address
	TRAPcc	If condition cc is true, then begin exception processing
	TST	Test an operand by comparing it to zero and setting flags
	UNLK	Deallocate local data and parameter area in the stack
External synchronization	cpxxx*	If condition holds, then branch or communicate with external coprocessor as specified by xxx
	RESET	Reset or restart external device (privileged instruction)
	TAS	Test-and-set instruction: Test operand and set one of its bits to 1 using an indivisible memory access cycle

*Instruction not in the original 68000 instruction set.

vector C. An indication of how computer instruction sets have evolved over the years can be obtained by comparing this with similar programs for the IAS (Fig. 1.19) and IBM 7094 (Fig. 1.22) computers. Here the vectors are assumed to be composed of 1-byte (2-digit) decimal numbers, and the desired addition is accomplished by executing the ABCD (add BCD) instruction 1000 times. The address registers A0, A1, and A2 are used as pointers to the current 1-byte operands, and they are initialized to the required starting values using the first three MOVE instructions. In these instructions,

Location	Operation	Operands	Comments
	MOVE.L	#2001, A0	Load address 2001 into register A0 (pointer to vector A).
	MOVE.L	#3001, A1	Load address 3001 into register A1 (pointer to vector B).
	MOVE.L	#4000, A2	Load address 4000 into register A2 (pointer to vector C).
START	ABCD	$-$(A0), $-$(A1)	Decrement contents of A0 and A1 by one, then add M(A0) to M(A1) using 1-byte decimal addition.
	MOVE.B	(A1), (A2)	Store the 1-byte result in vector C.
TEST	CMPA	#1001, A0	Compare 1001 to address in A(0). If equal, set the Z flag (condition code) to 1; otherwise reset Z to 0.
	BNE	START	Branch to START if Z is not equal to 1.

FIGURE 1.41
68020 assembly-language program for vector addition.

immediate addressing denoted by the prefix # is used to specify the actual address values, while a register name such as A0 indicates that the desired operand is the contents of the named register (this is direct addressing). In the ABCD and MOVE.B (move byte) instructions, *indirect addressing* indicated by parentheses is used. In this case, the data specified by (A0) is the contents of the main memory location whose address is stored in A0, i.e., the data in M(A0). Finally the minus prefix in the operand $-$(A0) means that the contents of A0 is first decremented by one before it is used to access main memory; this mode of addressing is called *autoindexing*; it eliminates the need for separate index registers (cf. Fig. 1.22).

The instruction repertoire of the 68020 is typical of later third-generation machines and includes fixed-point multiplication and division, and stack-based instructions for transferring control between programs. Hardware-implemented floating-point instructions are not available directly; however, they are provided indirectly by means of an auxiliary VLSI IC, the 68881 floating-point coprocessor. In general, a *coprocessor* P is a special instruction execution unit that can be coupled to a microprocessor in such a way that instructions to be executed by P can be included in programs fetched by the microprocessor. Thus the coprocessor serves as an extension to the microprocessor and forms part of the CPU as indicated in Fig. 1.42. The 68881 contains a set of eight 80-bit registers for storing floating-point numbers of various formats, including 32- and 64-bit numbers conforming to the widely used 754 standard format defined by the Institute of Electrical and Electronics Engineers (IEEE). Additional control registers in the 68881 allow it to communicate with the 68020. A set of coprocessor instructions are defined for the 68020 which contain command fields specifying floating-point operations that can be executed by the 68881. When such an instruction is fetched and decoded by the 68020, it transfers the command portion to the coprocessor, which then proceeds to execute it. Further information exchanges may take place between the main processor and the coprocessor until the coprocessor completes execution of its current operation, at which point the 68020 proceeds to its next instruction. The commands executed by the 68881 include the basic arithmetic operations (add, subtract, multiply, and divide), square root, logarithms, and trigonometric functions. Other types of coprocessors may be attached to the 68020 in similar fashion.

Several features of the 68020 are designed to support multiprogramming or multiprocessing. Like the S/360-370, the CPU has two main control states, a supervi-

THE EVOLUTION OF COMPUTERS

sor state intended for operating system use and a user state for use by application programs. As Figs. 1.39 and 1.40 indicate, certain control registers and instructions may only be used in the supervisor state. This allows a clear separation between user and supervisory programs—for example, they employ different stack pointers— thereby improving system security. 68020-based computers are also designed to allow easy implementation of virtual memory concepts. Many of the required address translation functions and demand paging control are implemented by the 68851 memory management unit (MMU), another coprocessor chip. While a typical 68020-based system has a much smaller physical memory than the 2^{32} bytes that its physical addressing capability allows, by using virtual memory techniques, the full 4G-byte memory can be made to appear available to each user in a multiuser environment.

An unusual feature of the 68020 shown in Fig. 1.39 is its use of two levels of microprogramming in its main control unit; this increases design flexibility while reducing chip area requirements compared with the more conventional one-level microprogrammed control illustrated in Fig. 1.25. Several special control mechanisms are also employed to speed up instruction execution by the 68020. For example, provided they satisfy certain independence conditions, up to three instructions can be processed simultaneously in an instruction pipeline, which, on average, introduces a modest amount of parallelism into program execution. Another speed-up feature is a 256-byte instruction cache memory. It allows the 68020 to prefetch instructions from main memory during times when the system bus would otherwise be idle and store them in the instruction cache. When subsequently needed for execution by the CPU,

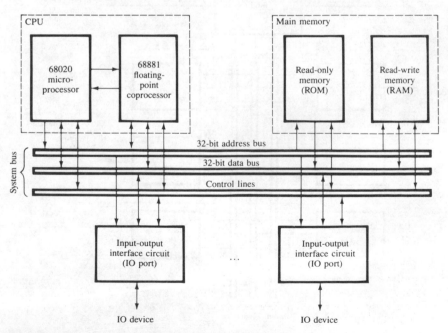

FIGURE 1.42
68020-based microcomputer with floating-point coprocessor.

the instructions can be obtained much more quickly from the on-chip cache than they can from the off-chip main memory.

Microcomputers. A powerful microcomputer with a large memory and many IO ports, such as that depicted in Fig. 1.42, can be typically implemented with 50 or so ICs (including SSI/MSI circuits that serve as interfacing logic or "glue" between the major LSI/VLSI chips) on a single printed-circuit board; the result is a single-board computer. A microcomputer with a relatively small main memory and limited IO connections can now be implemented on a single VLSI chip. The resulting one-chip microcomputer is, in many respects, a landmark development in computer techology because it reduces the computer to a small, inexpensive, and easily replaceable design component.

The production of single-chip microcomputers began in the mid-1970s, shortly after the appearance of the first microprocessors. They are typically used as programmable controllers for a wide range of devices and are consequently sometimes referred to as *microcontrollers*. A representative one-chip microcomputer, the Motorola 6801, is illustrated in Fig. 1.43. Introduced in 1979, this is a member of the 6800 8-bit microprocessor series. It consists of a 6800-like CPU, a main

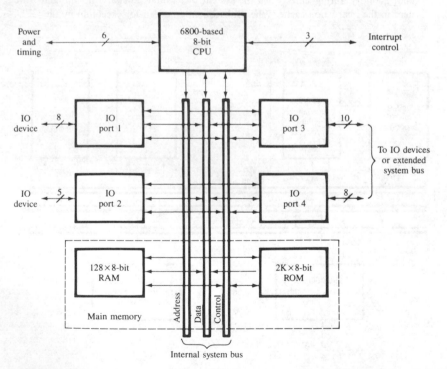

FIGURE 1.43
Structure of the Motorola 6801 one-chip microcomputer.

memory composed of 2K bytes of factory-programmable ROM and 128 bytes of RAM, and four general-purpose IO ports. The 6801 is contained in a DIP with 40 pins, most of which can be directly attached to IO devices. These IO pins are user-programmable so that they can be configured in various ways to match the characteristics of the particular IO devices being controlled. Most of the IO pins can be programmed to serve either as input data lines, output data lines, or IO control lines. The three ports 1, 3, and 4 are designed for parallel IO where data transmission is by 8-bit byte, whereas port 2 is intended for serial bit-by-bit data transmission. For simple applications the 6801 can function as a stand-alone one-chip controller. More complex applications may require additional ICs to increase memory capacity and the number of IO ports. To provide for this, IO ports 3 and 4 can be used as connections to, or extensions of, the 6801's internal system bus. In this mode of operation, the lines emerging from these ports constitute an external system bus to which additional memory chips and IO devices can be attached in straightforward fashion.

Microcomputers have given rise to a new class of general-purpose machines called *personal computers* [31]. These are small low-cost computers that are designed to sit on an ordinary office desk and, in some cases, to fold into a compact form that is easily carried. A typical personal computer has the organization shown in Figs. 1.42 and 1.43, with perhaps 1M bytes of main memory capacity, and the following IO devices: a keyboard; a video monitor consisting of a CRT or, in portable units, a flat screen employing liquid-crystal display (LCD) technology; a compact disk drive unit for removable floppy disks each having a storage capacity of around 1M bytes; and interface circuits for connecting the personal computer to telephone or computer networks. Personal computers have proliferated to the point that they have become as common as typewriters in business offices. Their main applications are word processing, where personal computers have assumed and greatly expanded many of the traditional typewriter's functions, accounting and similar data processing tasks, and as communication terminals with other computers. One of the most widely used personal computer families is the PC (*p*ersonal *c*omputer) series from IBM, which, following its introduction in 1981 and following precedents set by earlier IBM computers, has become a standard for this class of machine. The PC is based on the Intel 8086/286/386 families of 16/32-bit microprocessors, and is also distinguished by its use of the MS/DOS operating system developed by Microsoft Corp. under contract from IBM. A measure of the success of the PC series is the large number of compatible machines ("PC clones") produced by other manufacturers. Another noteworthy personal computer is Apple Computer's Macintosh, which employs microprocessors from the 68000 series.

Their small size and low cost have made it feasible to use microcomputers in many applications which previously employed special-purpose logic circuits, e.g., a traffic-light controller for a single intersection, or a domestic washing machine. The microcomputer is tailored to a particular application by means of programs which are frequently stored in ROM chips. Changes are made merely by replacing the ROM programs. Hence the task of designing special-purpose logic circuits can be replaced, often at substantial cost savings, by programming a standard microcomputer system. Logic designers must therefore be programmers and, to some extent, computer architects, since they must determine the microcomputer organization that best suits the application.

Figure 1.44 shows one of the earliest microprocessor applications: point-of-sale (POS) terminals to replace cash registers in retail stores. The computer architecture is based around a single bus comprising data, address, and control lines to which are attached the microprocessor (the CPU), one or more ROM chips for program storage, and one or more RAM chips for data and working storage. All IO devices are also connected to the main bus using IO interface chips which have also been standardized. The IO devices involved are the POS keyboard, printer, visual display, product code scanner, and a credit-card reader. The latter is used for credit authorization and requires a connection to the outside telephone system. Finally, there is a link to a central computer that can be used to obtain pricing information, perform inventory control, etc.

1.4.3   Recent Developments

The improvements in computer technology ushered in by VLSI are not without their limitations. The dramatic increase in IC density achieved over the years has not been accompanied by similar increases in raw computing speed as measured, for example, by CPU cycle times. This fact, coupled with the ultimate limitations on computing speed noted in Sec. 1.1.2, suggest that major speed improvements in the future will require extensive use of parallel processing techniques. Fortunately, the advent of low-cost but powerful microprocessors and microcom-

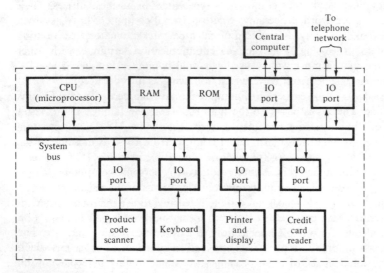

FIGURE 1.44
A microprocessor-controlled point-of-sale terminal.

puters makes it feasible to build supercomputers with extremely high levels of parallelism. However, the design and use of such parallel processors is poorly understood at present. Another problem is that software technology has not shared in the rapid improvements occurring in hardware technology. This problem has become more apparent as personal computers confront large numbers of naive users, such as schoolchildren, with computer programming for the first time. Traditional operating systems and programming languages are seen to be difficult to use or "unfriendly" by these users, and unhelpful in dealing with many important everyday computing tasks such as nonnumerical decision making. Some recent trends in computer architecture that address the foregoing issues, and are likely to influence future computer design, are discussed in this section.

Parallel processing. Supercomputers capable of executing many instructions in parallel have existed since the 1950s, but their high hardware cost and programming complexity have limited both their numbers and their range of applications. The first successful commercial supercomputers employed pipeline processing in which the CPU is organized as one or more multisegment pipelines. This organization allows a set of independent instructions to be in process simultaneously in each pipeline, resulting in a potential increase in performance or throughput (instructions executed per second) of a factor of n per n-segment pipeline. Typically n is not large, e.g., it is 4 in the case of the pipelined floating-point adder shown in Fig. 1.27. The Cray-1 supercomputer, first marketed by Cray Research Inc. in 1976, contains 12 pipeline processors for arithmetic-logic operations, several of which may operate in parallel. The Cray-1 can execute up to 160 million operations like floating-point addition per second. Machines of this type have been most successfully applied to scientific computations involving large amounts of vector and matrix calculations; consequently they are sometimes called *vector processors*. Vector calculations can be programmed fairly easily for these machines using standard languages like FORTRAN, and compilers have been developed that can generate object code which makes efficient use of the parallelism provided by pipeline processors.

An alternative approach to parallel processing with the potential of achieving higher degrees of parallelism is to use multiple independent processors, as in a multiprocessor with n separate CPUs. The task of writing parallel programs and optimizing compilers for these machines is far less well understood than the corresponding problem for pipeline processors. Nevertheless, machines of this type have been under consideration for many years, and in the 1980s powerful multiprocessors employing low-cost microprocessors as their CPUs began to be manufactured commercially. Two principal classes of multiprocessors can be distinguished: *shared-memory* machines in which all the processors have access to a common main memory through which they communicate to share programs and data; and *distributed-memory* machines where each processor has only a private or local main memory, and must communicate with other processors by sending them messages through an IO subsystem linking the processors. In each case a key issue is to design processor-to-memory or processor-to-processor interconnection networks that are of high-speed and low cost. Large crossbar networks like that used in the multiprocessor of Fig. 1.26 have been found too costly for most computer applications and are now rarely used. Figure 1.45 illustrates two alternative multiprocessor organizations used in more recent commercial multiprocessors. Both have been found to give very high throughput in certain (mainly scientific) applications, so that they constitute a possible alternative to the traditional vector supercomputer at a significantly lower price. Each has one or more host computers to manage IO devices and other operating-system functions.

BBN Laboratories Inc.'s Butterfly computer (Fig. 1.45a) is an example of a shared-memory machine composed of up to 256 CPUs (based on the Motorola

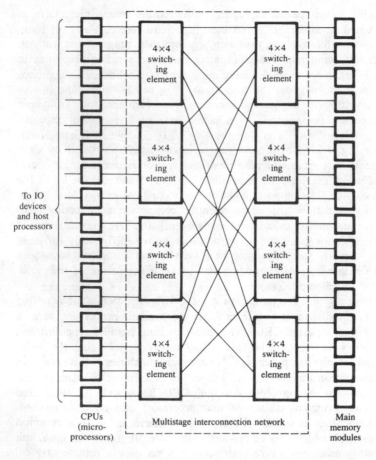

(a)

FIGURE 1.45
Two commercial multiprocessor organizations: (a) the BBN Butterfly; (b) the Intel iPSC.

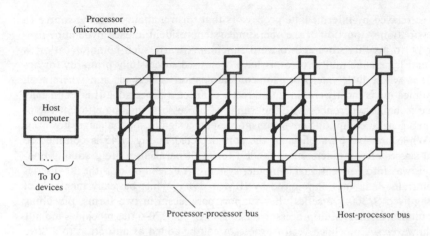

Processor
(microcomputer)

Host
computer

To IO
devices

Processor-processor bus

Host-processor bus

(b)

68000 microprocessor), a large global memory, and a multistage network of high-speed four-input four-output switching elements linking the processors to the memory. Each switch can, under program control, create a serial data-transfer path from any of its inputs to any of its outputs. The entire switching network is designed so that any processor can be connected to any part of main memory. Using packet-switching techniques, whereby information is transmitted between a processor and a memory module as a small fixed-length message, communication rates of 32M bits/s can be achieved through each switch. Of course, delays occur if several processors attempt to access the same region of memory simultaneously; therefore the system and application software must be designed to minimize this possibility.

Figure 1.45b illustrates the structure of another multiprocessor, the Intel iPSC (*Personal Supercomputer*) introduced in 1985. This can contain up to 128 microcomputer-class processors based on Intel's 80286 32-bit microprocessor; a small 16-processor version appears in the figure. The iPSC is the first commercial implementation of a class of distributed-memory computers called *hypercubes,* which are characterized by having 2^n processors which conceptually form vertices (corners) of an *n*-dimensional cube. For example, a three-dimensional hypercube contains eight processors corresponding to the vertices of an ordinary cube; the four-dimensional hypercube of Fig. 1.45b is composed of 2 three-dimensional cubes. In the *n*-dimensional case, each processor of the hypercube is directly linked to *n* other processors with which it communicates via a message-passing IO operation; it may also have a shared connection to a host processor. A processor can communicate with any processor to which it is not directly connected by having its message relayed by intermediate processors that form a chain from the source to the destination. A portion of the operating system resident in each hypercube processor performs this store-and-forward function. Clearly such communication is slow, and hypercube multiprocessors have been used successfully primarily for applications where little interprocessor communication is needed, and where such communication is mostly confined to directly connected processors. It is technically feasible to build hypercubes with thousands of processors; making efficient use of them in a general computing environment presents a significant challenge, however.

While massive parallelism of the sort depicted in Fig. 1.45 is confined to special classes of computers, more modest forms of parallelism are gradually finding their way into conventional computer systems. A case in point is the 3090 series of mainframe machines announced by IBM in 1985. While basically members of the long-lived S/360-370 series, they support parallelism in two forms, pipelining and multiprocessing. (Multiprocessor versions of S/360-370-series machines are not new, however.) A pipelined vector processor can be added as an option to a 3090 CPU in much the same way as the coprocessor of Fig. 1.42; this provides hardware to execute vector operations directly. To facilitate the programming of these operations, a "vector extension" to the S/360-370 architecture was also defined, which adds over 170 new vector instructions to the instruction set. (The original S/360-370 instructions can now be termed scalar.) Figure 1.46 shows the 3090 Model 400, which contains four CPUs each of which can have an optional vector processor.

Computer usability. Conventional computers are hard to use for several reasons. Humans cannot communicate with them by such natural means as speech or

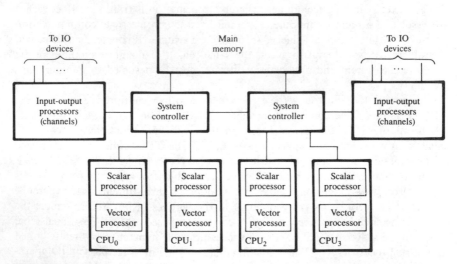

FIGURE 1.46
Structure of the IBM 3090 Model 400 computer.

graphic images; instead artificial languages (programming languages, operating-system command languages, etc.) of limited expressive power and unforgiving syntax must be used. Computers are normally designed to perform numerical calculations, or tasks such as word processing that can easily be couched in numerical terms; they therefore tend to be inefficient with most forms of non-numerical data processing. They also are unsuited to dealing with the ambiguity and heuristic reasoning that pervades human discourse. This is partly due to a computer's very limited knowledge of the world. For example, knowing the relative size of playpens, writing pens, and people makes it obvious which type of pen is referred to in such statements as: The pen is in Tom's pocket; the baby is in the pen. Knowledge of this kind that humans acquire often unconsciously as children is not easily given to computers, so that the intelligence of a computer, even a supercomputer, seems very far removed from that of human beings.

In the area of making computers easier to use, several techniques have been developed that minimize the user's need to learn specialized languages or protocols to communicate with the machine. One promising approach is illustrated by the operating system of the Apple Macintosh personal computer. This operating system, whose user interface is called the Finder, differs from traditional ones in that the user communicates with it not by typing in commands on a keyboard (although this is also an option), but by pointing to images (*icons*) on the screen of the Macintosh's video monitor using a hand-held pointing device called a *mouse*. The mouse moves a cursor on the screen and, when a switch on the mouse is depressed (clicked), an action associated with the image under the cursor is initiated. The mouse may also be used to select commands or parameters from predefined lists or "menus" that can be displayed on the Macintosh's screen. By pointing to a sequence of icons or menu items, relatively complex commands or programs can be generated. While a mouse is hardly a natural communication tool for humans, it is faster and easier to use than most keyed-in command languages.

Figure 1.47 shows a typical Macintosh screen image generated by the Finder. Two file directories named John and Tom are displayed, each in a separate "window" that can easily be manipulated via the mouse. The files, which include data sets and programs, are either in labeled file "folders" or identified by mnemonic icons, such as the writing-hand icon that marks the MacWrite word-processing program. To invoke execution of that program, the cursor (which appears as an arrowhead in the top lefthand corner of Figure 1.47) must be moved over the MacWrite icon, then the mouse must be clicked. In the figure, the cursor has been placed on a menu heading named File. On clicking the mouse, the indicated menu appears. This is a short list of Finder commands (starting with the command New Folder) for processing user files. If the command called Open is selected, by moving the cursor down the menu to the corresponding line, the Finder routine that opens a file is activated. This in turn creates a window with a list of the files currently stored in the Macintosh, and the user then selects the desired file by a mouse click. Thus the operating-system command "open file X" is reduced to a couple of clicks of the mouse.

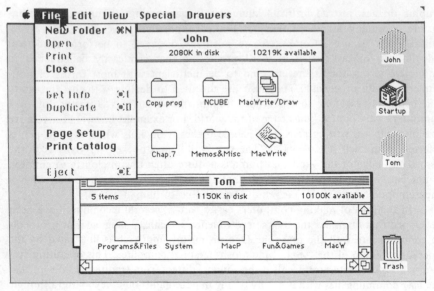

FIGURE 1.47
Screen image presented by the Macintosh Finder.

Efforts are also underway to extend the computers' abilities to store and process knowledge. The more ambitious of these projects have the goal of endowing computers with a humanlike artificial intelligence. For example, the Fifth-Generation Computer project, a long-term research project initiated in Japan in 1981, has the goal of developing a new class of intelligent computer systems which the project's founders expect to be in wide use by the year 2000 [23]. The main requirements for these machines are as follows: to be able to input and output information in the form of speech and graphic images; to process information conversationally in natural languages to store large amounts of everyday and expert knowledge in forms that can be put to practical use; to perform such high-level functions as learning and making inferences; to reduce the burden of software generation and programming. It is anticipated that the goals of the fifth generation will be achieved in several ways. Special (co)processors will be developed for such tasks as making logical inferences (inference engines), and managing massive amounts of stored knowledge (knowledge-base machines). These specialized functions will be realized using VLSI technology and, because of the huge amounts of computation they entail, will make considerable use of parallel processing techniques. Huge amounts of new system software will be required to support the fifth-generation hardware, and programming languages such as Prolog that have been designed for making logical inferences (logic programming languages) are expected to play a major role. Whether or not the ambitious goals outlined above will be achieved remains to be seen.

1.5 SUMMARY

The design of computers has evolved gradually over a long period of time. Calculators to perform the basic arithmetic operations were invented in the seventeenth century. The concept of a general-purpose program-controlled computer was conceived by Charles Babbage in the nineteenth century. Such a machine was not completed until the 1940s. Since then, progress has been rapid. The first major step was the abandonment of mechanical technology in favor of electronic. Four generations of electronic computers have been distinguished; their major characteristics are summarized in Fig. 1.48. Note that this classification by generation, while useful, is based on rather vague criteria. The evolution of computers has been strongly influenced by improvements in component technology. Often a design innovation must await the arrival of a suitable technology before it can be implemented. Babbage's vain attempts to realize his ideas provide a graphic illustration of this. Market forces also play an important part in the evolutionary process. The adoption of a particular design feature by an influential manufacturer can result in the appearance of that feature (which may be an old concept) throughout the computer industry.

The basic organization of electronic computers was defined by von Neumann and others in the 1940s. It comprises the following major components: a CPU responsible for fetching and executing instructions; a main memory external to, but

Generation	Technologies	Hardware features	Software features	Representative computers
First (1946–1954)	Vacuum tubes; acoustic memories; CRT memories	Fixed-point arithmetic	Machine language; assembly language	IAS; UNIVAC
Second (1955–1964)	Discrete transistors; ferrite cores; magnetic disks	Floating-point arithmetic; index registers; IO processors	High-level languages; subroutine libraries; batch monitors	IBM 7094; CDC 1604
Third (1965–1974)	Integrated circuits (SSI and MSI)	Microprogramming; pipelining; cache memory	Multiprogramming; multiprocessing; operating systems; virtual memory	IBM System/360; DEC PDP-8
Fourth (1975–	LSI/VLSI circuits; semiconductor memories	Microprocessors; microcomputers; massive parallelism	Parallel and problem-oriented languages	Motorola 68020; Intel iPSC

FIGURE 1.48
Milestones in the development of electronic computers.

directly accessible by, the CPU for instruction and data storage; and a set of input-output devices, such as user terminals, printers, and secondary storage devices (magnetic disk and tape units). The three main instruction categories are data-transfer, data processing, and program-control instructions. The data processing instructions perform arithmetic operations on fixed-point and floating-point numbers, and certain nonnumerical (logical) functions. The two major types of computer programming languages are assembly languages, which are symbolic forms of the machine languages actually executed by computers, and high-level languages such as FORTRAN and Pascal. The later generations of computers are distinguished by more powerful instruction sets, which are often implemented by microprogramming, autonomous IO processors for controlling input-output operations, and large physical and logical (virtual) memory spaces. Supervisory programs called operating systems are used to manage the resources of larger computers, so that they can be shared efficiently by many concurrent users. LSI/VLSI technology has had a far-reaching impact on computer design and application via the single-chip microprocessor, microcomputer, and main memory. These devices have made it feasible to build small low-cost computers for general use (personal computers), as well as supercomputers employing massive amounts of parallelism. Future (fifth-generation?) systems are likely to use this technology both to simplify the manner in which computers are programmed and to enable them to process knowledge in new, more humanlike, ways.

Despite rapid technological advances, the logical structure of computers has changed rather slowly. The following observation perhaps explains why this is so: "A frequent reason for a given (design) choice is that it is the same as, or the logical next step to a choice that was made once before" [2]. Thus in the ENIAC one finds a rather inefficient decimal representation of numbers; this representation is, however, essentially the same as that used in the ENIAC's mechanical predecessors. A particularly conservative influence on computer development is the high cost of writing programs. Once the software of a particular computer becomes widely used, there is a marked reluctance on the part of users to switch to computers requiring radically different software. A case in point is the S/360-370 series, which, because of the enormous amount of software written for it, has served as a world-wide standard longer than any comparable computer architecture. Its longevity is also due to the use of better implementation techniques such as VLSI and parallel processing in the newer members of the series.

PROBLEMS

1.1. Design a Turing machine that divides a unary natural number n by 2. n is stored on an otherwise blank tape in the following format:

$$\cdots b\,b\,A\,1\,1\,\underbrace{\cdots\,1\,1\,1}_{n \text{ ones}}\,B\,b\,b\,\cdots$$

where b denotes blank and A and B are delimiter symbols. The machine should compute $\lfloor n/2 \rfloor$, which is the integer part of $n/2$, and write the result in the format shown above. The only tape symbols allowed are b, A, B, and 1. Describe your machine by a state diagram or a "program listing," with comments similar to those in Example 1.1.

1.2. Repeat Prob. 1.1 for a Turing machine that subtracts a unary number n_2 from another unary number $n_1 \geq n_2$. Assume that n_1, n_2, and the result $n_1 - n_2$ are stored in the formats describe in Example 1.1. That is, the tape initially contains only n_1 and n_2 separated by a blank, while the final tape contains only $n_1 - n_2$. Again give your answer in the style of Fig. 1.3.

1.3. (a) Prove that a finite-state machine can be used to add two arbitrarily large binary numbers. Give a logic design for such a machine.

(b) Can a finite-state machine multiply two arbitrarily large binary numbers? Prove your answer.

1.4. Two instructions I_1 and I_2 in a computer program are "parallel" if the order of their execution does not affect the final results of the program for all input data sets. This means that I_1 and I_2 can be executed in parallel by independent processors. The identification of parallel instructions is very important in the design of systems for high-speed parallel processing. Prove that the problem of determining if any two instructions are parallel is unsolvable for arbitrary programs. (*Hint:* Prove that solving this problem is equivalent to solving the halting problem for Turing machines.)

1.5. Let A_1, A_2, A_3 be three algorithms that can be used to solve the same problem $Q(n)$ with input size n on a given computer. Let the exact time complexities of A_1, A_2, and A_3 be $100n$, $10^{-3}n^{10}$, and 2^n, respectively.

(a) Assuming that n is a positive integer, find the range of values of n for which each algorithm is best suited.

(b) Which algorithms provide the fastest solutions to $Q(1)$, $Q(10)$, and $Q(100)$?

1.6. Using the method of finite differences embodied in Babbage's Difference Engine, compute $x^2 - x + 41$ for all integer values of x in the range $0 \leq x \leq 9$.

1.7. Describe how a Difference Engine could be used to compute e^x where e is the base of the natural logarithms. e^x is to be calculated for values of x in the range $0 \leq x \leq 0.1$ at intervals of 0.01. The values computed should have an error not exceeding ± 0.0001.

1.8. Babbage estimated that his Analytical Engine could multiply two 50-digit numbers in 1 min. He also observed that, if greater precision were required, two $50k$-digit numbers, where $k \geq 1$ is an integer, could be multiplied in approximately k^2 minutes. Explain this observation.

1.9. Consider the problem of computing a table of the natural logarithms of the integers from 1 to 200,000 to 19 decimal places, a task carried out manually by the Prony group around 1795. Select any modern commercially available computer system with which you are familiar and estimate the total time it would require to compute and print this table. Define all the parameters used in your estimation.

1.10. Let r (for radix) denote the number of primitive symbols or digits used to represent numbers in a digital computer. Most mechanical computers used $r = 10$, whereas all modern computers use $r = 2$, i.e., binary notation.

(a) Suppose that the cost of using a particular radix r is proportional to r. This seems reasonable because the complexity of the circuits needed to store and process numbers increases with r. Then the cost $c(r)$ of using a radix-r representation for all $m = r^n$ possible n-digit integers can be expressed as

$$c(r) = Kmnr$$

where K is some constant. Show that the minimum value of r occurs when $r = 3$, assuming that m is fixed and r is an integer. This suggests that computers should use *ternary* ($r = 3$) instead of binary notation. Several experimental ternary computers have been built over the years based on arguments of this type.

(b) List all the arguments for *not* designing electronic computers to use values of r greater than 2, explaining why the argument of part (a) is usually rejected.

1.11. Discuss the advantages and disadvantages of storing programs and data in the same memory (the stored program concept). Under what circumstances is it desirable to store programs and data in separate memories?

1.12. Computers with separate program and data memories implemented in RAMs and ROMs, respectively, are sometimes called *Harvard-class* machines after the Harvard Mark 1 computer. Computers with a single (RAM) memory for program and data storage are then called *Princeton-class* after the IAS computer. The majority of currently installed microcomputers belong to one of these classes. Which one? Explain why the class you selected is the most widely used.

1.13. Consider the set S of 11 data transfer and branch instructions for IAS given in Fig. 1.16. Identify all the instructions in S that are "redundant" in the following sense: I is redundant if all the operations performed by I can be performed by a program that may contain any instructions from S except I.

1.14. Suppose that a vector of 10 nonnegative numbers is stored in consecutive locations beginning in location 100 in the memory of the IAS computer. Using the instruction set of Fig. 1.16, write a program that computes the address of the largest number in this array. If several locations contain the largest number, the smallest of their addresses should be specified.

1.15. Suppose that we wish to compare the IAS and IBM 7094 computers using the vector addition programs of Figs. 1.19 and 1.22, respectively, as representative, or *benchmark,* programs. For one complete execution of each program compute the following simple measures of performance: (a) the total number of references (read or write) made to main memory; (b) the total number of program and data bits transferred between the CPU and main memory.

1.16. Describe the functions performed by each of the following components of a computer system: CPU; main memory; IO processor; operating system; compiler.

1.17. Write an essay outlining the evolution of CPU register organization from the ENIAC to the Motorola 68020.

1.18. Discuss the significance of index registers. List as many applications of index registers as you can.

1.19. Explain the following statement: "In the early years all computers were crippled by their input and output devices" (M. V. Wilkes, 1972).

1.20. (a) Why is the 8-bit byte the basic unit for storing information in the main memory of the System/360 and most later machines?

(b) Why do the decimal number formats of the System/360 (see Fig. 1.31) and other computers place the sign of the number with the least significant digit, instead of the most significant digit as humans do?

1.21. After such popular languages as FORTRAN and COBOL, assembly languages as a group are the most widely used languages for programming computers. Explain this by constructing a list of general programming tasks where it is more advantageous to use assembly languages instead of high-level languages. For each of your examples, state why assembly-language programming is preferred.

1.22. List the functions performed by the operating system of a third-generation mainframe computer, such as a member of the S/360-370 series.

1.23. IBM has long held the largest share of the world market for medium and large computers. Explain how much smaller companies have successfully competed with IBM's S/360-370 series by only marketing computers that are fully hardware and software compatible with that series. (A number of manufacturers of IBM-compatible computers have not survived with this strategy, however.)

1.24. Define each of the following similar-sounding terms: microprogramming; multi-programming; microprocessor; multiprocessor; microcomputer.

1.25. Define the concepts of virtual memory and virtual machine, and explain briefly the differences between them.

1.26. Identify and briefly describe three distinct ways in which parallelism can be introduced into the design of a computer in order to increase its overall instruction execution rate.

1.27. Discuss the impact of developments in computer device technology on the evolution of each of the following:
   (a) The logical complexity of the smallest replaceable components
   (b) The operating speed of the smallest replaceable components
   (c) The formats used for data and instruction representation

1.28. Analyze the influence of pin limitations, i.e., the fact that the number of external connections to an IC package is limited, on the architecture of one-chip microprocessors and microcomputers.

1.29. What is meant by VLSI technology? Describe the influence of VLSI on the design and application of both special-purpose and general-purpose computers.

1.30. Compare and contrast the IAS computer and the Motorola 68020 microprocessor in terms of the complexity of writing assembly-language programs for them. Use the vector addition programs of Figs. 1.19 and 1.41 to illustrate your answer.

1.31. Write a brief note justifying the following statement made in Sec. 1.4.2: "Many of the distinctions made in the past between large (mainframe), mini-, and microcomputer systems are much less valid today."

1.32. Write an essay analyzing the validity of the following claim published in 1982: "With few exceptions, there have been no advances in the computer architectures of current systems since the 1950s."

REFERENCES

1. Aho, A. V., J. E. Hopcroft, and J. D. Ullman: *The Design and Analysis of Algorithms,* Addison-Wesley, Reading, Mass., 1974.
2. Alonso, R. L., H. Blair-Smith, and A. L. Hopkins: "Some Aspects of a Control Computer: A Case Study," *IEEE Trans. Electron. Comput.,* vol. EC-12, pp. 687–697, December 1963. (Reprinted in Ref. 4, pp. 146–156.)
3. Amdahl, G. M., G. A. Blaauw, and F. P. Brooks: "Architecture of the IBM System/360," *IBM J. Res. Develop.,* vol. 8, pp. 86–101, April 1964.
4. Bell, C. G., and A. Newell: *Computer Structures: Readings and Examples,* McGraw-Hill, New York, 1971.
5. Bell, C. G., et al.: "The IBM System/360, System/370, 3030, and 4300: A Series of Planned Machines that Span a Wide Range of Performance," in Ref. 27, pp. 856–892.
6. Blaauw, G. A., et al.: "The Structure of the System/360," *IBM Syst. J.,* vol. 3, pp. 119–195, April 1964 (5 papers).

7. Braun, E., and S. MacDonald: *Revolution in Miniature: The History and Impact of Semiconductor Electronics*, Cambridge University Press, Cambridge, England, 1978.
8. Bremermann, H. J.: "Optimization through Evolution and Recombination," in M. C. Yovits et al. (eds.): *Self-organizing Systems*, pp. 93–106, Spartan Books, Washington, D.C., 1962.
9. Burks, A. W., H. H. Goldstine, and J. von Neumann: "Preliminary Discussion of the Logical Design of an Electronic Computing Instrument," Report prepared for U.S. Army Ordnance Department, 1946. (Reprinted in Ref. 32, vol. 5, pp. 34–79, in Ref. 4, pp. 92–119, and Ref. 29, pp. 221–259.)
10. Chao, H. H., et al.: "Micro/370; a 32-bit single-chip microprocessor," *IEEE J. Solid-State Circuits*, vol. SC-21, pp. 733–740, October 1986.
11. Denning, P.: "Third Generation Computer Systems," *Comput. Surv.*, vol. 3, pp. 176–210, December 1971.
12. Estrin, G.: "The Electronic Computer at the Institute for Advanced Studies," *Mathematical Tables and Other Aids to Computation*, vol. 7, pp. 108–114, April 1953.
13. Gödel, K.: "Uber formal unentscheidbare Sätze der Principia Mathematica und vervandter Systeme I," *Monatsh. Math. Phys.*, vol. 38, pp. 173–198, 1931. (English translation in M. Davis (ed.): *The Undecidable*, pp. 4–38, Raven Press, Hewlett, N.Y., 1965.)
14. Goldstine, H. H., and J. von Neumann: "Planning and Coding Problems for an Electronic Computing Instrument," part II, vols. 1 to 3. Three reports prepared for U.S. Army Ordnance Department, 1947–1948. (Reprinted in Ref. 32, vol. 5, pp. 80–235.)
15. Intel Corp.: *MCS-4 Microcomputer Set User's Manual*, Santa Clara, Calif., 1974.
16. Intel Corp.: *MCS-80/85 Family User's Manual*, Santa Clara, Calif., 1979.
17. International Business Machines Corp.: *Reference Manual IBM 7094 Data Processing System*, publ. A22-6703, White Plains, N.Y., 1962.
18. International Business Machines Corp.: *IBM System/370 Principles of Operation*, publ. A22-6821-3, White Plains, N.Y., 1974.
19. MacGregor, D., D. Mothersole, and B. Moyer: "The Motorola MC68020," *IEEE Micro*, vol. 4, no. 4, pp. 101–118, August 1984.
20. Mead, C., and L. Conway: *Introduction to VLSI Systems*, Addison-Wesley, Reading, Mass., 1980.
21. Minsky, M.: *Computation: Finite and Infinite Machines*, Prentice-Hall, Englewood Cliffs, N.J., 1967.
22. Morrison, P., and E. Morrison (eds.): *Charles Babbage and His Calculating Engines*, Dover, New York, 1961.
23. Moto-Oka, T. (ed.): *Fifth-Generation Computer Systems*, North-Holland, Amsterdam, 1982.
24. Motorola Inc.: *MC68020 32-bit Microprocessor User's Manual*, 2d ed., Prentice-Hall, Englewood Cliffs, N.J., 1985.
25. Randell, B. (ed.): *The Origins of Digital Computers: Selected Papers*, 3d ed., Springer-Verlag, Berlin, 1982.
26. Samet, J. E.: *Programming Languages: History and Fundamentals*, Prentice-Hall, Englewood Cliffs, N.J., 1969.
27. Siewiorek, D. P., C. G. Bell, and A. Newell: *Computer Structures: Readings and Examples*, McGraw-Hill, New York, 1982.
28. Smith, D. E.: *A Source Book in Mathematics*, McGraw-Hill, New York, 1929.
29. Swartzlander, E. E. (ed.): *Computer Design Development: Principal Papers*, Hayden, Rochelle Park, N.J., 1976.
30. Turing A. M.: "On Computable Numbers with an Application to the Entscheidungsproblem," *Proc. Lond. Math. Soc.*, ser. 2, vol. 42, pp. 230–265, 1936.
31. Voelcker, J., P. Wallich, and G. Zorpette: "Personal Computers: Lessons Learned," *IEEE Spectrum*, vol. 23, no. 5, pp. 44–75, May 1986.
32. von Neumann, J.: *Collected Works* (ed. A. H. Taub), 6 vols., Pergamon, New York, 1963; vol. 5: *Design of Computers, Theory of Automata and Numerical Analysis*.
33. Wilkes, M. V.: "The Best Way to Design an Automatic Calculating Machine," Rept. of the Manchester University Computer Inaugural Conf., Manchester University, Electrical Engineering Department, pp. 16–18, 1951. (Reprinted in Ref. 29, pp. 266–270.)

CHAPTER TWO

DESIGN METHODOLOGY

The computer design process is the topic of this chapter. It is viewed as having three major levels of complexity: the gate, register, and processor levels. The two main aspects of gate-level design, combinational and sequential logic design, are reviewed first; then design at the register and processor levels is discussed. An introduction to computer performance evaluation is also presented.

2.1 INTRODUCTION

A complex object such as a digital computer is an example of a *system*, which may be defined informally as a collection of objects, called components, connected to form a coherent entity with a well-defined function or purpose. The function performed by the system is determined by those performed by its components and by the manner in which the components are interconnected. We are interested in information-processing systems whose function is to transform a set A of input information items, e.g., a program and its data sets, into output information B, e.g., the results computed by the program acting on the data sets. The transformation may be expressed formally by a mapping or mathematical function f from A into B denoted $f: A \rightarrow B$. If f maps $a \in A$ onto $b \in B$, we write $b = f(a)$ or $b \leftarrow f(a)$. We restrict membership of A and B to digital or discrete quantities defined only at discrete points of time.

2.1.1 System Modeling

A natural and very useful way of modeling a system is a graph. A (directed) *graph* consists of a set of objects V called nodes or vertices, and a set of edges E whose

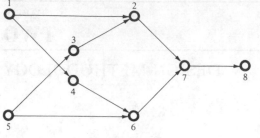

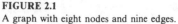

FIGURE 2.1
A graph with eight nodes and nine edges.

members are (ordered) pairs of nodes from V, that is, $E \subseteq V \times V$.* The edge (v_i, v_j) is said to join node v_i to node v_j. A graph is often defined by a diagram in which nodes are represented by circles or dots and edges are represented by lines; the diagram is taken to be synonymous with the graph (see Fig. 2.1). Note that the ordering implied by (v_i, v_j) is denoted by an arrowhead pointing from v_i to v_j.

We can view a system as comprising two classes of objects: a set of information-processing components C and a set of lines S that carry information signals between components. In modeling the system by a graph G, we can associate C with the nodes of G and S with the edges of G; the resulting graph is generally called a *block diagram*. This term stems from the fact that it is convenient to draw each node (component) as a block or box in which its name and/or its function can be written. Thus the various diagrams of computer structures presented in Chap. 1 are block diagrams. Figure 2.2 shows a block diagram representing a simple logic circuit, an EXCLUSIVE-OR circuit or modulo-2 adder. It can be seen that this circuit has the same general form as the abstract graph of Fig. 2.1. (It is convenient in this case to include nodes representing the external signal sources and destinations.) Several other graphical representations of systems are also possible. If the components are interpreted as edges and the signals as nodes, a *signal-flow graph* model is obtained. Signal-flow graphs are mainly of value for modeling linear analog systems and will therefore not be considered further.

Structure and behavior. Two central properties of any system are its structure and behavior. These very general concepts are not always defined precisely, and they are frequently confused with each other. We define the *structure* of a system as the abstract graph consisting of its block diagram with no functional information. Thus Fig. 2.1 shows the structure of the simple system of Fig. 2.2. A structural description merely names components and defines their interconnection. A behavioral description, on the other hand, enables one to determine for any given input signal a to the system the corresponding output $f(a)$. We define the function

---

* $P \times Q$ denotes the Cartesian product of the sets P and Q, that is, the set of all ordered pairs (p_i, q_j) where $p_i \in P$ and $q_j \in Q$.

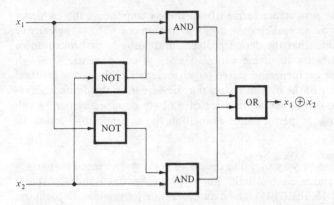

FIGURE 2.2
A block diagram representation of an EXCLUSIVE-OR logic circuit.

f to be the *behavior* of the system. The behavior f may be represented in many different ways. Figure 2.3 shows a specific behavioral description for the logic circuit of Fig. 2.2. This tabulation of all possible combinations of input-output values is called a *truth table*. Note that the structural and behavioral descriptions embodied in Figs. 2.1 and 2.3 are independent; neither can be derived from the other. The block diagram of Fig. 2.2 serves as both a structural and behavioral description for the logic circuit in question, since from it we can derive Figs. 2.1 and 2.3.

In general, a block diagram is used to convey structure rather than behavior. For example, in many of the block diagrams of computers in Chap. 1, blocks are identified as being arithmetic-logic circuits or control circuits. Such functional descriptions do not completely describe the behavior of the components in question; therefore, the behavior of the system as a whole cannot be deduced from the block diagram. If a more precise description of system behavior is needed, it is generally supplied separately. The description can be narrative text or a more formal description such as a state table or a flowchart.

The design problem. Having distinguished structure and behavior, we can now define in very general terms the problem facing the computer designer (or indeed any systems designer). Given a desired range of behavior and a set of available

Input a		Output
x_1	x_2	$f(a)$
0	0	0
0	1	1
1	0	1
1	1	0

FIGURE 2.3
Truth table for the logic circuit of Fig. 2.2

components, determine a structure formed from these components that achieves the desired behavior at an acceptable cost, e.g., a minimum cost. The complexity of computer systems is such that the design problem must usually be broken down into many smaller problems involving various classes of components. Although interrelated, the smaller problems are solved largely independently of one another. As a result, the behavior of the overall system may deviate from the desired behavior. The determination of the actual behavior of a newly designed system, which falls under the heading of performance evaluation, is an important aspect of computer-system design.

Data and control. It can be very useful to divide a digital system into two parts, a data processing unit and a control unit. For example, in the simple computer model shown in Fig. 1.1b, the CPU is the data processing part, while the memory, which contains the programs to be executed, is the control part (we are ignoring the IO equipment for simplicity). The CPU is neatly divided into an arithmetic-logic unit (the data processing part) and a program control unit (the control part). The distinction between data and control units is based on the implicit recognition of a subset of the information processed by the machine as its data. The components and connections (data paths) traversed by the data constitute the data processing unit. The rest of the machine is the control unit. The paths to be traversed by the data and the operations to be performed at each point of time by the data processing unit are specified by the control unit.

The distinction between control and data can be modeled using our functional definition $f: A \rightarrow B$ of machine behavior by decomposing f, A, and B into control and data parts indicated by the subscripts c and d, respectively. Letting $A \subseteq A_c \times A_d$ and $B \subseteq B_c \times B_d$, we can view f as consisting of a control function f_c: $A_c \rightarrow B_c$ and a data function f_d: $(A_d \times A_c) \rightarrow B_d$. If we implement the control and data functions separately, then the two-block diagram of Fig. 2.4 represents the system structure. This diagram clearly indicates the causal relationship implicit in the distinction between data and control; the control inputs A_c affect the behavior of the data processing unit, but the data inputs do not affect the control unit.

In practice, the distinction between data and control is usually less clear-cut than that given above. Often the data processing part of a network is permitted to influence the control unit. For example, an arithmetic operation within a CPU can result in overflow or underflow, and this fact may be used to alter the behavior of the program control unit. Thus f_c becomes dependent on both A_c and A_d, as indi-

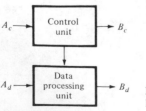

FIGURE 2.4
Idealized partition of a system into control and data processing units.

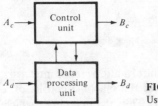

FIGURE 2.5
Usual partition of a system into control and data processing units.

cated in Fig. 2.5. This blurring of the causal relationship between the two components makes the boundary separating them somewhat arbitrary and subjective. The same signals may be viewed as control signals at certain times in the design process and as data signals at other times.

Suppose that a system is specified by a block diagram. If each block is divided into control and data processing parts, the resulting diagram can be viewed as containing two subdiagrams: one consisting of control units only, the other consisting of data processing units. It is then not difficult to visualize the system as comprising two distinct but interconnected subsystems: one for processing data, the other for processing control information. This division is important because control and data processing units are generally designed separately. Furthermore, systems may be classified by the way in which their (major) control function is implemented. If the control unit consists of fixed logic circuits so that f_c is essentially permanent, then the system is said to be *hardwired*. If f_c is implemented by storing control information in a memory, i.e., the control function resides in software rather than hardware, then the system is said to be *programmable*.

There is no standard notation for distinguishing data units and signals from control units and signals. It is not uncommon to use broken lines to indicate control signals and solid lines to indicate data signals, as shown in Fig. 2.6. The functions of the controls lines are usually indicated by labeling the lines themselves rather than the block they control.

Descriptive methods. A component or block in a block diagram has the general form shown in Fig. 2.7. It is a proverbial "black box" in that its internal structure is not specified. Only its behavior is defined, either wholly or in part. The components of interest here are finite-state machines; their behavior is thus state-determined. The total input states A of the machine which determine its behavior can be divided into two parts: the primary input signals X applied by an external

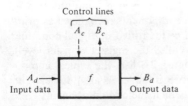

FIGURE 2.6
A block with distinguished control and data lines.

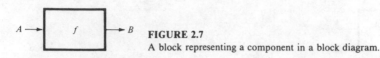

FIGURE 2.7
A block representing a component in a block diagram.

source, and the internal states Y, which comprise the information stored internally in the machine. Similarly, the total output states B of the machine consist of a primary output part Z and a new internal state part Y. Thus the mapping f which describes the function of the component in question has the general form $f: X \times Y \rightarrow Y \times Z$. If f maps $(x, y) \in X \times Y$ onto $(y', z) \in Y \times Z$, we write $y', z \leftarrow f(x, y)$. This mapping is represented explicitly by a function table called a *state table* whose rows and columns represent Y and X, respectively, and whose entries are the total output states $Y \times Z$. It is also common to represent the information in the state table by means of a graph, called a *state diagram*. The nodes of a state diagram denote internal states, and the edges, transitions between states. Unlike a block diagram, a state diagram contains no structural information; it is strictly a behavioral description.

Another way to represent state behavior is by means of a set of *state transitions* or equations of the form

$$y_1, z_1 \leftarrow f(x_0, y_0)$$
$$y_2, z_2 \leftarrow f(x_0, y_1) \tag{2.1}$$
$$\dots\dots\dots\dots\dots$$
$$y_p, z_q \leftarrow f(x_r, y_s)$$

(cf. the Turing machine description of Fig. 1.3). Each transition can be viewed as a statement about the machine which, in grammatical terms, can be interpreted as either indicative (a statement of what the machine does) or imperative (a statement of what the machine should do). In the latter case, the state transitions are viewed as orders or instructions. A sequence of transitions of this type that specifies a certain desired behavior is, of course, a program. Such program-like descriptions of digital systems have become popular in recent years; and a variety of special languages, known variously as *design languages*, *(hardware) description languages*, and *register transfer languages*, have been developed [10, 28]. Their characteristics are discussed further in Sec. 2.2.2.

2.1.2 Design Levels

Three major levels. The design of a complex system such as a computer can be viewed on many different levels, depending on the components recognized as primitive or indivisible. At least three major levels can be identified in digital computer design: the *processor* level, the *register* level (also called the register transfer level), and the *gate* level (also called the logic level). Figure 2.8 lists the typical components recognized at each level. The boundaries between the levels are not clear-cut, so it is quite common to encounter descriptions which include components from more than one level.

Design level	Components	IC density	Information units	Time units
Processor	CPUs, IOPs, memories, IO devices	LSI/VLSI	Blocks of words	$10^{-3}-10^3$ s
Register	Registers, combinational circuits, simple sequential circuits	MSI	Words	$10^{-9}-10^{-6}$ s
Gate	Logic gates, flip-flops	SSI	Bits	$10^{-10}-10^{-8}$s

FIGURE 2.8
The major computer design levels.

The processor level can be regarded as the computer-center manager's view of a computer system. The register level is approximately the level seen by an assembly-language programmer. The gate level, which is the subject of classical switching theory, is primarily the concern of the logic designer. These three design levels also correspond roughly to the major subdivisions of integrated-circuit technology into LSI/VLSI, MSI, and SSI components.

Figure 2.8 shows some further distinctions between the design levels. The type of information processed increases in complexity as one progresses from the gate to the processor level. At the gate level, individual or "random" bits are processed. At the register level, information is organized into words or vectors, usually of a small number of standard types. Such words represent numbers, instructions, character strings, and the like. At the processor level, the units of information are blocks of words, e.g., programs and data sets. Another important difference can be found in the time required for an elementary operation; successive levels typically differ by several orders of magnitude in this parameter. At the gate level, elementary operations, such as switching the output of a gate on or off, are typically measured in nanoseconds. At the processor level, an elementary operation might be the execution of a program whose execution time is measured in seconds or minutes.

Hierarchical design. It is customary to refer to design levels as high or low, depending on component complexity; the more complex the components, the higher the level. In this book we are primarily concerned with the two highest levels, the processor and register levels, which embrace what is generally regarded as computer architecture. The ordering of the levels suggested by the terms high and low is in fact quite strong. A component in any level L_i is equivalent to a network of components taken from the level L_{i-1} beneath it. This is illustrated in Fig. 2.9. Formally speaking, there is a one-to-one mapping h_i between components in L_i and disjoint subsystems in level L_{i-1}, a system with levels of this type is called a *hierarchical system*. Thus in Fig. 2.9, the subsystem composed of blocks 1, 3, and 4 in the low-level description maps onto block A in the high-level description.

Complex systems, both natural and artificial, tend to have a hierarchical organization; a profound explanation of this phenomenon has been given by Herbert A. Simon [26]. The components of a hierarchical system at each level are

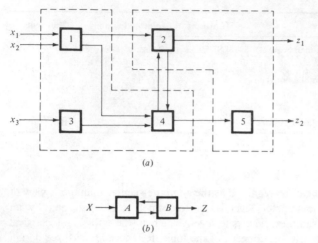

(a)

(b)

FIGURE 2.9
Two descriptions of a hierarchical system: (a) low-level; (b) high-level.

self-contained and stable entities. The evolution of systems from simple to complex organizations is greatly facilitated by, and perhaps requires, the existence of stable intermediate structures. Hierarchical organization also has important implications in the design of computer systems. It is perhaps most natural to proceed from higher to lower design levels because this corresponds to a progression to successively greater levels of detail. Thus, if a complex system is to be designed using SSI circuits, the design process might consist of the following three steps.

Step 1. Specify the processor-level structure of the system.

Step 2. Specify the register-level structure of each distinct component identified in step 1.

Step 3. Specify the gate-level structure of each distinct component identified in step 2.

This design approach has been termed "top down," or "structured," design; it is extensively used in both hardware and software design [9, 29].

A good hierarchical design may be defined as one in which the most appropriate components are chosen at each level. The following characteristics are desirable.

1. The components should be as independent as possible. This permits each component to be designed or analyzed, e.g., to verify its correctness, largely independently of the other components. A corollary of this is that the interfaces between components should be simple and involve relatively little information transfer.

2. The component boundaries should correspond to physical boundaries dictated by the current device technologies. Generally speaking, each design component

should be a physically replaceable component such as an integrated circuit, a printed-circuit board, or an entire cabinet. This is to facilitate the manufacture of the system and its subsequent modification or maintenance.

As might be expected, the design problems arising at each design level are quite different. Only in the case of gate-level design is there a substantial theoretical basis (switching theory). Register- and processor-level design is largely an art, so it is highly dependent on the designer's skill and experience. Computer architecture must therefore be treated mainly in descriptive terms at the present time. The need to establish a theoretical basis for computer architecture has been widely recognized [2].

2.2 THE GATE LEVEL

In this section the elements of switching theory and gate-level design are reviewed; it is assumed that the reader already has some familiarity with the subject. A knowledge of gate-level design is essential to the understanding of register-level design, which is the topic of Sec. 2.3. Our discussion will emphasize the design methodology employed at the gate level, since this may serve as a model for high-level design theories which have yet to be developed.

2.2.1 Combinational Circuits

Switching theory deals with binary variables $\{x_i\}$ whose two values are represented by the bits (binary digits) 0 and 1. A *combinational (switching) function* is a mapping $z: B^n \to B$, where $B = \{0, 1\}$ and B^n denotes the set of 2^n binary n-tuples. Any combinational function can, in principle, be defined by a truth table which specifies for every input combination $(x_1, x_2, \ldots, x_n)$ the corresponding output value $z(x_1, x_2, \ldots, x_n)$. Figure 2.10 gives an example of a truth table that defines two 3-variable functions $z_0(x_0, y_0, c_1)$ and $c_0(x_0, y_0, c_1)$.

Combinational functions do not involve time, and are contrasted with *sequential* switching functions in which the x_i's, and consequently $z(x_1, x_2, \ldots, x_n)$, are functions of time t. Sequential functions are therefore time-varying or dynamic quantities. A combinational function can represent the input-output behavior of a static logic system, or else it can represent a sequential system's behavior at a fixed instant of time. Figure 2.10, for example, describes the operation of a two-output logical system that adds three one-bit numbers represented by the input variables x_0, y_0, and c_1, with c_1 denoting an input carry signal. With this interpretation, the logical value 1 denotes the digit 1 and the logical value 0 denotes the digit zero. The output function z_0 is the sum digit, while c_0 is the output carry signal. Thus we see that Fig. 2.10 describes the following simple arithmetic operation (one-bit addition):

Zero + zero + zero = sum zero, carry zero

Zero + zero + one = sum one, carry zero

. . . .

One + one + one = sum one, carry one

Inputs			Outputs	
x_0	y_0	c_1	z_0	c_0
0	0	0	0	0
0	0	1	1	0
0	1	0	1	0
0	1	1	0	1
1	0	0	1	0
1	0	1	0	1
1	1	0	0	1
1	1	1	1	1

FIGURE 2.10
Truth table for two 3-variable combinational functions: z_0 (sum) and c_0 (carry).

In this manner, combinational functions can be used to represent the behavior of any logical operation or binary numerical operation.

Gates and circuits. A physical realization of a combinational function is called a *combinational circuit*. Combinational circuits are constructed from standard components called *gates*, which themselves realize very simple combinational functions. The most important gate types are listed in Fig. 2.11. The function performed by each gate is defined by a truth table. Gates will be represented in logic diagrams by the special logic symbols shown in Fig. 2.11. The symbols conform with several widely used standards and replace the more general block symbols used in Fig. 2.2. All the gate definitions except NOT can easily be generalized to allow any number of input lines k. Practical considerations limit k, which is called the gate *fan-in*, to a maximum value of 8 or so. Note that the NOT gate, or inverter, can also be regarded as a one-input NAND or NOR.

A set G of gate types is said to be *complete* if any combinational function can be realized by a circuit that contains gates from G only. Examples of complete sets of gates are {NAND}, {NOR}, {AND, NOT}, {OR, NOT}, {AND, OR, NOT}. NANDs and NORs are particularly important in logic design because they are easily manufactured using most IC technologies and are the only gate types that are complete by themselves.

Combinational circuits are formed by connecting gates according to certain rules. A *well formed* (*wf*) *combinational circuit* is defined recursively as follows [8].

1. A single line or gate is a wf circuit.
2. The juxtaposition of two wf circuits is wf.
3. Let C_1 and C_2 be disjoint wf circuits. The circuit obtained by connecting a set of output lines of C_1 to a distinct set of input lines of C_2 is wf.
4. If x_i and x_j are primary inputs to a wf circuit, the circuit obtained by connecting x_i and x_j to form a single primary input line x is wf.

The theory of combinational circuits, which has been extensively developed, deals almost exclusively with wf circuits.

Well-formed combinational circuits have several important properties. They

Name	Circuit symbol	Truth table			Equation

Name	Circuit symbol	x_1	x_2	z	Equation
AND	x_1 ⟩ z x_2	0 0 1 1	0 1 0 1	0 0 0 1	$z = x_1 x_2$ or $z = x_1 \wedge x_2$
OR	x_1 ⟩ z x_2	0 0 1 1	0 1 0 1	0 1 1 1	$z = x_1 + x_2$ or $z = x_1 \vee x_2$
NOT	x ▷∘ z	0 1		1 0	$z = \bar{x}$
NAND	x_1 ⟩∘ z x_2	0 0 1 1	0 1 0 1	1 1 1 0	$z = \overline{x_1 x_2}$
NOR	x_1 ⟩∘ z x_2	0 0 1 1	0 1 0 1	1 0 0 0	$z = \overline{x_1 + x_2}$
EXCLUSIVE-OR	x_1 ⟩ z x_2	0 0 1 1	0 1 0 1	0 1 1 0	$z = x_1 \oplus x_2$

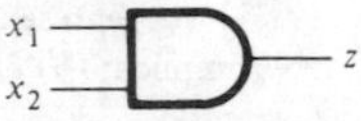

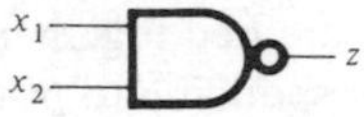

FIGURE 2.11
The major logic gate types.

are *acyclic*, i.e., they contain no closed loops or feedback. In a wf circuit the output lines of two gates may not be joined together as in Fig. 2.12a; such a structure implies a logical contradiction if the two gates generate different output signals. With certain logic device technologies, however, it may be possible to connect the outputs z_1 and z_2 of two *physical* gates to a common line z so that the signal on z is always well-defined. In such cases, the junction of the wires behaves like a logic gate defining a function

$$z = f(z_1, z_2)$$

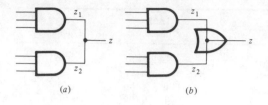

FIGURE 2.12
Two representations of a wired OR: (a)
implicit; (b) explicit.

Connections of this kind are referred to as *wired logic*. If the function $f(z_1, z_2)$ realized by the connection junction is AND or OR, it is called a wired AND or wired OR, respectively. Frequently, a wired gate is indicated on a logic diagram by joining gate outputs as in Fig. 2.12a. It is generally better to make the logical function explicit as in Fig. 2.12b, which shows a common representation of a wired OR.

Figure 2.13 shows two simple combinational circuits which demonstrate that the AND, OR, and NOT functions can be realized by means of NAND gates alone. The function of each circuit can be analyzed by determining the functions corresponding to all the signals in the circuit using the gate definitions of Fig. 2.11. For instance, in the circuit of Fig. 2.13a, the NAND function $p = \overline{x_1 x_2}$ appears on the internal line p, since p is the output line of a NAND gate with input signals x_1 and x_2. The second gate, whose two inputs are tied together, implements the NOT function, since if both its inputs are 0, corresponding to $p = 0$, then the definition of NAND requires the output z to be 1. If both inputs to the second NAND gate are 1 ($p = 1$), z must be 0. Thus z, considered as a function of the primary inputs x_1 and x_2, must have the behavior of an AND gate. In a similar fashion, it can be determined that, in the case of Fig. 2.13b, $q = \overline{x}_1$, $r = \overline{x}_2$, and $z = \overline{qr} = x_1 + x_2$, which is the OR function. Figure 2.14 shows a more complex circuit, which can readily be shown to implement the one-bit addition functions of Fig. 2.10. (Note that a k-input EXCLUSIVE-OR gate outputs a 1 if and only if an odd number of its input signals are 1.)

Because combinational functions are independent of time, the output signal of an ideal logic gate or combinational circuit responds instantaneously to a change in its input signals, i.e., its switching delay is zero. In a real logic circuit there is some delay between an input change and the corresponding output change due to the finite rate at which physical signals travel through the circuit. The circuit therefore has a nonzero signal propagation delay whose actual duration depends on the electrical characteristics of the physical circuits used to realize it. This delay is

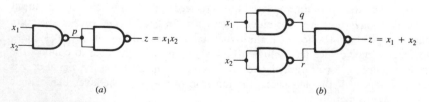

(a)   (b)

FIGURE 2.13
Using NAND gates to implement (a) AND and (b) OR.

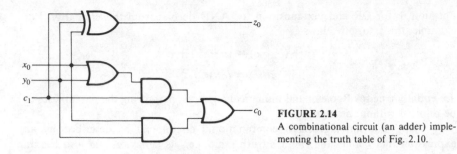

FIGURE 2.14
A combinational circuit (an adder) implementing the truth table of Fig. 2.10.

roughly proportional to the circuit's *depth* or *number of levels,* which is defined to be the maximum number of gates lying on any path from the circuit's input side to its output side. A single gate has depth 1, while the circuits of Figs. 2.13b and 2.14 have depths 2 and 3, respectively. A circuit of depth k is called a *k-level circuit.* In general, the fewer levels in a circuit, the faster it operates in its physical implementation.

Boolean algebra. The behavior of any combinational circuit can be derived by constructing the truth table for the entire circuit from the truth tables of its constituent gates. Since the truth table for an *n*-variable function contains 2^n rows, computation using truth tables may be very unwieldy, even for moderate values of *n*. An alternative approach is to represent the circuit by algebraic expressions in which the variables represent binary logic signals and the operators of the algebra represent gate functions. The algebra which models combinational circuits is a type of Boolean algebra which originated with the work of George Boole (1815–1864), a contemporary of Babbage's [5].

Boolean algebra, like any algebra, is defined by a set of elements K, a set of operators P over K, and a set of axioms or laws defining the properties of P and K. It is convenient to let $P = \{$**and, or, not**$\}$, where **and** and **or** are binary operations represented by juxtaposition and $+$, respectively, and **not** is a unary operation represented by an overbar. The more common and useful laws of Boolean algebra involving these operations are summarized in Fig. 2.15. Every Boolean algebra contains two special elements denoted 0 and 1; hence the simplest such algebra is two-valued, with $K = \{0, 1\}$. The operators **and** and **or** are closed, which means that if a and b are in K, $a + b$ and ab are also in K. This closure property and laws 1 through 4 of Fig. 2.12 form a complete set of axioms called *Huntington's postulates* for a Boolean algebra.

The significance of Boolean algebra in logic design derives from the fact that the set of all 2^{2^n} combinational functions of up to n variables is a Boolean algebra, where $P = \{$AND, OR, NOT$\}$ and AND, OR, and NOT are the standard gate operators. Combinational functions can also be defined using other operators such as NAND which correspond to the gate types actually being used. However, when analyzing or designing a circuit, it is generally convenient to use only the operators AND, OR, and NOT. This is because AND and OR obey many of the same laws as addition and multiplication in the ordinary algebra of real numbers. Indeed, the notation $+$ for OR and juxtaposition for AND derives from this similarity. For example, the associative laws

$$a + (b + c) = (a + b) + c$$

$$a(bc) = (ab)c$$

are equally true for Boolean and numerical algebras, permitting the parentheses to be omitted without ambiguity.

Using Boolean algebra, a combinational circuit can be described by an expression that defines the circuit's truth table, i.e., its behavior, and also has an algebraic structure that closely parallels that of the circuit. For example, the Boolean expression

$$z = \overline{\overline{x_1}\,\overline{x_2}}$$

describes the NAND circuit of Fig. 2.13b. Applying the first of De Morgan's laws (Fig. 2.15) to this expression yields the simple OR-gate form

$$z = x_1 + x_2$$

Thus Boolean algebra is useful for transforming Boolean expressions or the corresponding logic circuits into different, but functionally equivalent, forms. As

No.	Statement of axiom	Name
1	There exist elements $0, 1 \in K$ such that $$a + 0 = a$$ $$a1 = a$$	Existence of identity elements
2	$$a + b = b + a$$ $$ab = ba$$	Commutative laws
3	$$a(b + c) = ab + ac$$ $$a + (bc) = (a + b)(a + c)$$	Distributive laws
4	For every $a \in K$, there exists $\overline{a} \in K$ such that $$a\overline{a} = 0$$ $$a + \overline{a} = 1$$	Existence of inverse
5	$$a + (b + c) = (a + b) + c$$ $$a(bc) = (ab)c$$	Associative laws
6	$$a + a = a$$ $$aa = a$$	Idempotent laws
7	$$\overline{a + b} = \overline{a}\,\overline{b}$$ $$\overline{ab} = \overline{a} + \overline{b}$$	De Morgan's laws
8	$$\overline{\overline{a}} = a$$	Involution

FIGURE 2.15
The basic laws of Boolean algebra (a, b, and c are arbitrary elements of K).

another illustration, consider the lower portion of the circuit of Fig. 2.14 realizing the function c_0. This circuit is described by the Boolean equation

$$c_0 = (x_0 + y_0)c_1 + x_0y_0 \tag{2.2}$$

Applying the appropriate distributive law from Fig. 2.15 to (2.2) yields

$$c_0 = x_0c_1 + y_0c_1 + x_0y_0 \tag{2.3}$$

which corresponds to a two-level AND-OR circuit that is more desirable from a delay viewpoint than the three-level realization of c_0 in the figure.

Two-level circuits. The fundamental design problem for combinational circuits may be expressed as follows. Design a logic circuit to realize a given set of combinational functions using the minimum number of gates. Additional constraints are often imposed on the circuit structure, such as

1. The number of logic levels (which determines the circuit operating speed) should not exceed some number d.
2. The fan-in (number of input lines) of each gate should not exceed some specified value. Similarly, a gate's *fan-out*, which is the number of gate inputs to which the gate output line is connected, should not exceed a specified value. Fan-in and fan-out are mainly limited by circuit power constraints.

The classic Quine-McCluskey minimization procedure and its many variations solve the design problem for $d = 2$ with no fan-in or fan-out constraints [6, 19]. These techniques are based on the correspondence between two-level combinational circuits and Boolean equations of the form

$$f(x_1, x_2, \ldots, x_n) = \sum_i \dot{x}_{i1}\dot{x}_{i2} \cdots \dot{x}_{in_i} \tag{2.4}$$

and

$$f(x_1, x_2, \ldots, x_n) = \prod_i (\dot{x}_{i1} + \dot{x}_{i2} + \cdots + \dot{x}_{in_i}) \tag{2.5}$$

where Σ and Π denote the logical sum (OR) and product (AND) operations, and the *literal* $\dot{x}_{ij}$ denotes either x_{ij} or $\overline{x}_{ij}$. By analogy with ordinary algebra, the Boolean expressions on the right-hand side of Eqs. (2.4) and (2.5) are called *sum-of-products* (SOP) and *product-of-sums* (POS) expressions, respectively. Equation (2.3) gives an SOP expression for the carry function c_0, while a possible POS expression for the same function is

$$c_0 = (x_0 + y_0 + c_1)(\overline{x}_0 + y_0 + c_1)(x_0 + \overline{y}_0 + c_1)(x_0 + y_0 + c_1) \tag{2.6}$$

It is readily seen that if the input variables (literals) are available in both the *true* form x_{ij} and the *complemented* form $\overline{x}_{ij}$, then SOP and POS expressions correspond to two-level circuits composed of AND and OR gates. The two forms of literals are provided automatically by many input signal sources, e.g., flip-flops. If some of the required variables are not directly available, then an additional level of inverters (NOT gates or equivalent) is needed to generate them. The two-level circuit corresponding to an SOP expression is an AND-OR circuit in which each of the k product terms is implemented by an AND gate with appropriate fan-in, while the overall sum operation is implemented by a k-input OR gate. Similarly, a POS expression defines a two-level OR-AND circuit that realizes the corresponding function. Figure 2.16a shows a two-level AND-OR circuit corresponding to the SOP expression

$$f(x_1, x_2, x_3) = x_1 x_2 + x_1 x_3 + \overline{x}_1 \overline{x}_2 \overline{x}_3 \qquad (2.7)$$

while the OR-AND circuit of Fig. 2.16b corresponds to (2.6). POS and SOP expressions can thus be regarded as forming a simple but fairly precise design language for two-level combinational circuits.

As noted earlier, all-NAND and all-NOR circuits are generally preferable to those composed of AND, OR, and NOT gates. There is a simple correspondence between SOP and POS expressions and two-level all-NAND and all-NOR circuits, respectively, which makes it easy to construct the latter. Consider an SOP expression E and the corresponding two-level AND-OR circuit C. Replace each AND gate of C by the equivalent NAND circuit from Fig. 2.13a, and replace C's output OR gate by the NAND circuit from Fig. 2.13b. The resulting NAND circuit contains a pair of NANDs acting as inverters along each of its input-output paths. By the involution law $\overline{\overline{x}} = x$, the inverters in each path cancel, so the corresponding pairs of NANDs may be removed. This yields a two-level circuit C' which has exactly the same structure as the original circuit C with each AND or OR gate replaced by a NAND gate having the same fan-in as the gate it replaces. C' can also be obtained directly from E simply by mapping its AND and OR terms into NAND gates. In a similar way, it can be shown that a two-level OR-AND circuit corresponding to a POS expression is equivalent to a two-level all-NOR circuit obtained by replacing the AND and OR gates by NOR gates. Figure 2.17 shows

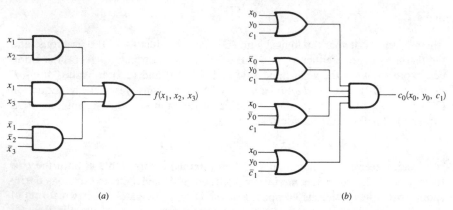

(a)   (b)

FIGURE 2.16
Two-level combinational circuits: (a) AND-OR circuit corresponding to SOP expression (2.7); (b) OR-AND circuit corresponding to POS expression (2.6).

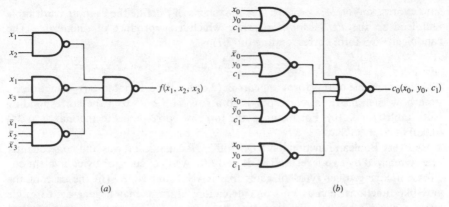

(a) (b)

FIGURE 2.17
(a) Two-level NAND circuit corresponding to the AND-OR circuit of Fig. 2.16a; (b) two-level NOR circuit corresponding to the OR-AND circuit of Fig. 2.16b.

two-level all-NAND and all-NOR circuits that are equivalent to the circuits of Fig. 2.16.

Let $m_i = \dot{x}_1 \dot{x}_2 \cdots \dot{x}_n$ be a product term in an SOP expression for $f(x_1, x_2, \ldots, x_n)$, where every variable of f appears in m_i either in true or complemented form. Such a term defines a Boolean function $m_i(x_1, x_2, \ldots, x_n)$, called a *minterm* of f. Minterm m_i assumes the value 1 for a unique combination of input variables corresponding to row i in the truth table of f. Specifically, $m_i(x_1, x_2, \ldots, x_n) = 1$ if and only if $x_j = 0$ (1) for $j = 1, 2, \ldots, n$, where the jth literal $\dot{x}_j$ in the product expression for m_i is $\bar{x}_j (x_j)$. For example, the term $m_0 = \bar{x}_1 \bar{x}_2 \bar{x}_3$ appearing in (2.7) is a minterm for which $m_0(0,0,1) = 1$; $m_0(x_1,x_2,x_3) = 0$ for all other input combinations. The other two product terms in (2.7) are not minterms since each has fewer than three literals. Since the positions of the 1s in its truth table uniquely define f, the function is also uniquely defined by its set of minterms. Consequently, an SOP expression like (2.4) for f, in which all the product terms are minterms, uniquely defines f, and therefore is said to be a *canonical SOP expression* for f. The canonical SOP form of the function defined by (2.7) is easily seen to be

$$f = x_1x_2x_3 + x_1x_2\bar{x}_3 + x_1\bar{x}_2x_3 + \bar{x}_1\bar{x}_2\bar{x}_3 \qquad (2.8)$$

It will be observed that the laws of Boolean algebra (Fig. 2.15) are listed in dual pairs that are related by the *Principle of Duality*, which states that any Boolean equation remains true if AND, OR, 0, and 1 are replaced by OR, AND, 1, and 0, respectively. This principle reflects the obvious symmetry existing among the operators and constants of Boolean algebra and allows many concepts to exist in dual forms. For example, NAND and NOR may be treated as dual operators. The dual concept for minterm is *maxterm*, which is defined as a sum term $M_i(x_1, x_2, \ldots, x_n) = \dot{x}_1 + \dot{x}_2 + \cdots + \dot{x}_n$ containing all n literals. In general, $M_i(x_1, x_2, \ldots, x_n) = 0$ if and only if $x_j = 0$ (1) for $j = 1, 2, \ldots, n$, where the jth literal x_j in the sum expression for M_i is $x_j (\bar{x}_j)$. The maxterms of f define the 0s in its truth table and lead to the *POS canonical form*, which is a product of maxterms. The canonical POS form corresponding to (2.7) is

$$f = (\bar{x}_1 + x_2 + x_3)(x_1 + x_2 + \bar{x}_3)(x_1 + \bar{x}_2 + \bar{x}_3)(x_1 + \bar{x}_2 + x_3)$$

Another example of this form appears in (2.6) for the 3-variable carry function c_0; note how each maxterm corresponds to a row with $c_0 = 0$ in the corresponding truth table (Fig. 2.10). For instance, the top row corresponds to the maxterm M_0 $(0,0,0) = x_1 + x_2 + x_3$.

Every Boolean function has POS and SOP canonical forms and consequently can be realized by two-level AND-OR and OR-AND circuits, or by equivalent circuits employing other types of gates like NAND and NOR. (In the case of the gate-like functions such as $x_1 + x_2$, the canonical forms may degenerate to single terms realizable by one-level circuits.) These circuits represent the fastest physical implementations for most functions. We now turn to ways of minimizing the number of gates needed to construct two-level combinational circuits.

Gate minimization. An SOP expression E for a function f is said to be *minimal* if it contains the smallest possible number of product terms among all SOP expressions defining f, and if, as a secondary condition, no literals can be deleted from any of the product terms without changing the function specified by E. A two-level circuit corresponding to E is also minimal in the sense that it contains the fewest gates among all AND-OR circuits realizing f, and the fan-in of none of the AND gates can be reduced. Minimal POS expressions and OR-AND circuits can be defined analogously. Canonical forms are generally nonminimal, as can be seen from comparing (2.7) and (2.8). In the sequel only the SOP case is considered in detail; dual arguments apply to the POS case.

A product term p is called an *implicant* of a function f if for any input combination $X = x_1, x_2, \ldots, x_n, p \cdot X) = 1$ implies that $f(X) = 1$. The implicant p is a *prime implicant* if the result of deleting any literal from the product term representing p is not an implicant of f. Every product in an SOP expression for f is obviously an implicant of f, but not necessarily a prime one. In (2.8), for example, the minterm $m_6 = x_1 x_2 \bar{x}_3$ is not prime, since deleting $\bar{x}_3$ results in the term $x_1 x_2$ that implies f. (This new term is a prime implicant, however.) The minterm $m_0 = \bar{x}_1 \bar{x}_2 \bar{x}_3$ of (2.8) is a prime implicant since if we delete any literal, the result is not an implicant of f. Deleting, say, the first literal $\bar{x}_1$ results in $m_0' = \bar{x}_2 \bar{x}_3$, for which we have $m_0'(0, 0, 1) = 1$ but $f(0, 0, 1) = 0$.

A minimal SOP expression for f must be a sum of prime implicants, hence prime-implicant identification is a basic part of any minimization procedure. Two product terms p_1 and p_2 are said to be logically *adjacent* if they differ in exactly one literal; that is, for some literal x_i, $p_1 = px_i$ and $p_2 = p\bar{x}_i$. Now

$$p_1 + p_2 = px_i + p\bar{x}_i = p(x_i + \bar{x}_i) = p \tag{2.9}$$

Clearly neither p_1 nor p_2 can be a prime implicant, but p may be one. Consequently, the sum $p_1 + p_2$ can be replaced by the single product term obtained by deleting the common literal x_i from either p_1 or p_2. Prime implicants can be computed by systematically constructing adjacent product terms, and replacing them by their common subterm p according to (2.9). The process can begin with the minterms of the function, and it terminates when none of the remaining product terms are adjacent.

The gate minimization problem (SOP case) may therefore be solved by the following two-step algorithm. (See Example 1.2 for a discussion of this algorithm's complexity.)

Step 1. Compute all prime implicants of the given function f.

Step 2. Select a minimal set of the prime implicants whose logical sum is f.

We now outline a well-known graphical version of the foregoing minimization algorithm suitable for small values of n. This technique was developed by Maurice Karnaugh at AT&T Bell Laboratories in the 1950s and is known as the *Karnaugh map* or *K-map* method [16]. A K-map of an n-variable function f is a rectangular array of 2^n cells in which all the 0 and 1 values generated by f are entered. It is basically a modified truth table in which the implicants of f correspond to rectangular groups of 1s (minterms); prime implicants correspond to the largest such groups. The K-map is drawn in such a way that logically adjacent implicants are approximately adjacent physically, thus allowing prime (and nonprime) implicants to be readily identified by inspection. Once all the prime implicant groups have been marked on the K-map, a minimal set is selected, also by inspection, that contains all the minterms of the function.

An example of a 4-variable K-map appears in Fig. 2.18. It contains 16 cells corresponding to the 16 rows of a 4-variable truth table. The rows and columns are labeled so that the labels of adjacent cells differ only in the value of one input variable. Note that the first and last rows and the first and last columns are labeled to make them adjacent in this sense. (Logical and physical adjacency would correspond completely if the K-map were drawn on the surface of a torus.) Every implicant $p = \dot{x}_a \dot{x}_b \cdots \dot{x}_k$ corresponds to a group G of 1-cells forming the intersection of all rows and columns whose labels are consistent with the literals of p. That is, if $\dot{x}_a = x_a (\overline{x}_a)$ is in the product expression for p, then every cell in G must have $x_a = 1 (0)$ in its label. Figure 2.18a shows the K-map representation of the prime implicants of the sample function. Note that each prime implicant corresponds to an encircled group of 2^i minterms, and is specified by a product term containing $n - i$ literals.

Once the prime implicants have been marked on the K-map, it remains to select a minimal subset S of them whose sum is the desired function f. S must be a *cover* of f in the sense that every minterm must be contained in at least one group included in S. If a particular minterm is included in only one prime implicant p of f, then p is said to be *essential*, and must be included in every cover, minimal or nonminimal, of f. The K-map method next identifies all essential prime implicant groups E of f and removes them from consideration since they must be included in S. In Fig. 2.18, there are five prime implicants, of which only $\overline{x}_2 \overline{x}_3 \overline{x}_4$ is not essen-

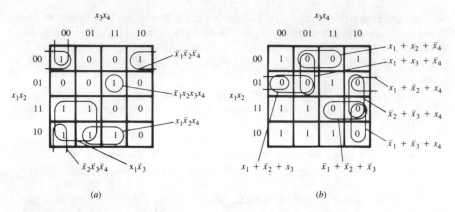

FIGURE 2.18
K-map of a 4-variable function showing (a) its prime implicants and (b) its prime implicates.

tial. For instance, $\bar{x}_1\bar{x}_2\bar{x}_4$ is essential because it is the only prime implicant that covers the minterm $\bar{x}_1\bar{x}_2x_3\bar{x}_4$ corresponding to the 1-cell in the top right-hand corner of the K-map. $\bar{x}_2\bar{x}_3\bar{x}_4$ is not essential because the two minterms it covers are also covered by other prime implicants, namely, $\bar{x}_1\bar{x}_2\bar{x}_4$ and $x_1\bar{x}_3$. Hence for this example, $E = \{\bar{x}_1\bar{x}_2\bar{x}_4, \bar{x}_1x_2x_3x_4, x_1\bar{x}_3, x_1\bar{x}_2x_4\}$.

It remains to select prime implicants to cover the minterms not covered by some member of E. A trial-and-error procedure based on inspection of all possibilities can be used to obtain a minimum cover S' for these minterms. Combining S' with E gives the desired minimal solution S. In the example of Fig. 2.18a, the four essential prime implicants cover all the minterms; hence the given function f has a unique minimal SOP expression containing the four corresponding product terms, viz.:

$$f = \bar{x}_1\bar{x}_2\bar{x}_4 + \bar{x}_1x_2x_3x_4 + x_1\bar{x}_3 + x_1\bar{x}_2x_4$$

This expression is easily mapped into a five-gate AND-OR or NAND-NAND circuit.

A dual approach involving grouping the 0s (maxterms) of the K-map into *prime implicates* is required to find the minimal POS forms. Figure 2.18b shows the seven prime implicates for the function under consideration, three of which ($x_1 + x_2 + \bar{x}_4$, $\bar{x}_1 + \bar{x}_2 + \bar{x}_3$, and $\bar{x}_1 + \bar{x}_3 + x_4$) are essential. The three maxterms not covered by the essential prime implicates can be covered in various ways by two of the nonessential ones, yielding several different five-term minimal POS solutions such as the following:

$$f = (x_1 + x_2 + \bar{x}_4)(\bar{x}_1 + \bar{x}_2 + \bar{x}_3)(\bar{x}_1 + \bar{x}_3 + x_4)(x_1 + \bar{x}_2 + x_4)(x_1 + \bar{x}_2 + x_3)$$

This corresponds to a six-gate OR-AND or NOR-NOR circuit; hence the five-gate SOP solution is better in this case. There seems to be no way of telling a priori which of the minimal forms, SOP or POS, is simpler.

Example 2.1 Design of a one-digit decimal incrementer. To illustrate the combinational design process further, we consider the task of designing a two-level circuit that increments a number N represented in 4-bit BCD form, producing (also in BCD form) the result $N + 1$. When $N = 9$, $N + 1$ is taken to be zero, so that the summation is modulo-10. Incrementers are a special form of adder and are used in the design of counters such as program counters. From the incrementer's functional description, we can immediately derive the truth table of Fig. 2.19. Since there are 16 possible input-output patterns but only 10 numbers to be represented, 6 of the possible patterns are never used. The corresponding output entries in the truth table are called *don't cares* and are denoted by the symbol d. The circuit designer may arbitrarily assign 0 or 1 to any don't-care value without violating the design specifications; because of the presence of don't cares the function is said to be *incompletely specified*. Our problem, therefore, is to design a four-input four-output two-level circuit with the behavior defined by Fig. 2.19.

The four K-maps for the incrementer's four output functions z_1:z_4 appear in Fig. 2.20; they were obtained directly from the truth table. The don't cares can be used to advantage in reducing both the number of prime implicants needed and the number of literals in individual prime implicants. If the d's are ignored (set to 0) in Fig. 2.20a, then the 1 in the lower left corner corresponds to the prime implicant $x_1\overline{x}_2\overline{x}_3\overline{x}_4$. However, if this 1 is grouped with three adjacent d's as depicted in the figure, i.e., if those d's are set to 1, we obtain the simpler prime implicant $x_1\overline{x}_4$. If the remaining d's are set to 0, we can then express z in the SOP form $x_1\overline{x}_4 + \overline{x}_1x_2x_3x_4$. Applying the same approach to the other three output functions, as illustrated by Fig. 2.20b–d, yields the following minimal SOP expressions defining the incrementer:

$$z_1 = x_1\overline{x}_4 + \overline{x}_1x_2x_3x_4$$

	Input					Output			
Number	x_1	x_2	x_3	x_4	Number	z_1	z_2	z_3	z_4
0	0	0	0	0	1	0	0	0	1
1	0	0	0	1	2	0	0	1	0
2	0	0	1	0	3	0	0	1	1
3	0	0	1	1	4	0	1	0	0
4	0	1	0	0	5	0	1	0	1
5	0	1	0	1	6	0	1	1	0
6	0	1	1	0	7	0	1	1	1
7	0	1	1	1	8	1	0	0	0
8	1	0	0	0	9	1	0	0	1
9	1	0	0	1	0	0	0	0	0
	1	0	1	0		d	d	d	d
	1	0	1	1		d	d	d	d
Don't-care	1	1	0	0		d	d	d	d
conditions	1	1	0	1		d	d	d	d
	1	1	1	0		d	d	d	d
	1	1	1	1		d	d	d	d

FIGURE 2.19
Truth table for the one-digit BCD incrementer.

$$z_2 = x_2\bar{x}_3 + x_2\bar{x}_4 + \bar{x}_2 x_3 x_4$$

$$z_3 = \bar{x}_1\bar{x}_3 x_4 + \bar{x}_1 x_3\bar{x}_4$$

$$z_4 = \bar{x}_4$$

Note that not all input variables appear in every equation. A direct NAND-NAND implementation of these equations is given in Fig. 2.21.

Simpler K-maps for fewer than four variables are easily derived from the 4-variable case by removing unneeded rows and columns. The K-map approach can also be extended to functions of five or six variables, but it becomes very difficult to visualize logical adjacencies among terms as the number of variables increases. Algebraic versions of the same approach, for example, the Quine-McCluskey algorithm, can be used for minimizing functions of up to about 10 variables. For very large numbers of variables, say 50, heuristic procedures such as those employed by the ESPRESSO program [6] can be used to obtain nearly minimal two-level designs. Large minimization problems of this kind are encountered in designing *programmable logic arrays* (PLAs), a class of two-level logic circuits

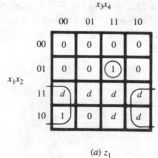

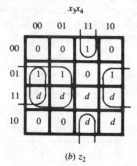

(a) z_1

(b) z_2

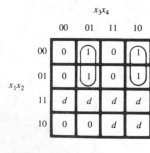

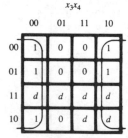

(c) z_3

(d) z_4

FIGURE 2.20
K-maps for the incrementer.

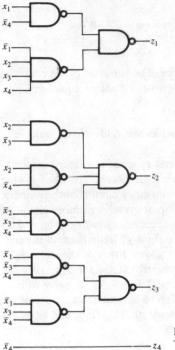

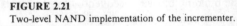

FIGURE 2.21
Two-level NAND implementation of the incrementer.

that can be efficiently realized by MOS ICs. In general, however, advances in IC device technology have greatly reduced the cost of manufacturing a gate, a fact which has tended to decrease the importance of gate minimization in logic design. In practice, a nearly minimal circuit devised using heuristic or ad hoc techniques is often acceptable. Other design objectives, e.g., minimizing the number of ICs used or simplifying the testing requirements of the circuit, may be more important than gate minimization.

2.2.2 Sequential Circuits

Sequential circuits are logic circuits whose present outputs depend on past inputs. Unlike combinational circuits, they are capable of storing or remembering information; sequential switching functions are therefore time-dependent. The gates of Fig. 2.11 are abstract models of physical gates in which the signal-propagation delay is ignored. A more accurate (but still idealized) gate model is shown in Fig. 2.22. A pure delay element characterized by the equation

$$z(t + \Delta) = y(t)$$

is placed in the gate-output line. The delay element has the property that it stores the signal on its input line for Δ time units before transferring it to its output line;

x_1

$\bar{x}_2$

y

z

Delay Δ

FIGURE 2.22
A more accurate model of a physical AND gate.

the delay element is therefore a simple storage device. The behavior of the circuit of Fig. 2.22 is described by the time-dependent or *sequential Boolean equation*:

$$z(t + \Delta) = x_1(t)\bar{x}_2(t)$$

The information stored in this gate may be defined as the value of the variable y, which is termed the internal *state variable*.

A simple delay element has only a finite memory span; the stored information y is lost after Δ time units. In order to obtain a logic circuit capable of storing information indefinitely, it is necessary to endow memory circuits with *feedback* paths that allow information to flow in a closed loop or cycle. A memory circuit of this type designed to store one bit of information is called a *flip-flop*. Figure 2.23 shows a very basic type of flip-flop in which the output y_1 feeds back to the first NOR gate. When $S = R = 0$, NOR-gate behavior allows either of the states $y_1 = \bar{y}_2 = 0$ or $y_1 = \bar{y}_2 = 1$ to be present indefinitely; these two states correspond to the flip-flop storing 0 or 1, respectively. The inputs S (set) and R (reset) serve to control the flip-flop's state. $SR = 10$ causes the flip-flop to assume the stored-1 or set state, while $SR = 01$ introduces the stored-0 or reset state. Flip-flops and gates are the basic building blocks of sequential logic circuits.

Circuit characteristics. The sequential circuits used in computer design have a structure which can be represented by the general *Huffman model*, defined in Fig. 2.24, which was proposed by David A. Huffman [15]. The sequential circuit is viewed as consisting of two parts, a combinational circuit C, and a memory M which is usually formed from a set of flip-flops. The information stored in M constitutes the *internal state*, or simply the *state*, of the circuit; the set of all the signal values in the circuit at any time is called the *total state*. Each primary output z_i generated by C is a function both of the primary inputs $x_1, x_2, \ldots, x_n$ and the secondary inputs (state variables) $y_1, y_2, \ldots, y_p$. There is also a set of secondary outputs $Y_1, Y_2, \ldots, Y_q$ from C, which determine the new values (next states) of $y_1, y_2, \ldots, y_p$ and enable the circuit to retain information derived from earlier input signals. Thus the circuit's primary output signals at any time depend not only on the current primary inputs but also on a sequence of earlier inputs.

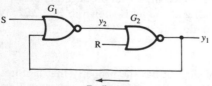

S

G_1

y_2

G_2

R

y_1

Feedback path

FIGURE 2.23
A simple SR (set-reset) flip-flop.

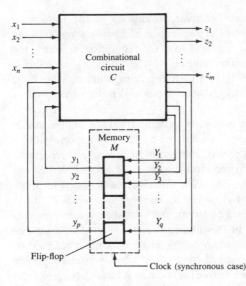

x_1
x_2
$\vdots$
x_n

Combinational
circuit
C

z_1
z_2

$\vdots$

z_m

Memory
M

y_1
y_2
$\vdots$
y_p

Y_1
Y_2
Y_3
$\vdots$
Y_q

Flip-flop

Clock (synchronous case)

FIGURE 2.24
Huffman model of a sequential circuit.

The sequential behavior of any gate-level logic circuit can, in principle, be analyzed if the delays associated with all its gates are known. In practice, however, these delays are not known with any accuracy; the individual gates of some particular type in a circuit may deviate from the "nominal" (average) delay for that type of gate by as much as 50 percent. Moreover, the number of gates lying along different input-output paths of a combinational circuit is not constant. Consequently, the times at which the individual output signals of C respond to some change on C's inputs can vary over quite a wide range. If precautions are not taken to control the times at which C's input-output signals change, then incorrect circuit behavior can result. For example, if some of the output signals of C change much faster than others, then the fast signals can feed back to the inputs of C via M and apply new values to the y_i lines before the circuit has had a chance to respond to the previous y_i values. This situation, where next states depend on the speed at which individual signals propagate through a circuit, is termed a *race* condition, and results in unpredictable behavior.

Suppose, for instance, that S and R are set to 1 in the SR flip-flop of Fig. 2.23. This causes both y_1 and y_2 to become 0 after a delay of approximately Δ, where Δ is the nominal delay of each NOR gate. Let the input combination SR then become 00 and be maintained indefinitely. After delay Δ, the signal-pair y_1y_2 changes from 00 to 11; after a further delay of Δ it changes back to 00; then it becomes 11 again, and so on. Hence if both gate delays are exactly Δ, the input sequence consisting of SR = 11 followed by SR = 00 causes the variables y_1y_2 to oscillate between 00 and 11 indefinitely. In practice, one gate, say G_1, is likely to have a delay Δ_1 that is appreciably less than the delay Δ_2 of the other gate G_2. As a result, y_1 can change from 0 to 1 while y_2 is still 0. This causes the SR flip-flop to assume the stable total state $SRy_1y_2 = 0010$. If, on the other hand, $\Delta_1 > \Delta_2$, the flip-flop is likely, after some oscillatory behavior, to end up in the total state $SRy_1y_2 = 0001$, which is also stable. Thus the application of 11 follow by 00 to the primary inputs SR of the SR flip flop can lead to a race condition in which the flip-flop's final state is indeterminate. The solution to the foregoing problem is either to avoid applying the input $SR = 11$ to SR flip-flops, thus making 11, a "forbidden" input combination, or else to use other types of flip-flops that are less prone to race conditions.

More generally, races and similar problems resulting from the unpredictable times at which key signals change value are eliminated by the use of special timing signals called *clocks*. A clock signal is derived from a central source (a clock generator) and is distributed to all points in the circuit where it is needed. It has the typical periodic waveform illustrated in Fig. 2.25. The clock is designed to allow the combinational part C of a sequential circuit to respond to one set of input changes and produce one unambiguous set of output and next-state values. Sequential circuits that employ clock signals in this manner are called *synchronous* circuits. Most sequential circuits encountered in computer design, are synchronous. For example, a typical CPU is synchronized by a clock signal whose frequency (defined as the reciprocal $1/T$ of its clock period) is taken as a basic measure of the CPU's speed of operation. Circuits that are not timed by central clock signals are termed *asynchronous*. Asynchronous circuits are difficult to design, and their reliability is reduced by their susceptibility to races and related problems. Asynchronous behavior is most frequently met when designing communication links between two or more synchronous circuits that are controlled by independent clocks; this issue is considered further in Chap. 6.

As indicated in Fig. 2.24, a clock signal is usually applied to the memory part of a sequential circuit, where it determines the times at which all the flip-flops respond to changes on their Y_i inputs and/or place new signal values on their y_i outputs. While the output signals of the combinational circuit C are changing values in response to some input change, the clock signal is used to disable M so that it does not respond to the changing, and temporarily ambiguous, Y_i signals. The manner in which this is done depends on the type of flip-flops used. When the outputs of C have stabilized at their new values, they are made available to M by enabling the clock. Thus a clock has two states: active or enabled, and inactive or disabled. The active and inactive states may be associated with the 1 or 0 levels of the clock, or they may correspond to certain points in the clock cycle, e.g., in many designs the active state is triggered by a 0-to-1 or 1-to-0 transition of the clock signal. The period during which the clock is inactive must be at least as long as the

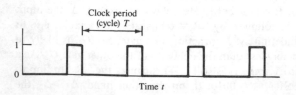

FIGURE 2.25
Waveform of a typical clock signal.

worst-case signal-propagation delay through C, while the active period must be long enough to allow M to make one complete state transition.

The design of a (synchronous) sequential circuit conforming to the Huffman model requires two major steps. First the states of M, the required state behavior of the circuit, and the flip-flop types to be used for M, are determined. The behavior of a sequential circuit is typically described by a *state table*, which defines the primary outputs and next states of the circuit for all possible combinations of primary inputs and current states; thus it is the sequential counterpart of a truth table. Then the combinational circuit C needed to produce the desired internal state transitions and primary output signals is designed. Thus the combinational design techniques discussed in the preceding section also play a central role in the design of sequential circuits.

Flip-flops. The asynchronous SR flip-flop depicted in Fig. 2.23, although rarely used by itself, is the basic circuit from which a variety of flip-flop types are derived by the addition of clock circuits and control inputs. It is usually drawn in the form shown in Fig. 2.26a, and represented by the special symbol of Fig. 2.26b. The signals denoted y_1 and y_2 in Fig. 2.23 can assume the four possible values 00, 01, 10, 11. As observed earlier the values 10 and 01 denote stored 1 and stored 0, respectively, and are maintained indefinitely as long as SR $= 00$. The combination $y_1 y_2 = 00$ occurs briefly during transitions between 01 and 10, while $y_1 y_2 = 11$ can lead to race conditions and therefore is never used. Thus considering only the normal stable states 10 and 01, the SR flip-flop is a two-state device, and its state may be represented by $y = y_1$, while y_2 may be denoted by $\bar{y}$, as in Fig. 2.26b.

If a delay Δ is assigned to each of its gates in Fig. 2.26a, the SR flip-flop's behavior is given by the following Boolean equation:

$$y(t + 2\Delta) = \overline{R(t + \Delta) + \overline{[S(t) + y(t + \Delta)]}}$$
$$= \bar{R}(t + \Delta)[S(t) + y(t + \Delta)] \tag{2.10}$$

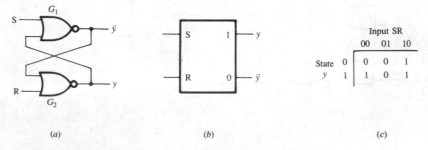

| | | (a) | | (b) | | (c) | |

(a)	(b)	(c)

FIGURE 2.26
Asynchronous SR flip-flop: (a) logic circuit; (b) circuit symbol; (c) state table.

It is often convenient to lump all the internal delays of a flip-flop together into a single parameter τ denoting the (nominal) time required for a single transition between stable states. In this case, $\tau \approx 2\Delta$ and (2.10) is replaced by

$$y(t + \tau) = \overline{R}(t)[S(t) + y(t)]$$

From this equation we obtain the state table of Fig. 2.26c, where the forbidden input combination $SR = 11$ is omitted. The table entries are the next-state values $y(t + \tau)$. Note that the state variables of flip-flops are also their primary outputs. More general state tables have separate entries for next states and primary output values. It will be observed that the input combination $SR = 00$ represents an inactive condition that has no effect on the flip-flop's state.

Two useful modifications to the basic SR flip-flop are illustrated by Fig. 2.27. A clock circuit has been added via a pair of AND gates inserted in the S and R input lines. These gates are connected to a control signal CLOCK with the behavior shown in Fig. 2.25. When $CLOCK = 0$, the inactive 00 input pattern is seen by the NOR gates no matter what signals are applied to S and R. This illustrates the clock's basic role in protecting a flip-flop from undesirable input changes. Once the S and R inputs have all reached their stable values, CLOCK is changed to the active value 1, allowing the SR signals to reach the NOR gates. The clock's active period when $CLOCK = 1$ must be long enough to allow the flip-flop time to change state. When a flip-flop is switched on, its state is uncertain unless it is explicitly brought to a known initial state. It is therefore desirable to be able to set or reset the flip-flop asynchronously, that is, independently of the clock signal, at the start of operation. To this end the basic SR flip-flop has been further modified by the addition of two unclocked inputs: P (preset), which sets y to 1, and C (clear), which resets y to 0; P and C function just like S and R in the original asynchronous case. Because of its use of a clock signal to control its main input signals, the flip-flop of Fig. 2.27 is known as a *clocked* SR flip-flop.

Figure 2.28 shows how two important flip-flop types, the JK and D flip-flops, are derived from the clocked SR type. A *JK flip-flop* (Fig. 2.28a)

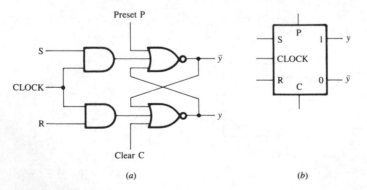

(a)   (b)

FIGURE 2.27
Clocked SR flip-flop: (a) logic circuit; (b) symbol.

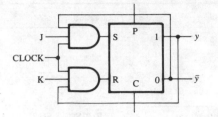

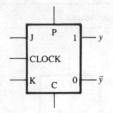

(a)

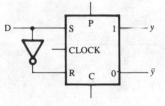
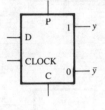

(b)

FIGURE 2.28
(a) JK flip-flop; (b) D (delay) flip-flop.

behaves like an SR flip-flop with J replacing S, and K replacing R, except that the input combination 11 is no longer forbidden. Again JK $= 00$ is the quiescent input combination, while JK $= 10$ and 01 take the flip-flop to the set and reset states, respectively. The JK flip-flop responds to JK $= 11$ by always changing state, since the 11 input is converted to 01 or 10 depending on the current state, before it is applied to the SR flip-flop part of the circuit. The D (*delay*) *flip-flop* also avoids the forbidden input problem, this time by deriving the S and R signals from a single input line with the property that D $=$ S $= \overline{R}$. It is easily seen that, when activated, the D flip-flop's output $y(t + \tau)$ always becomes D(t); in other words, y is a delayed version of the signal applied to the D line. Thus the D flip-flop resembles a clocked version of an ideal delay element (Fig. 2.22); hence its name.

Figure 2.29 summarizes the three flip-flop types discussed above. Since they are designed to have their effective state transition times controlled by an external clock signal rather than internal delays, it is convenient to consider state changes as taking place at unit time intervals, where the unit in question is one clock period. In general, a clock signal has the effect of quantizing time in a sequential circuit, so that successive events of interest (state changes) take place at discrete times $t, t + 1$, $t + 2, \ldots, t + n$, where n denotes n clock periods after the reference point of time t.

The memory part M of a synchronous sequential circuit (Fig. 2.24) is realized by a set of flip-flops connected to a common clock signal. The clock signal should ideally be enabled just long enough to allow all the flip-flops to respond to their new input values by making a single well-defined state transition. If the flip-flops

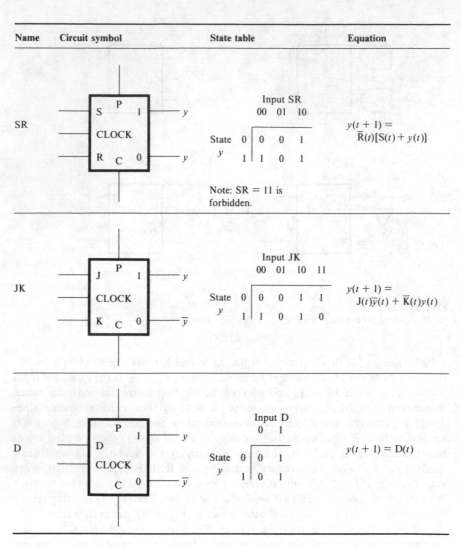

Name	Circuit symbol	State table	Equation

SR

Input SR
  00 01 10

State 0 | 0 0 1
y 1 | 1 0 1

$y(t+1) =$
$\overline{R}(t)[S(t) + y(t)]$

Note: SR = 11 is forbidden.

JK

Input JK
  00 01 10 11

State 0 | 0 0 1 1
y 1 | 1 0 1 0

$y(t+1) =$
$J(t)\overline{y}(t) + \overline{K}(t)y(t)$

D

Input D
  0 1

State 0 | 0 1
y 1 | 0 1

$y(t+1) = D(t)$

FIGURE 2.29
The major flip-flop types.

are enabled too long or, equivalently, some flip-flop outputs change too quickly, these output changes (representing new internal state signals) can propagate all the way around the circuit through C and back to M again, possibly causing some flip-flops to change state a second time during one clock cycle. This is a type of race condition that can occur if the feedback paths from M's outputs to its inputs are relatively short, and an unfavorable combination of gate delays and input signal changes is present.

To avert the foregoing problem, a more complex type of flip-flop termed a *master-slave* flip-flop is used. Like the flip-flops of Fig. 2.29, a master-slave flip-flop uses a clock signal to set the time at which it responds to changes on the Y_i lines feeding its main data inputs (SR, JK, or D). In addition, however, the master-slave unit uses the clock to control the time at which its y_i outputs change value. This behavior is achieved by connecting two simple clocked flip-flops in series in such a way that each can be enabled while the other is disabled. Figure 2.30 shows a master-slave JK-flip-flop; master-slave versions of other flip-flop types are similar. The Y_i signals from C are applied to the first flip-flop (the master) when the clock is first activated, e.g., when CLOCK goes from 0 to 1. At the same time the second flip-flop (the slave), from which the y_i signals are derived, is disabled. Changes occurring inside the master-slave flip-flop are then prevented from propagating outside the flip-flop back to its inputs. At a later point, e.g., when CLOCK returns from 1 to 0, the slave is enabled while the master is disabled. The slave then assumes the master's new state and propagates the new state information to C. Because the master is now disabled, the resulting signals cannot affect the master-slave flip-flop until the clock is again enabled during the following clock cycle. Many variants of the master-slave principle have been developed to decrease the likelihood of a flip-flop behaving improperly. Typically, the basic circuit symbols of Fig. 2.29 are used for all these variants.

Design techniques. A well-defined formal design methodology exists for gate-level synchronous sequential circuits, which may be summarized as follows:

Step 1. Construct a state table from the given specifications of the required circuit behavior. If desired, the state table may be reduced to a form having the minimum number of states using well-understood (but computationally complex) state minimization techniques.

Step 2. Select the flip-flop types to be used, and assign a binary code (the state assignment) to the states identified in step 1. For n states, at least $\log_2 n$ flip-flops are required.

Step 3. Construct a truth table (or equivalent representation) of a combina-

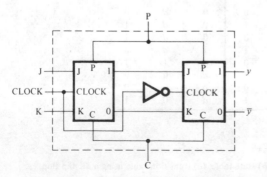

FIGURE 2.30
JK master-slave flip-flop.

tional circuit C defining the input signals $\{Y_i\}$ that must be applied to the flip-flops to produce the required state behavior; C should also define the primary output signals $\{z_i\}$.

Step 4. Design C using any appropriate design approach such as the K-map method.

We now illustrate the foregoing design methodology by applying it to a small but useful sequential circuit, a serial binary adder.

Example 2.2 Design of a serial binary adder. This circuit, which has the overall structure depicted in Fig. 2.31a, is required to add two binary numbers X_1 and X_2 of arbitrary length, producing the numerical sum $Z = X_1 + X_2$. The input numbers are entered into the adder serially, i.e., bit by bit, and the result is also sent out serially. In one clock cycle corresponding to time t, the adder can receive 2 bits $x_1(t)$ and $x_2(t)$ of X_1 and X_2 and compute 1 bit $z(t)$ of Z. Clearly each 1-bit addition can produce a carry signal $c(t)$ which affects the addition to be done in the next clock period. Thus two possible circuit states can exist: S_0, meaning no carry signal was produced in the preceding clock cycle, i.e., $c(t - 1) = 0$; and S_1, meaning $c(t - 1) = 1$. The addition performed at each step must then take the form $x_1(t) + x_2(t) + c(t - 1)$, where $c(t - 1)$ is determined from the state present at time t. These considerations lead to the two-state state table of Fig. 2.31b. Each entry in row $S(t)$ and column $I(t) = x_1(t)x_2(t)$

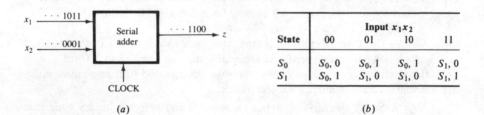

		Input x_1x_2		
State	00	01	10	11
S_0	$S_0, 0$	$S_0, 1$	$S_0, 1$	$S_1, 0$
S_1	$S_0, 1$	$S_1, 0$	$S_1, 0$	$S_1, 1$

(a) (b)

	Inputs		Outputs		
$y(t)$	$x_1(t)$	$x_2(t)$	$J(t)$	$K(t)$	$z(t)$
0	0	0	0	d	0
0	0	1	0	d	1
0	1	0	0	d	1
0	1	1	1	d	0
1	0	0	d	1	1
1	0	1	d	0	0
1	1	0	d	0	0
1	1	1	d	0	1

(c)

FIGURE 2.31
Serial binary adder: (a) overall structure; (b) state table; (c) transition table using a JK flip-flop.

of the state table has the form $S(t + 1)$, $z(t)$ where $S(t + 1)$ is the next internal state that the circuit must have in response to the present state $S(t)$ and the present primary input combination $I(t)$, while $z(t)$ is the corresponding primary output signal that must be generated.

Since there are only two states, one flip-flop suffices for M, with a (master-slave) JK flip-flop being a good choice. If y is the flip-flop's state variable, then there are only two possible state assignments; we select the more natural one with $y = 0$ for S_0 and $y = 1$ for S_1. We next construct a truth table, called a *transition table*, whose inputs are x_1, x_2, and y, and whose outputs are the input (excitation) signals J and K of the flip-flop, and also the primary output z. Here J and K are the quantities denoted $\{Y_i\}$ in the general sequential circuit model of Fig. 2.24. The entry in the first row and column of the state table (Fig. 2.31b) implies that if $y(t) = 0$ and $x_1(t)x_2(t)$ $= 00$, then $y(t + 1)$ must also be 0. Consequently, we must set the JK flip-flop's inputs to values that ensure that y goes from 0 to 0, i.e., the flip-flop remains in the reset state. Clearly, this will happen if JK = 00. However, it will also happen if JK = 01; consequently we can write JK = $0d$, where d denotes don't care. As we showed in Example 2.1, d's can be exploited to reduce the number of gates and the gate fan-in required to realize a combinational function. We therefore chose JK = $0d$ in this case, yielding the first row of the transition table of Fig. 2.31c. The remaining rows are constructed in similar fashion, taking advantage of don't cares wherever possible. For instance, the fourth row specifies a state change from $y = 0$ to $y = 1$. This can be produced either by JK = 10 or JK = 11; hence we use JK = $1d$. Note that if we were using an SR flip-flop we would have to use SR = 10, since SR = 11 is not permitted.

The transition table of Fig. 2.31c defines the behavior of the combinational part C of the serial adder. We now proceed to obtain a minimal two-level realization of C using the K-map method of Sec. 2.2.1. Figure 2.32 shows K-maps for J, K, and z which are derived directly from the transition table (and contain precisely the same information). Minimal SOP forms can be obtained immediately by inspection. The various prime implicants required, all of which are essential, are circled on the K-maps. Note that the d's reduce the fan-in of the gates generating the J and K signals to the flip-flop. A single two-input AND gate or equivalent suffices in each case. The resulting sequential circuit with C realized by AND, OR, and NOT gates appears in Fig. 2.33. Note how advantage is taken of the fact that the flip-flop provides both y and $\bar{y}$ directly. Before entering two new numbers to be added, it is necessary to reset the adder to the S_0 state. This is most easily accomplished by connecting a RESET control line directly to the flip-flop's asynchronous clear (C) input as indicated in Fig. 2.33.

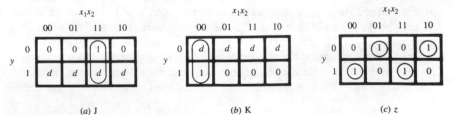

(a) J   (b) K   (c) z

FIGURE 2.32
K-maps for the serial adder.

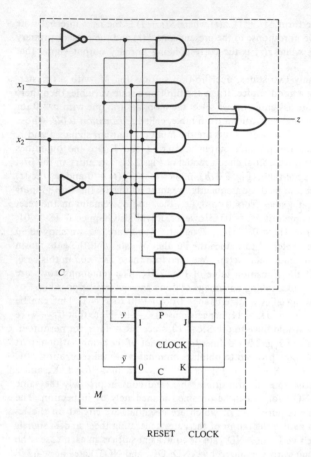

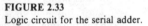

FIGURE 2.33
Logic circuit for the serial adder.

Minimizing the number of gates in a sequential circuit is very difficult because it is affected by the choice of flip-flops, the state assignment code, and, of course, the manner in which the combinational subcircuit C is designed. Other formal design techniques exist that attempt to simplify the design process at the expense of using more logic elements, e.g., the so-called *one-hot* technique that assigns one flip-flop to every state. A version of the one-hot approach (the delay-element method for designing small sequential control units) is discussed in Sec. 4.2; see also Prob. 2.12. Note that it is usually impractical to deal with complete binary descriptions like state tables if they contain more than, say, 20 states. Consequently, larger sequential circuits are designed by heuristic techniques which produce implementations that use reasonable but nonminimal amounts of hardware. These circuits are often best tackled at the register level rather than the gate level.

2.3 THE REGISTER LEVEL

The register level is a natural choice as the next highest level after the gate level in the computer design hierarchy. Related information bits are grouped into ordered sets called words or vectors. The primitive components are combinational or sequential circuits designed to process or store words. The complexity of these components corresponds approximately to the MSI range of IC density.

2.3.1 Introduction

Register-level circuits are composed of various types of word-oriented components, the more important of which are listed in Fig. 2.34. The key sequential component, from which this complexity level derives its name, is a (parallel) *register*, that is, a storage device for words. The other commonly used sequential elements are shift registers and counters, which are only a little more complex than basic registers. A larger number of combinational components exist, ranging from general-purpose components like Boolean word gates, to specialized circuits like decoders and adders. Register-level components are linked together to form circuits by means of word-carrying groups of lines, which are referred to as *buses*. Because a bus is treated as a primitive connection, it may be represented by a single line in a circuit diagram.

The components of Fig. 2.34 have been found generally useful in digital system design and are available as standard parts in various MSI IC series. It might be asked if they can be identified a priori based on some property analogous to the completeness property of gate-level Boolean operations. The answer appears to be no. For example, we will show that any combinational function can be realized by a network of multiplexers. This completeness property is incidental to their main application, which is signal selection or path switching. Similarly, a logic element, called a programmable logic array (PLA), is functionally complete. Either of these components in combination with registers (which are simply sets of flip-flops) could be used to realize any sequential machine according to the Huffman model of Fig. 2.24.

Circuit symbols. There are no widely accepted circuit symbols for the above components. They are generally represented in circuit diagrams by blocks containing an

Type	Component	Functions
Combinational	Word gates	Boolean operations
	Multiplexers	Data routing; general function generation
	Decoders and encoders	Code checking and conversion
	Programmable arrays	General function generation
	Arithmetic elements (adders, ALUs)	Numerical operations
Sequential	(Parallel) registers	Information storage
	Shift registers	Information storage; serial-parallel conversion
	Counters	Control/timing signal generation

FIGURE 2.34
The major component types at the register level.

appropriate written description of their behavior, as in Fig. 2.35. Similar to the format of Fig. 2.6, there is frequently an explicit or implicit separation of the input-output lines into data and control lines. Each such line may represent a bus transmitting $m \geq 1$ bits of information in parallel; m may be indicated in the block diagram by placing a slash ($/$) in the line and writing m next to it, as is done in Fig. 2.35.

Each m-bit line in a register-level block diagram is given a name which identifies the data transmitted over the line or, in the case of a control line, indicates the function initiated by the control line when it is in its "active," or "asserted," state. The active state of a line is usually that which exists when all the binary signals it transmits assume the logical 1 value. A small circle (representing logical inversion) placed at an input or output of a block indicates that the corresponding lines are active in the 0 state and inactive in the 1 state. Alternatively, the inversion circle may be omitted and an overbar placed over the line's name.

The control input lines associated with a block may be divided into two broad categories: "select" lines, which specify one of several possible operations that the circuit is to perform; and "enable" lines, which specify the time at which a selected operation is to be performed. Thus in Fig. 2.35, to perform the operation F_1, first activate the F_1 SELECT line by applying a logical 1 and then activate F_1 ENABLE by applying a logical 0. Enable lines are frequently connected directly to timing signals (clocks). The output control signals, if any, from a component may indicate the time that the component completes its processing or the completion state (normal or abnormal end). These control signals can then be used to select the next operation to be performed.

Word-based Boolean algebra. The two-valued Boolean algebra that forms the basis of switching theory has as its elements combinational functions of the form z: $B^n \rightarrow B$, where $B = \{0, 1\}$. We can extend this algebra in a straightforward way to a 2^m-valued Boolean algebra whose elements are word- or vector-based combina-

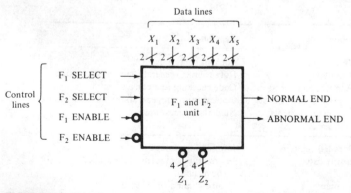

FIGURE 2.35
Typical block representation of a register-level component.

tional functions that perform the mapping $z: (B^m)^n \rightarrow B^m$. Let $z(x_0, x_1, \ldots, x_{n-1})$ be any two-valued Boolean function. Let $X_0, X_1, \ldots, X_{n-1}$ denote m-bit binary words, i.e., members of B^m, having the form

$$X_i = (x_{i,0}, x_{i,1}, \ldots, x_{i,m-1})$$

for $i = 0, 1, \ldots, n - 1$. We define $z: (B^m)^n \rightarrow B^m$ as follows:

$$z(X_0, X_1, \ldots, X_{n-1}) = [z(x_{0,0}, x_{1,0}, \ldots, x_{n-1,0}),$$
$$z(x_{0,1}, x_{1,1}, \ldots, x_{n-1,1}), \ldots$$
$$z(x_{0,m-1}, x_{1,m-1}, \ldots, x_{n-1,m-1})]$$

Using this definition, we can immediately extend the usual gate operations, AND, OR, NOT, NAND, etc., to word-gate operations. It is easily shown that the set K_n^m of all $2^{2^{mn}}$ combinational functions of up to n m-bit words is a Boolean algebra with respect to the m-bit word-gate operations {AND, OR, NOT}.

The extension of z to apply to m-bit vectors is achieved by operating on components of the vector with the same index. This is analogous to the extension of the algebra of real numbers to real vectors. Pursuing this analogy, we can regard 1-bit words as "scalars" and define scalar logical multiplication and addition by

$$yX = (yx_0, yx_1, \ldots, yx_{m-1})$$

and

$$y + X = (y + x_0, y + x_1, \ldots, y + x_{m-1})$$

respectively.

Although a word-based Boolean algebra is useful in analyzing certain aspects of register-level design, it does not by itself provide an adequate design theory. This may be attributed to several causes.

1. The operations performed by some of the basic components are numerical rather than logical and are not easily incorporated within the framework of a Boolean algebra.
2. Many of the logical operations associated with the basic components are complex and do not have the properties of the gate functions (associativity, commutativity, etc.) which simplify gate-level design.
3. Although a standard word length w is defined in many systems, based on the width of some important buses or registers, many lines carry signals with a different number of bits. For example, the outcome of a logical test on a set S of w-bit words (does S have property P?) is 1 bit rather than w. The lack of a uniform word size for all signals makes it difficult to define a useful algebra to describe operations on these signals.

Another perspective on the design problem may be obtained by noting that hardware design at the register level is analogous to the design of a program using an assembly language (a somewhat weaker analogy can be made with high-level language programming). In each case, the designer is concerned with processing words using a fixed set of elementary logical and arithmetic operations. Although assembly-language programming has been practiced for many years and has been the subject of intensive study, it remains more an art than a science. Lacking an adequate general theory, the useful goal of optimizing program design is, in practice, attacked mainly by heuristic and intuitive methods. The status of register-level hardware design is essentially the same.

Since many different word sizes are encountered in register-level design, it is desirable to be able to use k-input components of a given type to construct K-input components of the same type where $k \neq K$. The case where $K < k$ is usually quite simple. A single k-input component is taken and the superfluous $k - K$ inputs are deactivated by connecting them to appropriate logical constant values. In some circuit technologies it suffices to leave superfluous inputs unconnected, or "floating." When $K > k$, a circuit constructed from several copies of the basic k-input components, and possibly other types of components as well, is required. Register-level components are designed so that increasing the number of inputs is relatively easy. It will be seen in Sec. 2.3.2 that the control lines often play an important role in component expandability.

Description languages. Although block diagrams, state tables, and their many variations are, in principle, quite sufficient to describe the structure and behavior of any system, other descriptive methods have been developed which strive for the precision and conciseness of a set of equations or a computer program. The construction of such description languages can be traced back at least as far as Babbage [23]. Babbage's notation, of which he was very proud, centered around the use of various arrow symbols such as $\rightarrow$ to represent the transfer of mechanical motion. In modern times, the introduction of Boolean algebra as a descriptive method for logic circuits is due mainly to Claude E. Shannon [24]. The use of symbolic descriptions for high-level computer design was pioneered by Irving S. Reed [22]. These efforts are distinguished from developments in programming languages in that the objective is to describe the structure or behavior of a computer; they are not concerned with applications of the computer. Since a large number of description languages have been proposed in recent years [10, 28], we will therefore consider their relevance to computer design. As the common name "register transfer language" implies, these languages are primarily intended for describing computer systems at the register level.

The essential element of all computer description languages is the *register transfer statement*. This has the general form

$$Z \leftarrow f(X_1, X_2, \ldots, X_n) \tag{2.11}$$

where Z, X_1, X_2, $\ldots$, X_n denote registers or their contents, and f denotes a function, usually Boolean or numerical. Statement (2.11) has the following behavioral interpretation: compute the function f using the contents of registers X_1, X_2, $\ldots$, X_n as inputs, and place the result in register Z. It therefore specifies a (partial) state transition for the machine [cf. (2.1) in Sec. 2.1.1] and takes place during a single clock cycle. It is frequently useful to separate the data and control functions by explicitly naming the control conditions necessary for the register transfer to take place. Thus

$$c: \quad Z \leftarrow f(X_1, X_2, \ldots, X_n) \tag{2.12}$$

might be used to mean: when the Boolean expression c is 1, that is, when the control condition c is satisfied, perform the indicated transfer. Frequently, the format of a conditional statement in a programming language such as Pascal is adopted. An alternative notation for (2.12) might be

$$\textbf{if } c = 1 \textbf{ then } Z \leftarrow f(X_1, X_2, \ldots, X_n)$$

A natural starting point in developing a description language is an existing high-level programming language. Indeed, programming languages may be used directly to describe the behavior of a complex system; see, for example, the APL description of the IBM System/360, which represents one of the earliest and most ambitious efforts of this type [11]. Difficulties arise, however, when such languages are used to describe the hardware of the system in question. For this to be possible, it is necessary to provide a hardware interpretation for the language, i.e., to specify a correspondence between elements of the language and hardware components and signals. For example, the statement

$$c: \quad A \leftarrow A + B$$

could be used to describe the circuit of Fig. 2.36. In this interpretation, + represents the parallel adder. The input connections to the adder from registers A and B are inferred from the fact that A and B are the arguments of +, while the output connection from the adder to register A may be inferred from $A \leftarrow$. The role of the control signal c is unclear without further information.

High-level programming languages are, by definition, machine-independent. This implies that they are not necessarily capable of describing machine hardware. One finds, therefore, that most description languages are programming languages augmented by constructs that describe hardware features such as component types, signal-propagation times, and the like. Unfortunately, in many instances an adequate hardware interpretation is lacking, resulting in descriptions that may be ambiguous from a structural point of view. However, such languages are very suitable for behavioral or functional descriptions. They are particularly useful in two areas of system design: describing control unit behavior and simulation. In cases

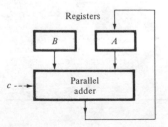

FIGURE 2.36
Hardware represented by the statement $c: A \leftarrow A + B$.

where the control function is implemented by programs, as in a microprogrammed control unit, the control programs themselves may constitute the most useful description of the control unit's behavior. The programming language used is then the natural description language. The second application of formal description languages is to define the input to simulation programs used for design verification and performance evaluation. Other potential applications exist in the area of design automation of digital systems [7]; however, these are limited by our lack of understanding of the design process itself.

A sample language. In this book use is made of the simple description language introduced in Sec. 1.2.3 to describe the IAS instruction set. The language is mainly employed as a shorthand notation for describing system behavior and is intended to be self-explanatory.

Figure 2.37 illustrates the use of this language to describe concisely the behavior of an 8-bit multiplication circuit that computes the product $Z = Y \times X$, where the numbers are binary fractions in sign-magnitude form. (The actual design of the multiplier is considered in more detail later in Example 2.3.) The multiplication algorithm used is a binary version of manual "long" multiplication and is based on iterated addition and shifting. The circuit employs three 8-bit data registers A, M, and Q, as well as a 3-bit control register COUNT that functions as an iteration or loop counter. The A and Q registers can be combined into a single 16-bit shift register denoted A.Q. Two 8-bit buses INBUS and OUTBUS link the multiplier to the outside world. The operands X (the multiplier) and Y (the multiplicand) are initially transferred from INBUS into the Q and M registers, respectively. The product is computed by multiplying Y by 1 bit of X at a time, and adding the result to A. After each addition step, the contents of A.Q are shifted 1 bit to the right, so that the next multiplier bit required is always in Q(7), the rightmost flip-flop in the Q register. (This means that the multiplier Y is eventually shifted out of Q and lost.) After seven iterations to multiply the magnitude parts of X and Y, the sign of the product is computed and placed in the leftmost flip-flop of A, that is, in

---

	declare register A(0:7), M(0:7), Q(0:7), COUNT(0:2)
	declare bus INBUS(0:7), OUTBUS(0:7)
BEGIN:	A ← 0, COUNT ← 0,
INPUT:	M ← INBUS;
	Q ← INBUS;
ADD:	A(0:7) ← A(1:7) + M(1:7) × Q(7);
RIGHTSHIFT:	A(0) ← 0, A(1:7).Q ← A.Q(0:6),
TEST:	COUNT ← COUNT + 1;
	if COUNT ≠ 7 **then go to** ADD,
FINISH:	A(0) ← M(0) ⊕ Q(7), Q(7), ← 0;
OUTPUT:	OUTBUS ← Q;
	OUTBUS ← A;
END:	

FIGURE 2.37
Formal language description of an 8-bit binary multiplier.

A(0). The 16-bit product ends up in A.Q, from which it is transferred 8 bits at a time to OUTBUS.

The description of the multiplier consists mostly of register transfer operations. The registers are defined by the initial **declare** statements, which give the names of the registers, their sizes, and the order in which their bits are indexed. For example,

$$\textbf{declare } M(0{:}7)$$

means that M is a register composed of eight flip-flops individually identified as M(i), where i runs from 0 to 7 from left to right. Equivalently, we could write

$$M = M(0).M(1).M(2).M(3).M(4).M(5).M(6).M(7)$$

Since buses are used in much the same way as registers, they are declared similarly. Register transfer operations that can take place simultaneously, i.e., during the same clock cycle, are separated by commas, while a semicolon separates sets of operations that must occur in successive clock cycles. Thus the statement

$$A \leftarrow 0, \text{COUNT} \leftarrow 0, M \leftarrow \text{INBUS};$$

appearing on the two lines labeled BEGIN and INPUT in Fig. 2.37, specifies three separate actions to take place simultaneously: transfer the all-0 operand into the accumulator A, i.e., reset or clear A; reset the COUNT register; and transfer the data on the bus INBUS into register M. Note that if a register is composed of master-slave flip-flops, it can be read from and written into in the same statement, as happens in the case of the Q register in the statement

$$A(0) \leftarrow M(0) \oplus Q(7), Q(7) \leftarrow 0;$$

The **if . . . then** construction is used in our language to make an action conditional on some circuit condition. The order in which the statements of a description (those terminating in semicolons) are written is the sequence in which the actions they define should occur. Deviations from this sequence are specified by conditional and unconditional **go to** statements, and by the use of statement labels. For example, the conditional branch statement

$$\textbf{if } \text{COUNT} \neq 7 \textbf{ then go to } \text{ADD}, \tag{2.13}$$

appearing in Fig. 2.37 means that the state of the 3-bit COUNT register should be tested. If COUNT is not equal to 7 (decimal), that is, 111 (binary), then the next action is specified by the statement labeled ADD. If COUNT = 7, then the next action is specified by the statement immediately following (2.13). Such tests can normally take place during the same clock cycle as a subsequent register transfer operation, and so may terminate in a comma instead of a semicolon.

2.3.2 Register-Level Components

Next we discuss the characteristics of the major combinational and sequential components used in design at the register level. These components are summarized in Fig. 2.34.

Word gates. Let $X = (x_0, x_1, \ldots, x_{m-1})$ and $Y = (y_0, y_1, \ldots, y_{m-1})$ be two m-bit binary words. It is often useful to perform gate operations (AND, OR, etc.) on X and Y to obtain another m-bit vector Z. We coin the term *word-gate operations* for functions of this type. More formally, if f is a Boolean operator, then we write $Z = f(X, Y)$ if $z_i = f(x_i, y_i)$ for $i = 0, 1, \ldots, m - 1$. As mentioned in Sec. 2.3.1, this represents an extension of the two-valued Boolean algebra used for gate-level design to a 2^m-valued Boolean algebra; it is therefore natural to use the same notation. Thus $Z = \overline{XY}$ denotes the m-bit NAND operation defined by

$$(z_0, z_1, \ldots, z_{m-1}) = (\overline{x_0 y_0}, \overline{x_1 y_1}, \ldots, \overline{x_{m-1} y_{m-1}})$$

This generalized NAND operation is realized by the circuit in Fig. 2.38a. We may represent this circuit by a single two-input NAND symbol, as shown in Fig. 2.38b, in register-level diagrams. It is also useful to represent scalar operations on words by a single gate. Thus the operation $y + X$ is realized by the circuit of Fig. 2.39a and will be represented by the OR gate of Fig. 2.39b.

Word gates are universal design components, i.e., they are logically complete, and word-gate circuits can be analyzed using Boolean algebra. In practice, their usefulness is limited because of the relatively simple or low-level operations they perform and because of the variability in word size discussed in Sec. 2.3.1.

Multiplexers. A multiplexer is a device intended to route data from one of several sources to a common destination; the source is determined by applying appropriate control (select) signals to the multiplexer. If the maximum number of data sources is k and each IO data line carries m bits, the multiplexer is referred to as a *k-input m-bit multiplexer* and may be represented by the symbol shown in Fig. 2.40. It is convenient to make $k = 2^p$, so that source selection is determined by an encoded pattern or address of p bits. Let $a_i = 1$ when input X_i is to be selected. If $a_i = 1$ when the binary number i is applied to the select bus S, then X_i is connected to Z when $e = 1$. The operation of the multiplexer can be defined formally by the m SOP Boolean equations

$$z_j = \sum_{i=0}^{k-1} x_{i,j} a_i e \qquad \text{for } j = 0, 1, \ldots, m - 1 \tag{2.14}$$

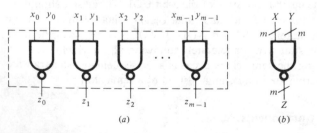

(a)

(b)

FIGURE 2.38
A two-input m-bit NAND word gate: (a) logic diagram; (b) symbol.

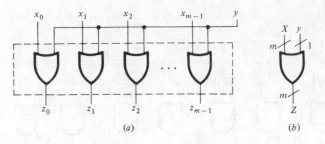

(a)   (b)

FIGURE 2.39
An OR word gate implementing scalar logical addition: (a) logic diagram; (b) symbol.

or by the single word-based Boolean equation

$$z = \sum_{i=0}^{k-1} x_i a_i e$$

Figure 2.41 shows a realization of a two-input 4-bit multiplexer.

k-input multiplexers can be used to route more than k data paths by connecting them in the treelike fashion shown in Fig. 2.42. A q-level tree circuit of this type forms a k^q-input multiplexer. A distinct set of select lines is associated with each level of the tree and is connected to all k-input multiplexers in that level. Thus each level performs a partial selection of the input line X_i to be connected to the output Z.

Multiplexers have the interesting property that they can be used to generate any combinational function and can therefore be viewed as a type of universal logic module. Specifically, any n-variable function z can be generated by a 2^n-input 1-bit multiplexer. This is accomplished by connecting the n input variables (s_0, s_1, ..., s_{n-1}) to the n select control lines of the multiplexer. If x_i denotes the ith data input line, then the output z, which is defined by (2.14), becomes

$$z = \sum_{i=0}^{2^n-1} x_i a_i e \qquad (2.15)$$

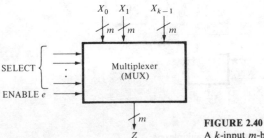

FIGURE 2.40
A k-input m-bit multiplexer.

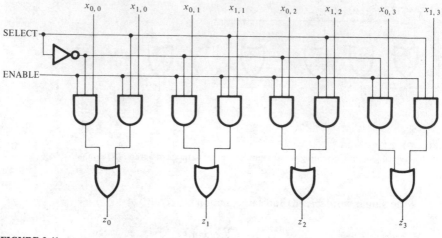

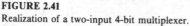

FIGURE 2.41
Realization of a two-input 4-bit multiplexer.

The term a_i, which is 1 when x_i is selected, corresponds to the ith minterm with respect to the select variables $s_0, s_1, \ldots, s_{n-1}$. By setting $e = 1$ and $x_i = 1$ (0) if a_i is a minterm (maxterm) of $z(s_0, s_1, \ldots, s_{n-1})$, then (2.15) becomes a canonical sum-of-minterms expression for z. Hence by connecting each input data line to the appropriate constant logic value 0 or 1, any of the 2^{2^n} functions of n variables can be realized. In fact, a 2^n-input 1-bit multiplexer can be used to realize any $(n + 1)$-variable function (see Prob. 2.14).

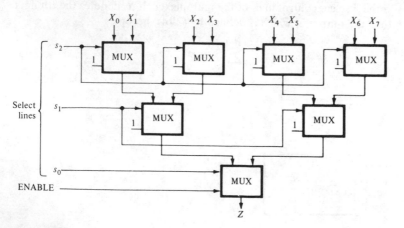

FIGURE 2.42
An eight-input multiplexer constructed from two-input multiplexers.

Decoders. A 1-out-of-2^n or *$1/2^n$ decoder* is a combinational circuit with n input data lines and 2^n output data lines such that each of the 2^n possible input combinations X_i activates (sets to 1) exactly one of the output lines z_i. Figure 2.43 shows a $1/4$ decoder.

The primary application of a decoder is that of addressing, where the n-bit input X is interpreted as an address used to select one of 2^n output lines. $1/2^n$ decoders can be used to decode more than n lines by connecting them in a tree circuit analogous to the multiplexer tree of Fig. 2.42. Another common application of decoders is that of routing data from a common source to one of several destinations. A circuit of this kind is called a *demultiplexer*, since it is, in effect, the inverse of a multiplexer. In this application the enable (control) input of the decoder is viewed as a 1-bit "data source" to be routed to one of 2^n destinations as determined by the address applied to the decoder. Thus a $1/2^n$ decoder is a 2^n-output 1-bit demultiplexer. A k-output m-bit demultiplexer can be constructed from a network of decoders. Figure 2.44 shows a four-output 2-bit demultiplexer that employs two $1/4$ decoders of the type in Fig. 2.43.

Encoders. An *encoder* is a circuit used to generate the address or name of an active input line; it is therefore the inverse of a decoder. A typical encoder has 2^k input data lines and k output address lines. An additional output control line may be used to indicate the presence or absence of an active input line. Figure 2.45 shows a simple 8-bit encoder of this type. Note that the control output is necessary to distinguish the input x_0 active and no input active states. A disadvantage of this type of encoder is that if more than one input line is active, an invalid address is generated. For example, if $x_1 = x_2 = 1$ in the circuit of Fig. 2.45, the output $Z = (0, 1, 1)$ is produced, which normally indicates that x_3 is active. To avoid this ambiguity, it is useful to assign priorities to the input lines and design the encoder so that the output address is always that of the active input line with the highest

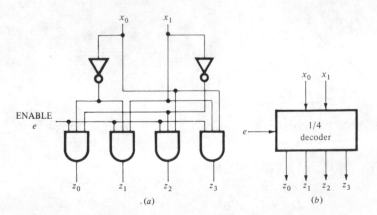

FIGURE 2.43
A $1/4$ decoder: (*a*) logic diagram; (*b*) symbol.

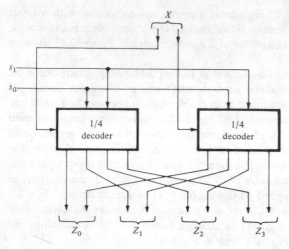

FIGURE 2.44
A four-output 2-bit demultiplexer.

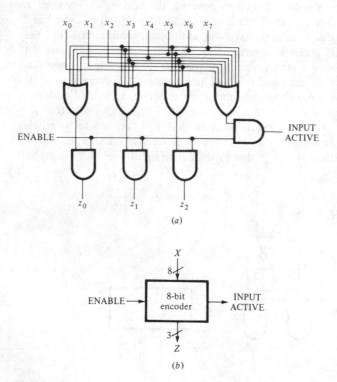

FIGURE 2.45
A simple 8-bit encoder: (*a*) logic diagram; (*b*) symbol.

priority; a circuit of this type is called a *priority encoder*. A fixed priority is assigned to each input line such that x_i has higher priority than x_j if $i > j$. The logic design of a priority encoder is left as an exercise (Prob. 2.16).

Array logic. There are many applications, especially in the design of control logic, where a set of combinational functions must be implemented that are essentially random, i.e., which cannot easily be classified. A number of general-purpose logic elements have been developed which permit efficient realization of complex random combinational functions. In general, such components have to meet the following requirements.

1. Each component should have a uniform underlying structure permitting efficient mass production using modern integrated-circuit techniques.
2. It should be possible to modify the basic structure during manufacture to implement the specific functions required by a designer.

These objectives can be achieved by a class of integrated circuits whose physical structure is that of a two-dimensional array of simple switching elements. We will discuss one representative type of array logic element here, the so-called programmable logic array or PLA. Another important array element is the read-only memory (see Prob. 2.18).

A PLA is a device that realizes a set of combinational functions by means of a two-level circuit corresponding to the SOP form given by Eq. (2.3). The physical structure of a PLA typically has the form of a grid of conductors arranged as p rows and q columns, with a coupling element such as a diode or transistor connecting the horizontal and vertical wires at each grid point. Figure 2.46a shows such an array which employs diodes. A subset of $2n$ columns are chosen as inputs; each of the n input variables and their complements are applied to these lines. The remaining $q - 2n$ columns may be used as output lines to realize a set of $q - 2n$ n-variable combinational functions. The functions to be realized are determined by breaking the connections to certain diodes. This may be done by either customizing the connector grid layout or else eliminating unwanted diodes during manufacture of the PLA.

The diodes in the $p \times 2n$ subarray connected to the input variables act as AND gates. Each row of this subarray generates a product term. These product terms are input to the $p \times (q - 2n)$ subarray connected to the output lines. The diodes in this output subarray act as OR gates so that the function on each output line is the logical sum of the product terms on the rows to which it is connected. In general, a $p \times q$ PLA can realize a set of $q - 2n$ functions of n variables provided the functions can collectively be expressed as sums of at most p product terms. Figure 2.46b shows a 4×8 array that has been specialized (programmed) to realize the two 3-variable functions:

$$f_1 = x_1\bar{x}_2 + \bar{x}_2 x_3 + x_1 x_3 \tag{2.16}$$

$$f_2 = x_1\bar{x}_2 + \bar{x}_1 x_2 x_3 \qquad (2.17)$$

The rules for programming the array to implement any given function can easily be deduced from this example. Note that the minimization techniques for two-level logic circuits discussed in Sec. 2.2.1 are directly applicable to PLA design.

Arithmetic elements. A few fairly simple arithmetic functions, notably addition and subtraction of fixed-point numbers, can be implemented by combinational register-level components. Most forms of fixed-point multiplication and division,

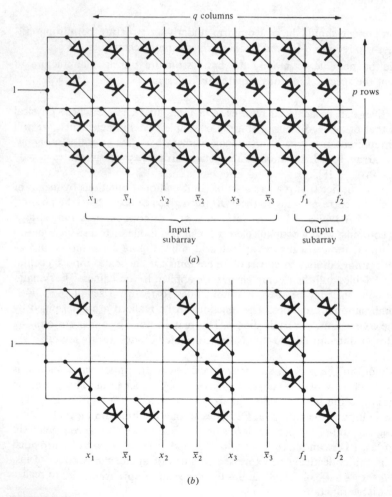

FIGURE 2.46
A 4 × 8 programmable logic array: (*a*) before and (*b*) after the modification to realize a pair of three-variable functions f_1, f_2.

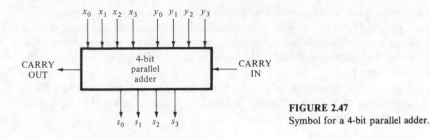

FIGURE 2.47
Symbol for a 4-bit parallel adder.

and all floating-point operations, are too complex to be realized by single components at this design level. Figure 2.47 shows a 4-bit version of a parallel adder for fixed-point binary numbers. The two carry lines allow multiple copies of this component to be chained together to add numbers of arbitrary size; however, it should be noted that the addition time increases with the number size. As will be discussed later, this type of adder is easily modified to perform both subtraction and addition if twos-complement number representation is used. The design of adders and more complex arithmetic circuits is covered in Chap. 3.

Another useful circuit is a *comparator* whose function is to compare the magnitudes of two numbers. Figure 2.48 shows our symbol for a 4-bit comparator. Comparators are relatively complex circuits requiring either many gates or many logic levels. (Readers may convince themselves of this by deriving a logic circuit for the 4-bit comparator of Fig. 2.48.) When large numbers are involved, it may be more efficient to implement the comparison operation by subtracting one number from the other and testing the sign of their difference.

Registers. An m-bit register is an ordered set of m flip-flops used to store an m-bit word $(z_0, z_1, \ldots, z_{m-1})$. Each bit of the word is stored in a separate flip-flop. Unless otherwise specified, the data lines of the flip-flops are assumed to be independent. Data may be transferred to or from all flip-flops simultaneously; this mode of operation is called *parallel input-output*. Since the stored information is treated as a single entity, common control signals (clock, preset, clear) are used for all flip-flops in the register. Registers can be constructed from any of the flip-flop types defined in Sec. 2.2.2. Master-slave configurations are often employed so that

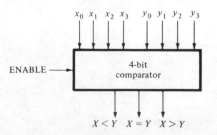

FIGURE 2.48
Symbol for a 4-bit comparator.

no restrictions have to be placed on feedback from the register's outputs to its inputs. Figure 2.49a shows a 4-bit register constructed from D flip-flops. Figure 2.49b shows a representative circuit symbol for this register. The register and its output signal (which also represents the register state, or contents) are frequently assigned the same name.

There are many situations in computer design where it is useful to be able to shift the contents of a register to the left or the right. A right-shift operation changes the register state as follows:

$$(0, z_0, z_1, \ldots, z_{m-2}) \leftarrow (z_0, z_1, \ldots, z_{m-1})$$

while a left shift performs the transformation

$$(z_1, z_2, \ldots, z_{m-1}, 0) \leftarrow (z_0, z_1, \ldots, z_{m-1})$$

A register organized to allow left- or right-shift operations of this kind is called a *shift register*. In its simplest form, an m-bit shift register consists of m master-slave flip-flops each of which is connected to its left or right neighbor. Data may be entered 1 bit at a time at one end of the register and may be removed (read) 1 bit at a time from the other end; this is called *serial input-output*. Figure 2.50 shows a simple 4-bit shift register using D flip-flops. A right shift is accomplished by activating the shift enable control line connected to the clock input of each flip-flop. It may also be useful to provide direct access to the internal flip-flops in an m-bit shift register. In addition to the serial data lines, m input or output lines may be provided to permit parallel data transfers to or from the shift register. Additional

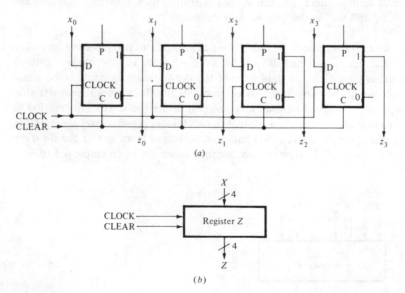

FIGURE 2.49
A 4-bit register with parallel input-output: (a) logic diagram; (b) symbol.

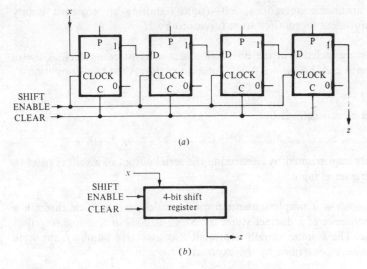

(a)

(b)

FIGURE 2.50
A 4-bit right-shift register: (a) logic diagram; (b) symbol.

control lines are required to select the serial or parallel input modes. A further refinement is to permit both left- and right-shift operations as in Fig. 2.51.

Shift registers are useful design components in a number of applications. These applications include:

1. Storage of serial data.
2. Serial-to-parallel and parallel-to-serial data conversion.

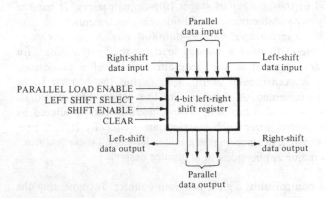

FIGURE 2.51
A 4-bit universal shift register.

3. Performing arithmetic operations; left- (right-) shifting an unsigned binary number is equivalent to multiplication (division) by 2.

Shift operations are included in the instruction sets of most computers. A useful related operation is called *rotation*. A left rotation performs the transformation

$$(z_1, z_2, \ldots, z_{m-1}, z_0) \leftarrow (z_0, z_1, \ldots, z_{m-2}, z_{m-1})$$

while a right rotation is defined by

$$(z_{m-1}, z_0, \ldots, z_{m-3}, z_{m-2}) \leftarrow (z_0, z_1, \ldots, z_{m-2}, z_{m-1}).$$

Rotation is easily implemented by connecting the serial output of a shift register to the corresponding serial input.

Counters. A counter is a simple sequential machine designed to cycle through a predetermined sequence of k distinct states $S_0, S_1, \ldots, S_{k-1}$ in response to pulses on an input line. The k states usually represent k consecutive numbers; the state transitions can thus be described by the expression

$$S_{i+1} \leftarrow S_i + 1 \ (\text{modulo } k)$$

Each input pulse increments the state by 1; the machine can therefore be viewed as counting the input pulses. Counters come in many different varieties depending on the number codes used, the modulus k, and the timing mode (synchronous or asynchronous).

The simplest counters can be obtained by minor modifications of an ordinary register or a shift register. Figure 2.52 shows a modulo-16 binary counter composed of four (master-slave) JK flip-flops. This circuit counts pulses on the count enable line. The output count is a 4-bit standard binary number. Note that the output of each flip-flop may alter the state of its right neighbor, so that "carry" signals ripple through the counter from left to right. This type of counter is therefore called a *ripple counter*. Its mode of operation is asynchronous, and its operating speed is proportional to the number of stages (flip-flops) present. It has the advantage that it is easily expandable without additional logic elements.

A counter is basically a serial-input parallel-output device. As in the case of shift registers, it can be useful to have a parallel load capability. (Consider, for example, the input modes required in the program counter of a processor.) Another refinement that is occasionally useful is to permit the counter to be decremented as well as incremented. A counter with this capability is called an *up-down counter*. Counters are also available whose modulus can be altered by means of modulus-select control lines; such counters are frequently termed *programmable*. Figure 2.53 shows a programmable counter having all these features. Counters have two major applications in computer design.

1. Storing the state of a control unit, e.g., a program counter. Incrementing the counter provides a convenient means of generating a sequence of control states.

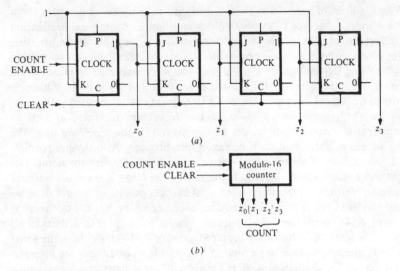

FIGURE 2.52
An asynchronous modulo-16 ripple counter: (*a*) logic diagram; (*b*) symbol.

2. Generating timing signals. Suppose that the count enable input is connected to a source of clock pulses. Then pulses appear on the output lines of the counter with frequencies which are directly related to the clock frequency. For example, if the modulo-16 counter of Fig. 2.52 is used, the pulses appearing on output z_0 have half the frequency of the clock source, the pulses on z_1 have one-quarter of the clock frequency, and so on. In this role, the counter is acting as a *frequency divider*. In general, if the period of the clock source is one time unit, then using a counter and, perhaps, some additional logic, pulses with a period of k time units can be obtained for any $k \geq 1$. Counters can therefore be used to introduce precise and controlled time delays into a system.

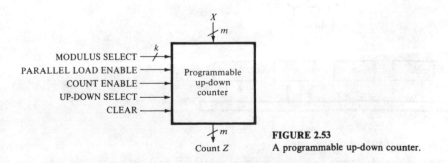

FIGURE 2.53
A programmable up-down counter.

Buses. A bus is a set of connectors (wires) designed to transfer all bits of a w-bit word from a specified source to a specified destination; the source and destination are typically registers. A bus may be unidirectional, i.e., capable of transmitting data in one direction only, or it may be bidirectional. A *dedicated bus* is one with a unique source and destination. If n units must be interconnected by buses in all possible ways, then the number of dedicated buses required is $n(n - 1)$. Although buses perform no logical functions, there is a significant cost associated with them, since they usually require logic circuits to control access to them, as well as signal amplification circuits (bus drivers and receivers). If the buses are long, the cost of the wires or cables used must be taken into account. Also the pin requirements and gate density of an integrated circuit increase rapidly with the number of external buses connected to the circuit. Because of these costs, it is common to use *shared buses*, which can connect one of several sources to one of several destinations. This results in fewer buses but requires more complex bus-control mechanisms. Figure 2.54a shows the use of dedicated buses to connect four units in all possible ways; a total of 12 buses are required. Figure 2.54b shows how the same units can be connected using a single shared bus. While shared buses are cheaper, they do not permit simultaneous transfers between different pairs of devices, which is possible with dedicated buses. Sharing buses, therefore, can result in a loss of performance. Bus structures are explored further in Chap. 6.

A bus frequently has some of the attributes of a register. It may store data temporarily, possibly in buffer registers associated with the bus. It may be assigned a name and be addressed by instructions in the same manner as a register or

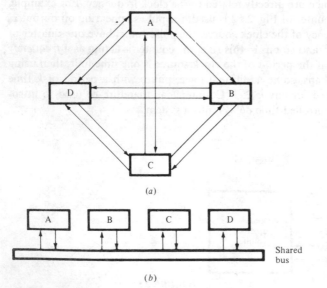

(a)

(b)

Shared
bus

FIGURE 2.54
Interconnection of four units via (*a*) dedicated buses and (*b*) a single shared bus.

memory location. The transfer of information between two registers via a bus is often broken down into a sequence of two "register" transfers thus:

$$c_1: \quad \text{DATABUS} \leftarrow \text{REGISTER A};$$

$$c_2: \quad \text{REGISTER B} \leftarrow \text{DATABUS};$$

2.3.3 Design Methods

The behavior of a register-level machine is defined by a finite set of operations or functions $F_1, F_2, \ldots, F_n$ to be performed on various types of words. Each operation is implemented by a sequence of elementary register transfer operations of the form

$$Z \leftarrow f(X_1, X_2, \ldots, X_k)$$

where f is an operation such as addition performed by one of the components of the machine. The sequence of register transfers that implements F_i constitutes the algorithm for F_i. The particular operation to be performed by the machine may be selected by an external control signal. The register-level machine of Fig. 2.36 performs only one operation, addition, so that no function selection is required. When multiple functions are involved, the function-selection signals are frequently organized into words called instructions; in such cases the machine is then referred to as an *instruction set processor*. The central processing units (CPUs) and input-output processors (IOPs) introduced in Chap. 1 are examples of instruction set processors.

Circuit specification. It is usually convenient to partition a register-level design into a data processing unit and a control unit. In the case of instruction set processors, the division between the two is relatively clear. The control unit is responsible for the interpretation of instructions and is called the program control unit or the instruction unit. The data processing part performs the actions specified by the control unit and is also called the execution unit. The program control unit may be further divided into a data and control part, in which case the second level of control corresponds to microprogramming. Further subdivisions are possible yielding a hierarchy of levels of control. Control concepts for instruction set processors are the topic of Chap. 4. In the case of simple machines such as the multiplier discussed later (Example 2.3), the control unit is usually a special-purpose hardwired sequential circuit that can be designed using standard gate-level-design techniques. In more complex cases, both the data processing and control units must be treated as register-level machines.

A register-level circuit is a network of register-level components. It is typically seen as a set of registers interconnected by combinational circuits. The simplest view of machine structure may be given by a block diagram that shows only the registers and functional components of the data processing part of the machine (see Fig. 2.55a for an example). The lines of such a diagram are called the *data paths* of the machine. Often the data paths shown are logical rather than physical. When several data paths enter or leave a component, control circuits must be introduced

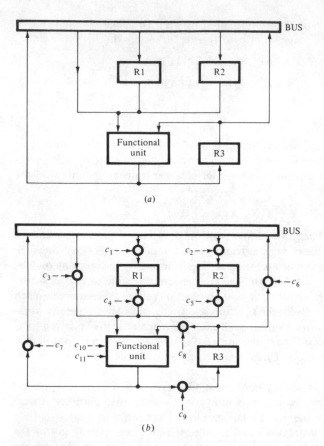

(a)

(b)

FIGURE 2.55
A register-level block diagram: (a) data paths and (b) data paths and control points.

to select one of the available data paths. This is indicated schematically in Fig. 2.55b, where control circuits, called control points, indicated by circles have been inserted. A *control point* is a data path switch which, when activated by a control signal, allows data to be transferred over the data path. When inactive, the data path is effectively blocked. A control point is primarily a conceptual device to aid in circuit design and description. Control points are implemented by logic circuits whose nature depends on the characteristics of the devices connected the data paths in question. For example, Fig. 2.56 shows how the input data paths to the "functional unit" of Fig. 2.55 might be controlled. A four-input multiplexer is used to select one of the three data paths that can be connected to the left input of the unit. Since the select inputs of the multiplexer are assumed to be encoded, an encoder may also be required to encode the control signals. The right input to the functional unit is connected to R3 only; hence an AND word gate may suffice to implement control point c_8. The control signals that activate the data path control points are generated by the control unit of the machine.

The behavior required of a register-level circuit can be described formally by description languages, state tables, or flowcharts, possibly used in some combination. An example of description-language usage appears in Fig. 2.37. If state tables are to be used, then the states chosen must be high-level to keep their number at manageable levels. Note that an m-bit register has 2^m distinct states. If m is large, then the 2^m possible states must be merged into a much smaller number of equivalent states in order for the state-table approach to be feasible.

Design techniques. The design problem for register-level circuits may be stated as follows. Given a set of algorithms or instructions, design a circuit using a specified set of register-level components which implements the desired functions while satisfying certain cost and performance criteria. No ways are known for imposing useful mathematical structures on the circuit behavior or structure corresponding to, say, Boolean algebra and the two-level constraint in gate-level design. Lacking appropriate mathematical tools, register-level-design methods tend to be heuristic and depend heavily on the designer's experience. It is possible, however, to identify some general approaches to the design problem, which we will now outline.

Step 1. Define the desired behavior by a set S of sequences of register transfer operations, such that each operation can be implemented directly using the available design components.

Step 2. Analyze S to determine the types of components and the number of each type required for the data processing unit.

Step 3. Construct a block diagram D for the data processing unit using the components identified in step 2. Choose the interconnections between the components so that all data paths implied by S are present, and the given performance and cost constraints are satisifed.

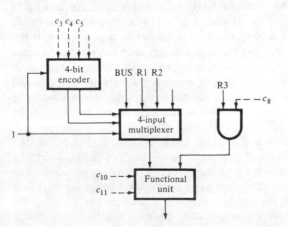

FIGURE 2.56
Implementation of some representative control points in the circuit of Fig. 2.55b.

Step 4. Analyze S and D to identify the control points and control signals needed. Introduce the necessary logic to implement the control points.

Step 5. Design the control unit for the machine so that the required control signals are generated in the order specified by S.

Step 6. Consolidate the design to eliminate duplication and simplify the circuit where possible.

The first step in the foregoing procedure involves a translation process analogous to writing an assembly-language program to implement the given set of algorithms. S therefore reflects the skill of the designer. The identification of data processing components in step 2 is straightforward. A statement such as

$$c: \quad A \leftarrow A + B;$$

implies the existence of two registers to store A and B, and an adder to which A and B must be connected via data paths. Complications arise when the possibility of sharing components exists. For example, the statement

$$c: \quad A \leftarrow A + B, C \leftarrow C + D;$$

defines two addition operations. Since the additions do not involve the same operands, they can be carried out in parallel if two independent adders are provided. However, the cost of the circuit can probably be lowered by sharing a single adder and performing the two additions sequentially:

$$c(t_0): \quad A \leftarrow A + B;$$
$$c(t_0 + 1): \quad C \leftarrow C + D;$$

This is a typical example of a cost-performance tradeoff. The identification of parallelism inherent in an algorithm can be exceedingly difficult.

The construction of the block diagram in step 3 requires defining an appropriate data bus structure. The performance of the machine in executing a particular algorithm A in S is proportional to the total delays of all the data paths and components traversed during the execution of A. The cost of the circuit may be taken to be $\Sigma_i n_i c_i$, where c_i is the cost of components of type i and n_i is the number of such components used. If a particular design does not meet a required performance criterion, e.g., some algorithm is executed too slowly, or if some maximum component cost is exceeded, it may be necessary to return to step 1 and redesign S. This points out the fact that the various design steps interact with one another, so that it may be necessary to modify repeatedly decisions made in earlier steps.

The design issues involved in step 4 are illustrated by Figs. 2.55 and 2.56. The design of the control unit (step 5) requires careful timing analysis of the algorithms in S. The final step recognizes that the heuristic nature of the design procedure can result in certain inefficiencies, some of which can be removed by minor modifications to the design. In practice, such improvements are made in every step of the design. We now present a detailed example that illustrates the foregoing design process.

Example 2.3   Design of a fixed-point binary multiplier. Fixed-point multiplication is often implemented in computers by a binary variant of the usual manual multiplication algorithm for decimal numbers, which is based on repeated addition and shifting. Consider the task of multiplying two 8-bit binary numbers $X = x_0x_1x_2x_3x_4x_5x_6x_7$ and $Y = y_0y_1y_2y_3y_4y_5y_6y_7$ to form the product $P = X \times Y$. Each number is assumed to be in sign-magnitude form, where the leftmost bit (with subscript 0) of the number denotes its sign (0 for positive and 1 for negative), and the remaining 7 bits represent the number's magnitude. The magnitude part is taken here to be a fraction, so that there is an implicit binary point between the two leftmost bits of each number. Hence $X = x_0x_1x_2x_3x_4x_5x_6x_7$ denotes the number $N = \sum\limits_{i=1}^{7} x_i 2^{-i}$ when $x_0 = 0$; it denotes $-N$ when $x_0 = 1$.

The multiplication algorithm first multiplies the magnitude parts X_M and Y_M of X and Y thus

$$P_M \leftarrow X_M \times Y_M \tag{2.18}$$

where $P_M = p_1p_2 \cdots p_{14}$ is the magnitude of the product P. It then computes the sign p_0 of the product via the operation

$$p_0 \leftarrow x_0 \oplus y_0$$

where $\oplus$ denotes EXCLUSIVE-OR. Note that the final result $P = p_0p_1p_2 \cdots p_{14}$ is 15 bits long. The magnitude multiplication (2.18), which is also referred to as *unsigned multiplication*, is the central design problem. The unsigned product P_M is computed in seven add-shift steps defined as follows:

$$P_i \leftarrow P_i + x_{7-i} \times Y \tag{2.19}$$

$$P_{i+1} \leftarrow 2^{-1}P_i \tag{2.20}$$

where $P_0 = 0$, $P_7 = P_M$, and i goes from 0 to 6. The quantities $P_0, P_1, \ldots, P_7$ are called *partial products*. When the current multiplier bit $x_{7-i} = 1$, (2.19) becomes $P_i \leftarrow P_i + Y$; when $x_{7-i} = 0$, (2.19) becomes $P_i \leftarrow P_i + 0$. Hence (2.19) requires adding either the multiplicand or 0 to the current partial product P_i. The factor 2^{-1} in (2.20) indicates that P_i is right-shifted by 1 bit after each addition; this is equivalent to division by 2. Note that add-shift step adds 1 bit to the partial product, which therefore grows from 7 to 15 bits in length over the course of the multiplication.

With these preliminaries, we can now specify the main components needed for the multiplier circuit. Two 8-bit registers, conventionally denoted Q (for multiplier-quotient) and M (for multiplicand), are required to store X and Y, respectively. A double-length 16-bit register A (for accumulator) is used to store the P_i's. (This standard length is more convenient than the actual 15-bit maximum size of P.) A 7-bit parallel adder (Fig. 2.47) is used for the addition specified by (2.19). Clearly it must have its output and its left input connected to A, while its right input must be connected either to M or to zero. (A serial adder of the kind discussed in Example 2.2 could also be used here, but it would be slower by a factor of 7 than the parallel adder.) The right-shift function can be very conveniently obtained by constructing A from a right-shift register with parallel input-output (Fig. 2.51). As specified by (2.19), addition is controlled by bit x_{7-i} which is stored in the Q register, so that it is necessary for the multiplier control unit to be able to scan the contents of Q from right to left in the course of the multiplication. If Q is also realized by a right-shift register, then the required multiplier bit x_{7-i} can always be obtained from Q's rightmost flip-flop, Q(7), if Q is right-shifted before the next x_{7-i} is needed. This means that X_M is gradually reduced from 7 to 0 bits, at the same time that P_i is gradually expanding from 7 to 14 bits, also by right-shifting. Hence we can combine the A and Q functions in a single 16-bit right-shift register, the left half of which is denoted A, while the right half is denoted Q. The multiplier is completed by the inclusion of external data buses INBUS and OUTBUS, and a control unit, which contains a 3-bit counter named COUNT that serves to determine the number of times (2.20) is executed. The resulting circuit has the structure depicted in Fig. 2.57.

A complete formal description of the multiplication algorithm developed above appears in Fig. 2.37. By way of contrast, the same algorithm is presented as a flow-chart in Fig. 2.58. In this format, a set of concurrent register transfer operations is placed in a rectangular box. The sequence in which nonconcurrent operations are executed is indicated by arrows between boxes. Conditional branching is indicated by diamond-shaped decision boxes, in which the condition to be tested is written. Flow-charts have the advantage of representing algorithm loops in clear visual form; they are, however, less concise and flexible than formal language descriptions.

At the core of the multiplication algorithm is the two-cycle add-shift step defined by (2.19) and (2.20) with P_i stored in A.Q. The addition of the two 7-bit quantities in A(1:7) and M(1:7) can produce an 8-bit sum, which is stored in A(0:7).

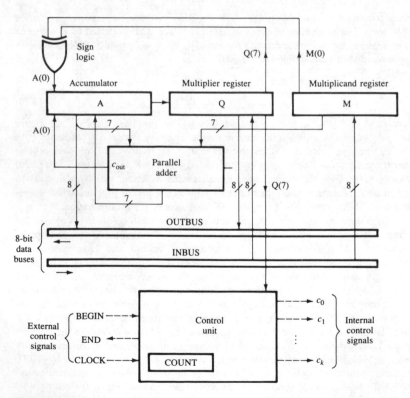

FIGURE 2.57
Block diagram of the binary multiplier.

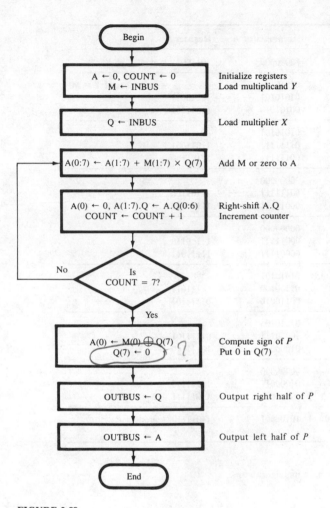

FIGURE 2.58
Flowchart of the binary multiplication algorithm.

The output carry signal c_{OUT} of the adder is the most significant bit of an 8-bit sum, and so is connected to the data input of $A(0)$. The counter COUNT is incremented and tested at the end of each add-shift step to determine if the add-shift phase should terminate. When COUNT is found to contain 7, P_M occupies bits 1:14 of the register-pair A.Q., i.e., $A(1:7).Q(0:6)$. The sign bit p_0 is then computed from x_0 and y_0, which are stored in $Q(7)$ and $M(0)$, respectively, and p_0 is placed in $A(0)$. At the same time, 0 is written into $Q(7)$ to expand the final product from 15 to 16 bits. Figure 2.59 shows the complete step-by-step multiplication process for two sample numbers $X = 10110011$ and $Y = 01010101$. The sign bit $x_0 = 1$ of X (indicating that it is a negative number) is marked by an underline in Fig. 2.59. The data in A.Q to the left of x_0 is the current partial product P_i.

Step	Action	Accumulator A	Register Q
0	Initialize registers	00000000	10110011 = multiplier X
1		01010101	= multiplicand Y = M
	Add M to A	01010101	10110011
	Shift A.Q	00101010	11011001
2		01010101	
	Add M to A	01111111	11011001
	Shift A.Q	00111111	11101100
3		00000000	
	Add zero to A	00111111	11101100
	Shift A.Q	00011111	11110110
4		00000000	
	Add zero to A	00011111	11110110
	Shift A.Q	00001111	11111011
5		01010101	
	Add M to A	01100100	11111011
	Shift A.Q	00110010	01111101
6		01010101	
	Add M to A	10000111	01111101
	Shift A.Q	01000011	10111110
7		00000000	
	Add zero to A	01000011	10111110
	Shift A.Q	00100001	11011111
8	Put sign of P in A(0) and set Q(7) to 0	10100001	11011110 = product P

FIGURE 2.59
Illustration of the binary multiplication algorithm.

The control unit of Fig. 2.57 is designed by first identifying from the formal description (Fig. 2.37 or 2.58) all the control signals and control points needed to implement the specified register transfer and related operations. Figure 2.60 lists a possible set of control signals for the multiplier. In some cases, several control signals implement a particular operation. For instance, the addition operation employs c_6 to select the adder's right input operand, c_9 to select c_{OUT} for loading into A(0), and c_2 and c_5 to actually load the 8-bit sum into A(0:7). The number of distinguished control signals will vary with the details of the logic used to implement the control unit. Figure 2.61 shows a straightforward implementation of the control logic associated with the accumulator and adder subcircuits using the control signals defined in Fig. 2.60.

Control signal	Operation controlled
c_0	Clear accumulator A (Reset to zero)
c_1	Clear counter COUNT (Reset to zero)
c_2	Load A(0)
c_3	Load multiplicand register M from INBUS
c_4	Load multiplier register Q from INBUS
c_5	Load main adder outputs into A(1:7)
c_6	Select M or zero to apply to right input of adder
c_7	Right-shift A.Q
c_8	Increment counter COUNT
c_9	Select c_{OUT} or $M(0) \oplus Q(7)$ to load into A(0)
c_{10}	Clear Q(0)
c_{11}	Transfer contents of A to OUTBUS
c_{12}	Transfer contents of Q to OUTBUS

FIGURE 2.60
Control signals for the binary multiplier.

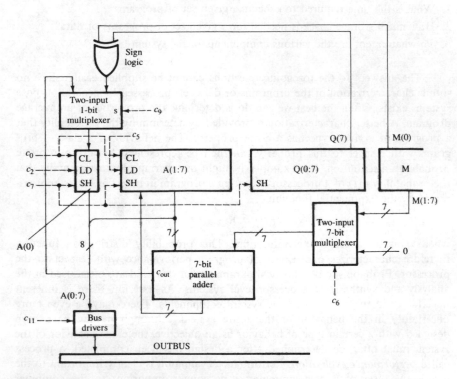

FIGURE 2.61
Implementation of some control points of the multiplier.

2.4 THE PROCESSOR LEVEL

The processor level is the highest in the computer design hierarchy. It is concerned with the storage and processing of blocks of information such as programs and data files. The design components at this level are complex, usually sequential, circuits that can be manufactured using LSI/VLSI technology.

2.4.1 Introduction

The component types recognized at the processor level fall into four main groups: (instruction set) processors; memories; input-output devices; and interconnection networks. For obvious reasons, information is transferred between the components in words or small groups of words. Thus the "signals" observable in a processor-level block diagram at any time are words rather than programs or data sets. However, the problems of interest at this level deal with the processing of programs and data sets. Typical questions of interest are

1. What is the time required to execute a given set of programs?
2. How much storage space is needed for a given set of programs or data?
3. To what extent are the various components of the system utilized?

The answers to the foregoing questions cannot be supplied easily, since no simple characterization of the programs or data sets processed by general-purpose systems exists. Often the best we can do is determine the properties of an average program. A better characterization is provided by determining the probability that a program of a given type has a given property. The behavior of a class of programs with respect to this property can then be represented by an appropriate probability distribution. For example, it might be determined experimentally that the probability $p(t)$ of a processor executing a program in time t or less is approximated by the exponential function

$$p(t) = 1 - e^{-t/T}$$

where T is an average execution time. This probability distribution function therefore characterizes one aspect of program performance with respect to the processor. Probabilistic or statistical parameters of this kind are often used in the analysis and synthesis of processor-level systems. As a result, there is inherent uncertainty in the behavior of the system components. There may be even more uncertainty in the behavior of the entire system. Although it may have been designed with a certain type of behavior as an objective, the exact behavior of the system must often be determined after a design has been completed, a process called *performance evaluation*. Performance evaluation is clearly important to the prospective user of a new computer; it is equally important to the computer designer.

Performance evaluation. The goal of performance evaluation is to determine functions of the form $\varphi(x_1, x_2, \ldots, x_n) = \varphi(X)$, where X is a set of design parameters (including input data characteristics) and φ is a performance measure such as processing time, waiting time, or resource utilization. It is generally desirable to be able to write φ as an algebraic expression involving X; such an expression is said to be an *analytic model* of φ. Tractable analytic models have been developed for certain aspects of computer performance evaluation, but accurate models of this kind are, in general, quite rare.

The difficulties of purely analytical approaches to performance evaluation arise from the fact that the components of a system can interact in complex ways. Communication between processor-level components is asynchronous, and contention for shared system resources frequently results. In cases where φ cannot be expressed in a tractable form, it may be possible to compute $\varphi(X)$ systematically for specific (numerical) values of X. Such approaches may be termed numerical or experimental and fall into two main groups: computer-based simulation and performance measurement on an actual system.

The mathematical discipline that appears to be most appropriate for performance evaluation at the processor level is queueing theory [18, 29]. *Queueing theory* is a branch of applied probability theory concerned with processes that involve sharing limited resources; the resource limitations result in waiting lines or queues forming at the resources. The origins of queueing theory are usually traced to the analysis of congestion in telephone systems made by the Danish engineer A. K. Erlang (1878–1929) in 1909. A queueing system is a collection of queues that are waiting for service by a set of servers. The manner in which the queues are formed and serviced is determined by suitable probability distributions. Figure 2.62 shows the simplest queueing system consisting of a single queue and a single server. The appropriateness of queueing theory for computer performance evaluation stems from the fact that a computer system consists of a set of limited resources such as memory space, IO channel capacity, and CPU time, which must be shared among competing programs. Unfortunately, the analysis of queueing systems is extremely difficult unless rather restrictive assumptions are made.

Frequently, a useful mathematical model of a computer can be constructed whose behavior cannot be determined analytically, but can be determined numerically by using simulation. Figure 2.63 shows the structure of a typical simulation system. A computer program S called a *simulator* is used to mimic the behavior of

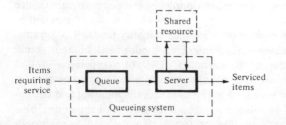

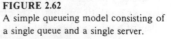

FIGURE 2.62
A simple queueing model consisting of a single queue and a single server.

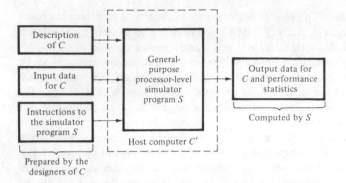

FIGURE 2.63
Computer-based simulation.

the system C whose performance is to be evaluated. S is supplied with a description of C, a set of input data for C, and a set of instructions concerning the performance parameters to be computed and reported. S is then executed on an appropriate host computer C'. During this execution, S computes all the relevant actions taken by C and prints a report on the performance of C. The value of this performance analysis depends on the accuracy of both the model used for C and the input data created for C. Accurate simulation may require elaborate modeling and extensive simulation runs. The cost of designing the model and the cost of the host computer time may be significant. These costs are usually primary limitations on the use of simulation in the design process. The great advantage of simulation is that minor modifications to the model C can easily and quickly be made and their effects evaluated. Simulation is also of value at the register and gate levels.

Another approach to performance evaluation is to construct a physical prototype or pilot model of the target system, run it under representative working conditions, and monitor its performance. This can be considered to be physical simulation, in contrast with the computer simulation discussed in the preceding paragraph. Performance information is obtained by physical measurement of the parameters of interest in real time. For example, a timer may be used to determine program execution times, and a counter may be used to determine the frequency of occurrence of an event of interest. These measuring techniques may also be software-implemented by inserting appropriate timing or counting instructions into the programs being executed. Such accounting routines are commonly included in operating systems to provide users with performance statistics for their programs. The main advantage of performance measurement via a pilot model is that actual programs for the target machine can be executed. It is not necessary to design artificial models for these programs as is usually the case when computer simulation or analytic methods are employed. In many instances the building and debugging of a physical model would introduce unacceptable delay into the design process, and computer simulation, perhaps at several levels of complexity, is preferred.

2.4.2 Processor-Level Components

CPUs. We define a central processing unit to be a general-purpose instruction set processor. Most computer systems have one such processor, which is assigned over-all responsibility for program interpretation and execution. The qualifier general-purpose distinguishes CPUs from other instruction set processors such as input-output processors whose functions are in some way restricted or special-purpose. An instruction set processor is characterized by the fact that it operates on word-organized instructions and data which are obtained by the processor from an external memory; results computed by the processor are also stored in this memory. Generally, only one CPU is present in a computer installation. A comput-er with one CPU is called a *uniprocessor* to distinguish it from a multiprocessor, which has two or more CPUs.

CPUs generally exhibit a clear-cut division into data processing and control parts. The more important considerations in CPU design are the following:

1. The types of instructions forming the CPU's instruction set and their execution times
2. The register-level organization of the data processing unit
3. The register-level organization of the program control unit
4. The manner in which the CPU communicates with external devices

CPU design problems are examined in detail in Chaps. 3 and 4. The evolution of CPU structure from the single accumulator organization of the IAS machine to the complex multiple-register organizations of modern CPUs is outlined in Chap. 1.

Figure 2.64 shows the simple block symbol used to represent a CPU in processor-level description. A one-word data bus is the main path by which infor-mation is transferred to and from the CPU. Note that the data bus is used to transfer both instructions and data words to the CPU. A second bus is generally, but not always, provided for transferring addresses from the CPU to main memory and, possibly, to IO devices. Finally, some control lines are present which are used by the CPU to control the other components of the system and synchronize their operations with those of the CPU.

Until VLSI manufacturing techniques made it possible to mass-produce inexpensive single-chip CPUs (microprocessors), CPUs were treated as design com-ponents only by a handful of computer architects, mostly employed by computer manufacturers. Microprocessors have vastly increased the number of situations where it is economically feasible to use CPUs. This expansion can be expected to result in changes in CPU architecture, so that CPUs can be used more easily by

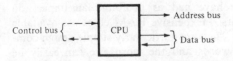

FIGURE 2.64
Symbol for a central processing unit.

designers who are not themselves computer architects. For example, in certain applications it may be desirable to have CPUs capable of operating on data words of nonstandard length. The introduction of CPUs that are expandable so that they can operate on words of any required length is a natural development; this can be accomplished by a technique called bit-slicing, which is discussed in Chap. 3.

Memories. CPUs and other instruction set processors are designed to operate in conjunction with external memory devices that store the programs and data required by the processors. Many different memory technologies are used, which vary greatly in cost and performance. Generally the cost of a memory device increases rapidly with the speed of operation required. The memory part of a computer system can be divided into two major subsystems:

1. Main memory, consisting of relatively fast storage devices connected directly to, and controlled by, the CPU
2. Secondary memory, consisting of slower and less expensive devices that communicate indirectly with the CPU via main memory

Secondary memory devices such as magnetic tape and disk units are used for storing large amounts of information needed relatively infrequently by the CPU. They are often controlled directly by special-purpose processors (memory control units or IOPs). Secondary memory devices are considered to be part of a computer's input-output system.

Main memory is, in most cases, a word-organized addressable random-access memory (RAM). This means that information can be accessed (read from or written into the memory) one word at a time. Each word storage location has associated with it an address that uniquely identifies it. To access a particular word in main memory, the CPU sends its address and appropriate control signals (read or write commands) to the memory. In a write operation, the CPU also places the word to be written into memory on the main memory data bus, from which it is transferred into the addressed location. In a read operation, the contents of the addressed location are transferred to the memory data bus and thence to the CPU. The term random access stems from the fact that the access time for every location is the same. Random access is contrasted with serial access, where access times vary with the location being accessed. Serial access memories are generally slower and less expensive than RAMs; most secondary memory devices use serial access. Because of their lower operating speeds and serial access modes, the manner in which the stored information is organized in secondary memories is more complex than the simple word organization of main memory. Memory technologies and the organization of stored information are covered in Chap. 5. Figure 2.65 shows a processor-level symbol for a main memory unit.

VLSI manufacturing technologies have had as profound an impact on memories as they have had on processors. Inexpensive RAM chips are available with capacities of a million or more bits. They are particularly simple design components, because both the number of words and the word size can easily be expanded.

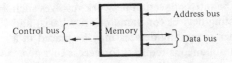

FIGURE 2.65
Symbol for a main memory unit.

IO devices. Input-output devices are the means by which a computer communicates with the outside world. A primary function of IO devices is to act as data transducers, i.e., to convert information from one physical representation to another. Unlike processors, IO devices do not alter the information content or meaning of the data on which they act. Since data is transferred and processed within a computer system in the form of digital electrical signals, input (output) devices transform other forms of information to (from) digital electrical signals. Figure 2.66 lists some typical IO devices and the information media they employ. Note that many of these devices make use of electromechanical technologies; hence their speed of operation is slow compared with processor and main-memory speeds. An IO device can be controlled directly by the CPU, but it is often under the immediate control of a special-purpose processor or control unit which directs the flow of information between the processor and main memory. The design of IO systems is examined in Chap. 6.

Interconnection networks. Processor-level components communicate by word-oriented buses. In systems with many components, this communication may be controlled by one or more devices, which we call interconnection networks (terms such as switching network, communications controller, and bus controller are also used in this context). The primary function of an interconnection network is to establish dynamic communication paths between the components via the buses under its control. For cost reasons, these buses are frequently shared. This can

IO device	Type		Medium to/from which IO device transforms digital electrical signals
	Input	Output	
Document reader	✔		Characters on paper
Line printer		✔	Characters on paper
Graphics plotter		✔	Visual images on paper
CRT video display		✔	Visual images on screen
Light pen	✔		Visual images on screen
Keyboard	✔		Characters on keyboard
Seven-segment digital display		✔	Characters on screen
Magnetic-tape unit	✔	✔	Characters on magnetic tape
Magnetic-disk unit	✔	✔	Characters on magnetic disk
Analog-digital converter	✔		Analog (continuous) electrical signals
Modem (modulator-demodulator)	✔	✔	Analog electrical signals
Voice synthesizer		✔	Spoken words

FIGURE 2.66
Representative IO devices.

result in contention for access to a bus. The interconnection network resolves such contention by selecting one of the requesting devices (on some priority basis) and connecting it to the desired bus. The other requesting devices may be placed in a queue by the interconnection network. Simultaneous requests for access to a given device or bus result from the fact that communication between processor-level components is generally asynchronous in that the components cannot be synchronized directly by a common clock signal. This can be attributed to several causes.

1. A high degree of independence exists among the components. For example, CPUs and IOPs execute different types of programs and interact relatively infrequently and at unpredictable times.
2. Component operating speeds vary over a wide range. For example, CPUs typically operate from 1 to 10 times faster than main-memory devices, while main-memory speeds may be many orders of magnitude faster than IO-device speeds.
3. The physical distance separating the components may be too large to permit synchronous transmission of information between them.

Asynchronous communication is frequently implemented by exchanging interlocked control signals, a technique referred to as *handshaking*. Suppose that a data word is to be transferred from device *A* to device *B*. *A* places the word in question on the data bus from *A* to *B* and then sends a control signal, often called a *ready* signal, to *B* to indicate the presence of the data on the data bus. When *B* recognizes the ready signal, it transfers the data from the data bus to a register within *B* and then activates an *acknowledge* control line to *A*. On receiving the acknowledge signal, *A* begins transmission of the next word. Thus a sequence of ready/acknowledge signals accompanies the data transfer, making it largely independent of the operating speeds of the two devices. The data and control lines connected to a device and the signal sequences required to communicate with the device constitute the device's *interface*. Clearly the more similar their interfaces, the more readily two devices can communicate. By using standard interfaces throughout a system, the ease with which it can be expanded or otherwise modified is greatly increased.

Bus control is often one of the functions of a processor such as a CPU or an IOP. For example, in the IBM S/360-370 series discussed in Sec. 1.3.3, an IOP controls a common IO bus to which many IO devices are connected. The IOP is responsible for selecting the device to be connected to the IO bus and from there to main memory. It also acts as a buffer between the relatively slow IO devices and the relatively fast main memory. Special processors whose sole function is to supervise data transfers over shared buses can be found in many large systems. Thus in the Burroughs B5000 system depicted in Fig. 1.26 (Sec. 1.3.2) an interconnection network called the memory exchange controls data transfers between the main-memory modules and the main processors. Another interconnection network, the IO exchange, connects the IOPs to the IO devices.

More difficult communications problems are encountered when a number of computers must be connected over long distances to form a computer network. Data transmission in such cases may be via shared telephone lines. Each host computer is typically connected to the network via a small processor whose function is to supervise the transmission of blocks of data (messages) to and from its host computer. Communications controllers of this type are often regarded as special-purpose IO devices. Inter- and intrasystem communication issues are explored further in Chap. 6.

2.4.3 Design Techniques

Processor-level design is even less amenable to formal analysis than design at the register level. This is mainly due to the difficulty of giving a sufficiently precise description of the desired system behavior. To say that the computer should execute efficiently all programs supplied to it is of little help to the designer. The usual approach to design at this level is to take a *prototype design* of known performance and modify it where necessary to accommodate new technologies or specific performance requirements. Performance specifications usually take the following form:

1. The computer should be capable of executing a instructions of type b per second.
2. The computer should be able to support c IO devices of type d.
3. The computer should be hardware and/or software compatible with computers of type e.
4. The total cost of the system should not exceed f.

Even when a new computer is closely based on a known design, it may not be possible to predict its performance accurately. This is due to our lack of understanding of the relation between the structure of a computer and its performance. Performance evaluation must generally be done experimentally, either by computer simulation or by measurement of the performance of a copy of the machine under actual working conditions. Thus we can view the design process as involving two major steps.

Step 1. Select a prototype design and adapt it to satisfy the given performance constraints.

Step 2. Determine the performance of the proposed system. If unsatisfactory, modify the design and repeat this step. Continue until an acceptable design is obtained.

This conservative approach to computer design has been widely followed and accounts in part for the relatively slow evolution of computer architecture. It is rare to find a computer structure that deviates substantially from the norm. The

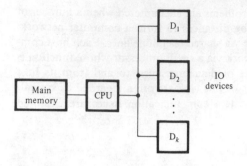

FIGURE 2.67
The simplest computer structure.

adherence to proven designs is also influenced by the need to remain compatible with existing hardware and software standards. Computer users are understandably reluctant to spend money retraining computer operators and programmers and replacing old software.

Prototype structures. The systems of interest here are general-purpose computers, which differ primarily in the number of components used and their autonomy. The variety of interconnection or communication structures used is surprisingly small. Figure 2.67 shows the simplest computer structure, which is typical of first-generation machines and many modern microprocessor-based systems. The addition of special-purpose IO processors typical of the second and subsequent generations is shown in Fig. 2.68. Here S denotes the interconnection (switching) network that controls memory-processor communication. Figure 2.69 shows one of the

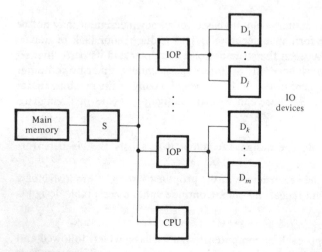

FIGURE 2.68
Computer with IOPs.

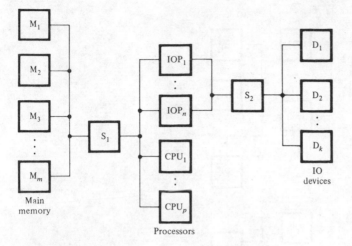

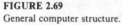

FIGURE 2.69
General computer structure.

most general single-computer prototype structures employing multiple CPUs (it is therefore a multiprocessor) and multiple main-memory banks. The preceding two uniprocessor systems are special cases of this general configuration.

More complex structures, called multicomputer systems or computer networks, may be obtained by connecting several copies of the foregoing prototype computer structures. The connection between the different computers is made via special IO devices that act as intercomputer communication controllers. Dedicated small computers are often used for this purpose. The computers are considered to be loosely coupled since their processors and memories are not directly connected. Figure 2.70 shows an example of two computers with the structure of Fig. 2.68 which have been connected to form a single system. This system has essentially the same structure as the ASP (*a*ttached *s*upport *p*rocessor) organization used in early S/360-370 installations. Here one computer acts as the main processor and overall system supervisor. The other computer manages input-output processing and other supporting tasks. The device D_i that couples the two computers is called a channel-to-channel adapter.

Simple performance measures. Several widely used performance parameters for a computer system are based on the performance of its major components, e.g., the main memory and the CPU. Two representative parameters of this type are main-memory bandwidth and CPU instruction execution speed.

The *main-memory bandwidth* is defined as the maximum rate in bits per second at which information can be transferred to or from main memory. This parameter clearly imposes a basic limitation on the computer's performance, since processing speed is ultimately determined by the rate at which instructions and data can be fetched from memory.

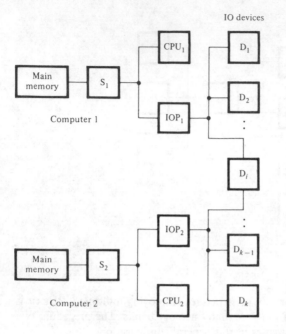

FIGURE 2.70
A multicomputer system similar to the IBM ASP organization.

Many performance measures are based on CPU behavior. The time required to execute an instruction is one such parameter. Since execution times vary from one instruction to another, the execution time of an instruction common to most processors, e.g., fixed-point addition, may be chosen as representative. A better measure is obtained by taking an average of all CPU instruction execution times weighted by their frequency of use. Let $I_1, I_2, \ldots, I_n$ be a set of representative instruction types. Let t_i denote the average execution time of an instruction of type I_i and let p_i denote the probability of occurrence of type I_i instructions in representative programs. Then the *average instruction execution time* t_E is given by

$$t_E = \sum_{i=1}^{n} p_i t_i$$

The set of instruction types selected and their frequency of occurrence constitute an *instruction mix*. A number of instruction mixes have been proposed as being representative of various system workloads. One of the best known is the *Gibson mix* [13], which is summarized in Fig. 2.71. An equivalent performance measure is $1/t_E$, the CPU *instruction execution rate* often measured in millions of instructions per second or *MIPS*.

The most serious limitation of the foregoing parameters is that they do not measure the performance of the system as a whole. In particular, the influence of IO operations is ignored. Perhaps the most satisfactory performance measure is the cost of executing a set of representative programs. This cost is typically the total

Instruction type	Probability of occurrence
Transfers to and from main memory	0.31
Indexing	0.18
Branching	0.17
Floating-point arithmetic	0.12
Fixed-point arithmetic	0.07
Shifting	0.04
Miscellaneous	0.11

FIGURE 2.71
Summary of the Gibson instruction mix.

execution time but may also include the use made of the various system components. A set of actual programs taken by a user to be representative of his computing environment may be chosen as the representative programs for performance evaluation. Such programs are called *benchmarks*, and are run by the user on a copy of the machine being evaluated. It is occasionally useful to devise an artificial benchmark, or *synthetic program*, whose sole purpose is to exercise the machine and provide data for performance evaluation.

Descriptive methods. Block diagrams supplemented by narrative descriptions are the most common ways of describing systems at the processor level. Most formal description languages that have been proposed are suitable for lower-level descriptions only (see Sec. 2.3.1). C. Gordon Bell and Allen Newell have developed a concise descriptive system called PMS (*p*rocessors *m*emories *s*witches) that can be used for representing systems at the processor level [3, 27]. They identify seven basic component types, which are listed in Fig. 2.72. Each component is denoted by a distinct symbol (a capital letter). These symbols may be qualified by appending additional (small) letters. For example, M denotes a memory and Mp denotes a primary memory, i.e., main memory. Further component information may be added in the form of a list of attributes in parentheses, e.g., Mp (technology: semiconductor; access time: 100 ns). A computer system is represented by a graph

Component name	Symbol	Examples
Processor	P	CPU, IOP
Control	K	Program control unit
Data operation	D	Arithmetic-logic unit
Memory	M	Main memory, secondary memory
Transducer	T	IO devices
Link	L	IO port
Switch	S	Multiplexer, crossbar switch

FIGURE 2.72
Basic components of Bell and Newell's PMS representation.

called a PMS diagram whose nodes are boxes containing PMS component symbols and whose edges are connections such as data and control buses. (The original version of PMS [3] omits the boxes around the component names.) Figure 2.73 shows the PMS diagram for the computer of Fig. 2.68. The symbol X denotes the external environment of the computer. It can be concluded from this example that a PMS diagram is essentially a formalized block diagram. It is mainly useful for structural descriptions since only a limited amount of behavioral information can reasonably be included among the component attributes.

Another class of formal description languages for processor-level designs can be found in the input languages for system simulators. They are intended for describing behavior and do not, in general, allow precise description of system structure. An example of such a language is ASPOL (*a* *s*imulator *p*rocess-*o*riented *l*anguage) [9, 25].

2.4.4 Queueing Models

In order to give the reader some flavor of analytic models of computer systems, we will consider a simple, but quite useful, queueing model. Our treatment is relatively informal; the interested reader is referred to Refs. 17 and 27 for further mathematical details.

M/M/1 model. The most basic queueing system is the single-queue single-server case depicted in Fig. 2.62. The parameters that define the behavior of this system are the rate at which items requiring service arrive and the rate at which items are serviced. It is assumed that items in the queue are serviced on a first-come first-served basis. The mean arrival and service rates are commonly denoted by λ and μ, respectively. The actual arrival and service rates vary randomly around these average values and are therefore characterized by probability distributions.

The way in which items arrive at the queueing system (the arrival process) is often modeled by a *Poisson probability distribution* function, which has the form

$$p_P(n,\, t) = \frac{(\lambda t)^n}{n!}\, e^{-\lambda t} \tag{2.21}$$

where $p_P(n,\, t)$ is the probability of exactly n items arriving in a time period of length t. If items are not removed from the queue, $p_P(n,\, t)$ represents the prob-

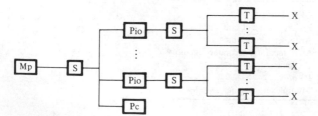

FIGURE 2.73
PMS diagram equivalent to Fig. 2.68.

ability that the queue length increases by n in time t. Figure 2.74 shows a plot of $p_P(n, t)$ as a function of t for fixed values of n and λ; this curve, which rises quickly to a peak and then goes asymptotically to zero, typifies the Poisson distribution. Many physical arrival processes, e.g., the arrival of calls at a telephone exchange, can be quite accurately modeled by a Poisson distribution.

Another important characteristic of an arrival process is the distribution of the time periods between two consecutive arriving items. The *interarrival time distribution* $p_I(t)$ is defined to be the probability that at least one item arrives during a period of length t. Clearly, for a Poisson arrival process

$$p_I(t) = 1 - p_P(0, t) \tag{2.22}$$

Therefore, on setting $n = 0$ in (2.21) and substituting into (2.22), we obtain

$$p_I(t) = 1 - e^{-\lambda t} \tag{2.23}$$

This is the (negative) *exponential distribution*, which has the form shown in Fig. 2.75. Hence the interarrival times of a Poisson arrival process are characterized by the exponential distribution (2.23). The probability density function corresponding to (2.23) is $\lambda e^{-\lambda t}$, while its mean value is $1/\lambda$. Exponential distributions are particularly simple and convenient to use in analytic models. It is therefore common to model the behavior of the server (the service process) by an exponential distribution also. Let $p_S(t)$ be the probability that the service required by an item is completed in time t or less after its removal from the queue. Then the service process is often characterized by the expression

$$p_S(t) = 1 - e^{-\mu t}$$

The performance of a queueing system can be measured by the following parameters:

1. The average number of items waiting in the system, including the items waiting for service and those actually being served. The parameter is called the *mean queue length* and is denoted by l_Q.

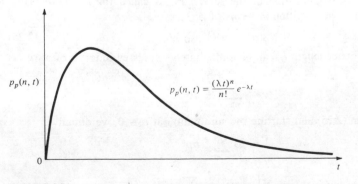

$$p_P(n, t)$$

$$p_P(n, t) = \frac{(\lambda t)^n}{n!} e^{-\lambda t}$$

FIGURE 2.74
Poisson distribution for fixed n and λ.

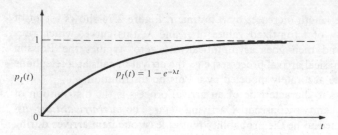

FIGURE 2.75
Exponential distribution for fixed λ.

2. The average time that arriving items spend in the system, both waiting for service and being served. This is called the *mean waiting time* and is denoted by t_Q. t_Q is sometimes called the system delay or response time.

We now consider the problem of calculating l_Q and t_Q for a single-queue single-server system in which the arrival distribution is Poisson (or, equivalently, the interarrival time distribution is exponential) and the service-time distribution is exponential. This type of queueing system is called the $M/M/1$ model, where the two Ms denote that the arrivals and service processes are Markov processes (essentially the same as Poisson processes) while the 1 denotes the number of servers. The state of the queue can be specified by $p_Q(n, t)$, which is the probability that at time t there are exactly n items in the queueing system either awaiting service or being served. When the system has been in operation for some time, the system can be expected to reach a state of equilibrium in which $p_Q(n, t)$ can be assumed to be independent of t, so we write $p_Q(n, t) = p_Q(n)$. It can be shown that under these conditions,

$$p_Q(n) = \left(\frac{\lambda}{\mu}\right)^n \left(1 - \frac{\lambda}{\mu}\right) \tag{2.24}$$

provided $\lambda < \mu$. If $\lambda > \mu$, then the queue grows indefinitely. Equation (2.24) is called the *steady-state* or *balance* equation for the queueing system. The quantity $\rho = \lambda/\mu$ is the mean utilization of the server and is called the *traffic intensity*. Equation (2.24) can be rewritten in terms of ρ thus:

$$p_Q(n) = \rho^n(1 - \rho) \tag{2.25}$$

The mean queue length l_Q can be immediately expressed in terms of $p_Q(n)$ as follows:

$$l_Q = \sum_{n \geq 1} n p_Q(n)$$

Substituting from (2.25) and starting the summation at $n = 0$, we obtain

$$l_Q = (1 - \rho) \sum_{n \geq 0} n\rho^n$$

$$= \rho(1 - \rho) \frac{d}{d\rho} \sum_{n \geq 0} \rho^n$$

The summation in this last expression is an infinite geometric progression equal to $1/(1 - \rho)$. Hence

$$l_Q = \rho(1 - \rho) \frac{d}{d\rho} \frac{1}{1 - \rho}$$

Using the formula

$$\frac{d}{dx} \frac{1}{u} = - \frac{1}{u^2} \frac{du}{dx}$$

we obtain

$$\frac{d}{d\rho} \frac{1}{1 - \rho} = \frac{1}{(1 - \rho)^2}$$

whence

$$l_Q = \frac{\rho}{1 - \rho} \tag{2.26}$$

which defines the mean queue length.

Finally, we turn to the parameter t_Q, which is the mean time items spend in the queueing system. t_Q and l_Q may be related intuitively as follows [19]. An average item X passing through the system should encounter the same number of waiting items l_Q when it enters as it leaves behind when it departs from the system. The number left behind is λt_Q, which is the number of items that enter the system at rate λ during the period t_Q when X is present. Hence we conclude that $l_Q = \lambda t_Q$, that is,

$$t_Q = \frac{l_Q}{\lambda} \tag{2.27}$$

Equation (2.27) is known as *Little's equation*. It is valid for all queueing systems, not just the M/M/1 model used here. Combining (2.26) and (2.27) yields the desired expression for t_Q:

$$t_Q = \frac{1}{\mu - \lambda} \tag{2.28}$$

The quantities l_Q and t_Q defined by (2.26) and (2.28) refer to items that are either waiting for access to the server or are actually being served. The mean number of items waiting in the queue excluding those being served is denoted by l_W, while t_W denotes the mean time spent waiting in the queue excluding service time. (The subscript W stands for waiting.) The mean utilization of the server in an M/M/1 system, i.e., the mean number of items being serviced, is $\rho = \lambda/\mu$; hence subtracting this from l_Q yields l_W thus:

$$l_W = l_Q - \rho \tag{2.29}$$

Using (2.26) to replace l_Q, we obtain

$$l_W = \frac{\rho^2}{1 - \rho} = \frac{\lambda^2}{\mu(\mu - \lambda)} \tag{2.30}$$

Similarly,

$$t_W = t_Q - \frac{1}{\mu}$$

where $1/\mu$ is the mean time it takes to service an item. Substituting for t_Q from (2.28) yields

$$t_W = \frac{\lambda}{\mu(\mu - \lambda)} \qquad (2.31)$$

Comparing (2.30) and (2.31) we see that $t_W = l_W/\lambda$, so that Little's equation holds for both the Q and the W subscripts.

To illustrate the use of the foregoing formulas, consider a computer that is processing jobs in a manner that can be approximated by the M/M/1 model. Arriving jobs are queued in main memory until they are fully executed in one step by the CPU, which therefore is the server. New jobs arrive at the system at an average rate of 10 per minute, and it is found that the computer is, on the average, idle 25 percent of the time. We ask two questions: What is the average time T that each job spends in the computer? What is the average number of jobs N in main memory that are waiting to begin execution? To answer them, we assume that steady state conditions prevail, from which it follows that T is t_Q, and N is l_W. Since the system is busy 75 percent of the time, $\rho = 0.75$. We are given that $\lambda = 10$ jobs/min; hence the service rate $\mu = \lambda/\rho$ is $\frac{40}{3}$ jobs/min. Substituting into (2.28) we get $T = t_Q = 0.3$ min. By Little's equation, $N = l_Q = \lambda t_Q = 3$; hence by (2.29), $l_W = 3 - 0.75 = 2.25$ jobs.

Extensions. The foregoing M/M/1 model can be generalized in many different directions, for example, by increasing the number of servers from one to c (the M/M/c model), by replacing the exponential service time distributions by the general service time distribution (the M/G/c model) or other distributions, by replacing the open system with its infinite population of arriving and departing items by a closed system around which a finite number of items flow (finite-population models), and so on. Some indication of the complexity of these extensions can be seen from Fig. 2.76, which shows the equations defining the standard M/M/c model. These equations reduce to those of the M/M/1 model when c is replaced by 1.

Large computer systems employing multiprogramming or multiprocessing can be modeled by interconnecting a set of queueing systems, so that items leaving one queue immediately enter another queue; the result is a *queueing network*. Figure 2.77 shows a particular example of a useful queueing network for computer performance analysis called the *central server model*. It is a closed network around which a fixed number of items (programs being executed) circulate. There are two component queues: a single-server queue, e.g., an M/M/1 model, representing the CPU; and a multiserver queue, e.g., an M/M/c model, representing a set of I/O devices and their controllers. The overall network models the behavior of a set of programs that alternate between CPU and IO processing in a manner that is typical of a multiprogramming environment. Note that the program queues for both the CPU and the IO subsystems are kept in main memory and/or secondary memory. Various analytic methods for solving this type of network are known.

Probability of zero items in system: $p_0 = \left[\dfrac{\rho^c}{c!(1 - \rho/c)} + \displaystyle\sum_{i=0}^{c-1} \dfrac{\rho^i}{i!} \right]^{-1}$

Probability of n items in system: $p_n = \begin{cases} \dfrac{\rho^n p_0}{n!} & \text{for } 0 \le n \le c \\[2ex] \dfrac{\rho^n p_0}{c!\, c^{n-c}} & \text{for } n \ge c \end{cases}$

Mean queue length (including server): $l_Q = \dfrac{\rho^{c+1} p_0}{(c - 1)!\,(c - \rho)^2} + \rho$

Mean time in queue (including service time): $t_Q = \dfrac{l_Q}{\lambda}$

FIGURE 2.76
Formulas for the standard $M/M/c$ model.

Example 2.4   Analysis of shared computer usage [1]. A small company has a computer with a single terminal that is shared by its engineering staff. It is used by an average of 10 engineers during an 8-hour working day, and each user occupies the terminal for an average of 30 min, mostly for fairly simple and routine calculations. The company manager feels that the computer is underutilized, since the system is idle an average of 3 hours a day. The users, however, complain that it is *over*utilized since they typically wait an hour or more to gain access to the terminal; they therefore request that new terminals be purchased and added to the system. We now attempt to analyze this apparent contradiction using queueing theory.

We assume that the computer system and its users are adequately represented by an $M/M/1$ queueing system. Since there are 10 users per 8 hours, on average, we set $\lambda = \frac{10}{8}$ users/hour $= 0.0208$ users/min. The system is busy an average of 5 out of 8 hours; hence $\rho = \frac{5}{8}$, implying that $\mu = \frac{1}{30} = 0.0333$. Substituting these values for λ and

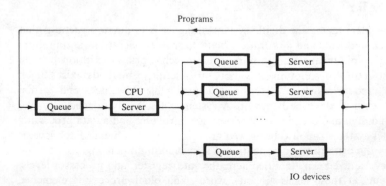

FIGURE 2.77
Queueing network model of a multiprogramming system.

μ into (2.31) yields $t_W = 50$ min, which confirms the users' estimate of their average waiting time for terminal access.

The manager is now convinced that additional terminals are needed and agrees to buy enough additional terminals to reduce t_W from 50 to 10 min. The question therefore arises: how many new terminals should he buy? There are several possible approaches to this problem. The first is to represent each terminal and its users by an independent M/M/1 queueing system. Let m be the minimum number of terminals needed to make $t_W \le 10$ or, equivalently, $t_Q \le 40$. The arriving users are assumed to divide evenly into m queues, one for each terminal. The arrival rate λ^* per terminal is taken to be $\lambda/m = 0.0208/m$ users/min. If, as indicated above, the computer's CPU is lightly utilized, then a few additional terminals should not affect the response time experienced at a terminal; hence we assume that each terminal's mean service rate is $\mu^* = \mu = 0.0333$ users/min. To meet the desired performance goal, we require

$$t_Q^* = \frac{1}{\mu^* - \lambda^*} = \frac{1}{\mu - \lambda/m} \le 40$$

from which it follows that $m \ge 2.5$. This implies that a total of three terminals are needed, i.e., two new terminals should be acquired. This result is pessimistic, since the users are unlikely to form three separate queues for three terminals, or to maintain the independence of the queues by not jumping from one queue to another whose terminal has become available. Nevertheless, this simple analysis gives the useful result that m must be 2 or 3.

A second, and more realistic approach, is to represent the entire computer system by a single M/M/m model. This model has a single queue with mean arrival rate λ^* and m independent servers, again corresponding to the m terminals, each with mean service time μ^*. It is reasonable to assume now that $\lambda^* = \lambda$ and that, as in the preceding case, $\mu^* = \mu$. If we substitute these parameters into the formulas for l_Q and t_Q in Fig. 2.76 with $m = c = 2$, we obtain $t_Q = 33.25$ min, which is less than the goal of 40 min. Hence this M/M/c model implies that one new terminal is sufficient, assuming of course, that the foregoing assumptions are reasonable. (Experience suggests they are.)

2.5   SUMMARY

The central problem facing the digital-systems designer is to devise structures that use available components and perform a specified range of operations at minimum cost. Abstractly, this means transforming a given behavioral description into an appropriate structural description. A variety of descriptive methods exist. Block diagrams are used primarily to describe structure, while flowcharts and formal languages are used to describe behavior. A system is frequently divided into two parts for both design and descriptive purposes, a control unit and a data processing unit. Computer systems can also be viewed at various levels of detail. Each level is determined by the primitive components and information units recognized at that level. Three levels have been identified here: the gate, register, and processor levels. The components at these levels are bit-, word-, and block-processing elements, respectively. Computer architecture deals with the register and processor levels. The gate level, which is the level of classical logic design, is characterized by a well-developed theory (switching theory) based on Boolean algebra. No equivalent theory exists at the register or processor level; hence heuristic design techniques must normally be used.

Register-level components include combinational devices such as word gates, multiplexers, decoders, and adders, as well as sequential devices such as (parallel) registers, shift registers, and counters. These components can be easily expanded to accommodate additional inputs. The behavior of register-level circuits can be described by register transfer languages, many of which have been proposed. The fundamental element of such languages is the register transfer statement

$$c: \quad Z \leftarrow f(X_1, X_2, \ldots, X_n)$$

where c denotes a control expression and $Z \leftarrow f(X_1, X_2, \ldots, X_n)$ denotes the transfer of data from registers $X_1, X_2, \ldots, X_n$ to register Z via a combinational processing circuit f. The first step in register-level design is to construct a formal description of the desired behavior. From this the required components and connections (data paths) for the data processing part can be determined and a block diagram constructed. The necessary control signals and control points are then identified. Finally, a control unit is designed to generate the required control signals in the correct sequence.

The primitive components identified at the processor level include processors, memories, and IO devices. The behavior of processor-level systems is complex and must often be specified in probabilistic terms. Performance evaluation is an important part of the design process. Queueing models of system behavior are particularly useful. Relatively few performance models can be solved analytically. Instead, experimental approaches using computer-based simulation, or performance measurements on an actual system may be used. Processor-level design is frequently based on the use of prototype structures. A prototype structure is selected and modified if necessary to meet the given performance specifications. The actual performance of the system is then evaluated, and the design is further modified until a satisfactory performance level is achieved.

PROBLEMS

2.1. Explain the difference between structure and behavior in the digital system context. Illustrate your answer by giving (a) a purely structural description and (b) a purely behavioral description of a simple three-input logic gate.

2.2. A useful gate type not included in Fig. 2.11 is EXCLUSIVE-NOR, which may be defined by the following equation:

$$z = \overline{x_1 \oplus x_2 \oplus \cdots \oplus x_n}$$

Construct truth tables for the EXCLUSIVE-NOR function with $n = 2$ and $n = 3$. What is the standard circuit symbol for an EXCLUSIVE-NOR gate?

2.3. Let $|$, the Sheffer stroke symbol, denote the binary NAND operation, that is, $a \mid b = \overline{ab}$. Determine whether or not $|$ obeys the commutative, associative, and idempotent laws of Boolean algebra.

2.4. A gate-level combinational circuit is said to be *well-behaved* if the logical value (state) of every line at time t can be determined from the circuit structure and the logical values of all its primary input lines at time t.

(a) Prove that every well-formed circuit is well behaved.

(b) Prove that some well-behaved circuits are not well formed.

2.5. (a) Construct a K-map for the function z defined by Fig. 2.78. List all the function's prime implicants and identify those that are essential.

(b) Design a minimal SOP-type two-level realization of z composed of NAND gates.

2.6. Obtain minimal SOP and POS expressions for the function of Fig. 2.78 when the values marked by asterisks are treated as don't cares.

2.7. Consider the 1-bit incrementer design discussed in the text (Example 2.1). It is to be modified by the addition of a fifth output signal z_5 that is normally 0, but becomes 1 if any of the six don't-care input combinations which do not represent BCD digits is applied to the circuit. z_5 thus serves to indicate the presence of erroneous input combinations. Design a minimal POS-type all-NOR implementation of the modified incrementer.

2.8. A useful flip-flop type not included in Fig. 2.29 is a T (*toggle*) *flip-flop*, which has a single data input denoted T and is characterized by the fact that T = 1 causes the flip-flop to change state, while T = 0 retains the current state. A T flip-flop has the same circuit symbol as a D flip-flop with the data input labeled T rather than D.

(a) Give a state table and Boolean equation defining the behavior of a (clocked) T flip-flop.

(b) Show how to convert an SR flip-flop to a T flip-flop by adding some logic to it.

2.9. Design a sequential circuit that multiplies an unsigned binary number N of arbitrary length by 3. N is entered serially via input line x with its least significant bit first. The result representing $3N$ emerges serially from the circuit's output line z. Construct a state table for your circuit and give a complete logic circuit that uses JK flip-flops and NAND gates only.

x_1	x_2	x_3	x_4	z
0	0	0	0	1
0	0	0	1	0
0	0	1	0	1*
0	0	1	1	0
0	1	0	0	1
0	1	0	1	1*
0	1	1	0	1
0	1	1	1	0*
1	0	0	0	1
1	0	0	1	1
1	0	1	0	1*
1	0	1	1	0
1	1	0	0	0*
1	1	0	1	1
1	1	1	0	0
1	1	1	1	0

FIGURE 2.78
Truth table for a four-variable function.

2.10. Redesign the serial adder of Example 2.2 using D flip-flops and NOR gates to implement the circuit. Give a description of circuit behavior in terms of sequential Boolean equations.

2.11. Carry out the gate-level design of a synchronous modulo-4 up-down counter. It is to have four input lines: a count enable line COUNT; an up-down select line DOWN; a clock line CLOCK; and a reset line CLEAR. There are two output lines $Z = (z_0, z_1)$. Use only NAND gates and D flip-flops in your circuit, and attempt to minimize the total number of logic gates.

2.12. A general method for designing small sequential machines, the one-hot method, uses one flip-flop per state. A particular state S_i is coded by setting the state variable y_i of the ith flip-flop to 1, and setting all y_j to 0 for $j \neq i$. Thus only one flip-flop is in the set or "hot" state at any time. Clearly, n rather than $\log_2 n$ flip-flops are being used to realize an n-state machine. This obvious disadvantage is countered by the fact that one-hot circuits are very easy to design and debug.

    (a) Use the one-hot approach to implement the modulo-4 up-down counter defined in Prob. 2.11.

    (b) Analyze the advantages and disadvantages of one-hot circuits, with your counter design serving as an illustration.

2.13. An important property of sets of gates is logical completeness, which ensures that a complete gate set is adequate for all types of digital computations.

    (a) It has been asserted that logical completeness is irrelevant when dealing with combinational components in the MSI range such as multiplexers, decoders, PLAs. Explain concisely why this is so.

    (b) Suggest a logical property of sets of MSI components that might be substituted for completeness as an indication of the components' general usefulness in digital design. Give a brief argument supporting your position.

2.14. (a) Prove that if the input variables are available in both true and complemented form (*double-rail logic*), a 2^n-input 1-bit multiplexer can be used to realize any $(n + 1)$-variable combinational function.

    (b) Show how a four-input 2-bit multiplexer can be used to realize a full adder circuit.

2.15. Describe how a $1/k^2$ decoder circuit can be constructed using $1/k$ decoders only.

2.16. Modify the logic diagram of the 8-bit nonpriority encoder given in Fig. 2.45 to obtain an 8-bit priority encoder.

2.17. Design a 16-bit priority encoder using two copies of an 8-bit priority encoder. Additional gates may also be used if needed.

2.18. A general-purpose logic element similar in concept to a PLA is a read-only memory (ROM). A ROM is used to generate a set of combinational functions $F(X)$ in the following way. X is treated as the ROM address and $F(X)$ is stored as data in the ROM location with address X. When X is applied to the ROM input (address) lines and the read operation is enabled, $F(X)$ appears at the ROM output (data) lines. The ROM thus stores a direct physical representation of the truth table for $F(X)$. ROMs are particularly useful in applications like code conversion where there is no simple logical relationship between the input and output variables.

    (a) Describe how a $p \times q$ diode array of the type shown in Fig. 2.46 can be used as a ROM for generating combinational functions. Explain how address decoding can be performed wholly or in part by the diode array.

    (b) Using the 4×8 array of Fig. 2.46, obtain an ROM realization of the functions f_1 and f_2 defined by Eqs. (2.16) and (2.17).

(c) Write a short note comparing the efficiency of the PLA and ROM organizations when the array dimensions p and q are fixed.

2.19. Design a comparator for two 10-bit numbers using only 4-bit comparators of the kind shown in Fig. 2.48.

2.20. Design a modulo-16 binary counter similar to that of Fig. 2.49 which operates synchronously, i.e., which allows all flip-flops to change state simultaneously.

2.21. A useful subcircuit in CPU design is a combinational *"barrel" shifter*, which is intended for high-speed shifting of a specified number of digits to the left or right. You are to design a barrel shifter for 8-digit (32-bit) BCD numbers. The inputs to the shifter are:
1. The 8-digit number X to be shifted
2. A 3-bit control word SIZE that specifies the length of the shift in digits
3. A direction bit DIR, where DIR $= 1$ denotes a right shift and DIR $= 0$ denotes a left shift
4. A bit FULL that specifies the logic value of all bits (trailing 0s or trailing 1s) introduced at the right (left) end of the number during a left (right) shift operation
5. A control bit ENABLE that enables the shifter

The shifter's output is a number Y that has been shifted in the specified manner.

Draw a register-level block diagram for your design. Use any appropriate components discussed in the text, such as word gates or multiplexers. Label all lines clearly, and give a brief narrative description of how your design works.

2.22. The following listing describes a familiar combinational circuit in an APL-based hardware description language. The variable names and identifiers have been chosen so that they do not provide mnemonic clues to circuit function.

1. SUBROUTINE WHATSIT (A, B)
2. X, Y $\leftarrow$ 19ρ0, 18ρ0
3. $X_{18} \leftarrow 0$
4. $i \leftarrow 17$
5. $X_i \leftarrow F(B_i, A_i, X_{i+1})$
6. $Y_i \leftarrow G(B_i, A_i, X_{i+1}, F)$
7. $i \leftarrow i - 1$
8. i: 0 $(\geq, <) \rightarrow (5, 9)$
9. $c \leftarrow (X_0 \oplus d)$
10. WHATSIT (A, B) $\leftarrow$ c, Y
11. RETURN

Draw a block diagram for the circuit described by this listing. Comment on any difficulties you encounter in interpreting the description. (*Note:* X $\leftarrow$ 19ρ0 means X is a 19-bit word that is initialized to zero. Statement 8 means if $i \geq 0$, go to statement 5; otherwise go to statement 9.)

2.23. Figure 2.79 is a flowchart describing an algorithm for multiplication that is used in some low-speed computer systems. The algorithm is implemented by three up-down counters, CQ, CM, and CP, which store the multiplier, multiplicand, and product, respectively, and the product P is formed by incrementing the counter CP a total of P times. Although this multiplication method is slow, it requires a fairly simple logic

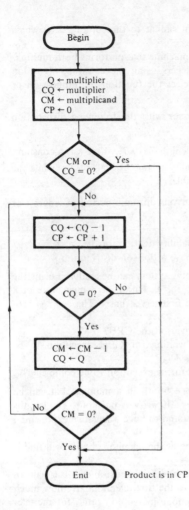

FIGURE 2.79
A multiplication algorithm using counters.

circuit and can easily accommodate complicated number codes. Construct a description of this multiplication algorithm using the formal language introduced in the text.

2.24. Consider the design of a multiplier that implements the multiplication algorithm of Fig. 2.79 (see also Prob. 2.23). The numbers to be multiplied are four-digit integers in sign-magnitude BCD code. For example, the number −1709 is represented by the bit sequence

$$1 \quad 0001 \quad 0111 \quad 0000 \quad 1001$$

CQ, CM, and CP are to be constructed from modulo-10 up-down counters with parallel input-output capability. Carry out the logic design of this multiplier at the register transfer level.

2.25. (a) Draw the flowchart of a counting algorithm similar to that of Fig. 2.79 which performs integer division.

(b) Carry out the register-level logic design of a machine that performs both multiplication and division on four-digit BCD integers using the counting algorithm approach. A single control signal should select the function (multiplication or division) to be performed.

2.26. Suppose that jobs arrive randomly at a processor with the following distribution properties:

1. The number of arrivals during any period of length T is λT, where λ is a constant.

2. In a small interval of length Δt, the probability of one arrival is $\lambda \Delta t$, while the probability of more than one arrival is negligible.

Let $p_0(t)$ be the probability that there are no arrivals during a period of length t or less.

(a) Prove that $p_0(t) = e^{-\lambda t}$.

(b) Prove that the interarrival time has the probability distribution $1 - e^{-\lambda t}$.

(Properties 1 and 2 also imply that the arrivals have a Poisson distribution.)

2.27. Suppose that CPU behavior in a multiprogramming system can be analyzed using the M/M/1 model. Programs are sent to the CPU for execution at a mean rate of 8 programs/min and are executed on a first-come first-served basis. The average program requires 6 s of CPU execution time.

(a) What is the mean time between program arrivals at the CPU?

(b) What is the mean number of programs waiting for CPU execution to be completed?

(c) What is the mean time a program must wait for its execution to be completed?

2.28. Suppose that people arrive at a public telephone booth in a manner that can be simulated by a Poisson process with an average of 10 arrivals per hour. The lengths of the telephone calls made from the booth are found to have a negative exponential distribution with a mean length of 2.5 min.

(a) What is the probability that someone arriving at the telephone booth will find it occupied?

(b) The telephone company will install a second booth if a customer must wait an average of 4 minutes or more to gain access to the first telephone. By how much must the flow of customers to the first telephone increase in order for the telephone company to install the second phone?

2.29. A certain computer executes a stream of programs in a manner that can be accurately modeled by an M/M/1 queueing system. It is found that the computer is busy 50 percent of the time, and that the average job spends 10 min in the computer.

(a) How many jobs are in the computer on average?

(b) What is the maximum rate at which jobs may arrive at the system before it becomes overloaded? State clearly your definition of overloaded.

2.30. Consider the problem of the shared computer terminal posed in Example 2.4. The reported average waiting time of $t_W = 50$ min applies to all users, including those whose waiting time is zero. Not surprisingly, most of the complaints come from users who experience nonzero waiting times. Determine, showing your reasoning, the average waiting time for this group of users.

2.31. Consider the $M/M/2$ queueing system model, which has two servers, each with a mean service rate of μ. Items arrive at the system at a mean rate of λ and enter a common queue for the two servers. Let p_n denote the steady-state probability that there are exactly n items in the system. It can be shown that, for $n \geq 1$,

$$p_n = \frac{\lambda}{\mu} \left(\frac{\lambda}{2\mu}\right)^{n-1} p_0 \qquad (2.32)$$

(a) Let $\nu = \lambda/2\mu = \rho/2$ denote the system utilization. From (2.32) prove that

$$p_n = 2\nu^n \left(\frac{1-\nu}{1+\nu}\right)$$

(b) Prove that the average number of items in the system is $2\nu/(1-\nu^2)$.

(c) Derive a general expression for the average time an item spends in the system.

Check that your results are consistent with the formulas of Fig. 2.76, but do not use those formulas in your proofs.

2.32. This problem involves manual simulation of a computer system that is executing a stream of jobs. The jobs arrive randomly, are queued until selected for execution, and depart immediately after execution is completed. The arrival and execution times for a particular job stream are given by the following table:

Job number:	1	2	3	4	5	6	7	8	9	10	11	12
Arrival time:	9:00	9:05	9:08	9:09	9:16	9:21	9:24	9:26	9:32	9:39	9:40	9:43 a.m.
Execution time (min):	2	5	8	1	6	5	8	2	4	1	3	7
Departure time:												
System response time (min):												

Assuming that jobs are executed on a first-come first-served (FCFS or FIFO) basis, find the mean response time t_Q of the system by completing the above table. What is the computer's utilization factor ρ from 9:00 a.m. until the last job departs?

2.33. Consider again the computer job stream in Prob. 2.32. Suppose that the FCFS method used to select jobs for execution is replaced by another scheduling discipline called *shortest-job first* (SJF), in which the next job selected for execution is the one in the queue with the shortest execution time. (It is assumed that all execution times are known in advance.) Using the data given in Prob. 2.32, determine the system utilization ρ and mean response time t_Q with SJF replacing FCFS. Provide a brief intuitive explanation for the difference (or lack of difference) in the values of ρ and t_Q obtained with the two methods.

2.34. A simulation program is to be written in a high-level programming language, e.g., FORTRAN. As part of that program, it is desired to generate a sequence of numbers $T = t_1, t_2, t_3, \ldots$, which represent consecutive interarrival times for a Poisson process. The available program library contains only one random number generating function, RANDOM(A, B), which produces a real number that is uniformly distributed between A and B. Describe how you would use RANDOM(A, B) to generate the sequence T.

2.35. A program is to be written in an ordinary high-level programming language that simulates the behavior of an $M/M/1$ queueing system. The program should be able to calculate the performance measures l_Q and t_Q under steady-state conditions for any given values of λ and μ.

(a) Draw a flowchart for the simulation program.

(b) Code your program and execute it for several sample queueing systems using any available computer. Explain any discrepancies observed between the simulated and analytic values of l_Q and t_Q.

REFERENCES

1. Allen, A. O.: "Queueing Models of Computer Systems," *IEEE Computer*, vol. 13, no. 4, pp. 13–24, April 1980.
2. Auerbach, I. L.: "Need for an Information Systems Theory," in H. Zemanek (ed.), *The Skyline of Information Processing*, pp. 9–21, North-Holland, Amsterdam, 1972.
3. Bell, C. G., and A. Newell: *Computer Structures: Readings and Examples*, McGraw-Hill, New York, 1971.
4. Blakeslee, T. R.: *Digital Design with Standard MSI and LSI*, 2d ed., Wiley, New York, 1979.
5. Boole, G.: *The Laws of Thought*, MacMillan, London, 1854. (Reprinted by Dover, New York, 1958.)
6. Brayton, R. K., et al.: *Logic Minimization Algorithms for VLSI Synthesis*, Kluwer, Boston, 1984.
7. Breuer, M. A. (ed.): *Digital System Design Automation: Languages, Simulation and Data Base*, Computer Science Press, Woodland Hills, Calif., 1975.
8. Burks, A. W., and J. B. Wright: "Theory of Logical Nets," *Proc. IRE*, vol. 41, pp. 1357–1365, October 1953.
9. Dahl, O. J., E. W. Dijkstra, and C. A. R. Hoare: *Structured Programming*, Academic, New York, 1972.
10. Dietmeyer, D. L., and J. R. Duley: "Register Transfer Languages and their Simulation," in Ref. 7, pp. 117–218.
11. Falkoff, A. D., K. E. Iverson, and E. H. Sussenguth: "A Formal Description of SYSTEM/360" *IBM Syst. J.*, vol. 3, pp. 198–263, 1964.
12. Ferrari, D.: *Computer Systems Performance Evaluation*, Prentice-Hall, Englewood Cliffs, N.J., 1978.
13. Gibson, J. C.: "The Gibson Mix," IBM Rep. TR00.2043, IBM Corp., Poughkeepsie, N.Y., June 1970.
14. Hayes, J. P.: *Digital System Design and Microprocessors*, McGraw-Hill, New York, 1984.
15. Huffman, D. A.: "The Synthesis of Sequential Switching Circuits," *J. Franklin Inst.*, vol. 257, pp. 161–190 and pp. 275–303, 1954.
16. Karnaugh, M.: "The Map Method for Synthesis of Combinational Logic Circuits," *Trans. AIEEE*, Pt. 1, vol. 72, pp. 593–599, 1953.
17. Kleinrock, L.: *Queueing Systems*, vol. 1: *Theory*, Wiley, New York, 1975.
18. Lucas, H. C.: "Performance Evaluation and Monitoring," *Comput. Surv.*, vol. 3, pp. 79–91, September 1971.
19. McCluskey, E. J.: *Logic Design Principles*, Prentice-Hall, Englewood Cliffs, N.J., 1986.
20. MacDougall, M. H.: "System Level Simulation," in Ref. 7, pp. 1–115.
21. Morrison, P., and E. Morrison (eds.): *Charles Babbage and his Calculating Engines*, Dover, New York, 1961.
22. Reed, I. S.: "Symbolic Design Techniques Applied to a Generalized Computer," MIT Lincoln Lab. Tech. Rep. TR-141, January 1956. (Reprinted with revisions in *IEEE Computer*, vol. 5, pp. 47–52, May/June 1972.)
23. Rosen, S.: *Lectures on the Measurement and Evaluation of the Performance of Computing Systems*, SIAM Reg. Conf. Series in Appl. Math., vol. 23, 1976.

24. Shannon, C. E.: "A Symbolic Analysis of Relay and Switching Circuits," *Trans. AIEE*, vol. 57, pp. 713–723, 1938.
25. Siewiorek, D., C. G. Bell, and A. Newell: *Computer Structures: Principles and Examples*, McGraw-Hill, New York, 1982.
26. Simon, H. A.: "The Architecture of Complexity," *Proc. Amer. Phil. Soc.*, vol. 106, pp. 467–482, December 1962. (Reprinted in H. A. Simon: *The Sciences of the Artificial*, 2d ed., pp. 193–229, M.I.T. Press, Cambridge, Mass., 1981.)
27. Trivedi, K. S.: *Probability and Statistics with Reliability, Queuing, and Computer Science Applications*, Prentice-Hall, Englewood Cliffs, N.J., 1982.
28. Van Cleemput, W. M.: "Computer Hardware Description Languages and their Applications," *Proc. 16th Design Autom. Conf.*, pp. 554–560, June 1979.
29. Van Tassel, D.: *Program Style, Design, Efficiency, Debugging, and Testing*, 2d ed., Prentice-Hall, Englewood Cliffs, N.J., 1978.

THREE
PROCESSOR DESIGN

This chapter is concerned with the data processing function of computers, as exemplified by the instruction execution unit of a central processing unit (CPU). Basic CPU organization is introduced, along with the methods used for representing numbers and instructions. The design of instruction sets and programming at the assembly-language level are then discussed. Finally, the implementation of arithmetic instructions is examined in detail.

3.1 INTRODUCTION

We begin by considering the general organization of instruction set processors and the methods used to represent the information they are intended to process.

3.1.1 Processor Organization

The primary function of a processor, such as the CPU of a computer, is to execute sequences of instructions stored in a memory (main memory), which is external to the CPU. The CPU must first fetch an instruction from this memory before it can be executed. The sequence of operations involved in processing an instruction constitutes an *instruction cycle*, which can be subdivided into two major phases: the *fetch cycle* and the *execution cycle*. The instruction is obtained from main memory during the fetch cycle. The execution cycle includes decoding the instruction, fetching any required operands, and performing the operation specified by the instruction's opcode. The behavior of the CPU during an instruction cycle is defined by a sequence of microoperations, each of which typically involves a register transfer operation. The time t_{CPU} required for the shortest well-defined CPU microoperation is defined to be the *CPU cycle time* and is the basic unit of time for measuring all CPU actions. The reciprocal of t_{CPU} is the CPU *clock rate*, generally measured in megahertz. The clock rate depends directly on the circuit technology used to fabricate the CPU.

In addition to executing programs, the CPU supervises the other system components, usually via special control lines. For example, the CPU directly or indirectly controls IO operations such as data transfers between IO devices and main memory. These operations require the CPU's attention relatively infrequently; it is therefore more efficient to allow the CPU to ignore IO devices and the like until they actively request service from the CPU. Such a request is called an *interrupt*. In the event of an interrupt, the CPU suspends execution of the program that it is executing and transfers to an appropriate interrupt handling program. Interrupts, particularly IO interrupts, frequently require a rapid response by the CPU. A test for the presence of interrupt signals is thus normally carried out at the end of each instruction cycle. The major functions of the CPU are summarized in the flowchart in Fig. 3.1.

Basic CPU organization. Despite the great improvements in circuit technology over the years, almost all CPU designs have been based on the following two premises.

1. The CPU should be as fast (measured by its cycle time t_{CPU}) as the available technology permits. Since cost invariably increases with speed, the number of components in the CPU must be kept relatively small.
2. A main memory of relatively large capacity is needed to store the programs and data required by the CPU. Because of the size of the main memory, it must be constructed using less expensive and therefore slower technology than that of the CPU.

Main memory speed may be measured by the *memory cycle time* t_M, which is the minimum time that must elapse between two successive read or write operations. The ratio t_M / t_{CPU} typically ranges from 1 to 10. The CPU contains a small number of storage devices called *registers*, used for temporary storage of instructions and operands. The transfer of information among these registers can proceed at a rate approximately t_M / t_{CPU} times that of a transfer between the CPU and main memory. Instructions whose operands are in fast CPU registers can be executed more rapidly than instructions whose operands are in main memory. Program execution is therefore frequently implemented as follows.

1. Transfer the required operands from main memory to CPU registers.
2. Compute the desired results in the CPU.
3. Transfer the results from the CPU to main memory.

The CPU communicates with IO devices in much the same way as it communicates with main memory. The IO devices have addressable registers called *IO*

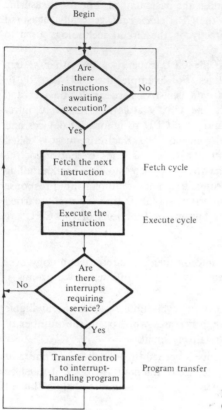

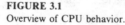

FIGURE 3.1
Overview of CPU behavior.

ports associated with them to which the CPU can write a word (an output operation) or from which it can read a word (an input operation). In some computers there are no IO instructions per se. All IO data transfers are implemented by memory-referencing instructions, an approach called *memory-mapped IO*. This requires that memory locations and IO ports share the same address space, so that an address bit pattern that is assigned to memory cannot also be assigned to an IO port, and vice versa. Other computers employ IO instructions that are distinct from memory-referencing instructions. These produce control signals to which IO ports, but not memory locations, respond; consequently, the main memory and IO address spaces are distinct and can use the same bit patterns for addresses. This second approach is called *IO-mapped* or *port-addressed IO*.

The design proposed by von Neumann and his colleagues for the IAS computer is the basis for almost all CPUs designed since then. It comprises a minimal set of registers and the necessary circuits to execute a small single-address instruc-

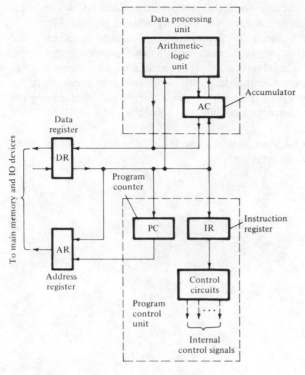

FIGURE 3.2
A simple accumulator-based CPU.

tion set. One of the CPU registers, called the *accumulator*,[1] plays a central role, being used to store an input or an output operand (result) in the execution of most instructions.

Figure 3.2 shows the essential structure of an accumulator-oriented CPU. This architecture is typical of first-generation machines such as IAS (cf. Fig. 1.13) and some modern computers in the mini and micro classes. The accumulator AC is the main operand register of the arithmetic-logic unit. The data register DR acts as a buffer between the CPU and main memory. It is used as an input operand register with the accumulator so that operations of the form $AC \leftarrow f(AC, DR)$ can be performed. The other major registers are the program counter PC, which stores

---

[1]The term "accumulator" originally meant a device that combined the functions of number storage and addition. Any quantity transferred to an accumulator was automatically added to its previous contents. The counter wheel memories of early mechanical computers had accumulators of this type.

the address of the next instruction word; the instruction register IR, which holds the opcode of the current instruction; and the memory address register AR.

Figure 3.3 shows the sequence of microoperations involved in fetching and executing some typical instructions in a machine with the foregoing architecture. The program counter PC is automatically incremented after an instruction has been fetched, under the assumption that instructions are normally executed in the sequence in which they are stored. PC may be subsequently modified during the instruction cycle by a jump instruction, as illustrated in Fig. 3.3.

Extensions. There are several ways in which the basic processor organization of Fig. 3.2 can be made more powerful.

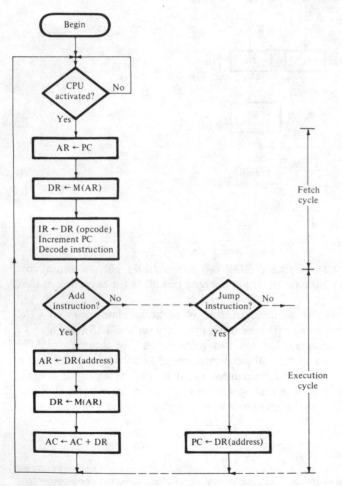

FIGURE 3.3
Operation of the CPU of Fig. 3.2.

1. Additional addressable registers can be provided for storing operands and addresses; this can be viewed as replacing the single accumulator by a set of registers. If the registers are multipurpose, the resulting machine is said to have the *general register organization* exemplified by the IBM S/360-370 (see Fig. 1.32). A set of general registers is sometimes referred to as a register file or a scratch-pad memory. A major function of these registers is to store operands needed for memory address construction. Sometimes special address registers, e.g., index or base registers, are provided for this purpose. The Motorola 68020 (Fig. 1.39) provides eight general-purpose data registers and a matching set of general-purpose address registers.

2. The capabilities of the arithmetic-logic circuits, particularly their arithmetic capabilities, can be extended. Many microprocessors, for example, can perform only addition and subtraction on fixed-point numbers. Relatively little extra circuitry is required for fixed-point multiplication and division. A substantial increase in hardware is required to implement floating-point arithmetic, however. Arithmetic function implementation is the topic of Secs. 3.3 and 3.4.

3. Special registers can be included to facilitate the transfer of control between instructions within a program. For example, a *status register* (also called a condition code or flag register) is used to indicate conditions resulting from the execution of the previous instruction, such as the sign (positive or negative) of a numerical result, the occurrence of an all-0 result, or an abnormal termination due to numerical overflow. The status register can be tested by a conditional branch instruction to alter the instruction execution sequence based on the outcome of the preceding instruction.

4. The transfer of control between different subprograms (subroutines or procedures) due to interrupts or subroutine calls and returns is also facilitated by special registers. For example, S/360-370 computers employ the PSW (program status word) register, whose contents include the program counter and flags, to record the execution status of a program. Control is transferred by saving the current PSW in a designated location in main memory and loading a new PSW into the CPU. Control is returned to the first program by retrieving the previously saved PSW from memory and restoring it to the CPU. Most computers now use a more flexible scheme for program-control transfer which is based on using a part of main memory as a pushdown stack. The stack is used to store program-status information and has a LIFO (last-in first-out) access discipline. It is controlled by a memory address register in the CPU called a *stack pointer* SP, which always indicates the current "top" or entry address of the stack. A word is transferred to or from the stack by carrying out a memory access with SP as the address register; SP is then adjusted automatically to point to the new stack top. A major advantage of a stack in this application is its ability to handle repeated (nested) program transfers efficiently.

5. Facilities can be provided for the simultaneous processing of two or more distinct instructions. As noted above, several instructions or operands can be fetched simultaneously by extending the memory addressing circuits and adding

sufficient buffer storage to the CPU. The execution of several instructions can also be overlapped in several ways. For example, the ALU can be divided into k parts or replicated k times to permit up to k instructions to be executed at once. An ALU or a portion thereof can be organized as a pipeline permitting several distinct operand sets to be processed simultaneously. Such parallel processing techniques are considered in detail in Chap. 7.

Figure 3.4 shows the register-level design of a typical CPU based on the foregoing considerations. It has the general register organization with a group of perhaps 16 registers for data and/or address storage. The ALU obtains most of its

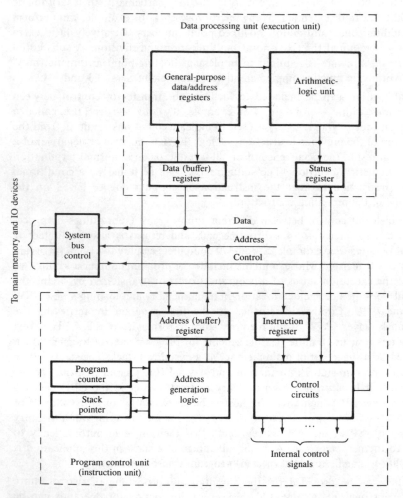

FIGURE 3.4
Typical CPU with general register organization.

operands from this register set and also stores most of its results there. A status register monitors the output of the ALU, recording key characteristics of the results being generated. The major special-purpose address registers are the program counter and the stack pointer. Some special logic (typical of a simple fixed-point ALU) is included for address computation; the main ALU may also be used for this purpose. The control circuits in the program control unit derive their inputs from the instruction register, which stores the opcode of the current instruction, and the status register. Communication with the outside world is via a system bus that is used for the transmission of address, data, and control information to and from the CPU. Various nonprogrammable buffer registers serve as intermediate temporary storage points between the system bus and the rest of the CPU. Parallelism may be present in the internal organization of the ALU or in the overlapping of the operations carried out by the data processing and program-control units.

3.1.2 Information Representation

Information is represented in a computer by means of binary sequences which are organized into words. A *word* is a unit of information of fixed length n, where n is primarily determined by hardware cost considerations. A word may be viewed as a sequence of binary coded characters. Early computers such as the IBM 7094 used 6-bit character codes, since 6 is the minimum number of bits needed to encode the 26 letters of the English alphabet, the 10 decimal digits, and a reasonable number (28) of special characters such as punctuation marks. In recent years, the use of 8-bit binary sequences, called *bytes*, for character representation has become universal. As well as allowing additional characters, e.g., both uppercase and lowercase alphabets, 8-bit characters permit efficient representation of BCD numbers. Two BCD digits can be stored in an 8-bit field with no wasted space. Only one BCD digit can be stored in a 6-bit field, thus wasting 2 bits. Most current computers have CPU word sizes which are multiples of 8; 8-, 16-, 32-, and 64-bit words are common choices. ASCII (*A*merican *S*tandards *C*ommittee on *I*nformation *I*nterchange) code is a widely used 8-bit character code.

Information types. Figure 3.5 shows the basic types of information represented in a computer. There is a fundamental division into instructions (control information) and data. Data may be further subdivided into numerical and nonnumerical. In view of the importance of numerical computation, a great deal of attention has been given to the development of number codes. Two major formats have evolved, fixed-point and floating-point. The binary fixed-point format is of the form

$$b_0 b_1 b_2 \cdots b_{n-1}$$

where $b_i \in \{0, 1\}$ and a binary point separating the integer and fraction parts is in some fixed but implicit position. A floating-point number, on the other hand, consists of a pair of fixed-point numbers

$$M, E$$

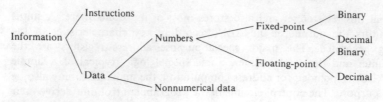

FIGURE 3.5
Some basic information types.

which represent the number $M \times B^E$, where B is a predetermined base. Floating-point corresponds to the so-called scientific notation. A variety of codes are used to represent fixed-point numbers. These codes may be classified as binary, e.g., twos-complement, or decimal, e.g., BCD. Large computers sometimes employ several different fixed-point and floating-point number formats. Nonnumerical data usually take the form of variable-length character strings encoded in ASCII or similar codes.

Tags. In stored-program computers, instructions and data are stored together in main memory. In the classic (von Neumann) stored-program machine, instructions and data words stored in main memory are indistinguishable from one another. In other words, a word chosen at random from memory cannot be identified as an instruction or a data word. Different data types such as fixed-point and floating-point numbers also cannot be distinguished. The meaning of the word is determined by the way a processor interprets it. Indeed the same word can be treated as an instruction and data at different times, e.g., the word X in the instruction sequence

$$X \leftarrow X + Y$$

go to X

Clearly it is the programmer's responsibility to ensure that data are not interpreted as instructions, and vice versa.

The reason for this deliberate indistinguishability of data and instructions can be clearly seen in the design of the first-generation IAS computer (see Sec. 1.2.3). The address modify instructions alter stored instructions in main memory. The ability to modify instructions in this way—in effect, treating them as data—is useful when processing indexed variables, as illustrated in Example 1.5. However, this type of instruction modification in main memory became obsolete with the introduction of indexing hardware. Most programmers, particularly those using high-level languages, have no need for programs that modify themselves; indeed it appears to be difficult to write a high-level language program that modifies itself in a useful way.

A number of computer designers have argued that the major information types should be assigned representations that identify them [11, 20]. This can be done by associating with each basic information unit a group of bits, called a *tag*, that identifies its type. The tag may be considered as a physical implementation of the **type** declaration found in many high-level programming languages. One of the first machines to use tags was the Burroughs B5000. It uses a single tag bit (called a flag) to distinguish two types of words called operands and descriptors. Its successors, the B6500 and B7500, employ a 3-bit tag field in every word, so that eight word types can be distinguished [9]. The 52-bit word format of the B6500/7500 is shown in Fig. 3.6.

The advantage of tagged information is that instruction sets and therefore the programming task can be simplified. In conventional von Neumann machines an instruction must specify the type of data on which it operates. It is therefore necessary to provide distinct instructions for each data type; see, for example, the list of different addition instructions for the S/360-370 given in Fig. 1.34. If the operand types are identified by tags, a single addition instruction suffices. The processor merely has to inspect the operand tags to determine the specific type of operation to be performed, e.g., a fixed-point double-precision addition. Furthermore, the tag inspection permits the hardware to check for software errors, such as an attempt to add operands whose types are incompatible. The disadvantage of tags is that they increase memory size and therefore add to the system hardware costs without increasing computing performance; this fact has restricted the use of tagged architecture in the past.

Error detection and correction. A variety of factors such as faulty components and inadequate design tolerances can result in errors appearing in the information being processed by a computer. Such errors frequently occur in information that is being transmitted between two relatively distant points within the system, or in information stored in a memory device. A bit x that is being transmitted from A to B may, due to "noise" in the communication channel, be corrupted so that $\bar{x}$ instead of x is received at the destination B. In order to guard against errors of this type, the information can be coded in such a way that the errors can be detected, and possibly even corrected, by special logic circuits. A general approach to this is to append check bits to each word, which can be used to detect or locate errors in the word.

One of the simplest and most widely used techniques for error control is the use of a single check bit c_0 called a *parity bit*. The parity bit is appended to an n-bit word $X = (x_0, x_1, \ldots, x_{n-1})$ to form the $(n+1)$-bit word $X^* = (x_0, x_1, \ldots, x_{n-1}, c_0)$; see, for example, Fig. 3.6. c_0 is assigned the value 0 or 1 that makes the number

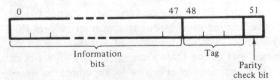

0   47 48   51

Information bits   Tag   **FIGURE 3.6**

Parity check bit   Word format of the Burroughs B6500/7500 computer series.

of 1s in X^* even in the case of even-parity codes, or odd in the case of odd-parity codes. Thus in the even-parity case c_0 is defined by the Boolean equation

$$c_0 = x_0 \oplus x_1 \oplus \cdots \oplus x_{n-1} \tag{3.1}$$

while in the odd-parity case

$$\overline{c}_0 = x_0 \oplus x_1 \oplus \cdots \oplus x_{n-1}$$

Suppose that the information X is to be transmitted from A to B. The value of c_0 is computed at the source point A using, say, (3.1), and X^* is sent to B. Let B receive the word $X' = (x_0', x_1' \ldots, x_{n-1}', c_0')$. B then determines the parity of the received word by recomputing the parity bit according to (3.1) thus:

$$c_0^* = x_0' \oplus x_1' \oplus \cdots \oplus x_{n-1}'$$

The received parity bit c_0' and the recomputed parity bit c_0^* are then compared. If $c_0' \neq c_0^*$, the received information contains an error. In particular, if exactly 1 bit of X^* has been inverted during the transmission process (a single-bit error), then $c_0' \neq c_0^*$. If $c_0' = c_0^*$, it can be concluded that no single-bit error occurred, but the possibility of multiple-bit errors is not ruled out. For example, if a 0 changes to 1 and a 1 changes to 0 (a double error), then the parity of X' is the same as that of X^* and the error will go undetected. The parity bit c_0 therefore provides *single-error detection*. It does not detect all multiple errors, much less provide any information about the location of the erroneous bits.

The parity-checking concept can be readily extended to the detection of multiple errors, or to the location of single or multiple errors. These goals are achieved by providing additional parity bits, each of which checks the parity of some subset of the bits in the word X^*. Suppose, for example, that we can deduce from the parity checks the identity of the bit x_i responsible for a single-bit error. It is then a simple matter to introduce logic circuits to replace x_i by $\overline{x}_i$, thus providing *single-error correction*. Let c be the number of check bits required to achieve single-error correction with n-bit data words. Clearly, the check bits have 2^n patterns which must distinguish between $n + c$ possible error locations and the single error-free case. Hence c must satisfy the inequality

$$2^c \geq n + c + 1 \tag{3.2}$$

For $n = 16$, (3.2) implies that $c \geq 5$, while for $n = 32$ we have $c \geq 6$. A variety of practical single-error correcting parity-check codes are known that meet the lower bound on c implied by (3.2). These codes also have the ability to detect double errors, and so are called *single-error correcting double-error detecting (SECDED)* codes.

As the main memories of computers have increased in storage capacity and decreased in physical size, they have become more prone to transient failures that are often correctable via SECDED codes. Such codes are used, for instance, in the IBM System/370 and its successors, and in the Data General ECLIPSE series of minicomputers. In all cases a set of c parity-check bits is appended to every memory word. Each check bit specifies the parity of a subfield of the word being protected. By appropriately overlapping these subfields, the correctness of every bit can be determined. Note that single-error correction assumes that no double errors are present; hence single-error correction and double-error detection cannot be performed simultaneously. Consider, for example, the ECLIPSE computer, which uses a type of SECDED code called a Hamming code for memory protection. When a 16-bit word $X = (x_0, x_1, \ldots, x_{15})$ is written into memory, five check bits $(c_0, c_1, c_2, c_3, c_4)$ are computed and stored with X. The check bits are specified by the following parity equations.

$$
\begin{aligned}
\bar{c}_0 &= & x_2 & & & \oplus\ x_5 & & & \oplus\ x_{10} \oplus x_{11} \oplus x_{12} \oplus x_{13} \oplus x_{14} \oplus x_{15} \\
c_1 &= & & & x_4 \oplus x_5 \oplus x_6 \oplus x_7 \oplus x_8 \oplus x_9 \oplus x_{10} & & & \oplus\ x_{15} \\
\bar{c}_2 &= & x_1 \oplus x_2 \oplus x_3 & & & \oplus\ x_7 \oplus x_8 \oplus x_9 & & & \oplus\ x_{14} \oplus x_{15} \\
c_3 &= x_0 & \oplus x_2 \oplus x_3 & & \oplus x_5 \oplus x_6 & & \oplus x_9 & & \oplus x_{12} \oplus x_{13} \\
\bar{c}_4 &= x_0 \oplus x_1 & \oplus x_3 \oplus x_4 & & \oplus x_6 & & \oplus x_8 & \oplus x_{11} & \oplus x_{13}
\end{aligned}
$$

When the word is subsequently read from memory, it may have been altered by errors to $(x'_0, x'_1, \ldots, x'_{15}, , c'_0, c'_1, c'_2, c'_3, c'_4)$. A new set of check bits $(c_0^*, c_1^*, c_2^*, c_3^*, c_4^*,)$ is then derived from $(x'_0, x'_1, \ldots, x'_{15})$ and the error vector

$$E = (c'_0 \oplus c_0^*, c'_1 \oplus c_1^*, c'_2 \oplus c_2^*, c'_3 \oplus c_3^*, c'_4 \oplus c_4^*)$$

is computed. If $E = 0$, then no detectable error has occurred. Every single and double error results in $E \neq 0$. Furthermore, each single error results in a distinct value of E, so that by including appropriate logic circuits, E can be used to complement, and therefore correct, the erroneous bit. For example, the fault causing x_0 to become $\bar{x}_0$ is detected by c_3 and c_4 and results in $E = (0, 0, 0, 1, 1)$. It can be seen from the parity-check equations that no other single fault is detected by c_3 and c_4 only; hence this value of E always indicates the presence of an error in bit x_0.

Many methods of designing error-detecting and error-correcting codes are known [12, 22, 30]. Any desired level of protection against errors can be obtained by using sufficient check bits. The cost increases rapidly with the level of protection required due to the added memory for storing the check bits and also the error detection or correction logic. Figure 3.7 shows the structure of a typical error detection and correction scheme.

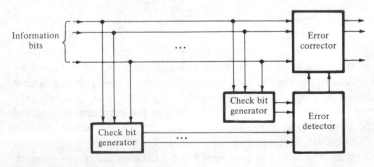

FIGURE 3.7
Error detection and correction logic.

3.1.3   Number Formats

In selecting a number representation to be used in a computer, the following factors should be taken into account

1. The types of numbers to be represented, e.g., integers, real numbers, complex numbers
2. The range of values likely to be encountered
3. The precision of the number, which refers to the maximum accuracy of the representation
4. The cost of the hardware required to store and process the numbers

The two principal number formats are fixed-point and floating-point. In general, fixed-point formats allow a limited range of values and have relatively simple hardware requirements. Floating-point numbers, on the other hand, allow a much larger range of values but require more costly processing hardware.

Binary numbers. The fixed-point format is derived directly from the ordinary (decimal) representation of a number as a sequence of digits separated by a decimal point. The digits to the left of the decimal point represent an integer; the digits to the right represent a fraction. This is a *positional notation* in which each digit has a fixed *weight* according to its position relative to the decimal point. If $i \geq 1$, the ith digit to the left (right) of the decimal point has weight 10^{i-1} (10^{-i}). Thus the five-digit decimal number 192.73 is equivalent to

$$1 \times 10^2 + 9 \times 10^1 + 2 \times 10^0 + 7 \times 10^{-1} + 3 \times 10^{-2}$$

More generally, we can assign weights of the form r^i, where r is the *radix* or *base* of the number system, to each digit. The most fundamental number representation used in computers employs a positional notation with 2 as the radix. A binary sequence of the form

$$b_N \cdots b_3 b_2 b_1 b_0 \, . \, b_{-1} b_{-2} b_{-3} b_{-4} \cdots b_M \qquad (3.3)$$

represents the number

$$\sum_{i=M}^{N} b_i 2^i$$

When not clear from the context, the radix r being used will be indicated by appending r as a subscript to the number. Thus 1010_2 denotes the binary equivalent of the decimal number 10_{10}, whereas 10_2 denotes 2_{10}. (3.3) is an example of a fixed-point binary number. The format of (3.3) is used for representing unsigned binary numbers. Several distinct methods used for representing signed (positive and negative) numbers are discussed below.

Suppose that an n-bit word is to be used to contain a signed binary number. One bit is reserved to represent the sign of the number, while the remaining bits indicate its magnitude. To permit uniform processing of all n bits, the sign is placed in the leftmost position, and the values 0 and 1 are used to denote plus and minus, respectively. Thus we obtain the format

$$x_0 \underbrace{x_1 x_2 \cdots x_{n-2} x_{n-1}}_{\text{Magnitude}} \qquad (3.4)$$
$$\underset{\text{Sign}}{\uparrow}$$

The precision allowed by this format is $n - 1$ bits, which is equivalent to $(n - 1)/\log_2 10$ decimal digits. The binary point is not explicitly represented; it is implicitly assigned to a fixed location within the word. The position of the binary point is not particularly important from the point of view of design. In many situations the numbers being processed are integers, so the binary point is assumed to lie immediately to the right of the least significant bit x_{n-1}. Monetary quantities are often expressed as integers, e.g., \$54.30 might be expressed as 5430 cents. Using an n-bit integer format, we can represent all integers N with magnitude $|N|$ in the range $0 \le |N| \le 2^n - 1$. The other most widely used format treats (3.4) as a fraction with the binary point lying between x_0 and x_1. The fraction format permits numbers with magnitudes in the range $0 \le |N| \le 1 - 2^{-n}$ to be represented.

Suppose that signed binary numbers are to be represented by an n-bit word $X = x_0 x_1 x_2 \cdots x_{n-1}$. The simplest and most common way of representing positive numbers is to use the format of (3.4) with the standard positional notation for the magnitude part. This means that each magnitude bit x_i has a fixed weight of the form 2^{k-i}, where k depends on the position of the binary point. Perhaps the most natural way to represent negative numbers is to employ the same positional notation for the magnitude and simply change the sign bit x_0 to 1 to indicate minus. This number code is called *sign magnitude*. Certain operations, notably subtraction, cannot be most efficiently implemented using sign-magnitude representation. However, multiplication and division of sign-magnitude numbers is almost as easy as the corresponding operation for unsigned numbers, as Example 2.3 in Sec. 2.3.3 illustrates for the case of multiplication.

Several number codes have been devised which use the same representation for positive numbers as the sign-magnitude code but represent negative numbers in various different ways. For example, in the *ones-complement* code, $-X$ is denoted by $\overline{X}$, the bitwise logical complement of X. In the *twos-complement* code, $-X$ is formed by adding 1 to the least significant bit of $\overline{X}$ and ignoring any carry bit generated from the most significant (sign) position. If X is an n-bit binary fraction, this may be expressed as follows:

$$-X = \overline{x}_0.\overline{x}_1\overline{x}_2 \cdots \overline{x}_{n-2}\overline{x}_{n-1} + 0.00 \cdots 01 \text{ (Modulo 2)} \qquad (3.5)$$
$$\qquad \uparrow \qquad\qquad\qquad\qquad\qquad \uparrow$$
$$\text{Implicit binary point} \qquad \text{Implicit binary point}$$

where the use of modulo-2 addition corresponds to ignoring carries from the sign position. If X is an integer, then (3.5) becomes

$$-X = \overline{x}_0\overline{x}_1\overline{x}_2 \cdots \overline{x}_{n-2}\overline{x}_{n-1}. + 1 \text{ (Modulo } 2^n) \qquad (3.6)$$
$$\qquad\qquad\qquad \uparrow$$
$$\text{Implicit binary point}$$

In each of the complement codes, x_0 retains its role as the sign bit, but the remaining bits no longer form a simple positional code when the number is negative. The primary advantage of these codes is that subtraction can be performed by logical complementation and addition only. Consider, for example, the twos-complement code. To subtract X from Y, add $-X$ to Y, where $-X$ is obtained by logical complementation and addition of a 1 bit as in (3.5) and (3.6). The sign bits do not require special treatment; consequently, as will be shown in Sec. 3.3.1, twos-complement addition and subtraction can be implemented by a simple n-bit parallel adder designed for unsigned numbers. The adder's carry-in line can then be used to introduce the 1 bit needed for subtraction.

Multiplication and division are somewhat more difficult to implement if twos-complement code is used rather than sign magnitude. The addition of ones-complement numbers is complicated by the fact that a carry bit from the most significant magnitude bit x_1 must be added to the least significant bit position x_{n-1}. Otherwise ones-complement codes have very similar properties to twos-complement codes and so will not be considered further.

Figure 3.8 illustrates how integers are represented using each of the three codes discussed above when $n = 4$. These are called binary codes to distinguish them from the so-called decimal codes discussed later. Note that in all cases, 0000 represents zero. Only in the case of twos-complement is the numerical complement of 0000 also 0000, which is an advantage in implementing instructions that test for zero.

If the result of an arithmetic operation involving signed n-bit numbers is too

Decimal representation	Binary code		
	Sign magnitude	Ones complement	Twos complement
+7	0111	0111	0111
+6	0110	0110	0110
+5	0101	0101	0101
+4	0100	0100	0100
+3	0011	0011	0011
+2	0010	0010	0010
+1	0001	0001	0001
+0	0000	0000	0000
−0	1000	1111	0000
−1	1001	1110	1111
−2	1010	1101	1110
−3	1011	1100	1101
−4	1100	1011	1100
−5	1101	1010	1011
−6	1110	1001	1010
−7	1111	1000	1001

FIGURE 3.8
Comparison of three 4-bit binary number codes.

large (small) to be represented by n bits, *overflow* (*underflow*) is said to occur. It is generally necessary to detect overflow and underflow since they are frequently an indication of a programming error.

Consider, for example, the addition operation

$$z_0 z_1 \cdots z_{n-1} \leftarrow x_0 x_1 \cdots x_{n-1} + y_0 y_1 \cdots y_{n-1}$$

using n-bit twos-complement operands. Assume that bitwise addition is performed with a carry bit c_i generated by the addition of x_i, y_i, and c_{i+1}. z_i and c_i for $1 \leq i \leq n-1$ can be computed according to the usual full-adder logic equations

$$z_i = x_i \oplus y_i \oplus c_{i+1}$$

$$c_i = x_i y_i + x_i c_{i+1} + y_i c_{i+1}$$

Let v be a binary variable indicating overflow or underflow when $v = 1$. Figure 3.9 shows how the sign bit z_0 and v are determined as functions of the sign bits x_0, y_0 and the carry bit c_1. The overflow-underflow indicator v is defined by the logic equation

$$v = \overline{x}_0 \overline{y}_0 c_1 + x_0 y_0 \overline{c}_1$$

If the combinations $(x_0, y_0, c_1) = (0,0,1)$ and $(1,1,0)$, which set v to 1, are removed from the truth table of Fig. 3.9, it can then be seen that z_0 is defined correctly for all the remaining combinations by the equation

$$z_0 = x_0 \oplus y_0 \oplus c_1$$

This has the important consequence that during twos-complement addition, the sign bits of the operands can be treated in the same way as the remaining (magnitude) bits.

A related issue in machine arithmetic is *roundoff error*, which results from the fact that every number must be represented by a limited number of bits. Frequently, an operation involving n-bit numbers produces a result of more than n bits. For example, the product of two n-bit numbers contains up to $2n$ bits, all but n of which must normally be discarded. Retaining the n most significant bits of the result without modification is called *truncation*. Clearly the resulting number is in

Input			Output	
x_0	y_0	c_1	z_0	v
0	0	0	0	0
0	0	1	0	1
0	1	0	1	0
0	1	1	0	0
1	0	0	1	0
1	0	1	0	0
1	1	0	1	1
1	1	1	1	0

FIGURE 3.9
Computation of the sign bit z_0 and the overflow-underflow indicator v in twos-complement addition.

error by the amount of the discarded digits. This error can be reduced by a process called *rounding*. One way of doing this is to add $r^j/2$ to the number before truncation, where r^j is the weight of the least significant retained digit. For instance, to round 0.346712 to three decimal places, add 0.0005 to obtain 0.347212 and then take the three most significant digits 0.347. Simple truncation yields the less accurate value 0.346. Successive computations can cause roundoff errors to build up unless countermeasures are taken. The number formats provided in a computer should have sufficient precision that roundoff errors are of no consequence to most users. It is also desirable to provide facilities for performing arithmetic to a higher degree of precision if required. Such high precision is usually achieved by using several words to represent a single number and writing special subroutines to perform multiword, or *multiple precision*, arithmetic.

Decimal numbers. Since individuals today normally use decimal arithmetic, numbers being entered into a computer must first be converted from decimal to some binary representation. Similarly, binary-to-decimal conversion is a normal part of the computer's output processes. In certain applications the number of decimal-binary conversions forms a large fraction of the total number of elementary operations performed by the computer. It is therefore important that number conversion be carried out rapidly. The various binary number codes discussed above do not lend themselves to rapid conversion. For example, to convert a binary number $x_0 x_1 x_2 \cdots x_{n-1}$ to decimal, a polynomial of the form

$$\sum_{i=1}^{n-1} x_i 2^{k-i}$$

must be evaluated.

Several number codes are used which allow very rapid binary-decimal conversion. This is achieved by encoding each decimal digit separately by a sequence of bits. Codes of this kind are called *decimal codes*. They should properly be called binary coded decimal, but the term is reserved for one of the most widely used decimal codes, the *binary coded decimal*, or BCD, code. In the BCD representation of a decimal number, each digit d_i is represented by its 4-bit equivalent $b_{i,3} b_{i,2} b_{i,1} b_{i,0}$ in standard binary form. Thus the BCD number representing 971 is 100101110001. BCD is a weighted (positional) number code, since $b_{i,j}$ has the weight $10^i 2^j$. BCD numbers are generally in sign-magnitude form. The 8-bit ASCII code represents the 10 decimal digits in a 4-bit field in the same way as BCD. The remaining 4 bits (the "zone" field) are essentially unused.

Two other decimal codes of moderate importance are shown in Fig. 3.10. The *excess-three* code can be formed by adding 0011_2 to the corresponding BCD number—hence its name. Excess-three code has the advantage that it may be processed using the same logic used for binary codes. If two excess-three numbers are added like binary numbers, the required decimal carry is automatically generated from the high-order bits. The sum must be corrected by adding ± 3. For example, consider the addition $5 + 9 = 14$ using excess-three code.

Decimal digit	Decimal code			
	BCD	ASCII	Excess-three	Two-out-of-five
0	0000	0011 0000	0011	11000
1	0001	0011 0001	0100	00011
2	0010	0011 0010	0101	00101
3	0011	0011 0011	0110	00110
4	0100	0011 0100	0111	01001
5	0101	0011 0101	1000	01010
6	0110	0011 0110	1001	01100
7	0111	0011 0111	1010	10001
8	1000	0011 1000	1011	10010
9	1001	0011 1001	1100	10100

FIGURE 3.10
Some important decimal number codes.

$$
\begin{array}{rl}
1000 & = 5 \\
+\ 1100 & = 9 \\
\hline
\text{Carry } 1 \leftarrow \quad 0100 & \quad \text{Binary sum} \\
+\ 0011 & \quad \text{Correction} \\
\hline
0111 & \quad \text{Excess-three sum}
\end{array}
$$

Binary addition of the BCD representations of 5 and 9 results in 1101 and no carry generation.[2] Some arithmetic operations are difficult to implement using excess-three code, mainly because it is a nonweighted code, that is, each bit position in an excess-three number does not have a fixed weight.

The final decimal code shown in Fig. 3.10 is the *two-out-of-five* code. Each decimal digit is represented by a 5-bit sequence containing two 1s and three 0s; there are exactly 10 distinct sequences of this type. The particular merit of the two-out-of-five code is that it is single-error detecting, since changing any one bit results in a sequence that does not correspond to a valid codeword. Its drawbacks are that it is a nonweighted code and uses 5 rather than 4 bits per decimal digit.

The main advantage of the decimal codes is ease of conversion between the internal computer representation that allows only the symbols 0, 1 and external representations using the 10 decimal symbols 0, 1, 2, . . . , 9. Decimal codes have two disadvantages.

1. They use more bits to represent a number than the binary codes. Decimal codes therefore require more memory space. An n-bit word can represent 2^n numbers

---

[2]The binary sum of two BCD numbers can also be corrected to give the proper BCD sum as described later in Sec. 3.3.1.

using binary codes; approximately $10^{n/4} = 2^{0.830n}$ numbers can be represented if a 4-bit decimal code such as BCD or excess-three is used.

2. The circuitry required to perform arithmetic using decimal operands is more complex than that needed for binary arithmetic. For example, in adding BCD numbers bit by bit, a uniform method of propagating carries between adjacent positions is not possible since the weights w_i and w_{i+1} of adjacent bits do not differ by a constant factor.

Floating-point numbers. The range of numbers that can be represented by a fixed-point number code is insufficient for many applications, particularly scientific computations where very large and very small numbers are frequently encountered. Scientific notation permits such numbers to be represented using relatively few digits. For example, it is easier to write a quintillion in the form

$$1.0 \times 10^{18} \tag{3.7}$$

than as the fixed-point integer

$$1\ 000\ 000\ 000\ 000\ 000\ 000$$

The floating-point codes used in digital processors are essentially binary versions of (3.7).

Three numbers are associated with a floating-point number, the *mantissa M*, the *exponent E*, and the *base B*. These three components together represent the number $M \times B^E$. For example, in (3.7), 1.0 is the mantissa. 18 is the exponent, and 10 is the base. For machine implementation the mantissa and exponent are encoded as fixed-point numbers with radix r, where r is usually 2 or 10. The base B is invariably some power of r for reasons that will be obvious later. Since the base is a constant, it need not be included in the number code; it can simply be built into the circuits that process the numbers. A floating-point number is therefore stored as a pair of fixed-point numbers—a mantissa M, which is usually a fraction or an integer; and an exponent E, which is an integer.

The precision of $M \times B^E$ is determined primarily by the number of digits used in M. The range is determined by B and E. Floating-point formats are used to represent real numbers over some continuous interval $\pm R$. Since only a finite set of numbers can be represented (at most 2^n, where n is the floating-point word size), these numbers are sparsely distributed over the interval $\pm R$. Increasing B greatly increases the range of the numbers that can be represented but results in a sparser distribution of numbers over that range.

Floating-point number representation is inherently redundant in the sense that the same number can be represented in more than one way. For example, 1.0 $\times 10^{18}$, 0.1×10^{19}, 1000000×10^{12}, and 0.000001×10^{24} are possible floating-point forms of a quintillion. It is generally desirable to specify a unique normal form for floating-point numbers in a computer implementation. Consider the case where the mantissa is a sign-magnitude fraction and a base of 2 is used. The mantissa is said to be *normalized* if the digit to the right of the binary point is not 0, that is, there are no leading 0s in the magnitude part of the number. Thus, for example, 0.1×10^{19} is the unique normal form of a quintillion using base 10 and decimal mantissa and exponent. A binary fraction in twos-complement code is normalized when the sign bit x_0 differs from the bit x_1 to its right. This implies that there are no leading 1s in negative numbers. Normalization restricts the magnitude $|M|$ of a fractional mantissa to the range

$$\tfrac{1}{2} \leq |M| < 1$$

Normal forms can be defined similarly for other number codes. An unnormalized floating-point number is easily normalized by shifting the mantissa to the right or left and appropriately incrementing or decrementing the exponent.

The representation of zero poses some special problems. The mantissa must, of course, be zero, but the exponent may have any value since $0 \times B^E = 0$ for all values of E. Often in attempting to compute zero, roundoff errors and the like result in a mantissa that is very small but not exactly zero. In order for the entire floating-point number to be close to zero, its exponent must be a very large negative number $-K$. This suggests that the exponent used for representing zero should be the negative number with the largest magnitude that can be contained in the exponent field of the number format. If k bits are allowed for the exponent (including its sign), then 2^k exponent bit patterns are available to represent signed integers, which can range either from -2^{k-1} to $2^{k-1} - 1$, or from $-2^{k-1} + 1$ to 2^{k-1}, so that K is 2^{k-1} or $2^{k-1} - 1$. A second complication arises from the desirability of representing zero by a sequence of 0 bits only. This gives zero the same representation in both fixed- and floating-point formats, which facilitates the implementation of instructions that test for zero. These considerations suggest that floating-point exponents be encoded in excess-K code similar to the excess-three code of Fig. 3.10, where the exponent field contains an integer that is the desired exponent value plus K. The quantity K is called the *bias*, and an exponent encoded in this way is called a *biased exponent* or *characteristic*. Figure 3.11 shows the possible values of an 8-bit exponent with bias 127 and 128.

Exponent bit pattern	Unsigned value E	Signed value	
		Bias = 127	Bias = 128
$111 \cdots 11$	255	+128	+127
$111 \cdots 10$	254	+127	+126
$\cdots$	$\cdots$	$\cdots$	
$100 \cdots 01$	129	+2	+1
$100 \cdots 00$	128	+1	0
$011 \cdots 11$	127	0	−1
$011 \cdots 10$	126	−1	−2
$\cdots$	$\cdots$	$\cdots$	
$000 \cdots 01$	1	−126	−127
$000 \cdots 00$	0	−127	−128

FIGURE 3.11
Eight-bit biased exponents with bias = 127 (excess-127 code) and bias = 128 (excess-128 code).

Example 3.1   The IEEE 754 standard floating-point number format [16, 27]. Until the 1980s, floating-point number codes varied from one computer family to the next, making it difficult to transport programs between different machines without encountering small but significant differences in such areas as roundoff errors, and the treatment of overflow, underflow, and other exceptional conditions. To deal with this problem, the Institute of Electrical and Electronics Engineers (IEEE) has sponsored a standard format for 32- and 64-bit floating-point numbers, known as the IEEE 754 standard, which has been widely adopted in new computer designs.

The 754 standard for 32-bit numbers is illustrated in Fig. 3.12. It comprises a 23-bit mantissa field M, an 8-bit exponent field E, and a sign bit S. The base B is 2. As in all signed binary number formats, both fixed-point and floating-point, S occupies the leftmost bit position. M is a fraction which with S forms a sign-magnitude binary number. For the reasons discussed earlier, floating-point numbers are usually normalized, meaning that the magnitude field should contain no insignificant leading bits. Hence the magnitude part of a normalized sign-magnitude number always has 1 as its most significant digit. There is no need to actually store this leading 1 in floating-point numbers, since it can always be inserted by the arithmetic circuits that process the numbers. Consequently, in the 754 standard the complete mantissa, which is called the *significand*, is actually $1.M$, where the 1 to the left of the binary point is an implicit or "hidden" leading bit that is not stored with the number. Use of the hidden 1 means that the precision of a normalized number is effectively increased by 1 bit. The exponent representation is the 8-bit excess-127 code of Fig. 3.11; hence the actual exponent value is computed as $E - 127$. The base B of the floating-point number is 2, so that a 1-bit left (right) shift of M corresponds to incrementing (decrementing) E by 1.

It follows from the above that a 32-bit floating-point number conforming to the IEEE 754 standard represents the real number given by the formula

$$N = (-1)^S 2^{E-127} (1.M) \tag{3.8}$$

provided $0 < E < 255$. For example, the number $N = -1.5$ is represented by

$$1\ 01111111\ 10000000000000000000000$$

where $S = 1$, $E = 127$, and $M = 0.5$, since from (3.8), we have $N = (-1)^1 2^{127-127}(1.5) = -1.5$. Nonzero floating-point numbers in this format have magnitudes ranging from $2^{-126}(1.0)$ to $2^{+127}(2 - 2^{-23})$, i.e., from 1.18×10^{-38} to 3.40×10^{38} approximately. In contrast, 32-bit fixed-point binary formats for integers can only represent nonzero numbers with magnitudes from one to $2^{31} - 1$ (approximately 2.15×10^9). The 64-bit version of the IEEE 754 standard is a straightforward extension of the 32-bit case. It employs an 11-bit exponent E and a 52-bit mantissa M, and defines the number

$$N = (-1)^S 2^{E-1023}(1.M) \tag{3.9}$$

where $0 < E < 2047$.

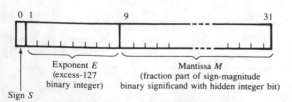

Exponent E
(excess-127
binary integer)

Mantissa M
(fraction part of sign-magnitude
binary significand with hidden integer bit)

Sign S

FIGURE 3.12
IEEE 754 standard 32-bit floating-point number format.

The IEEE floating-point standard addresses a number of subtle problems encountered in floating-point arithmetic. Well-defined formats are specified for the results of overflow, underflow, and other exceptional conditions, which often yield unpredictable and unusable numbers in computers employing other floating-point formats. The IEEE standard's exception formats are intended to set flags in the host processor, which can be used by subsequent instructions for error control, in many cases with little or no loss of accuracy. If the result of a floating-point operation is not a valid floating-point number, then a special code referred to as *not a number* (NaN) is used. Examples of operations that result in NaNs are dividing zero by zero, and taking the square root of a negative number. NaN formats are identified in the standard by $M \neq 0$, and $E = 255$ (32-bit format) or $E = 2047$ (64-bit format). When overflow occurs, meaning that a number has been produced whose magnitude is too big to represent by the usual format, the result is referred to as *infinity* or ∞, and is identified by $M = 0$, and $E = 255$ (32-bit format) or $E = 2047$ (64-bit format). The IEEE 754 standard stipulates that operations using the floating-point infinities $\pm\infty$ should follow the properties of infinity in real-number theory, such as $\infty + N = \infty$ and $-\infty < N < +\infty$ for any finite N. If underflow occurs, implying that a result is nonzero, but too small to represent as a normalized number, it is encoded in a *denormalized*[3] form characterized by $E = 0$ and a significand $0.M$ having a leading 0 instead of the usual leading 1. Denormalization reduces the effect of underflow to a systematic loss of precision equivalent to a roundoff error. Finally, floating-point zero is identified by an all-0 exponent and significand, but the sign S may be 0 or 1. Note that as the tiny denormalized numbers are diminished, they eventually reach zero. In summary, the number N represented by a 32-bit IEEE-standard floating-point number has the following set of interpretations.

If $E = 255$ and $M \neq 0$, then $N = $ NaN.

If $E = 255$ and $M = 0$, then $N = (-1)^S \infty$.

If $0 < E < 255$, then $N = (-1)^S 2^{E-127} (1.M)$.

If $E = 0$ and $M \neq 0$, then $N = (-1)^S 2^{-126} (0.M)$.

If $E = 0$ and $M = 0$, then $N = (-1)^S 0$.

The interpretation of 64-bit numbers is similar.

Typical of older floating-point number formats still in widespread use is that of the IBM S/360-370. It consists of a sign bit S, a 7-bit exponent field E, and a mantissa field M containing 24, 56, or 112 bits[4]; see Fig. 1.31. M is treated as a fraction, which with S forms a sign-magnitude number; there is also no hidden leading 1. E is an integer in excess-64 code, corresponding to an exponent bias of 64. Unlike the IEEE 754 format where the base B of the representation is 2, the S/360-370 has $B = 16$. Consequently, M is interpreted as a hexadecimal (base 16)

---

[3]The term *unnormalized* applies to numbers with any value of E, and a leading 0 instead of a leading 1 associated with their mantissas. Such numbers are only encountered as intermediate results during floating-point computations and are not relevant to the standard.

[4]Bits 64-71 are unused in the S/360-370's 128-bit extended floating-point format; hence the mantissa is 112 rather than 120 bits long.

number with every hexadecimal digit corresponding to 4 bits, and the exponent is treated as a power of 16. The value of a floating-point number in the normalized S/360-370 format is therefore given by

$$N = (-1)^S 16^{E-64}(0.M)$$

where M is a 6-, 14-, or 28-digit hexadecimal number. For example, the number 0.125×16^5 is encoded as

$$0\ 1000101\ 00100000 \cdots 0000$$

Note that the leftmost 4 bits 0010 of the mantissa represent the nonzero hexadecimal digit 2; hence this number is normalized. The number 0 is always represented by the all-0 word, making the floating-point representation of 0 identical to the S/360-370's fixed-point (twos-complement) representation. There are no equivalents of the IEEE 754 standard's NaN, infinity, and denormalized formats. While most floating-point instructions are performed with automatic normalization of the results, a few may be specified without normalization, thus providing some of the advantages of denormalization. Due to the larger value of B being used, the S/360-370's 32-bit format can represent numbers with magnitudes ranging from 5.40×10^{-79} to 7.24×10^{75} approximately.

3.2 INSTRUCTION SETS

Next we turn to the representation, selection, and application of instruction sets. This topic embraces opcode and operand specification, the design of the instruction types to include in a processor's instruction set, and finally the use of instructions in writing programs at the assembly-language level.

3.2.1 Instruction Formats

The purpose of an instruction is to specify an operation to be carried out and the set of operands or data to be used. Operands include the input data or arguments of the operation and the results that are produced. The operation and operands are usually described by specific "fields" of the instruction word. The operation is specified by a field called the *opcode* (*operation code*). The operand fields contain the *addresses* of storage locations in main memory or in the processor. The format of Fig. 3.13, comprising an opcode and a set of n operand addresses, is typical of processor instructions.

Most instructions specify a register transfer operation of the form

$$X_1 \leftarrow f(X_1, X_2, \ldots, X_n)$$

which involves n operands. The natural representation for this is the n-operand format of Fig. 3.13. To reduce instruction size and thereby reduce program storage space, it is common to specify only $m < n$ operands explicitly in the instruction; the remaining operands are implicit. The explicit address fields usually refer to main memory, while the implicit ones refer to registers. If m is the maximum

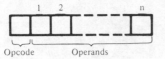

FIGURE 3.13
Basic instruction format.

number of explicit main-memory addresses allowed in any processor instruction, the processor may be called an *m-address machine*. Implicit input operands must be placed in locations known to the processor before the instruction that refers to them is executed.

Addressing modes. Every operand field of an instruction is associated with some piece of data X. In order to execute the instruction, the processor requires the current value of X. This value can be specified in several ways, termed *addressing modes*. If X is a constant, then its value can be placed in the instruction operand field, in which case X is called an *immediate* operand. This mode of operand specification is called *immediate addressing*. More often, the quantity of interest is a variable, and the corresponding operand field contains the address X of the storage location containing the required value. The operand value can then be varied without modifying any instruction addresses. Operand specification of this type is called *direct addressing*. It is frequently useful to change the location (as opposed to the value) of X without changing the address fields of any instructions that refer to X. This may be accomplished by *indirect addressing*, whereby the instruction contains the address W of a storage location which in turn contains the address X of the desired operand. By changing the contents of W, the address of the operand value required by the instruction is effectively changed. While direct addressing requires only one fetch operation to obtain an operand value, indirect addressing requires two. Figure 3.14 illustrates these different ways of specifying operands in the case of three load instructions which transfer the number 999 to the processor register AC.

The addressing modes of the operands appearing in a machine-language instruction, which may vary from operand to operand, are defined in the instruction's opcode. Many assembly languages allow addressing modes to be similarly defined by distinct opcodes. For example, the Intel 8085's assembly language has the opcode MOV (move) to specify data transfers involving direct addressing only, so that the register-to-register transfer $A \leftarrow B$, for instance, is specified by

$$\text{MOV} \quad \text{A, B} \qquad (3.10)$$

The A and B operands of (3.10) are considered to be directly addressed, since the contents of the named registers are the desired operand values. In contrast, to specify the operation $A \leftarrow 99$, where 99 is an immediate operand, the 8085 instruction

$$\text{MVI} \quad \text{A, 99} \qquad (3.11)$$

with the opcode MVI (*move immediate*) must be used. Note that (3.11) uses both the direct and immediate addressing modes.

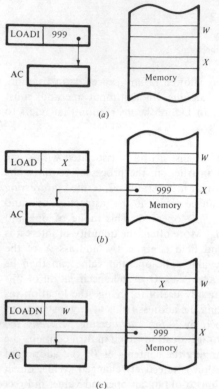

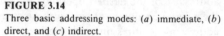

FIGURE 3.14
Three basic addressing modes: (*a*) immediate, (*b*) direct, and (*c*) indirect.

Other assembly languages, such as that of the Motorola 68000 series, take a different approach by specifying the addressing modes in the operand fields. For example, the 68000 equivalents of (3.10) and (3.11), with D1 = A and D2 = B are

$$\text{MOVE} \quad \text{D2, D1}$$

and
$$\text{MOVE} \quad \text{\#99, D1} \tag{3.12}$$

respectively; note that the Motorola operand order is reversed with respect to the Intel convention. In (3.12) the prefix # indicates that the immediate addressing mode is to be used for the operand in question. Deleting the # from (3.12) causes the first operand to refer to the data in memory location 99, i.e., M(99); this is an instance of direct memory addressing.

The ability to use all relevant addressing modes in a uniform and consistent way with all opcodes of an instruction set or assembly language is a desirable feature termed *orthogonality*. Orthogonal instruction sets simplify programming both by reducing the number of distinct opcodes needed and by simplifying the rules for operand address specification. Most computers have very little orthogonality since processor costs can be reduced (at the expense of programming costs) by restricting instructions to a few frequently used addressing modes that vary from instruction to instruction. As the foregoing MOVE example suggests, the 68000 has a more orthogonal instruction-set architecture than the 8085. However, unlike MOVE, most 68000 instructions cannot be used with all available addressing modes; so the 68000 series is by no means completely orthogonal, as a glance at its instruction set (Fig. 1.40) will confirm.

Absolute addressing, the simplest mode of (direct) address formation, requires the complete operand address to appear in the instruction operand field. This address is used without further modification to access the desired data item. Frequently, only partial addressing information is included in the instruction, so the complete (absolute) operand address must be constructed by the processor. One of the commonest techniques is *relative addressing*, in which the operand field contains a relative address or *displacement D*. The instruction also implicitly or explicitly identifies other storage locations $R_1, R_2, \ldots, R_k$ (usually processor registers) containing additional addressing information. The absolute or *effective* address A of an operand is then some function $f(D, R_1, R_2, \ldots, R_k)$. In most cases of interest, each operand is associated with a single address register R from a set of general-purpose address registers, and A is computed by adding D to the contents of R, that is,

$$A = R + D$$

R may also be a special purpose address register such as the program counter PC.

There are several important reasons for using relative addressing.

1. Since all the address information need not be included in the instructions, instruction length is reduced.
2. By changing the contents of R, the processor can change the absolute addresses referred to by a block of instructions B. This permits the processor to move (relocate) the entire block B from one region of main memory to another without invalidating the addresses in B. When used in this way, R may be referred to as a *base register* and its contents as a base address.
3. R can be used for storing indices to facilitate the processing of indexed data. In this role, R is called an *index register*. The indexed items $X(0), X(1), \ldots, X(k)$ are stored in consecutive addresses in main memory. The instruction address field D contains the address of the first item $X(0)$, while the index register R contains the index i. The address of item $X(i)$ is $D + R$. By changing the contents of the index register, a single instruction can be made to refer to any item $X(i)$ in the given data list.

The main disadvantages of relative addressing lie in the extra logic circuits and extra processing time required for address computation.

The instruction formats used in the IBM S/360-370 series are shown in Fig. 1.33. All aspects of relative addressing mentioned here are included. Some instructions require both an index register and a base register to construct an effective address.

Indexed items are frequently accessed sequentially, so that a reference to $X(k)$ stored in memory location A is immediately followed by a reference to $X(k + 1)$ or $X(k - 1)$ stored in location $A + 1$ or $A - 1$, respectively. To facilitate stepping through a sequence of items in this manner, addressing modes that automatically increment or decrement an address can be defined, and the resulting address-modification process is called *autoindexing*. For example, in the case of the Motorola 68000 series [13], the address field $-(A3)$ appearing in an assembly-language instruction indicates that the contents of the designated address register A3 should be decremented automatically before the instruction is executed; this is called predecrementing. Similarly, $(A3)+$ specifies that A3 should be incremented automatically after the current instruction has been executed (postincrementing). In each case, the amount of the address increment or decrement is the length in bytes of the indexed operands.

Autoindexing facilitates another important addressing mode called *stack addressing*, which is characterized by the use of part of main memory M as a pushdown stack. A *stack* is a logical sequence of items which are accessible from only one end referred to as the "top" of the stack. A write operation addressed to a stack, termed a *push* operation, stores a new item at the top of the stack, while a read operation, termed a *pop* operation, removes the item stored at the top of the stack. A push or a pop operation changes the position of the stack top by the length of the operand pushed or popped. A stack is controlled by an address register designated as the *stack pointer* SP. This register stores the address of the last operand placed in the stack; the address is automatically adjusted after a push or pop operation, so that SP contains the address of the new stack top. Suppose that address register A3 of the 68020 processor is designated by the programmer to be a stack pointer, and that the stack grows toward the low addresses of M. To push the contents of a data register, say D6, into the stack requires the instruction

$$\text{MOVE.L} \quad \text{D6}, -(A3) \tag{3.13}$$

This is a move instruction in which the .L modifier on the opcode MOVE indicates that the data to be moved is a "long" (4-byte) word. The input operand is the contents of D6 which is directly addressed in (3.13), while the output operand, which is the new contents of the top of the stack, is designated by indirect addressing with predecrementing. This push instruction is equivalent to the following operations in our formal description language:

$$A3 \leftarrow A3 - 4; \ M(A3) \leftarrow D6;$$

It is easily seen that the corresponding push instruction is

$$\text{MOVE.L} \quad (A3)+, D6 \tag{3.14}$$

which is equivalent to

$$D6 \leftarrow M(A3); \ A3 \leftarrow A3 + 4;$$

Processors frequently have a special autoindexed address register SP which serves as an implicit stack pointer for a stack used as a communication area by program-control instructions like call and return.

So far we have assumed that each operand is a single memory word and can therefore be specified by a single address. If variable-length data consisting of many words are to be processed by an instruction, each operand specification is divided into two parts: an address field, which points to the location of the first word of the operand; and a length field, which indicates the number of words in the operand. The instruction address field is automatically incremented by the processor as successive words of the operand are accessed. The access is complete when a number of words equal to the contents of the length field have been accessed.

Number of addresses. A source of some controversy since the early days of the first-generation computers is the question of how many explicit operand addresses to include in instructions. Clearly the fewer the addresses, the shorter the instruction. However, limiting the number of addresses also limits the range of functions each instruction can perform. Roughly speaking, fewer addresses mean more primitive instructions, and longer programs are therefore required to perform any given task. While the storage requirements of shorter instructions and longer programs tend to balance, larger programs require longer execution times. On the other hand, long instructions with multiple addresses usually require more complex decoding and processing circuits.

As noted earlier, processors are sometimes classified by the maximum number of main-memory address fields in their instructions. Computers generally have instructions of several different lengths containing varying numbers of addresses. Most instructions require no more than three operands. For example, the fundamental arithmetic operations—addition, subtraction, multiplication, and division—require three operands: two input operands and one output operand. In a three-address machine such as the CDC 6600, all three operands can be specified. For example, addition is defined by an assembly-language instruction with the format

$$\text{ADD} \quad Z, X, Y$$

meaning add the contents of memory locations X and Y and place the results in location Z, that is, $Z \leftarrow X + Y$. The add instruction in a one-address machine typically has the format

$$\text{ADD} \quad X$$

The unspecified operands are assumed to be stored in fixed locations, commonly in a processor register called the accumulator AC. The ADD instruction in this case results in the operation $AC \leftarrow AC + X$ being performed. In the case of a two-address machine, the accumulator may be used to store the result (the sum) only. Thus

$$\text{ADD} \quad X, Y$$

could be given the interpretation $AC \leftarrow X + Y$. An alternative implementation is to use one address, say X, to store both the addend X and the sum as follows: $X \leftarrow X + Y$. In the latter case the addition operand destroys the addend.

To illustrate the influence of the number of addresses on program length, we consider the execution of a high-level language arithmetic statement

$$X = A \times B + C \times C$$

where $\times$ denotes multiplication. The four operands A, B, C, and X are assumed to be stored in main memory. Let M_1, M_2, and M_3 denote one-address, two-address and three-address processors, respectively. Figure 3.15 shows typical assembly-language programs that implement the arithmetic statement above. Besides the obvious tradeoffs between instruction length and program size, certain other performance factors should be considered when comparing these machines. In particular, instruction execution time may be very dependent on the location of the operands. Operands stored in processor registers can generally be obtained much faster than those stored in the external main memory. But without further details on the way in which the three machines are implemented, we cannot really compare the execution time of the three programs appearing in Fig. 3.15.

Some computers have been designed so that most instructions contain no

Instruction	Comments
LOAD A	Transfer A to accumulator AC
MULTIPLY B	AC $\leftarrow$ AC $\times B$
STORE T	Transfer AC to memory location T
LOAD C	Transfer C to accumulator AC
MULTIPLY C	AC $\leftarrow$ AC $\times C$
ADD T	AC $\leftarrow$ AC $+ T$
STORE X	Transfer result to memory location X

(a) One-address machine M_1

Instruction	Comments
MOVE T, A	$T \leftarrow A$
MULTIPLY T, B	$T \leftarrow T \times B$
MOVE X, C	$X \leftarrow C$
MULTIPLY X, C	$X \leftarrow X \times C$
ADD X, T	$X \leftarrow X + T$

(b) Two-address machine M_2

Instruction	Comments
MULTIPLY T, A, B	$T \leftarrow A \times B$
MULTIPLY X, C, C	$X \leftarrow C \times C$
ADD X, X, T	$X \leftarrow X + T$

(c) Three-address machine M_3

FIGURE 3.15
Programs to execute the statement $X = A \times B + C \times C$ in one-address, two-address, and three-address processors.

explicit addresses; they are therefore sometimes termed *zero-address* machines. Addresses are eliminated by storing operands in a push-down stack. All operands used by a zero-address instruction are required to be in the top positions in the stack. For example, addition is invoked by an instruction such as

ADD

which causes the top two operands X and Y to be removed from the stack and added. The resulting sum $X + Y$ is placed at the top of the stack. A stack pointer is used to indicate the current position of the top of the stack. In order to transfer data to and from the stack, push and pop instructions are needed. PUSH X causes the contents of X to be placed at the top of the stack. POP X causes the topmost word in the stack to be transferred to location X. Note that PUSH and POP are not themselves zero-address instructions; as implemented by (3.13) and (3.14), they are two-address instructions. Figure 3.16 shows how a program to evaluate the arithmetic statement $X = A \times B + C \times C$ considered earlier might be written for a zero-address machine.

The order in which an arithmetic expression is evaluated in a stack machine corresponds to the order in the *Polish notation* for the expression, so-called after the Polish logician Jan Łukasiewicz (1878–1956), who first introduced it. The basic idea is to write a binary operation $X*Y$ either in the form $*XY$ (prefix notation) or $XY*$ (suffix or reverse Polish notation). The suffix Polish notation for the expression $A \times B + C \times C$ is thus $AB \times CC \times +$. Comparing this expression to the program of Fig. 3.16, we can see that every appearance of a variable X corresponds to PUSH X in the program, while every operator appears in the same position as the corresponding instruction in the program. Compilers for stack machines therefore convert ordinary infix arithmetic expressions into Polish form for execution in a stack. An important advantage of Polish notation is that no parentheses are needed. Thus while parentheses are essential in the infix expression $X(Y + Z)$, they are not required in the corresponding (suffix) Polish expression $XYZ + \times$.

Instruction	Comments
PUSH A	Transfer A to top of stack
PUSH B	Transfer B to top of stack
MULTIPLY	Remove A, B from stack and replace by $A \times B$
PUSH C	Transfer C to top of stack
PUSH C	Transfer second copy of C to top of stack
MULTIPLY	Remove C, C from stack and replace by $C \times C$
ADD	Remove $C \times C$, $A \times B$ from stack and replace by their sum
POP X	Transfer result from top of stack to X

FIGURE 3.16
Program to execute the statement $X = A \times B + C \times C$ in a stack-based zero-address processor.

Opcodes. In most computers, the opcode is a fixed-length field of k bits within each instruction permitting up to 2^k distinct operations to be specified. Typical values of k are 8 and 16 bits. Since the corresponding number of bit patterns (65,536 in the case of $k = 16$) is more than enough to specify all the distinct operation types performed by an instruction set, some addressing information may also be included in the opcode field, for example, the addresses of processor registers used to store operands. The number of such registers is small; hence they can be addressed using only a few bits. Figure 3.17 shows the instruction formats of the Intel 8085 microprocessor, whose internal organization appears in Fig. 1.38 [17]. An 8085 instruction can be 1, 2, or 3 bytes in length. In all cases the first byte is referred to as the opcode byte. The second and third bytes form a single 1-byte or 2-byte address field; hence the 8085 is considered to be a one-address machine. The contents of the address field can be a constant or an address; thus the 8085 supports the immediate and direct memory-addressing modes. One or two register addresses can be included in the opcode byte, since 3 bits suffice to address any of the 8-bit registers A, B, C, D, E, H, and L. In this way, direct register addressing (the required data is in a register) or indirect memory addressing (the register con-

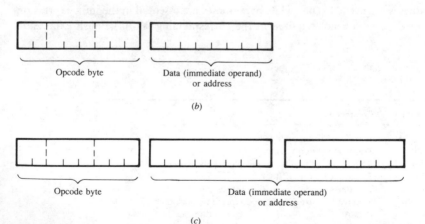

FIGURE 3.17
Instruction formats of the Intel 8085 microprocessor. (The fields marked with an asterisk are used only in some instructions.)

tains the address of the required data in main memory) is supported. An example of a 1-byte instruction is the register-to-register operation ADD r, meaning A ← A + r, where r is any 8-bit register. The add immediate instruction ADI d, meaning A ← A + d, where d is an 8-bit word, is 2 bytes long, while JMP *adr* meaning PC ← *adr* is a 3-byte branch instruction.

Since programs occupy a considerable amount of valuable storage space, it is desirable to reduce their length as much as possible. One way of doing so is to assign the shortest formats to the most frequently used instructions and the longest formats to the least frequently used. This is a common technique for encoding information. For example, in the Morse code, the shortest code, a single dot ·, is assigned to the most common letter in English (e), while the longest codes (up to four dots and dashes) are assigned to the least frequently occurring letters. The frequency with which operand addresses occur cannot be reasonably determined; all may be assumed to have equal probability. The frequency with which specific instruction types (determined by their opcodes) occur can be determined, however; it is the basis for instruction mixes such as the Gibson mix (see Fig. 2.71). One can therefore attempt to base opcode lengths on their probability of occurrence. This is done explicitly in such machines as the Burroughs B1700 and the Intel 432, which employ several different opcode lengths [20].

The foregoing idea is also used implicitly in many processors to allow register addresses to be placed in a fixed-length "opcode" field. For instance, the frequently used move register-to-register instruction of the Intel 8085 microprocessor, an example of which appears in (3.10), has the machine language format shown in Fig. 3.17a, where the required move operation is specified by the 2-bit pattern (01 in this case) in the leftmost two bit positions. This enables two 3-bit register addresses to be squeezed into the opcode byte. (Note that since an 8085 instruction can contain at most one memory address, the 8085 is regarded as a one-address machine.) This 1-byte instruction format can accommodate zero, one, or two register addresses, so that the effective opcode length ranges from 2 to 8 bits. In general, fixed-length opcodes (possibly including register addresses) are easier to decode and store than variable-length ones, and so are preferred. However, significant storage savings can result from the use of multiple opcode lengths.

Consider, for example, the hypothetical set of five instructions shown with their probabilities of occurrence in Fig. 3.18. If fixed-length opcodes are used, 3 bits are needed for every opcode. With the variable-length opcodes shown, the average number of opcode bits per instruction is

$$\sum_{i=1}^{5} p_i |c_i| = 1.82 \tag{3.15}$$

which implies a reduction of 39 percent in the memory space needed to store opcodes. If variable-length opcodes are used, they must be carefully chosen so that each opcode can be uniquely decoded. The opcodes in Fig. 3.18 can be decoded by scanning any given instruction from left to right, since no opcode is a prefix of any other opcode. Thus an instruction beginning 0100 · · · must be of type I_2. It would

Instruction	Probability of occurrence p_i	Opcode c_i
I_1	0.5	1
I_2	0.3	01
I_3	0.08	000
I_4	0.06	0011
I_5	0.06	0010

FIGURE 3.18
Variable-length opcodes based on instruction occurrence probabilities.

be impossible to uniquely identify this instruction if 0 were a valid opcode, since 0 is a prefix of 01.

A systematic method of constructing codes to minimize the average opcode length defined by (3.15) is due to David A. Huffman [12]. It involves two major steps.

Step 1. First, the probabilities associated with the instructions are formed into an ordered list $L_1 = p_{1,1}, p_{1,2}, \ldots, p_{1,n}$, where $p_{1,j} \geq p_{1,j+1}$. Then the two smallest members $p_{1,n-1}$ and $p_{1,n}$ of L_1 are replaced by their sum $p_{1,n-1} + p_{1,n}$. The resulting list of probabilities is reordered and called L_2. Next its two smallest members $p_{2,n-2}$ and $p_{2,n-1}$ are replaced by their sum in a new ordered list L_3, and so on. The process halts with the two-member list $L_{n-1} = p_{n-1,1}$, $p_{n-1,2}$, where $p_{n-1,1} \geq p_{n-1,2}$.

Step 2. The codes 1 and 0 (or vice versa) are assigned to $p_{n-1,1}$ and $p_{n-1,2}$ in L_{n-1}. If $p_{n-1,k}$ with code c_1 (0 or 1) was obtained by adding $p_{n-2,2}$ and $p_{n-2,3}$, then the 2-bit codes $c_1 1$ and $c_1 0$ are assigned to $p_{n-2,2}$ and $p_{n-2,3}$, respectively, in L_{n-2}. The remaining member $p_{n-2,1}$ of L_{n-2} is assigned the code, in this

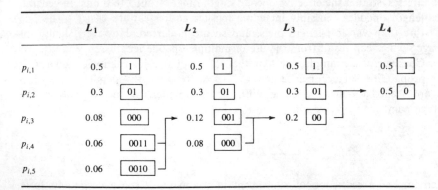

FIGURE 3.19
Construction of the optimal coding scheme of Fig. 3.18 by Huffman's method. (Codewords are enclosed in boxes.)

case c_1, of the corresponding member $p_{n-1,1}$ of L_{n-1}. Moving to L_{n-3}, again the last two members $p_{n-2,3}$ and $p_{n-2,4}$ are assigned $c_2 1$ and $c_2 0$, where c_2 is the code of the member of L_{n-2} formed by adding them. Each remaining member $p_{n-3,k}$ of L_{n-3} is assigned the code of the member of L_{n-2} from which it was derived, and which therefore has the same numerical value. The process terminates when each member p_k of the first list L_1 has been assigned a code; this is the opcode of the corresponding instruction I_k.

It is obvious that the opcodes formed by the foregoing algorithm are uniquely decodable; it is left as an exercise to prove that they minimize the average opcode length. Figure 3.19 shows its application to the example of Fig. 3.18, demonstrating that the code given there is optimal.

Many computers such as the Intel 8085 use instructions of several different lengths. The length of an instruction is determined by both the number and the types of operands it contains. It is generally desirable to restrict instruction lengths to multiples or submultiples of w, where w is the main-memory word size, i.e., the number of bits accessed in one memory cycle. This allows some saving in address bits by requiring instructions to begin at predetermined (sub) word boundaries in the memory address space. It also permits efficient transfer and processing of the instructions, since all buses and registers involved can be tailored to a particular word size. In the IBM S/360-370 series, for example, instructions may have length $w/2$, w, or $3w/2$, where $w = 32$ bits is the standard word size. (The actual number of bits accessed during a memory cycle depends on the S/360-370 model.) Several adjacent short instructions may be fetched simultaneously, which has the advantage of reducing the average instruction time. More than one memory cycle may be required to fetch long instructions.

3.2.2 Instruction Types

We now turn to the question: What types of instructions should be included in a general-purpose processor's instruction set? We are concerned here with the instructions that are in the processor's machine language. Almost all processors have a well-defined machine language, and some implement a lower-level "micromachine" language specified by microinstructions. A typical machine instruction defines one or two register transfer (micro) operations, and a sequence of such instructions is needed to implement a statement in a high-level programming language such as FORTRAN or Pascal. Because of the complexity of the operations, data types, and syntax of high-level languages, few successful attempts have been made to construct computers whose machine language directly corresponds to a high-level language [7]. There is thus a *semantic gap* between the high-level problem specification and the machine instruction set that implements it, a gap that a compiler must bridge.

The requirements to be satisfied by an instruction set can be stated in the following general, but rather imprecise, terms.

1. It should be *complete* in the sense that one should be able to construct a machine-language program to evaluate any function that is computable using a reasonable amount of memory space.
2. The instruction set should be *efficient* in that frequently required functions can be performed rapidly using relatively few instructions.
3. It should be *regular* in that the instruction set should contain expected opcodes and addressing modes, e.g., if there is a left shift, there should be a right shift. The instruction set should also be reasonably orthogonal with respect to the addressing modes.
4. To reduce both hardware and software design costs, the instructions may be required to be *compatible* with those of existing machines, e.g., previous members of the same computer family.

Because of the wide variation in CPU architectures between different computer families, there are no standard machine or assembly languages, although the need for standards in this area has been recognized [3]. There are, nevertheless, broad similarities between all instruction sets, which can be traced back to the IAS computer (Fig. 1.16) and other early machines.

Completeness. A function $f(x)$ is defined to be computable if it can be evaluated in a finite number of steps by a Turing machine (see Sec. 1.1.1). While real computers differ from Turing machines in having only a finite amount of memory, they can, in practice, be used to evaluate any computable function, at least to a reasonable degree of approximation. When viewed as instruction set processors, Turing machines use a very simple instruction set. In our discussion of Turing machines, four basic instruction types were defined (write, move tape one square to the left, move tape one square to the right, and halt). It follows that complete instruction sets can be constructed for finite-state machines using equally simple instruction types. Willem L. Van der Poel has designed a simple one-address computer that has only one instruction [28]; see Prob. 3.19. While simple instruction sets require simple, and therefore inexpensive, logic circuits to implement them, they can lead to excessively complex programs. There is therefore a fundamental tradeoff between processor simplicity and programming complexity.

Instructions are conveniently divided into the following five major types.

1. *Data-transfer* instructions, which cause information to be copied from one location to another either in the processor's internal memory or in the external main memory
2. *Arithmetic* instructions, which perform operations on numerical data
3. *Logical* instructions, which include Boolean and other nonnumerical operations
4. *Program control* instructions, such as branch instructions, which change the sequence in which programs are executed
5. *Input-output* (IO) instructions, which cause information to be transferred between the processor or its main memory and external IO devices

These types are not always mutually exclusive. For example, the arithmetic operation $A \leftarrow B + C$ can be used to implement the simple data transfer $A \leftarrow B$ by setting $C = 0$.

Figure 3.20 shows a representative set of instructions from the five basic types defined above, which have been culled from the instruction sets of a large number of different computers. The data-transfer instructions, particularly load and store, are the most frequently used instructions in computer programs, despite the fact that they involve no explicit computation. The arithmetic instructions cover a wide range of complexity as indicated by Fig. 3.21; consequently they are sometimes used as a rough measure of the complexity of an instruction set. The logical instructions usually include the basic word-based Boolean operations, as well as several types of shift operations. The major branch instructions are jump (un)conditionally, and the call and return instructions used for subroutine linkage. The simplest IO instructions are data-transfer instructions addressed to IO ports, which transfer one or more words between an IO port and either the CPU or main memory. If, as in the case of computers like the S/360-370, the CPU delegates control of IO operations to an IOP, the CPU instruction set contains instructions that enable it to supervise the execution of IO programs by an IOP. Instructions that are specific to particular IO devices like REWIND TAPE, PRINT LINE, and SCAN KEYBOARD, are treated as data by the CPU and IOP, and are only interpreted as instructions by the IO devices to which they are transferred.

The completeness of an instruction set can be demonstrated informally by showing that certain basic operations in each of these five groups can be programmed. It must be possible to transfer a word between the processor and any main-memory location. It must be possible to add two numbers, so an addition instruction is therefore included in most instruction sets. Other arithmetic operations can readily be programmed using addition. As pointed out in Sec. 3.1.3, subtraction of twos-complement numbers requires addition and logical complementation (NOT) only. More complex arithmetic operations such as multiplication, division, exponentiation, etc., can be programmed using addition, subtraction, and shifting, as in Example 2.3. If any complete set of Boolean operations such as AND and NOT are in the instruction set, then any other Boolean operation, e.g., EXCLUSIVE-OR, can be programmed. To implement branching, at least one conditional branch instruction is required which tests some stored quantity and alters the instruction execution sequence based on the test outcome. An unconditional branch can easily be realized using a conditional branch instruction.

RISC versus CISC. While an instruction set that is limited to two or three instructions is clearly impractical, there is no general agreement about what constitutes the appropriate size or membership of a general-purpose instruction set. Early computers like the IAS machine had small and simple instruction sets, forced by the need to minimize the amount of hardware used to implement them. These instruction sets included only the most frequently used operations such as load a register from memory, store a result in memory, add two fixed-point numbers. As hardware became cheaper, instructions tended to increase both in number and

Type	Operation name(s)	Description
Data transfer	MOVE (TRANSFER)	Transfer word or block from source to destination
	STORE	Transfer word from processor to external memory
	LOAD (FETCH)	Transfer word from external memory to processor
	EXCHANGE	Swap contents of source and destination
	CLEAR (RESET)	Transfer word of 0s to destination
	SET	Transfer word of 1s to destination
	PUSH	Transfer word from source to top of stack
	POP (PULL)	Transfer word from top of stack to destination
Arithmetic	ADD	Compute sum of two operands
	SUBTRACT	Compute difference of two operands
	MULTIPLY	Compute product of two operands
	DIVIDE	Compute quotient (and remainder) of two operands
	ABSOLUTE	Replace operand by its absolute value
	NEGATE	Change sign of operand
	INCREMENT	Add 1 to operand
	DECREMENT	Subtract 1 from operand
Logical	AND	
	OR	
	NOT (COMPLEMENT)	Perform the specified logical operation bitwise
	EXCLUSIVE-OR	
	EQUIVALENCE	
	SHIFT	Left- (right-) shift operand introducing constants at end
	ROTATE	Left- (right-) shift operand around closed path
	CONVERT (EDIT)	Change data format, e.g., from binary to decimal
Program control	JUMP (BRANCH)	Unconditional transfer; load PC with specified address
	JUMP CONDITIONAL	Test specified condition; depending on condition, either load PC with specified address or else do nothing
	JUMP TO SUBROUTINE (BRANCH-AND-LINK)	Place current program control information (PC, status register, etc.) in known location, e.g., in top of stack; jump to specified address
	RETURN	Replace contents of PC, status register, etc., with information from known location, e.g., from top of stack
	EXECUTE	Fetch operand from specified location and execute as instruction; note that PC is not modified
	SKIP	Increment PC to skip the next instruction
	SKIP CONDITIONAL	Test specified condition; depending on outcome, either increment PC or else do nothing
	TEST	Test specified condition; set flag(s) based on outcome
	COMPARE	Make logical or arithmetic comparison of two or more operands; set flag(s) based on outcome

FIGURE 3.20
List of common instruction types.

Type	Operation name(s)	Description
	SET CONTROL VARIABLES	Large class of instructions to set controls for protection purposes, interrupt handling, timer control, etc. (often privileged instructions)
	HALT	Stop program execution
	WAIT (HOLD)	Stop program execution; test a specified condition continuously; when the condition is satisfied, resume execution
	NO OPERATION	No operation is performed, but program execution continues
Input-output	INPUT (READ)	Transfer data from specified IO port to destination, e.g., main memory or processor register
	OUTPUT (WRITE)	Transfer data from specified source to IO port
	START IO	Transfer instructions to IOP to initiate IO operation
	TEST IO	Transfer status information from IO system to specified destination
	HALT IO	Transfer instructions to IOP to terminate IO operation

complexity, so that by 1960 a typical computer had a hundred or more types of instructions, with many instructions allowing a variety of different data types and addressing modes. These larger instruction sets contain infrequently used but hard-to-program operations like floating-point divide. Since such operations are primitives in high-level programming languages, they serve to reduce the semantic gap between the user and the machine languages. However, complex instructions lead to a number of complications in both hardware and software design, which we now examine.

Fixed-point +, −	Fixed-point ×, ÷	Floating-point (+, −, ×, ÷)	Vector arithmetic (floating-point +, −, ×, ÷)	Representative machine
✔				Intel 8085
✔	✔			Motorola 68020
✔	✔	✔		IBM System/360
✔	✔	✔	✔	Cray-1

FIGURE 3.21
Arithmetic operations included in the instruction sets of some representative computers.

Suppose that a particular operation F can be implemented either by a single complex instruction I_F, or by a multiinstruction routine P_F composed of simple instructions. Execution of P_F will generally be slower than that of I_F, due to the fact that more time must be spent fetching the instructions of P_F and, depending on the nature of F, handling the intermediate data that links these instructions. A further drawback of P_F is that it occupies more memory space than I_F. The obvious disadvantage of I_F is that it adds to the complexity of a processor's control unit, thereby increasing both the size of the processor and the time required to design it.

Clearly the writing of an assembly-language program involving F will be simplified by using I_F in place of P_F. When the program is written in a high-level language, however, as the vast majority of programs are, the improvements in execution speed discussed above that justify a complex instruction like I_F may not be fully realizable. A compiler will typically translate F into the corresponding machine instruction I_F, if available, which uses fixed CPU registers and has a fixed execution time. On the other hand, if I_F is not available, an efficient "optimizing" compiler may be able to generate object code Q_F corresponding to P_F that exploits information known at compilation time to reduce the execution time for F. The compiler can, for instance, vary the registers allocated to CPU to suit the particular occurrence of F, and introduce algorithm shortcuts that take advantage of specific operand values. Suppose that F is fixed-point multiplication and is implemented by both I_F and Q_F via a shift-and-add algorithm of the kind described in Example 2.3. (see Fig. 2.37). If one of the operands of F is a small constant or zero, then the compiler can easily generate a shorter form of P_F which can execute faster than the generic n-step multiply instruction I_F. The speed gap between I_F and P_F can also be narrowed by designing the small instruction set required for P_F to reduce the instruction fetch and execute cycle times as far as possible, e.g., to one CPU clock cycle each. Another speed advantage of P_F over I_F is that it can be interrupted in midoperation at an appropriate instruction boundary, whereas I_F must proceed to termination before the CPU can respond to an interrupt.

Motivated by considerations of the foregoing sort, a number of computer designers have advocated machines with small and relatively simple instruction sets, which have been dubbed *RISC* (*reduced instruction set computer*) machines. RISC architecture is contrasted with the *CISC* (*complex instruction set computer*) architecture found in most modern computers such as the S/360-370 and the Motorola 68020. The ideas underlying RISCs were first developed at IBM in the mid-1970s and implemented in an experimental minicomputer called the 801 [23]. The major attributes of RISCs have been more recently defined as follows [8].

1. Relatively few instruction types and addressing modes
2. Fixed and easily decoded instruction formats
3. Fast single-cycle instruction execution
4. Hardwired rather than microprogrammed control

5. Memory access limited mainly to load and store instructions

6. Use of compilers to optimize object code performance

Several of these RISC attributes are closely related. For example, the small size and regularity of the instruction set simplifies the design of a hardwired program control unit, which in turn facilitates the achievement of fast single-cycle execution. The stress placed on efficient compilation requires the machine architects and compiler writers to cooperate closely in the design process.

RISC architectures restrict the number of instructions that access main memory; in the most extreme case, they provide only the load instruction A ← M(adr) and the store instruction M(adr) ← A. Consequently, most RISC instructions involve only register-to-register operations that are internal to the CPU. To support them, a larger-than-usual number of registers may be placed in the CPU. This facilitates single-cycle execution, and allows the CPU cycle time and hardware complexity to be minimized. Since complex instructions are not in the instruction set and cannot be microcoded, they must be implemented by routines at the instruction level, which prompts the attention to efficient compilation. Machine code compiled for a RISC computer is likely to have more instructions than the corresponding CISC code, but as noted above, may execute more efficiently, especially if only fixed-point (integer) instructions are required. However, if the frequency of complex operations is high, then the performance of the CISC machine is likely to be better. In particular, CICSs outperform RISCs in scientific computing applications requiring lots of floating-point arithmetic.

Example 3.2   Architecture of the RISC I microprocessor [21]. We now outline the architecture of a microprocessor called the RISC I, which was designed by David A. Patterson and his colleagues at the University of California, Berkeley. This prototype RISC machine is a single-chip 32-bit CPU, containing a large set (138) of 32-bit general-purpose programmable registers which can be allocated to (sub)programs in overlapping groups of 32 registers denoted R0:R31. In addition to being reduced, the instruction set of RISC I was designed with the following objectives [21]: to achieve single-cycle execution with instructions of fixed size; to access main memory with load and store only; and to provide some support for high-level languages. The RISC I cycle time is the time required to read two CPU registers, add their contents, and store the result in a third register. Because it takes longer to access memory, two cycles are actually allowed for the load and store instructions.

All instructions in RISC I are 32 bits long and have the general format shown in Fig. 3.22. A complete list of the 31 instruction types of RISC I appears in Fig. 3.23. Most instructions are register-to-register types of the form

$$Rd \leftarrow F(Rs,S2) \tag{3.16}$$

where Rd is the destination register, Rs is the first source register, and the rightmost 5 bits of S2 define a second source register. If bit 18 of the instruction is set to 1, then S2 is interpreted as a 13-bit constant or immediate address. In this case, S2 is automatically expanded to 32 bits by sign extension before (3.16) is executed, that is, bit

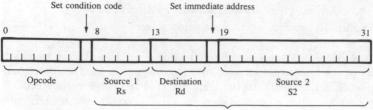

FIGURE 3.22
Instruction format of the RISC I.

19 of the instruction, which is the sign position of S2, is replicated to fill the remaining 19 bits of the 32-bit word. This allows the instructions to perform signed binary (twos-complement) arithmetic directly on numerical data with fewer than 32 bits. Memory is addressed by using Rs as an index (or base) register and S2 as a 13-bit offset, providing an indexed addressing mode with the effective address M(Rs + S2). Register R0 permanently stores the constant zero; hence setting Rs = R0 makes the effective address M(S2), which corresponds to direct or absolute memory addressing. Setting S2 to zero yields indirect memory addressing with Rs as the address register. Certain program-control instructions employ relative addressing, but stack addressing is not supported. There are also no explicit IO instructions; hence memory-mapped IO must be used.

Main memory can be accessed only by load and store instructions. These come in nine types, as described in Fig. 3.23, which depend on the operand length (1, 2, or 4 bytes), and whether or not sign extension is used when loading shorter operands. There are six arithmetic instructions, all variants of binary add and subtract. The add/subtract-with-carry instructions facilitate the extension of these operations to multiple-word operands. For example, the 64-bit addition $C \leftarrow A + B$ can be performed by first applying the ADD instruction to the right (less significant) halves of A and B, then applying ADDC to the left halves of these operands. Provided bit 7 of the ADD instruction is 1, its execution sets a condition code flag C in the program status register PSW. C is designed to store the carry-out signal resulting from all the add instructions. Since C is included as an input operand in the addition performed by ADDC, it produces the correct second half of the 64-bit result Z. When performing subtraction, C serves to store the borrow signals associated with multiple-precision subtractions.

The six logical instructions include AND, OR, and EXCLUSIVE-OR. The NOT operation can be obtained by executing XOR with S2 set to the all-1 bit pattern. The shift operations transfer data from Rs to Rd with a left or right shift by the number of bits specified by S2. The logical shift instructions use 0s to fill the data positions vacated by the shift operation. In the case of the arithmetic right-shift instruction SRA, the vacated positions are filled by sign extension. This makes an S2-bit right-shift equivalent to dividing a signed number by 2^{S2}.

The remaining RISC I instructions are intended for program control, and include (un)conditional jumps, subroutine calls and returns, and miscellaneous control instructions. These instructions involve some unusual design features which, however, are not directly related to RISC/CISC issues. We will confine our discussion to the

Type	Opcode	Operands	Description
Data transfer	STL	Rs, (Rd)S2	M(Rd + S2) ← Rs; store long (32-bit) word
	STS	Rs, (Rd)S2	M(Rd + S2) ← Rs(16:31); store short word
	STB	Rs, (Rd)S2	M(Rd + S2) ← Rs(24:31); store byte
	LDL	(Rs)S2, Rd	Rd ← M(Rs + S2); load long word
	LDSU	(Rs)S2, Rd	Rd(16:31) ← M(Rs + S2), Rd(0:15) ← 0; load short (16-bit) unsigned word
	LDSS	(Rs)S2, Rd	Rd(16:31) ← M(Rs + S2); Rd(0:15) ← Rd(16); load short (16-bit) word with sign extension
	LDBU	(Rs)S2, Rd	Rd(24:31) ← M(Rs + S2), Rd(0:23) ← 0; load unsigned byte
	LDBS	(Rs)S2, Rd	Rd(24:31) ← M(Rs + S2); Rd(0:23) ← Rd(24); load short (16-bit) word with sign extension
	LDHI	Rd, Y	Rd(0:18) ← Y, Rd(19:31) ← 0; load immediate high
Arithmetic	ADD	Rs,S2, Rd	Rd ← Rs + S2; fixed-point binary add
	ADDC	Rs,S2, Rd	Rd ← Rs + S2 + C; add with carry flag C
	SUB	Rs,S2, Rd	Rd ← Rs − S2; fixed-point binary subtract
	SUBC	Rs,S2, Rd	Rd ← Rs − S2 − C; subtract with carry flag C
	SUBR	Rs,S2, Rd	Rd ← S2 − Rs; fixed-point binary subtract
	SUBCR	Rs,S2, Rd	Rd ← S2 − Rs − C; subtract with carry flag C
Logical	AND	Rs,S2, Rd	Rd ← AND(Rs,S2)
	OR	Rs,S2, Rd	Rd ← OR(Rs,S2)
	XOR	Rs,S2, Rd	Rd ← EXCLUSIVE-OR(Rs,S2)
	SLL	Rs,S2, Rd	Rd ← Rs(S2:31).0; S2-bit logical left shift
	SRL	Rs,S2, Rd	Rd ← 0.Rs(0:31-S2); S2-bit logical right shift
	SRA	Rs,S2, Rd	Rd ← Rs(0).Rs(0). · · · .Rs(0).Rs(0:31-S2); S2-bit arithmetic right shift with sign extension
Program control	JMP	Cond, S2(Rs)	**if** Cond = 1 **then** PC ← Rs + S2; conditional jump
	JMPR	Cond, Y	**if** Cond = 1 **then** PC ← PC + Y; conditional jump with relative addressing
	CALL	Rd, S2(Rs)	Rd ← PC; PC ← Rs + S2, CWP ← CWP − 1; call and change register window
	CALLR	Rd, Y	Rd ← PC; PC ← PC + Y, CWP ← CWP − 1; call relative and change register window
	RET	Rs, S2	PC ← Rs + S2; CWP ← CWP + 1; return and change register window
	CALLINT	Rd	Rd ← PC; CWP ← CWP − 1; disable interrupts
	RETINT	Rs, S2	PC ← Rs + S2; CWP ← CWP + 1; enable interrupts
	GETLPC	Rd	Rd ← PC; restart delayed jump
	GETPSW	Rd	Rd ← PSW; load program status word
	PUTPSW	Rs	PSW ← Rs; set program status word

FIGURE 3.23
Instruction set of the RISC I.

most interesting feature of RISC I, namely, hardware support for parameter passing in high-level language programs. (See Ref. 21 for further details on the RISC I program-control instructions.) Because the passing of parameters during subroutine (procedure) calls and returns is a frequently occurring and slow operation, RISC I allows this operation to be done rapidly using its CPU registers. (Most computers employ a memory stack for this purpose.) Each subroutine is assigned from the 138 available CPU registers, a (virtual) set of 32 registers R0:R31 for storing its input and output parameters; this set is called a *register window*. When subroutine A calls subroutine B, the register window assigned to B is overlapped with that of A so that the output parameter part of A's window and the input parameter part of B's window are assigned to the same physical registers. Thus in most cases B has immediate access to the parameters it needs from the calling program. The call and return instructions manipulate the register windows automatically by incrementing and decrementing a special pointer register CWP. While register windows speed up the execution of programs that generate very large numbers of procedure calls, their impact on the performance of other programs is unclear.

Implementation. The design of circuits to implement an instruction set is primarily an exercise in register-level logic design. First it is necessary to devise an algorithm in terms of appropriate register transfers or other microoperations for each instruction. The particular component technology used to implement the processor determines the microoperations that can be used. The algorithms should be designed to provide an acceptable compromise between circuit cost and instruction execution speed. It is also common to choose algorithms that permit circuits used by different instructions to be shared.

Of the five major instruction types defined earlier (data transfer, arithmetic, logical, program control, and input-output), all but arithmetic and input-output are relatively easy to implement. Data-transfer instructions require the creation of a data path, such as a shared bus, from the source to the destination. A Boolean operation can be implemented by connecting the input operands to an appropriate word gate. Consider the implementation of the four logical operations AND, OR, EXCLUSIVE-OR, and NOT using n-bit operands. The inputs are stored in registers X and Y and the output is to be placed in register Z. The particular operation to be performed is specified by two control signals c_1 and c_2. It is easily seen that the logic circuit required to implement the four instructions is defined by the Boolean equation

$$Z = \bar{c}_1\bar{c}_2XY + \bar{c}_1c_2(X + Y) + c_1\bar{c}_2(X \oplus Y) + c_1c_2\bar{X}$$

where $c_1c_2 = 00$ specifies AND, $c_1c_2 = 01$ specifies OR, etc. This equation may be rewritten in the following sum-of-products form:

$$Z = \bar{c}_1\bar{c}_2XY + \bar{c}_1c_2X + \bar{c}_1c_2Y + c_1\bar{c}_2\bar{X}Y + c_1\bar{c}_2X\bar{Y} + c_1c_2\bar{X}$$

and implemented using the two-level NAND circuit of Fig. 3.24. Other common nonnumerical instructions such as shift and rotate are equally easy to implement. Branch instructions also present no serious difficulties. Figure 3.25 shows a possible implementation of two conditional branch instructions: SZA (*skip on zero*

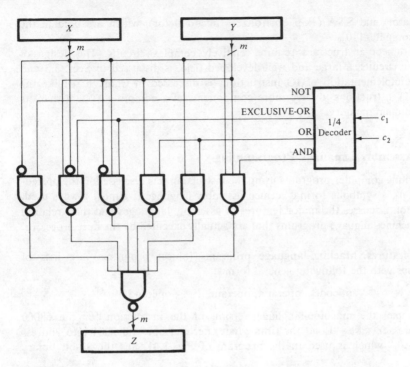

FIGURE 3.24
Implementation of four logical instructions: AND, OR, EXCLUSIVE-OR, and NOT.

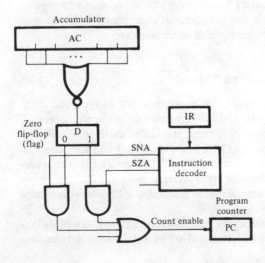

FIGURE 3.25
Implementation of two conditional branch instructions SZA (skip on zero accumulator) and SNA (skip on nonzero accumulator).

*a*ccumulator) and SNA (*s*kip on *n*onzero *a*ccumulator), which are used in the PDP-8 computer [10].

Arithmetic instructions require relatively complex circuits. The design of arithmetic circuits, a large and well-developed field, is discussed in Secs. 3.3 and 3.4. The implementation of IO instructions is discussed in Chap. 6. Unlike the others, IO instructions involve more components of a computer system than its CPU and main memory.

3.2.3 Assembly-Language Programming

When writing computer programs using the instruction sets discussed in the preceding sections, a symbolic format termed assembly language is almost always used. This section discusses the major features of assembly languages and their relation to the machine-language programs that are actually executed by the host processor.

General features. Machine-language programs (object programs) are lists of instructions with the following general form

$$\text{opcode} \quad \text{operand, operand, ... , operand}$$

For example, the machine-language version of the instruction for the 68000 microprocessor series "Load the (immediate) decimal operand 2001 into address register A0," which is used in the program of Fig. 1.41, has the 32-bit binary format

$$0010000001111000 \ 0000011111010001 \tag{3.17}$$

It may also be written more compactly in hexadecimal code thus:

$$2078 \ 07D1 \tag{3.18}$$

Here 2078 is the opcode word indicating "move long (32-bit) operand to register A0," while the operand field 07D1 is the hexadecimal equivalent of the decimal number 2001. Assembly-language versions of this instruction are

$$\text{MOVE.L} \quad \#2001, \text{A0} \tag{3.19}$$

and
$$\text{MOVE.L} \quad \#\$07D1, \text{A0} \tag{3.20}$$

where the opcode and one of the operands, A0, are represented in symbolic form. The prefix # denotes an immediate operand in the Motorola convention, while $ indicates that base 16 rather than base 10 is being used. Before they can be executed, assembly-language instructions like (3.19) and (3.20) must be translated into the equivalent machine-language form represented by (3.17) and (3.18). The translation or *assembly* process is carried out by a system program known as an *assembler*, which is analogous to a compiler that translates a high-level language program into machine code.

In addition to using symbolic names for opcodes and registers, assembly languages also allow symbolic names to be assigned to user-defined constants and variables, such as the immediate operand appearing in (3.19) and (3.20). For example, most assembly languages use the statement

$$A \quad EQU \quad 2001 \qquad (3.21)$$

to indicate that the symbol "A" is to be equivalent (EQU) to the (decimal) number 2001. If statement (3.21) is present in a program for the 68000/68020, then (3.19) and (3.20) can be replaced by

$$MOVE.L \quad A, A0$$

which is assembled into exactly the same machine code as before. Note that this last instruction also corresponds to the register-transfer operation denoted symbolically by A0 ← A. Statement (3.21) is considered to be an assembly-language instruction but, unlike the MOVE instructions, it is not translated into an executable instruction in machine language. Rather it is an instruction to the assembler telling it how to treat the symbol A during the program translation process. This type of nonexecutable assembly-language instruction is called a *directive* or *pseudoinstruction*.

The memory location to be assigned to an instruction can be indicated symbolically by means of a label at the beginning of an assembly-language statement. For example, the label L1 in

$$L1 \quad MOVE.L \quad A, A0 \quad ;\text{Load initial value into A0} \qquad (3.22)$$

is assigned to a physical memory address by the assembler, normally to the memory address immediately after the last address assigned to the preceding instruction. Labels are generally used in an assembly-language instruction only when another instruction needs to refer to the first one. For example, the 68000 instruction

$$JMP \quad L1 \quad ;\text{Branch unconditionally to instruction}$$
$$;\text{labeled L1} \qquad (3.23)$$

causes a branch to instruction (3.22) which has the label L1; this is the assembly-language equivalent of the high-level language statement **go to** L1. As discussed further below, certain assemblers (*macroassemblers*) also allow the programmer to assign a symbolic name to a sequence of instructions, permitting those instructions to be treated as a single instruction-like entity termed a *macroinstruction*, or simply a *macro*. Finally, assembly languages allow the programmer to introduce comments, which have no effect on the assembly process but are useful for documenting a program to improve its readability. As illustrated by (3.22) and (3.23), 68000 assembly language uses a semicolon as a prefix to mark comments.

Thus we conclude that assembly-language instructions have the following general format:

$$label \quad opcode \quad operand, operand, \ldots, operand \quad comments$$

where the opcode can either be an executable command corresponding to a machine-language opcode, a directive, or a macroinstruction. Like machine languages, assembly languages vary from computer to computer, and are usually defined (not always consistently) by a computer's primary manufacturer.

The input to the assembly process is a source program written in assembly language. The output is an object program in machine language, and an *assembly listing* which shows both the assembly-language and machine-language versions of the program, and the correspondence between them. The object code may be combined with other machine-language programs to produce a final composite executable program. The combining of different programs in this fashion is done by another system program called a *linker* or *link editor*. The use of symbolic names for shared data and labels plays an important role in allowing different assembly-language programs, perhaps the work of different programmers, to be merged by the linker. In particular, the linker can assign the same physical address to a shared parameter referred to symbolically in several different programs. Note that this ability to combine different programs into a single executable entity is the origin of the term "assembly" language.

Directives. Nonexecutable assembly-language instructions such as the EQU statement (3.21) are known as directives. They are used to define the values of program parameters, to assign programs and data to specific physical or symbolic memory locations, and to control the files and listings produced by the assembly process. In the case of macroassemblers, they are also used to define macros. Figure 3.26 lists a representative set of the directives found in most assembly languages.

The EQU directive tells the assembler to equate two different names for the same thing. As illustrated by (3.21) it may be used to assign a symbolic name to a constant; it may also be used to equate two symbolic names for variables, as in

ALPHA   EQU   BETA

Type	Opcode	Comments
Symbol definition	EQU	Equate symbolic name (in label position) to operand value
Memory assignment	ORG	Origin: use operand value as starting address for subsequent instructions
	DS	Define storage: reserve the specified number of consecutive locations (bytes) in memory
	DC	Define constant: store the operand values as constants
Macro definition	MACRO	Start of macro definition
	ENDM	End of macro definition
Miscellaneous	END	End of program(s) to be assembled
	TITLE	Use operand as title on each page of assembly listing
	IF	Start of conditional block of instructions to be assembled only if a specified condition is met
	ENDIF	End of conditional block

FIGURE 3.26
List of representative assembly-language directives.

which defines a new variable ALPHA that must always have the same value as a previously defined parameter BETA. The ORG (origin) directive is used to tell the assembler which memory address to assign for storing the subsequent executable code or data. For example, in

$$\text{ORG} \quad 100$$
$$\text{L1} \quad \text{MOVE.L} \quad \text{A, A0}$$

the ORG directive states that the MOVE instruction is to be assigned to memory location 100, which equates the symbolic address or label L1 to the physical address 100. Note that this address value is needed by the assembler in order to translate into machine code the address fields of any branch instructions that refer to L1. Once the start address of a block of code has been established, the assembler automatically keeps track of the memory locations to be assigned to all items in the block.

Sometimes it is useful to be able to reserve a block of memory for future use, e.g., as a buffer storage area for IO data, without specifying its contents. The DS (*d*efine *s*torage) instruction is provided for this purpose. Thus the directive

$$\text{L2} \quad \text{DS} \quad 500$$

states that a block of 500 memory words (usually bytes) should be reserved, beginning at the current location L2. If it is desired to actually define data to be placed in a program, the DC (*d*efine *c*onstant) directive is used. DS and DC typically exist in several versions depending on the word size to be used. For example, the 68000 directive

$$\text{L3} \quad \text{DC.B} \quad 1, 2, 3, 4, 5, 6, 7$$

causes the seven specified operand values to be placed in binary form in seven consecutive 1-byte memory locations starting with L3. If the same data is to be stored in the ASCII character code, then the format

$$\text{L3} \quad \text{DC.B} \quad \text{'1234567'}$$

is used. We now turn to an example that illustrates the directives discussed so far.

Example 3.3 A vector addition program for the Motorola 68000 microprocessor series. The particular programming task considered here, which also served as a running example to illustrate the assembly-language code for various computers (the IAS computer, the IBM 7094, as well as the 68000) in Chap. 1, is to add two 1000-element vectors A and B creating a sum vector C. For simplicity, we assume that the vector elements are bytes that store 2-digit BCD numbers. The 68000 series has a 1-byte add instruction called ABCD (*a*dd *BCD*) which must be placed in a program loop and executed 1000 times to accomplish the desired vector addition. The necessary program can be described abstractly in the following high-level language format:

$$\textbf{for } I = 1 \textbf{ to } 1000 \textbf{ do}$$
$$C(I) \leftarrow A(I) + B(I); \tag{3.24}$$

We assume that A, B, and C are stored in three consecutive 1000-byte blocks of memory as depicted in Fig. 3.27.

In order to determine how best to implement (3.24) in assembly language, the available instruction types and addressing modes must be examined carefully [13]. The ABCD instruction, in addition to being limited to byte operands, only allows two operand addressing modes: direct register addressing, and indirect register addressing with predecrementing. As explained in Sec. 3.2.1, the latter mode causes the contents of the designated address register to be automatically decremented just before the add operation is carried out. This is convenient for stepping through lists, in this case the elements of a vector, and hence it is selected here. Two of the address registers A0 and A1 are chosen to address or point to the current elements of A and B, respectively. Thus the basic addition step is implemented by the instruction

$$\text{ABCD} \quad -(A0), -(A1) \tag{3.25}$$

which is equivalent to

$$A0 \leftarrow A0 - 1, A1 \leftarrow A1 - 1;$$
$$M(A1) \leftarrow M(A0) + M(A1);$$

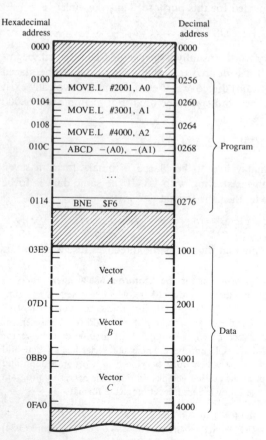

FIGURE 3.27
Memory allocation for the vector addition program.

A third address register A2 is used to point to vector C, and the result computed by (3.25) is stored in the C region by the 1-byte data-transfer instruction

$$\text{MOVE.B} \quad \text{(A1), (A2)} \tag{3.26}$$

Because addresses are predecremented, A0 and A1 must be initialized to values that are one greater than the highest addresses assigned to A and B. The foregoing instructions (3.25) and (3.26) are executed 1000 times, that is, until the lowest address (1001 in the case of vector A) is reached. This point can be detected by the CMPA (*compare address*) instruction

$$\text{CMPA} \quad \text{\#1001, A0}$$

which sets the zero status flag Z to 1 if A0 = 1001, and to 0 otherwise. When $Z \neq 1$, a branch is made back to (3.25) using the BNE (*branch if not equal to 1*) instruction. The resulting code, which appears with comments in Fig. 1.41, is as follows:

```
          MOVE.L   #2001, A0
          MOVE.L   #3001, A1
          MOVE.L   #4000, A2
START     ABCD     -(A0), -(A1)
          MOVE.B   (A1), (A2)
          CMPA     #1001, A0
          BNE      START
```

Figure 3.28 shows an assembly listing of a version of the foregoing code with various directives added for both illustrative purposes and also to complete the program. The assembly-language source program appears on the right-hand side of Fig. 3.28, while the assembled object program appears on the left in hexadecimal code. The leftmost column contains the memory addresses assigned by the assembler to the machine-language instructions and data, which are then listed to the right of these memory addresses. The first ORG directive causes the assembler to fix the start of the program at the hexadecimal address 100. The symbolic names A, B, and C are assigned by EQU directives to the addresses of the first elements of the three corresponding vectors. The subsequent MOVE.L (*move long*) instructions contain arithmetic expressions which are evaluated during assembly and replaced by the corresponding numerical value. For example, the expression A + 1000 appearing in the first MOVE.L instruction is replaced by 1001 + 1000 = 2001. In general, assembly languages allow arithmetic-logic expressions to be used as operands, provided the assembler can translate them to the form needed for the object program. The statement MOVE.L #2001, A0 is thus the first executable statement of the program and its machine-language equivalent 2078 07D1 is loaded into memory locations 0100:0103 (hex), as indicated in Figs. 3.27 and 3.28. The remainder of the short program is translated to machine code and allocated to memory in similar fashion.

Many of the 68000-series branch instructions use relative addressing, which means that the branch address is computed relative to the current address stored in the program counter PC. Consider, for instance, the conditional branch instruction BNE START, the last executable instruction in the vector addition program. As shown by Fig. 3.28, the corresponding machine-language instruction is 66F6 in which 66 is the opcode BNE and F6 is an 8-bit relative address derived from the operand START. Now $F6_{16} = 11110110_2$, which when interpreted as a twos-complement

Machine language			Assembly language			
Loc'n	Code/Data		; 68000/68020 program for vector addition			
			;			
			; The vectors are composed of a thousand 1-byte (two-digit)			
			; decimal numbers. The starting (decimal) addresses of A, B, C are			
			; 1001, 2001, and 3001, respectively.			
			;			
			;Define origin of program at hex address 100			
		0100		ORG	$100	
			;Define symbolic vector start addresses			
		03E9	A	EQU	1001	
		07D1	B	EQU	2001	
		0BB9	C	EQU	3001	
			;Begin executable code			
0100	2078 07D1			MOVE.L	A + 1000, A0	;Set pointer beyond end of A
0104	2278 0BB9			MOVE.L	B + 1000, A1	;Set pointer beyond end of B
0108	2478 0FA0			MOVE.L	C + 999, A2	;Set pointer to end of C
010C	C308		START	ABCD	−(A0), −(A1)	;Decrement pointers & add
010E	1491			MOVE.B	(A1), (A2)	;Store result in C
0110	B0F8 03E9			CMPA	A, A0	;Test for termination
0114	66 F6			BNE	START	;Branch to START if Z ≠ 1
			;End executable code			
			;			
			;Begin data definition			
		03E9		ORG	A	;Define start of vector A
03E9				DS.B	1000	;Reserve 1000 bytes for A
07D1	01 01 01			DC.B	1, 1, 1,	;Initialize elements 1:3 of B
07D4	16 16 16			DC.B	22,22,22	;Initialize elements 4:6 of B
				END		;End of program

FIGURE 3.28
Assembly listing of the Motorola 68000 program for vector addition.

number is -10_{10} or $-0A_{16}$. After BNE START has been fetched from memory locations 0114_{16} and 0115_{16}, PC is automatically incremented to point to the next consecutive memory location 0116_{16}. Hence at this point PC = 00000116_{16}. Now when the CPU executes the branch instruction BNE, it computes the branch address as PC + $(-0A)$ = $0000010C_{16}$ which, as required, is the physical address of the instruction (ABCD) with the symbolic address START.

The remainder of the vector addition program illustrates the assembly-language directives that define data regions. ORG is used again to establish a start address for the data region; in this case, the start address is $1001_{10} = 03E9_{16}$. A region of 1000 bytes is reserved by the DS.B (*define storage in bytes*) directive. Note that this directive merely causes the assembler's memory location counter, which it uses to keep track of memory addresses, to be incremented by the specified number of bytes. As indicated by Fig. 3.27, this action makes the location counter point to the start of the region storing vector B. The two DC.B (*define constant in bytes*) commands initialize six elements of B to the specified constant values. Finally the END directive indicates the end of the assembly-language program.

Macros and subroutines. Two useful tools for simplifying program design by allowing groups of instructions to be treated as single entities are macros and subroutines. A macro is defined by placing a portion of assembly-language code between appropriate directives as follows:

name   MACRO operand, . . . , operand

. . .   } Body of macro

ENDM

The macro is subsequently invoked by treating the user-defined macro name, which appears in the label field of the MACRO directive, as the opcode of a new (macro) instruction. Each time the macro opcode appears in a program, the assembler replaces it by a copy of the corresponding macro body. If the macro has operands, then the assembler modifies each copy of the macro body that it generates by inserting the operands included in the current macro instruction. Macros thus allow an assembly language to be augmented by new opcodes for all types of operations; they can also indirectly introduce new data types and addressing modes. A macro is typically used to replace a short sequence of instructions that occur frequently in a program. Note that although macros shorten the source code, they do not shorten the object code assembled from it.

Suppose, for example, that the following two-instruction sequence occurs in a program for the Intel 8085:

```
LDHL    ADR    ;Load M(ADR) into address register HL
MOV     A, M   ;Load M(HL) into register A
```

This code implements the operation $A \leftarrow M(M(ADR))$, which loads the accumulator treating ADR as an indirect memory address. We can define it as a macro named LDAI (*load a*ccumulator *i*ndirect) as follows:

```
LDAI  MACRO  ADR
      LHDL   ADR    ;Load M(ADR) into address register HL
      MOV    A, M   ;Load M(HL) into accumulator register A
      ENDM
```

With this macro definition present in an 8085 program, LDAI becomes a new assembly-language instruction for the programmer to use. The subsequent occurrence of a statement such as

$$\text{LDAI} \quad 1000\text{H} \tag{3.27}$$

in the same program causes the assembler to replace it by the macro body

```
LDHL    1000H
MOV     A, M
```

with the immediate address 1000_{16} from (3.27) replacing the macro's dummy input parameter ADR. Note that the macro definition itself is not part of the object program.

A subroutine is also a sequence of instructions that can be invoked by name, much like a single (macro) instruction. Unlike a macro, however, a subroutine definition is assembled into object code. It is subsequently used, not by replicating the body of the subroutine during assembly, but rather during program execution by establishing dynamic links between the subroutine object code and the points in the program where the subroutine is needed. The necessary links are established by means of two executable instructions named CALL or JUMP TO SUBROUTINE, and RETURN. Consider, for example, the following code segment:

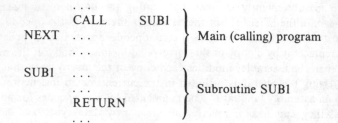

After CALL SUB1 has been fetched, the program counter PC contains the address NEXT of the instruction immediately following CALL; this *return address* must be saved to allow control to be returned later to the main program. Thus a call instruction first saves the contents of PC in a designated save area. It then transfers the address which forms the operand of the call statement, SUB1 in this case, into PC. This is the address of the first executable instruction in the subroutine and also serves as the subroutine's name. The processor then begins execution of the subroutine. Control is returned to the original program from the subroutine by executing RETURN, which simply retrieves the previously saved return address and restores it to PC.

Specific CPU registers or main-memory locations may be used by CALL and RETURN to store return addresses. RISC I, for instance, uses a CPU register from its current register window to save a return address on executing any of its call instructions; see Fig. 3.23. Most recent computers, however, use a memory stack for this purpose. CALL pushes the return address into the stack, from which it is subsequently retrieved by RETURN. The stack pointer SP automatically keeps track of the top of the stack where the last return address was pushed by CALL, and from which it will be popped by RETURN.

Figure 3.29 illustrates the actions taken by the CALL instruction in a typical stack implementation. For simplicity, we assume that opcodes and the addresses are each one memory word long. The instruction CALL SUB1 is stored in memory locations 1000 and 1001, and we assume that the assembler has replaced SUB1 by the physical address 2000. Immediately before the CALL instruction cycle begins, the program counter PC contains the address 1000 as shown in Fig. 3.29*a*. The CALL opcode is then fetched and decoded, and PC is incremented to 1001. On identifying the instruction as a subroutine call, the CPU fetches the address part

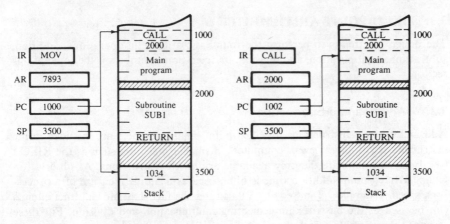

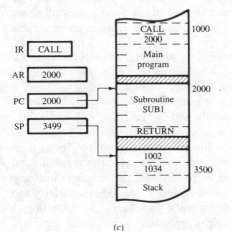

FIGURE 3.29
Processor and memory state during a CALL instruction cycle: (*a*) initial state; (*b*) state immediately after fetching the instruction; (*c*) final state.

2000 of the instruction and stores it in the (buffer) address register AR; again PC is incremented to 1002. At this point the system state is as shown in Fig. 3.29*b*, and PC contains the return address to the main program. Next the contents of PC are pushed into the stack. Then the contents of AR are transferred to PC, and the stack pointer SP is decremented by 1. The resulting state of the system is depicted in Fig. 3.29*c*.

3.3 FIXED-POINT ARITHMETIC

The design of circuits to perform the four basic arithmetic operations, addition, subtraction, multiplication, and division, on fixed-point numbers is the topic of this section.

3.3.1 Addition and Subtraction

Add and subtract instructions for fixed-point binary numbers are included in the instruction set of almost every computer. In smaller machines such as the RISC I (see Fig. 3.23), they are the only available arithmetic instructions. As observed in Chap. 2, fixed-point addition time is often used as a simple measure of a processor's speed. Example 2.3 in Sec. 2.3.3 illustrates the fact that add/subtract circuits can be used as the basis for implementing multiplication and division. For these reasons, considerable effort, beginning with Babbage, has been devoted to the design of high-speed addition and subtraction circuits. The complexity of an arithmetic circuit is determined in part by the number codes used. Twos-complement is perhaps the most widely used code for fixed-point binary numbers, since both addition and subtraction are easily implemented with this number code.

Basic adders. The fastest n-bit binary adder is, in principle, a two-level combinational circuit in which each of the n sum bits is expressed as a (logical) sum of products or product of sums of the input variables. In practice, such a circuit is feasible for very small values of n only, as it requires $c(n)$ gates with fan-in $f(n)$ where both $c(n)$ and $f(n)$ grow exponentially with n. Practical adders take the form of multilevel combinational circuits or, occasionally, sequential circuits. They therefore sacrifice operating speed for a reduction in circuit complexity as measured by the number and size of the components used. In general, the addition of two n-bit numbers X and Y is performed by subdividing the numbers into segments X_i and Y_i of length n_i, where $n \geq n_i \geq 1$. X_i and Y_i are added separately and the resulting partial sums are combined to form the total sum. The formation of the total sum involves assimilation of carry bits generated by the partial additions.

The sum z_i, c_i of two 1-bit numbers x_i and y_i can be expressed by the logic equations

$$z_i = x_i \oplus y_i$$
$$c_i = x_i y_i$$

Here z_i is the sum bit while c_i is the carry-out bit. The above equations define a *half adder*. It is useful to introduce a third input bit c_{i+1} denoting a carry-in signal leading to the following *full-adder* equations:

$$z_i = x_i \oplus y_i \oplus c_i$$
$$c_i = x_i y_i + x_i c_{i+1} + y_i c_{i+1} \tag{3.28}$$

A full-adder circuit can be directly implemented from these equations, as demonstrated by Fig. 2.14 in Sec. 2.2.1; it can also be constructed from two half adders and additional logic. Figure 3.30 shows a fast two-level AND-OR realization of a full adder, along with an appropriate circuit symbol for use in register-level designs.

Perhaps the simplest circuit for adding (unsigned) binary numbers is a serial adder, the design of which was covered in Example 2.2. A serial adder adds two numbers bit by bit, and so requires n clock cycles to compute the complete sum of two n-bit numbers. As Fig. 2.33 indicates, it consists of a combinational full adder realizing Eqs. (3.28), and a flip-flop to store c_i. One output bit is generated in each clock cycle; a carry is also computed and stored for use during the next clock cycle. Figure 3.31 presents a high-level view of a serial adder that employs a D flip-flop as its storage element. While a serial adder is slow, the amount of circuitry it contains is very small and is independent of n.

Circuits that add all bits of two numbers in one clock cycle are called parallel adders. A simple parallel adder can be formed by connecting n full-adder circuits in the series or cascade arrangement of Fig. 3.32. Each full-adder stage supplies a carry bit to the stage on its left. A carry appearing on the input of a full adder may cause it to generate a carry signal on its output carry line; thus carry signals can propagate serially through the adder from right to left giving rise to the name *ripple carry adder*. In the worst case, carries may ripple through all n stages of the adder; the maximum delay (which is synchronous circuit design determines the operating speed) is thus nd, where d is the delay of a full-adder stage. Note that unlike a serial adder, the amount of hardware required by a ripple carry adder increases linearly with n.

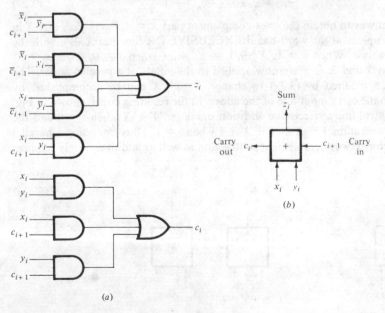

FIGURE 3.30
A full adder: (*a*) two-level AND-OR logic circuit; (*b*) symbol.

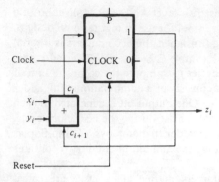

FIGURE 3.31
A serial binary adder.

Subtraction. Adders such as those of Figs. 3.31 and 3.32 operate correctly on unsigned numbers, and also on positive numbers because the 0 sign bit of a positive number has the same effect as the leading zero of an unsigned number. The appropriate way to add negative numbers, which have 1 as the sign bit, depends on the number code in use. Note that adding $-X$ to Y is equivalent to subtracting X from Y, so the ability to add negative numbers implies the ability to do subtraction. Subtraction is simple with twos-complement code since the negation operation is very easy to implement. As discussed in Sec. 3.1.3, if $X = x_0 x_1 \cdots x_{n-1}$ is a twos-complement integer, then negation is defined by

$$-X = \bar{x}_0 \bar{x}_1 \cdots \bar{x}_{n-1} + 1 \qquad (3.29)$$

A convenient way to obtain the ones-complement part $\bar{X} = \bar{x}_0 \bar{x}_1 \cdots \bar{x}_{n-1}$ of $-X$ in (3.29) is to implement the word-based EXCLUSIVE-OR function $X \oplus s$ with the control variable s. When $s = 1$, $X \oplus 1 = \bar{X}$, while when $s = 0$, $X \oplus s = X$. Suppose that Y and $X \oplus s$ are now applied to the inputs of a parallel adder. The addition of 1 required by (3.29) to change X to $-X$ can be accomplished by applying s to the carry input line of the adder. In the resulting circuit shown in Fig. 3.33, the control line s selects the addition operation $Y + X$ when $s = 0$ and the subtraction operation $Y - X = Y + \bar{X} + 1$ when $s = 1$. Thus extending a parallel adder to perform twos-complement subtraction as well as addition merely requires

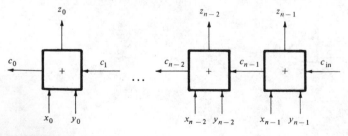

FIGURE 3.32
An n-bit ripple carry adder.

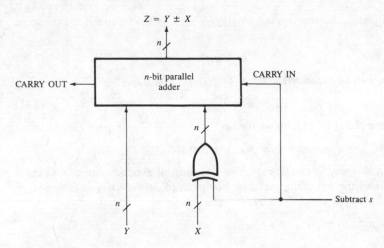

FIGURE 3.33
An n-bit twos-complement adder-subtracter.

connecting n two-input EXCLUSIVE-OR gates to the adder; these gates are represented by a word gate in Fig. 3.33.

Subtraction is not so readily implemented in the case of unsigned, or sign-magnitude, numbers. It is sometimes useful to construct a subtracter for such numbers based on the *full subtracter* function $z_i = y_i - x_i - b_i$. This operation is defined by the following logic equations:

$$z_i = x_i \oplus y_i \oplus b_{i+1}$$
$$b_i = x_i\overline{y_i} + x_ib_{i+1} + \overline{y_i}b_{i+1}$$

Here z_i is the difference bit, while b_{i+1} and b_i are the borrow-in and borrow-out bits, respectively. n-bit serial or parallel binary subtracters are constructed in essentially the same way as the corresponding adders with carry signals replaced by borrows. Subtracters are of minor interest compared with adders, since an adder suffices for both addition and subtraction when ones-complement or twos-complement number codes are used.

High-speed adders. The general strategy in designing fast adders is to reduce the time associated with carry propagation. One way of doing this is to generate the input carry bit of stage i directly from the inputs to the preceding stages $i + 1$, $i + 2, \ldots, i + k$ rather than allow carries to ripple from stage to stage. Adders designed using this principle are called *carry-lookahead adders*. An n-bit carry-lookahead adder can be formed from k stages, each of which is a full adder modified by replacing its carry output line c_i by two carry generate and propagate signals g_i and p_i defined by the logic equations

$$g_i = x_iy_i$$
$$p_i = x_i + y_i$$

The carry signal to be transmitted to stage $i - 1$ is then defined by the logic equation

$$c_i = g_i + p_i c_{i+1} \tag{3.30}$$

Similarly, c_{i+1} can be expressed in terms of g_{i+1}, p_{i+1}, and c_{i+2}:

$$c_{i+1} = g_{i+1} + p_{i+1} c_{i+2} \tag{3.31}$$

On substituting (3.31) into (3.30) we obtain

$$c_i = g_i + p_i g_{i+1} + p_i p_{i+1} c_{i+2}$$

Continuing in this way, c_i can be expressed as a sum-of-products function of the p and g outputs of the preceding k stages. For example, the carries in a four-stage carry-lookahead adder are defined by

$$
\begin{aligned}
c_3 &= g_3 + p_3 c_{in} \\
c_2 &= g_2 + p_2 g_3 + p_2 p_3 c_{in} \\
c_1 &= g_1 + p_1 g_2 + p_1 p_2 g_3 + p_1 p_2 p_3 c_{in} \\
c_0 &= g_0 + p_0 g_1 + p_0 p_1 g_2 + p_0 p_1 p_2 g_3 + p_0 p_1 p_2 p_3 c_{in}
\end{aligned} \tag{3.32}
$$

Figure 3.34 shows the corresponding circuit. The lookahead circuit is a two-level logic circuit that generates c_0, c_1, c_2, c_3 according to the equations above. If d is the propagation delay of a two-level circuit, then the total delay of this carry-lookahead adder is $3d$; with further minor modifications the total delay can be reduced to $2d$. Since the complexity of the carry-generation equations increases with the number of stages, practical considerations limit the number of carry-lookahead stages to $k \leq 8$ or so.

The carry-lookahead principle can be extended to handle mk bits by performing carry-lookahead addition on groups of k adjacent bits and transferring the output carry bit of each group to the carry input of its left neighbor. Thus carries ripple through the m groups. Figure 3.35 shows a 12-bit adder designed in this way using three 4-bit carry-lookahead adders of the type given in Fig. 3.34. In this kind of adder, each group can generate an output carry d time units (where d

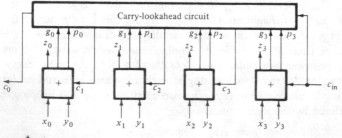

FIGURE 3.34
A 4-bit carry-lookahead adder.

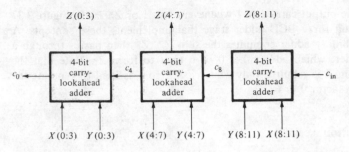

FIGURE 3.35
A 12-bit adder with group carry lookahead and ripple carry between groups.

is the two-level delay) after it receives its input carry. Hence if there are m groups, the total addition time is $(m + 2)d$. The 12-bit adder of Fig. 3.26 has a delay of $5d$ compared with $12d$ for a simple ripple carry adder.

Decimal adders. Adders that handle numbers in decimal codes such as BCD or excess-three are, as might be expected, more complex than binary adders. Decimal adders can often be regarded as binary adders with "correction" logic added to transform the sum to the required decimal format. As an example, we consider the design of an n-digit ripple carry BCD adder analogous to the binary adder of Fig. 3.32. Speedup methods such as carry lookahead can readily be extended from the binary to the decimal case.

The general structure of an n-digit BCD ripple carry adder is illustrated in Fig. 3.36. There are n stages, each of which adds a pair of 4-bit BCD digits and is connected via 1-bit carry lines to its neighbors. As a first approximation, one might attempt to implement each stage by a 4-bit binary adder and add X_i and Y_i as if they were binary numbers. Let Z_i^* denote the resulting 4-bit binary sum and let c_i^* be the output carry. Let Z_i be the correct BCD sum and let c_i be the correct carry. If $X_i + Y_i + c_{i+1} < 10$, $Z_i^* = Z_i$, otherwise $Z_i^* \neq Z_i$ and Z_i^* must be "corrected" to change it to Z_i. As the reader can readily verify, this correction can be made by adding 6 to Z_i^*, since the low-order 4 bits of $Z_i^* + 6$ are equal to Z_i whenever $X_i +$

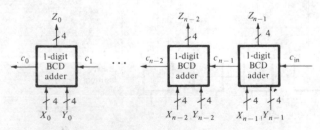

FIGURE 3.36
An n-digit ripple carry BCD adder.

$Y_i + c_{i+1} \geq 10$. The output carry c_i is 1 whenever $c_i^* = 1$ or $Z_i^* \geq 10$. Figure 3.37 shows a logic circuit for a BCD adder stage that implements these concepts. A 4-bit ripple carry binary adder computes the sum Z_i^*. Z_i^* then passes through a second binary adder, which adds either 0 or 6 to it to form Z_i. Note that the correction by adding 6 is required only when $c_i = 1$, so c_i is used to generate the required correction factor 0 or 6.

3.3.2   Multiplication

Multiplication requires substantially more hardware than addition and, as a result, may not be included in the instruction sets of smaller processors such as microprocessors or RISCs. It is usually implemented by some form of repeated addition. One of the simplest but slowest multiplication methods is to add the multiplicand Y to itself X times, where X is the multiplier. An implementation of this technique using counters is discussed in Prob. 2.23. More commonly, multiplication is implemented by multiplying Y by X k bits at a time and adding the resulting terms. Figure 3.38 shows how this is done for unsigned binary numbers in pencil-and-paper calculations with $k = 1$. The main operations involved are shifting and addition. The algorithm of Fig. 3.38 is inefficient in that the 1-bit products $x_j 2^i Y$ must be stored until the final addition step is completed. In machine implementations, it is desirable to add each $x_j 2^i Y$ term as it is generated to the sum of the preceding terms to form a number P_{i+1} called the partial product. Figure 3.39 shows the calculation in Fig. 3.38 implemented in this

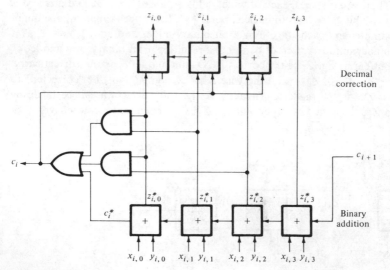

FIGURE 3.37
A 1-digit BCD adder stage.

```
1010      Multiplicand Y
1101      Multiplier X = x₀x₁x₂x₃
1010      x₃Y
0000      x₂2Y
1010      x₁2²Y
1010      x₀2³Y
```

$$10000010 \quad \text{Product } P = \sum_{j=0}^{3} x_j 2^{3-j} Y$$

FIGURE 3.38
Typical pencil-and-paper method for multiplication of unsigned binary numbers.

way. The computation involved in processing one multiplier bit x_j can be described by a register transfer statement of the form

$$P_{i+1} \leftarrow P_i + x_j 2^i Y \tag{3.33}$$

where $2^i Y$ is equivalent to Y shifted i positions to the left. In the version of this multiplication algorithm presented in Example 2.3, the partial product P_i is shifted right with respect to a fixed multiplicand Y, so that (3.33) is replaced by the equivalent operations

$$P_i \leftarrow P_i + x_j Y; \ P_{i+1} \leftarrow 2^{-j} P_i; \tag{3.34}$$

The multiplication of sign-magnitude binary numbers requires a straightforward extension of the unsigned case. The magnitude part of the product $P = Y \times X$ is computed by the unsigned multiplication algorithm, and the sign p_0 of P is computed from the signs of X and Y thus:

$$p_0 \leftarrow x_0 \oplus y_0$$

The implementation of the sign-magnitude multiplication is covered in detail in Example 2.3.

Twos-complement multipliers. The multiplication of twos-complement numbers presents some difficulties in the case of negative operands. (Recall that the sign-magnitude and twos-complement codes employ exactly the same representations for positive numbers.) For example, when a negative P_i is right-shifted as in (3.34), leading 1s rather than leading 0s must be introduced at the left end of the number.

```
1010       Y
1101       X
00000000   P₀ = 0
1010
00001010   P₁ = P₀ + x₃Y
0000
00001010   P₂ = P₁ + x₂2Y
1010
00110010   P₃ = P₂ + x₁2²Y
1010
10000010   P₄ = P₃ + x₀2³Y = P
```

FIGURE 3.39
The multiplication of Fig. 3.38 modified for machine implementation.

More seriously, the multiplication process may need to treat positive and negative operands differently.

A conceptually simple approach to twos-complement multiplication is to negate all negative operands at the beginning, perform unsigned multiplication on the resulting (positive) numbers, then negate the result if necessary. Twos-complement negation for fractions is specified by

$$-X = \overline{x}_0.\overline{x}_1\overline{x}_2 \cdots \overline{x}_{n-2}\overline{x}_{n-1} + 0.00 \cdots 01 \text{ (Modulo 2)} \tag{3.35}$$

and can easily be implemented by an adder (the one already present in an unsigned multiplier circuit) and an EXCLUSIVE-OR word gate; cf. Fig. 3.33. However, as many as four extra clock cycles may be needed to negate X and Y and the double-length product P. Several faster schemes have been proposed to handle negative operands. Since these hinge on certain properties of the twos-complement representation, we consider the latter first.

Clearly $\overline{x}_i = 1 - x_i$ (modulo 2), so we can rewrite (3.35) as follows:

$$-X = 1.11 \cdots 11 - x_0.x_1x_2 \cdots x_{n-2}x_{n-1} + 0.00 \cdots 01$$

$$= 10.00 \cdots 00 - x_0.x_1x_2 \cdots x_{n-2}x_{n-1} \tag{3.36}$$

or more briefly,

$$-X = 2 - X$$

which, incidentally, indicates the origin of the term twos-complement.

Now if X is positive ($x_0 = 0$), we can express its value as

$$X = \sum_{i=0}^{n-1} 2^{-i}x_i = \sum_{i=1}^{n-1} 2^{-i}x_i \tag{3.37}$$

If X is negative ($x_0 = 1$), then (3.37) does not hold. We can, however, rewrite (3.35) as

$$-X = 10.00 \cdots 00 - 0.x_1x_2 \cdots x_{n-2}x_{n-1} + 1.00 \cdots 000$$

$$= 1.00 \cdots 00 - 0.x_1x_2 \cdots x_{n-2}x_{n-1} \text{ (modulo 2)}$$

which with (3.37) implies

$$-X = 1 - \sum_{i=1}^{n-1} 2^{-i}x_i \tag{3.38}$$

Replacing 1 by 2^0x_0 in (3.38) and transposing yields

$$X = -2^0x_0 + \sum_{i=1}^{n-1} 2^{-i}x_i \tag{3.39}$$

For example, suppose that $n = 4$ and $X = 1.011$, which represents -0.625_{10}. Evaluating it according to (3.39), we obtain

$$X = -2^0 \times 1 + 2^{-1} \times 0 + 2^{-2} \times 1 + 2^{-3} \times 1$$
$$= -1.000 + 0.250 + 0.125$$
$$= -0.625$$

Equation (3.39) states that we can treat bits $x_1:x_{n-1}$ of a negative twos-complement fraction X in the same way as the corresponding (magnitude) bits of a positive number, provided we assign the negative weight $-2^0 = -1$ to the sign bit x_0. If X is the multiplier operand in a shift-and-add multiplication algorithm, then this suggests that when multiplying by the sign bit, we perform subtraction rather than addition in a special "correction" step associated with a negative x_0. This observation is the basis of a twos-complement multiplication algorithm due to James E. Robertson, which has been widely used in computer design [5, 25]. We now consider how the multiplication circuit developed in Example 2.3 for sign-magnitude numbers might be adapted to deal with the twos-complement case.

Example 3.4 Design of a multiplier for twos-complement numbers. Consider again the task of multiplying the two 8-bit binary numbers $X = x_0x_1x_2x_3x_4x_5x_6x_7$ and $Y = y_0y_1y_2y_3y_4y_5y_6y_7$ to form the product $P = X \times Y$, this time using twos-complement representation. We assume that the multiplier will have a register-level structure similar to that shown in Fig. 2.57, with registers A, M, and Q storing the various operands, and A.Q forming a right-shift register. Since sign bits will be included in additions and subtractions, an 8-bit adder is needed rather than the 7-bit magnitude-only multiplier used in the earlier design. The adder will also be modified as in Fig. 3.33 to provide twos-complement subtraction as well as addition.

To develop the required twos-complement multiplication algorithm for this machine, we consider the four cases determined by the signs of X and Y.

1. $x_0 = y_0 = 0$, that is, both X and Y are positive. The computation in this case follows that of Example 2.3, with the product P computed in a series of add-and-shift steps of the form

$$P_i \leftarrow P_i + x_{7-i}Y; \quad P_{i+1} \leftarrow 2^{-1}P_i;$$

Note that all partial products P_i are nonnegative, so leading 0s are introduced into A during right shifting.

2. $x_0 = 0$, $y_0 = 1$, that is, X is positive and Y is negative. The partial product P_i will be zero, and leading 0s should be shifted into A as before, until the first 1 in X is encountered. Multiplication of Y by this 1, and addition of the result to A, causes P_i to become negative, from which point on leading 1s rather than 0s must be shifted into A. These rules ensure that in all cases a right shift corresponds to division by 2 in twos-complement code.

3. $x_0 = 1$, $y_0 = 0$, that is, X is negative and Y is positive. This follows case 1 for the first seven add-and-shift steps yielding the partial product

$$P_7 = \sum_{i=1}^{7} 2^{-i}x_iY$$

For the final step, often referred to as a correction step, the subtraction

$$P \leftarrow P_7 - Y$$

is performed. The result P is then given by

$$P = -Y + \sum_{i=1}^{7} 2^{-i}x_iY = \left(-x_0 + \sum_{i=1}^{7} 2^{-i}x_i\right)Y$$

which is XY by (3.39).

4. $x_0 = y_0 = 1$, that is, both X and Y are negative. The procedure used here follows case 2, with leading 0s (1s) being introduced into the accumulator whenever its contents are zero (negative). The correction step of case 3 is also performed, which ensures that the final product in A.Q is nonnegative.

Each addition/subtraction step can be performed in the usual twos-complement fashion treating the sign bits like any other and ignoring overflow. As noted above, care is needed in the shift step to ensure that the correct new value is placed in A(0). This must be a leading 0 if the current partial product in A.Q is positive or zero, and 1 if it is negative. To control the values assigned to A(0), we introduce a flip-flop F whose value determines A(0). F is initially set to 0. It is then defined by

$$F \leftarrow y_0 \wedge x_i \vee F$$

where $\wedge$ and $\vee$ denote AND and OR, respectively, y_0 is the sign of the multiplicand stored in M(0), and x_i is the current multiplier bit being tested in Q(7). Thus F is set to 1 if Y is negative and at least one nonzero x_i is encountered. Once set to 1, it remains at that value. A negative Y and a positive or negative X therefore produce a series of negative partial products. This is to be expected since bits $x_1:x_{n-1}$ of the multiplier X are always treated as if they were positive. A positive Y, or $X = 0$, will cause F to remain permanently at 0. Note that the sign p_0 of the product P requires no separate computational step. As in Example 2.3, bit p_{15} of P is set to 0 to make the product exactly 16 bits long.

Figure 3.40 presents a formal description of the twos-complement multiplication algorithm which summarizes the foregoing analysis; cf. the corresponding sign-magnitude algorithm in Fig. 2.37. An application of the algorithm to the case $X = 10110011$ and $Y = 11010101$ appears in Fig. 3.41. Observe how F becomes 1 in step 1, when the negative multiplicand is first added to the accumulator. F continues to supply leading 1s to the A register until step 8. Then because $Q(7) = x_0 = 1$, a subtraction is performed which produces the proper sign $p_0 = 0$ in A(0). Setting $Q(7) = p_{15}$ to 0 completes the multiplication process. The necessary changes for the multiplier circuit of Fig. 2.57 to implement the algorithm of Fig. 3.40 appear in Fig. 3.42.

---

	declare register A(0:7), M(0:7), Q(0:7), COUNT(0:2), F
	declare bus INBUS(0:7), OUTBUS(0:7)
BEGIN:	A $\leftarrow$ 0, COUNT $\leftarrow$ 0, F $\leftarrow$ 0,
INPUT:	M $\leftarrow$ INBUS;
	Q $\leftarrow$ INBUS;
ADD:	A(0:7) $\leftarrow$ A(0:7) + M(0:7) $\times$ Q(7),
	F $\leftarrow$ M(0) $\wedge$ Q(7) $\vee$ F;
RIGHTSHIFT:	A(0) $\leftarrow$ F, A(1:7).Q $\leftarrow$ A.Q(0:6);
TEST:	**if** COUNT = 6 **then go to** CORRECTION,
	COUNT $\leftarrow$ COUNT + 1, **go to** ADD;
CORRECTION:	A(0:7) $\leftarrow$ A(0:7) $-$ M(0:7) $\times$ Q(7), Q(7) $\leftarrow$ 0;
OUTPUT:	OUTBUS $\leftarrow$ A;
	OUTBUS $\leftarrow$ Q;
END:	

FIGURE 3.40
Formal description of an 8-bit twos-complement multiplier.

Step	Action	F	Accumulator A	Register Q
0	Initialize registers	0	00000000	10110011 = multiplier X
1			11010101	= multiplicand Y = M
	Add M to A	1	11010101	10110011
	Shift A.Q	1	11101010	11011001
2			11010101	
	Add M to A	1	10111111	11011001
	Shift A.Q	1	11011111	11101100
3			00000000	
	Add zero to A	1	11011111	11101100
	Shift A.Q	1	11101111	11110110
4			00000000	
	Add zero to A	1	11101111	11110110
	Shift A.Q	1	11110111	11111011
5			11010101	
	Add M to A	1	11001100	11111011
	Shift A.Q	1	11100110	01111101
6			11010101	
	Add M to A	1	10111011	011111101
	Shift A.Q	1	11011101	101111110
7			00000000	
	Add zero to A	1	11011101	10111110
	Shift A.Q	1	11101110	11011111
8			11010101	
	Subtract M from A	1	00011001	11011111
	Set Q(7) to 0		00011001	11011110 = product P

FIGURE 3.41
Illustration of the twos-complement multiplication algorithm.

Booth's algorithm. Another interesting and widely used scheme for twos-complement multiplication was designed by Andrew D. Booth [4]. Like Robertson's method used in Example 3.4, it employs both addition and subtraction, but unlike the earlier method, it treats both positive and negative operands uniformly. It also allows n-bit multiplication to be done using fewer than n additions or subtractions, thereby making possible faster multiplication.

The preceding multiplication algorithms involve scanning the multiplier X from right to left and using the value of the current multiplier bit x_i to determine which of the following operations to perform: add the multiplicand Y, subtract Y, or add zero, i.e., no operation. In Booth's approach two adjacent bits $x_i x_{i+1}$ are examined in each step. If $x_i x_{i+1} = 01$, then Y is added to the accumulated partial product P_i, while if $x_i x_{i+1} = 10$, Y is subtracted from P_i. If $x_i x_{i+1} = 00$ or 11, then

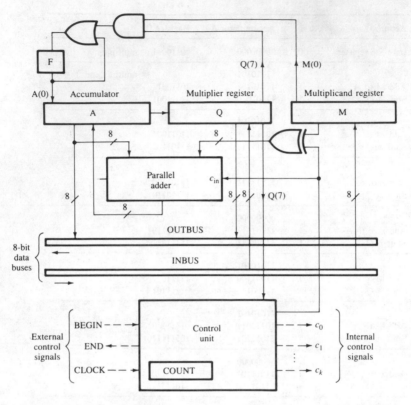

FIGURE 3.42
Block diagram of a twos-complement multiplier.

neither addition or subtraction is performed; only the subsequent right shift of P_i takes place. Thus Booth's algorithm effectively skips over runs of 1s and runs of 0s that it encounters in X. It is this skipping that reduces the average number of add-subtract steps and allows faster multipliers to be designed, although at the expense of more complex timing and control circuitry.

The validity of Booth's algorithm may be seen as follows. Suppose that X is a positive fraction and contains an internal subsequence X^* consisting of a run of k 1s flanked by two 0s.

$$X^* = x_i x_{i+1} x_{i+2} \cdots x_{i+k-1} x_{i+k} x_{i+k+1}$$
$$= 0\,1\,1\,\cdots\,1\,1\,0$$

In a direct add-and-shift multiplication algorithm such as Robertson's, Y is multiplied by each bit of X^* in sequence and the results are summed, so that X^*'s contribution to the product $P = X \times Y$ is

$$\sum_{j=i+1}^{i+k} 2^{-j} Y \qquad (3.40)$$

Now when Booth's algorithm is applied to X^*, it performs an addition when it encounters $x_i x_{i+1} = 01$ which contributes $2^{-i} Y$ to P, and it performs a subtraction at $x_{i+k} x_{i+k+1} = 10$ which contributes $-2^{-(i+k)} Y$ to P. Thus the net contribution of X^* to the product P in this case is

$$2^{-i} Y - 2^{-(i+k)} Y = 2^{-(i+k)} (2^k - 1) Y$$

$$= 2^{-(i+k)} \sum_{m=0}^{k-1} 2^m Y$$

$$= \sum_{m=0}^{k-1} 2^{m-i-k} Y \tag{3.41}$$

If the index m is replaced by $j = m - i - k$, then it is obvious that (3.40) and (3.41) are the same; hence Booth's algorithm correctly computes the contribution of X^*, and hence of the entire multiplier X, to the product P. Equation (3.39) implies that the contribution of a negative X^* to P can also be expressed in the formats of (3.40) and (3.41); therefore a similar argument demonstrates the correctness of the algorithm for negative multipliers.

The Booth approach results in a reduction in the number of additions and subtractions needed for runs of k 1s or 0s, provided $k > 1$. If $k = 1$, i.e., X^* corresponds to an isolated 1 flanked by 0s, then no such reduction results. In fact, if $X = 010101..01$, where there are $n/2$ isolated 1s, then $n/2$ additions and $n/2$ subtractions are required if the basic Booth algorithm is used. This is worse than the earlier multiplication algorithms which only perform $n/2$ additions corresponding to the $n/2$ 1s in such cases. Thus the basic Booth method can be improved by identifying isolated 1s in the multiplier X and only performing a single addition and no subtraction at the corresponding point in the multiplication process. Similarly, at an isolated 0 only a single subtraction need be performed. The resulting *modified* Booth algorithm always requires fewer addition-subtraction steps than the other multiplication methods considered.

The twos-complement multiplication circuit of Fig. 3.42 can also be adapted to implement the (modified) Booth algorithm. Two bits $x_{i-1} x_i$ of the multiplier register Q are scanned at a time, beginning with Q(6)Q(7), to determine the operation (add Y, subtract Y, or skip) to be performed, instead of examining bit x_i alone, as in the earlier multiplication schemes. An extra flip-flop Q(-1) is also appended to the left end of Q. To identify isolated 1s and 0s in X, a *mode* flip-flop F is introduced which is set to 1 when a run of two or more 1s is encountered, and is reset to 0, when the run ends with two or more 0s. Thus when a multiplier subsequence $X^* = 010$ is identified, $F = 0$ and only a single add is performed; $X^* = 001..10$ causes F to be set to 1 and a subtraction and an addition are performed at the start and end of the run of 1s, respectively. If $X^* = 101..10$, then at the end of the run of 1s, 10 is encountered with $F = 1$, and at the isolated 0 only a subtraction is carried out. Figure 3.43 presents a complete description of an implementation of the Booth algorithm using the above approach with $n = 8$ and a circuit based on Fig. 3.42. To simplify the handling of zero operands, X and Y are both tested for

	declare register $A(0:7)$, $M(0:7)$, $Q(-1:7)$, COUNT$(0:2)$, F
	declare bus INBUS$(0:7)$, OUTBUS$(0:7)$
BEGIN:	$A \leftarrow 0$, COUNT $\leftarrow 0$, $F \leftarrow 0$,
INPUT:	$M \leftarrow$ INBUS;
	$Q(0:7) \leftarrow$ INBUS, $Q(-1) \leftarrow$ INBUS(0);
ZEROTEST:	if $M = 0 \lor Q = 0$ then go to OUTPUT,
LOOP:	if $F = 0$ then begin
ADD1:	if $Q(6)Q(7) = 01$ then $A(0:7) \leftarrow A(0:7) + M(0:7)$; else
SUBTRACT1:	if $Q(6)Q(7) = 11$ then $A(0:7) \leftarrow A(0:7) - M(0:7)$, $F \leftarrow 1$; else go to TEST; end
	if $F = 1$ then begin
ADD2:	if $Q(6)Q(7) = 00$ then $A(0:7) \leftarrow A(0:7) + M(0:7)$, $F \leftarrow 0$; else
SUBTRACT2:	if $Q(6)Q(7) = 10$ then $A(0:7) \leftarrow A(0:7) - M(0:7)$; end
TEST:	if COUNT $= 7$ then go to OUTPUT,
RIGHTSHIFT:	$A(0) \leftarrow \overline{M}(0) \land F \lor M(0) \land A(0)$, $A(1:7).Q \leftarrow A.Q(-1:6)$,
INCREMENT:	COUNT $\leftarrow$ COUNT $+ 1$, go to LOOP;
OUTPUT:	$Q(6) \leftarrow 0$, OUTBUS $\leftarrow A$;
	OUTBUS $\leftarrow Q(-1:6)$;
END:	

FIGURE 3.43
Formal description of an 8-bit (modified) Booth multiplier.

zero at the start; if either is found to be zero, the main algorithm is skipped, resulting in the correct result $P = 0$ in A.Q$(-1:6)$. The value initially placed in $Q(-1)$ is the sign of X, i.e., the sign in $Q(0)$ is effectively extended to $Q(-1)$. The new value of $A(0)$ in each step depends in a somewhat complex way on the sign $M(0)$ of the multiplicand, the previous value of $A(0)$, and the mode flag F; it is specified by the statement RIGHTSHIFT in Fig. 3.43. If Y is negative, indicated by $M(0) = 1$, then A.Q is always sign-extended into $A(0)$ during right shifts, i.e., $A(0) \leftarrow A(0)$. If Y is positive, then $A(0)$ is set to 1 when skipping over runs of 1s; otherwise it is set to 0. The application of this algorithm to the example solved by Robertson's method in Fig. 3.41 appears in Fig. 3.44.

The process of inspecting the multiplier bits required by the Booth algorithm can be viewed as encoding the multiplier using three digits 0, 1, $\bar{1}$, where 0 means shift the multiplicand relative to the accumulator, while 1 $(\bar{1})$ means add (subtract) the multiplicand before shifting. Thus the binary integer

$$X = 0111\ 1011\ 0010\ 0011 \tag{3.42}$$

which represents $+31,523$, can be replaced by

$$X^* = 1000\ \bar{1}10\bar{1}\ 01\bar{1}0\ 010\bar{1} \tag{3.43}$$

where each 1 $(\bar{1})$ in X^* indicates that an addition (subtraction) should be performed. X^* is an example of a *signed digit* number. It is a variation of the usual positional notation which allows a bit to have weight -2^i (indicated by $\bar{1}$ in that bit position) as well as the usual values of 0 and 2^i. Hence (3.43) can be expressed as

$$X^* = 2^{15} - 2^{11} + 2^{10} - 2^8 + 2^6 - 2^5 + 2^2 - 2^0$$

$$= 31,523$$

The process of converting a multiplier X to signed digit form to simplify the multiplication process is called *multiplier recoding*.

Figure 3.45 gives the rules for a multiplier recoding scheme that takes isolated 0s and 1s into account. Called *canonical signed digit* recoding, it is incorporated into the Booth multiplication algorithm described above (Fig. 3.43). First $x_{-1} = x_0$ is appended to the left end of the input number $x_0 x_1 \cdots x_{n-1}$ to form $X = x_{-1} x_0 x_1 \cdots x_{n-1}$. X is then scanned from right to left and the pair of bits $x_{i-1} x_i$ is used to determine bit x_i^* of the output number X^*. A flag f, which is initially 0, is set to 1 (0) while a run of 1s (0s) is being traversed. Note that f is not altered when an isolated 1 (0) is encountered in a sum of 0s (1s). Applying these rules to the number X defined by equation (3.42) yields the canonical signed digit form

$$X^* = 1000\ 0\bar{1}0\bar{1}\ 0010\ 010\bar{1}$$

which contains more 0s than (3.43). On the average, an n-bit twos-complement number contains $n/2$ 0s. The canonical signed digit representation, however, con-

Step	Action	F	Accumulator A	Register Q
0	Initialize registers	0	00000000	010110011 = multiplier X
	Extend Q(0) to Q(−1)	0	00000000	110110011
1			11010101	= multiplicand Y = M
	Subtract M from A	1	00101011	110110011
	Shift A.Q	1	00010101	111011001
2	Skip add/subtract	1	00010101	111011001
	Shift A.Q	1	00001010	111101100
3			11010101	
	Add M to A	0	11011111	111101100
	Shift A.Q	0	11101111	111110110
4	Skip add/subtract	0	11101111	111110110
	Shift A.Q	0	11110111	111111011
5			11010101	
	Subtract M from A	1	00100010	111111011
	Shift A.Q	1	00010001	011111101
6	Skip add/subtract	1	00010001	011111101
	Shift A.Q	1	00001000	101111110
7			11010101	
	Subtract M from A	1	00110011	101111110
	Shift A.Q	1	00011001	110111111
8	Skip add/subtract	1	00011001	110111111
	Set Q(6) to 0	1	00011001	110111101
			00011001	11011110 = product P

FIGURE 3.44
Illustration of the modified Booth multiplication algorithm.

Input			Output		
x_{i-1}	x_i	f	x_i^*	f	Comments
0	0	0	0	0	
0	1	0	1	0	x_i is an isolated 1
1	0	0	0	0	
1	1	0	$\bar{1}$	1	x_i begins a run of 1s
0	0	1	1	0	x_i begins a run of 0s
0	1	1	0	1	
1	0	1	$\bar{1}$	1	x_i is an isolated 0
1	1	1	0	1	

FIGURE 3.45
Rules for forming the canonical signed-digit representation of a number.

tains an average of $2n/3$ 0s, indicating that one-third fewer add-subtract operations are required.

Combinational array multipliers. Advances in VLSI technology have made it possible to build combinational circuits that perform $n \times n$-bit multiplication for relatively large values of n. An example is the Advanced Micro Devices (AMD) 29323 multiplier chip introduced in 1985, which can multiply two 32-bit numbers in less than 80 ns [1]. These multipliers resemble the n-step sequential multipliers discussed above, but have n times as much logic circuitry to allow the product to be computed in one step instead of n. They are typically composed of large arrays of simple combinational elements, each of which implements an add/subtract-and-shift operation for small, e.g., 1-bit, portions of the multiplication operands.

Suppose that two binary numbers $X = x_0 x_1 \cdots x_{n-1}$ and $Y = y_0 y_1 \cdots y_{n-1}$ are to be multiplied. For simplicity assume that X and Y are unsigned integers. The product $P = X \times Y$ can be expressed as

$$P = \sum_{i=0}^{n-1} x_i 2^{n-1-i} Y \qquad (3.44)$$

corresponding to the usual bit-by-bit multiplication (cf. Fig. 3.38). Now (3.44) can be rewritten as

$$P = \sum_{i=0}^{n-1} 2^{n-1-i} \left(\sum_{j=0}^{n-1} x_i y_j 2^{n-1-j} \right) \qquad (3.45)$$

Each of the n^2 1-bit products $x_i y_j$ in (3.45) may be computed by a two-input AND gate. (Note that the arithmetic and logical products coincide in the 1-bit case.) Hence an $n \times n$ array of two-input ANDs of the type shown in Fig. 3.46 can compute the $x_i y_j$ terms. The summation of these terms is accomplished according to (3.45) by an array of $n(n - 1)$ full adders, as illustrated in Fig. 3.47. The full-adder array is essentially a two-dimensional ripple carry adder. The shifts implied by the 2^{n-1-i} and 2^{n-1-j} factors in (3.45) are implemented by the spatial displacement of the full adders.

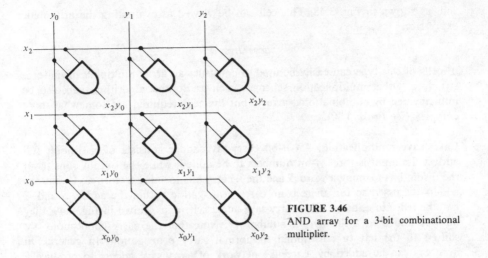

FIGURE 3.46
AND array for a 3-bit combinational multiplier.

The multiplication time for this array multiplier is clearly determined by the worst-case carry propagation and can be expressed as

$$2(n - 1)d + d'$$

where d and d' are the propagation delays of a full adder and an AND gate, respectively. Note that the component cost of this multiplier increases as the square of n. However, the array organization makes it suitable for manufacture using VLSI circuits.

The functions of the AND gates and full adders may be combined in a single

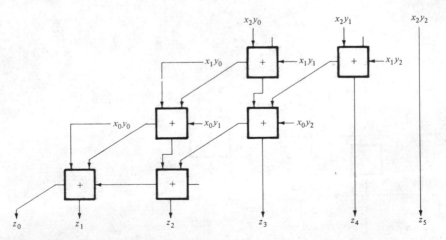

FIGURE 3.47
Full-adder array for a 3-bit combinational multiplier.

cell, as shown in Fig. 3.48. This cell can be viewed as evaluating the arithmetic expression

$$ac + b + d$$

n^2 cells of this type can easily be used to construct an array multiplier of uniform structure. Other multiplication schemes, such as Booth's algorithm, can also be implemented by combinational arrays, but the cells required are somewhat more complex (see Prob. 3.30).

Carry-save multiplication. An n-bit carry-save adder consists of n disjoint full adders. Its input is three n-bit numbers to be added, while the output consists of the n sum bits forming a word S and the n carry bits forming a word C. Unlike the adders discussed so far, there is no carry propagation within the adder. S and C may be fed into another n-bit carry-save adder where, as shown in Fig. 3.49, they may be added to a third n-bit number W. Note that the carry connections are shifted to the left to correspond to normal carry propagation. In general, m numbers can be added by a treelike network of carry-save adders to produce a result in the form (S, C). To obtain the final sum, S and C must be added by a conventional adder with carry propagation.

Multiplication can be performed using a multistage carry-save adder circuit of the type shown in Fig. 3.50. The inputs to the carry-save adder tree are n terms of the form $M_i = x_i Y 2^{k-i}$. M_i represents the multiplicand Y multiplied by the ith multiplier bit weighted by the appropriate power of 2. For simplicity, assume that M_i is represented by $2n$ bits and that the full double-length product is required. The desired product P is given by

$$\sum_{i=0}^{n-1} M_i$$

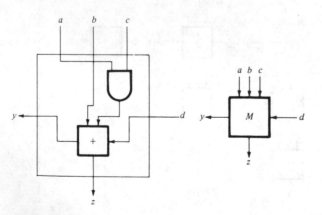

FIGURE 3.48
Cell for an array multiplier.

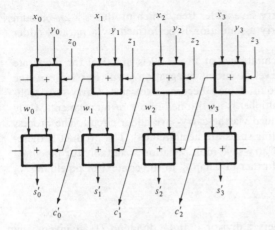

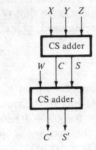

FIGURE 3.49
A two-stage carry-save adder.

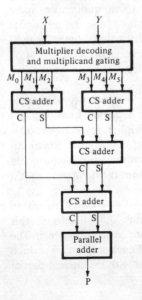

FIGURE 3.50
A carry-save multiplier.

This sum is computed by the carry-save adder tree, which produces a $2n$-bit sum and a $2n$-bit carry. The final carry assimilation is performed by a parallel adder with internal carry propagation.

The strictly combinational multiplier of Fig. 3.50 is practical for moderate values of n, depending on the level of circuit integration used. For large n, the number of carry-save adders required may become excessive. Carry-save techniques may still be used if the multiplier is partitioned into k m-bit segments. Only m terms M_i are generated and added via the carry-save adder circuit. The process is repeated k times and the resulting sums are accumulated. The product is therefore obtained after k iterations. Carry-save multiplication is suitable for pipelined implementation and is discussed further in Chap. 7 in the context of pipelining.

3.3.3 Division

In fixed-point division two numbers, a divisor V and a dividend D, are given. The object is to compute a third number Q, called the quotient, such that $Q \times V$ equals or is close to D. For example, if integer formats are being used, Q is computed so that

$$D = Q \times V + R$$

where R, the remainder, is required to be of smaller magnitude than V, that is, $0 \leq |R| < V$. If fraction formats are used, the number of bits in the quotient is not necessarily bounded a priori. For example, $0.2000 \div 0.3000 = 0.66666 \cdots$, a repeating fraction. It is necessary, therefore, to limit the number of quotient bits generated by the division process. Division of 0.2000 by 0.3000 might thus be required to yield a four-digit quotient Q with truncation or rounding determining the final digit of Q. Division circuits are usually designed to yield quotients of some specified length. In most cases only the quotient Q is required, and the remainder R, which is generated as a by-product of the division, is discarded. R may be used to generate additional quotient digits if required via a second division operation $R \div V$. In this way successive fixed-length division instructions can be used to generate a more accurate quotient.

The relationship $D \approx Q \times V$ suggests that there is a close correspondence between division and multiplication, specifically that the dividend, quotient, and divisor correspond to the product, multiplicand, and multiplier, respectively. This correspondence means that similar algorithms and circuits can be used for multiplication and division. In multiplication the shifted multiplicand is added to yield the product. In division the shifted divisor is subtracted from the dividend to yield the quotient.

One of the simplest division methods is the sequential digit-by-digit algorithm similar to that used in pencil-and-paper methods. Figure 3.51 illustrates this approach. Suppose that the divisor V and dividend D are positive integers. The quotient $Q = q_0 q_1 q_2 \cdots$ is computed one bit at a time. At each step i, $2^{-i}V$, which represents the divisor shifted i bits to the right, is compared with the current partial

```
          0111        Quotient Q = q₀q₁q₂q₃
Divisor V   101 |100110    Dividend D = R₀
          000         q₀V
          100110      R₁
          101         q₁2⁻¹V
          10010       R₂
          101         q₂2⁻²V
          1000        R₃
          101         q₃2⁻³V
          011         R₄ = remainder R
```

$$\text{Quotient } Q = q_0q_1q_2q_3$$

FIGURE 3.51
Typical pencil-and-paper method for division of unsigned integers.

remainder[5] R_i. The quotient bit q_i is set to 1 (0) if $2^{-i}V$ is less (greater) than R_i; and a new partial remainder R_{i+1} is computed according to the relation

$$R_{i+1} \leftarrow R_i - q_i 2^{-i}V \tag{3.46}$$

In machine implementations it is usually more convenient to shift the partial remainder to the left relative to a fixed divisor, in which case (3.46) is replaced by

$$R_{i+1} \leftarrow 2R_i - q_iV$$

Figure 3.52 shows the calculation of Fig. 3.51 modified in this way. Note that the final partial remainder is the required remainder R shifted to the left, so that in Fig. 3.52, $R = 2^{-3}R_4$.

A central problem in division is determining the quotient digit q_i. If radix-r numbers are being represented, then q_i must be chosen from among r possible values. When $r = 2$, q_i may be generated by comparing V and $2R_i$ in the ith step; cf. Fig. 3.52. If $V > 2R_i$, then $q_i = 0$; otherwise $q_i = 1$. If V is long, a combinational comparator circuit may be impractical, in which case q_i is usually determined by subtracting V from $2R_i$ and examining the sign of $2R_i - V$. If $2R_i - V$ is negative, $q_i = 0$; otherwise $q_i = 1$.

Basic algorithms. The circuit used for multiplication in Example 3.3 (Fig. 3.42) can easily be modified to perform division, as shown in Fig. 3.53. The pair of n-bit shift registers A.Q is used to store the partial remainders. Initially the dividend (which may be up to $2n$ bits in length) is placed in these registers. The divisor V is placed in the M register where it remains throughout the division process. In each step A.Q is shifted to the left. The cells vacated at the rightmost end of the Q register can be used to store the quotient bits as they are generated. When the division process terminates, Q contains the quotient while A contains the (shifted) remainder.

---

[5] R_i is also termed the partial dividend because it is used as the dividend in step $i + 1$.

Divisor V			Quotient Q	
101	100110	Dividend $= 2R_0$		
	000	$q_0 V$	0	
	100110	R_1		
	1001100	$2R_1$		
	101	$q_1 V$	01	
	100100	R_2		
	1001000	$2R_2$		
	101	$q_2 V$	011	
	100000	R_3		
	1000000	$2R_3$	0111	**FIGURE 3.52**
	101	$q_3 V$		The division of Fig. 3.51 modified for
	011000	$R_4 = 2^3 R$		machine implementation.

As noted already, the quotient bit q_i may be determined by a trial subtraction of the form $2R_i - V$. This trial subtraction also yields the new partial remainder R_{i+1} when $2R_i - V$ is positive, i.e., when $q_i = 1$. Clearly, the process of determining q_i and R_{i+1} may be integrated. Two major division algorithms are distinguished by the way in which they combine the computation of q_i and R_{i+1}. If $q_i = 0$, then the result of the trial subtraction is $2R_i - V$; however, the required new partial remainder R_{i+1} is $2R_i$. R_{i+1} may be obtained by adding V back to the result of the

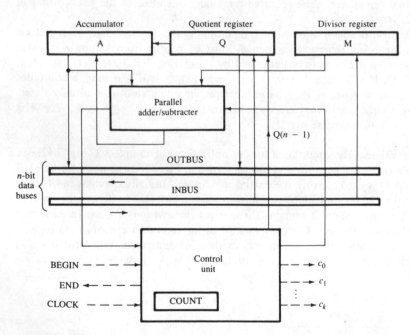

FIGURE 3.53
Block diagram of a sequential n-bit binary divider.

trial subtraction. This straightforward technique is called *restoring division*. In every step the operation

$$R_{i+1} \leftarrow 2R_i - V$$

is performed. When the result of the subtraction is negative, a restoring addition is performed as follows:

$$R_{i+1} \leftarrow R_{i+1} + V$$

If the probability of $q_i = 1$ is $1/2$, then this algorithm requires n subtractions and an average of $n/2$ additions.

The restoration step of the foregoing algorithm is eliminated in a slightly different technique called *nonrestoring division*. It is based on the observation that a restoration of the form

$$R_i \leftarrow R_i + V \tag{3.47}$$

is followed in the next step by a subtraction

$$R_{i+1} \leftarrow 2R_i - V \tag{3.48}$$

(3.47) and (3.48) can be merged into the single operation

$$R_{i+1} \leftarrow 2R_i + V \tag{3.49}$$

Thus when $q_i = 1$, which is indicated by a positive value of R_i, R_{i+1} is computed using (3.48). When $q_i = 0$, R_{i+1} is computed using (3.49). Each quotient bit calculation requires either an addition or a subtraction but not both. Nonrestoring division therefore requires n additions or subtractions, whereas restoring division requires an average of $3n/2$ additions and subtractions.

Figure 3.54 presents a nonrestoring division algorithm for unsigned integers designed for the circuit of Fig. 3.53. The divisor V and quotient Q are n bits long (with leading 0s if necessary), while the dividend D is $2n - 1$ bits long, which is the maximum length of the product of two n-bit integers. The flip-flop S is appended to the accumulator A to record the sign of the result of an addition or subtraction operation and to determine the quotient bit. Each new quotient bit is placed in $Q(n - 1)$, and the final values of the quotient Q and the remainder R are in the Q and A registers, respectively. An application of this algorithm when $n = 4$ appears in Fig. 3.55, with $D = 1100001_2 = 97_{10}$ and $V = 1010_2 = 10_{10}$.

The foregoing restoring and nonrestoring division techniques can be extended to signed numbers in much the same way as multiplication. Sign-magnitude numbers present few difficulties since the magnitudes of the quotient and remainder can be computed as in the unsigned number case, while their signs are determined separately. As noted in [5], there are no simple division algorithms for handling negative numbers directly in twos-complement code. This is primarily due to the difficulty of selecting the quotient bits in such a way that the quotient has the correct positive or negative representation. The most straightforward approach to signed division is to negate any negative operands, perform division on the resulting positive numbers, and then negate the results, as needed.

declare **register** S, A(0:n−1), M(0:n−1), Q(0:n−1), COUNT(0:$\lceil \log_2 n \rceil$ − 1)
declare **bus** INBUS(0:n−1), OUTBUS(0:n−1)

BEGIN: COUNT ← 0, S ← 0,
INPUT: A ← INBUS; {Input the left n bits of the dividend D}
                 Q(0:n−1) ← INBUS(0:n−1); {Input the right n−1 bits of D}
                 M ← INBUS, {Input the divisor}
SUBTRACT: S.A ← S.A − M; {S is the sign of the result}
TEST: **if** S = 0 **then**
                   begin Q(n−1) ← 1;
                   if COUNT = n−1 **then go to** CORRECTION; **else**
                     begin COUNT ← COUNT + 1, S.A.Q(0:n−2) ← A.Q; **end**
                   S.A ← S.A − M, **go to** TEST; **end**
                 else {S = 1}
                   begin Q(n−1) ← 0;
                   if COUNT = n−1 **then go to** CORRECTION; **else**
                     begin COUNT ← COUNT + 1, S.A.Q(0:n−2) ← A.Q; **end**
                   S.A ← S.A + M, **go to** TEST; **end**
CORRECTION: **if** S = 1 **then** S.A ← S.A + M;
OUTPUT: OUTBUS ← Q; {Output the quotient}
                 OUTBUS ← A; {Output the remainder}
END:

FIGURE 3.54
Nonrestoring division algorithm for unsigned integers.

Step	Action	S	A	Q
0	Initialize registers	0	1100	0010 = dividend D
1			1010	= divisor V = M
	Subtract M from A	0	0010	0010
	Set Q(3)	0	0010	0011
	Left shift S.A.Q	0	0100	0110
2			1010	
	Subtract M from A	1	1010	0110
	Set Q(3)	1	1010	0110
	Left shift S.A.Q	1	0100	1100
3			1010	
	Add M to A	1	1110	1100
	Set Q(3)	1	1110	1100
	Left shift S.A.Q	1	1101	1000
4			1010	
	Add M to A	0	0111	1000
	Set Q(3)	0	0111	1001
				1001 = quotient Q
			0111	= remainder R

FIGURE 3.55
Illustration of the nonrestoring division algorithm.

Figure 3.56 illustrates one way of adapting the nonrestoring division algorithm to accommodate twos-complement numbers directly. Here a positive dividend $D = 0.1011_2 = 0.6875_{10}$ is being divided by a negative divisor $V = 1.0001_2 = -0.9375_{10}$ using the nonrestoring algorithm of Fig. 3.54 with suitable changes. Since V is negative, a trial addition is used to determine the quotient bit q_i. If $q_i = 1$, V is subtracted from $2R_i$ in step $i + 1$. Note that it is necessary to correct the quotient by adding 1 to the least significant bit position. The final contents of the A register is the remainder multiplied by 2^4. Thus we conclude that $0.1011 \div 1.0001 = 1.0101 + 0.00001011$. An efficient general division algorithm for twos-complement numbers was devised independently in 1958 by Dura W. Sweeney, James E. Robertson, and Keith D. Tocher, and is called the SRT method in their honor; see Refs. 5 and 25 for details.

Another problem with division not encountered in multiplication is overflow, which occurs when the divisor V is so small relative to the dividend D that the quotient Q lies outside the range of representable numbers. For example, if a fraction format is employed and the magnitude of D exceeds that of V, the correct quotient has a magnitude greater than 1, and so is not representable as a fraction. In the extreme case where $V = 0$, the quotient is undefined. Special circuits are normally appended to dividers to test the input operands before division begins to

Step	Action	A	Q
0	Initialize registers	0.1011	$0.0000 =$ dividend D
1		1.0001	$=$ divisor $V = M$
	Add M to A	1.1100	0.0000
	Set Q(4)	1.1100	0.0001
	Left shift A.Q	1.1000	0.0010
2		1.0001	
	Subtract M from A	0.0111	0.0010
	Set Q(4)	0.0111	0.0010
	Left shift A.Q	0.1110	0.0100
3		1.0001	
	Add M to A	1.1111	0.0100
	Set Q(4)	1.1111	0.0101
	Left shift A.Q	1.1110	0.1010
4		1.0001	
	Subtract M from A	0.1101	0.1010
	Set Q(4)	0.1101	0.1010
	Left shift A.Q	1.1010	1.0100
5	Add 1 to Q(4) to		0.0001
	correct Q		$1.0101 =$ quotient Q
		1.1010	$=$ remainder $R \times 2^4$

FIGURE 3.56
Illustration of nonrestoring division for twos-complement fractions.

see if an overflow or a divide-by-zero condition exists. If so, an appropriate error flag is set, and the division process is aborted. Since the length of the exact quotient is not necessarily bounded, the normal division process terminates when a sufficient number of quotient bits have been generated. The quotient may then be rounded off, which involves an extra addition or subtraction step.

Combinational array dividers. Combinational arrays can be used for division as well as multiplication. Figure 3.57 shows a cell D suitable for implementing a version of the restoring division algorithm. The cell is basically a full subtracter with t and u being the borrow-in and borrow-out bits, respectively. The main output z is controlled by input a. When $a = 0$, z is the difference bit defined by the arithmetic equation $z = x - (y + t)$; when $a = 1$, $z = x$. Thus the behavior of the cell D is defined by the logic equations

$$z = x \oplus \bar{a}\,(y \oplus t)$$

$$u = \bar{x}y + \bar{x}t + yt$$

Figure 3.58 shows an array of D cells that divides two 3-bit positive integers and generates a 5-bit quotient. Each row of the array subtracts the divisor V from the shifted partial remainder $2R_i$ generated by the row above it. The sign of the result, and therefore of the quotient bit, is indicated by the borrow-out signal from the leftmost cell in the row. This signal u_i is connected to the control inputs a of all cells in the same row. If $u_i = 0$, then the output from the row is $2R_i - V$ and $q_i = \bar{u}_i = 1$. If $u_i = 1$, then the output from the row is restored to $2R_i$ and again $q_i = \bar{u}_i = 0$. Thus the output of each row is initially $2R_i - V$, but it is restored to $2R_i$ if required. Note that restoration is achieved by overriding the subtraction performed by the row rather than by explicitly adding back the divisor.

Let d and d' be the carry propagation and restore times of a cell, respectively. Let the divisor and dividend be n bits long. Each row of the divider array functions as an n-bit ripple borrow subtracter; hence the maximum time required to compute one quotient bit is $nd + d'$. The time required to compute an m-bit quotient and the corresponding remainder is therefore $m(nd + d')$, and the number of cells required is $m(n + 1) - 1$.

Division by repeated multiplication. In systems containing a high-speed multiplier, division can be performed efficiently and at low cost using repeated multiplication. In each iteration, a factor F_i is generated and used to multiply both the divisor V

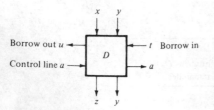

FIGURE 3.57
A cell for array implementation of restoring division.

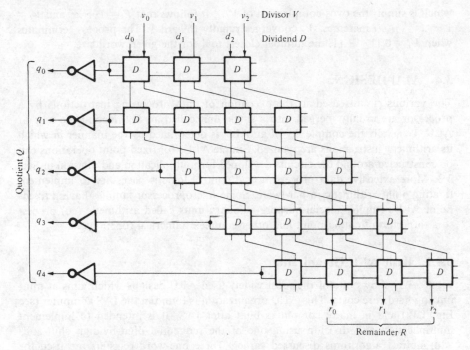

FIGURE 3.58
A divider array for 3-bit positive numbers using the cell of Fig. 3.57.

and the dividend D. F_i is so chosen that the sequence $V \times F_0 \times F_1 \times F_2 \cdots$ converges rapidly toward 1. This implies that $D \times F_0 \times F_1 \times F_2 \cdots$ converges toward the desired quotient Q, since

$$Q = \frac{D \times F_0 \times F_1 \times F_2 \cdots}{V \times F_0 \times F_1 \times F_2 \cdots}$$

If the denominator converges toward 1, the numerator must also converge toward Q.

The convergence of the method depends on the selection of the F_i's. For simplicity, assume that D and V are positive normalized fractions so that $V = 1 - x$, where $x < 1$. Set $F_0 = 1 + x$. We can now write

$$V \times F_0 = (1 - x)(1 + x) = 1 - x^2$$

Clearly $V \times F_0$ is closer to 1 than V. Next set $F_1 = 1 + x^2$. Hence

$$V \times F_0 \times F_1 = (1 - x^2)(1 + x^2) = 1 - x^4$$

and so on. Let V_i denote $V \times F_0 \times F_1 \times \cdots \times F_i$. The multiplication factor at each stage is computed as follows:

$$F_i = 2 - V_{i-1}$$

which is simply the twos-complement of V_{i-1}. It follows that $F_i = 1 + x^{2^i}$ and $V_i = 1 - x^{2^{i+1}}$. As i increases, V_i converges rapidly toward 1. The process terminates when $V_i = 0.11 \cdots 11$, the number closest to 1 for the given word size.

3.4   ALU DESIGN

The various circuits used in the execution of data processing instructions by a processor are usually merged into a single unit called an arithmetic-logic unit or ALU. Generally the complexity of an ALU is determined by the manner in which its arithmetic instructions are realized. Simple ALUs for fixed-point operations can be constructed around the circuits developed for multiplication and division in Sec. 3.3. More extensive data processing and control logic is necessary to implement floating-point arithmetic in hardware. Some microprocessor families having fixed-point ALUs employ special-purpose auxiliary units called arithmetic (co) processors to perform floating-point and other complex numerical functions.

3.4.1   Basic ALU Organization

Figure 3.59 shows one of the most widely used ALU designs which aims at minimizing hardware costs. This ALU organization is found in the IAS computer (see Fig. 1.13) and in many computers built after IAS. It is intended to implement multiplication and division using one of the sequential digit-by-digit shift-and-add/subtract algorithms discussed earlier. Three one-word registers are used for operand storage: the accumulator AC, the multiplier-quotient register MQ, and the data register DR. AC and MQ are organized as a single register AC.MQ capable of left- and right-shifting. The main additional data processing capability is provided by a parallel adder that derives its inputs from AC and DR and places its results in AC. The MQ register is so called because it stores the multiplier during multiplication and the quotient during division. DR stores the multiplicand or divisor, while the result (product or quotient and remainder) is stored in AC.MQ.

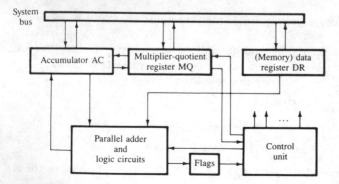

FIGURE 3.59
Structure of a basic fixed-point ALU.

The use typically made of these registers may be defined concisely as follows:

Addition:	$AC \leftarrow AC + DR$
Subtraction:	$AC \leftarrow AC - DR$
Multiplication:	$AC.MQ \leftarrow DR \times MQ$
Division:	$AC.MQ \leftarrow MQ \div DR$
AND:	$AC \leftarrow AC \wedge DR$
OR:	$AC \leftarrow AC \vee DR$
EXCLUSIVE-OR:	$AC \leftarrow AC \oplus DR$
NOT:	$AC \leftarrow \overline{AC}$

In many instances, DR serves as a memory buffer register to store data addressed by an instruction address field ADR. Then DR can be replaced by M(ADR) in the above list of ALU operations, resulting in a one-address memory-referencing format. Processors with the general register organization, like the RISC I and the 68020, have sets of general-purpose registers associated with their ALUs, any members of which can serve as AC, DR, or MQ.

Bit-sliced ALUs. It is quite feasible to manufacture an entire fixed-point ALU on a single IC chip, especially if the word size m is kept fairly small, e.g., 4 or 8 bits. Moreover, such an m-bit ALU can readily be designed to be expandable in that k copies of the ALU chip can be connected to form a single ALU capable of processing km-bit words directly. The resulting arraylike circuit is said to be *bit-sliced*, because each component chip processes an independent "slice" of m bits from each km-bit operand. Bit-sliced ALUs have the advantage that any desired word size, or even several different word sizes, can be handled efficiently simply by selecting the appropriate number of components (bit slices) to use.

Figure 3.60 shows how a 16-bit ALU can be constructed from four 4-bit ALU slices. The data buses and registers of the individual slices are effectively juxtaposed to increase their size from 4 to 16 bits. The control lines that select and sequence the operations to be performed are connected to every slice, so that all slices execute the same actions in step with one another. Each slice thus performs the same operation on a different 4-bit part (slice) of the input operands, and produces only the corresponding part of the results. The required control signals are derived from an external control unit, which is usually microprogrammed. Certain operations require information to be exchanged between slices. For example, if a shift operation is to be implemented, then each slice must send a bit to, and receive a bit from, its left or right neighbors. Similarly, when performing addition or subtraction, carry bits must be transmitted between neighboring slices. For this purpose, horizontal connections are provided between the slices as shown in Fig. 3.60.

Example 3.5 The Advanced Micro Devices 2901 bit-sliced ALU [1, 18]. The 2900 series of bit-sliced components was introduced by AMD in 1976 and has become

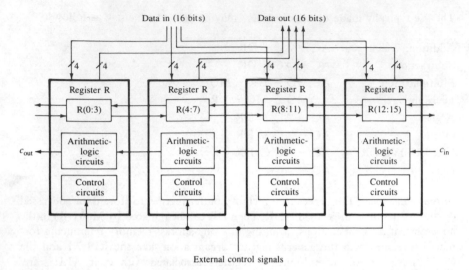

FIGURE 3.60
A 16-bit bit-sliced ALU composed of four 4-bit slices.

widely used in the design of bit-sliced processors. The 2901 IC is the simplest of several 4-bit slices in this family. It has the internal organization depicted in Fig. 3.61 and executes a small and simple set of (micro) instructions. A combinational arithmetic-logic circuit C performs three arithmetic operations (twos-complement addition and subtraction) and five logical operations on 4-bit operands. The particular operation to be carried out by C is defined by a 9-bit (micro) instruction bus I, which is driven by an external microprogram control unit. A pair of combinational shifters allow results generated by C to be left- or right-shifted, in order to facilitate the implementation of multiplication, division, etc., via shift-and-add/subtract algorithms. The 2901 has a general-register organization, with 16 4-bit registers organized as a 16×4-bit RAM. An additional register designated Q is designed to act as the multiplier-quotient register when implementing multiplication or division. C obtains its inputs either from the RAM, Q, or an external input data bus D; all-0 constant input operands may also be specified. The RAM registers to be used as operand sources or destinations are specified by the 4-bit A and B address buses, which are also derived from an external microinstruction. The results generated by C can be stored internally in the 2901 and/or placed on the external output data bus Y.

A set of k 2901s may be interconnected in the one-dimensional array structure of Fig. 3.60 to form a processor with essentially the same properties as the 2901, but handling $4k$-bit instead of 4-bit data. The instruction bus I and the RAM address buses A and B are the main control lines that are connected in common to all slices. Direct connections between the shifters on adjacent slices permit shifting to be extended across the entire processor array. Each slice produces a carry-out signal c_{out} that can be connected to the carry-in line c_{in} of the slice on its left, allowing the arithmetic operations to be extended across the array via the intergroup ripple-carry scheme of Fig. 3.35. (Note that the latter is also a bit-sliced circuit with 4-bit slices).

This design has the disadvantage that carry-propagation times increase rapidly with k. Consequently, the 2901 and other bit-sliced ALUs also support the implementation of carry lookahead in the manner of in Fig. 3.34. To this end, each slice produces (in complemented form) the g and p signals required for carry lookahead, and an external carry-lookahead circuit is used to generate the c_{in} signals for the slices (except the rightmost one) from the g's and p's of all preceding slices. The 2900 series contains an IC for this purpose, namely, the 2902 4-bit carry-lookahead generator, which is a fast two-level logic circuit that implements Eqs. (3.32). The 2901 also produces three flag signals providing status information on the current result F from the arithmetic-logic

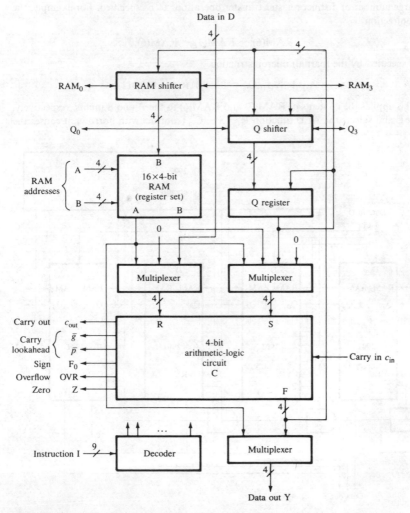

FIGURE 3.61
Structure of the 2901 4-bit ALU slice.

circuit C: the zero flag Z indicates whether the all-zero result $F = 0000$ occurred; the overflow flag OVR indicates whether overflow occurred during arithmetic operations; and the sign flag F_0 is the value of the leftmost bit of F. A 16-bit ALU composed of four copies of the 2901 appears in Fig. 3.62. This circuit employs carry lookahead, and also shows how the flag signals for the array are obtained.

The 9-bit control bus I contains three 3-bit fields, I_S, I_F, and I_D, which specify the operand sources, the ALU function, and the result destinations, respectively; see Fig. 3.63. I_D is also used to control shifting of the result; this is indicated by multiplication by 2 (left shift) or division by 2 (right shift) in the figure. The various possible combinations of the three I fields define the 2901's microinstruction set and enable a large number of distinct register transfer operations to be specified. For example, the subtraction

$$RAM(6) \leftarrow RAM(7) - RAM(6)$$

is specified by the (partial) microinstruction

$$A,B,I_S,I_F,I_D,C_{in} = 0111,0110,001,010,011,0$$

This applies the contents of RAM(7) and RAM(6) to the R and S inputs, respectively, of C and selects the ALU function $R - S - \overline{C}_{in}$ (subtract with borrow); it causes the

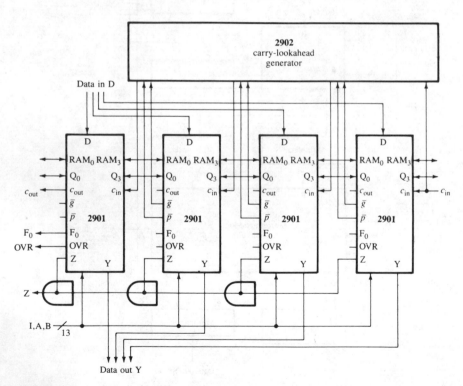

FIGURE 3.62
A 16-bit 4-slice array of 2901s employing carry lookahead.

result on F to be stored back into RAM(6). Although no data-transfer operations are explicitly specified in Fig. 3.63, they are easily obtained from the specified functions. For instance, the operation

$$Q \leftarrow D$$

which loads register Q from an external data source, can be realized via the logical OR operation $Q \leftarrow D \vee 0$ as follows:

$$A,B,I_S,I_F,I_D,C_{in} = dddd,dddd,111,011,000,d \qquad (3.50)$$

where d denotes a don't-care value.

Multiplication and division cannot be bit-sliced in the same way as addition, subtraction, or shifting. However, these operations can be obtained in a bit-sliced

$I_S = I_0 I_1 I_2$	ALU sources	
	R	S
000	RAM(A)	Q
001	RAM(A)	RAM(B)
010	0	Q
011	0	RAM(B)
100	0	RAM(A)
101	D	RAM(A)
110	D	Q
111	D	0

$I_F = I_3 I_4 I_5$	ALU function
000	$R + S + C_{in}$
001	$S - R - \overline{C}_{in}$
010	$R - S - \overline{C}_{in}$
011	$R \vee S$ (OR)
100	$R \wedge S$ (AND)
101	$\overline{R} \wedge S$ (COMPLEMENT-AND)
110	$R \oplus S$ (EXCLUSIVE-OR)
111	$\overline{R \oplus S}$ (EXCLUSIVE-NOR)

$I_D = I_6 I_7 I_8$	ALU destinations and shifts		
	Y	RAM(B)	Q
000	F	—	F
001	F	—	—
010	RAM(A)	F	—
011	F	F	—
100	F	$F \div 2$	$Q \div 2$
101	F	$F \div 2$	—
110	F	$2 \times F$	$2 \times Q$
111	F	$2 \times F$	—

FIGURE 3.63
Microoperations performed by the 2901.

ALU under the control of a microprogram that implements one of the shift-and-add/subtract algorithms described in the preceding section. Figure 3.64 shows how a 4-slice 2901 array can be configured to multiply 16-bit (unsigned) numbers via the basic shift-and-add approach, using three registers: an accumulator A, a multiplicand register M, and a multiplier register Q, as in the multiplication circuit of Fig. 2.57. The roles of the A, M, and Q registers are assigned to the 2901's RAM(B), RAM(A), and Q registers, respectively, where A and B may have any values determined by external signals placed on the corresponding RAM address buses. The shift lines Q_0 and Q_3 serve to link Q registers in the four 2901s to form a 16-bit Q register that can be right-shifted. In the same fashion, the RAM_0 and RAM_3 shift lines effectively link the slices of RAM(B) allowing it to serve as the 16-bit accumulator. Finally, a connection from RAM_3 on the rightmost slice to Q_0 on the leftmost slice links the 16-bit RAM(B) and Q registers to form the 32-bit shift register (A.Q in the original design) where the product is stored.

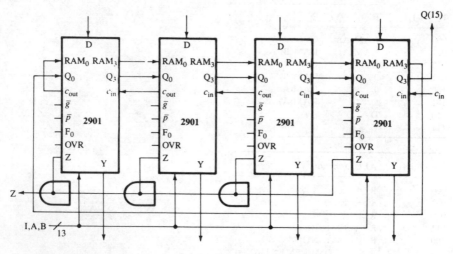

(a)

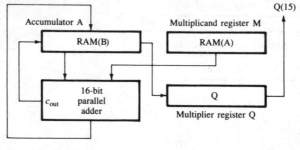

(b)

FIGURE 3.64

A 2901 array configured for 16-bit multiplication: (a) interconnections; (b) register assignments.

Multiplication is initiated by clearing RAM(B) and loading the multiplier X and the multiplicand Y into registers Q and RAM(A), respectively, using appropriate microinstructions. For example, (3.50) is a suitable microinstruction for loading Q. The product P is obtained by executing 16 add-shift steps of the form

> **if** Q(15) = 1 **then** RAM(B) ← RAM(B) + RAM(A);
>
> RAM(B).Q ← RAM(B).Q ÷ 2

(3.51)

We can easily implement (3.51) using one or two microinstructions. If Q(15), which is the output Q_3 from the rightmost slice, can be applied as a variable to line I_2 of the I bus, then (3.51) can be specified by a single microinstruction thus:

$$I_S, I_F, I_D = 0\overline{Q}(15)1{,}000{,}100$$

(3.52)

Note that changing I_S from 001 to 011 changes the ALU function from F ← RAM(A) + RAM(B) to F ← 0 + RAM(B), effectively skipping the addition step. The value of I_D in (3.52) causes the result F to be right-shifted before loading into RAM(B); it also right-shifts Q as specified in Fig. 3.63.

3.4.2 Floating-Point Arithmetic

Let (X_M, X_E) be the floating-point representation of a number X. Hence $X = X_M \times B^{X_E}$. To simplify the discussion, the following realistic assumptions are made:

1. X_M is an n_M-bit binary (twos-complement or sign-magnitude) fraction.
2. X_E is an n_E-bit integer in excess-2^{n_E-1} code, implying an exponent bias of 2^{n_E-1}.
3. $B = 2$.

It is also assumed that floating-point numbers are stored in normalized form only; hence the results of all floating-point arithmetic operations should be normalized.

Basic operations. The formulas to perform floating-point addition, subtraction, multiplication, and division are given in Fig. 3.65. Multiplication and division are relatively simple, since the mantissas and exponents can be processed independently. Floating-point multiplication requires a fixed-point multiplication of the mantissas and a fixed-point addition of the exponents. Floating-point division requires a fixed-point division involving the mantissas and a fixed-point subtraction involving the exponents. Thus multiplication and division are not significantly more difficult to implement than the corresponding fixed-point operations. Floating-point addition and subtraction are complicated by the fact that the exponents of the two input operands must be made equal before the corresponding mantissas can be added or subtracted. As suggested by Fig. 3.65, this can be done by right-shifting the mantissa X_M associated with the smaller exponent X_E a total of $Y_E - X_E$ digit positions to form a new mantissa $X_M 2^{X_E - Y_E}$ which can then be combined with Y_M. Thus addition and subtraction require the following three steps.

Addition:	$X + Y = (X_M 2^{X_E - Y_E} + Y_M) \times 2^{Y_E}$
Subtraction:	$X - Y = (X_M 2^{X_E - Y_E} - Y_M) \times 2^{Y_E}$
Multiplication:	$X \times Y = (X_M \times Y_M) \times 2^{X_E + Y_E}$
Division:	$X \div Y = (X_M \div Y_M) \times 2^{X_E - Y_E}$

where $X_E \leq Y_E$

FIGURE 3.65
The four basic arithmetic operations for floating-point numbers.

1. Compute $Y_E - X_E$ (a fixed-point subtraction).
2. Shift X_M $Y_E - X_E$ places to form $X_M 2^{X_E - Y_E}$.
3. Compute $X_M 2^{X_E - Y_E} \pm Y_M$ (a fixed-point addition or subtraction).

An extra step is needed for each of the four floating-point arithmetic operations in order to normalize the result. A number $X = (X_M, X_E)$ is normalized by left-shifting (right-shifting) X_M and decrementing (incrementing) X_E by 1 for each one-digit shift. As observed earlier, a twos-complement fraction is normalized when the sign bit x_0 differs from the bit x_1 on its right. This fact may be used to terminate the normalization process. A sign-magnitude fraction is normalized by left-shifting the magnitude part until there are no leading 0s, that is, until $x_1 = 1$. (The normalization rules are different if the base B differs from 2.) The leftmost bit of the mantissa may be hidden, since normalization fixes its value; see the discussion of the IEEE 754 floating-point standard in Example 3.1.

Several minor problems are associated with the use of exponent biasing. If exponents are added or subtracted using ordinary integer arithmetic in the course of a floating-point calculation, the resulting exponent is doubly biased and must be corrected by subtracting the bias. For example, let the exponent length be 4, and let the bias be $2^{4-1} = 8$. Suppose that $X_E = +7$ and $Y_E = -3$ are to be added. If ordinary integer addition is used, we obtain the following (ignoring the sign bits).

	Unbiased equivalent
$X_E = 1111$	$15 = 7 + 8$
$X_Y = 0101$	$5 = -3 + 8$
10100	$20 = 4 + 8 + 8$

The integer sum 10100 is now corrected by subtracting the bias 1000 to produce 1100, which is the correct biased representation of $X_E + Y_E = 4$. Of course, the correction step could be avoided by using an excess-eight adder. Another problem arises from the all-0 representation usually required of zero. If $X \times Y$ is computed as $(X_M \times Y_M) \times 2^{X_E + Y_E}$ and either X_M or Y_M is zero, the resulting product has an all-0 mantissa but may not have an all-0 exponent. A special step is then required to set the exponent bits to 0.

All the floating-point operations can lead to overflow or underflow if the result is too large or too small to be represented. Overflow or underflow resulting from mantissa operations can usually be corrected by shifting the mantissa of the result and modifying its exponent. This is done automatically during floating-point processing. If, however, the exponent ever overflows or underflows, an appropriate error signal indicating floating-point overflow or underflow is generated. A floating-point result that has overflowed may be retained in denormalized form as discussed in Example 3.1.

To preserve accuracy during floating-point calculations one or more extra bits called *guard bits* are temporarily attached to right end of the mantissa $x_0.x_1x_2 \cdots x_n$. For example, a guard bit x_{n+1} is needed when results are to be rounded rather than truncated to n bits; rounding is accomplished by adding 1 to x_{n+1} and then truncating the result to n bits. When a mantissa is right-shifted during the alignment step of addition or subtraction, the bits shifted from the right end may be retained as guard bits. In the case of floating-point multiplication, bits from the right half of the $2n$-bit result of multiplying two n-bit (unsigned) mantissas serve as guard bits. Suppose, for instance, that $X_M = 0.1 \cdots$ and $Y_M = 0.1 \cdots$ are normalized positive mantissas (fractions). Multiplying them by a standard fixed-point multiplication algorithm yields an unnormalized double-length result of the form

$$P_M = X_M \times Y_M = 0.01 \cdots \tag{3.53}$$

which contains a leading 0. If P_M is now truncated or rounded to n bits, then the precision of the result is only $n - 1$ bits. It is clearly desirable to retain an additional bit from the double-length product so that when (3.53) is normalized by a left shift, the result contains n significant bits. We may therefore employ two guard bits in this case, one to maintain precision during normalization and one for rounding purposes.

Floating-point ALUs. Floating-point arithmetic can be implemented by two loosely connected fixed-point arithmetic circuits, an exponent unit and a mantissa unit, as suggested in Fig. 3.66. The mantissa unit is required to perform all four basic operations on the mantissas; hence a general-purpose fixed-point arithmetic unit such as that of Fig. 3.59 can be used. A simpler circuit capable of only adding, subtracting, and comparing exponents suffices for the exponent unit. Exponent comparison may be performed by a comparator or else by subtracting the exponents. Figure 3.67 shows the general structure of a floating-point arithmetic unit

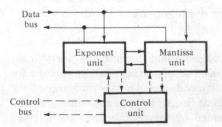

FIGURE 3.66
A floating-point arithmetic unit viewed as two fixed-point arithmetic units.

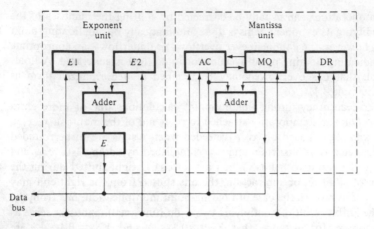

FIGURE 3.67
Data processing part of a simple floating-point arithmetic unit.

employing the latter approach. The exponents of the input operands are placed in registers $E1$ and $E2$, which are connected to a parallel adder that permits $E1 \pm E2$ to be computed. The exponent comparison required for floating-point addition and subtraction is performed by computing $E1 - E2$ and placing it in a counter E. The larger exponent is then determined by the sign of E. Furthermore, the shifting of one mantissa required before the mantissa addition or subtraction can take place is easily controlled by E. The magnitude of E is sequentially decremented to zero. After each decrement, the appropriate mantissa (whose location in the mantissa unit varies with the operation being performed) is shifted one digit position. Once the mantissas have been aligned, they are processed in the normal manner. The exponent of the result is also computed and placed in E.

Although the scheme of Fig. 3.67 is conceptually simple, it has the disadvantage that it can be used for n-bit (one-word) floating-point operations only, even though it has most of the facilities required for n-bit fixed-point operations. Since all computers with floating-point instructions also have fixed-point instructions, it is often desirable to design a single unit for both fixed-point and floating-point instruction execution. In principle, this is not difficult, although a more complicated control unit is needed. Essentially it has the form of a one-word fixed-point arithmetic unit in which the registers and the adder can be partitioned into exponent and mantissa parts when floating-point operations are being performed.

Addition. We now consider the implementation of floating-point addition in more detail. Figure 3.68 describes a basic addition algorithm intended for use with the ALU of Fig. 3.67. With minor modifications, this algorithm can also be used for floating-point subtraction. The mantissa is assumed to be a binary fraction, and the exponent a biased integer. The base B is 2. The first step of the algorithm is equalization of the exponents, which is implemented by subtracting them and aligning the mantissas by shifting one of them until the difference between the exponents has been reduced to zero. Next the aligned mantissas are added. Finally the result is normalized, if necessary, by again shifting the mantissa and making a compensating change in the exponent. The mantissa and exponent of the final result are placed in the AC and E registers, respectively. Tests are also performed for floating-point overflow and underflow; if either occurs, the flag ERROR is set to 1. A separate test is made for a zero result which, if indicated by AC = 0, causes E to be set to 0 also.

Several improvements could be made to this algorithm, which are left as an exercise (Prob. 3.34). Time can be saved by checking if one of the input operands X or Y is zero at the start, and simply making the nonzero operand the result. If both X and Y are 0, either operand may be used as the result. If the difference E between exponents is very large ($|E| > n_M$), then the shifting process to align one of the mantissas, say X_M in AC, will result in AC = 0 after n_M steps; continued shifting to make $E = 0$ will not affect the result, which in this case will be Y_M. Note also that it would be more efficient to terminate the shifting after n_M steps instead of $|E|$ steps, as is done in Fig. 3.68. A shift counter could be included in the design to implement this.

---

	declare register AC(0:n_M−1), DR(0:n_M−1), E1(0:n_E−1),
	E2(0:n_E−1), E(0:n_E−1), AC_OVERFLOW, ERROR
BEGIN:	AC_OVERFLOW←0, ERROR ← 0,
LOAD:	E1 ← X_E, AC ← X_M;
	E2 ← Y_E, DR ← Y_M;

[Compare and equalize exponents]

COMPARE:	E ← E1 − E2;
EQUALIZE:	if E < 0 then AC ← **right-shift**(AC), E ← E + 1,
	go to EQUALIZE; **else**
	if E > 0 then DR ← **right-shift**(DR), E ← E − 1,
	go to EQUALIZE;

{Add mantissas}

ADD:	AC ← AC + DR, E ← **max**(E1,E2);

{Adjust for mantissa overflow and check for exponent overflow}

OVERFLOW:	if AC_OVERFLOW = 1 **then begin**
	if E = E_{MAX} **then go to** ERROR;
	AC ← **right-shift**(AC), E ← E + 1, **go to** END; **end**

{Adjust for zero result}

ZERO:	if AC = 0 **then** E ← 0, **go to** END;

{Normalize result}

NORMALIZE:	if AC is normalized **then go to** END;
UNDERFLOW:	if E > E_{MIN} **then begin**
	AC ← **left-shift**(AC), E ← E − 1, **go to** NORMALIZE;

{Set error flag indicating overflow or underflow}

ERROR:	ERROR ← 1;
END:	

FIGURE 3.68
Algorithm for floating-point addition.

We conclude with a description of the floating-point adder used in a high-performance scientific computer, the IBM System/360 Model 91. (This machine was withdrawn by IBM shortly after its announcement in 1965, but it influenced a number of later S/360-370 models). Two separate floating-point arithmetic units are employed, one for addition and subtraction (the add unit), the other for multiplication and division (the multiply-divide unit). For a description of the multiply-divide unit, see Refs. 2 and 24.

Example 3.6 Floating-point adder of the IBM System/360 Model 91 computer [2]. The data processing part of the adder (with minor simplifications) is shown in Fig. 3.69. It is designed to add or subtract floating-point numbers with the 32-bit and 64-bit formats of Fig. 1.31. The general algorithm of Fig. 3.68 is used with some changes to increase speed. In particular, the shifting required to align the mantissas and subsequently to normalize their sum is carried out by combinational (barrel) shifters. These shifters allow k hexadecimal digits (recall that base 16 rather than base 2 is used in the S/360-370 series) to be shifted simultaneously. The corresponding subtraction of k from the exponent required in normalization is also achieved in one step by using an additional adder (adder 3).

    The operation of this unit will now be described. The exponents of the input operands are placed in registers $E1$ and $E2$ and the corresponding mantissas are placed in $M1$ and $M2$. Next $E2$ is subtracted from $E1$ using adder 1, and the result is

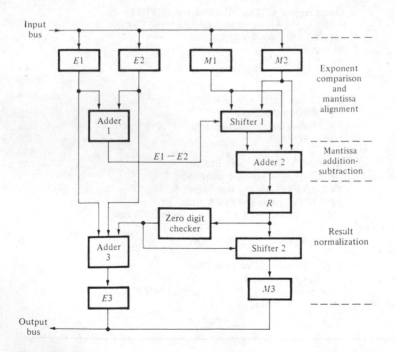

FIGURE 3.69
Floating-point adder of the IBM System/360 Model 91.

used to select the mantissa to be right-shifted by shifter 1, and also to determine the length of the shift. For example, if $E1 > E2$ and $E1 - E2 = k$, $M2$ is right-shifted by k digit positions, that is, $4k$ bit positions. The shifted mantissa is then added to or subtracted from the other mantissa using adder 2, a 56-bit parallel adder with several levels of carry lookahead. The resulting sum or difference is placed in a temporary register R where it is examined by a special combinational circuit called the zero digit checker. The output z of this circuit indicates the number of leading zero digits (or leading F's in the case of negative numbers) of the number in R. z is then used to control the final normalization step. The output of R is left-shifted z digits by shifter 2 and the result is placed in register $M3$. The corresponding adjustment is made to the exponent by subtracting z using adder 3. In the event that $R = 0$, adder 3 can be used to set all bits of $E3$ to 0, which denotes an exponent of -64.

3.4.3 Arithmetic Processors

A typical CPU devotes a considerable amount of control and data processing hardware to implementing nonarithmetic functions. Consequently, the hardware costs in terms of IC count or chip area associated with implementing the more complex arithmetic operations like floating-point instructions often prevent their inclusion in the CPU's instruction set. Such CPUs must rely on much slower software routines to provide the missing arithmetic operations. If, however, a processor is devoted exclusively to arithmetic functions, then a full range of numerical operations can be implemented in hardware at relatively low cost, e.g., in a single IC. An example of this is found in the one-chip processors used in pocket calculators. This concept can be applied to CPU design by providing auxiliary special-purpose *arithmetic processors* that are physically separate from the CPU, but are used by it to execute a class of arithmetic instructions which are not executable by the CPU itself. Auxiliary processors of this kind speed up program execution by replacing software routines with hardware; they can also reduce programming complexity. The instructions assigned to arithmetic processors include the basic add, subtract, multiply, and divide operations on fixed-point and floating-point operands of various lengths, as well as exponentiation, logarithms, and trigonometric functions.

There are two general ways of introducing arithmetic processors into a computer. In the first approach, the arithmetic processor is simply treated as a peripheral or IO device to which the CPU sends (outputs) data and processing instructions, and from which it receives (inputs) results; we term this a *peripheral processor*. A peripheral processor therefore has a number of registers for communication with the CPU which are assigned addresses in the CPU's memory or IO address space. The CPU and the peripheral processor are quite independent, and they exchange information via data-transfer instructions that must be explicitly programmed into the CPU's instruction stream. In the second approach, the arithmetic processor is closely coupled to the CPU so that its instructions and register set are extensions to those of the CPU. The CPU's instruction set contains a special subset of opcodes reserved for the auxiliary processors. These instructions are fetched by the CPU, jointly decoded by the CPU and the auxiliary processor, and finally executed directly by the auxiliary processor in a manner that is transparent to the programmer. Arithmetic processors of this type form a logical extension to the CPU and are termed *coprocessors.*

Peripheral processors. Peripheral arithmetic processors such as the AMD 9511/12 one-chip floating-point processors [6] have the advantage that they can be used with any host CPU. Their main disadvantage compared with coprocessors is their need for explicitly programmed and relatively slow communication links with the host. Peripheral processors are used in the following fashion.

1. The CPU executes a series of data-transfer instructions that send a set of input operands and command information, e.g., the type of arithmetic operation to be performed, to registers in the peripheral processor. Note that the command to the peripheral processor is simply treated as data by the host CPU.
2. The peripheral processor decodes and executes the command received from the CPU, generating a result that it places in registers accessible to the CPU.
3. The CPU determines that the peripheral processor has completed its task either by checking its status, e.g., by polling a predetermined status register, or else by receiving an interrupt signal from the peripheral processor.
4. The CPU then obtains the results from the peripheral processor by executing more data-transfer instructions.

Note that the CPU may proceed to other tasks while the peripheral processor is busy. In many cases, however, the CPU must wait for the result of the peripheral processor's computations, in which case the CPU can be idle for an extended period.

Coprocessors. Unlike a peripheral processor, a coprocessor is tailored to a particular CPU family. Each CPU is designed with a coprocessor interface that includes special control circuits linking the CPU with the coprocessor, and special instructions designated for execution by the coprocessor. The communication between the CPU and coprocessor to initiate and terminate execution of instructions by the coprocessor is implemented automatically in hardware, so that coprocessor instructions appear in assembly- or machine-language programs just like any other CPU instructions. Even if no coprocessor is present, coprocessor instructions can be included in CPU programs, since if the CPU knows that no coprocessor is available, it can transfer program control to a predetermined memory location where a software routine implementing the desired operation can be stored. This type of CPU-generated interruption of normal program flow is termed a (coprocessor) trap. Thus the coprocessor approach makes it possible to provide either hardware or software support for certain instructions without altering the source or object code of the program being executed.

   The general structure of the hardware side of a CPU-coprocessor interface is depicted by Fig. 3.70. The coprocessor sits idly until a coprocessor instruction is encountered. It is directly linked to the CPU by a small number of control lines

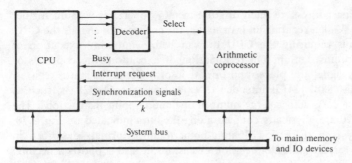

FIGURE 3.70
Typical connections between a CPU and an arithmetic coprocessor.

that allow the activities of the two processors to be rapidly synchronized. Both processors are connected to the system bus, which therefore can be used in normal fashion for interprocessor data transfers. The coprocessor may be a passive or slave device whose registers can be written into and read by the CPU in the same manner as main memory. It is also useful to permit the coprocessor to control the system bus, so that it can initiate data transfers to and from the CPU and, for that matter, to and from main memory.

Coprocessor instructions typically contain the following three fields: a unique opcode F_0 that identifies coprocessor instructions, the address F_1 of the particular coprocessor to be used if several coprocessors can be attached to the system, and finally the type F_2 of the particular instruction or command to be executed by the coprocessor. The F_2 field may also include (partial) operand addressing information. By having the coprocessor monitor the system bus, it can decode and identify coprocessor instructions at the same time as the CPU, and can then proceed to execute them directly. This approach is taken by the 8087 arithmetic coprocessor of the Intel 8086 series. Alternatively, the CPU alone can decode the coprocessor instructions, as is done in systems employing the 68881 floating-point coprocessor of the Motorola 68000 series. After decoding the F_0 and F_1 fields of a coprocessor instruction, the CPU "wakes up" the required coprocessor P by sending it certain control signals. The CPU then transmits F_2 to a predefined location in P that serves as the latter's command register. F_2 is decoded by P, and execution of the specified operation is initiated.

Usually it is necessary for the CPU to provide P with the addresses of the operands or, perhaps, the actual operand values, needed by the coprocessor. Several approaches to this are possible. The host CPU can read a special status register in P that specifies P's operand requirements, which the CPU can then proceed to satisfy by performing effective address calculations and/or initiating data transfers. In the 8087 case, for example, the CPU automatically responds to a coprocessor opcode by initiating a dummy memory read cycle (one making no use of the data bus), which places a memory address on the system address bus. This address is then read by the coprocessor, which subsequently uses it and other addresses derived from the first address, to fetch or store memory operands without further CPU involvement. While executing an instruction, the coprocessor signals the CPU that it is busy, thus requiring the CPU to wait before initiating execution of another coprocessor instruction. On termination of execution, the coprocessor deactivates its busy signal and places appropriate information in its status register.

The Motorola 68881 [14] is intended to extend 68000-series CPUs, such as the 68020 (Example 1.7), with a large number of floating-point instructions. The 68881 and the 68020 are physically coupled along the lines indicated by Fig. 3.70. The 68881 employs the IEEE 754 floating-point number formats described in Example 3.1, with certain multiple-precision extensions; it also supports a decimal floating-point format. From the programmer's perspective, the 68881 adds the following registers to the CPU: a set of eight 80-bit floating-point data registers FP0:FP7, and several 32-bit control registers including command and status registers. Besides providing a complete range of arithmetic operations for floating-point numbers, the 68881 has instructions for transferring data to and from its registers, and for branching on conditions it encounters during instruction execution. The 68881's instructions are summarized in Fig. 3.71. They are distinguished by the prefix F (floating-point) in their mnemonic opcodes and are used in assembly-language programs just like regular 68000-series instructions; see Fig. 1.40. The status information (condition codes) generated by the 68881 in executing floating-point instructions include invalid operation, overflow, underflow, division by zero, and inexact result. Coprocessor status is recorded in a control register, which is read by the host CPU at the end of a set of calculations, enabling the CPU to initiate the appropriate exception-processing response. Because some of its instructions have relatively long execution times, the 68881 can be interrupted in the middle of instruction execution. Its state must then be saved in main memory and subsequently restored to complete execution of the interrupted instruction at a later time.

3.5 SUMMARY

The primary purpose of an instruction set processor such as a CPU is to fetch instructions from an external memory and execute them. The functions performed by a CPU are defined by its instruction set. An instruction specifies an opcode and a set of operands or data words. A variety of different techniques (addressing modes) are used to specify operands, including immediate, direct, indirect, indexed, and stack addressing. Operands may be located in main memory or in registers in the processor itself; the latter can be accessed more rapidly by the processor. To reduce instruction length, operand addresses, especially those referring to registers, are often implicitly included in an instruction's opcode. If m is the maximum number of explicit memory addresses allowed in a processor's instruction formats, then the processor is called an m-address machine.

Precise criteria for the design of instruction sets are difficult to formulate, but the instruction set should be complete, efficient, and easy to use in some broad sense. Instructions may be grouped into five major types: data transfer, arithmetic,

Opcode	Operation specified	Opcode	Operation specified
FADD	Add	FABS	Absolute value
FSUB	Subtract	FNEG	Negate
FMUL	Multiply	FSQRT	Square root
FDIV	Divide	FNOP	No operation
FCMP	Compare	FGETEXP	Get exponent
FREM	Remainder (IEEE format)	FGETMAN	Get mantissa
FMOD	Modulo remainder	FINT	Integer
FSGLMUL	Single-precision multiply	FTEST	Test
FSGLDIV	Single-precision divide	NSCALE	Scale exponent by integer
		FMOVE	Move word to/from coprocessor data or control register
FACOS	Arc cosine		
FASIN	Arc sine		
FATAN	Arc tangent	FMOVEM	Move multiple words to/from coprocessor
FATANH	Hyperbolic arc tangent		
FCOS	Cosine	FMOVECR	Move word to/from ROM storing constants
FCOSH	Hyperbolic cosine		
FETOX	e to the power of x		
FETOXM1	(e to the power of x) minus 1	FSAVE	Save coprocessor data
FLOG10	Logarithm to the base 10	FRESTORE	Restore coprocessor data
FLOG2	Logarithm to the base 2		
FLOGN	Logarithm of x to the base e		
FLOGNP1	Logarithm of $x + 1$ to the base e	FBcc	Branch if condition code (status) cc is 1
FSIN	Sine		
FSINCOS	Simultaneous sine and cosine	FDBcc	Test, decrement count, and branch on cc
FSINH	Hyperbolic sine		
FTAN	Tangent	FScc	Set ($cc = 1$) or reset ($cc = 0$) a specified byte
FTANH	Hyperbolic tangent		
FTENTOX	Ten to the power of x	FTcc	Conditional trap
FTWOTOX	Two to the power of x	FTPcc	Conditional trap with parameter

FIGURE 3.71
Instruction set of the Motorola 68881 floating-point arithmetic coprocessor.

logical, program control, and input-output. All practical computers contain at least a few instructions of each type, although in theory one or two instructions suffice to perform all computations. RISCs (reduced instruction set computers) are characterized by small instruction sets that have fast hardwired implementations, and are supported by efficient compilers. While the more commonly used CISC instruction sets are larger and in some ways more complex, they simplify the programming of complex functions like floating-point operations and reduce their execution time. Programming of all types of processors can be simplified by the use of subroutines and macroinstructions. The power of a processor's instruction set is sometimes measured by the arithmetic instructions it contains. The arithmetic functions of simpler machines such as RISCs is limited to the addition and subtraction of fixed-point numbers. More powerful processors are capable of multiplication and division, and in many cases floating-point arithmetic.

The two major number formats are fixed-point and floating-point. Fixed-point numbers may be binary or decimal, where decimal means a binary code such as BCD that preserves the decimal weights found in ordinary (radix 10) decimal numbers. The most common binary number codes are sign magnitude and twos complement. Each code simplifies the implementation of certain arithmetic operations. Twos complement, for example, simplifies the implementation of subtraction, so it is preferred in most applications. A floating-point number comprises a pair of fixed-point numbers, a mantissa M, and an exponent E, and is used to represent numbers of the form $M \times B^E$, where B is an implicit base. Floating-point numbers greatly increase the range obtainable using a given word size but require much more complex arithmetic circuits than fixed-point numbers. In order to provide a unique representation for every number, floating-point numbers are normalized.

Arithmetic circuit design is a well-developed field. Fixed-point addition is easily implemented using a variety of combinational circuits. One of the simplest is a ripple carry adder. High-speed adders attempt to reduce carry propagation time by techniques such as carry lookahead. Fixed-point multiplication and division are generally implemented by algorithms that are similar to manual methods. The product or quotient of two km-bit numbers may be formed in k sequential steps, where each step involves an m-bit shift and, possibly, a km-bit addition or subtraction. Division is inherently more difficult than multiplication due to the problem of determining the quotient digit. Both multiplication and division can be implemented by combinational logic circuits, but at a substantial increase in the amount of hardware required.

An ALU to execute all the basic fixed-point instructions can be constructed from a few (shift) registers, a parallel adder-subtracter, and some control logic. A complete ALU for m-bit operands can be placed in a single IC in such a way that k copies of the ALU can be connected to form a km-bit ALU, which is termed bit-sliced. ALUs to execute floating-point instructions typically comprise a pair of fixed-point ALUs to process exponents and mantissas, with special circuits for normalization and, in the case of addition and subtraction, exponent comparison and mantissa alignment. Floating-point and other complex numerical operations may be implemented in an arithmetic processor, which can either be a special-purpose peripheral device or else a program-transparent extension to the CPU called a coprocessor.

PROBLEMS

3.1. Define the role of each of the following components in the operation of an instruction set processor: program counter, flag (status) register, stack pointer register.

3.2. The usual objection to tagged architecture is that the presence of tags in stored data increases memory size and cost. It has been argued, however, that tags can actually reduce storage requirements by decreasing program size. Analyze the validity of this argument.

3.3. Figure 3.72 lists all the 16 code words of a Hamming code designed to check 4-bit words using three check bits. Prove that all single-bit errors can be corrected and all double-bit errors detected by this code.

3.4. Developments in LSI/VLSI technology have made it feasible to build computers with identical CPU and memory cycle times. Presumably this makes it also feasible to treat a large main memory as a set of CPU registers and to eliminate all the operand registers usually included in the CPU such as the accumulator. Discuss the advantages and disadvantages of doing this.

3.5. Using 32-bit integer formats, give the sign-magnitude, twos-complement, and BCD representation of each of the following decimal numbers: $+999$, -999, $+1000$, -1000, zero. State your assumptions concerning sign representation.

3.6. Let $X = x_0 x_1 \cdots x_{n-1}$ be a negative twos-complement integer. Prove that the following relation holds:

$$X = -2^n + \sum_{i=1}^{n-1} 2^{n-i-1} x_i$$

3.7. Discuss the relative advantages of sign-magnitude and twos-complement number codes in representing the mantissa of floating-point numbers.

3.8. Consider the 64-bit IEEE floating-point number format defined in Sec. 3.1.3. Determine the largest positive number, the smallest nonzero positive number, and the negative number with the largest magnitude that can be represented in this format. Assume that the three numbers are to be normalized, and give your answers in the form of 16-digit hexadecimal strings.

3.9. Repeat Prob. 3.8 for the 64-bit IBM S/360-370 floating-point number format which is also defined in Sec. 3.1.3.

3.10. Write a brief note comparing and contrasting the IEEE 754 and IBM S360/370 32-bit floating-point number formats from the viewpoints of range, precision, and handling of exceptions.

3.11. A 32-bit floating-point number format is defined as follows. The leftmost bit is the sign of the number. The next 10 bits form an exponent with bias 2^9. The remaining 21

Information bits				Check bits		
0	0	0	0	0	0	0
0	0	0	1	1	1	1
0	0	1	0	1	1	0
0	0	1	1	0	0	1
0	1	0	0	1	0	1
0	1	0	1	0	1	0
0	1	1	0	0	1	1
0	1	1	1	1	0	0
1	0	0	0	0	1	1
1	0	0	1	1	0	0
1	0	1	0	1	0	1
1	0	1	1	0	1	0
1	1	0	0	1	1	0
1	1	0	1	0	0	1
1	1	1	0	0	0	0
1	1	1	1	1	1	1

FIGURE 3.72
Hamming SECDED code for 4-bit words.

bits constitute a mantissa that represents a fraction in twos-complement code. All numbers are required to be normalized. Determine the correct representation of the following four numbers, giving your answer in the form of a 32-bit binary string: plus 10; minus 10; n_{MAX}, which is the largest positive number that can be represented; minus n_{MAX}.

3.12. Computers such as the IBM S360/370 allow the results of some floating-point instructions to be retained in unnormalized form; see, for example, Fig. 1.34. What are the advantages of giving the programmer unnormalized results?

3.13. A floating-point processor is being designed with a number format that must meet the following requirements.

1. Numbers in the range $\pm 1.0 \times 10^{\pm 50}$ must be represented.
2. The precision required is six decimal digits, i.e., the six most significant digits of the decimal equivalent of every number in the required range must be representable.
3. The representation of each number should be unique. Zero is to be represented by a sequence of 0s.
4. Binary arithmetic is to be used throughout with $B = 2$, where B is the floating-point number base.

Design a number format that satisfies these requirements and uses as few bits as possible. Indicate clearly the number codes used and why they were chosen.

3.14. Discuss the advantages and disadvantages of choosing 2^k where $k > 1$ rather than 2 as the base B for floating-point number representation.

3.15. Consider a set of four processors P_0, P_1, P_2, and P_3, where P_i is an i-address machine. P_0 is a zero-address stack machine similar to the Burroughs B5000 (see also Prob. 3.20), while $P_1:P_3$ are conventional computers each with 16 general-purpose registers R0:R15 for data and address storage. All four processors have instructions with the (assembly-language) opcodes ADD, SUB, MUL, and DIV to implement the operations $+$, $-$, $\times$, and $/$, respectively.

(a) Using as few instructions as you can, write a program for each of the four machines to evaluate the following arithmetic expression:

$$X \leftarrow (A/B + C \times D)/(D \times E - F + C/A) + G$$

Use standard names for any additional instructions that you need, e.g., LOAD, PUSH, etc.

(b) Calculate the total object program size in bits for each of your four programs assuming the following data on machine-language instruction formats: opcodes (which contain no addressing information) are 8 bits long; memory address length is 16 bits; and register address length is 4 bits. (For example, the two-address instruction LOAD R7,B for P_2, which denotes R7 $\leftarrow$ M(B), occupies $8 + 4 + 16 = 28$ bits.)

3.16. In most processors with k-bit opcode fields there are fewer than 2^k distinct instruction types; consequently some opcode patterns are *invalid*, that is, they do not correspond to defined instructions. The processor may occasionally fetch and attempt to decode and execute invalid opcodes due to programming errors or hardware failures. Describe a suitable course of action for the processor to take when it detects an invalid opcode. (Many microprocessors have no mechanism for handling invalid opcodes, and their attempted execution results in unpredictable behavior.)

3.17. A new microprocessor is being designed with a conventional architecture employing single-address instructions and 8-bit words. Due to physical size constraints, only eight distinct 3-bit opcodes are allowed. The use of modifiers or the address field to extend the opcodes is forbidden.

(*a*) What eight instructions would you implement? Specify the operations performed by each instruction as well as the location of its operands.

(*b*) Demonstrate that your instruction set is functionally complete in some reasonable sense; or if it is not, describe an operation that cannot be programmed using your instruction set.

3.18. Many computers contain the instruction NOP, meaning no operation, which has no effect on the CPU state other than causing the program counter to be incremented. List as many uses for NOP as you can.

3.19. Consider a simple hypothetical computer with a main memory M having a capacity of 2^{n-1} n-bit words. The CPU contains an n-bit accumulator AC and an $(n - 1)$-bit program counter PC. It has a repertoire of two n-bit instructions in which the leftmost bit is the opcode and the remaining bits form an address in M. The first instruction is called SUBS (subtract and store). SUBS X causes the following microoperations to take place:

$$AC \leftarrow AC - M(X);$$

$$M(X) \leftarrow AC, PC \leftarrow PC + 1;$$

The second instruction is an unconditional branch JUMP X, which causes the following operation to take place:

$$PC \leftarrow M(X(0:n - 2));$$

A word in M may be either an instruction (SUBS or JUMP) or a fixed-point binary number in twos-complement code. Prove informally that this instruction set is complete by demonstrating that the following operations can be programmed.

(*a*) The memory data transfers $AC \leftarrow M(X)$ and $M(X) \leftarrow AC$

(*b*) The addition operation $AC \leftarrow AC + M(X)$

(*c*) Conditional branching

(*d*) The logical OR operation $AC \leftarrow AC \lor M(X)$

(*e*) Input-output transfers

3.20. A hypothetical stack-oriented computer called HAYSTACK has a pushdown stack S in its CPU in place of the usual data and address registers. HAYSTACK employs the following seven zero-address data processing instructions: ADD, SUBTRACT, MULTIPLY, DIVIDE, AND, OR, and NOT. It also has the instructions PUSH X and POP X, where X is a main memory address. Instruction sequencing is controlled by three instructions BT X (branch if true), BF X (branch if false), and the zero-address instruction COMP (compare), which make use of two special words (constants) denoted TRUE and FALSE. Let S(TOP) and S(TOP − 1) denote the top and next-to-top words, respectively, in S. BZ X tests S(TOP) and causes a branch to X if S(TOP) = TRUE, while BZN X also tests S(TOP) and causes a branch to X if S(TOP) = FALSE. The third program-control instruction COMP pops S(TOP) and S(TOP-1) and compares them. If S(TOP) = S(TOP − 1), then COMP pushes TRUE; otherwise it pushes FALSE. Using as few instructions as you can, write HAYSTACK programs to implement each of the following high-level language statements:

(*a*) $Z \leftarrow (A - B/C) + D;$

(*b*) **if** $A \oplus B \neq C$ **then** $C \leftarrow D$ **else go to** E;

3.21. Compare and contrast RISC and CISC architectures, illustrating your answer with the RISC I (Example 3.2) and any CISC machine of your choosing.

3.22. List the types of branch instructions commonly found in (CISC) instruction sets, and give one general application for which each instruction you name is well suited.

3.23. A computer's performance is often improved by prefetching the next instruction while executing the current instruction. This technique is ineffective when the current instruction causes a branch to a nonconsecutive instruction address. To deal with this, several RISCs have a special type of branch instruction JUMPX L called a *delayed branch* or *branch with execute* which, unlike a normal branch, always causes the CPU to execute the instruction I′ immediately following the delayed branch instruction while the instruction at the branch target address L is being fetched. The effect of the branch is thus delayed until immediately after I′ has been executed, but the CPU is no longer idle while branch instructions are being processed. Discuss, using a simple example to illustrate your answer, how a compiler might be designed to replace normal branches automatically by delayed branches in order to improve the performance of the compiled code.

3.24. There are few well-defined general principles concerning hardware-software tradeoffs in processor design. Two recently proposed principles of this type are given below. Write a brief note on each, illustrating it with examples.

(*a*) "Whenever there is a system function that is expensive and slow in all its generality, but where software can recognize a frequently occurring degenerate case (or can move the entire function from run time to compile time) that function [should be] moved from hardware to software, resulting in lower cost *and* improved performance." (George Radin, 1983)

(*b*) "Simple, frequent, and highly-skew conditional branches [e.g., tests for arithmetic overflow] should be implemented in hardware [rather than software]." (Brian Randell, 1985)

3.25. (*a*) Explain how directives differ from other assembly-language instructions.

(*b*) List the criteria for using macros instead of subroutines to structure assembly-language programs.

3.26. Consider the processor and memory state depicted in Fig. 3.29, and suppose that execution of the subroutine continues to completion. Let the subroutine's RETURN instruction be stored in memory location 2500 (decimal). Draw a diagram similar to Fig. 3.29 that shows the system state at the same three points during the execution of RETURN.

3.27. Write a note comparing and contrasting ripple-carry, carry-lookahead, and carry-save adders in terms of speed, hardware complexity, and the handling of signed binary numbers. (Note that addition of a negative number corresponds to subtraction of a positive number.)

3.28. Let X^* be the canonical signed-digit representation of a fixed-point n-bit number defined by Fig. 3.45. Prove each of the following.

(*a*) Every two nonzero digits in X^* are separated by at least one zero.

(*b*) The average number of nonzero digits in n-bit canonical signed-digit numbers is $n/3$.

3.29. Design a combinational array circuit to multiply two 4-bit positive binary numbers using the cell M of Fig. 3.48.

3.30. Figure 3.73 shows a cell $M′$ intended for a twos-complement combinational array multiplier that implements Booth's algorithm. $M′$ is capable of acting as a full adder or a full subtracter. The particular operation to be performed by M' is specified by the control lines a and b in the following way.

a	b	Operation
0	—	None
1	0	Addition
1	1	Subtraction

The main data inputs are x and y. During addition z is the sum bit, while t and u are the carry in and carry out, respectively. During subtraction, z is the difference bit, while t and u are the borrow in and borrow out, respectively. The cell functions are expressed concisely by the following logic equations:

$$z = x \oplus u(y \oplus t)$$
$$u = (x \oplus b)(y + t) + yt$$

The input signals a, b, and y are connected directly to cell outputs in order to simplify interconnection of the cells.

Design a combinational array multiplier for 3-bit twos-complement numbers using these cells. (Additional elements may also be included in the circuit to generate the control signals a and b.) Estimate the multiplication time of your array assuming a gate delay of d seconds.

3.31. Describe how the adder-subtracter cell M' of Fig. 3.73 can be used to construct an array divider using the nonrestoring division principle. Give the block diagram of an array that divides 3-bit positive numbers and computes the quotient to 6 significant bits.

3.32. Modify the algorithm for restoring division given in Fig. 3.54 to handle both positive and negative integers in twos-complement code.

3.33. Design a 12-bit bit-sliced ALU using three copies of the AMD 2901 4-bit slice. Carry lookahead is to be used, and the necessary carry-generation logic should be designed by you using NOR gates. Give a block diagram of your design, and a set of Boolean equations that specify the carry-lookahead function.

3.34. Modify the algorithm for floating-point addition given in Fig. 3.68 to make the following improvements:

(*a*) Perform either addition or subtraction as specified by an opcode in the instruction register IR.

(*b*) Test for zero operands at the start, and skip as much computation as possible when X and/or Y is zero.

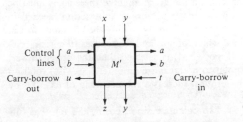

FIGURE 3.73
Cell M' for an array multiplier.

(c) Modify the mantissa assignment strategy to reduce the amount of shifting when $|E| > n_M$.

(d) Introduce separate flags OVR_ERROR and UND_ERROR to indicate overflow and underflow, respectively; these flags replace ERROR.

3.35. The CORDIC (COordinate Rotation Digital Computer) technique due to James E. Volder [29] has been widely used in scientific calculators for computing trigonometric functions. It is relatively fast and can be implemented by very simple circuits. In the CORDIC system, a number Z is treated as a vector represented by its Cartesian coordinates (X, Y), and the required functions of Z are calculated by operations that are analogous to vector rotation. Suppose that the vector Z is rotated through an angle θ. The resulting vector $Z' = (X', Y')$ is defined by the equations

$$X' = X \cos \theta \pm Y \sin \theta$$

$$Y' = Y \cos \theta \mp X \sin \theta \tag{3.54}$$

where the upper and lower signs correspond to clockwise and counterclockwise rotation, respectively. These equations imply that

$$X'' = \frac{X'}{\cos \theta} = X \pm Y \tan \theta$$

$$Y'' = \frac{Y'}{\cos \theta} = Y \mp X \tan \theta \tag{3.55}$$

$Z'' = (X'', Y'')$ can be interpreted as the original vector Z after rotation through an angle θ and a magnitude increase by the factor $K = 1/\cos \theta$. If $\tan \theta$ is a power of 2, then the multiplication by $\tan \theta$ required in (3.55) can be realized by shifting. The essence of CORDIC is to implement the rotation described by (3.55) as a sequence of $n + 1$ rotations through angles α_i such that

$$\theta = \alpha_0 \pm \alpha_1 \pm \alpha_2 \pm \cdots \pm \alpha_n \tag{3.56}$$

and

$$\alpha_1 = \tan^{-1}(2^{-i}) \tag{3.57}$$

Then if we set $Z = (X_0, Y_0)$, each rotation through angle α_i is defined by (3.55) and (3.57) and has the form

$$X_{i+1} = X_i \pm Y_i 2^{-i}$$

$$Y_{i+1} = Y_i \mp X_i 2^{-i} \tag{3.58}$$

The resulting vector Z_n has magnitude $Z_n = K_n |Z_0|$, where $K_n = \Pi_{i=0}^n (\cos \alpha_i)^{-1}$. K_n is a constant depending on n and it converges toward 1.6468. Note that the only operations required in (3.58) are addition, subtraction, and shifting.

The signs appearing in (3.56) depend on the given angle θ; these signs must be computed in order to determine the operations (addition or subtraction) needed in evaluating (3.58). The sign computation is carried out by storing the constants $\{\alpha_i\}$ in a table. In each iteration it is determined which of $+\alpha_i$ and $-\alpha_i$ causes $|\theta + (\pm\alpha_0 \pm\alpha_1 \cdots \pm\alpha_i)|$ to converge toward zero. If $+\alpha_i$ ($-\alpha_i$) is selected then the upper (lower) signs in (3.58) are used which correspond to a clockwise (counterclockwise) rotation through the angle α_i. Note that each iteration increases the accuracy of (X_i, Y_i) by approximately one bit.

The CORDIC method can be used to calculate $\sin \theta$, $\cos \theta$, and $\tan \theta$ as follows. Let $X_0 = K_n^{-1} \approx 0.6073$ and $Y_0 = 0.0$, where n has been chosen to achieve the desired accuracy. Compute (X_n, Y_n) according to (3.58). From (3.54) and (3.55) we see that $X_n = K_n X_0 \cos \theta$ and $Y_n = K_n X_0 \sin \theta$, hence X_n and Y_n are the required values of $\cos \theta$ and $\sin \theta$, respectively. $\tan \theta$ can now be computed by a single division since $\tan \theta = Y_n / X_n$.

(a) Give in tabular form all the calculations required to compute $\cos 37°$ to three decimal places using the CORDIC method.

(b) Draw a register level logic circuit for a simple CORDIC arithmetic unit that computes $\sin \theta$ and $\cos \theta$.

3.36. Describe how the CORDIC technique presented in Prob. 3.35 can be adapted to compute the inverse trigonometric functions $\sin^{-1}x$, $\cos^{-1}x$, and $\tan^{-1}x$.

3.37. Many methods of computing trigonometric functions, logarithms, and the like are based on power series expansions. In Example 1.3, $\sin x$ is obtained from a power series using the method of finite differences in the manner of Babbage's Difference Engine. In modern computers the trigonometric functions are often computed by subroutines that evaluate the power series directly using addition, subtraction, multiplication, and division. Let machine M_1 compute $\sin x$ using the CORDIC approach with parallel addition. Let machine M_2 compute $\sin x$ by power series evaluation. Assume that M_2 has efficient hardware implementations of the four basic arithmetic operations. If M_1 and M_2 employ the same logic technologies, estimate their relative speeds in computing $\sin x$ to 16 binary places.

3.38. Compare and contrast peripheral processors and coprocessors in the hardware implementation of floating-point instructions, considering programming requirements, processing speed, and communication with the host CPU.

REFERENCES

1. Advanced Micro Devices Inc.: *Bipolar Microprocessor and Logic Interface (Am2900 Family) Data Book*, Sunnyvale, Calif. 1985.
2. Anderson, S. F., et al.: "The IBM System/360 Model 91: Floating-Point Execution Unit." *IBM J. Res. Develop.*, vol. 11, pp. 34–53, January 1967.
3. Baldwin, G.: "Towards an Assembly Language Standard," *IEEE Micro*, vol. 4, no. 4, pp. 81–85, August 1984.
4. Booth, A. D.: "A Signed Binary Multiplication Technique," *Quart. J. Mech. Appl. Math.*, vol. 4, pt. 2, pp. 236–240, 1951.
5. Cavanagh, J. J. F.: *Digital Computer Arithmetic*, McGraw-Hill, New York, 1984.
6. Cheng, S.: *Am9511A/Am9512 Floating-Point Processor Manual*, Advanced Micro Devices Inc., Sunnyvale, Calif. 1981.
7. Chu, Y. (ed.): *High-Level Language Architecture*, Academic, New York, 1975.
8. Colwell, R. P., et al.: "Computers, Complexity, and Controversy," *IEEE Computer*, vol. 18, no. 9, pp. 8–19, September 1985.
9. Creech, B. A.: "Architecture of the Burroughs B-6500," in J. Tou (ed.): *Software Engineering*, pp. 29–43, Academic, New York, 1970.
10. Digital Equipment Corp.: *Small Computer Handbook (PDP-8)*, Maynard, Mass., 1973.
11. Feustel, E. A.: "On the Advantages of Tagged Architecture," *IEEE Trans. Comput.*, vol. C-12, pp. 644–656, July 1973.
12. Hamming, R. W.: *Coding and Information Theory*, 2d ed., Prentice-Hall, Englewood Cliffs, N.J., 1986.
13. Harman, T. L., and B. Lawson: *The Motorola MC68000 Microprocessor Family*, Prentice-Hall, Englewood Cliffs, N.J., 1985.

14. Huntsman, C., and D. Cawthron: "The MC68881 Floating-Point Coprocessor," *IEEE Micro,* vol. 3, no. 6, pp. 44–54, December 1983.
15. Hwang, K.: *Computer Arithmetic,* John Wiley & Sons, New York, 1979.
16. IEEE Inc.: *IEEE Standard for Binary Floating-Point Arithmetic (ANSI/IEEE Std 754-1985),* New York, August 1985.
17. Intel Corp.: *MCS-80/85 Family User's Manual,* Santa Clara, Calif. 1979.
18. Mick, J., and J. Brick: *Bit-Slice Microprocessor Design,* McGraw-Hill, New York, 1980.
19. Motorola Inc.: *MC68020 32-Bit Microprocessor User's Manual,* 2d ed., Prentice-Hall, Englewood Cliffs, N.J., 1985.
20. Myers, G. J.: *Advances in Computer Architecture,* 2d ed., Wiley-Interscience, New York, 1982.
21. Patterson, D. A., and C. H. Séquin: "A VLSI RISC," *IEEE Computer,* vol. 15, no. 9, pp. 8–21, September 1982.
22. Peterson, W. W., and E. J. Weldon: *Error-Correcting Codes,* 2d ed., MIT Press, Cambridge, Mass., 1972.
23. Radin, G.: "The 801 Minicomputer," *IBM J. Res. & Dev.,* vol. 27, pp. 237–246, May 1983.
24. Ramamoorthy, C. V., and H. F. Li: "Pipeline Architecture," *Comput. Surv.,* vol. 9, pp. 61–102, March 1977.
25. Robertson, J. E.: "Twos Complement Multiplication in Binary Parallel Computers," *IRE Trans. Electron. Comput.,* vol. EC-4, pp. 118–119, September 1955.
26. Robertson, J. E.: "A New Class of Division Methods," *IRE Trans. Electron. Comput.,* vol. EC-7, pp. 218–222, September 1958.
27. Stevenson, D.: "A Proposed Standard for Binary Floating-Point Arithmetic," *IEEE Computer,* vol. 14, no. 3, pp. 51–62, March 1981.
28. Van der Poel, W. L.: "The Essential Types of Operations in an Automatic Computer," *Nachrichtentechnische Fachberichte,* vol. 4, pp. 144–145, 1956.
29. Volder, J. E.: "The CORDIC Trigonometric Computing Technique," *IRE Trans. Electron. Comput.,* vol. EC-8, pp. 330–334, September 1959.
30. Wakerly J.: *Error Detecting Codes, Self-Checking Circuits and Applications,* North-Holland, New York, 1978.

CONTROL DESIGN

The implementation of the control part of a processor is studied in this chapter using two basic design approaches—hardwired and microprogrammed. Hardwired control is discussed briefly, whereas microprogramming is examined in detail.

4.1 INTRODUCTION

In Sec. 2.1.1, we noted that it is generally useful to separate a digital system into two parts, a data processing unit and a control unit. The data processing unit is a network of functional units capable of performing certain operations on data. The purpose of the control unit is to issue control signals or instructions to the data processing part. These control signals select the functions to be performed at specific times and route the data through the appropriate functional units. In other words, the data processing unit is logically reconfigured by the control unit to perform certain sets of (micro) operations. The sequence in which these micro-operations are performed is very important, so the control unit is intimately involved in the sequencing and timing of the data processing unit.

In this chapter we are concerned with the design of control units for digital systems. Of particular interest is the design of control units for instruction set processors such as the CPU of a computer. The function of the control unit in such cases is to fetch instructions from a memory and interpret them to determine the control signals to be sent to the data processing units. Two central aspects of this process can be identified.

1. *Instruction sequencing*, that is, the methods by which instructions are selected for execution or, equivalently, the manner in which control of the processor is transferred from one instruction to another

2. *Instruction interpretation*, or the methods used for activating the control signals that cause the data processing unit to execute the instruction.

4.1.1   Instruction Sequencing

Conceptually, the simplest method of controlling the sequence in which instructions are executed is to have each instruction explicitly specify the address of its successor (or successors, if more than one possibility exists). This was done in some early computers such as EDVAC (see Sec. 1.2.2). Explicit inclusion of instruction addresses in all instructions has the disadvantage of substantially increasing instruction length, which in turn increases the cost of the memory where the instructions are stored.

Most instructions in a typical program have a unique successor. If an instruction I is stored in memory location A, and I has a unique successor I', then it is natural to store I' in the location that immediately follows A. Let PC denote a *program counter* or *instruction address register* containing the address A of instruction I. The address of I' can then be determined by incrementing PC thus:

$$PC \leftarrow PC + k$$

where k is the length in words of I. If I must be fetched from main memory one word at a time, then PC is automatically incremented by one before each new instruction word is read. Consequently, after all words of I have been fetched, PC points to I'. A program counter therefore makes it unnecessary for an instruction to specify the address of its successor.

In order to select one of several possible courses of action or to repeat instructions, it is necessary to provide some instructions that transfer control between instructions at nonconsecutive addresses. Such instructions, called *branch* instructions, specify implicitly or explicitly an instruction address X. An *unconditional* branch always alters the flow of program control by causing the operation

$$PC \leftarrow X$$

to take place. A *conditional* branch instruction first tests for some condition C within the processor; C is typically a property of a result generated by an earlier instruction and stored in a status register. If C is present, then $PC \leftarrow X$, otherwise PC is incremented to point to the next consecutive instruction.

Program control transfer. Conditional and unconditional branch instructions are adequate to direct the flow of control within a single program or procedure. Very often it is necessary to implement a temporary transfer of control from a program P_1 to a (sub)program P_2. There are two major situations where this occurs: subroutine calls and interrupts. A subroutine call is a temporary transfer of control from P_1 to P_2 initiated by P_1. An interrupt is a temporary transfer of control from P_1 to P_2 initiated by P_2 or some device associated with P_2.

The transfer of control from P_1 to P_2 required by a subroutine call is accomplished by a call or jump-to-subroutine branch instruction. A typical mnemonic expression for such an instruction is

CALL X

where X (or some address computed from X) is the address of the first instruction of P_2. CALL X is executed in two steps. First the contents of PC after fetching the CALL instruction, which is the address of the next instruction of P_1, is saved in some predetermined location S, typically a processor register or a main-memory location. Then X is loaded into PC causing P_2 to begin execution. In order for control to be transferred back to the main program P_1, the last instruction from P_2 that is executed should transfer the contents of S, called the return address, to PC. Special return instructions are often designed for this purpose. An interrupt is processed in essentially the same fashion except that the call instruction is replaced by an interrupt signal. The interrupt branch address is either fixed a priori, or is supplied with the interrupt request by the interrupting device.

A common way of implementing subroutine calls in early computers is illustrated by the PDP-8 [9]. The instruction

JMS SUB

where JMS stands for jump to subroutine, causes the current contents of the program counter PC (the return address) to be stored in main-memory location SUB. The address SUB is loaded into PC, which is then incremented, implying that the first instruction of the subroutine SUB should have address SUB + 1. Control can be transferred from the subroutine back to the calling program by executing the statement

JMP I SUB

which is an indirect (specified by the modifier I) jump to location SUB, corresponding to PC ← M(SUB). This method of subroutine calling has the disadvantage that a subroutine cannot be allowed to call itself, since a second call to the subroutine results in the second return address overwriting the first return address and thus destroying it. One subroutine may call another, however, and thereby permit the nesting of distinct subroutines.

Control stacks. Pushdown stacks, which we already encountered in Chap. 3, provide a particularly powerful mechanism for transferring control between programs. In this application, a stack is used primarily to store return addresses. The stack may also be used to pass variables (parameters) from P_1 to P_2, and to store variables that are local to P_2. Each time a call is executed, the return address is entered into the top of the stack and the program counter is loaded with the subroutine address. Thus the statement

CALL SUB

results in the following sequence of actions:

$$\text{PUSH PC;}$$

$$\text{PC} \leftarrow \text{SUB}$$

which are illustrated in Fig. 3.29 (Sec. 3.2.3) for the case of the Motorola 68000. A return from the subroutine may be effected by the instruction RETURN, which is equivalent to POP PC and causes the topmost entry in the stack to be transferred to the program counter.

The last-in first-out (LIFO) organization of a pushdown stack is well suited to transferring control among nested subroutines, since the last calling program is the first program to which control must be returned. Furthermore, there is no restriction on the use of recursive subroutine calls as there is in the case of the PDP-8 JMS instruction discussed above. Because the location where return addresses are saved is the top of the stack, which varies dynamically, successive PUSH operations to save return addresses do not interfere with one another. Consider, for example, the following segment of recursive code.

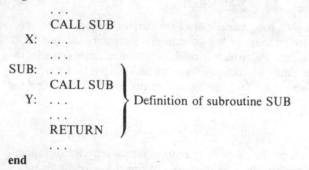

When SUB is first called from the main program, the return address X is saved in the stack, as shown in Fig. 4.1a. Control is then transferred to the subroutine, where the statement CALL SUB is encountered. This causes a new return address Y to be pushed into the stack, as shown in Fig. 4.1b. If CALL SUB is again executed, Y is pushed into the stack, as shown in Fig. 4.1c, and so on. This process continues until eventually RETURN is executed. If a total of k calls to SUB are made, then $k-1$ returns must be made to the instruction at location Y in SUB, with an additional RETURN transferring control back to the main program.

Stack implementation. A stack with a capacity of n k-bit words is easily constructed from k n-bit shift registers having left- and right-shift capabilities. The shift registers are arranged as shown in Fig. 4.2 to form an n-word shift register. One end of this shift register, say the left end, is defined as the "top" of the stack. To perform a push operation, the word X to be written into the stack is applied to

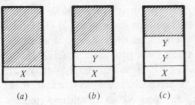

FIGURE 4.1
Use of a pushdown stack to control recursive subroutine calls.

the left inputs of the shift register and the right-shift control line is activated. Conversely, a pop operation is performed by activating the left-shift control line, which transfers the word at the top of the stack to the output data bus.

Two possible error conditions may arise in stack operation. An attempt to push an additional word into a stack containing n words results in *stack overflow*. An attempt to pop a word from an empty stack results in *stack underflow*. Both the overflow and underflow conditions can be detected by including a counter in the stack circuitry to indicate the number of words currently in the stack. This counter is incremented (decremented) by each push (pop) operation. The combination of a push (pop) signal and a count of n (zero) results in an overflow (underflow) indication.

Shift registers, which are serial access memories, are only suitable for constructing stacks of limited capacity, such as those found in microprogram control

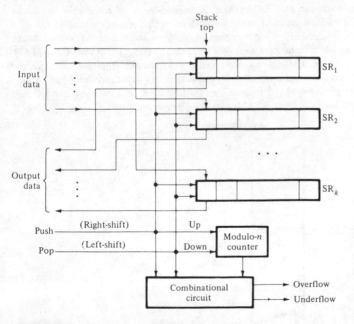

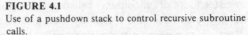

FIGURE 4.2
A stack constructed from shift registers.

units. When large stacks are required, it is generally more economical to use a contiguous region of random access memory as the main stack area [5]. The push and pop operations are then implemented by memory write and read operations, respectively. A simple way of controlling the stack is to provide a special control register (actually a counter) called a *stack pointer* SP. This register typically contains the address of the memory location that is currently acting as the top of the stack. A pop operation is performed by reading M using SP as an address register. Then SP is decremented to point to the new top element. Similarly, to perform a push operation, SP is first incremented and a write operation is·performed using SP as an address register.

Stack overflow and underflow can be detected by including additional registers in the processor to store the highest and lowest addresses of the stack region. The register containing the highest stack address is called the *limit register* L: the register containing the lowest stack address is called the *base register* B. B, L, and SP define the boundaries of the stack, as indicated in Fig. 4.3. If an attempt is made to access a stack word whose address SP is such that SP > L (SP < B), an overflow (underflow) signal is issued.

Example 4.1 Stack control in the Motorola 68000 series [17]. CPUs in this series, such as the 68020 microprocessor (Fig. 1.39), have conventional call and return instructions with the mnemonic names JMS (jump to subroutine) and RTS (return from subroutine). When executed in ordinary user programs, JMS and RTS employ a stack pointer denoted A7 which controls a pushdown stack in main memory. If the CPU is in the supervisor state rather than the user state, as indicated by a flag bit in the status register SR, a second stack pointer denoted A7' is used instead of A7. The supervisor state is intended for use by operating systems and allows the control stacks of an operating system to be kept separate from those of user programs. Data can be added or removed from stacks via push and pop operations implemented with the 68000's MOVE instructions and autoindexed addressing mode, as described in Sec. 3.2.1. For example, a word (16 bits) can be pushed from, say, data register D0 into the stack controlled by A7 (or A7') by executing the instruction

$$\text{MOVE} \quad \text{D0}, -(\text{A7})$$

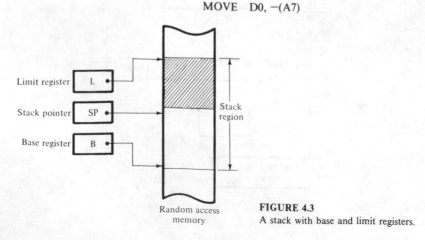

FIGURE 4.3
A stack with base and limit registers.

The corresponding pop instruction is

$$\text{MOVE} \quad (A7)+, D0$$

Interrupt signals to the CPU, which indicate an exceptional condition requiring the attention of the operating system, are handled in 68000-series CPUs by switching to the supervisor state (which implies changing the status word SR) and pushing the original contents of both the program counter PC and the status register SR into the stack controlled by A7'. The CPU creates a new status word indicating that it is in the supervisor mode, and loads PC with an address X that is either supplied by the source of the interrupt request, or else is predetermined (wired into the CPU) for that particular interrupt. X is the starting address of a program designed to service the interrupt in question. To return control to the original interrupted program, the special return instruction RTE (return from exception) may be executed by the interrupt service program, which pops the previously saved status word and return address from the A7' stack into SR and PC, respectively. Thus RTE is functionally equivalent to the two-instruction sequence

$$\text{MOVE} \quad (A7)+, SR$$
$$\text{RTS}$$

Stacks are very convenient both for storing parameters to be passed between programs, and as working storage for local variables during a computation. For this purpose, it is convenient for users to be able to allocate and deallocate blocks of storage at the top of the stack when needed. The 68000 family provides two special stack-control instructions LINK (link) and UNLK (unlink) for this purpose. These instructions control an address register (one of A0:A6) termed a *frame pointer* FP, which with the stack pointer SP = A7 or A7', delimit a working area or *frame* in the stack. FP thus corresponds approximately to the stack base register B of Fig. 4.3.

The 68000's link instruction has the following assembly-language format:

$$\text{LINK} \quad Ai, \#-k \qquad\qquad (4.1)$$

where the specified register Ai is the frame pointer FP. Execution of (4.1) first causes the 4-word contents of FP (the old frame pointer FP_1) to be pushed into the stack. The new contents $SP_1 - 4$ of SP are then transferred to FP. The frame pointer FP now points to the bottom of the frame area being allocated. At this point the number k in the link instruction is subtracted from the contents of SP, so that the stack top is moved k bytes beyond the location addressed by FP. The k-byte frame delimited by FP and SP is typically employed as the working storage area for a subroutine. Local variables of the subroutine can therefore be addressed relative to FP, while the stack top can move up and down independently of FP. The effect of LINK is illustrated in Fig. 4.4. The space allocated by (4.1) can be subsequently deallocated by executing the unlink instruction

$$\text{UNLK} \quad Ai$$

UNLK moves the contents of FP = Ai to the stack pointer SP and then pops the stack into Ai, thereby restoring the original state of Fig. 4.4a. The use of LNK and UNLK in this fashion makes it simple to allow repeated use of a common stack by multiple calls to the same or different subroutines, without the working storage (frames) associated with the calls interfering with one another.

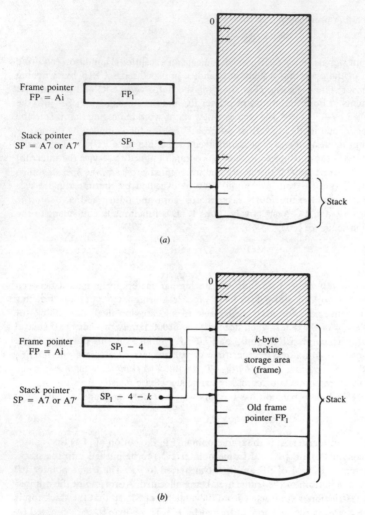

(a)

(b)

FIGURE 4.4
Processor and memory state (a) immediately before and (b) immediately after execution of the LINK instruction.

4.1.2   Instruction Interpretation

We now turn to the manner in which a control unit interprets an instruction in order to determine the control signals to be issued. The control signals are transmitted from the control unit to the outside world via control lines. Figure 4.5 shows the main control lines connected to a typical control unit. They are sometimes indicated by broken lines to distinguish them from (unbroken) data lines. Again it should be emphasized that control and data are relative rather than absolute concepts; it may be convenient, therefore, to view the same physical lines as either data or control lines at different complexity levels.

Control specification. The four groups of control signals distinguished in Fig. 4.5 have the following functions.

1. C'_{out}: These signals directly control the operation of the data processing unit. The main function of the control unit is to generate C'_{out}.
2. C'_{in}: These signals enable the data being processed to influence the control unit, allowing data-dependent decisions to be made. A frequent function of C'_{in} is to indicate the occurrence of unusual conditions such as errors, e.g., overflow, in the data processing unit.
3. C''_{out}: These signals are transmitted to other control units and may indicate status conditions such as "busy" or "operation completed."
4. C''_{in}: These signals are received from other control units, e.g., from a supervisory controller. They typically include start and stop signals and timing information. C''_{in} and C''_{out} are primarily used to synchronize the control unit with the operation of other control units.

Flowcharts and description languages, separately or in combination, appear to be the most useful formal tools for describing the behavior of a control unit. A flowchart describes the microoperations to be performed and indicates graphically the way in which they are to be sequenced. Once the data processing unit design has been completed and the control points identified, each microoperation $Z \leftarrow f(X)$ can be identified with a set of control lines $\{c_{ij}\}$ that must be activated in order to execute that microoperation. If these control-signal sets are entered into the description, then we obtain a formal specification of the input-output behavior of the control unit. In this chapter, a flowchart description identifying the control lines to be activated will be the usual starting point in the control-unit design process.

Implementation methods. Historically, two general approaches to control-unit design have evolved. The first of these views the control unit as a sequential logic circuit to generate specific fixed sequences of control signals. As such, it is designed with the usual goals of minimizing the number of components used and maximizing the speed of operation. Once constructed, changes in behavior can be imple-

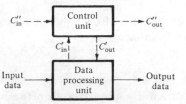

FIGURE 4.5
A control unit and its input-output lines.

mented only by redesigning and physically rewiring the unit. Such a circuit is therefore said to be a hardwired control unit.

Processor control units are among the most complex logic circuits in computers. Different instructions are executed by the activation of control-signal sequences which may have little resemblance to one another. As a result, a hardwired control unit often has little apparent structure and is frequently said to contain random logic. This lack of structure makes complex hardwired control units costly to design and debug.

Around 1950 several computer designers, notably Maurice V. Wilkes, observed the need for a flexible and systematic way of designing control circuits [12, 22]. The technique proposed by Wilkes, which he named *microprogramming*, treats a statement of the form

$$\text{Activate control lines } \{c_{i,j}\}$$

as a (micro)instruction stored in a special addressable memory called a control memory. The sequence of microinstructions needed to execute a particular operation constitutes a microprogram for that operation. The operation is performed by fetching the microinstructions one at a time from the control memory and using them to activate the control lines directly. A control unit designed around a control memory is called a microprogrammed control unit.

Microprogramming clearly makes control-unit design more systematic by organizing control signals into words (microinstructions) having a well-defined format. These signals are implemented by a kind of software (firmware) rather than by hardware; consequently, design changes can easily be made by altering the contents of the control memory. Furthermore, a microprogrammed CPU can, if the necessary microprograms are available, execute programs written in the machine languages of several different computers—a process called emulation. On the negative side, microprogrammed control units are often more costly than hardwired units due to the presence of the control memory and its access circuitry. They may also be slower because of the extra time required to fetch microinstructions from the control memory. Microprogramming did not become widely used until its appearance in the smaller models of the IBM System/360 series in the mid-1960s. (Microprogramming was not used in the larger faster System/360 models because of the decrease in operating speed it entails.) Since then improvements in memory technology have greatly lowered the cost of control memories, and microprogramming has become a standard method of designing control units.

4.2   HARDWIRED CONTROL

In this section we examine the design of control units that use fixed logic circuits to interpret instructions and generate control signals from them.

4.2.1   Design Methods

The design of a hardwired control unit involves various complex tradeoffs between the amount of hardware used, its speed of operation, and the cost of the design process itself. Because of the large number of control signals used in a typical CPU and their dependence on the particular instruction set being implemented, the design methods employed in practice arc often ad hoc and heuristic in nature, and therefore cannot easily be formalized. To illustrate the main issues involved, we consider three simplified and systematic approaches to the design of hardwired controllers. These methods are representative of those used in practice, but by themselves are suitable only for small control units such as might be encountered in nonprogrammable controllers or RISC processors.

Method 1: The standard algorithmic approach to sequential circuit design covered in Sec. 2.2.2, which is called the state-table method, since it begins with the construction of a state table for the control unit.

Method 2: A heuristic method based on the use of clocked delay elements for control-signal timing.

Method 3: A related method that uses counters, which we call sequence counters, for timing purposes.

Method 1, the most formal of these design approaches, may incorporate systematic techniques for minimizing the number of gates and flip-flops. Methods 2 and 3, which are less formal, attempt to derive a logic circuit directly from the original (flowchart) description of the control-unit behavior. The resulting designs may not contain the minimum number of gates and flip-flops, but they are often obtained with much less effort. Furthermore, these designs are usually easier to comprehend and are therefore easier to maintain. Our main emphasis will be on methods 2 and 3.

The foregoing design methods are by no means unrelated, nor are they the only systematic approaches to hardwired control design. In practice, CPU control units are often so complex that no one design method by itself can yield a satisfactory circuit at an acceptable design cost. For example, the most efficient design may consist of several linked, but largely independent, sequential circuits.

State-table method. The behavior required of a control unit, like that of any finite-state sequential machine, can be represented by a state table of the type shown in Fig. 4.6. Let C_{in} and C_{out} denote the input and output variables of the control unit. The rows of the state table correspond to the set of internal states $\{S_i\}$ of the machine. An internal state is determined by the information stored in the unit at discrete points of time (clock periods). The columns correspond to the set of external signals to the control unit, that is, C_{in}. The entry in row S_i and column I_j has the form $S_{i,j}$, $z_{i,j}$, where $S_{i,j}$ denotes the next state of the control unit, and $z_{i,j}$ denotes the set of output signals $z_{i,j}$ from C_{out} that are activated by the application of I_j to the control unit when it is in state S_i.

A state-table description is a suitable starting point for the implementation of small control units. A well-defined design methodology exists using the state-table approach [14]. This method was discussed in Sec. 2.2.2 and will be illustrated by an example in Sec. 4.2.2. There are several practical disadvantages to using state tables.

	Input combinations C_{in}			
States	I_1	I_2		I_m
S_1	$S_{1,1}, z_{1,1}$	$S_{1,2}, z_{1,2}$	$\cdots$	$S_{1,m}, z_{1,m}$
S_2	$S_{2,1}, z_{2,1}$	$S_{2,2}, z_{2,2}$	$\cdots$	$S_{2,m}, z_{2,m}$
S_n	$S_{n,1}, z_{n,1}$	$S_{n,2}, z_{n,2}$	$\cdots$	$S_{n,m}, z_{n,m}$

FIGURE 4.6
State table for a control unit.

1. The number of state and input combinations may be so great that the state-table size and the amount of computation needed become excessive.
2. State tables tend to conceal useful information about a circuit's behavior, e.g., the existence of repeated patterns or loops.

Control circuits designed from state tables also tend to have a random structure, which makes design debugging and subsequent maintenance of the circuit difficult.

Delay-element method. Consider the problem of generating the following sequence of control signals at times $t_1, t_2, \ldots, t_n$ using a hardwired control unit.

$$t_1: \quad \text{Activate } \{c_{1,j}\};$$

$$t_2: \quad \text{Activate } \{c_{2,j}\};$$

$$\ldots\ldots\ldots\ldots$$

$$t_n: \quad \text{Activate } \{c_{n,j}\};$$

Suppose that an initiation signal called $\text{START}(t_1)$ is available at t_1. $\text{START}(t_1)$ may be fanned out to $\{c_{1,j}\}$ to perform the first microoperation. If $\text{START}(t_1)$ is also entered into a time delay element of delay $t_2 - t_1$, the output of that circuit, $\text{START}(t_2)$ can be used to activate $\{c_{2,j}\}$. Similarly, another delay element of delay $t_3 - t_2$ with input $\text{START}(t_2)$ can be used to activate $\{c_{3,j}\}$ and so on. Thus a sequence of delay elements can be used to generate control signals in a very straightforward manner. To ensure synchronous operation, the delay elements are implemented by D (delay) flip-flops and controlled by a common clock signal. Since normally only one flip-flop is set or "hot" at any time and all other flip-flops are reset, this approach incorporates a version of the one-hot state assignment technique mentioned in Chap. 2.

A control unit using delay elements can be constructed directly from a flow-chart that specifies the control-signal sequences required. The circuit thus formed has essentially the same structure as the flowchart, a consequence of the fact that the circuit simply mirrors the flow of control through the flowchart. A few simple rules illustrated in Fig. 4.7 indicate the way in which the control circuit is derived from the flowchart.

1. Each sequence of two successive microoperations requires a delay element. The signals that activate the control lines are taken directly from the input and out-

put lines of the delay, as shown in Fig. 4.7a. Signals that are intended to activate the same control line c_i are fed to an OR gate whose output is c_i. This line may then be connected to the control point it activates.

2. k lines in the flowchart that merge to a common line are transformed into a k-input OR gate, as shown in Fig. 4.7b.

3. A decision box (which indicates a branch in the control flow based on a condition test) can be implemented by two AND gates, as shown in Fig. 4.7c. This AND circuit forms a simple 1-bit demultiplexer controlled by the test variable x. Note that x may be replaced by a Boolean function $f(x)$, so that condition tests of arbitrary complexity can be used to determine the flow of control.

Figure 4.8 shows a portion of a typical flowchart indicating the control signals $\{c_{i,j}\}$ that must be activated at each step. Figure 4.9 shows the control circuit obtained using these transformation rules. Note that the AND gates derived from the two decision boxes have been merged in an obvious manner.

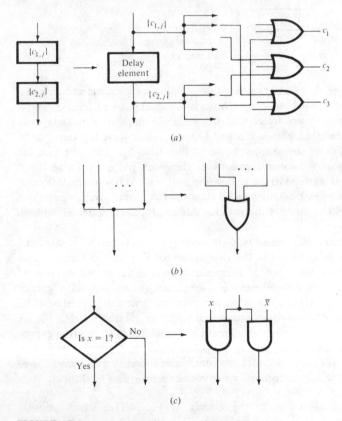

FIGURE 4.7
Rules for transforming a flowchart into a control circuit using delay elements.

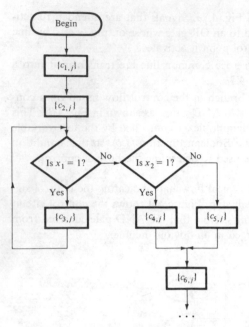

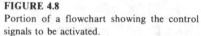

FIGURE 4.8
Portion of a flowchart showing the control signals to be activated.

The delay element required in control circuits of this type is more than just a passive two-terminal delay line. Its output must be a signal pulse of precise magnitude and duration that is synchronized with the main system clock. If all delays are one clock period in duration, then a clocked D-type master-slave flip-flop can be used to construct the delay element, as shown in Fig. 4.10. The control pulses are assumed to be of about the same durations as the clock pulse. When an input control pulse arrives, it is stored in the D flip-flop and is gated out by the following clock pulse. A more complex circuit may be required if an input control pulse can become appreciably out of phase with the clock due to propagation delays between delay elements.

Despite the conceptually simple way that control circuits can be constructed from flowcharts using delay elements, this design method has the disadvantage that the number of delay elements needed is approximately equal to the number of states n_s. Furthermore, each delay element is a sequential circuit of equal or greater complexity than a flip-flop [11]. Using the classical state-table design method (Sec. 2.2.2), one can design a synchronous sequential circuit of n_s states with no more than $\lceil \log_2 n_s \rceil$ flip-flops. Thus the delay-element approach tends to produce expensive circuits in which timing is controlled by pulses traveling through cascades of clocked delay elements. (These cascades are sometimes called *timing chains*.) Synchronization of many widely distributed delay elements may also be difficult.

Sequence-counter method. Consider the circuit of Fig. 4.11a, which consists basically of a modulo-k counter whose output is connected to a $1/k$ clocked

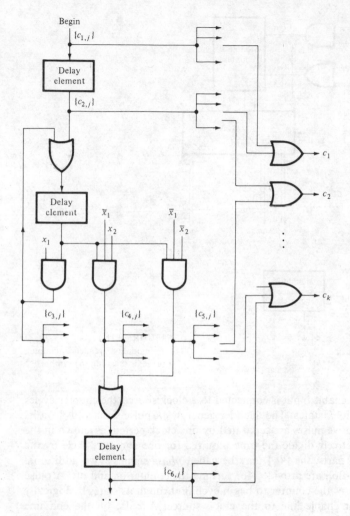

FIGURE 4.9
Control unit using delay elements, which corresponds to the flowchart of Fig. 4.8.

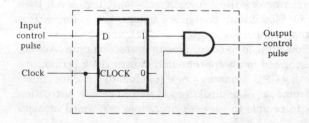

FIGURE 4.10
A synchronous delay element for
control unit design.

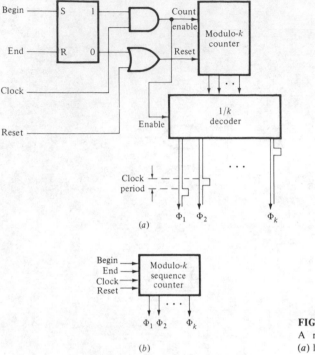

(a)

(b)

FIGURE 4.11
A modulo-k sequence counter:
(a) logic diagram; (b) symbol.

decoder. If the count enable input is connected to a clock source, the counter cycles continually through its k states. The decoder generates k pulse signals $\{\Phi_i\}$ on its output lines. Consecutive pulses are separated by one clock period, as shown in the figure. The $\{\Phi_i\}$ effectively divide the time required for one complete cycle by the counter into k equal parts; the $\{\Phi_i\}$ may be called *phase* signals. Two additional input lines and a flip-flop are provided for turning the counter on and off. A pulse on the begin line causes the counter to begin cycling through its states by logically connecting the count enable line to the clock source. A pulse on the end line disconnects the clock and resets the counter. The circuit of Fig. 4.11a will be called a *sequence counter* and will be represented by the circuit symbol of Fig. 4.11b.

The usefulness of control counters of this type stems from the fact that many digital circuits are designed to perform a relatively small number of actions repeatedly. This type of behavior can be described (usually at a fairly high level) by a flowchart consisting of a single closed loop containing k steps. For example, Fig. 4.12 shows a one-loop flowchart containing six steps that describes the behavior of a typical CPU. Each pass through the loop constitutes an instruction cycle. Assuming that each step can be performed in an appropriately chosen clock period, one may build a control unit for this CPU around a single (modulo-6) sequence counter. Each signal Φ_i activates some set of control lines in step i of every instruction cycle. It is usually necessary to be able to vary the operations performed in step i

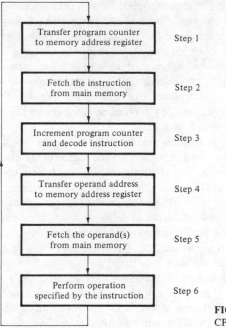

Transfer program counter to memory address register	Step 1
Fetch the instruction from main memory	Step 2
Increment program counter and decode instruction	Step 3
Transfer operand address to memory address register	Step 4
Fetch the operand(s) from main memory	Step 5
Perform operation specified by the instruction	Step 6

FIGURE 4.12
CPU behavior represented as a single closed loop.

depending on certain control signals or condition variables applied to the control unit. These are represented by the signals $C_{in} = \{C'_{in}, C''_{in}\}$ in Fig. 4.13. A logic circuit N is therefore needed which, as shown in Fig. 4.13, combines C_{in} with the timing signals $\{\Phi_i\}$ generated by the sequence counter.

Relationships. Most of the state information in a control unit of the type shown in Fig. 4.13 resides in the sequence counter. If the logic circuit N is combinational, then the entire circuit has the form of the Huffman model of a sequential circuit shown in Fig. 2.24. This, of course, is also the type of circuit produced by the state-table design method.

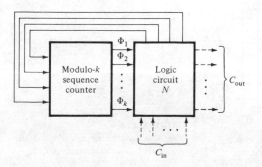

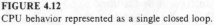

FIGURE 4.13
A control unit based on a sequence counter.

A strong relationship exists between the sequence counter and delay-element methods. A modulo-k sequence counter can easily be made to behave like a cascade of $k - 1$ delay elements. This is accomplished by connecting the kth output line Φ_k to the end line, as shown in Fig. 4.14b, so that the counter shuts itself off after one complete cycle. Thus the control-unit design method with delay elements described earlier can, in principle, be directly modified to apply to sequence counters if every cascade of $k - 1$ delay elements is replaced by the circuit of Fig. 4.14b. However, the resulting design would generally be very inefficient compared with a sequence counter design of the type shown in Fig. 4.13.

Conversely, a cascade of $k - 1$ delay elements can be made to behave like a sequence counter by connecting its output to its input via an additional delay element and an OR gate, as shown in Fig. 4.15. The resulting circuit, which behaves like a free-running modulo-k sequence counter, is called a (modulo-k) *ring counter*. It is a useful component for control design. A ring counter is most easily constructed from a shift register, since a cascade of identical delay elements is essentially a shift register. A single control pulse propagates around the ring counter, so that at any time only one delay element is in the set state. No decoding circuitry is required, unlike the usual type of counter, and this is perhaps its most useful feature. On the other hand, a modulo-k ring counter requires k flip-flops, whereas an ordinary modulo-k counter requires only $\lceil \log_2 k \rceil$ flip-flops. In the sequel, sequence counters will be assumed to have the general form of Fig. 4.11. However, any such counter can be replaced by an equivalent modulo-k ring counter.

In the next two sections, some examples are presented to illustrate the foregoing methods for designing hardwired control units. Section 4.4.2 examines in detail the design of a control unit for a sequential multiplier. This can be viewed as a specialized control unit to interpret a single instruction, namely, multiply. In Sec. 4.2.3, the design of a CPU control unit which must interpret a variety of instructions is briefly considered. These examples will be used again in our discussions of

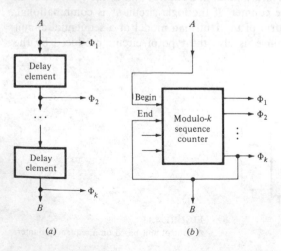

(a)

(b)

FIGURE 4.14
(a) A delay-element cascade; (b) the equivalent sequence-counter circuit.

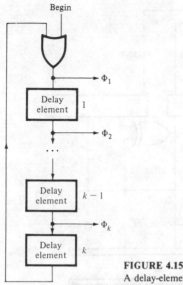

Begin

Φ_1

Delay element 1

Φ_2

...

Delay element $k-1$

Φ_k

Delay element k

FIGURE 4.15
A delay-element circuit (ring counter) that behaves like a sequence counter.

microprogramming, thus providing some concrete comparisons between hardwired and microprogrammed control.

4.2.2 Multiplier Control Unit

In this section we study the design of a hardwired control unit for the two-complement multiplier introduced in Example 3.4. The block diagram of the multiplier (Fig. 3.42) is redrawn in Fig. 4.16, to show a set of possible control points. The corresponding control signals and their functions are derived from the multiplication algorithm appearing in Fig. 3.40, and are listed in Fig. 4.17. In general, a control point is associated with each distinct action (register transfer operation) S appearing in the algorithm being implemented. Its control signal c_i is inserted into the device or the data path(s) associated with S. Operations that take place simultaneously may be able to share control signals. (Procedures to eliminate redundant control signals are considered later.) The statement labeled BEGIN in Fig. 3.43, for instance, requires the registers A, COUNT, and F to be reset simultaneously to the all-0 state. A single control signal c_{10} is therefore provided for this purpose. It can be connected directly to the CLEAR inputs of the three registers in question, so no additional logic is needed to implement the c_0 control points. Control signals c_8 and c_9 transfer a data word from the input bus INBUS to registers Q and M, respectively, and are shown in the corresponding data paths of Fig. 4.16; these signals may be connected to the registers' (parallel) LOAD inputs. Control signal c_5 serves to change the function performed by the parallel adder from addition to subtraction for the correction step; it also resets Q(7) to 0. The remaining control signals of Fig. 4.17 are defined similarly. Figure 4.16 introduces a control signal

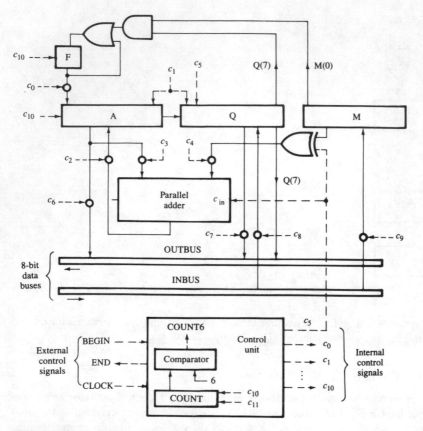

FIGURE 4.16
Twos-complement multiplier with control points.

Control signal	Operation controlled
c_0	Set sign bit of A to F.
c_1	Right-shift register-pair A.Q.
c_2	Transfer adder output to A.
c_3	Transfer A to left input of adder.
c_4	Transfer M to right input of adder.
c_5	Perform subtraction (correction). Clear Q(7).
c_6	Transfer A to OUTBUS.
c_7	Transfer Q to OUTBUS.
c_8	Transfer word on INBUS to Q.
c_9	Transfer word on INBUS to M.
c_{10}	Clear A, COUNT, and F registers.
c_{11}	Increment COUNT.

FIGURE 4.17
Control signals for the twos-complement multiplier.

called COUNT6, which is set to 1 when $COUNT = 110_2$, and is set to 0 otherwise. COUNT6, the rightmost bit $Q(7)$ of the multiplier register Q, and the external BEGIN signal, serve as the primary inputs to the control unit.

The twos-complement multiplication algorithm of Fig. 3.40 is redrawn as a flowchart in Fig. 4.18, which indicates when the control signals from Fig. 4.17 are activated. We now apply the three design techniques from the preceding section to this example, taking the flowchart of Fig. 4.18 as the starting point.

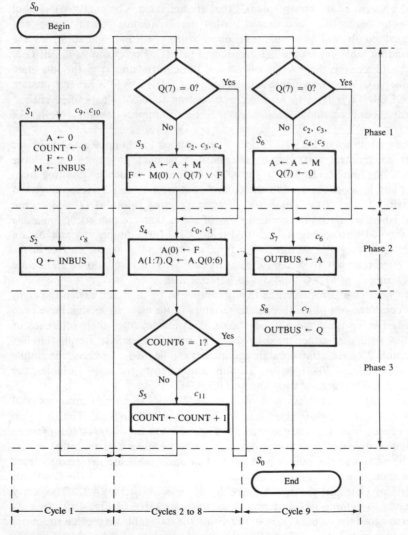

FIGURE 4.18
Flowchart for twos-complement multiplication.

State-table method. The multiplier control unit is sufficiently small and simple so that the state-table design approach is feasible. First it is necessary to construct a state table for the control unit. We can associate a state S_i with every microoperation block in Fig. 4.18, giving eight states labeled S_1 through S_8. S_0 will denote an additional state representing the idle or waiting state of the control unit. There are three primary input signals BEGIN, Q(7), and COUNT6, hence there are eight possible input combinations. Figure 4.19 shows a state table for the control unit which is derived directly from the flowchart. Each entry indicates the next state followed by a list of the control signals that are activated. The empty set symbol $\varnothing$ means no control line is activated in that particular state. Certain state- and input-signal combinations should not occur during normal operation, so the corresponding table entries are left unspecified (blank). For example, the BEGIN signal should assume the 1 value only when the control unit is in the idle state S_0. Similarly, COUNT6 (which becomes 1 when COUNT = 6) is never 1 in state S_2, since COUNT is reset to zero in the preceding state S_1. Unspecified entries, which correspond to don't cares, may be used to simplify the logic design of the unit.

The techniques of Sec. 2.2.2 can now be applied to obtain a gate-level logic design for the control unit. First an attempt may be made to reduce the number of states in the state table. Let O_i and O_j be the output sequences resulting from applying any input sequence I to the control unit with S_i and S_j, respectively, as initial states. S_i and S_j are *compatible* if corresponding values of O_1 and O_2 are identical whenever both are specified. Sets of states that are pairwise compatible can be merged into a single state. In Figure 4.19, for example, S_2 and S_8 are compatible, so they can be merged to form a new state S_2' whose entries in the reduced state table are the union of rows S_2 and S_8. This results in an eight-state table requiring $\lceil \log_2 8 \rceil = 3$ flip-flops to implement it.

The next step is to select the flip-flop types to be used and assign the eight possible combinations of the three state variables to the eight states that have been identified. JK flip-flops are a good choice, if available, since their tolerance of unspecified values on either the J or the K inputs often leads to simpler circuits (see Example 2.2). An arbitrary state assignment can be made; we chose the simple assignment of Fig. 4.20. If we use JK flip-flops to store the state variables, the control unit has the general form shown in Fig. 4.21.

The remaining problem is to design the 6-input 19-output combinational logic circuit N, a straightforward but, in this case, a tedious task. The first step is to construct a transition table as shown in Fig. 4.22. The transition table represents the various outputs of N as functions of the state variables and the other inputs to N. The entries in the output part of the transition table are determined from the state table, the state assignment, and the defining equations of the flip-flops. Consider, for example, the row marked by an asterisk in Fig. 4.22. This entry corresponds to column 001 and row S_4 in the state table of Fig. 4.19, since S_4 has been assigned the values $y_1 y_2 y_3 = 100$. From the state table we see that the corresponding next state is $S_7 = 111$ and that the output variables c_0 and c_1 should be activated. The output values are entered directly into the transition table as shown. The

Input combination (BEGIN, Q(7), COUNT6)

State	000	001	010	011	100	101	110	111
S_0	$S_0, \varnothing$	$S_0, \varnothing$	$S_0, \varnothing$	$S_0, \varnothing$	$S_1, \varnothing$	$S_1, \varnothing$	$S_1, \varnothing$	$S_1, \varnothing$
S_1	S_2, c_9, c_{10}	S_2, c_9, c_{10}	S_2, c_9, c_{10}	S_2, c_9, c_{10}				
S_2	S_4, c_8		S_3, c_8					
S_3			S_4, c_2, c_3, c_4	S_4, c_2, c_3, c_4				
S_4	S_5, c_0, c_1	S_7, c_0, c_1	S_5, c_0, c_1	S_6, c_0, c_1				
S_5	S_4, c_{11}	S_4, c_{11}	S_3, c_{11}	S_3, c_{11}				
S_6				S_7, c_2, c_3, c_4, c_5				
S_7		S_8, c_7		S_8, c_7				
S_8		$S_0,$ END	$S_0,$ END	$S_0,$ END				

FIGURE 4.19
State table for the multiplier control unit.

	State variable		
States	y_1	y_2	y_3
S_0	0	0	0
S_1	0	0	1
S_2'	0	1	0
S_3	0	1	1
S_4	1	0	0
S_5	1	0	1
S_6	1	1	0
S_7	1	1	1

FIGURE 4.20
State assignment for the multiplier control unit.

state transition $S_4 \rightarrow S_7$ implies that flip-flop $FF1$ should be left in the set state ($y_1 = 1$), while the other two flip-flops must be changed from the reset state ($y_2 = y_3 = 0$) to the set state ($y_2 = y_3 = 1$). Knowing the behavior of JK flip-flops, we can immediately specify the values required by flip-flop inputs $\{J_i\ K_i\}$ to cause these state changes. $J_1 = d$ and $K_1 = 0$ leaves $FF1$ unchanged, while $J_2 = J_3 = 1$ and $K_2 = K_3 = d$ (don't care) set both $FF2$ and $FF3$. These values are then entered into the transition table. A realization of N can then be obtained using any combinational circuit design method.

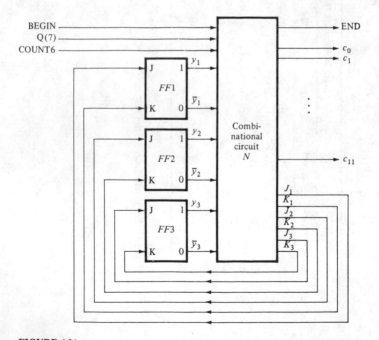

FIGURE 4.21
Multiplier control unit obtained by the state-table method.

Inputs						Outputs											
BEGIN	Q(7)	COUNT6	y_1	y_2	y_3	END	c_0	c_1	$\cdots$	c_{11}	J_1	K_1	J_2	K_2	J_3	K_3
0	0	0	0	0	0	0	0	0		0	0	d	0	d	0	d
0	0	0	0	0	1	0	0	0		0	0	d	1	d	d	1
*0	0	:	1	0	0	0	1	1	:	0	d	0	1	d	1	d
1	1	1	1	1	1	d	d	d		d	d	d	d	d	d	d

FIGURE 4.22
Transition table for the multiplier control unit.

Delay-element method. We can design the multiplier control unit directly from the flowchart of Fig. 4.18 by using the transformation rules defined in Fig. 4.7. The result is shown in Fig. 4.23. Nine delay elements are used, a consequence of the approximately one-to-one correspondence between the states and the delay

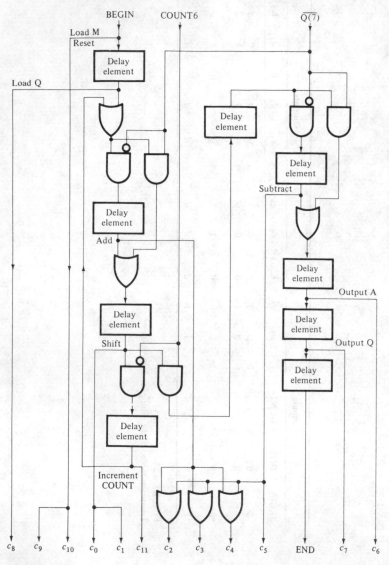

FIGURE 4.23
Multiplier control unit using delay elements.

elements. This circuit has the advantage of closely reflecting the structure of the flowchart being implemented, a fact that greatly simplifies the design process as well as subsequent maintenance of the circuit. It is also worth noting that very few combinational components are required, fewer than can be expected using the state-table approach. This is largely due to the fact that no decoding is required to identify the control-unit state.

Sequence-counter method. The essence of this approach is the organization of the multiplication algorithm into cycles of k repetitive actions that can be timed by a modulo-k sequence counter. Inspection of the flowchart for the multiplication algorithm reveals that it contains a single closed loop involving three steps—add, shift, and increment. This loop is traversed seven times. (In the general case where n-bit numbers are involved, it is traversed $n - 1$ times.) Thus we can attempt to design the control unit around a modulo-3 sequence counter.

The algorithm also involves some steps which are not part of the main closed loop. Two clock periods are required at the beginning to reset the control unit and load the input operands. At the end of the algorithm, three clock periods are required for correcting the final result and for transferring the product to the output bus. These initiation and termination steps can be performed in two extra cycles of the sequence counter, as indicated in Fig. 4.18. Thus the execution of a single multiplication instruction can be performed in nine cycles organized as follows.

Step 1 (cycle 1): Initialize the control unit and load the multiplier and multiplicand.

Step 2 (cycles 2 to 8): Form the product, multiplying by one multiplier bit per cycle.

Step 3 (cycle 9): Correct the product if necessary, and output the result.

In order to distinguish these three steps, it is necessary to introduce flip-flops that can be set to identify the current step. Figure 4.24 shows a design based on the foregoing principles. The modulo-3 sequence counter provides the main timing signals. Three SR flip-flops have been included to identify the three steps of the algorithm. (Actually two flip-flops would suffice, but would require additional decoding logic.) Each is set at the beginning of the corresponding step and reset at the end. A set of AND gates identify the particular microoperations to be performed in each clock period. The inputs to these AND gates come from three sources: the sequence counter, the three flip-flops, and the external control signals to the control unit. The inputs required by each AND gate are easily determined from the flowchart. For example, to load the Q register from the input bus, the control unit must be in step 1 with $\Phi_2 = 1$. Hence, the corresponding AND gate is connected to $FF1$ and Φ_2. Finally, the control signals c_0 through c_{11} and END are derived from the AND gates outputs via OR gates when two or more distinct microoperations require the same control lines to be activated.

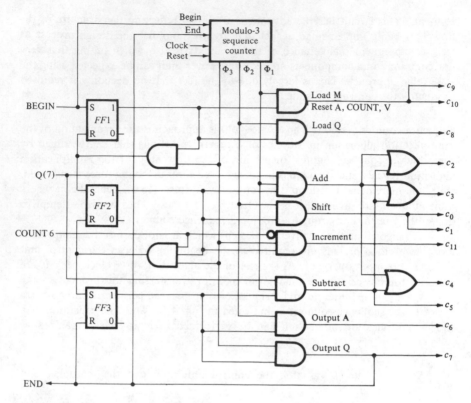

FIGURE 4.24
Multiplier control unit using a sequence counter.

4.2.3 CPU Control Unit

The design of the control logic for a CPU differs in degree but not in kind from the multiplier control unit of the preceding section. A CPU may contain several hundred control lines, which makes control-unit design quite complex. In this section we briefly examine some of the design issues involved, using the simplest possible RISC-style CPU as an example.

Consider the hypothetical CPU organization depicted in Fig. 3.2. Assume that it is required to execute the set of eight one-address instructions listed in Fig. 4.25. The algorithms needed to implement each instruction using the given hardware are easily derived. Figure 4.26 is a flowchart describing the instruction fetch cycle common to all instructions, as well as the distinct execution cycle required for each of the specified instructions. The microoperations in this flowchart determine the control signals and control points needed in the CPU. Figure 4.27 lists a suitable set of control signals and their functions, while Fig. 4.28 shows the approximate positions of the corresponding control lines in the CPU.

Mnemonic	Description
LOAD X	$AC \leftarrow M(X)$ (transfer contents of memory location X to the accumulator)
STORE X	$M(X) \leftarrow AC$
ADD X	$AC \leftarrow AC + M(X)$ (twos-complement addition)
AND X	$AC \leftarrow AC \wedge M(X)$ (logical AND)
JUMP X	$PC \leftarrow X$ (unconditional branch)
JUMPZ X	**if** $AC = 0$ **then** $PC \leftarrow X$ (conditional branch)
COMP	$AC \leftarrow \overline{AC}$ (complement accumulator)
RSHIFT	Right-shift accumulator

FIGURE 4.25
Instruction set to be implemented.

Implementation. The microoperations performed by the CPU can be viewed as forming a six-step closed loop as depicted in Fig. 4.12. The first three steps form the fetch cycle, and are identical for all instructions. The remaining execution steps vary with the instruction, which suggests that the control unit can be designed efficiently around a sequence counter. This is the only method we will consider here.

Let us suppose that every microoperation except READ M and WRITE M can be performed in one time unit of suitable length. Further suppose that READ M and WRITE M can be completed in two time units. Inspection of the CPU flowchart reveals that a "slow" instruction such as ADD requires eight time units, which are divided evenly between the fetch and execute cycles. An instruction such as JUMP requires only five time units, four in the fetch cycle and one in the execute cycle. We will therefore use a modulo-8 sequence counter driven by a clock whose period is equal to one time unit.

Figure 4.29 shows the general structure of a simple hardwired control unit. From the CPU flowchart it is determined which control signals must be activated for each instruction at every point of time in the instruction cycle. For example, c_3, which causes a memory read operation to take place, is activated when $\Phi_2 = 1$ to fetch an instruction. It is also activated when $\Phi_6 = 1$ to fetch an operand provided that the LOAD, ADD, or AND output of the instruction decoder is 1. c_3 can therefore be defined by the following logic equation

$$c_3 = \Phi_2 + \Phi_6 \, (\text{LOAD} + \text{ADD} + \text{AND})$$

which is implemented by the combinational circuit N in Fig. 4.29. In general, each control signal c_i can be defined by a logic equation of the form

$$c_i = \sum_j \left(\Phi_j \sum_m I_m \right)$$

where I_m is an output of the instruction decoder. In the case of an instruction requiring $j < k$ steps where k is the sequence counter modulus, the sequence counter may be reset after the jth step.

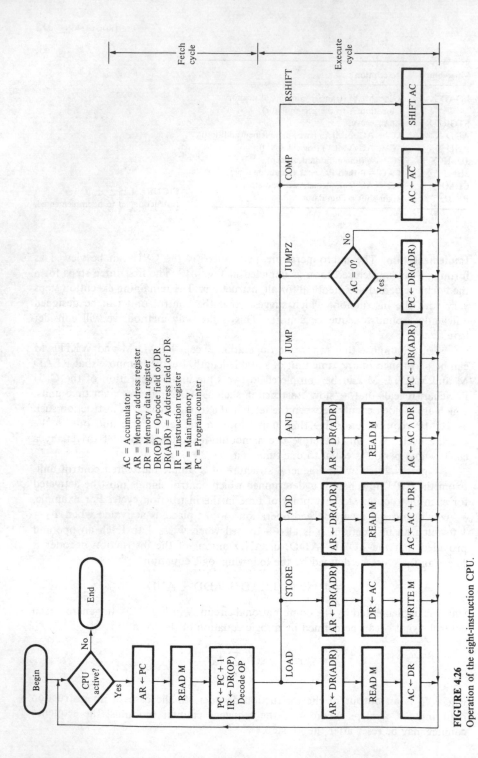

FIGURE 4.26
Operation of the eight-instruction CPU.

AC = Accumulator
AR = Memory address register
DR = Memory data register
DR(OP) = Opcode field of DR
DR(ADR) = Address field of DR
IR = Instruction register
M = Main memory
PC = Program counter

Control signal	Operation controlled
c_0	$AC \leftarrow AC + DR$
c_1	$AC \leftarrow AC \wedge DR$
c_2	$AC \leftarrow \overline{AC}$
c_3	$DR \leftarrow M(AR)$ (READ M)
c_4	$M(AR) \leftarrow DR$ (WRITE M)
c_5	$DR \leftarrow AC$
c_6	$AC \leftarrow DR$
c_7	$AR \leftarrow DR(ADR)$
c_8	$PC \leftarrow DR(ADR)$
c_9	$PC \leftarrow PC + 1$
c_{10}	$AR \leftarrow PC$
c_{11}	$IR \leftarrow DR(OP)$
c_{12}	RIGHT-SHIFT AC

FIGURE 4.27
Control signals of the simple CPU.

4.3 MICROPROGRAMMED CONTROL

We turn next to the design of control units that use microprograms to interpret and execute instructions.

4.3.1 Basic Concepts

Every instruction in a CPU is implemented by a sequence of one or more sets of concurrent microoperations. Each microoperation is associated with a specific set

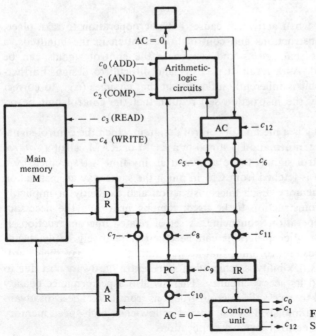

FIGURE 4.28
Structure of the simple CPU.

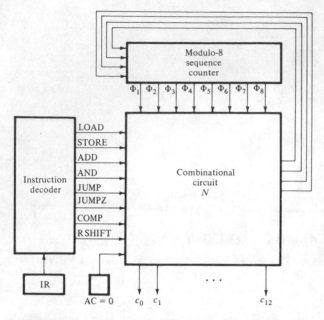

FIGURE 4.29
Hardwired CPU control unit using a sequence counter.

of control lines which, when activated, cause that microoperation to take place. Since the number of instructions and control lines is often in the hundreds, a hardwired control unit that selects and sequences the control signals can be exceedingly complicated. As a result, it is costly and difficult to design. Furthermore, such a control unit is inherently inflexible in that changes (e.g., to correct design errors or modify the instruction set) require that the control unit be redesigned.

Microprogramming is a method of control design in which the control-signal selection and sequencing information is stored in a ROM or RAM called a *control memory* CM. The control signals to be activated at any time are specified by a *microinstruction*, which is fetched from CM in much the same way an instruction is fetched from main memory. Each microinstruction also explicitly or implicitly specifies the next microinstruction to be used, thereby providing the necessary information for microoperation sequencing. A set of related microinstructions is called a *microprogram*. Microprograms can be changed relatively easily; hence microprogramming yields control units that are far more flexible than their hardwired counterparts. This flexibility is achieved at some extra hardware cost due to the control memory and its access circuitry. There is also a performance penalty due to the time required to access the microinstructions from CM. These disadvantages have been greatly diminished by the advent of low-cost, high-speed memory technologies suitable for control memory applications.

In a microprogrammed CPU, each machine instruction is executed by a microprogram which acts as a real-time interpreter for the instruction. The set of microprograms that interpret a particular instruction set or language L is sometimes called an *emulator* for L. A microprogrammed computer C_1 can often be used to execute programs written in the machine language L_2 of some other computer C_2 by placing an emulator for L_2 in the control memory of C_1. C_1 is then said to be capable of emulating C_2.

As a design activity microprogramming can be compared with assembly-language programming; however, the microprogrammer requires a more detailed knowledge of the processor hardware than the assembly-language programmer. Symbolic languages similar to assembly languages are normally used to write microprograms: these are referred to as *microassembly languages*. A *microassembler* is required to translate such microprograms into executable programs that can be stored in the control memory.

Wilkes' design. A microinstruction in its simplest form has two major parts: a set of *control fields* which indicate the control lines to be activated, and an *address field* which indicates the address in the CM of the next microinstruction to be executed. In the original scheme proposed by M.V. Wilkes in 1951 [22], each bit k_i of the control fields corresponds to a distinct control line c_i. When $k_i = 1$ in the current microinstruction, c_i is activated; otherwise c_i remains inactive.

Figure 4.30 shows an example of Wilkes' original proposal for microprogrammed control unit design [12, 22]. The control memory, organized as a ROM, is composed of a PLA-like diode matrix of the type discussed in Sec. 2.3.2. The left part of the ROM (called matrix A in Ref. 22) contains the control fields of every

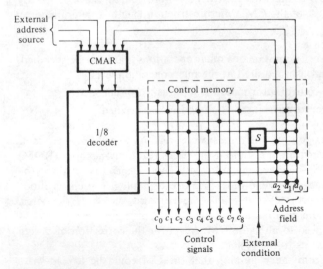

FIGURE 4.30
A microprogrammed control unit based on Wilkes' original design.

microinstruction, while the right part (matrix B) contains the (3-bit) address fields. The rows of CM represent microinstructions. The columns of CM represent either control lines or address lines. A register, called the *control memory address register* (CMAR), stores the address of the current microinstruction. This address is decoded, causing one of the horizontal lines of the diode matrix to become active. All vertical lines connected by a black dot (denoting the presence of a diode) to any given horizontal line are activated when the horizontal line becomes active. For example, when the topmost horizontal line in the CM of Fig. 4.30, which represents the microinstruction with address 000, is selected, control lines c_0, c_2, c_3, and c_7 are activated. At the same time the address field contents (001) are sent to the CMAR, where they are stored and used to address the next microinstruction.

As Fig. 4.30 indicates, the CMAR may be loaded from an external source as well as from the address field of a microinstruction. Typically this external source provides the starting address of a microprogram stored in the CM. For example, in a typical microprogrammed CPU, each instruction is executed by (or interpreted by) a specific microprogram. The instruction opcode after suitable encoding provides the starting address for its microprogram.

A requirement of any control unit is the ability to respond to external signals or conditions. This requirement is satisfied in the Wilkes scheme by introducing a switch S controlled by an "external condition" flip-flop which allows one of two possible address fields to be selected. Thus in Figure 4.30, the fourth microinstruction may be followed by the microinstruction with address 011 or 100 as specified by the external condition. This feature makes conditional jumps within a microprogram possible.

Many modifications to this basic design have been proposed over the years. A major area of concern is the microinstruction word length, since it greatly influences the size and cost of the CM. Microinstruction length is determined by three major factors:

1. The maximum number of simultaneous microoperations that must be specified, i.e., the degree of parallelism required at the microoperation level
2. The way in which the control information is represented or encoded
3. The way in which the next microinstruction address is specified

In the early years, control memories were read-only devices, i.e., their contents could not be altered on-line. Indeed the terms read-only memory (ROM) and read-only store (ROS) were synonymous with control memory. Among the reasons for this is the fact that read-only memory technologies such as diode matrices provide faster access rates than read-write memories such as ferrite cores. Furthermore, the instruction set of a microprogrammed processor was viewed as permanent, implying no need to alter the CM except for the correction of design errors or minor enhancements to the system.

It was recognized from the beginning that the CM could be a read-write memory. Wilkes observed that such a device, usually called a *writable control memory* (WCM), would have a number of "fascinating possibilities," but doubted that its cost could be justified [22]. The most interesting feature of a WCM is that it allows the instruction set of a machine to be changed, simply by changing the microprograms that interpret the instruction opcodes. Thus we can provide the same machine with different instruction sets which may be tailored to specific applications. Computers with WCMs are often considered to have no instruction set in the usual sense. A computer with a WCM is called *dynamically micropro-grammable* because the control memory contents can be altered under program control.

Parallelism in microinstructions. Microprogrammable processors are frequently characterized by the maximum number of microoperations that can be specified by a single microinstruction. This number can vary from one to several hundred.

Microinstructions that specify a single microoperation are quite similar to conventional machine instructions. They are relatively short, but due to the lack of parallelism, more microinstructions may be needed to perform a given operation. The format of the IBM System/370 Model 145, which is shown in Fig. 4.31, is representative of this type of microinstruction [13]. It consists of 4 bytes (32 bits). The leftmost byte (shaded) is an opcode that specifies the microoperation to be performed. The next 2 bytes specify operands. In most cases, these bytes are addresses of CPU registers. The rightmost byte contains information used to construct the address of the next microinstruction.

Microinstructions are often designed to take advantage of the fact that at the microprogramming level, many operations can be performed in parallel. If all useful combinations of parallel microoperations were specified by a single opcode, the number of opcodes would, in most cases, be enormous. Furthermore, a microinstruction decoder of considerable complexity would be needed. To avoid these difficulties it is usual to divide the microoperation specification part of the microinstruction into k disjoint control fields. Each control field is associated with a set of microoperations, any one of which can be performed simultaneously with the microoperations specified by the remaining control fields. A control field usually specifies the control-line values for a single device such as an adder, a register, or a bus. In the extreme case represented by Fig. 4.30, there may be a 1-bit control field for every control line in the system.

A more typical example is shown in Fig. 4.32, which is the microinstruction format used in the IBM System/360 Model 50 [12]. A total of 90 bits are used, which are partitioned into separate fields for various purposes. There are 21 fields, shown shaded in Fig. 4.32, which constitute the control fields. The remaining fields

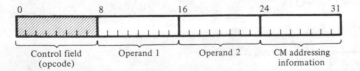

FIGURE 4.31
Microinstruction format of the IBM System/360 Model 145.

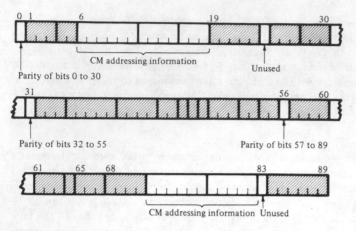

FIGURE 4.32
90-bit microinstruction format of the IBM System/360 Model 50 (shaded areas are control fields).

are used for generating the next microinstruction address and for error detection by means of parity bits. For example, the 3-bit control field consisting of bits 65 to 67 controls the right input to the main CPU adder. This field indicates which of several possible registers should be connected to the right input of the adder. The control field comprising bits 68 to 71 identifies the particular function to be performed by the adder. The possible functions include binary addition and decimal addition with various ways of handling input and output carry bits. (For further details, see Ref. 12.)

The scheme of Fig. 4.30, in which there is a control field for every control line, is wasteful of CM space, since many combinations of control signals that can be specified by the microinstruction are never used. Consider, for instance, the register R of Fig. 4.33, which may be loaded from one of four independent sources using the control lines c_0, c_1, c_2, c_3. Suppose that there is 1 bit for each of these control lines in a microinstruction control field. Only the 5 bit patterns shown in Fig. 4.34a are valid, since any other patterns will cause an erroneous attempt to load R from two independent sources simultaneously. These five patterns can be encoded into a field of width $\lceil \log_2 5 \rceil = 3$ bits, as shown in Fig.

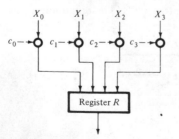

FIGURE 4.33
A register that can be loaded from four independent sources.

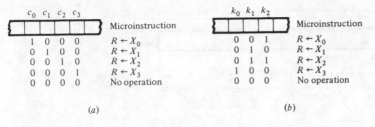

FIGURE 4.34
Control field for the circuit of Fig. 4.33: (*a*) unencoded format; (*b*) encoded format.

4.34*b*. In general, any n independent control signals or microoperations can be encoded in a control field of $\lceil \log_2(n + 1) \rceil$ bits, assuming that it is necessary to be able to specify a no-operation condition when no control signals are to be activated.

The unencoded format of Fig. 4.34*a* has the advantage that the control signals may be derived directly from the microinstruction. Suppose that the microinstruction is loaded into a register, e.g., the CM data register, which is usually referred to as the *microinstruction register* μIR. The outputs of the control part of this register are the control lines, as shown in Fig. 4.35*a*. When encoded control fields are used, each control field must be connected to a decoder from which the control signals are derived, as shown in Fig. 4.35*b* and *c*.

Microinstructions are commonly classified as horizontal or vertical. *Horizontal* microinstructions have the following general attributes:

1. Long formats
2. Ability to express a high degree of parallelism
3. Little encoding of the control information

Vertical microinstructions, on the other hand, are characterized by

1. Short formats
2. Limited ability to express parallel microoperations
3. Considerable encoding of the control information

The format of the IBM System/360 Model 50 shown in Fig. 4.32 is representative of horizontal microinstructions, while that of the System/370 Model 145 shown in Fig. 4.31 is representative of vertical microinstructions.

The reader will encounter more rigid definitions of horizontal and vertical in the literature on microprogramming than those given above. One definition is based entirely on the degree of encoding. A horizontal microinstruction format allows no encoding of control information, whereas a vertical format does. An alternative definition is based on the degree of parallelism possible. A vertical microinstruction can specify only one microoperation (no parallelism), while a

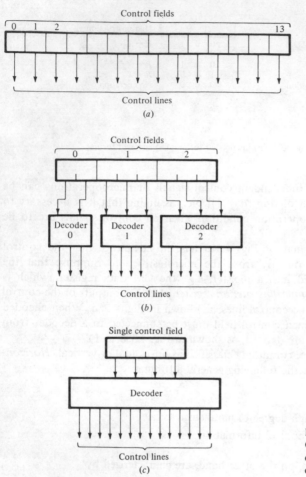

FIGURE 4.35
Control-field formats: (a) no encoding; (b) some encoding; (c) complete encoding.

horizontal microinstruction can specify many microoperations. These definitions are not entirely independent, since a large amount of parallelism implies little encoding, and vice versa. Thus the format of Fig. 4.35a is horizontal and that of Fig. 4.35c is vertical under both definitions. The intermediate case represented by Fig. 4.35b may be called horizontal by some authors and vertical by others.

Microinstruction addressing. In the Wilkes design of Fig. 4.30, each microinstruction contains the CM address of the next microinstruction to be executed. In the case of branch microinstructions, two possible next addresses are included. This explicit address specification has the advantage that no time is lost in microinstruction address generation, but it is wasteful of CM space.

The address fields can be eliminated from all but branch instructions by using a *microprogram counter* μPC as the primary source of microinstruction addresses. Its role is analogous to that of the program counter PC at the instruction level. Since only instructions have to be fetched from CM, the μPC is also used as the CM address register.

Conditional branching, clearly a desirable feature in microprograms, is implemented in a variety of ways. The condition to be tested is generally a condition variable or flag generated by the data processing unit. If several such conditions exist, a *condition select* subfield is often included in the microinstruction to indicate which of the possible condition variables is to be tested. The branch address may be contained in the microinstruction itself, in which case it is loaded into the CM address register when a branch condition is satisfied. CM space can be conserved by not storing a complete address field in the microinstruction, but by storing instead, say, some low-order bits of the address. This restricts the range of branch instructions to a small region of the CM, and may therefore increase the difficulty of writing some microprograms.

An alternative approach to branching is to allow the condition variables to modify the contents of the CM address register directly, thus eliminating wholly or in part the need for branch addresses in microinstructions. For example, let the condition variable v indicate an overflow condition when $v = 1$, and the normal no-overflow condition when $v = 0$. Suppose that we want to execute a SKIP ON OVERFLOW microinstruction. This can be done by logically connecting v to the count enable input of μPC at an appropriate point in the microinstruction cycle. This allows the overflow condition to increment μPC an extra time, thus performing the desired skip operation.

Microoperation timing. So far we have assumed that each microinstruction generates a set of control signals which are active for the duration of the microinstruction's execution cycle. A single clock pulse therefore synchronizes all the control signals; the clock period can be the same as the microinstruction cycle period. This mode of control is termed *monophase*. The number of microinstructions needed to specify a particular operation can often be reduced by dividing the microinstruction cycle into several sequential *phases* or subperiods. Each control signal is typically active during only one of the phases. This mode of operation, which is called *polyphase*, permits a single microinstruction to specify a sequence of microoperations. An increase in the complexity of the microinstruction format can be expected, since it is necessary to specify the phases during which a control signal is to be activated.

Consider a microinstruction that implements the register transfer operation

$$R \leftarrow f(R_1, R_2)$$

where R can be R_1 or R_2. Depending on the implementation, this operation might be performed in several phases. The following four-phase interpretation is common [12].

Phase Φ_1: Transfer the contents of registers R_1 and R_2 to the inputs of the f unit.

Phase Φ_2: Store the result generated by the f unit in a temporary register or latch L.

Phase Φ_3: Transfer the contents of L to the destination register R.

Phase Φ_4: Fetch the next microinstruction from CM.

Figure 4.36 shows the timing signals associated with these four phases.

The time required to fetch a microinstruction from CM is often a significant portion of the total microinstruction cycle time. The microinstruction fetch and execute steps can be overlapped in much the same way that the instruction fetch and execute steps are overlapped at the machine-language level. A fairly simple way of doing this is to replace the microinstruction register μIR by a pair of registers forming a two-segment pipeline, as shown in Fig. 4.37. While one microinstruction in μIR1 is being executed, the next microinstruction can be fetched and placed in μIR0. The equivalent behavior may also be achieved by using a single register composed of master-slave flip-flops.

So far we have assumed that the influence of a microinstruction control field is limited to the period during which the microinstruction is executed. This restriction can be lifted by storing the control field in a register which continues to exercise control until it is modified by a subsequent microinstruction. This technique is called *residual control* and is particularly useful when microinstructions are used to allocate the resources of a system. For example, a connection between two units may be established by a microinstruction and maintained for an arbitrarily long period of time via residual control.

Control unit organization. We now consider the structure of a typical modern microprogrammed control unit. Suppose that the microinstruction format shown in Fig. 4.38 is used. Each microinstruction has three main parts.

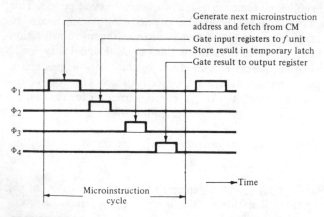

FIGURE 4.36
Timing diagram for a typical four-phase microinstruction.

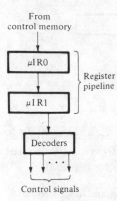

From control memory

μIR0

Register pipeline

μIR1

Decoders

· · ·

Control signals

FIGURE 4.37
Register pipeline allowing overlap of microinstruction fetching and execution.

1. A condition select field is used to specify the external condition to be tested in the case of conditional branch microinstructions.
2. An address field contains the next address field to be used when a branch condition is satisfied. It is assumed that a microprogram counter μPC is used to provide the next microinstruction address when no branching is required.
3. The rest of the microinstruction specifies in encoded or unencoded format the control signals that must be activated to perform the desired microoperations.

Figure 4.39 shows a control unit designed around this microinstruction format. The counter μPC is the address register for the control memory CM. The contents of the addressed word in CM are transferred to the microinstruction register μIR. The control fields are decoded (if necessary) and used to generate control signals for the data processing unit. μPC is then incremented. If a branch is specified by a microinstruction in μIR, the contents of the microinstruction address field are loaded in μPC.

In the scheme of Fig. 4.39, the microinstruction condition select field is used to control a multiplexer which activates the parallel-load control input of μPC based on the status of external condition variables. Suppose, for example, that two condition variables v_1, v_2 must be tested. A condition select field $s_0\, s_1$ of 2 bits suffices, with the following interpretation.

s_0	s_1	Meaning
0	0	No branching
0	1	Branch if $v_1 = 1$
1	0	Branch if $v_2 = 1$
1	1	Unconditional branch

The multiplexer has four inputs x_0, x_1, x_2, x_3, where x_i is routed to the multiplexer output when $s_0\, s_1 = i$. Hence we require $x_0 = 0$, $x_1 = v_1$, $x_2 = v_2$, and $x_3 = 1$ to control the loading of microinstruction branch addresses into μPC in this case.

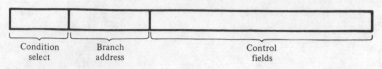

| Condition select | Branch address | Control fields |

FIGURE 4.38
Typical microinstruction format.

Finally, a provision is also made for loading μPC with an address from an external source. This is used for loading the starting address of the desired microprogram in cases where CM contains more than one microprogram.

Example 4.2   The Advanced Micro Devices 2909 microprogram sequencer [1,16]. Like the 2901 4-bit processor (Example 3.5), the 2909 is an early member of the AMD 2900 family of microprocessor components. It is designed to generate microinstruction addresses for a control memory CM, and comprises a microprogram counter μPC and all the logic needed for next address generation. Devices of this type are termed *microprogram sequencers*. The 2909 thus replaces μPC and the multiplexer MUX appearing in Fig. 4.39; it also adds a stack to implement subroutine calls at the microprogram level. Figure 4.40 shows the internal organization of the 2909. Reflect-

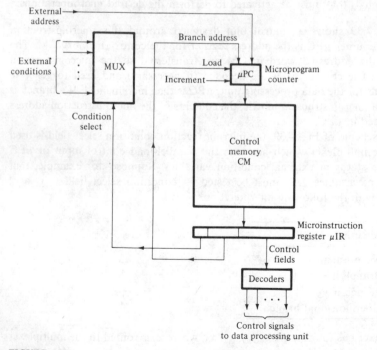

FIGURE 4.39
Typical microprogrammed control unit.

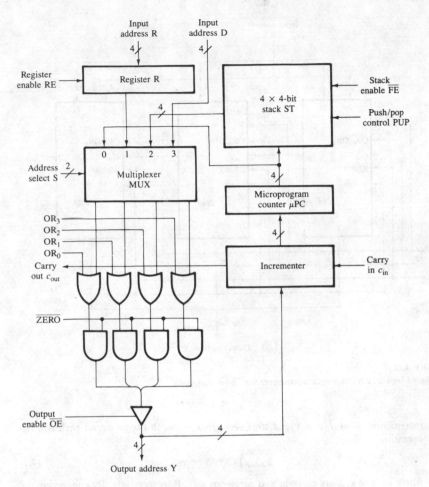

FIGURE 4.40
Structure of the 2909 microprogram sequencer slice.

ing the LSI technology of the late 1970s, it handles only addresses that are 4 bits long, thus limiting a single 2909 IC to controlling a 16-word CM. However, the 2909 also has the bit-sliced organization of the 2901, which allows k copies of the 2909 to be cascaded to form a microprogram sequencer for $4k$-word addresses. Thus three copies of the 2909 connected as shown in Fig. 4.41 can process 12-bit addresses and accommodate a 4096-word control memory.

The main function of a microprogram sequencer is to transfer an address from one of several internal and external address sources to an output bus (the 4-bit bus Y in the 2909 case) that is connected to the address bus of CM. The 2909 has four separate address sources: its microprogram counter μPC, an external bus D, a register R that is attached to a second external bus, and a 4-word internal pushdown stack ST. μPC is actually implemented by a 4-bit register of the same name, and a separate

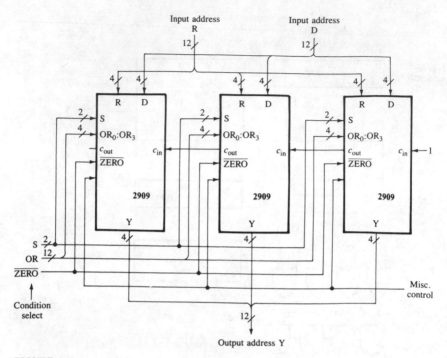

FIGURE 4.41
2909-based bit-sliced microprogram sequencer for 12-bit addresses.

incrementer, as shown in Fig. 4.40. Every clock cycle, this logic circuit performs the operation

$$c_{out} \cdot \mu PC \leftarrow Y + c_{in} \qquad (4.2)$$

where c_{in} and c_{out} are carry-in and carry-out signals, respectively. By connecting the c_{out} output line of each 2909 in an array of k 2909s to the c_{in} input of the 2909 to its left, the operation (4.2) can be extended to addresses of arbitrary length. No provision is made in the 2909 for carry lookahead since, in practice, $k = 3$ or 4 is adequate for most CPU designs.

If a sequence of microinstructions without branches (a so-called *straight-line microprogram* or *SLM*) is being executed, then (4.2) alone suffices for microinstruction sequencing. Most microprograms, however, involve some branching to nonconsecutive addresses in CM. A branch address may be made available as the address of the next microinstruction by connecting the appropriate address field of the current microinstruction in the external microinstruction register μIR to the 2909's D or R bus in the manner of Fig. 4.39. The stack ST serves as the remaining address source. ST, which is constructed along the lines of Fig. 4.2, is intended to support subroutine calls within microprograms. A microsubroutine call operation of the form CALL X is implemented by pushing the contents of μPC into ST and taking the next address X from the D or R source. A subsequent return from the microsubroutine requires popping ST into μPC. Four addresses can be stored in ST, which allows up to four subroutine calls to be nested within a microprogram.

The four possible address sources μPC, D, R, and ST are connected to a multiplexer MUX which, as shown in Fig. 4.40, is controlled by the two external select lines S. These lines are typically driven from a two-bit condition select field in the current microinstruction; they may also be connected to CPU flags or interrupt request lines. The 2909 provides five additional control lines, denoted $OR_0{:}OR_3$ and $\overline{\text{ZERO}}$, that allow external conditions to modify the address selected by MUX. For example, if $\overline{\text{ZERO}}$ is activated ($\overline{\text{ZERO}} = 0$) then Y becomes 0000. This line is typically connected to a reset signal which forces the control unit to begin execution of a microprogram whose starting address is all 0s. The OR_i lines can force selected bits of Y to 1 to implement conditional branches relative to the current address, e.g., to skip the next microinstruction. The stack ST is enabled by the $\overline{\text{FE}}$ (file enable) line, while the push-pop select line PUP causes a push (pop) to be performed when PUP $= 1$ (0).

Thus microinstruction sequencing by the 2909 is controlled by signals that are derived from a combination of microinstruction control fields and external conditions. For example, suppose the address X is applied to the 2909s input bus D. The following microinstruction control fields

$$S,\overline{\text{FE}},\text{PUP},\text{OR},\overline{\text{ZERO}} = 11,1,d,0000,1 \qquad (4.3)$$

implement the operation **go to** X. The effect of (4.3) is to disable ST and the OR-AND address-modification logic while routing the desired branch address X from D to Y. The microoperation CALL X, where X is stored in the R register, is specified by

$$S,\overline{\text{FE}},\text{PUP},\text{OR},\overline{\text{ZERO}} = 01,0,1,0000,1$$

while RETURN is implemented by

$$S,\overline{\text{FE}},\text{PUP},\text{OR},\overline{\text{ZERO}} = 10,0,0,0000,1$$

4.3.2 Control-Memory Optimization

The control memory CM is a major contributor to the total cost of a microprogrammed control unit. The cost of CM itself may be measured by two parameters: its width W, which is the number of bits per microinstruction; and its height H, which is the number of microinstructions it stores. As indicated in the preceding section, W can be reduced systematically by encoding control fields, while H can be reduced by including many parallel microoperations (active control fields) within each microinstruction. While the problems of minimizing W and H with respect to a given set of microinstructions are not computationally feasible—they are, in fact, intractable in the sense of Sec. 1.1.2—they are among the few general design problems in the microprogramming area that are amenable to precise analysis. We first examine the problem of minimizing W, which is related to the gate-minimization problem covered in Sec. 2.2.2. Then we briefly discuss the minimization of H.

Minimizing W. Suppose that a set of microinstructions $I_1, I_2, \ldots, I_m$ has been defined for a given processor. Each microinstruction specifies a subset of the available control lines $c_1, c_2, \ldots, c_n$ which must be activated. Our objective is to derive a format for the microinstruction control fields of the type depicted in Fig. 4.35b such that the total number of bits in the control fields is a minimum. In other words, we want a control-field encoding method that uses as few bits as possible.

An encoded control field can activate only one control signal at a time. Two control signals can be included in the same control field only if they are never simultaneously activated by a microinstruction; such control signals are said to be compatible. More formally, let $c_i \in I_j$ denote that control signal c_i is to be activated by microinstruction I_j. Two control signals c_1 and c_2 are *compatible* if $c_1 \in I_j$ implies that $c_2 \notin I_j$, and vice versa. A *compatibility class* is a set of control signals that are pairwise compatible. Clearly the control signals included in any one control field must form a compatibility class. The minimum number of bits needed to encode a compatibility class C_i is $\lceil \log_2(|C_i| + 1) \rceil$. We will assume that the control-field decoder must produce $|C_i| + 1$ distinct outputs, including the no-operation case where no control line is activated.

The minimization problem can now be defined formally as follows. Find a set of compatibility classes $\{C_i\}$ such that

1. Every control signal is contained in at least one member of $\{C_i\}$.
2. The width cost function $W = \sum_i \lceil \log_2(|C_i| + 1) \rceil$ is a minimum.

Note that only the microinstruction control field width is being minimized. Other fields such as the next address or condition select fields are not considered.

We now describe a minimization algorithm for W due to Sunil R. Das, Dilip K. Banerji, and A. Chattopadhyay [6]. The *maximal compatibility classes* (MCCs) are defined as compatibility classes to which no control signals can be added without introducing a pair of incompatible control signals. Clearly the compatibility classes that minimize W are subsets of the MCCs. The minimization process involves three major steps.

Step 1. Determine the set of MCCs.

Step 2. Determine all minimal sets of MCCs that include each control signal. Each of these sets is called a *minimal MCC cover*. (Note that a minimal MCC cover does not in general yield a minimum value of the cost function W.)

Step 3. Inspect each minimal MCC cover $\{C_i\}$ in turn and determine all ways of including each control signal in exactly one subset of some C_i. Calculate the cost W of the resulting solutions and select one with the minimum cost.

It is interesting to note that the first two steps are closely related to well-known procedures in switching theory [14]. The problem of minimizing the number of states in an incompletely specified sequential machine involves finding maximal compatibility classes among the states. Step 2 requires solving a covering problem similar to the prime implicant covering problem which forms part of most two-level gate minimization methods (see Sec. 2.2.1). The MCCs correspond to prime implicants and the control signals correspond to minterms. Many of the methods developed for simplifying the prime-implicant covering problem may be used in step 2. Step 3 also involves a similar covering problem.

The MCCs may be derived systematically by first determining all compatibility classes containing two control signals, then determining all compatibility classes containing three control signals, and so on. Let S_i denote the set of compatibility classes $\{C_{ij}\}$ such that C_{ij} contains i control signals and $i \geq 1$. The members of S_1 are simply the n original control signals. S_{i+1} is constructed from S_i as follows. Consider each member C_{ij} of S_i in turn. Add a new control signal to C_{ij} to form C. Test C to determine if it is a compatibility class. If it is, add C to S_{i+1} and delete C_{ij} and any other subsets of C from S_i. Form all possible $(i + 1)$-member compatibility classes in this way, then move on to S_{i+2}. The process terminates when no new compatibility classes can be formed, i.e., when $S_k = \varnothing$, the empty set, for some $k \leq n + 1$. The compatibility classes that have not been deleted from the list $S_1, S_2, \ldots, S_k$ are the MCCs. Figure 4.43 shows the computation of the MCCs for the four microinstructions defined in Fig. 4.42. For brevity, a compatibility class $\{a, b, c, \ldots\}$ is denoted by $abc. \ldots$ It can be seen that there are eight MCCs in this case: a, cd, bde, bdh, deg, dgh, efg, and fgh.

Minimal MCC covers. The minimal MCC covers are most easily obtained by constructing a *cover table* containing a row for each MCC C_i and a column for each control signal c_j. An x is placed at the intersection of the ith row and jth column if $c_j \in C_i$, or, in other words, if C_i *covers* c_j. Figure 4.44 shows the cover table corresponding to the microinstruction set of the running example (Fig. 4.42).

Certain rows and columns can be deleted from a cover table to simplify determination of the minimal MCC covers.

1. Suppose that column c_j contains only one x, which occurs in row C_i. C_i is said to be an *essential MCC* and must appear in every minimal MCC cover, since it is the only MCC that covers c_j. All rows corresponding to essential MCCs can be deleted from the cover table. In the case of Fig. 4.44, C_1 and C_2 are the essential MCCs and can be deleted. Furthermore, all columns with x's in essential rows can be deleted. This implies that the columns a, c, and d can be deleted from Fig. 4.44.

2. If the cover table contains two or more identical columns, then all but one of those columns can be deleted.

Microinstruction	Control signals
I_1	a, b, c, g
I_2	a, c, e, h
I_3	a, d, f
I_4	b, c, f

FIGURE 4.42
A set of microinstructions and the control signals they activate.

S_1: a, b̸, f̸, d̸, e̸, f̸, g̸, h̸

S_2: b̸d̸, b̸e̸, b̸h̸, cd, d̸e̸, d̸g̸, d̸h̸, e̸f̸, e̸g̸, f̸g̸, f̸h̸, g̸h̸

S_3: bde, bdh, deg, dgh, efg, fgh

S_4: ∅

FIGURE 4.43
Computation of the MCCs for the microinstructions of Fig. 4.42.

3. Column c_i is said to *dominate* column c_j if c_i contains an x in every row where c_j contains an x, and c_i contains more x's than c_j. The dominating column c_i can be deleted since every MCC that covers c_j automatically covers c_i. In Fig. 4.44, d dominates b and c, while g dominates f.

4. Row C_i is said to dominate row C_j if C_i contains an x in every column where C_j contains an x, and C_i contains more x's than C_j. In this case, the dominated row C_j can be deleted, since C_i covers all the control signals that are covered by C_j. Figure 4.44 contains no row domination.

Figure 4.45 shows the result of deleting essential rows, the columns covered by essential rows, and dominating columns from the example cover table. It can be seen immediately that a minimal cover for this table contains two MCCs, and the possible choices are $\{C_3, C_8\}$ and $\{C_4, C_7\}$. Combining these with the essential MCCs C_1 and C_2, we conclude that the desired MCC solutions are $\{C_1, C_2, C_3, C_8\}$ and $\{C_1, C_2, C_4, C_7\}$.

While minimal MCC covers can be obtained by inspection from very small cover tables, more formal methods are needed for large tables. A conceptually simple approach is to derive the minimal MCC cover from a logical expression that embodies the covering conditions. This is known as *Petrick's method*. Let $\mathbf{C}_i$ be a Boolean variable which is 1 if C_i is selected for inclusion in a set of MCCs that cover all columns of a cover table; $\mathbf{C}_i$ is 0 otherwise. Let $C_{j1}, C_{j2}, \ldots, C_{jn_j}$ be the MCCs that cover column f_j. To ensure that f_j is covered, the Boolean equation

$$\mathbf{C}_{j1} + \mathbf{C}_{j2} + \cdots + \mathbf{C}_{jn_j} = 1$$

must be satisfied. This equation says, in effect, that C_{j1} must be selected or C_{j2} must be selected or C_{j3} must be selected, etc. In order that every column be

MCCs	Control signals							
	a	b	c	d	e	f	g	h
$C_1 = a$	x							
$C_2 = cd$			x	x				
$C_3 = bde$		x		x	x			
$C_4 = bdh$		x		x				x
$C_5 = deg$				x	x		x	
$C_6 = dgh$				x			x	x
$C_7 = efg$					x	x	x	
$C_8 = fgh$						x	x	x

FIGURE 4.44
Cover table for the microinstructions of Fig. 4.42.

MCCs	Control signals			
	b	e	f	h
$C_3 = bde$	x	x		
$C_4 = bdh$	x			x
$C_5 = deg$		x		
$C_6 = dgh$				x
$C_7 = efg$		x	x	
$C_8 = fgh$			x	x

FIGURE 4.45
Reduced cover table obtained from Fig. 4.44.

covered, the expression $C_{j1} + C_{j2} + \cdots + C_{jn_j}$ must be 1 for $j = 1, 2, \ldots, n$. In other words, the product-of-sums Boolean equation

$$\prod_{j=1}^{n} (C_{j1} + C_{j2} + \cdots + C_{jn_j}) = 1 \qquad (4.4)$$

must be satisfied. Every solution to (4.4) defines a cover for the original cover table.

To solve (4.4) we can simply multiply it out, using the distributive laws of Boolean algebra to convert it to a sum-of-products expression of the form

$$\sum_{k=1}^{p} (C_{k1} C_{k2} \cdots C_{kn_k}) = 1 \qquad (4.5)$$

Every product term $C_{k1} C_{k2} \cdots C_{kn_k}$ in (4.5) implies that $\{C_{k1}, C_{k2}, \ldots, C_{kn_k}\}$ is a distinct solution to the covering problem. The product terms containing the fewest C_i variables define the minimal MCC covers.

Let us apply Petrick's method to the reduced cover table of Fig. 4.45. The initial product-of-sums expression is

$$(C_3 + C_4)(C_3 + C_5 + C_7)(C_7 + C_8)(C_4 + C_6 + C_8) = 1 \qquad (4.6)$$

This expression is reduced to a sum-of-products by applying the two distributive laws from Fig. 2.15:

$$a(b + c) = ab + ac \qquad (4.7)$$

$$(a + b)(a + c) = a + bc \qquad (4.8)$$

in any order. It is desirable to apply (4.8) as often as possible, since it eliminates an a term, whereas (4.7) adds an a term. Applying (4.8) twice to (4.6) yields

$$(C_3 + C_4(C_5 + C_7))(C_8 + C_7(C_4 + C_6)) = 1$$

Two applications of (4.7) yield

$$(C_3 + C_4C_5 + C_4C_7)(C_8 + C_4C_7 + C_6C_7) = 1$$

Using (4.8) again we obtain

$$C_4C_7 + (C_3 + C_4C_5)(C_8 + C_6C_7) = 1$$

and finally

$$C_4C_7 + C_3C_8 + C_3C_6C_7 + C_4C_5C_8 + C_4C_5C_6C_7 = 1 \qquad (4.9)$$

From inspection of (4.9) it can be seen that the only minimal MCC covers for the reduced cover table are $\{C_4, C_7\}$ and $\{C_3, C_8\}$. Combining these with the essential MCCs C_1 and C_2, we conclude that $\{C_1, C_2, C_4, C_7\}$ and $\{C_1, C_2, C_3, C_8\}$ are the minimal MCC covers for the original cover table.

The amount of computation required by Petrick's method for large tables is substantial. It may be more efficient to derive the minimum covers using other algorithmic or heuristic techniques [2, 7]; see Prob. 4.17.

The number of MCCs in each minimal MCC cover is the minimum number of control fields required to encode the given microinstructions. If control signal c_i is covered by two MCCs C_1 and C_2, then c_i can be deleted from C_1 or C_2 to yield a new non-MCC cover of potentially lower cost. In the final step of the algorithm, we consider all possible ways of deleting control signals from the MCC covers so that in the resulting cover each control signal is covered once, i.e., the cover is a partition of the set of control signals. The final solution is obtained by computing W for each partition and selecting one with the minimum value of W.

The partitions may be derived manually from each minimal MCC cover by setting up a cover table whose rows are the members of the MCC cover. Then for each control signal c_i, select a row C_j containing c_i and delete c_i from the covers defining the remaining rows. (Note that if C_j is an essential row it is the only possible cover for c_i.) The process is repeated until all control signals have been covered. The resulting compatibility classes form a partition. All possible partitions of the set of microoperations are obtained and their cost functions W are calculated. This procedure is repeated for every MCC solution, and a partition with the minimum value of W is selected.

Consider one of the two minimal MCC covers $\{C_1, C_2, C_3, C_8\}$ obtained for the running example. Figure 4.46 shows the corresponding cover table. There is only one way in which a, b, c, e, f, g, and h can be covered. d may be covered by either C_2 or C_3. If we decide to cover it by C_2, we delete d from C_3 obtaining the partition $\{a, cd, be, fgh\}$ for which $W = 7$. If, however, we cover d using C_3, we obtain the partition $\{a, c, bde, fgh\}$ for which $W = 6$. Similarly, the other minimal MCC cover $\{C_1, C_2, C_4, C_7\}$ yields the two partitions $\{a, cd, bh, efg\}$ and $\{a, c, bdh, efg\}$, for which $W = 7$ and 6, respectively. Hence there are two possible assignments of the control signals to four control fields yielding the minimum cost of $W = 6$ bits. Figure 4.47 shows one of the many possible ways of coding the control

	a	b	c	d	e	f	g	h
$C_1 = a$	x							
$C_2 = cd$			x	x				
$C_3 = bde$		x		x	x			
$C_8 = fgh$						x	x	x

FIGURE 4.46
Cover table for the minimal MCC cover $\{C_1, C_2, C_3, C_8\}$.

Control field	Bits used	Code	Control signal activated
0	0	0	No operation
		1	a
1	1	0	No operation
		1	c
2	2,3	00	No operation
		01	b
		10	d
		11	e
3	4,5	00	No operation
		01	f
		10	g
		11	h

FIGURE 4.47
Optimal encoding scheme for the microinstructions of Fig. 4.42.

fields using the minimum-cost partition $\{a, c, bde, fgh\}$. Figure 4.48 gives the corresponding control bit patterns for the four original microinstructions.

Minimizing H. We turn next to the problem of minimizing the number of microinstructions H stored in the control memory CM. This is of interest in horizontally microprogrammed machines, where it is possible to reduce H by merging two or more microinstructions into a single one, provided the microinstructions in question do not specify conflicting microoperations. The merging process is often referred to as *microcode compaction*. Conflicts arise when the microoperations being merged use such shared items as common operands and functional units in incompatible ways. Nonconflicting microinstructions can be executed simultaneously or in parallel during the same microinstruction cycle; consequently the task of compacting microcode to minimize H corresponds to maximizing the parallelism in microprograms.

A number of methods have been developed [7] to compact a simple class of straight-line microprograms (SLMs) that are expressed as a sequence of microoperations (single-operation microinstructions) $m_1, m_2, \ldots, m_k$ and, as the term straight-line implies, involve no branching. Each microoperation m_i in such a microprogram P may be characterized by the data variables (corresponding to

Microinstruction	Control bits					
	0	1	2	3	4	5
I_1	1	1	0	1	1	0
I_2	1	1	1	1	1	1
I_3	1	0	1	0	0	1
I_4	0	1	0	1	0	1

FIGURE 4.48
Control-field codes for the microinstructions of Fig. 4.42.

temporary or stored signal values) it uses as operand sources and destinations, the shared resources (buses, ALUs, etc.) it controls, and, in the case of polyphase operation, the clock phases it requires for its execution. Two microoperations m_i and m_j in P, where $i < j$, will be said to be *parallel*, denoted $m_i \| m_j$, if no data, resource, or time conflicts arise during their execution. In general, parallel microoperations can be combined in a single microinstruction. Nonparallel microoperations cannot be so combined, and the microinstruction containing m_i must be executed before that of m_j.

The parallelism present in a set of microoperations can be determined by examining their data dependencies and resource conflicts. Two microoperations m_i and m_j are said to be *directly data dependent* if any of the following situations occurs.

1. m_i computes output data required as input by m_j.
2. m_i and m_j compute the same output variables.
3. m_j alters a variable used as input by m_i.

The microoperations are *indirectly data dependent* if they are linked by a chain of two or more direct data dependencies. For example, consider the following SLM of three microoperations:

$$m_1: \quad R2 \leftarrow F(R1)$$
$$m_2: \quad R3 \leftarrow F(R2)$$
$$m_3: \quad R4 \leftarrow F(R3)$$

By the above definition, m_1 and m_2 are directly data dependent, as are m_2 and m_3. However, m_1 and m_3 are only indirectly data dependent, and obviously cannot be executed in parallel. Microoperations that are either directly or indirectly data dependent are referred to as *data dependent*. Data-dependent microoperations m_i and m_j can never be placed in the same monophase microinstruction. They may appear in the same polyphase microinstruction if they are associated with different phases such that, when $i < j$, m_i is executed in one or more phases that precede those used for the execution of m_j. In effect, the data-dependent microoperations can be executed sequentially in the proper time sequence within a single microinstruction cycle. Data-dependent microoperations of the latter kind are said to be *weakly data dependent*. In addition to data dependencies, microoperations can be nonparallel due to conflicts over shared resources. For example, two microoperations might require use of an ALU circuit at the same time. A similar resource conflict occurs if the microoperations must be encoded in the same control field of the particular microinstruction format being used. We conclude then that for m_i and m_j to be parallel, they must have no (strong) data dependencies or resource conflicts.

Consider, for instance, the SLM P listed in Fig. 4.49, which is designed for a control unit where microinstructions are executed in three consecutive phases Φ_1, Φ_2, and Φ_3. The indicated system resources, the adder, shifter, and bus, can per-

Name	Microoperation	Resources used	Phases used
m_1	RLEFT $\leftarrow$ AC		Φ_1
m_2	RRIGHT $\leftarrow$ 1		Φ_1
m_3	ROUT $\leftarrow$ RLEFT + RRIGHT	Adder	Φ_2
m_4	MAR $\leftarrow$ RIGHTSHIFT(ROUT)	Shifter	Φ_3
m_5	M(MAR) $\leftarrow$ MDR	Bus	Φ_2, Φ_3
m_6	RLEFT $\leftarrow$ 1		Φ_1
m_7	RRIGHT $\leftarrow$ RO		Φ_1
m_8	ROUT $\leftarrow$ RLEFT + RRIGHT	Adder	Φ_2
m_9	AC $\leftarrow$ ROUT		Φ_3
m_{10}	R1 $\leftarrow$ F1(R1)	Adder,bus	Φ_2, Φ_3
m_{11}	R2 $\leftarrow$ 0		Φ_1
m_{12}	AC $\leftarrow$ 0		Φ_1

FIGURE 4.49
Example of a straight-line microprogram.

form only one microoperation at a time. Clearly $m_1 \parallel m_2$, since they involve no common data or resource conflicts. Now m_1 computes an input variable RLEFT used by m_3, implying the existence of a data dependency between these microoperations. However, m_1 is executed in the phase Φ_1 preceding the phase Φ_2 during which m_3 is executed; hence they are only weakly data dependent and $m_1 \parallel m_3$. In contrast, while m_4 computes the output variable MAR, which is an input variable of m_5, both microoperations use phase Φ_3. Hence they are strongly data dependent, and $m_4 \nparallel m_5$. In the case of m_3 and m_8, we also have $m_3 \nparallel m_8$, not only because of strong data dependencies, but also because both require use of the adder.

FCFS compaction. We now outline a representative SLM compaction approach called *first-come first-served* (*FCFS*), which is based on the work of Subrata Dasgupta and others [7, 8]. It is a heuristic technique that involves sequentially scanning the microoperations $m_1, m_2, \ldots, m_k$ in the given SLM and assigning each one to the first microinstruction where it can be placed without conflict, starting with the most recent microinstruction I_i. If the current microoperation m_j cannot be assigned to any microinstruction in the list $L = I_1, I_2, \ldots, I_i$ created so far, then a new microinstruction $I = \{m_j\}$ is introduced to accommodate it. If m_j is not data dependent on any member of L, but cannot be placed in L due to resource conflicts, I is put at the beginning of the list as I_1, and the other members of L are renumbered by the operation $I_h \leftarrow I_{h+1}$. Otherwise, I is placed at the end of the list as I_{i+1}.

Figure 4.50 illustrates the foregoing compaction technique applied to the example of Fig. 4.49. The first microoperation m_1 forms the initial microinstruction I_1. Subsequent microinstructions m_2, m_3, and m_4 are assigned to I_1 until a strong data dependency is encountered in the case of m_5, whose input variable MAR in phase Φ_3 is computed in Φ_3 by the microoperation m_4. A second microin-

m_j	Microinstruction list $L = I_1, I_2, \ldots, I_i$	Comments
m_1	$I_1 = \{m_1\}$	
m_2	$I_1 = \{m_1, m_2\}$	
m_3	$I_1 = \{m_1, m_2, m_3\}$	m_1, m_3 and m_2, m_3 are weakly data dependent
m_4	$I_1 = \{m_1, m_2, m_3, m_4\}$	m_3, m_4 are weakly data dependent
m_5	$I_1 = \{m_1, m_2, m_3, m_4\}$ $I_2 = \{m_5\}$	m_4, m_5 are strongly data dependent
m_6	$I_1 = \{m_1, m_2, m_3, m_4\}$ $I_2 = \{m_5, m_6\}$	m_1, m_6 are strongly data dependent
m_7	$I_1 = \{m_1, m_2, m_3, m_4\}$ $I_2 = \{m_5, m_6, m_7\}$	m_2, m_7 are strongly data dependent
m_8	$I_1 = \{m_1, m_2, m_3, m_4\}$ $I_2 = \{m_5, m_6, m_7, m_8\}$	m_3, m_8 are strongly data dependent; m_6, m_8 and m_7, m_8 are weakly data dependent
m_9	$I_1 = \{m_1, m_2, m_3, m_4\}$ $I_2 = \{m_5, m_6, m_7, m_8, m_9\}$	m_8, m_9 are weakly data dependent
m_{10}	$I_1 = \{m_{10}\}$ $I_2 = \{m_1, m_2, m_3, m_4\}$ $I_3 = \{m_5, m_6, m_7, m_8, m_9\}$	m_{10} has no data dependencies but has resource conflicts with m_3 and m_8
m_{11}	$I_1 = \{m_{10}, m_{11}\}$ $I_2 = \{m_1, m_2, m_3, m_4\}$ $I_3 = \{m_5, m_6, m_7, m_8, m_9\}$	m_{11} has no data dependencies or resource conflicts
m_{12}	$I_1 = \{m_{10}, m_{11}\}$ $I_2 = \{m_1, m_2, m_3, m_4\}$ $I_3 = \{m_5, m_6, m_7, m_8, m_9\}$ $I_4 = \{m_{12}\}$	m_9, m_{12} are strongly data dependent

FIGURE 4.50
Application of FCFS compaction to the SLM of Fig. 4.49.

struction I_2 must therefore be introduced to accommodate m_5. Now an attempt is made to assign subsequent microoperations to I_2, and, failing that, to I_1. The data dependencies allow m_6, m_7, m_8, and m_9 to be placed in I_2, but not in I_1. Microoperation m_{10} involves a data variable R1 which does not appear elsewhere in the SLM, and therefore could be assigned either to I_1 or I_2 without data conflicts. However, its use of the adder in Φ_2 and the bus in Φ_3 cause resource conflicts with I_1 and I_2. We therefore create a new microinstruction consisting of m_{10} alone, and place it at the beginning of the list L, renumbering the members of L as indicated in the figure. The next microoperation m_{11} has no conflicts with any of I_1, I_2, and I_3; it is therefore placed in I_1. The final microoperation m_{12} has a strong data-dependency relation with I_3, and so is assigned to a new microinstruction I_4 placed at the end of the list. Thus the 12-element SLM of Fig. 4.49 can be compacted into the (horizontal) microprogram

$$I_1 = \{m_{10}, m_{11}\}$$
$$I_2 = \{m_1, m_2, m_3, m_4\}$$
$$I_3 = \{m_5, m_6, m_7, m_8, m_9\}$$
$$I_4 = \{m_{12}\}$$

of length 4.

Name	Microoperation	Resources used	Phases used
m_1	$A \leftarrow R1$		Φ_1
m_2	$C \leftarrow A + R2$	Adder	Φ_2
m_3	$R3 \leftarrow D$		Φ_2
m_4	$R6 \leftarrow R6 + 1$	Adder	Φ_2
m_5	$R7 \leftarrow R3 \wedge R6$	ALU	Φ_2

FIGURE 4.51
An SLM that is not optimized by FCFS compaction.

It might be expected from its sequential nature that the foregoing FCFS compaction procedure does not always generate an SLM with the minimum number of microinstructions. This is illustrated by the SLM appearing in Fig. 4.51. It is easily verified that the FCFS approach yields three microinstructions ($H = 3$), as demonstrated in Fig. 4.52. However, the five microinstructions in this SLM can be compacted into

$$I_1 = \{m_1, m_3, m_4\}$$
$$I_2 = \{m_2, m_5\}$$

which form a solution with $H = 2$ that is easily seen to be optimal. Thus the optimizing capability of the heuristic FCFS method is limited to ensuring that each microinstruction contains at least one microoperation that cannot be placed in any microinstruction that precedes it. Nevertheless, it has been found experimentally to yield optimal results in most cases [8], and is much faster than any strictly optimal microcode compaction algorithm.

4.3.3 Multiplier Control Unit

Consider once more the twos-complement multiplication circuit introduced as Example 3.4. Several hardwired control-unit designs for this multiplier were presented in Sec. 4.2.2; here we consider the design of a microprogrammed control unit for it. Again the flowchart of Fig. 4.18, which defines the flow of control and

m_j	Microinstruction list $L = I_1, I_2, \ldots, I_i$	Comments
m_1	$I_1 = \{m_1\}$	
m_2	$I_1 = \{m_1, m_2\}$	
m_3	$I_1 = \{m_1, m_2, m_3\}$	
m_4	$I_1 = \{m_4\}$	m_4 has no data dependencies but
	$I_2 = \{m_1, m_2, m_3\}$	has a resource conflict with m_2
m_5	$I_1 = \{m_4\}$	m_3, m_5 are strongly data dependent
	$I_2 = \{m_1, m_2, m_3\}$	
	$I_3 = \{m_5\}$	

FIGURE 4.52
Application of FCFS compaction to the SLM of Fig. 4.51.

identifies the control signals to be activated (see also Figs. 4.16 and 4.17), is taken as the starting point of the design process.

As a first attack, we employ the straightforward microinstruction format of Fig. 4.38 consisting of three parts: a condition select field, a branch address, and a set of control fields. Initially, no encoding will be used, so that there are thirteen 1-bit control fields, one for each of the control lines $c_0, c_1, \ldots, c_{11}$ and one for the END signal. The control unit will have the general organization of Fig. 4.39, which uses a microprogram counter μPC as the control-memory address register. During each microinstruction cycle, μPC is incremented to form the address of the next microinstruction. In the case of a branch microinstruction, the address stored in the microinstruction itself is used as the next address. The need for an external address input will be eliminated by storing the first microinstruction in CM address zero and simply resetting μPC to zero at the start of every multiplication.

It may be helpful to rewrite the flowchart of Fig. 4.18 using our formal description language, since the resulting description is essentially the microprogram we require in abstract symbolic form. This description is given in Fig. 4.53. Each nonbranching statement in Fig. 4.53 corresponds to a distinct microinstruction, implying that a microprogram of approximately 10 microinstructions is required. An address field of 4 bits should therefore suffice.

Every microinstruction may contain a branch address if desired and thus implement a conditional or unconditional **go to**. The condition select field is required to indicate four conditions:

1. No branching

2. Branch if $Q(7) = 0$

Address	Microoperations	Control signals
BEGIN:	Activate the control unit;	{BEGIN}
	$A \leftarrow 0$, COUNT $\leftarrow 0$, $F \leftarrow 0$, $M \leftarrow$ INBUS;	{c_9, c_{10}}
	$Q \leftarrow$ INBUS;	{c_8}
TEST1:	**if** $Q(7) = 0$ **then go to** RSHIFT;	
	$A \leftarrow A + M$, $F \leftarrow M(0) \wedge Q(7) \vee F$;	{c_2, c_3, c_4}
RSHIFT:	$A(0) \leftarrow F$, $A(1{:}7).Q \leftarrow A.Q(0{:}6)$;	{c_0, c_1}
	if COUNT6 $= 1$ **then go to** TEST2;	
	COUNT $\leftarrow$ COUNT $+ 1$,	{c_{11}}
	go to TEST1;	
TEST2:	**if** $Q(7) = 0$ **then go to** OUTPUT;	
	$A \leftarrow A - M$, $Q(7) \leftarrow 0$;	{c_2, c_3, c_4, c_5}
OUTPUT:	OUTBUS $\leftarrow A$;	{c_6}
	OUTBUS $\leftarrow Q$;	{c_7}
END:	Halt;	{END}

FIGURE 4.53
Formal language description of the twos-complement multiplication algorithm.

3. Branch if COUNT6 $= 1$

4. Unconditional branch

Hence a 2-bit condition select field suffices. We conclude that a 19-bit microinstruction having the horizontal format shown in Fig. 4.54 is to be used.

It is now quite easy to write the microprogram that implements multiplication. The symbolic microprogram of Fig. 4.53 is converted line by line into the bit patterns shown in Fig. 4.55. Consecutive microinstructions are assigned to consecutive addresses, and the appropriate condition select bits are inserted (00 denotes no branching; the remaining condition codes can easily be deduced from Fig. 4.55). When the multiplication is completed, the microprogram enters a waiting state by repeatedly executing the no-operation microinstruction in CM location 1011. It remains in this state until μPC is reset by the arrival of a new external BEGIN signal. Alternatively, we could introduce a flip-flop to enable CM operation, which is set (reset) by the BEGIN (END) control signal. The structure of the resulting control unit is shown in Fig. 4.56.

Very few of the 2^{13} possible control-field patterns allowed by the microinstruction format of Fig. 4.54 are actually needed. From Fig. 4.55 it can be seen that several sets of control signals are always activated simultaneously; hence it suffices to reserve a single 1-bit control field for these signals. Thus the 7 bits reserved for the three sets $\{c_0, c_1\}$, $\{c_2, c_3, c_4\}$, and $\{c_9, c_{10}\}$ can be replaced by 3 bits yielding the shorter microinstruction shown in Fig. 4.57.

Control-field encoding. A further reduction in control-field size can be achieved by encoding the control fields. Since there are 12 distinct microinstructions in the multiplication microprogram, we can encode the control information in a single 4-bit control field or opcode yielding a purely vertical microinstruction format. However, this severely limits our ability to modify the microinstruction set. Let us suppose that the microinstruction format we are designing will be used for more applications than the control of multiplication. (Note that the multiplier circuit being controlled has all the essential components of a general-purpose arithmetic-logic unit.) Thus it is of interest to encode the microinstructions in such a way that microinstructions as yet unspecified can readily be accommodated.

One possible approach is to divide the control information into compatible control fields using the method of Sec. 4.3.2. This method minimizes the number of control bits while maintaining the maximum degree of parallelism inherent in the

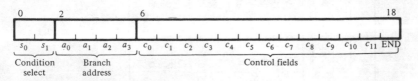

FIGURE 4.54
Unencoded (horizontal) microinstruction format for the twos-complement multiplier.

Microinstruction

Address in CM	Condition select	Branch address	Control fields												E N D	Comments
			c_0	c_1	c_2	c_3	c_4	c_5	c_6	c_7	c_8	c_9	c_{10}	c_{11}		
0000	00	0000	0	0	0	0	0	0	0	0	0	1	1	0	0	$A \leftarrow 0$, COUNT $\leftarrow 0$, $F \leftarrow 0$, $M \leftarrow$ INBUS;
0001	00	0000	0	0	0	0	0	0	0	0	1	0	0	0	0	$Q \leftarrow$ INBUS;
0010	01	0100	0	0	0	0	0	0	0	0	0	0	0	0	0	**if** $Q(7) = 0$ **then go to 4;**
0011	00	0000	0	1	0	1	1	0	0	0	0	0	0	0	0	$A \leftarrow A + M$, $F \leftarrow M(0) \land Q(7) \lor F$;
0100	10	0110	1	1	0	1	0	0	0	0	0	0	0	0	0	$A(1:7).Q \leftarrow A.Q(0:6)$, $A(0) \leftarrow F$; **if** COUNT6 $= 1$ **then go to 6;**
0101	11	0010	0	0	0	0	0	0	0	0	0	0	0	1	0	COUNT $\leftarrow$ COUNT $+ 1$, **go to 2;**
0110	01	1000	0	0	0	0	0	0	0	0	0	0	0	0	0	**if** $Q(7) = 0$ **then go to 8;**
0111	00	0000	0	0	1	1	1	0	1	0	0	0	0	0	0	$A \leftarrow A - M$, $Q(7) \leftarrow 0$;
1000	00	0000	0	0	0	0	0	1	0	1	0	0	0	0	0	OUTBUS $\leftarrow A$;
1001	00	0000	0	0	0	0	0	1	0	0	0	0	0	0	0	OUTBUS $\leftarrow Q$
1010	00	0000	0	0	0	0	0	0	0	0	0	0	0	0	1	Issue completion signal;
1011	11	1011	0	0	0	0	0	0	0	0	0	0	0	0	0	Halt;

FIGURE 4.55

Multiplication microprogram using the microinstruction format of Figure 4.54.

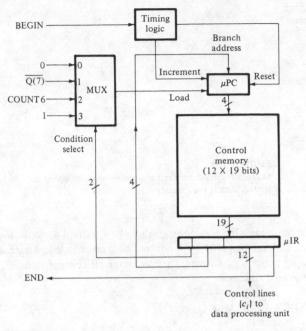

FIGURE 4.56
Microprogrammed control unit for the twos-complement multiplier.

original microinstruction set. Let $\{I_j\}$ denote the microinstructions in the multiplication microprogram, where j is the CM address of I_j. After the elimination of redundant bits from the control field, we are left with nine microoperations to be specified; these can be represented by the control signals c_0, c_2, c_5, c_6, c_7, c_8, c_9, c_{11}, and END. Figure 4.58 lists the 12 microinstructions and the control signals they specify.

The first step is to determine the MCCs. This is easy because there are only two incompatible microoperations c_2 and c_5. The only two MCCs are $C_0 = c_0 c_2 c_6 c_7 c_8 c_9 c_{11} \text{END}$ and $C_1 = c_0 c_5 c_6 c_7 c_8 c_9 c_{11} \text{END}$, each containing eight members. C_0 and C_1 are also the minimal MCC covers, so a format containing two encoded

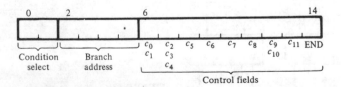

FIGURE 4.57
Unencoded microinstruction format for the twos-complement multiplier after removal of redundant control fields.

Microinstruction	Control signals
I_0	c_9
I_1	c_8
I_2	
I_3	c_2
I_4	c_0
I_5	c_{11}
I_6	
I_7	c_2, c_5
I_8	c_6
I_9	c_7
I_{10}	END
I_{11}	

FIGURE 4.58
Microinstructions for the twos-complement multiplier and the control signals they specify.

control fields suffices. Since there are nine control signals to be specified as well as the no-operation condition, at least $\lceil \log_2 10 \rceil = 4$ control bits are needed. There exist several ways of choosing subsets of C_0 and C_1 that cover all control signals and yield a value of 5 for the cost function

$$W = \sum_{i=1}^{2} \lceil \log_2 (|C_i| + 1) \rceil$$

which is clearly the minimum cost. For example, we can set $C_0' = c_0 c_2 c_6$ and $C_1' = c_5 c_7 c_8 c_9 c_{11}$ END. The resulting microinstruction has the format shown in Fig. 4.59 and requires a pair of decoders to generate the control signals. The fact that there are only two control fields indicates that there is very little inherent parallelism in the multiplication algorithm.

Encoding by function. A disadvantage of the minimum-bit control format of Fig. 4.59 is that functionally unrelated control signals are combined in the same control

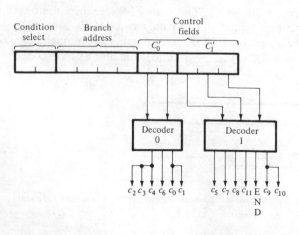

FIGURE 4.59
Encoded microinstruction format with maximum parallelism and the minimum number of control bits.

field, while related signals are derived from different control fields. For example, both C_0' and C_1' control the transfer of information to OUTBUS. This lack of functional separation makes the writing of microprograms more difficult, since the microprogrammer must associate several unrelated opcodes with each control field. An encoded format in which each control field specifies the control signals for one component or for a related set of operations is usually preferred, even though more control bits may be needed.

On examining the multiplier design, we see that there are five major components to be controlled: the adder, the A.Q register pair, the external iteration counter COUNT, and the two data buses INBUS and OUTBUS; this suggests the encoded microinstruction format of Fig. 4.60. Figure 4.61 indicates possible control-field bit assignments and their interpretation. Note that this ad hoc encoding has combined the "incompatible" control signals c_2 and c_5; this is unlikely to be of concern, however, if the microinstruction set is later enlarged, since there is no obvious functional advantage in keeping these control signals in separate fields. The assignment of a separate control field to INBUS is of questionable wisdom. It prevents INBUS from transferring data to two or more destinations, for example, Q and M, simultaneously. This capability could be useful, for example, to clear both registers at once. Thus it might be better to associate a control field with each register that is a potential destination of INBUS rather than with INBUS itself.

Multiple microinstruction formats. In the original multiplication microprogram of Fig. 4.53, several microinstructions are used only for next-address generation and do not activate any control lines. This suggests that microinstruction size could be reduced by using a single field to contain either control information or address information. This results in two distinct microinstruction types—branch microinstructions, which specify no control information, and action (or "operate") microinstructions, which activate control lines but have no branching capability. Note that this approach is almost always used at the instruction level. The division of microinstructions into the branch and action types is a rather natural one, since the branch instructions directly control the internal operations of the control unit, while the action instructions directly control the external data processing unit.

Suppose that we wish to use unencoded control fields for the multiplier, since that allows a maximum of flexibility. Nine control bits are required, as demonstrated in Fig. 4.57. Now let us define a microinstruction format consisting of two parts, a 2-bit condition select field with the same meaning as before, and a 9-bit

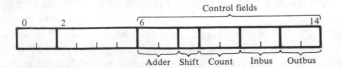

FIGURE 4.60
Microinstruction format with control fields encoded by function.

Control field	Bits used	Code	Microoperations specified	Control signals activated
ADDER	6, 7	00	No operation	
		01	$A \leftarrow A + M$	c_2, c_3, c_4
		10	$A \leftarrow A - M, Q(7) \leftarrow 0$	c_2, c_3, c_4, c_5
		11	Unused	
SHIFT	8	0	No operation	
		1	Right-shift A.Q and load A(0)	c_0, c_1
COUNT	9, 10	00	No operation	
		01	Clear COUNT, A, F	c_{10}
		10	COUNT $\leftarrow$ COUNT $+ 1$	c_{11}
		11	Unused	
INBUS	11, 12	00	No operation	
		01	Q $\leftarrow$ INBUS	c_8
		10	M $\leftarrow$ INBUS	c_9
		11	Unused	
OUTBUS	13, 14	00	No operation	
		01	OUTBUS $\leftarrow$ A	c_6
		10	OUTBUS $\leftarrow$ Q	c_7
		11	Unused	

FIGURE 4.61
Interpretation of the microinstruction control fields with encoding by function.

field which can contain either a branch address or control information. The condition select code 00, which means no branching, serves to identify the action microinstructions. The remaining three select field codes identify conditional and unconditional branches. We thus obtain the 11-bit microinstruction formats of Fig. 4.62. Note that the additional address bits make it possible to write microprograms containing up to $2^9 = 512$ instructions. Because we have destroyed the ability of every microinstruction to implement a two-way branch, more microinstructions may be needed to perform certain functions.

Figure 4.63 shows a microprogram for twos-complement multiplication using the formats of Fig. 4.62. This microprogram is somewhat easier to derive from the flowchart (Fig. 4.18) than the earlier microprogram (Fig. 4.55), since we can now transform decision blocks directly into branch microinstructions, while activity boxes are transformed into action microinstructions. There is also a one-to-one correspondence between the microinstructions and statements in the formal-language description given in Fig. 4.53. The control-unit design of Fig. 4.56 is easily modified to handle these new microinstruction formats. The condition select field can be used to control a demultiplexer which routes bits 2:10 either to external control lines (action microinstructions) or to the branch address loading circuitry (branch microinstructions).

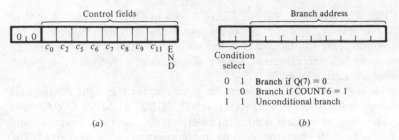

FIGURE 4.62

Example of multiple microinstruction formats: (a) action microinstruction; (b) branch microinstruction.

4.4 MICROPROGRAMMED COMPUTERS

This section examines the design of the microprogrammed control units for the CPUs of general-purpose computers, including several commercial machines with one or two levels of microprogramming.

4.4.1 CPU Control Units

First we reconsider the control part of the hypothetical CPU introduced in Sec. 4.2.3. The use of general-purpose microprogram sequencers such as the AMD 2909 (Example 4.2) as building blocks for CPU design is also discussed further.

Address in CM	Condition select 0 1	Branch address or control bits 2 3 4 5 6 7 8 9 10	Comments
0000	0 0	0 0 0 0 0 0 1 0 0	$A \leftarrow 0$, COUNT $\leftarrow 0$, $F \leftarrow 0$, $M \leftarrow$ INBUS;
0001	0 0	0 0 0 0 0 1 0 0 0	$Q \leftarrow$ INBUS;
0010	0 1	0 0 0 0 0 0 1 0 0	**if** $Q(7) = 0$ **then go to 4**;
0011	0 0	0 1 0 0 0 0 0 0 0	$A \leftarrow A + M$, $F \leftarrow M(0) \wedge Q(7) \vee F$;
0100	0 0	1 0 0 0 0 0 0 0 0	$A(1{:}7).Q \leftarrow A.Q(0{:}6)$, $A(0) \leftarrow F$;
0101	1 0	0 0 0 0 0 1 0 0 0	**if** COUNT6 $= 1$ **then go to 8**;
0110	0 0	0 0 0 0 0 0 0 1 0	COUNT $\leftarrow$ COUNT $+ 1$;
0111	1 1	0 0 0 0 0 0 0 1 0	**go to 2**;
1000	0 1	0 0 0 0 0 1 0 1 0	**if** $Q(7) = 0$ **then go to 10**;
1001	0 0	0 1 1 0 0 0 0 0 0	$A \leftarrow A - M$, $Q(7) \leftarrow 0$;
1010	0 0	0 0 0 1 0 0 0 0 0	OUTBUS $\leftarrow A$;
1011	0 0	0 0 0 0 1 0 0 0 0	OUTBUS $\leftarrow Q$;
1100	0 0	0 0 0 0 0 0 0 0 1	Issue completion signal;
1101	1 1	0 0 0 0 0 1 1 0 1	Halt;

The table above has the column group header "Microinstruction" spanning the Condition select and Branch address columns.

FIGURE 4.63

Multiplication microprogram using the microinstruction formats of Fig. 4.62.

A small CPU. The structure of this CPU is shown in Fig. 4.28. The 13 control signals listed in Fig. 4.27 define the microoperations that are available to the microprogrammer. (We will later extend this to a more realistic set.) To simplify the discussion, we will only represent the microinstructions in symbolic form using our hardware description language.

Suppose that it is desired to write an emulator for the eight instructions considered earlier: LOAD, STORE, ADD, AND, JUMP, JUMPZ, COMP, and RSHIFT. The microoperations needed to interpret the various instructions are shown in Fig. 4.26, from which the required microprograms are easily derived. The microprogram to be selected for each instruction is determined by the instruction opcode; hence the contents of the instruction register IR are used to determine the microprogram starting address. We will use the unmodified contents of IR as the microprogram address. We will further assume that each microinstruction can specify a branch condition, a branch address used only if the branch condition is satisfied, and a set of control fields defining the microoperations to be performed.

Figure 4.64 shows a complete emulator for the given instruction set in symbolic form; the conversion of each microinstruction to binary form is easy. The emulator contains a distinct microprogram for each of the eight instruction execution cycles and a microprogram called FETCH which implements the instruction fetch cycle. The **go to** IR statement can be implemented as $\mu PC \leftarrow$ IR, which transfers control to the first microinstruction in the microprogram that interprets the current instruction.

```
FETCH:     AR ← PC;
           READ M;
           PC ← PC + 1, IR ← DR(OP);
           go to IR;

LOAD:      AR ← DR(ADR);
           READ M;
           AC ← DR, go to FETCH;

STORE:     AR ← DR(ADR);
           DR ← AC;
           WRITE M, go to FETCH;

ADD:       AR ← DR(ADR);
           READ M;
           AC ← AC + DR, go to FETCH;

AND:       AR ← DR(ADR);
           READ M;
           AC ← AC ∧ DR, go to FETCH;

JUMP:      PC ← DR(ADR), go to FETCH;

JUMPZ:     if AC ≠ 0 then go to FETCH;
           PC ← DR(ADR), go to FETCH;

COMP:      AC ← AC̄, go to FETCH;

RSHIFT:    RIGHT-SHIFT(AC), go to FETCH;
```

FIGURE 4.64

A microprogrammed emulator in symbolic form for a small instruction set.

Suppose that because of a design error, we have forgotten to implement a required instruction called CLEAR whose function is to reset all bits of the accumulator AC to zero. Although no control line to clear AC was included in the CPU, we can still write a microprogram to implement the CLEAR instruction as follows:

$$\text{CLEAR:} \quad \begin{array}{l} \text{DR} \leftarrow \text{AC}; \\ \text{AC} \leftarrow \overline{\text{AC}}; \\ \text{AC} \leftarrow \text{AC} \wedge \text{DR, } \textbf{go to } \text{FETCH}; \end{array}$$

Thus by adding this microprogram to CM, CLEAR can be added to the instruction set without changing any hardware. This flexibility is a key advantage of microprogramming over hardwired control.

Extensions. We will now add to the basic CPU structure of Fig. 4.28 the necessary circuits to implement fixed-point multiplication and division using iterative algorithms of the type discussed in Chap. 3. Two new registers are required, a multiplier-quotient register MQ and a counter called COUNT, which can be used for counting the number of iterations (add/subtract and shift steps) used during multiplication or division. The memory data register DR will be assigned the role of multiplicand or divisor register when required.

Figure 4.65 shows the extended CPU in which the number of control lines has been approximately doubled. The complete set of control lines defined for this unit is given in Fig. 4.66. Note that lines c_0 through c_{12} are the control lines for the original circuit of Fig. 4.28. A number of the control lines in Fig. 4.66 implicitly cause the flag bits to be set or reset. For example, if overflow occurs during addition or subtraction, which are controlled by c_0 and c_{23}, respectively, then OVR is set to 1; otherwise OVR is reset to 0.

Figure 4.67 lists the microprogram that implements twos-complement multiplication using the algorithm first given in Example 3.4. A special-purpose microprogrammed controller for this type of multiplication was developed in Sec. 4.2.3. The microprogram MULT given here is essentially the same as the one defined previously (Fig. 4.53). It is assumed that before MULT is executed, the multiplier is in MQ and the multiplicand is in DR. Each statement in Fig. 4.67 corresponds to a single microinstruction.

The general three-part microinstruction format comprising a condition select field, a branch address field, and a set of control fields will be used. Five conditions to be tested are identified in Fig. 4.65, specifically $AC = 0$, $AC < 0$, $MQ(n-1)$, $COUNT = n - 2$ and OVR, the overflow-underflow indicator. Adding the possibilities of an unconditional branch and no branching, we obtain seven branch condition codes which can be represented by a 3-bit condition select field.

Various control signals can be grouped together in common encoded fields to reduce microinstruction size. Many of these can be identified from the list of control signals, without reference to the actual microinstructions that are to be implemented. For example, there are three control signals c_3, c_5, and c_{19} that transfer data to DR. Since they are mutually exclusive (compatible), we can encode them in

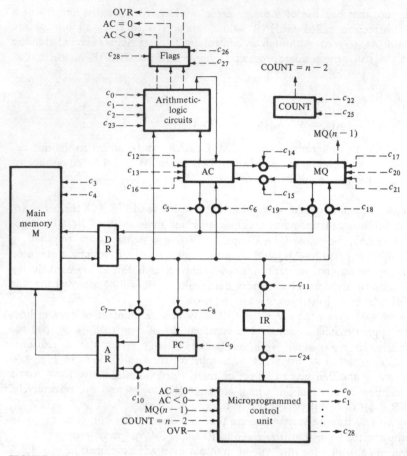

FIGURE 4.65
Structure of the extended CPU.

a 2-bit field. (Note that one bit pattern must be reserved for the no-operation case.) Similarly, the many control signals that alter the contents of AC can be combined.

Let us suppose that it has been decided not to encode the control signals. This implies that the condition select and control fields occupy 32 bits of each microinstruction. Let us further suppose that an 8-bit branch address representing a complete CM address is included in each microinstruction. A CM with a capacity of 256 40-bit words is therefore to be used. Figure 4.68 shows a possible organization for the CPU control unit with the foregoing design assumptions. As in our previous designs, external conditions are used to load branch addresses into the μPC. In addition, the μPC may be loaded from the instruction register IR via a logic circuit K (possibly a ROM) which maps instruction opcodes onto microinstruction addresses.

Control signal	Operation controlled
c_0	$AC \leftarrow AC + DR$
c_1	$AC \leftarrow \overline{AC} \wedge DR$
c_2	$AC \leftarrow \overline{AC}$
c_3	$DR \leftarrow M(AR)$
c_4	$M(AR) \leftarrow DR$
c_5	$DR \leftarrow AC$
c_6	$AC \leftarrow DR$
c_7	$AR \leftarrow DR(ADR)$
c_8	$PC \leftarrow DR(ADR)$
c_9	$PC \leftarrow PC + 1$
c_{10}	$AR \leftarrow PC$
c_{11}	$IR \leftarrow DR(OP)$
c_{12}	RIGHT-SHIFT AC
c_{13}	LEFT-SHIFT AC
c_{14}	RIGHT-SHIFT AC.MQ
c_{15}	LEFT-SHIFT AC.MQ
c_{16}	$AC \leftarrow 0$
c_{17}	$AC(0) \leftarrow F$
c_{18}	$MQ \leftarrow DR$
c_{19}	$DR \leftarrow MQ$
c_{20}	$MQ(n - 1) \leftarrow 1$
c_{21}	$MQ(n - 1) \leftarrow 0$
c_{22}	$COUNT \leftarrow COUNT + 1$
c_{23}	$AC \leftarrow AC - DR$
c_{24}	$\mu PC \leftarrow IR$
c_{25}	$COUNT \leftarrow 0$
c_{26}	$F \leftarrow 0$
c_{27}	$F \leftarrow 1$
c_{28}	$FLAGS \leftarrow 0$

FIGURE 4.66
Control signals of the extended CPU.

Microprogram sequencers. Developments in VLSI technology have resulted in components which allow a microprogrammed control unit for a CPU to be designed using a very small number of IC chips. In particular, all the circuitry required to generate microinstruction addresses can be placed in a single package called a microprogram sequencer, a simple example of which, the AMD 2909, was discussed earlier (Example 4.2). A microprogram sequencer is a general-purpose building block for microprogrammed control units, and can greatly simplify CPU

```
MULT:   AC ← 0, COUNT ← 0, F ← 0;
TEST1:  if MQ(n −1) = 0 then go to SHIFT;
        AC ← AC + DR, F ← DR(0) ∧ MQ(n − 1) ∨ F;
SHIFT:  AC.MQ ← RIGHT-SHIFT (AC.MQ), AC(0) ← F
            if COUNT = n − 2 then go to TEST2;
        COUNT ← COUNT + 1, go to TEST1;
TEST2:  if MQ(n − 1) = 0 then go to FETCH;
        AC ← AC − DR, MQ(n − 1) ← 0, go to FETCH;
```

FIGURE 4.67
Twos-complement multiplication microprogram for the extended CPU.

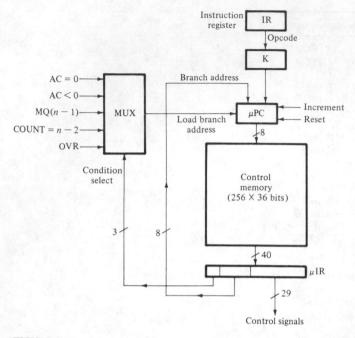

FIGURE 4.68
Microprogrammed CPU control unit.

design. It typically contains a microprogram counter μPC, as well as the logic required for conditional branching and the transfer of control between microprograms. A microprogrammed control unit can be constructed from three major components: a RAM or ROM used as the control memory, a microinstruction register, and a microprogram sequencer. Figure 4.69 shows a microprogrammed CPU designed in this way. The microinstruction register can be implemented as a two-stage pipeline register to allow microinstruction fetching and execution to be overlapped.

Microprogram sequencers are primarily an outgrowth of microprocessor technology. Many microprocessors, but by no means all, employ microprogram control; an example to be considered later is the Motorola 68000 one-chip CPU. (Note again that the terms microprogramming and microprocessor are unrelated.) In particular, bit-sliced microprocessor component families like the AMD 2900 series, are intended for the design of general-purpose CPUs that have microprogrammed control units built around microprogram sequencers. Because of IC component density and pin restrictions, early microprogram sequencers like the 2909 were relatively simple and had to be bit-sliced to allow control units of practical size to be constructed from them. Subsequent advances in VLSI technology have enabled much more powerful and self-contained devices of this kind to be

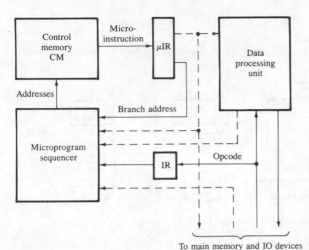

FIGURE 4.69
Microprogrammed CPU employing a microprogram sequencer.

built. The following example is representative of this newer class of microprogram sequencers.

Example 4.3 The Texas Instruments 8835 16-bit microprogram sequencer [20]. This device, whose full designation is the SN74AS8835, is a member of the Texas Instruments (TI) 88xx (micro) processor component family, which was introduced in 1986 and is aimed at the design of high-performance 32-bit CPUs. It may be considered a natural evolution of the 2909-class microprogram sequencers developed a decade earlier, to accommodate larger address sizes (and hence larger control memories), more address sources, and more flexible operating modes. The 8835 also incorporates a number of useful features to simplify the development and debugging of microprograms. The address size is 16 bits, enabling a single 8835 to control a 64K-word CM; several 8835s can be cascaded to produce even longer addresses if desired. To handle the large address size, a 156-pin PGA package is used, and microinstruction cycle times in the range of 50 ns can be supported.

The internal organization of the 8835 appears in Fig. 4.70. Like the AMD 2909 (Fig. 4.40), the main CM address sources are external buses, internal registers including a microprogram counter μPC, and a stack ST. A 16-bit μPC, which is implemented as a register and a separate incrementer in the fashion of the 2909, is the usual address source. There are two main external sources of branch addresses, the input buses DRA and DRB, and one output address bus Y. (The DRA, DRB, and Y buses may be compared with the 2909's D, R, and Y buses.) The DRA and DRB buses have registers/counters A and B, respectively, associated with them. These can be used as independent address sources, or else as iteration counters when executing a loop in a microprogram. The 8835 has a 65 $\times$ 20-bit stack ST to implement subroutine calls and interrupts. The 20-bit stack word allows 4 bits of internally or externally supplied status information to be stored along with a 16-bit return address. Roughly corresponding to the 2909's OR-AND gates for address modification via status bits, etc., the 8835 has a group of 16 input lines B0:B15 to modify the addresses appearing on the DRA or DRB buses. Under control of the

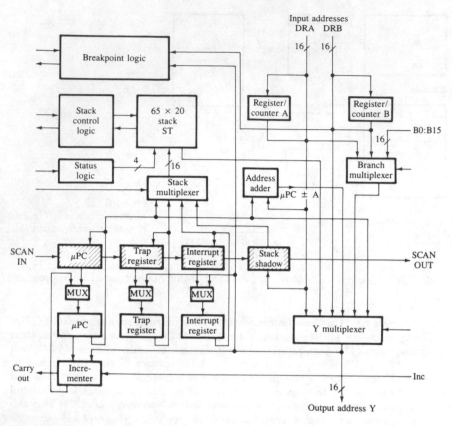

FIGURE 4.70
Structure (simplified) of the Texas Instruments 8835 microprogram sequencer.

branch multiplexer, a group of 4 bits from the 16-bit B bus, e.g., B12:B15, may be used to replace the four low-bits of DRA and DRB before they reach the Y multiplexer.

A new feature of the 8835 is relative addressing, which is implemented by a 16-bit adder that can add the contents of the DRA bus to (or subtract it from) the contents of μPC. This addressing mode makes it possible to write relocatable microcode that is executable anywhere in CM. There are also several registers designed to provide rapid response to external interrupts and traps (internally generated interrupts). As indicated in Fig. 4.70, two registers, the trap and interrupt registers, automatically store the return addresses of interrupted programs. If it is desired to save these return addresses in the stack ST, they must be explicitly pushed into ST via push microoperations in the interrupt-handling microprograms.

The 8835 has external lines that are connected to the control inputs of all the major components in Fig. 4.70, including the multiplexers, the stack, the registers, etc. As might be expected, the signals applied to these control lines define a large number of microoperations for the 8835, which are useful in constructing microprograms. These include a variety of conditional and unconditional branches, calls, and returns. Loops can readily also be specified by a single microinstruction. An example is the "loop until zero" operation, which has the following interpretation:

LOOP: $A \leftarrow A - 1$; **if** $A = 0$ **then** $\mu PC \leftarrow ST(SP)$ **else go to** LOOP;

The 8835 has a number of interesting features to simplify microprogram debugging. In addition to the usual stack pointer SP for automatically tracking the top of the stack, there is a second pointer register, the *read pointer* RP, which may be used to read out the contents of the stack word by word to external ports of the 8835. This readout process, which does not alter the contents of the stack or SP, may be used to backtrack through a sequence of subroutine calls or interrupts to identify the cause, e.g., overflow, and the location in CM of a problem occurring during microprogram execution. Another useful debugging aid is a pair of *breakpoint registers* designed to generate an external signal whenever the address appearing on the Y bus lies in a specified range of values. The limits of this range are loaded via the DRB bus into the breakpoint registers and are continuously compared to the address on Y. Whenever Y is found to be within the breakpoint range, an output signal BKPT is activated. If this signal is connected to the trap enable line TEN, then a trap sequence is executed automatically when the breakpoint condition is satisfied.

Certain registers in the 8835 have *shadow registers* associated with them for diagnostic purposes. Several such registers are shown shaded in Fig. 4.70. A shadow register R_s is basically similar to its companion register R (unshaded), but has both serial and parallel input-output connections, thereby resembling a universal shift register. R may be loaded in parallel from R_s, and vice versa, by appropriate multiplexing of the stored data. The contents of the shadow R_s can also be set serially via an external data input line called SCAN IN. Similarly, the contents of R_s may be transferred out serially (without affecting the contents of R) via a data output line called SCAN OUT. Thus the state of R can be controlled and observed via its shadow register R_s, independently of the other circuits connected to R. This provides direct access to R for diagnostic purposes, no matter how deeply it is buried in the system. Moreover, it does so using very few pins, basically those needed for the SCAN IN/OUT lines and one or two control lines. The SCAN IN/OUT lines of several shadow registers can be chained together as shown in Fig. 4.70, so that they all share the same pins. The 8835 has a second shadow-register chain (not shown in the figure) that contains the breakpoint registers.

We conclude this chapter with detailed descriptions of the microprogramming methods used in some commercial computers. There is a remarkable diversity to be found in the microinstruction formats and microoperation types of these machines. Even within the same computer family, different CPUs may be microprogrammed in entirely different ways, e.g., the CPUs of different models in the IBM System/360 series [12, 21]. It is therefore difficult to select a microprogrammed computer that is typical in any general sense. The examples given serve to indicate the range of the approaches taken to microprogrammed control design.

4.4.2 A Conventional Computer

This section examines a microprogrammed 16-bit minicomputer of conventional design, the Hewlett-Packard (HP) 21MX, which was introduced in 1974 [10]. Its instruction set was intended to emulate that of its predecessor, the HP 2100. The HP 21MX was also designed to execute user-defined microprograms and therefore contains a writeable control memory. (Although compatible at the instruction level, the HP 2100 and HP 21MX are incompatible and quite different at the microinstruction level.)

The architecture of the HP 21MX is shown in Fig. 4.71. The main-memory word size is 16 bits and the CPU is organized around two 16-bit buses: the S bus, which is connected to main memory and the input side of the ALU; and the T bus, which is connected to the output side of the ALU. The two registers A and B fill the role of main accumulators in the HP 21MX. The L (latch) register is used to store one ALU operand; the other is obtained directly from the S bus. Sixteen additional registers are connected to the S and T buses. Thirteen of these registers, designated S, S1, S2, . . . , S12, are general-purpose or scratch-pad registers. The X and Y registers are used as index registers, while PC is a standard program counter. The 8-bit counter COUNT is intended for controlling loops within a microprogram, e.g., counting the number of iterations performed during multiplication. The arithmetic-logic unit ALU directly implements a set of fixed-point operations including add, subtract, increment, shift, NAND, and EX-CLUSIVE-OR, which are typical of a small computer. More complex functions such as fixed-point multiply and divide and floating-point arithmetic operations are implemented by microprograms.

Information is processed in the HP 21MX in the following way. Operands are transferred from the memory data register, IO devices, or the CPU registers to the S bus, and from there they enter the ALU. The result generated by the ALU is placed on the T bus from which it may be loaded into any of the 18 CPU registers connected to the T bus.

Microinstruction types. Microinstructions in the HP 21MX are 24 bits long, and the control memory CM has a capacity of 4K (2^{12}) microinstructions. A conventional control unit organization is used. A special 12-bit SAVE register is provided, as its name indicates, to save a microinstruction address. This permits a one-level subroutine call capability within microprograms. Semiconductor RAMS are used for both M and CM with cycle times of 650 and 140 ns, respectively. The microinstructions of the HP 21MX are relatively short and highly encoded and have limited ability to define parallel microoperations. As such, they may be considered to be of the vertical type. (They are called "diagonal" in Ref. 3.) Four main formats, illustrated in Fig. 4.72, are available, which are designated common, immediate, conditional jump, and unconditional jump.

The common format is used mainly to specify data transfers and arithmetic-logic operations. The opcode field specifies the general type of the microinstruction, while the ALU field indicates the operation, if any, to be performed by the

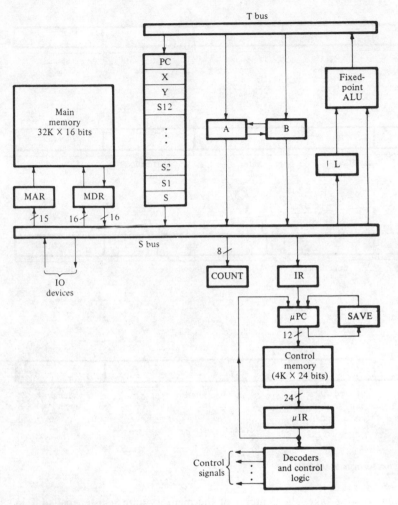

FIGURE 4.71
Structure of the Hewlett-Packard 21MX computer.

arithmetic-logic circuits. The source and destination fields contain the names of registers that store the operands to be used. The "special" field performs a variety of control functions, including specification of the next microinstruction address. Consider, for example, the following microinstruction whose control fields are defined symbolically in the manner of the HP 21MX microassembly language.

Opcode	ALU function	Source register	Destination register	Special field
NOP	INC	T	A	RTN

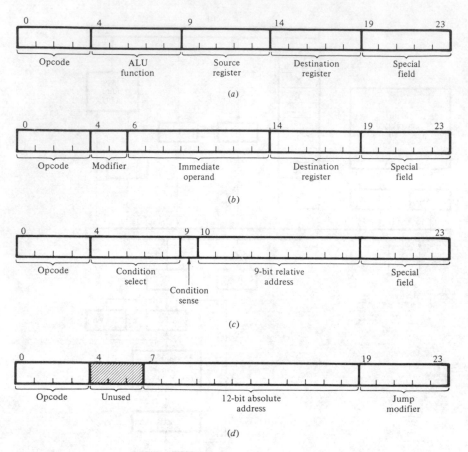

FIGURE 4.72
Microinstruction formats of the 21MX.

This microinstruction takes the contents of the memory data register (called T in 21MX terminology), passes it through the arithmetic-logic circuits where it is incremented, and places the result in the A register. The opcode NOP means no operation, indicating that no additional function is specified by this field. The code RTN in the special field means return, indicating that this is the last microinstruction in a subroutine and that the next microinstruction address should be taken from the SAVE register. In terms of our description language, the foregoing microinstruction corresponds to

$$A \leftarrow T + 1, \textbf{ go to } SAVE;$$

Note that the opcode, ALU function, and special fields are largely independent and permit up to three microoperations to be specified.

The second format is used to load immediate operands into registers. The opcode field is (in symbolic form) IMM, while 2 modifier bits indicate which half of the destination register is to be used, and whether the immediate operand is to be stored in true or complemented form. For example, the microinstruction

Opcode	Modifier	Immediate operand	Destination field	Special field
IMM	CMLO	8	S4	

causes the logical complement (CM) of the number 8 to be placed in the low-order (LO) half of the scratch-pad register S4.

The remaining two formats are used for jump instructions. A conditional jump instruction (Fig. 4.72c) can test for a variety of conditions such as overflow resulting from the preceding ALU operation, or external conditions such as pending interrupts. Bit 9 indicates if the jump is to take place when the condition is true or when the condition is false. Only 9 address bits are specified restricting conditional jumps to a 512-word page within the control memory. An example of a conditional jump is

Opcode	Condition select	Condition sense	Address	Special field
JMP	OVFL	RJS	200	CNDX

which means branch to address 200 within the current page if the overflow flag OVFL = 0. Omitting the RJS (reverse jump sense) term causes the jump to take place only if OVFL = 1, that is, when the selected condition is satisfied.

The final instruction format is the unconditional branch, which can specify a jump to any of the 4096 control-memory addresses. There are two types of instructions which use this format: a simple unconditional jump with opcode JMP, and an unconditional jump to subroutine or subroutine call with opcode JSB. JSB causes the contents of the microprogram counter μPC to be placed in the SAVE register. The jump modifier field can be used to indicate that the branch address is to be taken from the microinstruction address field (bits 7 to 18), the instruction register IR, or the SAVE register. The jump modifier field therefore acts as a condition select field. The microinstruction

Opcode	Address	Jump modifier
JSB	SUB1	UNCD

causes a jump to the subroutine with starting address SUB1, while the return address (the address of the JSB instruction plus one) is placed in the SAVE register.

The multiple microinstruction formats of the HP 21MX require a two-level process to decode each microinstruction. First the opcode field is decoded to identify the instruction type. This determines the meaning of the remaining fields, which can then be decoded. Microinstructions of this kind, in which the meaning of a field depends on another field, are said to have *two-level encoding*. This is to be contrasted with the *single-level encoding* schemes depicted in Fig. 4.35b and c.

Microprogramming. Microprograms for the 21MX can be written using a microassembly language whose structure is shown in Fig. 4.73 [10]. Mnemonics are provided for specifying the control fields, and symbolic names may be used for operands and addresses. A statement in the 21MX microprogramming language defines one microinstruction. Each statement is divided into seven fields. Field 1 is used to specify an optional label, which is the symbolic address to be assigned to the microinstruction; field 2 specifies the opcode. In all cases except the common format, only one or two opcodes are defined. The remaining fields are self-explanatory. Note that while there is a one-to-one correspondence between fields 2 to 6 in the microassembly-language format and the binary formats given in Fig. 4.72, the positions of the corresponding fields are not the same.

Figure 4.74 shows an HP 21MX microassembly-language version of the simple emulator described in Fig. 4.64. (Some minor liberties have been taken with the microassembly language in order to simplify this example.) As before, the emulator comprises an instruction fetch microprogram called FETCH and a separate microprogram for each of the eight instructions to be emulated. The FETCH routine in this case also fetches the operand for all memory-referencing instructions. The special field command JTAB used in the last microinstruction of FETCH causes the control-memory address register to be loaded with an address obtained from a "jump table" using the opcode part of the current instruction IR(OP) to address that table. JTAB also causes the SAVE register to be set to zero. It is assumed that the microinstruction labeled FETCH is in control-memory location zero, that is, FETCH = 0. Hence after the specific operations required by each instruction have been performed, another FETCH cycle can be initiated by giving the return-from-subroutine command RTN.

Consider, for example, execution of the ADD instruction. JTAB causes a branch to the microinstruction labeled ADD, which transfers the contents of the memory data register T (containing the prefetched ADD operand) to the L register. The command PASS in this microinstruction indicates that no function is to be performed by the ALU. The next microinstruction contains the command ENV, which enables the overflow indication flip-flop and specifies the addition

Microinstruction type	Field 1	Field 2	Field 3	Field 4	Field 5	Field 6	Field 7
Common		Opcode	Special	ALU function	Destination register	Source register	
Immediate	Label (address in CM)	IMM	Special	Modifiers	Destination register	Operand	Comment
Conditional jump		JMP	CNDX	Condition select	Condition sense	Branch address	
Unconditional jump		JMP or JSB	Jump modifier	Unused	Unused	Branch address	

FIGURE 4.73
Format used for microinstructions in the 21MX microassembly language.

```
*  HP 21MX Emulator for a Simple Computer
*  A = Accumulator
*  L = ALU latch
*  M = Memory address register
*  P = Program counter
*  T = Memory data register
*
```

1	2	3	4	5	6	7 (Comments)
FETCH	READ		INC	PNM	P	M ← P. Read instruction into T. P ← P + 1.
			PASS	IR	T	IR ← T
	READ	JTAB		CM	ADR	If IR contains a memory reference instruction,
*						M ← IR(ADR) and read data into T. Jump to
*						CM address specified by IR(OP) and jump table.
*						Clear SAVE register.
*						
LOAD		RTN	PASS	A	T	A ← T. Return.
*						
STORE	WRITE	RTN	PASS	T	A	T ← A. Write T into memory. Return.
*						
ADD			PASS	L	T	L ← T.
	ENV	RTN	ADD	A	A	Enable overflow flag. A ← A + L. Return.
*						
AND			PASS	L	T	L ← T.
		RTN	AND	A	A	L ← A ∧ L. Return.
*						
JUMP		RTN	PASS	P	ADR	P ← IR(ADR). Return.
*						
JUMPZ			PASS	S1	A	Set test for A = 0.
	JMP	CNDX	TBZ	RJS	FETCH	If A ≠ 0 then go to FETCH.
		RTN	PASS	P	ADR	P ← IR(ADR). Return.
*						
COMP		RTN	CMPS	A	A	A ← $\overline{A}$. Return.
*						
RSHIFT	ARS	RTN	PASS	B	B	Right-shift the A.B register pair. Return.

FIGURE 4.74
Emulator for a small computer in 21MX microassembly language.

A ← A + L. Note that L is an implicit operand register for this microinstruction. The addition is carried out and the overflow flip-flop is set if overflow occurs. Finally, the RTN (return) operation transfers the SAVE register contents to the microprogram counter, which results in another FETCH cycle being executed.

4.4.3 Nanoprogrammed Computers

In conventional microprogrammed computers like the HP 21MX, each instruction fetched from main memory is interpreted by a microprogram stored in a single control memory CM. In some machines, however, the microinstructions do not directly issue the signals that control the hardware. Instead, they are used to access a second control memory termed a *nanocontrol memory* nCM that directly controls the hardware. Thus there are two levels of control memories, a higher-level one termed a *microcontrol memory* μCM whose contents are termed microinstructions, and the lower level nCM which stores *nanoinstructions;* see Fig. 4.75. The nanoprogramming concept was first used in the QM-1 computer designed around 1970 by Nanodata Corp. [18]. It is also employed in the more recent Motorola 68000-series of microprocessors, including the 68020 (Example 1.7).

Nanoprogramming. Consider a nanoprogrammed computer, in which μCM and nCM have dimensions $H_m \times W_m$ and $H_n \times W_n$, respectively. A major advantage of this two-level control design technique is that it can reduce the total size $S_2 = H_m \times W_m + H_n \times W_n$ of the control memories needed; this translates to smaller chip area in the case of one-chip CPUs like the 68020. Typically, the microprograms are encoded in a narrow vertical format so that although H_m is large, W_m is small. Nanoinstructions, on the other hand, usually have a highly parallel horizontal format making W_n large. If many microinstructions can be interpreted by the same nanoprogram, then H_n can be kept relatively small, so that $S_2 < S_1 = H_m \times W_n$, which is very roughly the size of a comparable single-level control unit. This potential for optimizing the total size of the control memories is the major motivation for the use of nanoprogramming in the design of the 68000-series microprocessors. Another advantage is the greater design flexibility resulting from loosening the bonds between instructions and hardware with two intermediate levels of control rather than one. This motivated the QM-1, which had the goal of efficiently emulating the instruction sets of a wide variety of different computers. The major disadvantages of the two-level approach are some reduction in

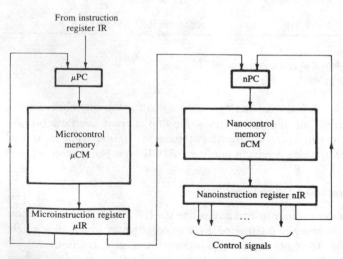

FIGURE 4.75
Two-level control store organization for nanoprogramming.

speed due to the extra memory access for nCM, and a more complex control-unit organization.

To see the savings in control-memory size that can result from the use of nanoprogramming, we consider the analysis carried out by the designers of the 68000 microprocessor [19]. Suppose that one- and two-level control stores are characterized by the parameters shown in Fig. 4.76. A one-level conventional CM is assumed to store H_m horizontal microinstructions each with a simple format consisting of N control bits and $\lceil \log_2 H_m \rceil$ next-address bits. The size of this memory is therefore

$$S_1 = H_m(N + \lceil \log_2 H_m \rceil) \tag{4.10}$$

In the two-level organization (Fig. 4.76b), the microcontrol memory μCM again stores H_m microinstructions, but the N-bit control fields are transferred to nCM. In place of the latter, each microinstruction in μCM contains a $\lceil \log_2 H_n \rceil$-bit address to specify any nanoinstruction location in nCM. It is assumed that little or no branching takes place among nanoinstructions, so no explicit address bits are included in the model of nCM. Thus the size of the two-level control store is

$$S_2 = H_m(\lceil \log_2 H_m \rceil + \lceil \log_2 H_n \rceil) + NH_n \tag{4.11}$$

Suppose that all control-bit patterns in nCM are different, so that each represents a unique control state associated with the given instruction set. We can write $H_n = rH_m$, where r is the ratio of the number of unique control states to the total number H_n of control states needed to implement all instructions. Substituting into (4.11) yields

$$S_2 = H_m(\lceil \log_2 H_m \rceil + \lceil \log_2 rH_m \rceil + rN)$$

$$= H_m(2\lceil \log_2 H_m \rceil + \lceil \log_2 r \rceil + rN) \tag{4.12}$$

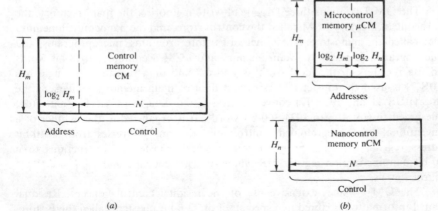

(a)

(b)

FIGURE 4.76
Control memory models: (a) one-level; (b) two-level.

The following parameters are cited for the 68000 [19]: $N = 70$, $H_m = 650$, and $r = 0.4$, so that $H_n = 260$. Substituting into (4.10) and (4.12), we obtain $S_1 = 52,450$ and $S_2 = 30,550$. Consequently, a total of $52,450 - 30,550 = 21,850$ bits of control storage (42 percent of S_1) are saved by the use of nanoprogramming. In general, two levels of control memory require less memory space if $S_2 < S_1$. Hence from (4.10) and (4.12) the following inequality must be satisfied.

$$N > \lceil \log_2 H_m \rceil + \lceil \log_2 r \rceil + rN$$

Nanodata QM-1. The QM-1 was developed as a universal emulation machine for research into new computer architectures [3, 18]. Its overall structure is depicted in Fig. 4.77. The QM-1's standard word size for its main memory and major buses is 18 bits, but it can also be operated in a 16-bit mode in which 2 bits are not used. These 16- and 18-bit formats make it easy to emulate architectures employing many different word sizes, for example, the 36-bit architectures of early machines such as the IBM 7094, and those of modern computers whose word size is a multiple of 8 or 16.

The CPU of the QM-1 is designed around a set of 32 registers called the local store. Most of these are general purpose, and four are implemented as counters to facilitate their use as program counters at the instruction or microinstruction levels. One local store register is used exclusively as a microinstruction register, i.e., as the output register of the microcontrol memory. The unit designated the main ALU in Fig. 4.77 is the major data processing component of the system. It is a fixed-point ALU capable of performing addition, subtraction, and all standard logic operations. Operations requiring shifting are performed in a separate shift circuit which may, if required, be integrated with the main ALU. The second ALU, called the index ALU, is used primarily for high-speed indexing and similar address-manipulation functions. A second set of 32 registers, called the external store, contains index registers and buffer registers for IO operations.

The QM-1 contains three large read-write memories: the main memory, the microcontrol memory μCM called the control store, and the nanocontrol memory nCM called the nanostore. These memories store programs, microprograms, and nanoprograms, respectively. Main memory and μCM accommodate 18-bit words and use registers in the local store as address and data registers. A single bus (BUS 7) is used to transfer addresses and data to main memory, while separate buses (BUS 11 and BUS 12) convey addresses and data to μCM. The nanostore is designed to store up to 1024 360-bit words. It is organized in the manner of a conventional microprogrammed control unit, deriving addresses from a 10-bit address register (the nanoprogram counter) and transferring instructions to a 360-bit nanoinstruction register nIR where they are decoded and used to activate control signals.

The QM-1 makes extensive use of the residual control concept. Residual control information is stored in a special set of 32 6-bit registers called the F store. These registers, which are under nanoprogram control, specify the way in which

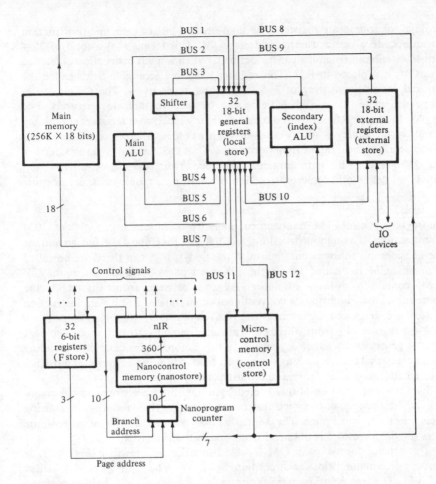

FIGURE 4.77
Structure of the Nanodata QM-1.

certain resources are to be allocated. For example, the name of the local store register to be used as the microprogram counter is stored in the F register FMPC. A major function of the F registers is to specify the local stores that are currently connected to the main QM-1 buses. There are 12 such buses labeled BUS 1 through BUS 12 in Fig. 4.77. At any time only one local store register is connected to each bus as determined by the F store. The 12 buses are quite independent, so up to 12 data transfers can take place simultaneously.

The microprogram control unit is composed of the microcontrol memory μCM and the local store registers used as its microprogram counter and microinstruction register. The four registers R24:27 have a special increment feature to facilitate their use as microprogram counters, while R31 is dedicated to the role of microprogram register. The high-order 7 bits of each microinstruction form an opcode which is used to address nCM. This means that a total of $2^7 = 128$ distinct microinstructions can be defined. When a microinstruction is fetched from μCM, it is placed in R31. This register has three accessible fields called the *C, A,* and *B* fields consisting of 7, 5, and 6 bits, respectively. The *C* field stores the opcode, while the *A* and *B* fields can be used to indicate operands. For example, the *A* and *B* fields can be used to identify local store registers containing operands or the addresses of operands in main memory. Microinstructions of this type are clearly vertical rather than horizontal. Thus the "natural" microinstruction of the QM-1 is an 18-bit word containing an opcode and two addresses. However, the user can define other microinstruction formats, e.g., multiword microinstructions.

Nanoprogram control. The nanocontrol memory nCM has a capacity of 1024 nanoinstructions. The nanoinstructions are 360 bits long and take full advantage of the considerable inherent parallelism of the QM-1; they can therefore be called horizontal. nCM is divided into eight 128-word pages, each of which may, if desired, contain a distinct emulator. As can be seen from Fig. 4.77, the nanoprogram control unit has a conventional organization. 10-bit nanoinstruction addresses are generated by a nanoprogram counter and nanoinstructions are placed in a register nIR from which control signals are directly obtained. The next address is generated by either incrementing the nanoprogram counter or loading it from an external source such as the branch field within the current nanoinstruction or an address derived from a microinstruction opcode.

Each microinstruction is interpreted by a nanoprogram stored in the nanostore. The 7-bit opcode of the microinstruction is used as the nanoprogram starting address relative to some page. The 3-bit page address needed to form an absolute address for the nanostore is obtained from one of the F registers.

The general format of a QM-1 nanoinstruction is shown in Fig. 4.78. It consists of five major fields, each containing 72 bits. The leftmost field is called the *K* field. The remaining four fields are called *T* fields. The *K* field contains a 10-bit branch address, condition select fields, and some control fields. Most of the specific control functions to be performed are specified by the *T* fields which have a common format consisting of 41 separate control subfields. Most of these control fields contain 1 bit, implying that very little encoding is used.

A nanoinstruction is executed in four phases, where each phase is normally one machine clock cycle (80 ns) in duration. The *K* field is active during all four phases, but only one *T* field is active during each phase. Thus during the first

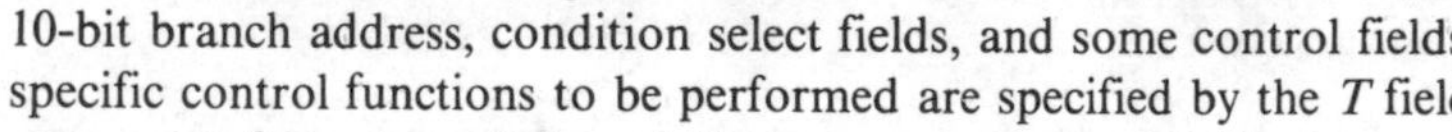

0	72	144	216	288	359
K	T_1	T_2	T_3	T_4

FIGURE 4.78
Nanoinstruction format of the QM-1.

phase of executing a nanoinstruction, K and T_1 control the machine, during the second phase K and T_2 control it, and so on. Each 360-bit nanostore word can be thought of either as a single polyphase nanoinstruction or else as four distinct nanoinstructions (K, T_1), (K, T_2), (K, T_3), and (K, T_4) which are executed in sequence. In the assembly language defined for QM-1 nanoinstructions [18], each nano-instruction is specified by five statements which define the K field and four T fields as follows.

Statement identifier	Operations
. . . .	K field
x . . .	T_1 field
. x . .	T_2 field
. . x .	T_3 field
. . . x	T_4 field

As an example we will now describe a nanoprogram consisting of a single nanoinstruction that interprets the microinstruction

ADD   R3, R6

which adds the contents of local store registers R3 and R6 and places the result in R3. The microinstruction is assumed to be in the microinstruction register R31, with the operands R3 and R6 in the A- and B-fields of R31, respectively. As noted earlier, these fields may be accessed by nanoprograms. The following nanoinstruction, written in the QM-1 nanoassembly language, implements ADD.

. . . .	KALC = ADD
x . . .	A → FAIR, B → FAIL, A → FAOD, MPC PLUS 1
. x . .	GATE ALU, READ CS(MPC)
. . x .	READ NS(CS)
. . . x	GATE NS

The first statement specifies that the control field called KALC in the nanoinstruc-tion K field be set to indicate the ADD operation. The second statement causes the registers R3 and R6 identified by the microinstruction A and B fields to be connected to the ALU. This is done by loading A and B into the three F registers FAIR, FAIL, and FAOD that control the input and output buses of the ALU. For example, the contents of FAIR control BUS 5 (ALU $i$nput $r$ight AIR), FAIL controls BUS 6 (ALU $i$nput $l$eft AIL), while FAOD controls BUS 2 (ALU $o$utput $d$ata AOD). Thus the microoperation A → FAIR effectively causes BUS 5 to connect local store register R3 to the rightmost input of the ALU. Figure 4.79 shows the bus connections produced by the ADD R3, R6 microinstruction.

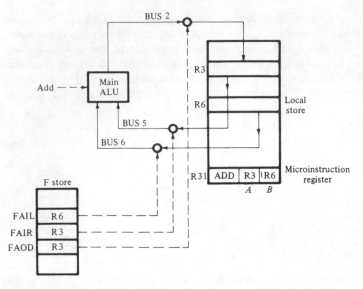

FIGURE 4.79
Effective QM-1 bus connections during execution of the microinstruction ADD R3,R6.

At this point the sum is computed and placed on BUS 2. The final microoperation MPC PLUS 1 in T_1 increments the local store register being used as the microprogram counter MPC.

Moving to T_2, the microoperation GATE ALU causes the result on BUS 2 to be loaded into the local store register currently connected to BUS 2, that is, R3. This completes the addition operation. The remaining parts of the nanoinstruction cause the next microinstruction to be fetched and decoded. The statement READ CS(MPC) in T_2 causes the microcontrol memory (control store) to be read using the address in the microprogram counter MPC. This results in a new microinstruction being placed on BUS 8. T_3 then causes the opcode part of the microinstruction (7 bits) to be loaded into the nanoprogram counter nPC; the remaining 3 bits of the 10-bit nanostore address are obtained from F register FIDX. The final statement GATE NS causes the nanostore to be read using the address in nPC. The nanoinstruction obtained is placed in the nanoinstruction register nIR where it is decoded and executed.

Emulation firmware has been written to enable the QM-1 to emulate numerous computers ranging from the Intel 8080, an 8-bit microprocessor, to the IBM S/360-370. To make the QM-1 behave like a System/360-series machine requires 124 nanoinstructions and about 9000 microinstructions.

4.5 SUMMARY

A complex digital system is usually partitioned into control and data processing units. The function of the control unit is to issue to the data processing unit control signals that select and sequence the data processing operations. Processors such as a CPU are controlled by instructions obtained from an external program memory. In such cases, the control unit has two main functions, instruction sequencing and instruction interpretation.

Instructions are normally obtained from consecutive locations in the program memory, and a program counter is used to generate instruction addresses. Deviations from the normal instruction sequence within a program are indicated by conditional and unconditional branch instructions. Two methods are used for temporary transfer of control between distinct programs—subroutine calls and interrupts. A pushdown stack is a particularly convenient mechanism for controlling subroutines and interrupts.

Two general techniques for interpreting instructions have been identified: hardwired control and microprogrammed control. Hardwired control units employ fixed special-purpose logic circuits to generate control signals. In a microprogrammed control unit, control signals are stored in the form of microinstructions in a special addressable memory called the control memory. Microprogramming has two major advantages:

1. It provides a systematic method for control unit design.
2. Since instructions are interpreted by microprograms, an instruction set can easily be changed by changing the microprograms.

Thus the behavior of a microprogrammed control unit can be altered by software rather than by hardware changes. On the other hand, microprogrammed control units are generally somewhat larger and slower than the corresponding hardwired units.

We have defined three systematic approaches to hardwired control design, which we term the state-table, delay-element, and sequence-counter methods. The state-table method, a formal-design approach derived from switching theory, attempts to minimize the number of gates and flip-flops used. It is computationally very difficult, thereby limiting its usefulness to small control units. The delay-element method yields a circuit whose structure mirrors the flow of control in a flowchart specification of the control-unit behavior. Clocked delay elements are used for timing purposes and constitute the memory part of the control unit. While this design approach is relatively simple to use, it may yield circuits containing an excessive number of memory elements. The third method uses a counter as a centralized source of timing signals. It is particularly useful for implementing control in processors whose behavior is cyclic in nature. Many processors within a computer have such behavior and can be controlled efficiently by sequence counters.

A microprogrammed control unit is designed around a control memory which stores microprograms. It contains logic for generating microinstruction addresses, fetching microinstructions, and decoding them to determine the control signals to be activated. The address-generation logic is often implemented by a (bit-sliced) component termed a microprogram sequencer. The control signals are specified by the control fields of the microinstructions. Microinstructions also contain control memory addresses which allow branches within a microprogram to be implemented. Branching may be made dependent on an external condition specified in a condition select field. All the methods used for program control at the instruction level, e.g., subroutine calls, can also be implemented at the microinstruction level.

The formats used for microinstructions vary greatly from computer to computer. These formats may be divided into two groups, horizontal and vertical. Horizontal microinstructions are typically characterized by long formats, little encoding of the control fields, and the ability to control many microoperations in parallel. Vertical microinstructions have short formats, considerable encoding of the control fields, and limited ability to control parallel microoperations. In practice, control fields are often identified with specific data paths or components of the system being controlled. Formal methods exist for reducing control-memory size by designing microinstructions which contain as few control bits as possible, and for compacting microprograms into as few microinstructions as possible.

A much greater variability exists among computers at the microinstruction level than at the instruction level. Some microprogrammed machines use a read-only memory as the control memory and thus execute a fixed-set of microprograms. This is usually the case in a microprogrammed CPU with a fixed instruction set. The microprograms then constitute an emulator for that instruction set. If a writeable control store is employed, many emulators may be used, thus enabling the computer to interpret dynamically a variety of instruction sets. Some computers use two levels of microprogramming; microinstructions are interpreted by nanoinstructions which directly control the hardware. Nanoprogramming increases a control unit's flexibility, while allowing the total size of the control memories to be reduced.

PROBLEMS

4.1. Programming languages like Pascal allow variables to be defined as local to a particular block of instructions such as a subroutine. The local variables are only required to exist, i.e., to have memory space allocated to them, when the block in question is actually being executed. Describe how a stack organization that is embedded in a random access memory can be used
   (a) To allow storage space for the local variables of a subroutine to be allocated when the subroutine is entered, and be deallocated when the subroutine is left
   (b) To allow a subroutine S to have access to the local variables of another subroutine when those variables are global variables of S

4.2. A useful program structure closely related to a stack is a queue, which replaces the stack's LIFO access mechanism by FIFO. Describe how a region of main memory can be managed as a software-implemented queue in a typical general-purpose computer. Specify the instructions needed to write a word into the queue or read a word from it.

4.3. Write an essay comparing the three hardwired control design approaches (state table, delay element, sequence counter) discussed in this chapter, paying particular attention to component cost and design difficulty.

4.4. A hardwired control unit is to be designed for a 32-bit fixed-point multiplier that implements the version of Booth's algorithm given in Fig. 3.43.

(a) Select what you think is the most appropriate design method for the control unit, when the major design objective is to specify a complete correctly functioning logic circuit in the shortest possible time. (Component cost and complexity are secondary considerations.) Give the reasons for your choice.

(b) Using the method you have selected, construct a logic circuit for this control unit. Use the control signal names given in Fig. 4.17, making any necessary modifications.

4.5. Consider the twos-complement multiplication algorithm appearing in Fig. 4.18. Redesign it so that incrementing the counter (state S_5) is done in parallel with shifting (S_4), thereby increasing the multiplier's speed. The modified algorithm is to be implemented using the circuit of Fig. 4.16, with any necessary changes. Design a hardwired control unit for the multiplier using the delay-element approach. Your answer should include an algorithm flowchart, a list of control signals based on those of Fig. 4.17, and a logic diagram for the control unit.

4.6. Repeat Prob. 4.5 using the sequence-counter approach in place of the delay-element method. The logic diagram should follow the style of Fig. 4.24.

4.7. Some commercial microprocessors like the Intel 8086 and Motorola 68000 employ microprogrammed control; others like the Zilog Z8000 series do not. Analyze the effects, both positive and negative, of using hardwired control in the design of general-purpose one-chip microprocessors.

4.8. Define each of the following terms: frame pointer, microprogram counter, microprogram sequencer, monophase, nanoprogram, residual control, shadow register.

4.9. Write a brief essay comparing and contrasting horizontal and vertical microinstruction formats from the viewpoints of hardware cost, speed, and ease of microprogramming.

4.10. A certain processor has a microinstruction format containing 10 separate control fields $C_0:C_9$. Each C_i can activate any one of n_i distinct control lines, where n_i is specified as follows:

$$i = 0 \quad 1 \quad 2 \quad 3 \quad 4 \quad 5 \quad 6 \quad 7 \quad 8 \quad 9$$

$$n_i = 4 \quad 4 \quad 3 \quad 11 \quad 9 \quad 16 \quad 7 \quad 1 \quad 8 \quad 22$$

What is the minimum number of control bits needed to represent the 10 control fields? What is the maximum number of control bits needed if a purely horizontal format is used for all the control information?

4.11. Draw a logic diagram showing how to construct a microprogram sequencer for (a) a 64 × 12-bit control memory, and (b) a 12 × 64-bit control memory, using one or more copies of the AMD 2909.

4.12. Using the format of Eq. (4.3), specify the control signals needed to perform the following microoperations in a 2909-based microprogram sequencer:

(a) CALL X, where X is the address on the D bus

(b) **go to** 0 if external condition $C_i = 1$

(c) Repeat the last microinstruction

4.13. Find a method of encoding the microinstructions described by Fig. 4.80 so that the minimum number of control bits is used and all inherent parallelism among the microoperations is preserved.

Microinstruction	Control signals activated
I_1	a, b, c, d, e
I_2	a, d, f, g
I_3	b, h
I_4	c
I_5	c, e, g, i
I_6	a, h, j
I_7	c, d, h
I_8	a, b, i

FIGURE 4.80
A set of microinstructions for Prob. 4.13.

4.14. Repeat Prob. 4.13 for the microinstructions specified in Fig. 4.81.

4.15. Let $\{C_i\}$ be a compatibility class cover for a set of microinstructions. $\{C_i\}$ is called a *minimum-cost cover* if

$$W = \sum_i \lceil \log_2(|C_i| + 1) \rceil$$

is a minimum. A compatibility class C_i is called a *principal* compatibility class if $|C_i| \neq 2^j$ for every integer $j \geq 1$. Prove that for any set of microinstructions there exists a minimum-cost cover whose members are principal compatibility classes. (This means that only principal compatibility classes need to be considered when constructing a minimum-cost cover.)

4.16. A compatibility class C_i is called *prime* if it satisfies either of the following conditions:

1. C_i is nonmaximal and $|C_i| = 2^h - 1$ for some integer $h \geq 1$.
2. C_i is maximal, that is, C_i is an MCC, and $|C_i| \neq 2^h$ for any integer $h \geq 1$.

Prove that for any set of microinstructions there exists a minimum-cost cover whose members are prime compatibility classes.

4.17. Integer linear programming is a useful mathematical technique for solving many optimization problems. An *integer linear program* is defined as follows. Find a set of values of the n integer variables $x_1, x_2, \ldots, x_n$ which maximizes or minimizes a linear expression (called the objective function) of the form

$$\sum_{i=1}^{n} c_i x_i$$

Microinstruction	Control signals activated
I_1	a, c, e, g, i
I_2	a, b, d, f, h, j
I_3	a, d, e, f
I_4	a
I_5	a, d, j

FIGURE 4.81
Microinstruction set for Prob. 4.14.

while satisfying a set of m linear inequalities of the form

$$\sum_{i=1}^{n} a_{i,j} x_i \approx b_j \quad j = 1, 2, \ldots, m$$

where the quantities a_{ij}, b_j, and c_i are constant real numbers and $\approx$ denotes either $\leq$ or $\geq$. Although the term programming in this context has nothing to do with computer programming, efficient computer routines are commercially available for solving integer linear programs.

Consider the problem of determining a minimal MCC cover, which forms part of the microinstruction size minimization technique discussed in Sec. 4.3.2. Show how this covering problem can be formulated as an integer linear program.

4.18. (a) Identify the SLMs in the microcode listed in Fig. 4.82, and use the FCFS compaction technique of Sec. 4.3.2 to reduce the length of the SLMs as much as possible.

(b) Show that this microprogram can be further shortened by (heuristic) consideration of the relations between the SLMs.

4.19. Define each of the following terms: horizontal microcode compaction; indirectly data dependent microoperations; weakly data dependent microoperations.

4.20. A number of practical considerations severely limit the applicability of control-memory optimization algorithms of the type discussed in Sec. 4.3.2. Analyze these considerations in detail.

4.21. Design a microprogrammed control unit for the Booth multiplier specified in Prob. 4.4. Draw a block diagram of the control unit and give a binary listing (with suitable comments) of the multiplication microprogram to be used.

4.22. Repeat Prob. 4.5 using microprogrammed rather than hardwired control.

4.23. You are to design a microprogrammed controller for a fixed-point divider that uses the circuit of Fig. 3.53 and the nonrestoring division algorithm of Fig. 3.54. The divider should handle both positive and negative integers having a 16-bit sign-magnitude format.

(a) List all the required control signals and the microoperations they control.

Name	Microoperation	Phases used
m_1	RLEFT ← R1	Φ_1
m_2	ROUT ← RLEFT + RRIGHT	Φ_2
m_3	R1 ← ROUT	Φ_3
m_4	**if** R1 = R2 **then go to** L	Φ_3
m_5	RLEFT ← R1	Φ_1
m_6	RRIGHT ← R3	Φ_1
m_7	ROUT ← RLEFT + RRIGHT	Φ_2
m_8	R2 ← ROUT	Φ_3
m_9	L: MAR ← PC	Φ_1
m_{10}	MDR ← M(MAR)	Φ_1, Φ_2, Φ_3
m_{11}	R4 ← MDR	Φ_1
m_{12}	RLEFT ← R4	Φ_1

FIGURE 4.82
Microprogram for Prob. 4.18.

(b) Design a microinstruction format of the type shown in Fig. 4.60 in which the control fields are encoded by function in an efficient manner.

(c) Using Fig. 4.48 as a model, draw a block diagram of the microprogrammed control unit for the divider.

4.24. A microprogrammed control unit is to be designed for a floating-point adder with the general structure shown in Fig. 3.69. A number of the form $M \times B^E$ is represented by a 32-bit word comprising a 24-bit mantissa, which is a twos-complement fraction, and an 8-bit exponent, which is a biased integer. The base B is 2.

(a) Using our description language, give a complete listing of a symbolic microprogram to control this adder.

(b) Derive a suitable microinstruction format that uses unencoded control fields.

4.25. In some microinstruction formats no address fields are used. Instead all control-memory addresses are obtained from the microprogram counter μPC. To implement microprogram branches, external condition signals are allowed to increment μPC. Design a microprogrammed control unit that uses this type of addressing, giving your answer in the style of Fig. 4.68. Assume that the control memory CM has a capacity of 512 words. There are six external condition signals $S_0:S_5$ to be tested, where the existence of condition i is indicated by $S_i = 1$. If a specified condition is present the next sequential microinstruction should be skipped, otherwise it should be executed.

4.26. A microprogrammed emulator is required for the CPU of Fig. 4.65. It should implement the eight instructions defined in Fig. 4.25 as well as the instructions SUB and MULT, which perform fixed-point subtraction and multiplication, respectively.

(a) Give in symbolic form a complete listing of a suitable emulator.

(b) Design a microinstruction format for the emulator with control fields encoded by function. Use the control signals listed in Fig. 4.66, making any necessary modifications.

4.27. Modify the CPU design of Fig. 4.27 to allow dynamic microprogramming using a writeable control memory. Draw a block diagram showing the structure of the microprogrammed control unit and all changes made to the original design.

4.28. A number of computers have microinstructions containing an "emit" field, in which the microprogrammer can place an arbitrary constant for use as an immediate operand. Give some general reasons for including an emit field in microinstructions.

4.29. An important aspect of the operation of any digital computer is *fault diagnosis,* which is the process of identifying or locating faulty components. Fault diagnosis is accomplished by applying input sequences (test sequences) to the unit under test and observing the resulting output responses at appropriate observation points. When an observed response differs from the known correct response, a fault has been detected in the unit in question. By applying many test sequences, one can usually isolate faults to the smallest replaceable components. Fault diagnosis is generally implemented by diagnostic (micro) programs, which carry out the necessary test generation and response analysis in a systematic manner.

Consider the problem of diagnosing faults in the CPU of a computer where it is desired to isolate faulty components at the register level. Discuss the relative merits of hardwired and microprogrammed control for the CPU from the viewpoint of implementing on-line fault-diagnosis procedures.

4.30. A conventional microprogrammed CPU is being redesigned for implementation as a one-chip microprocessor. At present it has a single 256×80-bit control memory, and employs a highly parallel horizontal microinstruction format in which every instruction contains one 8-bit branch address. It is estimated that in a two-level organization of the control unit, only about 64 300-bit nanoinstructions would be needed to implement the current instruction set. If the total size of the control memories is the major cost consideration, should the new microprocessor have one- or two-level control? Show your calculations and state all your assumptions.

4.31. Analyze in terms of hardware cost, computational speed, and microprogramming complexity the advantages and disadvantages of using two levels of microprogramming in the manner of the QM-1.

REFERENCES

1. Advanced Micro Devices Inc.: *Bipolar Microprocessor and Logic Interface (Am2900 Family) Data Book,* Sunnyvale, Calif. 1985.
2. Agerwala, T.: "Microprogram Optimization: A Survey," *IEEE Trans. Comput.,* vol. C-25, pp. 962–973, October 1976.
3. Agrawala, A. K., and T. G. Rauscher: *Foundations of Microprogramming: Architecture, Software, and Applications,* Academic, New York, 1976.
4. Andrews, M.: *Principles of Firmware Engineering in Microprogram Control,* Computer Science Press, Potomac, Md., 1980.
5. Carlson, C. B.: "The Mechanization of a Push-down Stack," *AFIPS Conf. Proc.,* vol. 24, pp. 243–250, 1963.
6. Das, S. R., D. K. Banerji, and A. Chattopadhyay: "On Control Memory Minimization in Microprogrammed Computers," *IEEE Trans. Comput.,* vol. C-23, pp. 845–848, September 1973.
7. Dasgupta, S.: "The Organization of Microprogram Stores," *Comput. Surv.,* vol. 11, pp. 39–65, March 1979.
8. Davidson, S., et al.: "Some Experiments in Local Microcode Compaction for Horizontal Machines," *IEEE Trans. Comput.,* vol. C-30, pp. 460–477, July 1981.
9. Digital Equipment Corp.: *Small Computer Handbook* (PDP-8), Maynard, Mass., 1973.
10. Hewlett-Packard Co.: *Microprogramming 21MX Computers: Operating and Reference Manual,* Manual 02102-90008, Cupertino, Calif., 1974.
11. Hill, F. J., and G. R. Peterson: *Digital Systems: Hardware Organization and Design,* 2d ed., Wiley, New York, 1978.
12. Husson, S. S.: *Microprogramming: Principles and Practices,* Prentice-Hall, Englewood Cliffs, N.J., 1970.
13. International Business Machines Corp.: *An Introduction to Microprogramming,* Publ. GF20-0385-0, White Plains, N.Y., 1971.
14. Kohavi, Z., *Switching and Finite Automata Theory,* 2d ed., McGraw-Hill, New York, 1978.
15. Kraft, G. D., and W. N. Toy: *Microprogrammed Control and Reliable Design of Computers,* Prentice-Hall, Englewood Cliffs, N.J., 1981.
16. Mick, J., and J. Brick: *Bit-Slice Microprocessor Design,* McGraw-Hill, New York, 1980.
17. Motorola Inc.: *MC68020 32-Bit Microprocessor User's Manual,* 2d ed., Prentice-Hall, Englewood Cliffs, N.J., 1985.
18. Nanodata Corp.: *QM-1 Hardware Level User's Manual,* 3d ed., Buffalo, N.Y., 1979.
19. Stritter, S., and N. Tredennick: "Microprogrammed Implementation of a Single-chip Computer," *Proc. 11th Microprog. Workshop,* pp. 8–16, December 1978.
20. Texas Instruments Inc.: *SN74AS8835 16-bit Microsequencer,* Dallas, Tex., 1986.
21. Tucker, S. G.: "Microprogram Control for System/360," *IBM Syst. J.,* vol. 6, pp. 222–241, 1967.
22. Wilkes, M. V.: "The Best Way to Design an Automatic Calculating Machine," Rept. Manchester University Computer Inaugural Conf., pp. 16–18, 1951 [Reprinted in E. E. Swartzlander (ed.): *Computer Design Development: Principal Papers,* pp. 266–270, Hayden, Rochelle Park, N.J., 1976.]

MEMORY ORGANIZATION

This chapter considers the organization of a computer's memory system. The characteristics of the most important storage-device technologies are surveyed. Hierarchical memory systems including virtual memory are studied, as well as some high-speed memory organizations.

5.1 MEMORY TECHNOLOGY

Every computer system contains a variety of devices to store the instructions and data required for its operation. These storage devices plus the algorithms (either implemented by hardware or software) needed to control or manage the stored information constitute the memory system of the computer. In general, it is desirable that processors should have immediate and uninterrupted access to memory, so the time required to transfer information between a processor and memory should be such that the processor can operate at, or close to, its maximum speed. Unfortunately, memories that operate at speeds comparable to processor speeds are relatively costly. It is not feasible (except for very small systems) to employ a single memory using just one type of technology. Instead the stored information is distributed in complex fashion over a variety of different memory units with very different physical characteristics.

The memory components of a computer system can be divided into three main groups:

1. *Internal processor memory.* This comprises a small set of high-speed registers used as a working memory for temporary storage of instructions and data.

2. *Main memory* (also called primary memory). This is a relatively large fast memory used for program and data storage during computer operation. It is characterized by the fact that locations in main memory can be accessed directly and rapidly by the CPU instruction set. The principal technology used for main memory is based on semiconductor integrated circuits (ICs).

3. *Secondary memory* (also called auxiliary or backing memory). This is generally much larger in capacity but also much slower than main memory. It is used for storing system programs, large data files, and the like which are not continually required by the CPU; it also serves as an overflow memory when the capacity of the main memory is exceeded. Information in secondary storage is accessed indirectly via input-output programs that first transfer the required information to main memory. Representative technologies used for secondary memory are magnetic disks and tapes.

An increasing number of machines employ another type of memory called a *cache,* which serves as an intermediate temporary storage unit logically positioned between the processor registers and main memory. Unlike the other memory levels mentioned above, caches are transparent to the programmer.

The major objective in designing any memory system is to provide adequate storage capacity with an acceptable level of performance at a reasonable cost. Four important interrelated ways of approaching this goal can be identified.

1. The use of a number of different memory devices with different cost/performance ratios organized to provide a high average performance at a low average cost per bit. The individual memories form a hierarchy of storage devices.

2. The development of automatic storage-allocation methods to make more efficient use of the available memory space.

3. The development of virtual-memory concepts to free the ordinary user from memory management, and make programs largely independent of the physical memory configurations used.

4. The design of communication links to the memory system so that all processors connected to it can operate at or near their maximum rates. This involves increasing the effective memory processor bandwidth and also providing protection mechanisms to prevent programs from accessing or altering one another's storage areas.

5.1.1 Memory-Device Characteristics

The computer architect is faced with a bewildering variety of different memory devices to use [14, 16]. However, all memories are based on a relatively small number of physical phenomena and employ relatively few organizational principles. In this section, we examine the functional characteristics that are common to the devices used to build main and secondary computer memories. A knowledge of these general properties is essential in evaluating any memory technology. The characteristics and underlying physical principles of some specific representative technologies are also discussed.

Cost. The cost of a memory unit is most meaningfully measured by the purchase or lease price to the user of the complete unit. The price should include not only the cost of the information storage cells themselves but also the cost of the peripheral equipment or access circuitry essential to the operation of the memory. Let C be the price in dollars of a complete memory system with S bits of storage capacity. We define the *cost* c of the memory as follows:

$$c = \frac{C}{S} \text{ dollars/bit}$$

Access time. The performance of a memory device is primarily determined by the rate at which information can be read from or written into the memory. A convenient performance measure is the average time required to read a fixed amount of information, e.g., one word, from the memory. This is termed the *read access time* or, more commonly, the *access time* of the memory and is denoted by t_A. (The write access time is defined similarly; it is typically, but not always, equal to the read access time.) Access time depends on the physical characteristics of the storage medium, and also on the type of access mechanism used; a precise general definition of t_A is difficult. It is usually calculated from the time a read request is received by the memory unit to the time at which all the requested information has been made available at the memory output terminals. The *access rate* b_A of the memory defined as $1/t_A$ and measured in words per second is another widely used performance measure for memory devices.

Clearly, low cost and high access rates are desirable memory characteristics; unfortunately they appear to be largely incompatible. Memory units with high access rates are generally expensive, while low-cost memories are relatively slow. Figure 5.1 shows the relation between cost c and access time t_A for the major current (1987) memory technologies. This relation can be approximated by the straight line AB. If we write $t_A = 10^y$ and $c = 10^x$, then $y \approx mx + k$, where m denotes the slope of AB and k is a constant. Hence $t_A \approx 10^{mx+k'} \approx kc^m + k''$. From the data provided in Fig. 5.1, it can be concluded that $m \approx -0.5$. Thus to decrease t_A by a factor of 10, the cost c must increase by about 100. In other words, $b_A = 1/t_A$ grows roughly as the square of the cost per bit c.

Improvements in manufacturing techniques are continually reducing c and, at a much slower rate, t_A, for most memory technologies. Especially striking have been the achievements in semiconductor RAM ICs. For example, a 4K-bit (dynamic) RAM chip representing the state of the art of VLSI technology circa 1975 initially cost about \$40, making $c \approx 0.01$ \$/bit; the same device 10 years later cost about \$4. The state of VLSI technology in 1985 is represented by the 256K-bit RAM chip, which, at roughly the same introductory price of \$40, has $c \approx 0.00015$ \$/bit. Similar developments have taken place in other memory technologies, e.g., magnetic disk memories, as storage density has increased steadily with relatively little overall cost change. Thus while the scales of Fig. 5.1 will inevitably shift over

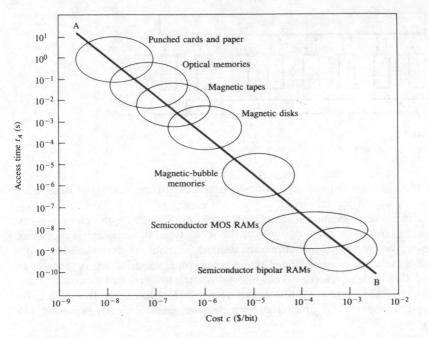

FIGURE 5.1
Access time vs cost for representative memory technologies.

time, it is expected that the relative positions of the various memory technologies, and the slope m of the line AB, will remain fairly constant.

Access modes. An important property of a memory device is the order or sequence in which information can be accessed. If locations may be accessed in any order and access time is independent of the location being accessed, the memory is termed a *random-access memory* (RAM). Ferrite-core and semiconductor memories are usually of this type. Memories where storage locations can be accessed only in certain predetermined sequences are called *serial-access memories*. Magnetic-tape, magnetic-bubble, and optical memories employ serial access methods.

In a random-access memory each storage location can be accessed independently of the other locations. There is, in effect, a separate access mechanism, or read-write head, for every location, as illustrated in Fig. 5.2. In serial memories, on the other hand, the access mechanism is shared among different locations. It must be assigned to different locations at different times. This is accomplished by moving the stored information, the read-write head, or both. Many serial-access memories operate by continually moving the storage locations around a closed path or track, as shown in Fig. 5.3. A particular location can be accessed only when it passes the fixed read-write head; thus the time required to access a

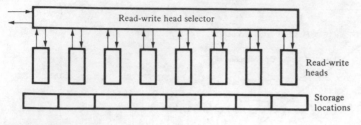

FIGURE 5.2
Conceptual model of a random-access memory.

particular location depends on its position relative to the read-write head when the access request is received.

Since every location has its own addressing mechanism, random-access memories tend to be more costly than the serial type. In serial-access memories, however, the time required to bring the desired location into correspondence with a read-write head increases the effective access time, so serial access tends to be slower than random access. Thus the access mode employed contributes significantly to the inverse relation between cost and access time. In Fig. 5.1, for example, random-access and serial-access technologies are clearly separated into two groups.

Some memory devices such as magnetic disks contain a large number of independent rotating tracks. If each track has its own read-write head, the tracks may be accessed randomly, although access within each track is serial. In such cases the access mode is sometimes called *semirandom* or, rather misleadingly, *direct access*. It should be noted that access mode is a function of memory organization as well as the inherent characteristics of the storage technology used.

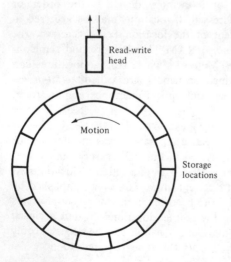

FIGURE 5.3
Conceptual model of a serial-access memory.

Memory technologies, e.g., semiconductor, that are primarily used to construct random-access memories can also be used to construct serial-access memories. The converse is not usually true, however.

Alterability; ROMs. The method used to write information into a memory may be irreversible, in that once information has been written, it cannot be altered while the memory is in use, i.e., on-line. Punching holes in cards and printing on paper are examples of essentially permanent storage techniques. Memories whose contents cannot be altered on-line (if they can be altered at all) are called *read-only memories* (ROMs). A ROM is therefore a nonerasable storage device. ROMs are widely used for storing control programs such as microprograms. ROMs whose contents can be changed (usually off-line and with some difficulty) are called *programmable read-only memories* (PROMs).

Memories in which reading or writing can be done with impunity on-line are sometimes called *read-write* memories to contrast them with ROMs. All memories used for temporary storage purposes are read-write memories. Unless otherwise specified, we will use the term memory to mean a read-write memory.

Permanence of storage. The physical processes involved in storage are sometimes inherently unstable, so that the stored information may be lost over a period of time unless appropriate action is taken. There are three important memory characteristics that can destroy information: destructive readout, dynamic storage, and volatility. Some memories have the property that the method of reading the memory destroys the stored information; this phenomenon is called *destructive readout* (DRO). Memories in which reading does not affect the stored data are said to have *nondestructive readout* (NDRO). In DRO memories, each read operation must be followed by a write operation that restores the original state of the memory. This restoration is usually carried out automatically using a buffer register, as shown in Fig. 5.4. The word at the addressed location is transferred to the buffer register where it is available to external devices. The contents of the buffer are automatically written back into the location originally addressed.

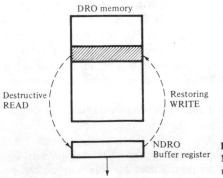

FIGURE 5.4
Memory restoration in a destructive readout (DRO) memory.

Certain memory devices have the property that a stored 1 tends to become a 0, or vice versa, due to some physical decay process. For example, in several memory technologies, a stored 1 is represented by an electric charge in a capacitor; the absence of a stored charge represents a 0. Over a period of time, a stored charge tends to leak away, causing a loss of information unless the charge is restored. The process of restoring is called *refreshing*. Memories which require periodic refreshing are called *dynamic* memories, as opposed to *static* memories, which require no refreshing. (Note that the terms dynamic and static in this context do not refer to the presence or absence of physical motion in the storage device.) Most memories using magnetic storage techniques are static. Refreshing in dynamic memories can be carried out in the same way data is restored in a DRO memory. The contents of every location are transferred periodically to buffer registers and then returned, in suitably amplified form, to their original locations.

Another physical process that can destroy the contents of a memory is the failure of its power supply. A memory is said to be *volatile* if the stored information can be destroyed by a power failure. Most semiconductor memories are volatile, while most magnetic memories are nonvolatile.

Cycle time and data-transfer rate. We defined the access time t_A of a memory as the time between the receipt of a read request by the memory and the delivery of the requested information to its external output terminals. In DRO and dynamic memories, it may not be possible to initiate another memory access until a restore or refresh operation has been carried out. This means that the minimum time that must elapse between the initiation of two different accesses by the memory can be greater than t_A; this rather loosely defined time is called the *cycle time* t_M of the memory.

It is generally convenient to assume that t_M is the time needed to complete any read or write operation in the memory. Hence the maximum amount of information that can be transferred to or from the memory every second is $1/t_M$; this quantity is called the *data-transfer rate* or *bandwidth* b_M. The data-transfer rate is measured in bits or words per second. A factor limiting memory bandwidth is the *memory bus width w,* which is the number of bits that can be transferred simultaneously over the memory bus. w is generally, but not necessarily, the same as the internal memory word size. Clearly $b_M = w/t_M$ bits/s.

In cases where $t_A \neq t_M$, both are used to measure memory speed. The access time may be more important in measuring overall computer-system performance since it determines the length of time a processor must wait after initiating a memory access request; during the remainder of the memory cycle, both processor and memory can operate simultaneously. On the other hand, if $t_A \neq t_M$, then $b_A \neq b_M$ and b_A does not represent the actual number of accesses that can be carried out per second, whereas b_M does.

Physical characteristics. Many different physical properties of matter are used for information storage. The more important properties used for this purpose can be classified as electronic, magnetic, mechanical, and optical. A basic requirement for a storage medium is that it have two well-defined physical states that can be used to represent the logical 0 and 1 values. The access rate of a particular memory device depends on the rate at which its physical states can be measured and altered. Figure 5.5 contains a table showing representative physical characteristics of some major modern memory technologies.

There are several other attributes of memories that may significantly affect the cost of a memory technology in a particular application. A factor determining the physical size of a memory unit is the *storage density* measured, perhaps, in bits per unit area, or volume. The physical size also determines the portability of the memory. The energy consumption of the memory units may contribute significantly to the running costs of a computer system. Large energy consumption combined with high storage density may require expensive cooling equipment.

Finally, some mention should be made of *reliability,* which can be measured by the mean time to failure (MTTF). In general, memories with no moving parts have much higher reliability than memories such as magnetic disks, which involve considerable mechanical motion. Even in memories that involve no moving parts, reliability problems arise, particularly when very high storage densities or high data-transfer rates are used. The reliability of any memory can be increased by using error detecting and error correcting codes (see Sec. 3.1.2).

5.1.2 Random-Access Memories

Random-access memories (RAMs) are characterized by the fact that every location can be accessed independently. The access and cycle times for every location

Technology	Access time t_A, s	Access mode	Alterability	Permanence	Physical storage medium
Bipolar semiconductor	10^{-9}	Random	Read/write	NDRO, volatile	Electronic
Metal-oxide-semiconductor (MOS)	10^{-8}	Random	Read/write	DRO or NDRO, volatile	Electronic
Magnetic disk	10^{-2}	Semirandom	Read/write	NDRO, nonvolatile	Magnetic
Magnetic tape	10^{-1}	Serial	Read/write	NDRO, nonvolatile	Magnetic
Compact disk ROM	1	Semirandom	Read only	NDRO, nonvolatile	Optical
Punched cards	10	Serial	Read only	NDRO, nonvolatile	Mechanical

FIGURE 5.5
Characteristics of some major memory technologies.

are constant and independent of its position. Figure 5.6 shows the main components of a random-access memory unit. The storage cell unit comprises N cells each of which can store 1 bit of information. The memory operates as follows. The address of the required location (a set of $w \geq 1$ cells) is transferred via the address bus to the memory address register. The address is then processed by the address decoder which selects the required location in the storage cell unit. A read-write select control line specifies the type of access to be performed. If read is requested, the contents of the selected location is transferred to the output data register. If write is requested, the word to be written is first placed in the memory input data register and then transferred to the selected cell. Since it is not usually desirable to permit simultaneous reading and writing, the input and output data registers are frequently combined to form a single data register (also called the memory buffer register). The input and output parts of the data bus may then be merged to form a single bidirectional data bus.

Figure 5.7 shows an idealized model of a RAM cell and its external connections. The address lines are used to select the cell for either reading or writing, as determined by the read-write control lines. A set of data lines is used for transferring data to and from the memory. The actual number of physical lines connected to a storage cell is very much a function of the technology being used. Frequently one physical line has several functions, e.g., it may be used as both an address and a data line. Thus the cell connections depicted in Fig. 5.7 should be viewed as logical rather than physical. In each line connected to the storage cell unit one can expect to find a driver which acts as either an amplifier or a transducer of physical signals. Thus we find in Fig. 5.6 a set of address line drivers and a set of data line drivers. The various drivers, decoders, and control circuits are collectively referred to as the *access circuitry* of the memory unit.

RAM organization. The access circuitry needed has a very significant effect on the total cost of any memory unit. A general approach to reducing the access

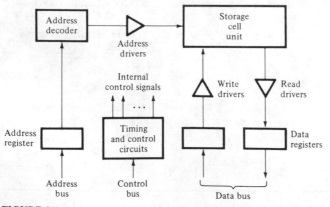

FIGURE 5.6
A random-access memory unit.

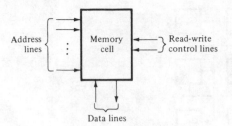

Address lines

Memory cell

Read-write control lines

Data lines

FIGURE 5.7
General model of a random-access memory cell.

circuitry cost in random-access memories is called *matrix*, or *array*, *organization* [16]. It has two essential features:

1. The storage cells are physically arranged as rectangular arrays of cells. This is primarily to facilitate layout of the connections between the cells and the access circuitry.
2. The memory address is partitioned into d components so that the address A_i of cell C_i becomes a d-dimensional vector $(A_{i,1}, A_{i,2}, \ldots, A_{i,d}) = A_i$. Each of the d parts of an address word goes to a different address decoder and a different set of address drivers. A particular cell is selected by simultaneously activating all d of its address lines. A memory unit with this kind of addressing is said to be a *d-dimensional memory*.

The simplest array organizations have $d = 1$ and are called *one-dimensional,* or 1-D, memories. Each cell is connected to one address line, as shown in Fig. 5.8. If the storage capacity of the unit is N bits, then the access circuitry typically contains a one-out-of-N address decoder and N address drivers. In the *two-dimensional* (2-D) organization shown in Fig. 5.9, the address field is divided into two components, called X and Y, which consist of a_x and a_y bits, respectively. The cells

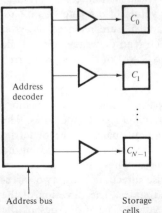

Address decoder

C_0

C_1

C_{N-1}

Address bus

Storage cells

FIGURE 5.8
One-dimensional addressing scheme.

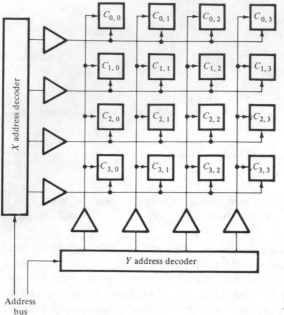

FIGURE 5.9
Two-dimensional addressing scheme.

Address
bus

are arranged in a rectangular array of $N_x \leq 2^{a_x}$ rows and $N_y \leq 2^{a_y}$ columns so that the total number of cells is $N = N_x N_y$. A cell is selected by the coincidence of signals on its X and Y address lines. The 2-D organization requires substantially less access circuitry than the 1-D for a fixed amount of storage. For example, if $N_x = N_y = \sqrt{N}$, the number of address drivers needed is $2\sqrt{N}$. Instead of one one-out-of-N address decoder, two one-out-of-$\sqrt{N}$ address decoders are required. In addition, the 2-D memory organization matches well the inherently two-dimensional circuit structures allowed by IC technology. These advantages diminish or disappear with larger numbers of dimensions; hence values of d greater than 2 are rarely used. If the 1-bit storage cells of Figs. 5.8 and 5.9 are replaced by w-bit registers, then an entire word can be accessed in each read or write cycle but the bits within a word are not individually addressable. A RAM of this sort is referred to as an $N \times w$-bit *word-organized* memory.

Ferrite-core memories. Until the advent of high-capacity semiconductor memory ICs in the 1970s, most main memories in computers employed ferrite cores. The basic storage cell in this technology is a tiny doughnut-shaped piece of ferrite material called a *core*, through which several wires are threaded. By passing an electric current called a drive current through these wires, the core can be magnetized in either a clockwise or counterclockwise direction; these two directions of magnetization represent the logical 0 and 1 states. The direction of the drive current determines the direction of magnetization. The properties of the ferrite material are such that when this current is reduced to zero, the core retains its previous magnetized state. This implies that ferrite-core memories are non-volatile.

Large random-access memories can be constructed from multidimensional arrays of ferrite cores. While ferrite-core memories have been widely used, they have several disadvantages. They are basically incompatible with processor technologies. They are also difficult to manufacture due to the complex wiring patterns needed. The memory cycle time achievable is primarily a function of core size; the smaller the core, the shorter the cycle time but the more difficult the wiring problem.

To employ a ferrite core as a read-write memory cell at least two conductors are required, a drive line and a sense line, as shown in Fig. 5.10. The drive line is used for changing the state of the core (writing) and the sense line is used for sensing the state (reading). Suppose that a current of magnitude I is passed through the drive line, as shown in Fig. 5.10a. This produces a magnetic flux φ in the direction indicated, which can be taken to represent the 0 state. If I exceeds a certain threshold or saturation level and is then reduced to zero, the core remains in the 0 state. If a current of $-I$ amperes is passed through the drive line, as shown in Fig. 5.10b, the direction of the magnetic flux is reversed and the core enters the 1 state. Again this state remains if the drive current is switched off.

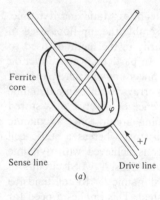

(a)

Ferrite core

Sense line

Drive line

$+I$

φ

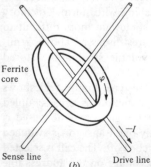

(b)

Ferrite core

Sense line

Drive line

$-I$

φ

FIGURE 5.10
Switching a ferrite core to (a) the 0 state and (b) the 1 state.

The readout process requires using both the drive and sense lines. A current I is passed through the drive line in a fixed direction, say that of Fig. 5.10a. If the core is in the 0 state, there is no change in its direction of magnetization. If, however, the core is in the 1 state, the magnetic flux in the core reverses direction and, as described by Faraday's law, a voltage pulse is induced in the sense line. This pulse is detected by a sense amplifier and transferred to the memory data register. Thus the state of the cell is determined by the presence or absence of a signal on the sense line. The reading method used is clearly destructive (DRO), so the cell state must be restored before a second read operation can take place.

Semiconductor RAMs. Semiconductor memories in which the basic storage cells are transistor circuits have been used for high-speed CPU registers since the 1950s. It was not until the development of VLSI ICs in the 1970s that it became economical to produce large RAM chips suitable for main-memory applications. Single-chip RAMs are manufactured in a wide range of sizes from a few hundred bits to a megabit (2^{20} bits) or more. Both bipolar and MOS transistor circuits (see Sec. 1.1.4) are used, with MOS being the dominant circuit technology for larger RAM chips. The present limitations of IC manufacturing makes it impossible to manufacture, say, a gigabit (2^{30}-bit) RAM on a single chip. Consequently, very large semiconductor RAMs must be constructed by interconnecting a number of smaller RAM ICs.

Semiconductor memories fall into two main categories, static and dynamic. Static RAMs are composed of memory cells that resemble the flip-flops used in processor registers. They differ from the latter primarily in the methods used to address the cells and transfer data to and from them. In particular, multifunction lines are used to minimize the number of external connections to each RAM cell and so facilitate the manufacture of large planar (2-D) arrays of cells. In a dynamic RAM cell, the 1 and 0 states correspond to the presence or absence of a stored charge in a capacitor controlled by a transistor switching circuit. Since a dynamic RAM cell can be constructed around a single transistor, whereas a static cell requires up to six transistors, higher storage density is achieved with dynamic RAM designs. Indeed, dynamic RAMs are among the densest VLSI circuits in terms of transistors per chip. The charge stored in a dynamic RAM cell tends to decay with time, and so it must be periodically refreshed. This implies a need for extra control circuitry and a need to interleave refreshing with normal memory access operations. Consequently, dynamic RAMs are somewhat more difficult to use than their static counterparts. Unlike the ferrite cores discussed above, semiconductor memories, both static and dynamic, are volatile so that the stored information is lost when the power source is removed.

Bipolar RAM cells are usually of the static flip-flop type. Figure 5.11 shows an example. The two bipolar transistors T_0 and T_1 function as cross-coupled NAND gates (or NOR gates, depending on whether the logic convention used is positive or negative); cf. Fig. 2.26a. At any time exactly one transistor is switched on, i.e., conducting current, while its companion is switched off. The cell is selected for either the read or write operation by changing the voltage on the address line

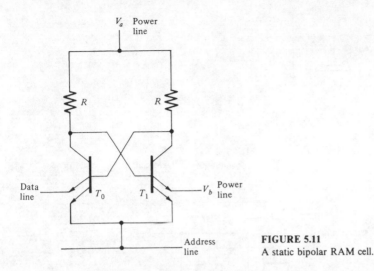

FIGURE 5.11
A static bipolar RAM cell.

from low to high. The data line can be considered to have three distinct states represented by three voltage levels V_0, $V_{1/2}$, and V_1. V_0 and V_1 are used for writing, while the intermediate voltage level $V_{1/2}$ is used in reading. V_a and V_b are the circuit power lines. V_b is held at the voltage level $V_{1/2}$. To read the cell, the data line is held at $V_{1/2}$ and the address line voltage is raised. This causes the current flowing through the on transistor to transfer from its lower emitter to its upper emitter. The resulting signal indicating the state of the cell is detected by a sense amplifier connected to the data line. A 0 (1) is written into the cell by again activating its address line and applying V_0 (V_1) to its data line.

MOS storage cells may be either static or dynamic. Figure 5.12 shows a particularly simple and useful MOS cell based on the dynamic charge-storage approach. It comprises a field-effect MOS transistor T, which acts as a switch, and a capacitor C, which stores the data. It has only two external connections: a data line and an address line. To write information into the cell, a voltage (either high or low, representing 1 and 0, respectively) is placed on the data line. A voltage is then applied to the address line to switch T on. This causes a charge to be transferred to C if the data line is in the 1 state; no charge is transferred otherwise. To read the cell, the address line is again activated, causing the charge stored in C, if any, to be transferred to the data line, where it is detected by a sense amplifier. Since the readout process is destructive, the information read out is amplified and subsequently rewritten into the cell; this may be combined with the periodic refreshing operation required by dynamic memories of this type. The advantages of this memory cell are its small size, which means that ICs with very high cell density can be built, and its low power consumption.

A semiconductor RAM IC typically has a word-organized array structure and contains all required access circuitry, including address decoders, drivers, and control circuits. Figure 5.13 shows a simple 4 × 2-bit RAM that incorporates eight

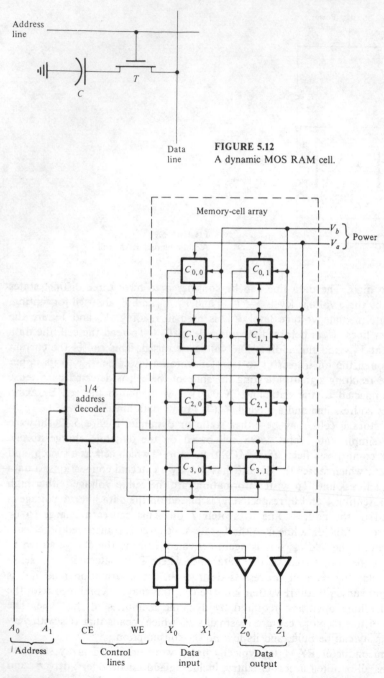

FIGURE 5.12
A dynamic MOS RAM cell.

FIGURE 5.13
Structure of a 4 × 2-bit RAM.

static bipolar cells of the type shown in Fig. 5.11. The more important access circuitry is also shown. WE is the *write enable* line; a write (read) operation can take place only if WE = 1 (0). A second control line, the *chip enable* CE or *chip select* line CS, is also needed. A word can be accessed for either reading or writing only if CE = 1. The behavior of the bidirectional data lines connected to each cell is determined by the underlying device physics.

RAM design. A memory design problem that the computer architect may encounter is the following: given that certain $m \times n$-bit RAM ICs, denoted $M_{m \times n}$, are available, design an $m' \times n'$-bit RAM where $m' \geq m$ and/or $n' \geq n$. A general approach is to construct a $p \times q$ array of the $M_{m \times n}$ modules where $p = \lceil m'/m \rceil$ and $q = \lceil n'/n \rceil$, and $\lceil x \rceil$ denotes the smallest integer greater than or equal to x. In this IC array, each row stores m words (except possibly the last row), while each column stores a fixed set of n bits from every word (except possibly the last column). When $m' \geq m$, additional external address decoding circuitry may be required.

Consider the design of a 16×4-bit memory using 4×2-bit ICs of the type shown in Fig. 5.13. It is convenient to represent each IC by a single block with its external connections labeled as in Fig. 5.14. Clearly eight of these ICs are needed. They can be arranged as a 4×2 array as shown in Fig. 5.15. The left column of ICs stores the two low-order data bits, while the right column stores the two high-order data bits. Since there are four address lines, some additional decoding circuitry is needed. We therefore introduce a one-out-of-four decoder with an address enable input similar to the decoder shown in Fig. 5.13. Two of the incoming address lines are connected to every IC; the remaining two address lines are inputs to the external decoder. Each of the output lines of this decoder is connected to the address enable inputs of the ICs in the same row. Thus each row of cells in the resulting array has a unique address. The output data lines of all cells in the same column are connected together under the assumption (which is valid for many semiconductor technologies) that this connection forms a wired-OR.

Example 5.1 The Intel 2186 64K-bit dynamic RAM chip [10]. This commercial RAM chip, which was introduced in 1983, contains 64K one-transistor MOS storage

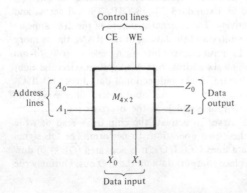

Control lines

FIGURE 5.14
Symbol for the 4×2-bit RAM of Fig. 5.13.

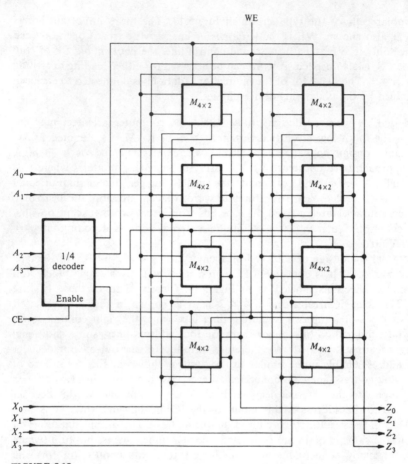

FIGURE 5.15
A 16 × 4-bit RAM.

cells of the kind shown in Fig. 5.12. Its stored information is organized as 8K (2^{13}) 8-bit bytes, and the RAM is housed in a standard 28-pin DIP. Typical access and cycle times are 250 and 500 ns, respectively. The internal structure of the 2186 appears in Fig. 5.16. To simplify the access circuitry and the layout of the RAM, the memory cells form a 2-D array. Seven of the 13 input address bits A_0:A_6 select a row R from the 128 rows of this array; the remaining six address bits A_7:A_{12} then select the eight columns of R containing the desired word. Eight bidirectional data lines I/O_0:I/O_7 transfer data to or from the RAM chip. There are three input control lines $\overline{WE}$ (write enable), $\overline{CE}$ (chip enable), and $\overline{OE}$ (output enable); as the overbars indicate, these lines are all active in the 0 state. $\overline{CE}$ serves to activate the chip for a read or write cycle, while $\overline{WE}$ specifies which of these two operations to perform. The $\overline{OE}$ signal controls the bidirectional (tristate) data lines I/O_0:I/O_7; it is activated ($\overline{OE}$ = 0) during read cycles to allow the RAM to place (output) data on the I/O bus. During write cycles $\overline{OE}$ is inactive ($\overline{OE} = 1$), causing the I/O bus to be placed in the high-impedance state Z which permits it to be driven by external data sources.

The 2186 contains all the control logic needed for refreshing, which must be done at least once every 2 ms. It is accomplished by internally reading all 128 rows of the memory-cell array in sequence. The automatic write-back associated with the DRO read operation serves to recharge all 512 cells (64 bytes) in the addressed row simultaneously. Refreshing is triggered automatically by an internal timer, and to completely refresh the memory takes 128 memory cycles, or about 64 μs. Since no more than 64 μs out of every 2 ms need be devoted to refreshing, i.e., about 3 percent of the available time, refreshing has little impact on the performance of the memory. Normal memory accesses cannot take place during refreshing. However, refresh cycles and normal access cycles are interleaved by the 2186, so that an external read or write request is delayed by no more than one cycle period (500 ns) if it is received after a refresh cycle has begun. The RAM chip informs the external devices that it is busy with a refresh cycle by deactivating the RDY (ready) control line. An arbiter circuit in the on-chip refresh logic selects the row address to be supplied to the memory-cell array from either the externally supplied row address $A_0:A_6$ or a 7-bit address generated by an internal (refresh) counter. A memory read cycle proceeds as follows. First $\overline{WE}$ must be deactivated ($\overline{WE} = 1$) to indicate a read operation. The requesting device initiates the read cycle at t_0 by activating $\overline{CE}$; it must then activate $\overline{OE}$ within a specified period of time. If no refresh cycle is in progress, the word addressed by $A_0:A_{12}$ is read out and placed on the I/O data lines at time $t_0 + t_A$, where t_A is the normal access time. If refreshing is underway at t_0, the 2816 immediately changes RDY to 0. After the refresh cycle has been completed, RDY returns to 1 and the requested read cycle is executed. In the case of a write cycle,

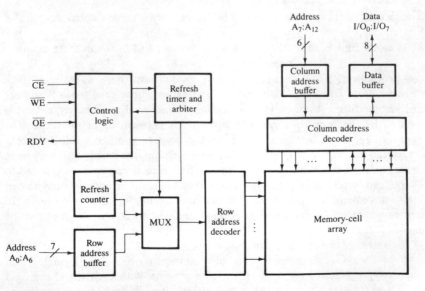

FIGURE 5.16
Structure of the Intel 2186 8K $\times$ 8-bit dynamic RAM chip.

$\overline{WE}$ must be activated a specified time after $\overline{CE}$ has been activated to start the write cycle. The falling edge of the $\overline{WE}$ signal is used to transfer the input data on the I/O bus into the addressed RAM cells. An ongoing refresh cycle will cause RDY to be deactivated as in the read cycle, and the write cycle to be delayed by up to one cycle period.

5.1.3   Serial-Access Memories

Serial-access memories are characterized by the fact that the read-write circuitry is shared among different storage locations. Large serial memories are usually designed so that the stored information moves continuously along a set of fixed paths or tracks. A track consists of a sequence of cells each capable of storing 1 bit of information. Each track has a number of fixed access points at which a read-write "head" may transfer information to or from the track. A specific stored item is accessed by moving either the stored information, the read-write heads, or both. From a functional point of view, the storage tracks in serial memories are shift registers with a limited number of input-output points. Thus the transfer of information to and from any one track is essentially serial.

Serial-access memories find their main application as secondary or bulk on-line computer memories because of their low cost per bit and relatively long access times. Low cost per bit is obtained by using very simple and very small storage cells. The long access time is due to several factors:

1. The read-write head positioning time
2. The relatively slow speed at which the tracks move
3. The fact that data transfer to and from the memory is serial rather than parallel

Because access time is so important, we now consider this factor in more detail.

Access procedures. Serial memories may be divided into those where each track has one or more fixed read-write heads, and those whose read-write heads are shared among different tracks. In memories that share read-write heads, a delay is introduced by the need to move read-write heads between different tracks. The average time required to move a head from one track to another is called the *seek time* t_S of the memory unit. Once the head is in position, the desired cell may be in the wrong part of the moving storage track. Some time is required for this cell to reach the read-write head so that data transfer can begin. The average time needed for this movement to take place is called the *latency* t_L of the memory. In memories where information rotates around a closed track, t_L is also called the *rotational delay*.

Each storage cell in a track stores a single bit. A w-bit word may be stored in two different ways. A word may consist of w consecutive bits along a single track. Alternatively, w tracks may be used to store a word, with each track storing a different bit. By synchronizing the w tracks and providing a separate read-write head for each track, all w bits can be accessed simultaneously. In either case it may be inefficient to access just one word per access since so much time is consumed by the seek time and latency. Words are normally grouped into larger units called *blocks*. All the words in a block are stored in consecutive locations, so that the time required to access an entire block includes only one seek and one latency period.

Once the read-write head is positioned at the start of the requested word or block, data is transferred at a rate which depends primarily on the speed at which the stored information is moving and the storage density along the track. The speed at which information can be transferred continuously to or from the track under these circumstances is called the *data-transfer rate*. If a track has a storage density of T bits per centimeter and moves at a velocity of V centimeters per second past the read-write head, the data-transfer rate is TV bits per second.

The time t_B required to access a block of information in a serial-access memory may be estimated as follows. Assume that the memory has closed rotating tracks of the type shown in Fig. 5.3. Let each track have a capacity of N words and rotate at a rate of r revolutions per second. Let n be the number of words per block. The data rate of the memory is rN words per second. Hence once the read-write head is positioned at the start of the desired block, it can be transferred in approximately $n(rN)^{-1}$ seconds. The average latency is $(2r)^{-1}$ seconds, which is the time needed for half a revolution. If t_S is the average seek time, an appropriate formula for t_B is

$$t_B = t_S + (2r)^{-1} + n(rN)^{-1}$$

Memory organization. Figure 5.17 shows the general organization of a serial memory unit. Assume that each word is stored along a single track and that each access results in transfer of a block of $n \geq 1$ words. The address of the information to be accessed is applied to the address decoder, whose output determines the track to be used (the track address) and the location of the desired block of information within the track (the block address). The track address determines the particular read-write head to be selected. Then, if necessary, the selected head is moved into position to transfer data to or from the target track. The desired block cannot be accessed until it reaches the selected head. To determine when this occurs, some type of track position indicator is needed which generates the address of the block that is currently passing the read-write head. The generated address is compared with the block address produced by the address decoder. When they match, the selected head is enabled and data transfer between the storage track and the memory data buffer registers begins. The read-write head is disabled when a complete block of information has been transferred. The memory input and output data registers are generally shift registers of the parallel-in/series-out and series-in/parallel-out types, respectively.

The number of different types of storage media and access mechanisms used to construct serial memories is quite large. In many serial memories the read-write heads and/or the storage locations are moved through space by electromechanical devices such as electric motors, in order to perform an access. The most widely

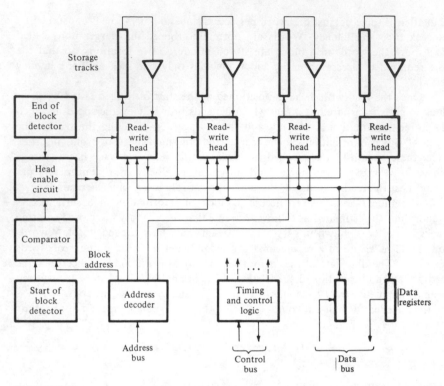

FIGURE 5.17
A serial-access memory unit.

used group of secondary memory devices, magnetic-disk and -tape units, fall into this category, as do many optical memories. No mechanical motion is required to access some types of serial memories. The long obsolete mercury delay line memory was of this type, as are magnetic-bubble memories.

Magnetic memories with electromechanical access have had many years of development. The storage media (disks and tapes) used are inexpensive and also portable. However, electromechanical equipment is relatively unreliable and a major source of computer-system failures. Memories with no moving parts are therefore very attractive from the point of view of reliability. We will discuss representative examples of both types of serial-access memory.

Magnetic-surface recording. In magnetic-disk and -tape memories, information is stored in tracks on the surface of a magnetic medium, usually ferric oxide. Each cell in a track has two stable magnetic states that represent the logical 0 and 1 values. The magnetic states are typically defined by the direction or magnitude of the magnetic flux in the cell (many different methods of encoding information in magnetic states are used). Each cell is therefore similar in principle to a ferrite core. As in the case of ferrite cores, electric currents are used for altering and sensing the magnetic state. In surface magnetic storage, however, an external read-write head of the type shown in Fig. 5.18 is employed. The read and write currents pass through coils around a ring of soft magnetic material. There is a gap in this ring which permits magnetic flux to pass into the surrounding air. A very narrow space separates the ring gap from a cell on the storage track, so that their respective magnetic fields can interact. This interaction permits information transfer between the read-write head and the storage medium.

In order to write information, the addressed cell is moved under the read-write gap. A pulse of current is then transmitted through the write coil, which alters the magnetic field at the ring gap; this in turn alters the state of magnetization of the cell under the gap. The direction or magnitude of the write current determines the resulting cell state. To read a cell, it is moved past the read-write head, causing the magnetic field of the cell to induce a magnetic field in the core material of the read-write head. Since the cell is in motion, this magnetic field varies and so induces an electric voltage pulse in the read coil. This voltage, which is then fed to a sense amplifier, identifies the state of the cell. The readout process is nondestructive. In addition, magnetic-surface storage is nonvolatile.

Electromechanically accessed magnetic memories are distinguished by the shapes of the surfaces in which the storage tracks are embedded. In disk memories, the tracks form concentric circles on the surface of a disk. In tape memories, the tracks form parallel lines on the surface of a long narrow plastic tape.

Magnetic-disk memories. A magnetic disk is similar in appearance to a phonograph record. It may be made of aluminum or plastic with a thin coating of magnetic material on its surface. On each surface of the disk there are up to several

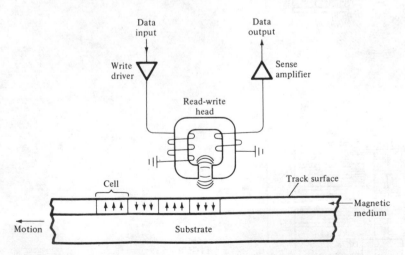

FIGURE 5.18
Magnetic-surface recording mechanism.

hundred tracks which are arranged in concentric circles as shown in Fig. 5.19a. Several disks may be attached to a common spindle. During operation of a disk memory, the disks are rotated continuously at a constant speed. In modern disk units, each recording surface is supplied with at least one read-write head. The read-write heads may be connected to form a read-write "arm," as shown in Fig. 5.19b, so that all heads move in unison. This arm may then be moved in a fixed linear path to select a particular set of tracks. Disk memories have also been designed with one head per track, thus eliminating the need for a moving read-write arm and effectively reducing the seek time to zero. Small flexible magnetic disks referred to as *floppy* disks form a compact, inexpensive, and portable medium for off-line storage of moderate amounts of data, e.g., 1M bytes. They are contrasted with *hard* disks, which are usually sealed into their drive units and have higher storage capacity and reliability.

Example 5.2   The NEC Model D2257 disk drive. This hard-disk memory manufactured by NEC Corp. was introduced in the mid-1980s. It employs the "Winchester" disk-drive technology originally developed by IBM, which places the magnetic disks and their read-write head assembly in a hermetically sealed unit. Winchester drives, which are typical of hard-disk units, reduce head-to-track alignment problems by allowing the read-write heads to rest on the recording surface (which is specially lubricated) when the drive is stopped. These features result in high recording density, as well as high reliability. The D2257 is housed in a rectangular box whose

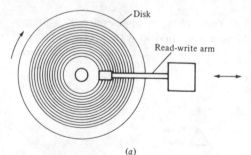

(a)

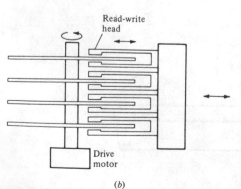

(b)

FIGURE 5.19
(a) Top view and (b) side view of a magnetic-disk unit.

dimensions are approximately $42 \times 22 \times 14$ cm. It contains five 8-in. (20.3 cm) disks or platters supplying a total of eight recording surfaces, each with its own read-write head. Figure 5.20 summarizes the major characteristics of this device.

Magnetic-tape memories. Magnetic-tape memory units are essentially similar to domestic tape recorders; instead of storing analog information, they store binary digital information. The storage medium has as its substrate a flexible plastic tape. Information is generally stored in nine parallel longitudinal tracks. A read-write head that can simultaneously access all nine tracks is used; hence the basic memory "word" is 9 bits. This usually comprises 8 bits (1 byte) of information and 1 parity check bit. Magnetic tapes are stored on reels and provide a compact, inexpensive, and portable medium for storing large information files. They are also packaged in cartridges or cassettes which resemble audio tape cassettes.

Figure 5.21 shows the main components of a large tape drive unit. Two reels are used to store the tape. Unlike disk memories, the storage medium is not in continuous motion. When an access request is received, the tape is moved forward or backward to the desired location; it is stopped at the end of the data transfer. In order to permit rapid starting and stopping, two large loops of tape are permitted to hang freely on each side of the read-write head. The rotating drums (called capstans) that pull the tape past the read-write head are here only to accelerate the tape in these loops while the reels themselves are brought up to speed. This procedure reduces the influence of the inertia of the reels. After its initial acceleration, the tape moves at a constant velocity, called the tape speed.

Data transfer takes place only when the tape is moving at constant velocity; hence the data-transfer rate of a particular tape unit is determined by the storage density and the tape speed. For example, if the tape storage density is 1600 bytes/in. and the tape speed is 18.75 in./s (these figures are representative of low-speed tape systems), the data-transfer rate is $1600 \times 18.75 = 30,000$ bytes/s. Information stored on magnetic tapes is organized into blocks of various sizes. Relatively large gaps must be inserted at the end of each block to permit the tape to start and stop between blocks. Note that the time required to rewind an entire tape is of the order of 1 min.

Number of recording surfaces	8
Number of tracks per recording surface	1024
Number of read-write heads per recording surface	1
Track recording density (max)	9420 bits/in.
Storage capacity of track	20,480 bytes
Total storage capacity of disk drive	167.7M bytes
Disk rotation speed	3510 r/min
Average seek time	20 ms
Average latency	8.55 ms
Data-transfer rate	1.198M bits/s

FIGURE 5.20
Characteristics of the NEC D2257 disk memory.

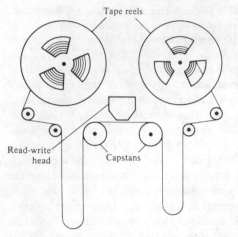

FIGURE 5.21
A large magnetic-tape drive unit.

Magnetic-bubble memories. In thin plates of certain materials such as garnets, the natural directions of magnetization are perpendicular to the surface of the plates. When no external magnetic field is present, serpentine areas called *domains* form spontaneously in the plate; see Fig. 5.22a. The material within each domain is magnetized in one of the two possible directions, and adjacent domains are magnetized in opposite directions. Suppose that an external magnetic field H_b, called a *bias field,* is applied perpendicular to the plate surface, as shown in Fig. 5.22b. As the magnitude of H_b is increased, the domains whose direction of magnetization is opposite to that of H_b contract in size until eventually they are cylindrical in shape. These cylindrical domains are called *magnetic bubbles.* Typical bubble diameters are around 1 μm.

Bubbles can be moved at high velocity through the plate if an additional

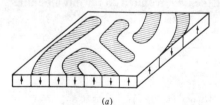

(a)

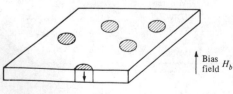

↑ Bias
  field H_b

(b)

FIGURE 5.22
Formation of magnetic bubbles.

external magnetic field called a *drive field* H_d is applied whose direction is parallel to the plate surface. Usually the drive field is rotated at a fixed rate. This rotating field is generated by an electromagnet, so no mechanical motion is involved. By depositing linear tracks of a soft magnetic material called permalloy on the plate surface, the bubbles can be moved along predetermined paths. The permalloy tracks are designed so that they constrain the bubbles to remain under the tracks. They also convert the drive field into magnetic fields that force the bubbles trapped under the track to move continuously in a fixed direction. Bubble propagation tracks can also be created in a surface layer of the garnet substrate by ion implantation.

Figure 5.23 shows a *T-bar* track used in early bubble-memory systems, which consists of T- and bar-shaped permalloy elements in an alternating linear sequence. The rotating drive field H_d induces a magnetic field in the permalloy elements parallel to H_d. Thus, depending on the orientation of H_d, the extremities of the T's and bars and the junctions of the T's become north (N) or south (S) magnetic poles at various times. Each magnetic bubble is like a small magnet, one of whose poles (the S pole in Fig. 5.23) is at the surface on which the permalloy track has been laid. According to the classic law of magnetism (like poles attract, unlike poles repel), a bubble is attracted to the nearest N pole in either a T or a bar. Figure 5.23 shows how one revolution of H_d causes a bubble to move in a straight line from one T to the corresponding position under a neighboring T. Many other equally ingenious permalloy track designs exist for bubble propagation [16]; see Prob. 5.6.

Bubble-memory devices are constructed by forming closed tracks around which bubbles can be circulated continuously at a fixed rate. In the case of the T-bar track of Fig. 5.23, each pair of adjacent T's and bars constitutes a storage cell. The presence (absence) of a bubble in a cell denotes the logical 1 (0) state. In order to be able to write data into a cell, two special devices are needed; a *bubble generator* to introduce bubbles into a track and a *bubble annihilator* to remove bubbles. For reading purposes, a *bubble detector* is required that can produce an electrical signal indicating the presence or absence of a bubble. The structure of a bubble-memory chip organized as a single N-bit shift register is shown in Fig. 5.24. The average access time for 1 bit (which in this case is the same as the latency) is the time required to propagate a bubble through $N/2$ cells. The access time can be decreased by a factor of k by the common stratagem of using k independent bubble shift registers that can be accessed in parallel.

An example of a relatively fast bubble-memory system is the *major-minor loop* organization shown in Fig. 5.25. Data is stored in k bubble shift registers called the minor loops, which are rotated in synchronism by a common magnetic-drive field. Data is transferred to or from the minor loops via another bubble shift register called the major loop. Each minor loop is connected to the major loop by a device called a transfer gate. An external control signal applied to the transfer gates causes one bit of information to be transferred between the major loop and each of the minor loops. The major loop is attached to the input-output circuitry (bubble annihilators, generators, and detectors) and acts as a communication link between the minor storage loops and the outside world.

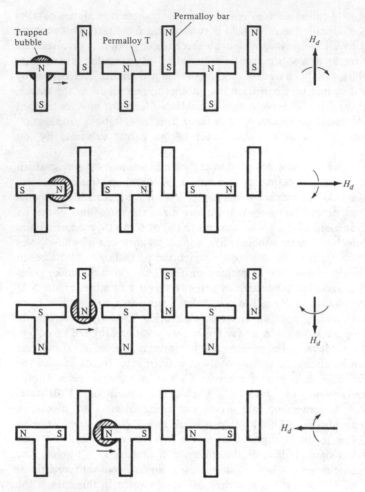

FIGURE 5.23
Propagation of magnetic bubbles along a T-bar track.

Magnetic bubble memories have been manufactured with capacities of 1M or more bits per chip. As Fig. 5.1 suggests, they fall somewhere between semiconductor RAMs and magnetic disks in terms of cost and performance. If a permanent magnet is used to generate the bias field, a bubble memory is nonvolatile, an advantage compared with semiconductor RAMs. Their lack of moving parts gives bubble memories a reliability advantage over magnetic disks. On the negative side, bubble memories are more difficult to manufacture than competing technologies, and are harder to interface with conventional processors. As a result, bubble memories have been mainly used in specialized applications such as the secondary memories of air- or spaceborne computers, where extremely high reliability is required.

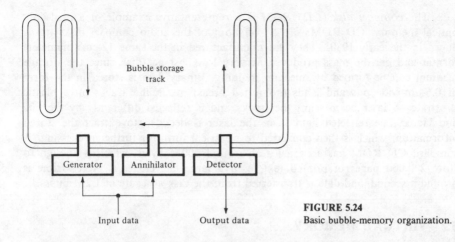

FIGURE 5.24
Basic bubble-memory organization.

Optical memories. Optical techniques for data storage have been the subject of intensive research for many years. Optical memories usually take the form of optical disks, which resemble magnetic disks in that they store binary information in concentric tracks on a mechanically rotated disk. The information is read or written optically, however, with a laser replacing the mechanical read-write arm of a magnetic-disk drive. Optical memories offer the potential of extremely high storage capacities. Read-only optical memories are well developed, but read-write memories have proven difficult to build due to the fact that the physical effects underlying easily alterable optical storage media are poorly understood at present.

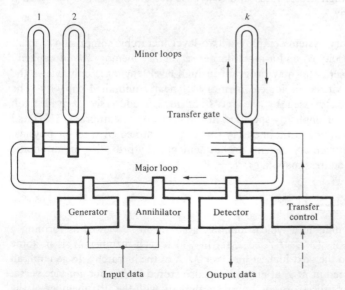

FIGURE 5.25
Major-minor loop bubble-memory organization.

The *compact disk* (*CD*) *ROM* is a representative example of a read-only optical memory. CD ROMs are an offshoot of the audio compact disks introduced in the early 1980s. They are manufactured in the same 12-cm (diameter) format and can be mass produced at very low cost per disk since the storage medium can be formed by injection molding. Binary data is stored in the form of 0.6-μm-wide pits and lands (nonpitted areas) in circular tracks on a plastic substrate. A laser beam scans the tracks and is reflected differently by the pits and lands. The reflected light from the laser is decoded to extract the stored information, which is then converted to electrical form for further processing. A standard CD ROM has a capacity of around 500M bytes, which is enough to store 200,000 pages of printed text, e.g., a large encyclopedia. Access time is around a second, and data is transferred from the disk at a rate of 1.2M bits/s.

5.2 VIRTUAL MEMORY

Virtual memory loosely describes a hierarchical storage system of at least two levels, which is managed by an operating system to appear to a programmer like a single large directly addressable main memory. There are three main reasons for using virtual memory.

1. To free programmers from the need to carry out storage allocation and to permit efficient sharing of memory space among different users
2. To make programs independent of the configuration and capacity of the memory systems used during their execution
3. To achieve the high access rates and low cost per bit that is possible with a memory hierarchy

Most virtual memory systems employ a two-level hierarchy comprising a main memory M_1 of capacity S_1 and a much larger secondary memory M_2 of capacity S_2. The ordinary user, who may program in high-level languages only, views the system as a single virtual or logical memory of nearly unlimited capacity. The virtual memory is addressed by the set L of logical addresses derived from identifiers explicitly or implicitly specified in the user's object program. The fixed physical storage locations in the memory units are identified by a set of physical addresses P. Virtual memory systems are implemented by providing an automatic mechanism for the address mapping $f: L \to P$.

5.2.1 Memory Hierarchies

The various major units in a typical memory system can be viewed as forming a hierarchy of memories $(M_1, M_2, \ldots, M_n)$ in which each member M_i is in some sense subordinate to the next highest member M_{i-1} of the hierarchy. In general, all the information stored in M_{i-1} at any time is also stored in M_i, but not vice versa. The CPU and other processors communicate directly with the first member of the hierarchy M_1, M_1 can communicate directly with M_2, and so on. Let c_i, t_{A_i}, and S_i denote the cost per bit, access time, and storage capacity, respectively, of M_i. The following relations normally hold between the memory levels M_i and M_{i+1}:

$$c_i > c_{i+1}$$

$$t_{A_i} < t_{A_{i+1}}$$

$$S_i < S_{i+1}$$

Figure 5.26 shows the two most common memory hierarchies. Typical technologies used in these hierarchies are bipolar semiconductor RAMs for cache memory, MOS semiconductor RAMs for main memory, and magnetic-disk units for secondary memory.

During the execution of programs, the CPU generates a continuous stream of logical memory addresses. At any time these addresses are distributed in some fashion throughout the memory hierarchy. If an address is generated which is currently assigned only to M_i where $i \neq 1$, the address must be reassigned to M_1, the level of the memory hierarchy that the CPU can access directly. This relocation of logical addresses generally requires the transfer of information between levels M_i and M_1, a relatively slow process. In order for a memory hierarchy to work efficiently, the addresses generated by the CPU should be found in M_1 as often as possible. This requires that future addresses be to some extent predictable, so that information can be transferred to M_1 before it is actually referenced by the CPU. If the desired information cannot be found in M_1, then execution of the program originating the memory request must be suspended until an appropriate reallocation of storage is made.

Locality of reference. The predictability of logical memory addresses which is essential to the successful operation of a memory hierarchy is based on a common characteristic of computer programs called locality of reference. This describes the fact that over the short term, the addresses generated by a typical program tend to be confined to small regions of its logical address space, as illustrated in Fig. 5.27. The items of information whose addresses are referenced during the time interval from $t - T$ to t, denoted $(t - T, t)$, constitute the *working set* $W(t, T)$ [6]. It has been found that $W(t, T)$ tends to change rather slowly; hence by maintaining all of $W(t, T)$ in the fastest level of memory M_1, the number of

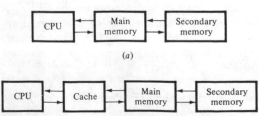

(a)

(b)

FIGURE 5.26
Common memory hierarchies: (a) two-level; (b) three-level.

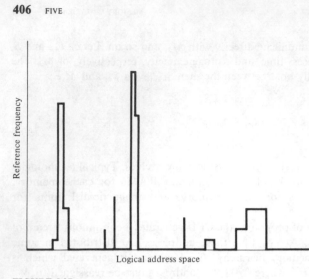

FIGURE 5.27
Typical nonuniform distribution of address references.

references to M_1 can be made considerably greater than the number of references made to the other levels of the memory hierarchy.

One reason for locality of reference is that instructions and, to a lesser extent, data are written down and subsequently stored in the computer's memory in approximately the order in which they are needed during program execution. Suppose that a request is made for a one-word instruction I stored at address A, and this address is currently assigned to $M_i \neq M_1$. The instruction most likely to be required next by the CPU is the one immediately following I whose address is $A + 1$. Thus instead of simply transferring the instruction I to M_1, it is desirable to transfer a block of consecutive words containing I. A common way of implementing this is by subdividing the information stored in M_i into pages, each containing a fixed number S_{p_i} of consecutive words. Information is then transferred one page or S_{p_i} words at a time between levels M_i and M_{i+1}. Thus if the CPU requests word I in level M_i, the page of the length $S_{p_{i-1}}$ in M_i containing I is transferred to M_{i-1}, then the page of length $S_{p_{i-2}}$ containing I is transferred to M_{i-2}, and so on. Finally, the page P of length S_{p_1} containing I is transferred to M_1, where it can be accessed by the CPU. Subsequent memory references are likely to refer to addresses in P, so that the single transfer to M_1 anticipates future memory requests by the CPU.

A second factor in locality of reference is the presence of program loops. Statements within a loop may be executed repeatedly, resulting in a high frequency of reference to their addresses. When a loop is being executed, it is desirable to store the entire loop in M_1 if possible.

Design objectives. The overall goal in memory hierarchy design is to achieve a performance close to that of the fastest device M_1 and a cost per bit close to that of the cheapest device M_n. The performance of a memory hierarchy depends on a variety of factors, which are related in a complex manner. The more important of these are the following.

1. The address reference statistics, i.e., the order and frequency of the logical addresses generated by programs that use the memory hierarchy
2. The access time t_{A_i} of each level M_i relative to the CPU
3. The storage capacity of each level
4. The size of the blocks of information transferred between successive levels
5. The strategy, called the allocation algorithm, used for determining the regions of memory to which blocks of information are transferred by the swapping process

These design factors interact in a complex manner which is by no means fully understood. A number of simple analytic models exist, however, which reveal the general way in which some of these factors are related. Some representative models of this kind are discussed in the present chapter. It should be emphasized that simulation is still the major tool for memory-system design. Simulation is used for determining such program-dependent design parameters as address reference frequencies. It is also the main technique for evaluating memory-system performance.

Cost and performance. For simplicity we restrict our attention to the most common form of memory hierarchy, a two-level hierarchy (M_1, M_2). It is not difficult to generalize the cost and performance measures discussed here to n-level hierarchies. The average cost per bit of memory is given by

$$c = \frac{c_1 S_1 + c_2 S_2}{S_1 + S_2} \tag{5.1}$$

where c_i denotes the cost per bit of M_i and S_i denotes the storage capacity in bits of M_i. To achieve the goal of making c approach c_2, S_1 must be very small compared with S_2.

The performance of a two-level memory hierarchy is frequently measured in terms of the *hit ratio H*, which is defined as the probability that a logical address generated by the CPU refers to information stored in M_1. Since references to M_1 (hits) can be satisfied much more quickly than references to M_2 (misses), it is desirable to make H as close to 1 as possible. Hit ratios are generally determined experimentally as follows. A set of representative programs is executed or simulated. The number of address references satisfied by M_1 and M_2, which are denoted by N_1 and N_2, respectively, are recorded. H is then given by the equation

$$H = \frac{N_1}{N_1 + N_2} \tag{5.2}$$

Clearly H is highly program-dependent. The quantity $1 - H$ is called the *miss ratio*.

Let t_{A_1} and t_{A_2} denote the access times of M_1 and M_2, respectively, relative to the CPU. The average time t_A for the CPU to access a word in the memory system is given by the equation

$$t_A = Ht_{A_1} + (1 - H)t_{A_2} \qquad (5.3)$$

In most two-level hierarchies, a request for a word not in main memory causes a block of information containing the requested word to be transferred to main memory. When the block transfer has been completed, the requested word is accessed in main memory. The time t_B required for the block transfer is called the *block-replacement,* or *block-transfer,* time. Hence we have $t_{A_2} = t_B + t_{A_1}$. Substituting into Eq. (5.3) yields

$$t_A = t_{A_1} + (1 - H)t_B \qquad (5.4)$$

Block transfer requires a relatively slow IO operation; therefore t_B is usually much greater then t_{A_1}. Hence $t_{A_2} \gg t_{A_1}$ and $t_{A_2} \approx t_B$.

Let $r = t_{A_2}/t_{A_1}$ denote the access-time ratio of the two levels of memory. Let $e = t_{A_1}/t_A$, which is the factor by which t_A differs from its minimum possible value; e is called the *access efficiency* of the virtual memory. From Eq. (5.3) we obtain

$$e = \frac{1}{r + (1 - r)H} \qquad (5.5)$$

In Fig. 5.28, e is plotted as a function of H. This graph shows the importance of achieving high values of H in order to make $e \approx 1$, that is, $t_A \approx t_{A_1}$. For example, suppose that $r = 100$. In order to make $e > 0.9$, we must have $H > 0.998$.

Memory capacity is limited by cost considerations; it is therefore desirable that as little memory space as possible be wasted. The efficiency with which space is being used at any time can be loosely defined as the ratio of the memory space S_u occupied by "active" parts of user programs to the total amount of memory space available S. We call this the *space utilization u* and write

$$u = \frac{S_u}{S}$$

Since main-memory space is more valuable than secondary-memory space, it is useful to restrict u to measuring main-memory space utilization. In that case, the $S - S_u$ words of M_1 which represent "wasted" space can be attributed to several sources.

1. Empty regions. The blocks of instructions and data occupying M_1 at any time are generally of different lengths. As the contents of M_1 are changed, unoccupied regions or holes of various sizes tend to appear between successive blocks. This phenomenon is called *fragmentation.*

2. Regions occupied by the memory management part of the operating system. A certain amount of main-memory space is required to store memory management routines and memory maps.

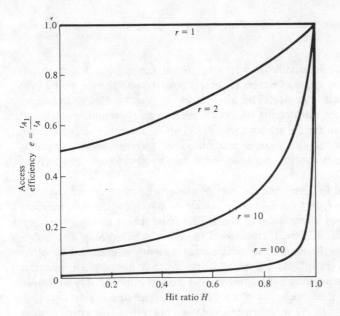

FIGURE 5.28
Access efficiency e of a two-level memory as a function of hit ratio H for various values of $r = t_{A2}/t_{A1}$.

3. Regions occupied by inactive user information. Certain words may be transferred to M_1, for example, as part of a page, and may be subsequently transferred back to M_2 without ever being referenced by a processor. Some superfluous transfers of this kind are unavoidable since exact address references are unpredictable. However, superfluous transfers can also be caused by an inefficient memory-allocation strategy.

The efficiency with which a given program Q utilizes main memory can be measured by its *memory space-time* function defined as

$$q = \int_0^T S(t) \, dt$$

where $(0, T)$ is a real-time interval and $S(t)$ is the amount of main-memory space assigned to Q at time t. $(0, T)$ includes time spent actively executing Q, as well as waiting time while memory swapping and other IO operations take place.

The major operation involved in any virtual memory system is the swapping of blocks of information between the levels of memory in accordance with processing demands. There are three central questions to be answered.

1. When should swapping take place?
2. Where should the block being transferred into main memory be placed?

3. How many words are transferred during each swap, i.e., what is the block size to be used?

The first question is usually answered by *demand swapping*, which means initiating a swap when a memory access request is received and the requested item is not currently in main memory. The alternative is some kind of *anticipatory swapping*, which implies transferring blocks to main memory in anticipation that they will be required in the future by the CPU. This is not easily implemented, since it requires relatively long-range predictions of memory access requests. Short-range prediction is possible because of the locality-of-reference property of programs.

The method used to determine the part of main memory where an incoming block is to be placed is called the *allocation policy*. In systems with static memory allocation, each block of information is bound to a fixed region of main memory. When dynamic allocation is used, the region to which a block K is assigned is variable: it depends on the manner in which main memory is occupied by other blocks when K is to be placed in main memory. Two methods of dynamic allocation may be distinguished: preemptive and nonpreemptive. An allocation strategy is *preemptive* if an incoming block can be assigned to a region occupied by another block required by a currently executing program. This entails either moving the preempted block to another part of main memory or else expelling it entirely from main memory. In *nonpreemptive* allocation, an incoming block can be placed only in an unoccupied region that is large enough to accommodate it. A successful allocation algorithm results in a high hit ratio and a low average access time. If the hit ratio is very low, an excessive amount of swapping occurs; this phenomenon is called *thrashing*.

Address mapping. The set of all abstract locations that can be referenced by a program is loosely defined as its logical address space L. Logical addresses may be explicitly named by identifiers assigned by the programmer. Many addresses are implicit or relative to other addresses. In order to execute the program on a particular machine, the logical addresses must be mapped onto the physical address space P of the machine's main memory. This process is called *address mapping* or, occasionally, *address binding*. The physical address space is represented by a linear sequence of numbers $0, 1, 2, \ldots, n - 1$. Main memory is therefore a one-dimensional array of word locations. The mathematical structure of a program represented by L is usually more complex; it can include multidimensional arrays, trees, linked lists, and other nonlinear structures. Before the program can be executed, it and its data sets must be "linearized," which means, in effect, transforming them into a set of contiguous word sequences, each of which can fit in main memory.

Address mapping can be viewed abstractly as a function $f: L \to P$. This function is not easily determined, since address mapping can be carried out wholly or in part at various stages in the life of a program, specifically:

1. By the programmer while writing the program
2. By the compiler during program compilation
3. By the loader at initial program load time
4. By the operating system while the program is being executed

Specification of physical addresses by the user was necessary in the earliest computers, which had neither operating systems nor the facilities to support any programming languages except assembly language. It is only used nowadays in very simple computers. It is generally not permittted in systems where memory space is shared by different users. In modern computer systems, the user is limited to specifying relative addresses within the program. The final physical addresses are determined by the compiler, the loader, or the operating system.

The compiler transforms all user identifiers into binary addresses. If the program is sufficiently simple, the compiler may be able to make a complete transformation of logical to physical addresses, especially if the program in question contains no concurrent or recursive procedures, i.e., it is strictly sequential and nonrecursive. In general, the output of the compiler is a set of program and data blocks each of which is a sequence of contiguous words. Each word within a block can be identified by a logical address which comprises a *base address* and a *displacement* (also called a relative address or offset), as shown in Fig. 5.29.

Address mapping can be completed when the program is first loaded by assigning fixed values to the base address of each block. This is called *static allocation,* since the physical address space of the program is fixed for the duration of its execution. In systems that support recursive or concurrent procedures, the logical space of a program may vary dynamically during execution. For example, a recursive procedure is typically controlled by a stack containing the linkage between successive calls to the procedure. The size of this stack cannot be predicted before execution, because it depends on the number of times the procedure is invoked. In such cases it is desirable to be able to allocate storage during execution. In multiprogramming systems where a common store is

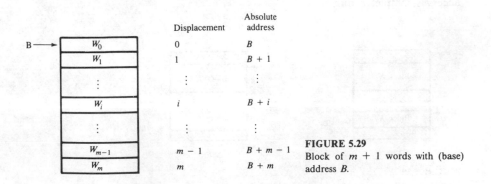

FIGURE 5.29
Block of $m + 1$ words with (base) address B.

shared by many programs, it is also useful to be able to alter storage allocation, i.e., vary f, while programs are being executed. The ability to do this is called *dynamic allocation*.

The fundamental method of implementing both static and dynamic storage allocation is by giving the operating system control over the addresses assigned to each program and data block. This can be accomplished by storing base addresses in a special *memory map* or *memory address table* in main memory and/or a set of high-speed CPU registers. In the latter case, the registers may be called *base*, or *relocation*, registers. The address-generation circuitry of the CPU computes relative addresses within a block from the specifications contained in a program. A physical address A_p is obtained by adding the displacement A_r to the contents of the corresponding base register B_i. Often B_i contains only the high-order bits of A_p, while A_r contains the low-order bits. A_p can then be formed by concatenating B_i and A_r, a process that does not significantly increase the time required for address generation.

Blocks are relocated in main memory by altering their base addresses. Base-address modification may therefore be a privileged operation that is restricted to the operating system. Figure 5.30 illustrates block relocations using base-address modification. Suppose that two blocks are allocated to main memory M as shown in Fig. 5.30a. It is desired to load a third block K_3 into M; however, a contiguous empty space, or "hole," of sufficient size is not available. A solution to this problem is to move block K_2, as shown in Fig. 5.30b, by assigning it a new base address B_2' and reloading it into memory. This creates a gap into which block K_3 can be loaded by assigning to it an appropriate base address.

In systems with dynamic memory allocation, it is necessary to control the references made by a block to locations outside the memory area currently assigned to it. (The block may be permitted to read from certain locations, but writing outside its assigned area must be prevented.) A common way of implementing this is by specifying the highest address, L_i, called the *limit address*, that the block may access. Equivalently, the size of the block may be specified. The base address B_i and the limit address L_i are stored in the memory map. Every physical address A_p generated by the block is compared to B_i and L_i; the memory access is completed only if

$$B_i \le A_p \le L_i$$

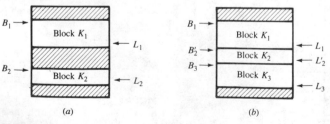

(a)   (b)

FIGURE 5.30
Memory relocation using base and limit addresses.

Figure 5.31 shows the main components of a virtual memory system and their logical interconnections. The physical addresses assigned to each block of information are stored in a set of tables called the memory map. This map is used to translate logical (virtual) block addresses into physical addresses and to maintain priority information for the blocks if preemptive allocation is used. The logical address includes a displacement part which is typically the effective address computed in accordance with the program-defined addressing mode (direct, indirect, indexed, etc.) for the memory item being accessed. The memory map for logical-to-physical address translation may be quite large and may therefore need to be stored in a block of its own within main memory M. To speed up the address translation process, part of the memory map is placed in a high-speed memory in the CPU termed a *translation lookaside buffer* TLB. The TLB is a special type of cache whose input L is a virtual address, or a portion thereof, and whose output is the corresponding physical address $f(L) = P$. (Cache operation is discussed later in Sec. 5.3.) If the current logical address L is not assigned to TLB, then the part of the memory map that contains L is transferred from M into TLB. The contents of TLB thus vary dynamically during program execution.

Example 5.3 Memory address mapping in the DEC VAX-11/780 [3,21] The VAX-11 minicomputer series, of which the 11/780 is one of the larger models, was introduced by Digital Equipment Corp. (DEC) in 1978. It enhances the earlier, and very successful, DEC PDP-11 series by the addition of a large virtual address space (VAX stands for virtual *address extension*), which is achieved by increasing the address size of the PDP-11 from 16 to 32 bits. This allows the VAX-11/780 to have a virtual address space of 2^{32} bytes, or 4 gigabytes. The address space is composed of 512-byte pages and is partitioned into four quadrants, two of which form the system region SM devoted to operating system functions, while the other two form

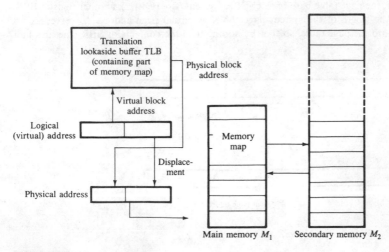

FIGURE 5.31
Structure of a virtual memory system.

the process (user) region PM where user programs and control stacks are stored. PM is assigned to one user at a time, and each user has a memory map or page table which defines the manner in which that user's virtual page addresses are translated into physical page addresses. Thus the system has a set of page tables for the various users, which it stores in SM. A translation lookaside buffer TLB which can accommodate 128 entries provides high-speed logical-to-physical address translation.

The format of a VAX-11/780 logical address is shown in Fig. 5.32a. It consists of 2 bits identifying a quadrant of virtual address space, a 21-bit virtual page address, and a 9-bit displacement or offset which specifies the address of a byte within the virtual page. The virtual page address is used to access a 32-bit entry in the corresponding page table, which, as shown in Fig. 5.32b, contains a 21-bit physical address (page frame number). This physical page address is then substituted for the virtual page address to obtain the desired 32-bit physical address. Note that a typical VAX configuration will have much less than 4 gigabytes of physical memory, so that not all the available physical address combinations are used and physical memory will be smaller than virtual memory. Other information stored in the page table entry is a *presence* or *valid* bit P, which indicates whether or not the referenced address is presently assigned to main memory M_1 (if not, secondary memory M_2 must be accessed), and a 4-bit protection mask, which indicates the current program's access rights (read and write, read only, or no access) to the addressed physical page. An access request to a page that is not present in M_1, or an access attempt without the proper access rights, results in a trap that aborts the current microinstruction and transfers control to an appropriate operating system microprogram.

The basic VAX mechanism for translating a virtual address L to a physical address P is illustrated by Fig. 5.33. First we consider a memory access addressed to the system space SM; such an access is normally requested only by the operating system. A single system page table stored in a contiguous region of SM serves as a memory map for all of SM. The physical location of this table is held in a CPU register, the page-table base register SBR (*system base register*); another register SLR stores the length of the system page table. A virtual page address L_p serves as an index into the page table, so that by adding it to the contents of SBR, the absolute

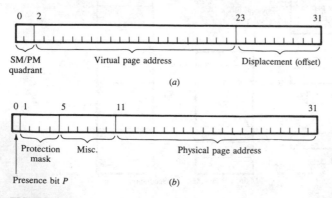

FIGURE 5.32
(a) Logical address and (b) page-table entry for the VAX-11/780.

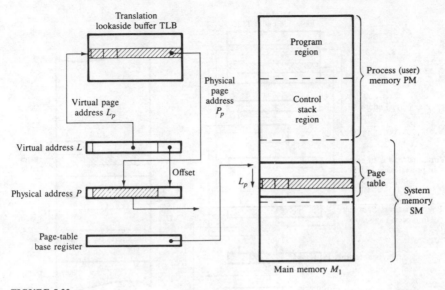

FIGURE 5.33
Basic address translation method in the VAX-11/780.

physical address of the required page-table entry E is obtained. E is then fetched, and the physical page address P_p it contains is extracted and substituted for the page field in the virtual address to complete the translation process. Note that the CPU always "looks aside" into the translation buffer TLB to see if a copy of E is there, and E is fetched from TLB rather than M_1. If E is not in TLB, a set of 32 entries including E, is read from the page table in M_1 into TLB. This 32-word "page" replacement is typical of address translation buffer operation and, indeed, of cache operation in general.

Address translation for items stored in the process memory is more complex. One half PM_0 of process memory is used to store the program being executed, while the other half PM_1 stores the user and system control stacks associated with that program's execution. PM_0 and PM_1 are specified by setting bits 0 and 1 of a virtual address (Fig. 5.32a) to 00 and 01, respectively. A page table for each of PM_0 and PM_1 is stored in SM, and the page table's *virtual* address is placed in base registers PBR_0 and PBR_1, respectively. (Observe that SBR stores the *physical* base address of the system page table.) The use of PBR_1 to store virtual addresses means that the corresponding page table can be relocated anywhere in virtual address space, and is not limited by the available amount of physical memory space. However, this feature also implies that an extra address translation step is needed to determine the physical address of a process page table. Thus address translation requires two page-table look-up operations as illustrated in Fig. 5.34. First, the virtual page address of L is added to the appropriate process base register PBR_0 or PBR_1 to form a virtual page address L' pointing to the page-table entry E' of the current process page table. E' is included in the system page table whose physical address is stored in SBR. The entry E' is then fetched (from TLB or M_1) and the physical page address it contains

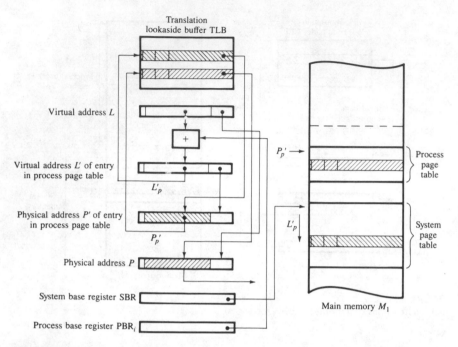

FIGURE 5.34
Translation of an address for process memory PM_1.

is used to construct the physical address P' of the desired page-table entry E in the process page table. Next E is fetched (again from TLB or M_1) and another logical-to-physical address translation is made, yielding the final physical address P of the desired item. Note the relevant portions of the system and/or the process page tables can be stored simultaneously in the translation lookaside buffer TLB. Sixty-four of the 128 entries in TLB are assigned to the system memory, while the other 64 are assigned to the process memory.

Address translation and related virtual-memory support functions are sometimes assigned to a specialized processor called a *memory management unit* (*MMU*). The MMU, which may be incorporated into the CPU, is positioned between the effective-address generation unit EAU of the CPU and main memory M. It receives logical addresses from the EAU and converts them to physical addresses for transmission to M (or to a cache, if one is present). The MMU is also responsible for handling such exceptional conditions as memory protection violations and the swapping of data between main and secondary memory. An example of a single-chip MMU is the 68851 chip for the Motorola 68000 microprocessor series, which supports a virtual memory environment with demand paging and 32-bit logical/physical addresses [4]. Like the 68881 floating-point processor (Sec. 3.4.3), the 68851 is designed for use as a coprocessor of the CPU.

Operating with the 68020 CPU and a 16-MHz clock, a logical-to-physical address translation can be carried out by the 68851 in at most 45 ns.

5.2.2 Main-Memory Allocation

It is convenient to view main memory as divided into sets of contiguous word locations called *regions,* each of which can store a block of information. In a paging system, the regions are nonoverlapping page frames, and each region has a base address which is a multiple of the page size. The process of determining the region to which a particular block is to be assigned is called *main-memory allocation.* The information needed for memory allocation is maintained by the operating system in the memory map. It can be expected to contain the following information.

1. An *occupied space list,* each entry of which specifies a block name, the (base) address of the region it occupies, and the block size. The block size may be omitted if a fixed block size is used. In systems using preemptive allocation, additional information is associated with each block to determine when and how it may be preempted.
2. An *available space list,* each entry of which specifies the address of an unoccupied region and, if necessary, its size.
3. A secondary-memory *directory* or a list specifying the secondary-memory devices which contain the directories for all the blocks associated with currently executing programs. These directories define the regions of the secondary-memory space to which each block is assigned.

When a block is transferred from secondary to main memory, the operating system makes an appropriate entry in the occupied space list. When a block is no longer required in main memory, it is *deallocated,* and the region it occupies is transferred from the occupied space list to the available space list. A block is deallocated when the programs using it terminate execution, or when it is replaced to make room for a block with higher priority.

A variety of preemptive and nonpreemptive algorithms have been developed for dynamic memory allocations. The mathematical analysis of the performance of these algorithms is generally very difficult. Simulation is the most widely used performance evaluation tool. The performance of an allocation algorithm can be measured by the various parameters introduced in Sec. 5.2.1; specifically, hit ratio H, memory access time t_A, and space utilization u.

Nonpreemptive allocation. Suppose that a block K_i of n_i words is to be transferred from secondary to main memory. If none of the blocks already occupying main memory may be preempted (overwritten or moved) by K_i, then it is necessary to find or create an unoccupied "available" region of n_i or more words to accommodate K_i. This process is termed nonpreemptive allocation. The problem is simple in a paging system where all blocks (pages) comprise S_p words, and main store is divided into fixed S_p-word regions (page frames). The memory map (page table) is searched for an available page frame; if one is found, it is assigned to the incoming block K_i. This ease of space allocation is one of the primary reasons for using paging. If memory space is divisible into regions of variable length, however, then it becomes much more difficult to allocate incoming blocks efficiently.

Two of the more widely used algorithms for nonpreemptive allocation of variable-length blocks are first fit and best fit. The *first-fit* method scans the memory map sequentially until an available region R_j of n_i or more words is found, where n_i is the number of words in the incoming block K_i. It then allocates K_i to R_j. The *best-fit* approach requires searching the memory map sequentially and then assigning K_i to a region of $n_j \geq n_i$ words such that $n_j - n_i$ is minimized.

Suppose, for example, that at some time main memory is storing three blocks, as illustrated in Fig. 5.35a. There are three available regions, and the available space list might have the form:

Region address	Size (words)
0	50
300	400
800	200

Suppose that two additional blocks K_4 and K_5 whose sizes are 100 and 250 words, respectively, are to be assigned to main memory. Figures 5.35b and c show the results obtained using the first-fit and best-fit methods, respectively, when the memory scan starts at address 0.

The first-fit algorithm has the advantage that it requires less time to execute than the best-fit approach. If the best-fitting available region can be found by scanning k entries of the available space list, the first fit can always be found by

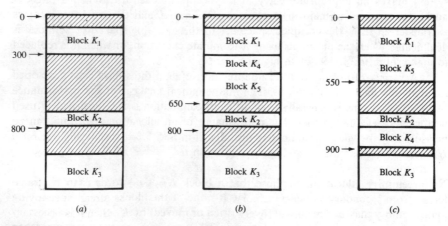

FIGURE 5.35
(a) Initial memory state; (b) allocation of K_4 and K_5 by the first-fit method; (c) allocation of K_4 and K_5 by the best-fit method.

scanning k or fewer entries. The relative efficiency of the two techniques has been a subject of debate, since both have been implemented with satisfactory results [11, 19]. The performance obtained in a given environment depends on the distribution of the sizes of the blocks being allocated. Simulation studies suggest that in practice, first fit outperforms best fit.

Preemptive allocation. Nonpreemptive allocation techniques cannot make efficient use of memory in all situations; overflow, i.e., rejection of a memory allocation request due to insufficient space, can be expected to occur with main memory only partially full. Much more efficient use of the available memory space is possible if the occupied space can be reallocated to make room for incoming blocks. This may be done in two ways:

1. The blocks already in main memory can be relocated in main memory to make a gap large enough for the incoming information; this is illustrated in Fig. 5.30.
2. One or more occupied regions can be made available by deallocating or expelling the blocks they contain. This requires a rule for selecting blocks to be replaced. A distinction must also be made between "dirty" blocks, which have been modified since being loaded into main memory, and "clean" blocks, which have not been modified. Blocks of instructions generally remain clean, whereas blocks of data generally become dirty. To replace a clean block, the operating system can simply overwrite it with the new block, and update its entry in the memory map. Before a dirty block can be overwritten, it must be copied onto secondary memory, which involves a time-consuming IO operation.

The relocation of the blocks already occupying main memory can be accomplished by a technique called *compaction*, which is illustrated in Fig. 5.36. The blocks currently in memory are combined into a single block placed at one end of the memory. This creates a single available region of the maximum possible size. The main disadvantage of this technique is the time required for compacting. If t_M is the cycle time of main memory, then the time required to compact the S-word memory is at least $2uSt_M$, where u is the fraction of the memory that is occupied.

A simple allocation technique can be based on compacting alone [11]. After each compaction, incoming blocks are assigned to contiguous regions at the unoccupied end of the memory. The memory is therefore viewed as having a single available region; new available regions due to freed blocks are ignored. When the hole at the end of the memory is filled, compaction is again carried out. The advantage of this scheme is that it eliminates the problem of selecting an available region; it may, however, result in the system's spending an excessive amount of time compacting memory.

Replacement policies. The second major approach to preemptive allocation involves preempting a region R occupied by block K and allocating it to an incoming block K'. The criteria used for selecting K as the block to be replaced constitute the *replacement policy*. The major objective in choosing a replacement

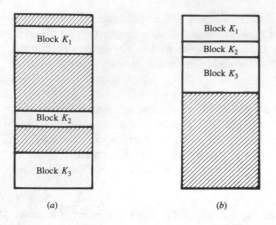

FIGURE 5.36
Main-memory allocation (*a*) before and
(*b*) after compacting.

policy is to maximize the hit ratio or, equivalently, minimize the number of times a referenced block is not in main memory, a condition called a *memory fault*.

It is generally believed that the hit ratio tends to a maximum if the time intervals between successive memory faults are maximized. An *optimal replacement strategy* would therefore at time t_i determine the time $t_j > t_i$ at which the next reference to block K is to occur; the K to be replaced is the one for which $t_j - t_i$ has the maximum value t_K. This ideal strategy has been called OPT [15]. OPT can be implemented by making two passes through the program. The first is a simulation run to determine the sequence S_B of distinct logical block addresses generated by the program; the sequence is called the *block address stream* or *block address trace*. The values of t_K at each point in time can be computed from S_B and used to construct the optimal sequence S_B^{OPT} of blocks to be replaced. The second run is the execution run, which uses S_B^{OPT} to specify the blocks to be replaced. OPT is not a practical replacement policy because of the cost of the simulation run and the fact that S_B may be extremely long, making S_B^{OPT} very expensive to compute. A practical replacement policy attempts to estimate t_K using statistics it gathers on the past references to all blocks currently in main memory.

Two of the most commonly implemented replacement policies are *first-in first-out* (FIFO) and *least recently used* (LRU). FIFO selects for replacement the block least recently loaded into main memory. FIFO has the advantage that it is easily implemented. A loading sequence number is associated with each block in the occupied space list. Each time a block is transferred to or from main memory, the loading sequence numbers are updated. By inspecting these numbers, the operating system can easily determine the oldest (first-in) block. FIFO has the defect, however, that a frequently used block, e.g. one containing a program loop, may be replaced because it is the oldest block.

The LRU policy selects for replacement the block that was least recently accessed by the processor. It is based on the very reasonable assumption that the least recently used block is the one least likely to be referenced in the future. The LRU policy avoids the replacement of frequently used blocks, which can occur with FIFO. It is slightly more difficult to implement than FIFO, however, since the operating system must maintain statistics on the times of references to all blocks in main memory. LRU can be implemented by associating a hardware or software counter, called an *age register,* with every block in main memory (see also Prob. 5.19). Whenever a block is referenced, its age register is set to a predetermined positive number. At fixed intervals of time, the age registers of all the blocks are decremented by a fixed amount. The least recently used block at any time is the one whose age register contains the smallest number.

The performance of a replacement policy in a given memory organization can be analyzed using the block address stream generated by a set of representative computations. Let N_1^* and N_2^* denote the number of references to M_1 and M_2, respectively, in the block address stream. The *block hit ratio H^** is defined by

$$H^* = \frac{N_1^*}{N_1^* + N_2^*}$$

which is analogous to the (word) hit ratio H defined by Eq. (5.2). Let n^* denote the average number of consecutive word address references within each block. H can be estimated from H^* using the following relation:

$$H = 1 - \frac{1 - H^*}{n^*}$$

In a paging system, H^* is the page hit ratio. $1 - H^*$, the page miss ratio, is also called the *page fault probability.*

Example 5.4 Comparison of replacement policies. Consider a paging system in which main memory has a capacity of three pages. The execution of a program Q requires reference to five distinct pages P_i, where $i = 1, 2, 3, 4, 5$, and i is the page address. The page address stream formed by executing Q is

$$2\ 3\ 2\ 1\ 5\ 2\ 4\ 5\ 3\ 2\ 5\ 2$$

which means that the first page referenced is P_2, the second is P_3, etc. Figure 5.37 shows the manner in which the pages are assigned to main memory using FIFO, LRU, and the ideal OPT replacement policies. The next block to be selected for replacement is marked by an asterisk in the FIFO and LRU cases. It will be observed that LRU recognizes that P_2 and P_5 are referenced more frequently than other pages, whereas FIFO does not. Thus FIFO replaces P_2 twice but LRU does so only once. The highest page hit ratio is achieved by OPT, the lowest by FIFO. The page hit ratio of LRU is quite close to that of OPT, a property which seems to be generally true.

Stack replacement policies. As discussed in Sec. 5.2.1, the cost and performance of a memory hierarchy can be measured by average cost per bit c and average access time t_A. Equations (5.1) and (5.4) repeated below are convenient expressions for c and t_A:

$$c = \frac{c_1 S_1 + c_2 S_2}{S_1 + S_2} \tag{5.1}$$

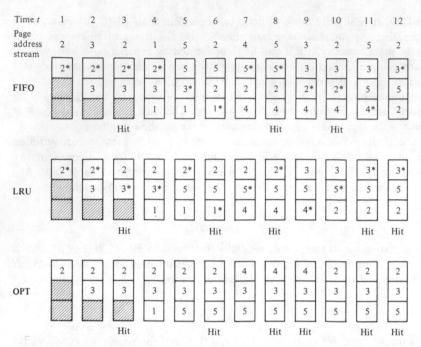

FIGURE 5.37
Action of three replacement policies on a common address stream.

$$t_A = t_{A_1} + (1 - H)t_B \tag{5.4}$$

The quantities c, t_{A_1}, and t_B are determined primarily by the memory-device technologies used for M_1 and M_2. Once these have been chosen, the hit ratio H must be computed for various possible system configurations. The major variables on which H depends are

1. The types of address streams encountered
2. The average block size
3. The capacity of main memory
4. The replacement policy

Simulation is perhaps the most practical technique used for evaluating different memory system designs. H is determined for a representative sample of address streams, memory technologies, block sizes, memory capacities, and replacement policies. Figure 5.37 shows a sample point in this simulation process. In this example, the block address stream, block size, and main-memory capacity are fixed, and three different replacement strategies are being tested.

Due to the large number of alternatives that exist, the amount of simulation required to optimize the design of a virtual memory system can be very great. A number of analytic models for optimizing memory design have been proposed. Notable among these is a technique called *stack processing*, which is applicable to paging systems that use a class of replacement algorithms called stack algorithms [15]. Let A be any page address stream of length L to be processed using a replacement policy R. Let t denote the point in time when the first t pages of A have been processed. Let n be a variable denoting the page capacity of M_1. $B_t(n)$ denotes the set of pages in M_1 at time t, and L_t denotes the number of distinct pages that have been encountered at time t. R is called a *stack algorithm* if it has the following *inclusion property:*

$$B_t(n) \subset B_t(n+1) \qquad \text{if } n < L_t$$

$$B_t(n) = B_t(n+1) \qquad \text{if } n \geq L_t$$

LRU retains in M_1 the n most recently used pages. Since these are always included in the $n + 1$ most recently used pages, it can be immediately concluded that LRU is a stack algorithm. Many other replacement policies are also of this type. FIFO is a notable exception, however. Consider the following page address stream:

$$1 \ 2 \ 3 \ 4 \ 1 \ 2 \ 5 \ 1 \ 2 \ 3 \ 4 \ 5$$

Figure 5.38 shows how this address stream is processed using FIFO and main-memory capacities of three and four pages. It can be seen that at various points of time the conditions for the inclusion property are not satisfied. For example, when $t = 7$, $B_7(3) = \{1, 2, 5\}$ and $B_7(4) = \{2, 3, 4, 5\}$; therefore $B_7(3) \nsubseteq B_7(4)$. Hence FIFO is not a stack algorithm.

The usefulness of stack replacement algorithms lies in the fact that the hit

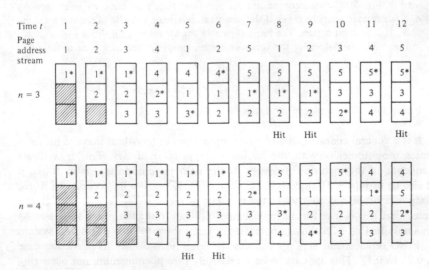

FIGURE 5.38
FIFO replacement with two different M_1 capacities.

ratios for different capacities of M_1 can be easily determined by processing the address stream once, and representing M_1 by a list, or "stack." The stack S_t at time t is an ordered set of L_t distinct pages $S_t(1), S_t(2), \ldots, S_t(L_t); S_t(1)$ is referred to as the top of the stack at time t. The inclusion property of stack algorithms implies that the stack can always be generated so that

$$B_t(n) = \{S_t(1), S_t(2), \ldots, S_t(n)\} \qquad \text{for } n < L_t$$

$$B_t(n) = \{S_t(1), S_t(2), \ldots, S_t(L_t)\} \qquad \text{for } n \geq L_t$$

In other words, the behavior of a system in which M_1 has capacity n is determined by the top n entries of the stack. By scanning S_t, we can easily determine whether or not a hit occurs for all possible values of n. This type of analysis therefore permits the simultaneous determination of hit ratios for various main-memory capacities.

The procedures for updating the stack depend on the particular stack algorithm R being used. There may be little resemblance between the order of the elements in S_t and S_{t+1}; the stack should not be confused with simple LIFO pushdown stacks. We now describe the stack updating process for LRU replacement.

Example 5.5   Determination of hit ratios with LRU replacement. Let $S_t = S_t(1)$, $S_t(2), \ldots, S_t(k)$ denote the stack contents at time t. The strategy used is to place the most recently used page addresses in the top of stack so that the least recently used page gets pushed to the bottom. More formally, let x be the new page reference at time t. If $x \notin S_t$, x is pushed into the stack, so that x becomes $S_{t+1}(1); S_t(1)$ becomes $S_{t+1}(2)$; and so on. If $x \in S_t$, x is removed from S_t and then pushed into the top of the stack to form S_{t+1}. Figure 5.39 illustrates this for the address stream used in Fig. 5.38. To determine if a hit occurs at time t for memory page capacity n, it is necessary only to check if the new page reference x is one of the top n entries of S_t; if it is, a hit occurs. The hit occurrences for all values of $n \leq 5$ are also shown in Fig. 5.39. The values for the various page hit ratios H^* are seen to be as follows:

$n =$	1	2	3	4	5	> 5
$H^* =$	0.00	0.17	0.42	0.50	0.58	0.58

Figure 5.40 shows a plot of H^* against n.

It is a general characteristic of stack replacement algorithms that the hit ratio increases monotonically with the available capacity n of M_1. This is a direct consequence of the inclusion property. If the next page address x is in $B_t(n)$, it must also be in $B_t(n + 1)$, since $B_t(n) \subseteq B_t(n + 1)$. Hence if a hit occurs with M_1 of capacity n, a hit also occurs when the capacity is increased to $n + 1$. It might be expected that this is true for all replacement policies, but such is not the case. As the example in Fig. 5.38 shows, increasing n from three to four pages in a system using FIFO replacement actually reduces the page hit ratio in this particular case from 0.25 to 0.17. This appears to be a relatively rare phenomenon, not occurring for most address streams.

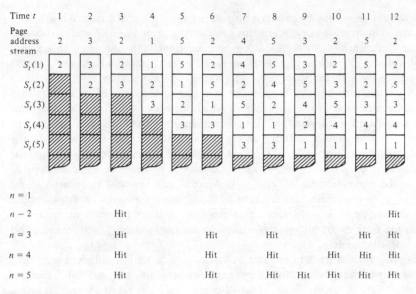

Time t	1	2	3	4	5	6	7	8	9	10	11	12
Page address stream	2	3	2	1	5	2	4	5	3	2	5	2
$S_t(1)$	2	3	2	1	5	2	4	5	3	2	5	2
$S_t(2)$		2	3	2	1	5	2	4	5	3	2	5
$S_t(3)$				3	2	1	5	2	4	5	3	3
$S_t(4)$					3	3	1	1	2	4	4	4
$S_t(5)$							3	3	1	1	1	1

$n = 1$												
$n - 2$		Hit									Hit	
$n = 3$		Hit			Hit		Hit			Hit	Hit	
$n = 4$		Hit			Hit		Hit		Hit	Hit	Hit	
$n = 5$		Hit			Hit		Hit	Hit	Hit	Hit	Hit	

FIGURE 5.39
Stack processing of a page address stream using LRU.

5.2.3 Segments, Pages, and Files

We consider next the principal techniques used for organizing programs and data in virtual memory systems.

Segmentation. The smallest or most primitive elements of a computation are instruction and data words. A well-written program, however, exhibits a substantial amount of high-level structure. A sequence of instructions, for instance, may be defined as a subroutine or procedure and be given an appropriate name. Similarly,

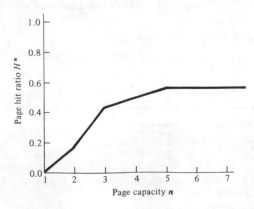

FIGURE 5.40
Page hit ratio vs page capacity for Example 5.5.

primitive data items may be grouped into stacks, arrays, and the like. We will refer to groups of instructions or data of this general type as *modules*. A well-structured program has clearly defined modules whose relations with one another are also clearly defined. Programming languages, such as Pascal, which are "block-structured" have a syntax that yields a high degree of modularity.

A module may be loosely regarded as a named sequence of statements that are usually processed in the sequence in which they are written by the programmer. Compilation transforms this into a machine-executable module with essentially the same sequential ordering as the original module; this type of module is termed a segment. Formally, a *segment* is a set of logically related contiguous words generated by a compiler or a programmer. It is therefore a special type of block in the sense defined in Sec. 5.2.1. A word in a segment is referred to by specifying a base address (the segment address) and an address or displacement within the segment. The displacements are derived from program identifiers at compilation time. Segment addresses may be assigned during program execution by the operating system.

A program and its data sets can be viewed as a collection of linked segments. The links arise from the fact that a program segment may use, or "call," another program or data segment. Since segments contain logically related words, it seems reasonable to maintain complete segments in main memory. A memory management technique that allocates main memory by segments is called *segmentation*. When a segment not currently resident in main memory is required, the entire segment is transferred from secondary memory. The physical addresses assigned to the segments are maintained in a memory map called a *segment table,* which may itself be a relocatable segment.

An early computer series whose memory allocation is based on segmentation is the Burroughs B5500. Each main program has associated with it a segment called its program reference table (PRT), which serves as a segment table. Each segment associated with a program is defined by a word called a descriptor in the corresponding PRT. As shown in Fig. 5.41, a *descriptor* contains the following information:

1. A presence bit P, which is set to 1 if the segment in question is currently assigned to main memory, and to 0 otherwise
2. A size field Z, which is the number of words in the segment
3. An address field S, which is the segment's physical address in main memory if $P = 1$, or in secondary memory if $P = 0$

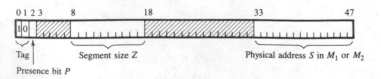

FIGURE 5.41
Segment-table entry (data descriptor) for the Burroughs B5500.

A program refers to a word within a segment by specifying the segment descriptor word W in its PRT and the displacement D (called an index in Burroughs literature). W is fetched and examined by the central processor. If the presence bit $P = 0$, then an interrupt occurs, and execution of the requesting program is suspended while the operating system transfers the required segment from secondary to main memory. If $P = 1$, the CPU compares the displacement D to the segment size field Z in the descriptor. If $D \geq Z$, D is invalid and an interrupt occurs. If $D < Z$, the address field S of the descriptor is added to the displacement D. The result, $S + D$, is the absolute physical address of the required word in main memory, which may then be accessed.

The main advantage of segmentation is the fact that segment boundaries correspond to natural program and data boundaries. Consequently, information that is shared among different users is organized into segments. Because of their logical independence, a program segment can be changed and recompiled at any time without affecting other segments. Certain properties of programs such as the scope (range of definition) of a variable and the access rights to a program are specified by segment. These properties require that accesses to segments be checked to protect against unauthorized use; this protection is most easily implemented when the units of allocation are segments. Certain segment types, most notably stacks and queues, can vary in length during program execution. A segmentation system can vary the region assigned to such a segment as it expands and contracts, thus efficiently using the available memory space. On the other hand, the fact that segments can be of different lengths requires a relatively complex main-memory allocation method to avoid excessive fragmentation of main-memory space. This problem can be alleviated by combining segmentation with paging, as discussed later.

Paging. Paging systems use fixed-length blocks called pages and assign them to fixed regions of physical memory called page frames. The flowchart of a typical demand paging system can be found in Fig. 1.28 in Sec. 1.3.2. The main advantage of paging is that memory allocation is greatly simplified, since an incoming page can be assigned to any available page frame. Each logical address consists of two parts: a page address and a displacement (sometimes called a line address). The memory map, now called a page table, contains the information shown in Fig. 5.42. For each (logical) page address there is the corresponding (physical) address of a page frame in main or secondary memory. When the presence bit P is 1, the page in question is present in main memory, and the page table contains the base address of the page frame to which the page has been assigned. If $P = 0$, a page fault occurs, and a page swap ensues. The change bit C is used to specify whether or not the page has been changed since last being loaded into main memory. If a change has occurred, indicated by $C = 1$, the page must be copied onto secondary memory when it is preempted. The page table may also contain memory protection information that specifies the access rights of the program requesting the memory access to read from, write into, or execute the page in question. An example of the page-table format used by the VAX-11/780 appears in Fig. 5.42.

Page address	Page frame	Presence bit P	Change bit C	Access rights
A	0	1	0	R, X
C	D6C7T9	0		R, W, X
E	24	1	1	R, W, X
F	16	1	0	R

FIGURE 5.42
Representative organization of a page table.

Page tables differ from segment tables primarily in the fact that they contain no block size information.

As noted earlier, paging requires a simpler memory allocation system than segmentation, since block size is not a factor in paging. On the other hand, pages have no logical significance; they do not correspond to program elements. It can be useful to regard segmentation as partitioning the logical address space, while paging partitions the physical address space [23]. The two techniques can also be compared from the point of view of memory fragmentation. In systems with segmentation, holes of different sizes tend to proliferate throughout main memory; they can be eliminated only by the time-consuming process of memory compaction. Unusable space between occupied regions is called *external fragmentation*. Since page frames are contiguous, no external fragmentation occurs in paged systems. However, if k words are divided into p n-word pages, and k is not a multiple of n, the last page will not be filled. When this page is assigned to a page frame, part of the page frame is empty; this is called *internal fragmentation*.

Paged segments. Paging and segmentation can be combined in an attempt to gain the advantages of both. This is done by dividing each segment into pages. A word then has a logical address with three components: a segment address, a page address, and a displacement (line address). The memory map consists of a segment table and a set of page tables, one for each segment. The segment table contains for each segment address a pointer to the base of the corresponding page table. The page table is used in the usual way to determine the required physical address.

The great advantage of breaking a segment into pages is that it eliminates the need to store the segment in a contiguous region of main memory. Instead, all that is required is a number of page frames equal to the number of pages into which the segment has been broken. Since these page frames need not be contiguous, the task of placing a large segment in main memory is simplified. In particular, the various space allocation strategies such as best fit and first fit discussed earlier can be dispensed with.

The page size S_p has a significant impact on both storage utilization and the memory-access rate. Let us first consider the influence of S_p on the space-utilization factor u introduced in Sec. 5.2.1. If S_p is too large, excessive internal fragmentation results; if it is too small, the page tables become very large and tend to reduce space utilization. A good value of S_p should achieve a balance between these two difficulties. Let S_s denote the average segment size in words. If $S_s \gg S_p$, it can be expected that the last page assigned to a segment contains, on the average, $S_p/2$ words. The size of the page table associated with each segment is approximately S_s/S_p words, assuming each entry in the table is a word. Hence the memory space overhead associated with each segment is

$$S = \frac{S_p}{2} + \frac{S_s}{S_p}$$

The physical memory space utilization u can be defined as

$$u = \frac{S_s}{S_s + S} = \frac{2S_sS_p}{S_p^2 + 2S_s(1 + S_p)} \tag{5.6}$$

The optimum page size S_p^{OPT} may be defined as the value of S_p which maximizes u or, equivalently, which minimizes S. Differentiating S with respect to S_p, we obtain

$$\frac{dS}{dS_p} = \frac{1}{2} - \frac{S_s}{S_p^2}$$

S is a minimum when $dS/dS_p = 0$, from which it follows that

$$S_p^{\text{OPT}} = \sqrt{2S_s} \tag{5.7}$$

The optimum space utilization u^{OPT} is given by

$$u^{\text{OPT}} = \frac{1}{1 + \sqrt{2/S_s}}$$

Figure 5.43 shows the space utilization u defined by Eq. (5.6) plotted against S_s for representative values of S_p.

The influence of page size on hit ratio is complex, depending on the program reference stream and the amount of main-memory space available. Let the logical address space of a program be a sequence of numbers $A_0, A_1, \ldots, A_{L-1}$. Let A_i be the logical address referenced at some point in time; and let A_{i+d} be the next address generated, where d is the "distance" between A_i and A_{i+d}. For example, if both addresses point to instructions, $A_i + d$ points to the $(d + 1)$st instruction either preceding or following the instruction whose logical address is A_i. Let S_p be the page size, and suppose that an efficient replacement policy such as LRU is being used. The probability of A_{i+d} being in M_1 is high if one of the following conditions is satisfied.

1. d is small compared with S_p, so that A_i and A_{i+d} are in the same page P. The probability of this being true increases with the page size.
2. d is large relative to S_p, but A_{i+d} is associated with a set of words that are frequently referenced. A_{i+d} is therefore likely to be in a page $P' \neq P$ which is also in M_1. The probability of this being true tends to increase with the number of pages that can be stored in M_1; it therefore tends to decrease with the size of S_p.

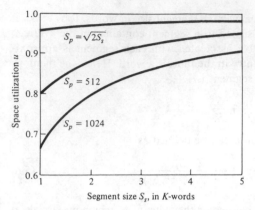

FIGURE 5.43
Influence of page size S_p and segment size S_s on space utilization u.

Thus H is influenced by two opposing forces as S_p is varied. The result is that when S_p is small, H increases with S_p. However, when S_p exceeds a certain value, H begins to decrease. Figure 5.44 shows some typical curves relating H and S_p for various main-memory capacities. Simulation studies indicate that in large systems, the values of S_p yielding the maximum hit ratios can be much greater than the "optimum" page size given by Eq. (5.7). Since high H is important in achieving small t_A (due to the relatively slow rates at which page swapping takes place), values of S_p that maximize H are preferred. The first computer with a paging system (the Atlas) uses a 512-word page, as does the VAX-11/780. The Intel 80386 discussed below has a page size of 4096 words.

Example 5.6 Virtual memory organization of the Intel 80386 [7]. The 80386 is a high-performance 32-bit microprocessor introduced in 1985, which provides direct hardware support for both segmentation and paging. It is a member of Intel's extensive 8086 microprocessor family, and maintains compatibility at the object code-level with the original (1976-vintage) 8086 CPU, one of the first 16-bit microprocessors. This family also provides the CPUs for the IBM Personal Computer (PC) series introduced in 1981. Like the VAX-11/780 (Example 5.3), the 80386's physical address

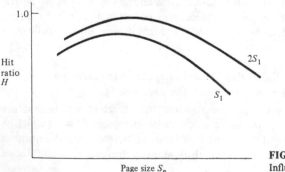

FIGURE 5.44
Influence of page size S_p on hit ratio H.

space can be as large as 4G bytes (2^{32} bytes); however, the logical address space is an exceptionally large 64 terabytes (2^{46} bytes). There is an on-chip MMU containing a segmentation unit that performs address translation for segments that can range in size from 1 to 2^{32} bytes. A separate paging unit handles address translation for 4K-byte pages. The programmer can effectively bypass either unit (see Prob. 5.23), thus allowing any of the following four memory organizations to be used in an 80386-based system: unsegmented and unpaged, segmented and unpaged, unsegmented and paged, segmented and paged. The output of the paging unit is a 32-bit physical address, while that of the segmentation unit is a 32-bit word called a *linear* address. If both segmentation and paging are used, every memory address generated by a program goes through the two-stage translation process

$$\text{Virtual address } L \rightarrow \text{linear address } N \rightarrow \text{physical address } P$$

depicted in Fig. 5.45. Without segmentation $L = N$, while without paging $N = P$. The segmentation and paging units both contain high-speed caches to store the active portions of the various memory maps needed for address translation, so the delay associated with the translation process is small. The effect of this delay is further diminished by overlapping (pipelining) the formation of the virtual, linear, and physical addresses, as well as by overlapping memory addressing and fetching, so that the next physical address is ready by the time the current memory cycle is completed.

An active process controlled by an 8086-series processor has several segments associated with it, such as the object program, a program control stack, and one or

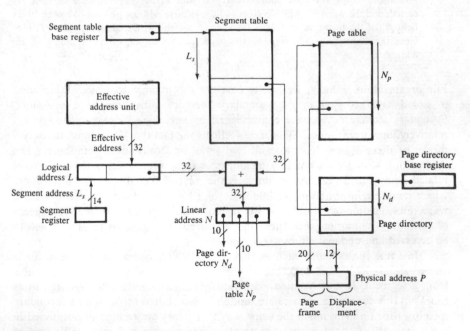

FIGURE 5.45
Address translation with segmentation and paging in the Intel 80386.

more data sets. The 80386 contains six segment registers which store the addresses of these segments. For example, the segment registers CS and SS address a code (program) and stack segment, respectively. These registers are typically used in a manner that is transparent to the applications programmer. For instance, when an instruction fetch is initiated, a 32-bit (effective) address obtained from the program counter PC is appended to a 14-bit segment address L_s obtained from the CS register forming a 46-bit logical address L. As Fig. 5.45 indicates, L_s serves as a relative address for an 8-byte segment descriptor in one of several segment tables. The descriptor specifies the base address and length of the segment S referred to by L_s. It also indicates S's type and access rights, and whether or not S is present in main memory. The required linear address N is constructed by adding the base address obtained from the descriptor to the program-derived effective address.

Figure 5.45 also shows how the linear address N is processed by the paging unit to produce a physical address P. As in the VAX-11/780 (see Fig. 5.34), a two-step translation process is employed to obtain P; the implementation here is rather different, however. The rightmost 12 bits of N form a relative address within the 4K-byte page containing the desired information. The remaining 20 bits of N are used to derive a physical page address as follows. First a page directory, corresponding to the VAX's system page table, is accessed, which contains entries defining up to 1024 page tables. The leftmost 10 bits N_d of N serve as the relative address of a 32-bit entry E in the page table directory. E contains the 20-bit base address of a page table T, as well as such standard information as a presence bit, a change bit (indicating whether or not the page has been written into), and some protection information. Using the base address derived from E, the page table T is then accessed, and the word E', which is stored at the relative address pointed to by the 10-bit field N_p of the linear address N, is fetched. E', which has the same format as E, provides the 20-bit page address, i.e., the page frame number, of the desired physical address P.

File organization. Finally, we briefly consider the manner in which information is stored and accessed in the secondary memory subsystem of a computer. Secondary storage devices are characterized by very high storage capacities and relatively long access times. Slow access reflects the fact that, in general, the access modes of these devices have a significant serial or semirandom component. The information stored on secondary memories is usually grouped into large sets of related items called *files*. An example is the payroll file of a large corporation, which contains information on hundreds of employees: their names, addresses, wage rates, income tax status, etc. Because of their large size and the slow speeds of secondary memories, such files must be carefully organized to allow them to be accessed and updated efficiently.

In some file systems, such as that of the UNIX operating system, a file is viewed simply as a word sequence of arbitrary length and so is indistinguishable from a segment. It may be subdivided into pages, which are often referred to as *blocks* in this context, and these are randomly distributed throughout a secondary memory (disk) unit in much the same way that pages are randomly positioned in main memory. A page is then the smallest addressable and relocatable unit of secondary storage.

Files are also frequently composed of logical addressable units of fixed or variable length called *records*, which may, in turn, be further subdivided into *fields*. The size and structure of the records and fields are application-dependent. For example, in a payroll file, the information about each employee may constitute a record. The individual items of information about the employee—his or her name, address, wage rate, etc.—form the fields. Every item that has to be accessed independently—the entire file, a record, or a field within a record—must be identified by means of a name called a *key*. The key therefore constitutes the logical address of the item in question. There are three general ways in which the data can be accessed.

1. The file can be searched sequentially comparing the given key to the stored keys until the desired one is found. This is normally done with tape files, which can only be accessed serially.
2. A memory address map, called a directory, can be used to translate the key onto a physical storage address. This is used when the memory permits random or semirandom access.
3. The physical address is generated by a simple transformation of keys according to some algorithm. Again this is suitable only for random- or semirandom-access memories.

The most important secondary storage device in most computer systems is the magnetic-disk unit. As discussed in Sec. 5.1.3, information is stored in a disk memory by means of concentric circular tracks on a set of rotating disks. A set of tracks with the same radius is referred to as a *cylinder*. The smallest addressable unit of storage will be assumed to be a record whose length may be fixed or variable. A track may therefore store a fixed or variable number of records. Each record contains a key which serves as its logical address. It is convenient to view a disk unit as a two-dimensional storage device with the structure suggested by Fig. 5.46. A particular track is accessed randomly by specifying a cylinder and a track number. The required record is then accessed serially by scanning the track until a record whose key matches the given key is found.

Sequential files. The simplest type of file organization requires storing records in some fixed sequence and performing all access and modification operations by

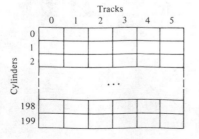

FIGURE 5.46
Storage organization in a magnetic-disk memory.

serial processing. The record sequence may be arbitrary, in which case the organization is called *unordered sequential.* More commonly, the records are ordered by a key and stored in that order; this is called (*ordered*) *sequential* organization. This type of organization therefore has the structure of a linear list. Sequential files are most useful when all records must be accessed in sequence and processed. For example, a payroll file is processed in this manner to produce employees' paychecks. More generally, records that are processed in batch mode may be organized sequentially. If real-time access to any record is required, then other file organizations with shorter access time are more suitable. A second disadvantage of sequential organization is that it is necessary to move large amounts of data in order to make insertions or deletions. This organization is therefore inefficient if the file must be updated frequently. Updating can be simplified by leaving gaps between records or groups of records into which insertions can be made.

Magnetic-tape files are invariably organized sequentially. Magnetic-disk files are sometimes sequential also. Figure 5.47*a* shows a possible file organization of this kind. The file consists of fixed-length records with the format

key, data

stored in ascending numerical order determined by the keys. The file is filled cylinder by cylinder and track by track. Changes are made by transferring an

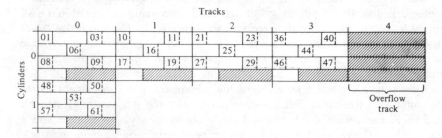

(a)

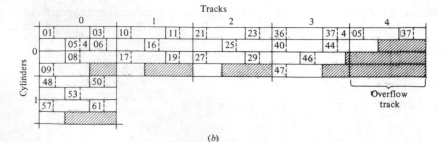

(b)

FIGURE 5.47
A sequential disk file (*a*) before and (*b*) after inserting two records.

entire track into main memory, making the required changes, and then writing the information back onto the same track. To facilitate the insertion of new records, overflow areas are included in every track, and an overflow track is included in every cylinder. New records may be inserted directly into a track until its overflow area is filled. Further insertions can be made using the overflow track. Instead of inserting an entire record into a track, a short pointer of the form

key, overflow track

is inserted in the correct position in the logical sequence of records. Figure 5.47*b* shows how the records with keys 05 and 37 are placed on the disk file when pointers and the overflow track are used. The use of overflow areas permits insertion and deletions to be made rapidly without moving large amounts of data. Note that when pointers are introduced, the physical sequence of the records is no longer the same as the logical sequence. The file must be processed from time to time to eliminate the pointers and restore the records to their proper physical sequence.

Indexed sequential files. A popular method for organizing disk files so that individual items can be accessed rapidly is called the *indexed sequential* organization. It is characterized by the use of directories or indexes which specify the location of each record. The records are ordered sequentially by key as in sequential file organization, so that records can also be accessed sequentially without using the directories. The directories, however, permit rapid semirandom access.

The simplest kind of directory stores the entire physical address, specified by a disk-unit number, a cylinder number, and a track number for every record. It thus consists of a list of items of the form

record key, physical address

A record is located by sequentially searching the directory until a matching key is found. If the number of records is very large, this type of directory is impractical due to both its size and the time required to search it. In such cases, several levels of directories are employed where each directory provides a part of the physical address.

Figure 5.48 shows a three-level directory system. The first directory, called the unit directory, indicates the disk unit where each record can be found. Each disk unit stores a cylinder directory that specifies the cylinder address of every record in the unit. Finally, each cylinder contains a track directory indicating the track addresses of every record in the cylinder. The size of the directories can be minimized by storing only the highest record key associated with each level of storage (unit, cylinder, or track). This is done in Fig. 5.48. The unit directory contains one entry for each unit. It specifies, for example, that unit 0 stores all records with keys between 0 and 9999, while unit 1 stores all records with keys between 10,000 and 17,426. The structure of the cylinder and track directories is similar. The physical address of a given record is found by first examining the

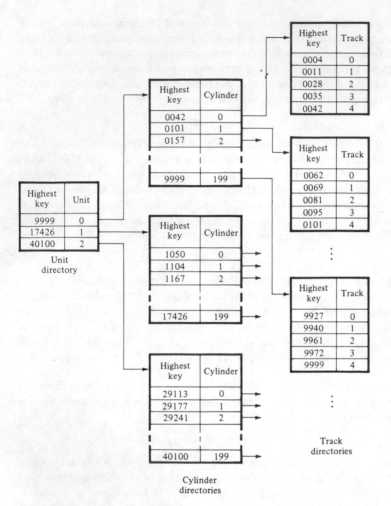

FIGURE 5.48
Multilevel indexed sequential file directory.

unit directory. This points to the appropriate cylinder directory, which in turn points to a track directory. For example, suppose that record 0087 is to be accessed. The unit directory indicates that it can be found in unit 0. The cylinder directory for unit 0 indicates that the record is in cylinder 1. Finally, a search through the track directory for cylinder 1 of unit 0 reveals that the desired record is in track 3.

Let n_u, n_c, and n_t denote the number of units, the number of cylinders per unit, and the number of tracks per cylinder, respectively. The number of possible physical (track) addresses is $n_u n_c n_t$. Using the three-level directory of Fig. 5.48, we see that the maximum number of directory entries that must be scanned to locate a record is $n_u + n_c + n_t$. The various directories are generally stored along with the data they define. Figure 5.49 shows how directories are often stored within a disk unit. The first track of cylinder 0 contains the cylinder directory for that unit. The first item stored in each cylinder is its track directory. Information in the disk unit is typically processed in the following way:

1. The required cylinder directory is read into main memory and searched to identify the cylinder storing the desired information.
2. The track directory stored in this cylinder is transferred to main memory and searched to determine the required track.
3. The contents of this track are read into main memory, where they are searched to obtain the required records. The records can then be processed. If records are inserted or deleted, the cylinder and track directories are also updated.
4. All modified records and directories are transferred from main memory back to the disk unit.

Random-access files. A number of so-called random file organizations have been devised, where the word random refers to the fact that there is no apparent logical connection between records. Records with consecutive keys are not necessarily in consecutive physical locations, nor are there links between the records. The physical address $f(X)$ of record X is determined by processing its key X using some well-defined algorithm. Two major techniques for doing this have been distinguished [18]:

1. *Compression.* The physical address is formed by selecting a subset of the characters forming the key and (possibly) rearranging them. An example of

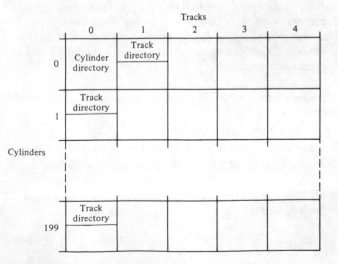

FIGURE 5.49
Storage of file directories in a disk memory unit.

this approach is truncation of the key. Compression is particularly suitable for processing nonnumerical keys because it can be designed to produce physical addresses that resemble the keys.

2. *Hashing.* The key X is treated as a number and an arithmetic function f, called a *hash function,* is used to compute the physical address $f(X)$. Many hash functions have been devised [9]. One technique is to divide X by a constant n and use the remainder as the address, i.e.,

$$f(X) = \text{remainder}(X) \quad \text{(Modulo } n)$$

The number of possible valid record keys is generally much larger than the number of physical addresses available. Thus two distinct keys may yield the same value of $f(X)$. A good choice of f should generate addresses that are distributed uniformly over the available file storage area. If each addressable unit of storage, e.g., a track, can accommodate several records, then records with the same address are assigned sequentially to consecutive locations within the track. Once the track is filled, subsequent items with the same address must be assigned to an overflow area.

The function f which is used to determine where a record is written in a file is also used to retrieve that record, thus eliminating the need for directories. This type of addressing is very suitable for large files that must be accessed randomly in real time. Because there is no logical sequence among the records, batch processing of randomly organized files is difficult.

5.3   HIGH-SPEED MEMORIES

A major problem in achieving high-speed computation is the disparity in operating speeds between processors (CPUs, IOPs, etc.) and main memory M. Typically the cycle time of M is greater by a factor of 5 or so than the cycle time of a processor. Furthermore, several memory words may be required during a processor cycle. To eliminate processor idle time while waiting for memory accesses to be completed, special measures may be taken to increase the effective processor-memory interface bandwidth. Several approaches are possible:

1. Decrease the memory access time by using a faster (and more expensive) technology for main memory.
2. Access more than one word during each memory cycle.
3. Insert a fast cache memory between the processor and main memory.
4. Use associative addressing in place of the normal random-access method.

In this section, we study the role of the last three approaches in the design of high-performance computer systems.

5.3.1   Interleaved Memories

In order to carry out m independent accesses simultaneously, main memory must be partitioned into m separate *memory modules* or *banks* $M_0, M_1, \ldots, M_{m-1}$, as shown in Fig. 5.50. Each module must be provided with its own independent addressing circuitry. If the physical buses between the processors and memory are shared by the modules, an appropriate bus-control mechanism must also be introduced. Finally, sufficient buffer storage must be included in the processors to accommodate the increased flow of information. A modular memory organization is particularly useful in multiprocessor systems where several processors require access to a common memory. Different processors can access memory simultaneously provided that they reference separate modules.

In order for this memory organization to be utilized efficiently, the memory references generated by the processors should be distributed evenly among the m modules. Ideally, every member of a set of m consecutive memory references should address a separate module. Any set of m or fewer memory accesses, no two of which refer to the same module, can be carried out simultaneously. The processor-memory bandwidth is then m words per memory cycle.

Address interleaving. Let $X_0, X_1, \ldots, X_{k-1}$ be k words that are known (or expected) to be required in sequence by a processor, for example, k consecutive instructions in a program. They will normally be assigned k consecutive physical addresses $A_0, A_1, \ldots, A_{k-1}$ in main memory. The following rule can be employed to distribute these addresses among the memory modules.

Interleaving rule. Assign address A_i to module M_j if $j = i$ (Modulo m).

Thus $A_0, A_m, A_{2m}, \ldots$ are assigned to M_0; $A_1, A_{m+1}, A_{2m+1}, \ldots$ are assigned to M_1, etc. This technique for distributing addresses among memory modules is termed *interleaving*. The interleaving of addresses among m modules is called *m-way* interleaving. It is convenient to make m, the number of modules, a power of 2, say $m = 2^p$. Then the least significant p bits of every (binary) address immediately identify the module to which the address belongs.

The number of memory modules m is determined by comparing the cycle time of the main-memory technology to that of the processors. Consider the case of the Cray-1 supercomputer which is described in Sec. 7.2. It employs a CPU with a cycle time of 12.5 ns, and semiconductor main memory M composed of modules with a cycle time of 50 ns and a word size of 64 bits. Although the number of main-memory accesses associated with each CPU cycle varies from

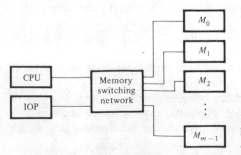

FIGURE 5.50
A modular memory organization.

cycle to cycle, a reasonable estimate is that when operating at maximum speed one instruction word and two input operand words will be read from M, and one result word will be written into M. This implies that a memory bandwidth of 4 words per CPU cycle, or 16 words per memory cycle, is required. Consequently the Cray-1 has 16 memory modules and uses 16-way address interleaving.

The efficiency with which any interleaved memory system can be used is highly dependent on the order in which memory addresses are generated; this order is clearly determined by the programs being executed. If two or more addresses require simultaneous access to the same module, then there is said to be memory *interference* or *contention*. The memory accesses in question cannot be executed simultaneously. In the worst case, if all addresses refer to the same module, the advantages of memory modularity are entirely lost.

Interleaving is frequently applied to program addresses in order to increase the rate at which instructions can be fetched from memory. The instructions of a program are normally assigned consecutive addresses and executed in the sequence in which they are written. Only program control instructions such as branch instructions cause a deviation in the execution sequence. Since the proportion of instructions that result in branching is small (typically around 20 percent of the instructions executed), the CPU can reasonably assume that the current instruction will be followed by the instructions in the next consecutive instruction addresses. Thus the CPU can fetch instructions in advance and store them in an instruction buffer. With m-way interleaving m consecutive instruction words can be fetched during one memory cycle.

A performance model. A model for measuring the efficiency of interleaved memory systems has been studied by G. J. Burnett and E. G. Coffman, Jr. [2]. It is assumed that there are m independent memory modules and that the CPU maintains a "request queue" of memory addresses $A_1, A_2, \ldots, A_q$ that it needs to access. Before each memory cycle, the request queue is scanned and a sequence called the request sequence $A_1, A_2, \ldots, A_k$ of $k \leq m$ addresses is selected from the head of the queue. $A_1, A_2, \ldots, A_k$ is the longest sequence with the property that no two of its members are in the same module. During the next memory cycle, these addresses are used to carry out k simultaneous memory accesses.

The efficiency of this system clearly depends on the average length of the request sequences—the closer to m the better. Following Ref. 2, let $p(k)$ denote the probability density function of the request sequence lengths, where $k = 1, 2, \ldots, m$. The mean value of k is denoted by b_m and is given by the equation

$$b_m = \sum_{k=1}^{m} k \, p(k) \tag{5.8}$$

b_m is the average number of words that can be accessed per cycle and therefore represents the memory bandwidth.

Since $p(k)$ depends on the programs being executed, $p(k)$ and b_m may be difficult to determine. Consider the case where the request queue contains only instruction addresses. An instruction request queue can be characterized by the *branching probability* λ, defined as the probability that any given instruction causes a jump to a nonconsecutive address. $p(k)$ can then be defined as follows:

$$p(1) = \lambda$$
$$p(k) = (1 - \lambda)^{k-1}\lambda \qquad \text{for } 1 < k < m$$
$$p(m) = (1 - \lambda)^{m-1}$$

Substituting into Eq. (5.8), we obtain

$$b_m = \lambda + 2(1 - \lambda)\lambda + 3(1 - \lambda)^2\lambda + \cdots + m(1 - \lambda)^{m-1} \tag{5.9}$$

It can easily be shown by induction on m, that (5.9) implies

$$b_m = \sum_{i=0}^{m-1} (1 - \lambda)^i$$

which is a simple geometric progression. Hence

$$b_m = \frac{1 - (1 - \lambda)^m}{\lambda} \tag{5.10}$$

It can be seen from (5.10) that $b_m = 1$ when $\lambda = 1$, while $b_m = m$, its maximum value, when $\lambda = 0$. Figure 5.51 shows b_m plotted as a function of λ for

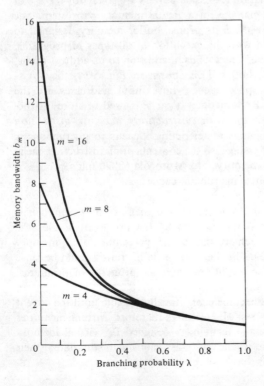

FIGURE 5.51
Memory bandwidth b_m as a function of branching probability in an m-way interleaved memory.

several values of m. These curves suggest that λ must be reasonably small for b_m to approach its maximum value.

5.3.2   Caches

A cache is a small fast memory placed between a processor and main memory as illustrated in Fig. 5.26b. The cache is then the fastest component in the memory hierarchy. It can be viewed as a buffer memory for the main memory, so that the cache M_1 and main memory M_2 form a two-level hierarchy. It is common to manage the three-level system of Fig. 5.26b as two largely independent two-level hierarchies (M_1, M_2) and (M_2, M_3). The main–secondary system (M_2, M_3) may be organized as a virtual memory system of the type examined in Sec. 5.2. The cache–main-memory system (M_1, M_2) is organized along essentially similar lines; hence (M_1, M_2) has many of the properties of a virtual memory system. In a system with multiple processors (CPUs or IOPs), each processor can have its own separate cache.

Caches are used in various forms to reduce the effective time required by a processor to access addresses, instructions, or data that are normally stored in main memory. The translation lookaside buffers found in segmentation and paging units—see, for instance, Fig. 5.34—are special-purpose *address caches* designed to store segment or page tables. Translation lookaside buffers are solely for the use of the operating system in its role as manager of a virtual memory subsystem. The term cache is usually reserved for a general-purpose buffer memory designed to store instructions or data associated with the execution of all types of programs, and we will use the word cache in this sense. Thus in addition to its address cache, the 128-entry translation lookaside buffer TLB shown in Fig. 5.34, the VAX-11/780 has an 8K-byte general-purpose cache whose input addresses are the physical addresses derived from TLB. Sometimes a cache is used to store instructions but not data, in which case the term *instruction cache* or *instruction lookaside buffer* are used. The advantage of restricting a cache to instructions is that, unlike data, instructions do not change, so the contents of an instruction cache need never be written back to main memory. The Motorola 68020 microprocessor (Fig. 1.39) employs an on-chip 256-byte instruction cache.

Cache design. The performance goal of adding a cache memory to a computer is to make the average memory access time t_A seen by the processor as close as possible to that of the cache t_{A_1}. To achieve this, a high percentage of all memory references should be satisfied by the cache, i.e., the cache hit ratio should be close to 1. This is possible because of the locality-of-reference property of programs. Although small instruction caches were used to store prefetched instructions in some early machines, caches did not become economically feasible until the advent of LSI/VLSI semiconductor memories. Historically, therefore, virtual memories preceded cache memories. Many of the techniques designed for virtual memory management have been applied to cache systems and have stimulated their development.

There are, nevertheless, some important differences between the cache–main-memory hierarchy (M_1, M_2) and main–secondary-memory hierarchy (M_2, M_3); these differences are summarized in Fig. 5.52. Because it is higher in the memory hierarchy, the pair (M_1, M_2) functions at a higher speed than (M_2, M_3). The access time ratio t_{A_2}/t_{A_1} is typically 5 or less, while t_{A_3}/t_{A_2} is typically 1000 or more. These differences in operating speed require (M_1, M_2) to be managed by high-speed logic circuits or firmware rather than software routines. (M_2, M_3), on the other hand, is controlled mainly by programs within the operating system. Thus while the (M_2, M_3) hierarchy may be transparent to the applications programmer but visible to the systems programmer, (M_1, M_2) is transparent to both. Another important difference is in the block size used. Communication within (M_1, M_2) is paged, but the page size is much smaller than that used in (M_2, M_3). Finally, we note that the processor generally has direct access to both M_1 and M_2, so that Fig. 5.53 is a more accurate representation of the logical data paths in a cache system. For this reason, caches are also called lookaside memories.

The structure of a cache memory unit is outlined in Fig. 5.54. It stores a set of main memory addresses A_i and the corresponding (data) words $M(A_i)$. The data entries are grouped into blocks (cache pages, often rather misleadingly called "lines"), each of which is a subblock of some main-memory page; the corresponding stored address is therefore a block address. The contents of the cache array are thus copies of a set of small noncontiguous main-memory blocks tagged with addresses. A cache typically operates as follows. A physical address A is sent to it from the CPU at the start of a read (load) or write (store) memory access cycle. The cache compares the relevant part of A, sometimes called the address *tag*, to all the addresses it currently stores. If there is a match, i.e., a cache hit, then the cache selects the desired word $M(A)$ from the data entry corresponding to A. It completes the memory cycle by transferring data from the CPU to its copy of $M(A)$ (read operation), or else retrieving its copy of $M(A)$ and routing it to the CPU (write operation). If A fails to match any of the stored addresses, i.e., a cache miss occurs, then the cache usually initiates a sequence of one or more main-memory read cycles to copy into the cache the main-memory block $P(A)$ containing the desired item $M(A)$. If necessary, the cache

Two-level hierarchy (M_{i-1}, M_i)	Cache–main memory (M_1, M_2)	Main–secondary memory (M_2, M_3)
Typical access time ratios $t_{A_i}/t_{A_{i-1}}$	5/1	1000/1
Memory management system	Implemented by special hardware	Mainly implemented by software
Typical page size	4 to 128 bytes	64 to 4096 bytes
Access of processor to second level M_i	Has direct access to M_2	All access to M_3 is via M_2

FIGURE 5.52
Major differences between cache–main-memory and main–secondary-memory hierarchies.

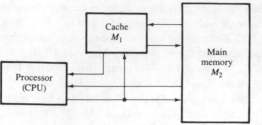

FIGURE 5.53
Data flow in a system with a cache.

controller first saves in main memory the old contents of the cache page frame $P'(A)$ it selects in which to place $P(A)$. $P'(A)$ is determined by a standard replacement policy such as LRU. The cache page size is often designed so that an entire page can be fetched in one main-memory cycle. Consequently, the effective access time on a cache miss is the main-memory cycle time, plus the short time needed to check the cache. The actual cache-main-memory transfer procedures vary from cache to cache, and read and write operations are usually handled differently, as explained later.

The design of a cache involves many of the issues encountered earlier in connection with virtual memory design, such as the selection of allocation strategy,

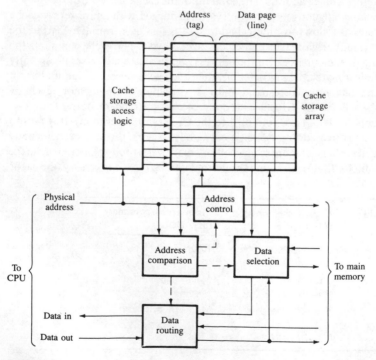

FIGURE 5.54
Basic design of a cache.

replacement policy, and page size. We now examine two other important issues that are peculiar to cache design.

1. The manner in which main-memory addresses are mapped into cache addresses
2. The policy on updating main memory when a write operation changes the contents of the cache

Address mapping. First we consider the mapping of main-memory addresses into a cache. This must be done in such a way that an address A presented to the cache by a processor can be quickly compared to all the addresses stored in the cache to determine whether or not A is currently assigned to the cache. The obvious approach of scanning all the cache entries serially is unacceptably slow. The fastest technique is to implement the cache's address store as a single associative memory, which permits the input address A to be compared simultaneously to all the addresses stored in the cache. Pure associative memories are extremely expensive, however, so it is only feasible to use them in very small caches. A variety of less costly techniques have been proposed to solve this problem, some of which make limited use of associative addressing.

An example of a pure associative cache is found in Data General Corp.'s ECLIPSE, a 16-bit minicomputer family introduced in the early 1970s. This series employs a modular memory design in which each memory board contains an 8K-word main-memory module M_1 and a 16-word 4-page cache M_2. Main memory M_1 is constructed from MOS RAM chips with a 700-ns access time, while M_2 uses bipolar RAMs with an access time of 200 ns. The main-memory addresses of the 16 words stored in the cache are placed in an associative or content-addressable memory CAM. When a memory address A is generated by the CPU, it is sent to the CAM, which compares it to all addresses currently stored in the cache. If the CAM indicates a match, M_2 responds to the memory request directly by either reading or writing the data $M(A)$. If $M(A)$ is not currently assigned to M_1, then the CAM forwards A to the main memory M_2, which responds to the original CPU memory request by executing a read or write cycle. At the same time, M_2 sends a block of four words, i.e., a cache page, containing $M(A)$ to M_1, which uses it to replace the least recently used cache page. The cache's LRU replacement policy is implemented by special hardware that constantly monitors cache usage. Note that making a cache part of the main memory as here, rather than making it part of the CPU, increases the time it takes the CPU to access the cache. Moreover, it does not reduce the traffic on the CPU-memory bus, an important consideration if there are multiple processors sharing the memory system. Consequently memory-based caches of the foregoing type are much less common than processor-based caches.

One of the simplest memory mapping techniques is called *direct mapping*. Let M_1 be divided into $S_1 = 2^k$ regions $M_1(0), M_1(1), \ldots, M_1(S_1 - 1)$, each of which stores a block of n consecutive words. Main memory M_2 is similarly divided into one-block regions $M_2(0), M_2(1), \ldots, M_2(S_2 - 1)$. Each region $M_2(i)$ in M_2

is mapped onto a fixed region $M_1(j)$ in M_1. The address j is determined from i by the rule

$$j = i \quad \text{(Modulo } S_1\text{)}$$

For example, if $S_1 = 2$ as illustrated in Fig. 5.55a, every even (unshaded) block in M_2 is mapped onto $M_1(0)$, while every odd (shaded) block in M_2 is mapped onto $M_1(1)$. The hardware needed to implement direct mapping is very simple. The low-order k bits of each block address identify the cache region that may

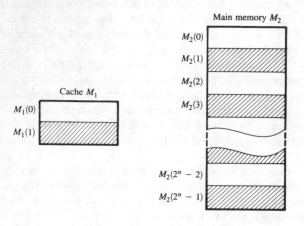

(a)

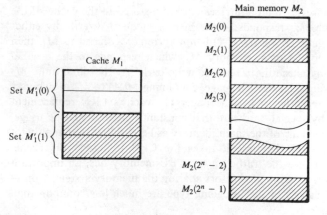

(b)

FIGURE 5.55
Cache address mapping techniques: (a) direct mapping with cache size 2; (b) two-way set-associative mapping.

contain the block. These k bits therefore constitute the cache address. If there are 2^p words per block, then the low-order $k + p$ bits of each effective address generated by the CPU constitute the cache address of the word in question. Thus, unlike associative mapping, there is no need to store the addresses of items in the cache. A disadvantage of direct mapping is that the cache hit ratio drops sharply if two or more frequently used blocks happen to map onto the same region in the cache. This possibility is minimized by the fact that such blocks are relatively far apart in the logical address space.

There is a more general mapping method called *set associative* which includes pure associative and direct mapping as special cases. As in direct mapping, blocks in main memory are grouped into equivalence classes determined by their addresses. $M_2(i)$ and $M_2(j)$ are in the same equivalence class E if $i = j$ (modulo S_1'). The cache is divided into S_1' regions $M_1'(0)$, $M_1'(1)$, . . . , $M_1'(S_1' - 1)$ called *sets*, each of which accommodates $k = 2^s$ blocks. A block $M_2(i)$ in M_2 is mapped into the set $M_1'(h)$ satisfying $i = h$ (modulo S_1'). Each set $M_1'(h)$ is controlled by a small associative memory, so that mapping within each set is associative. This k-*way* associative mapping permits up to k members of the same equivalence class E to be stored in the cache simultaneously, which is not possible with direct mapping. Figure 5.55b illustrates set associative mapping with cache size $S_1 = 4$ and set size $k = 2$; this therefore is an example of 2-way associative mapping. Every shaded (unshaded) page in M_2 can be mapped into either of the two shaded (unshaded) page frames in M_1. Set associative mapping reduces to direct mapping when the set size $k = 1$; it reduces to pure associative when $k = S_1$, the cache's page capacity. Intermediate set sizes lead to address mapping methods requiring an intermediate amount of associative hardware; see also Prob. 5.34.

Updating main memory. As noted earlier, the CPU generally has direct physical access to main memory, so that when a required item is not found in the cache, the CPU can access it in main memory with minimal delay. The existence of direct communication links between the CPU and M_2 permits some different schemes for updating M_2 when information in M_1 is altered. For example, the approach used in virtual memory systems to update secondary memory can also be employed here. In that case, each cache block in M_1 has a change bit C attached to it, which is set to zero when the block is first placed in M_1. Any subsequent write operation into that block sets C to 1. When a block with $C = 1$ is deallocated, its data contents are copied back into M_2. This technique for updating main memory is called *write-back* or *copy-back*. It has the disadvantage that M_1 and M_2 can be inconsistent, i.e., have different data associated with the same physical address. This leads to problems if there are several processors with independent caches sharing a common main memory, since their cache data can become inconsistent. Write-back also complicates recovery from system failures or other exceptional conditions.

An alternative to the write-back policy is to transfer the data word to both M_1 and M_2 during every memory write cycle, even when the target address is already assigned to the cache. This policy, which is called *write-through*, is easily implemented, and ensures that M_2 never contains obsolete information. It is especially useful in this regard when M_2 is shared by multiple processors. On the other hand, write-through results in more writes to M_2 than write-back. Since the time needed for each write is then the slower (write) access time of M_2, the processor's performance may suffer slightly. Note, however, that typically only a small fraction, perhaps one tenth, of all memory accesses are for write operations.

Example 5.7   Design of the VAX-11/780 cache [17]. The VAX- 11/780 introduced in Example 5.3 has a general-purpose cache with a capacity of 8K bytes. A cache page (line) contains 8 bytes, and 2-way set-associative mapping is used with 512 2-page sets. This results in the storage-array organization appearing in Fig. 5.56. The VAX's 32-bit physical address format A is interpreted as shown in Fig. 5.57 for addressing the cache. Bits 20:29 of A constitute a 9-bit set address (termed the index in VAX literature), which is used to directly map A into one of the cache's 512 sets. Bits 29:31 are subsequently used to select one of the 8 bytes in a cache page after the page has been selected. Only the 18-bit tag field composed of bits 2:19 of A actually needs to be stored in the cache. (Since all addresses will be assumed to be confined to a fixed quadrant of the physical address space, bits 0 and 1 are ignored here.)

The VAX cache is used in the following way. A physical address A is generated via the translation buffer TLB as discussed in Example 5.3, and is presented to the cache. Suppose that a request to read 1 byte from memory has been generated in some (micro) instruction cycle. The index bits 20:29 are decoded and used directly to

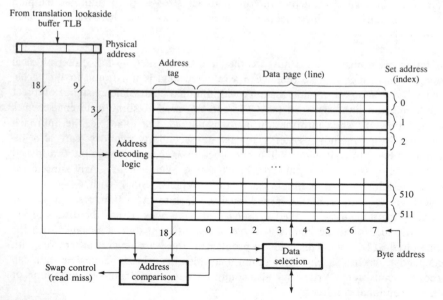

FIGURE 5.56
Organization of VAX-11/780 8K-byte cache.

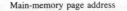

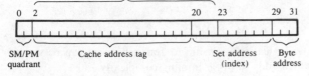

FIGURE 5.57
The VAX-11/780 physical address as interpreted by the cache.

select the correct set S in the cache. Next, the tag bits 2:19 of A are compared simultaneously to the address fields of the two cache pages currently assigned to S. If there is a hit, then the matching page P in S is marked, and one of its bytes is selected using the byte-address bits of A to control the selection. The contents of the selected byte are then read out. If a miss occurs, indicated by a no-match outcome from the address-tag comparison, the cache initiates an 8-byte page swap with main memory to bring the desired data into the cache. The page to be replaced is selected randomly from the two available candidates. (See Prob. 5.20). Once the new page is present in the cache, the memory read request is completed.

Write requests are handled as follows by the VAX-11/780. The incoming memory address A is directly mapped into a set whose address tags are compared associatively to the tag field of A as before. If there is a hit, the new data is written into the cache and, at the same time into the corresponding location in M_2; thus the VAX cache implements the write-through memory updating policy. When a miss occurs, the data is written into M_2 only. Unlike a read miss, a write miss does not initiate a page swap. The newly written data thus remains in M_2 until it subsequently has a read operation addressed to it, at which time its page is swapped into the cache as described above.

5.3.3 Associative Memories

Consider the table shown in Fig. 5.58, which is to be stored in a computer's memory. It consists of a list of records, each containing three (major) subfields: a person's name, an identification number, and an age. Many information storage and retrieval problems involve accessing certain subfields within a set of one or more records in answer to questions such as: "What are A. Jones's ID number and age?" If a conventional random-access memory is being used, it is necessary to

Name	ID number	Age
J. Smith	124	24
J. Bond	007	40
A. Jones	106	50
R. Roe	002	19
J. Doe	009	28

FIGURE 5.58
A table to be stored in a computer's memory.

specify exactly the physical address of the Jones entry in the table, e.g., by the instruction

READ ROW 3

The address ROW 3 has no logical relationship to Jones; hence it can be viewed as an artificial construct which adds to programming complexity.

An alternative approach is to search the entire table using the name field as an address. In such a system, the request for the Jones data would be in the form of an instruction such as

READ NAME = A. JONES

The conventional method of implementing this approach involves scanning all entries in the table sequentially and comparing their NAME fields to the given address, A. JONES, until a match is found. Sequential searching of this type is easily implemented with serial-access memories, but it is very slow. An associative memory eliminates this difficulty by simultaneously examining all entries in the table and selecting the one that matches the given address. It is clearly useful to be able to select other fields of the record to use as an address. For example,

READ ID = 106

uses the ID number field as an address and also accesses the Jones entry in the table.

In general, an *associative memory* is one in which any stored item can be accessed directly by using the contents of the item in question, generally some specified subfield, as an address. Associative memories are also commonly known as *content addressable memories (CAMs)*. The subfield chosen to address the memory is called the *key*. Items stored in an associative memory can be viewed as having the format

KEY, DATA

where KEY is the address and DATA is the information to be accessed. For example, if a page table of the kind shown in Fig. 5.42 is placed in an associative memory, the page address forms the key; and the page frame, presence bit, etc., form the data.

Word-organized memory. Figure 5.59 shows the structure of a simple associative memory. Each unit of stored information is a fixed-length word. Any subfield of the word may be chosen as the key. The desired key is specified by the *mask register*. The key is compared simultaneously with all stored words; those which match the key emit a match signal, which enters a *select circuit*. The select circuit enables the data field to be accessed. If several entries have the same key, then the select circuit determines which data field is to be read out; it may, for example, read out all matching entries in some predetermined order. Since all words in the memory are required to compare their keys with the input key simultaneously, each must have its own *match circuit*. The match and select circuits make

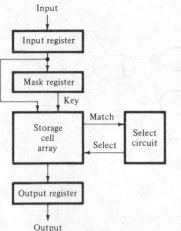

Input

FIGURE 5.59
Output
Structure of a word-organized associative memory.

associative memories much more complex and expensive than conventional memories. The advent of VLSI techniques has made associative memories economically feasible. However, cost considerations still limit them to applications where a relatively small amount of information must be accessed very rapidly, e.g., memory address mapping.

The logic circuit for a 1-bit associative memory cell appears in Fig. 5.60; designs of this type have been used in several commercial associative memory devices, including the 16-cell Fairchild F100142 CAM chip [22] on which Fig. 5.60 is based. It comprises a D-type flip-flop for data storage, a match circuit (the EXCLUSIVE-NOR gate) for comparing the flip-flop's contents to an external data bit D, and circuits reading from and writing into the cell. The results of a comparison appear on the match line M, with M = 1 denoting a match and M = 0 denoting no match. The cell is selected or addressed for both read and write operations by setting the select line S to 1. New data is written into the cell by setting the write enable line WE to 1, which in turn enables the D flip-flop's CLOCK input. The stored data is read out via the Q line. For both input and output operations to take place, the mask control line MK must be disabled (MK = 0); when MK = 1, the D flip-flop is disabled (CLOCK = 0) and the output data line Q is forced to 0. A typical cell like that of Fig. 5.60 can be implemented with about a dozen transistors; note that this is greater by an order of magnitude than the single transistor required for a dynamic RAM cell (Fig. 5.12). This greater hardware cost is one reason why large associative memories are rarely used. Hardware costs are further aggravated by the fact that fast, but low-density, bipolar technologies are preferred to the slower MOS designs used for RAM design. The F100142 chip, for instance, stores only 16 bits; however, its operating speed as measured from the time that input data is presented until the match output value M is established is a mere 3.2 ns.

Associative cells of the foregoing design can easily be combined into

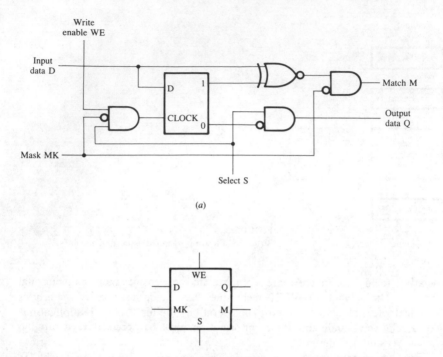

FIGURE 5.60
Associative memory cell: (a) logic circuit; (b) symbol.

word-organized associative memory arrays. Figure 5.61 shows the organization of the F100024 16-bit associative memory chip, which stores four words (columns) of 4 bits each. The words are individually addressable via their S lines. All words share a common set of data, match and mask lines for each bit position. Consequently, an external data bit D_i can be compared simultaneously to the ith stored bit of every word in the associative memory. The output lines of the cells are designed so that they can be wire-ORed together as indicated in the figure.

In some applications, the key assigned to every word is unique. Any attempt to address the memory results in either no match or a single match indicated by a single M line in the 1 state. If the keys are not unique, then a *multiple match* may occur. Note that a multiple match could result from an error in the system, even when all keys are intended to be unique. An important function of the select circuit of Fig. 5.59 is to resolve multiple matches. It can do so by storing all match signals in a register, then scanning this register to access the matching words one by one. Figure 5.62 shows such a design for the 4×4-bit memory of Fig. 5.60. The match signals $M_0:M_3$ produced by the associative-cell array are stored in a match register F composed of individually resettable SR flip-flops. After the

WE

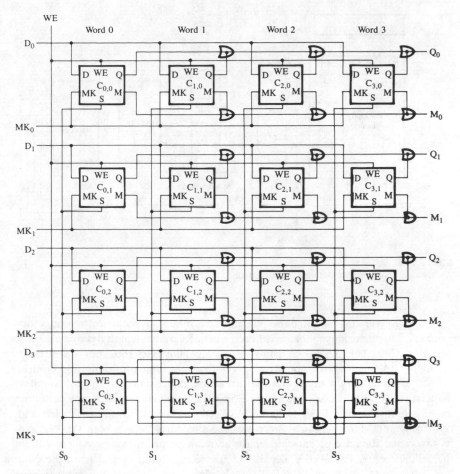

FIGURE 5.61
A 4×4-bit associative memory array.

associative match has been performed in the cell array, the SEARCH control line is activated to transfer $M_0{:}M_3$ to F; SEARCH is then deactivated. The outputs of F go to a priority encoder which therefore encodes the address i of a unique flip-flop F_i storing an active match signal. (No significance is being attached to the fixed order in which the match signals are selected.) The encoder's 2-bit output is applied to a 1-out-of-4 decoder, which then activates the output line Z_i corresponding to the current active match line M_i. Z_i in turn activates the select line S_i in the cell array, allowing the first matching data word to be read out. Z_i also resets the flip-flop F_i, so that in the next clock cycle the encoder selects the matching word of second-highest priority. This process is repeated up to four times until all words with $M_i = 1$ have been accessed.

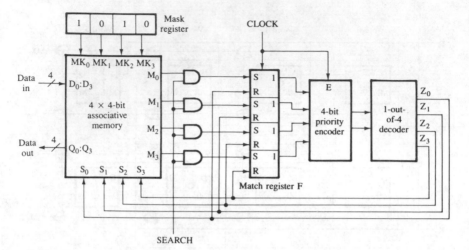

FIGURE 5.62
An associative memory with multiple-match resolution circuit.

Memory for variable-length data. We now describe a hypothetical memory organization for associative storage and retrieval of variable-length data based on a design by C. Y. Lee and M. C. Paull [13]. It also illustrates the types of functions typically implemented in associative processors, and their programming requirements. The memory can be viewed as a one-dimensional array of complex associative storage cells as shown in Fig. 5.63. Each cell is connected to a common set of data and control lines. In addition, a cell can communicate with its left and right neighbors. Information is stored in key-data form, where both the key and its associated data are of variable length and can be positioned anywhere within the cellular array. Each cell is capable of transferring data to and from the data bus in response to external control signals placed on the common control bus. The source of these control signals is a small processor which executes (micro) programs that specify the desired storage or retrieval operation.

The cell array may be of arbitrary length; hence it is not possible to provide individual match lines which would immediately pinpoint matching cells. All cell match lines are combined into a single line which tells the processor when, but not where, a match occurs. Two special flip-flops M and C are included in each cell. They are used to mark cells so that read and write operations can be localized within the memory array. These control flip-flops therefore correspond to the mask register of a word-organized associative memory. In addition, every cell contains a data register S used to store a single alphanumeric symbol.

The instructions executed by the control processor have the format

operation (condition)

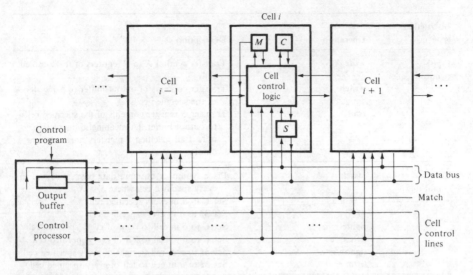

FIGURE 5.63
Associative memory for variable-length strings.

The condition field of an instruction specifies the values that C and M must have in order for the operation to be performed. For example,

write A $(C = 1)$

instructs all cells having $C = 1$ to store A in their S registers. An unconditional instruction such as

write A

is executed by every cell in the memory. Figure 5.64 lists the operations performed by the cells and the control processor. The "specified cells" are those that satisfy the condition, if any, appended to the operation.

In order to store or retrieve data, an appropriate program for the control processor must be written. Consider the problem of reading a specific data item from the memory. Assume that information is stored in the format

... # KEY1\$DATA1#KEY2\$DATA2# ...

where the symbols # and \$ act as delimiters. The given key is applied character by character to the input data bus and the match instruction as issued. The C flip-flop in the cell to the right of each matching cell is marked using the instruction

rightc $\leftarrow 1$ $(M = 1)$

Instruction type	Operation	Description
Input-output	**write** X	Transfer symbol X to S registers of the specified cells
	writeb	Transfer contents of output buffer to S registers of the specified cells
	read	Transfer S register contents of the specified cells to output buffer. (A meaningful instruction only if all specified S registers store the same data)
Cell marking	**match** X	Place symbol X on input data bus; set $M = 1$ in every specified cell where $S = X$
	$C \leftarrow a$	Set C to a in every specified cell
	$M \leftarrow a$	Set M to a in every specified cell
	rightc $\leftarrow a$	Set C to a in cell to right of every specified cell
	leftc $\leftarrow a$	Set C to a in cell to left of every specified cell
	rightm $\leftarrow a$	Set M to a in cell to right of every specified cell
	leftm $\leftarrow a$	Set M to a in cell to left of every specified cell
Program control	**go to** LABEL	Unconditional branch to instruction LABEL
	if X **then go to** LABEL	Conditional branch; compare symbol X to output buffer contents: if they match go to LABEL, otherwise go to next consecutive instruction
	if MATCH **then go to** LABEL	Conditional branch; if $M = 1$ in some cell go to LABEL, otherwise go to next consecutive instruction
	halt	Stop program execution

FIGURE 5.64
Instruction set for the associative memory of Fig. 5.63.

The next match instruction has the condition $C = 1$ appended to it, which restricts matching cells to those that lie on the right of a previous match. In this way a complete key can be matched and its data field uniquely marked. Figure 5.65 shows a program implementing this approach where the key is AZ. The frequently used sequence of three instructions that sets C to 1 in the right neighbor of a matching cell has been defined to be the macroinstruction MARKRIGHTC. The state of the memory after the execution of the first few instructions in this program is shown in Fig. 5.66. For clarity, M and C cells in the 0 state are shown blank. It will be observed that initially many cells are marked by the presence of 1 in their M or C flip-flops. The number of marked cells diminishes rapidly as the key is read in. Ultimately, if the key is unique, only one cell is marked and readout can commence.

A number of practical limitations of this system can readily be discerned. The very great cell complexity probably makes its cost prohibitive. The management of space in such a memory is also difficult. For example, items no longer needed result in gaps of varying lengths appearing in the memory. Locating such

Location	Instruction	Comment
SEARCH:	match #	Mark beginning of key
	$C \leftarrow 0$	Macroinstruction MARKRIGHTC,
	rightc $\leftarrow 1$ $(M = 1)$	which sets $C = 1$ in cell to right
	$M \leftarrow 0$	of cell with $M = 1$
	match A $(C = 1)$	
	MARKRIGHTC	
	match Z $(C = 1)$	
	MARKRIGHTC	
	match $\$$ $(C = 1)$	
	MARKRIGHTC	Mark beginning of data
READ:	read $(C = 1)$	
	if # then go to END	If output buffer contains #, go to END
	$M \leftarrow 1$ $(C = 1)$	
	MARKRIGHTC	
	go to READ	
END:	halt	

FIGURE 5.65
Program to read data with key AZ from the associative memory of Fig. 5.63.

gaps for reuse is not easy. An obvious solution is to eliminate gaps by periodic compaction (see Prob. 5.36). Further refinements in the design may be needed to solve the multiple match problem.

The storage cells of associative memories have certain logical capabilities, so that "distributed logic memory" is yet another term for an associative memory. By providing additional logical functions within each cell, it is possible to perform many standard arithmetic and nonnumerical operations in the memory [5, 12]. In such cases it is more appropriate to refer to the system as an associative processor. An associative processor called ALAP (Associative Linear Array Processor), with a one-dimensional organization resembling that of Fig. 5.63, has been built [8].

A more recent computer based on associative processing techniques is the Massively Parallel Processor (MPP) developed by Goodyear Aerospace Corp. [1]. At its heart is a set of 16,384 cells or small processing elements (PEs) organized as a 128 × 128 array. The PE array resembles a 2-D associative memory in which each PE can be accessed associatively and is capable of communicating with its four (north, south, east, and west) nearest neighbors. Like the 1-D associative memory for variable-length strings discussed above, the MPP is designed to process many variable-length items, in this case numbers as well as character strings. Thus the PEs can perform arithmetic-logic operations associatively, as well as the storage, retrieval, and control functions considered here. Although each PE is limited to 1-bit operations, and consequently individual numbers are processed serially rather than in parallel, the MPP is capable of very high performance because so many different sets of operands can be handled simultaneously by its large number of PEs.

While associative memories allow very fast access to large information files,

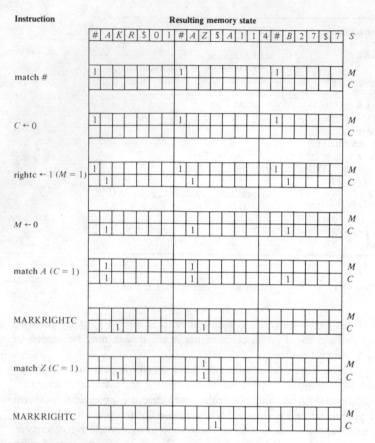

FIGURE 5.66
Memory states during execution of part of the program in Fig. 5.65.

it should be noted that fast access methods also exist for conventional nonassociative memories. In particular, if the hash addressing method defined in Sec. 5.2.5 is used, access times close to that of an associative memory can be achieved at a much lower hardware cost.

5.4 SUMMARY

No one technology can be used to supply all the memory needs within a computer system. This is mainly because the cost per bit of storage increases as the access time is decreased. As a result, several different memory technologies with widely varying characteristics can be found in a typical computer system. Besides cost per bit and access time, important properties of storage devices are alterability, storage permanence, reliability, and compatibility with processor technologies.

Main memories are usually of the random-access type, wherein the access time of every location is constant. Such memories are organized as multidimensional arrays to reduce the cost of their access circuitry and facilitate manufacture. The dominant technologies for this application are MOS semiconductor RAM ICs. In secondary memories, lower cost per bit and higher storage density are required. These are frequently achieved by using serial-access memories, which are characterized by the use of shared access mechanisms, serial data transfer, and an access time that varies with location. Serial-access memories store information on tracks which behave like shift registers. The most widely used technologies in this group are magnetic-surface memories with electromechanical access mechanisms, e.g., magnetic-disk and -tape units. Serial-access memories with static access mechanisms include magnetic-bubble devices.

The memory units of a computer are generally organized as a multilevel hierarchy $(M_1, M_2, \ldots, M_n)$ in which M_1 is connected to the CPU and other processors, M_2 is connected to M_1, and so on. M_i has less capacity, higher cost, and a shorter access time than M_{i+1}. The objective of using a hierarchical memory system is to achieve a cost per bit close to that of the least expensive memory M_n and an access time close to that of the fastest memory M_1. A virtual memory is a hierarchical memory, generally of two levels, which is managed by an operating system to appear like a single large memory to the applications programmer. This is achieved by automatically transferring blocks of information between M_1 and the other levels of the hierarchy. The locality-of-reference property of programs makes it possible to ensure that data is generally in M_1 when referenced by a processor. A fundamental measure of the performance of a virtual memory system is the hit ratio, the fraction of all memory references that are satisfied by M_1. The performance of a virtual memory is highly program-dependent; hence simulation is the principal design tool.

Memory space is generally a limited resource of a computer and therefore must usually be shared by different programs. Dynamic allocation means determining the regions of memory assigned to programs while they are being executed. Two allocation techniques have been distinguished: nonpreemptive and preemptive. Nonpreemptive methods assign space to incoming blocks only if an available region of sufficient size exists. Best fit and first fit are two possible allocation methods of this type. Preemptive methods can assign incoming blocks to occupied regions of M_1 and thereby permit more efficient use of memory space. Blocks to be preempted are selected according to a replacement policy. Least recently used (LRU) and first-in first-out (FIFO) are among the most widely used replacement policies. LRU is an example of a stack replacement algorithm. Stack algorithms permit rapid analysis of the effect of varying the capacity of M_1 on memory performance.

The block types used in memory allocation are also important. Segments are blocks of arbitrary size which correspond to logical units of a program. Pages are fixed-sized blocks with no logical significance. Memory space may be allocated by segments (segmentation) or pages (paging) or a combination of both, i.e., by using paged segments. The use of fixed-size pages greatly simplifies memory management. Information in secondary storage systems is organized into files. Because of their relatively large size, file access techniques have been developed that aim at various tradeoffs between access speed and ease of updating.

Several methods for decreasing the average access time for memory requests have been discussed. Main memory can be divided into a number of independently addressable modules to permit simultaneous access to several words. Efficient use of a modular memory requires addresses to be distributed throughout the modules in an interleaved fashion. Another approach is to insert a high-speed buffer memory or cache between the processors and main memory. The cache–main-memory pair approximates a two-level hierarchy, and many of the techniques used to manage a virtual memory are applicable to cache-based systems. A very different approach to high-speed storage and retrieval is associative or content addressing. In an associative memory, data is accessed by comparing the logical address or key of the required item to the keys of all stored items. Data and their keys are stored together in the memory. Very fast access is achieved by comparing the input key to all stored keys simultaneously. Associative memories require complex storage cells and therefore tend to be expensive.

PROBLEMS

5.1. A 2-D RAM has N storage cells organized as N_x rows and N_y columns. The number of address drivers needed is $N_x + N_y$.
    (a) If $N = M^2$, where M is an integer, that is, N is a perfect square, show that the number of address drivers needed is a minimum if and only if $N_x = N_y = M$.
    (b) If N is not a perfect square, provide an algorithm for determining values of N_x and N_y that minimize the number of address drivers.

5.2. A 16K-byte RAM is to be designed from 256×4-bit RAM ICs. Assume that 1-out-of-8 decoder ICs are also available, as well as ICs containing standard logic gates. The main design goal is to minimize the total number of ICs used.
    (a) Carry out the design assuming that each RAM chip has a single chip-enable line CE. Give your answer in the style of Fig. 5.15.
    (b) Repeat the design assuming that the RAM IC has two chip-enable lines CE_1 and CE_2, and is enabled if and only if $CE_1 = CE_2 = 1$.

5.3. Using the Intel 2186 dynamic RAM (Example 5.1) as the basic component, design a $64K \times 16$-bit RAM, giving your answer in the style of Fig. 5.15.

5.4. A certain moving-arm disk-storage device has the following specifications:

Number of tracks per recording surface	200
Disk rotation speed	2400 r/min
Track storage capacity	62,500 bits

Estimate the average latency and the data-transfer rate of this device.

5.5. A magnetic-tape system accommodates 2400-ft reels of standard nine-track tape. The tape is moved past the recording head at a rate of 200 in./s.
    (a) What must the linear tape-recording density be in order to achieve a data-transfer rate of 10^7 bits/s?

(*b*) Suppose that the data on the tape is organized into blocks each containing 32K bytes. A gap of 0.3 in. separates each block. How many bytes may be stored on the tape?

5.6. An array of closely packed permalloy chevrons of the form shown in Fig. 5.67 is used in bubble-memory chips in place of the T-bars of Fig. 5.23. As in the T-bar case, a rotating magnetic drive field H_d causes bubbles to propagate in a straight line under the chevrons. Determine the path taken by the bubble B, assuming that the north pole of B is closest to the chip surface, and that the drive field rotates counterclockwise.

5.7. Write a short essay comparing and contrasting the following memory technologies in terms of access time, alterability, cost per bit, and data-transfer rate: dynamic semiconductor RAMs, static semiconductor RAMs, magnetic-bubble memories, magnetic-disk memories, CD ROMs.

5.8. A computer has a two-level virtual memory system. The main memory M_1 and the secondary memory M_2 have average access times of 10^{-6} and 10^{-3} s, respectively. It is found by measurement that the average access time for the memory hierarchy is 10^{-4} s, which is considered unacceptably high. Describe two ways in which this memory access time could be reduced from 10^{-4} to 10^{-5} s and discuss the hardware and software costs involved.

5.9. In a two-level virtual memory, $t_{A_1} = 10^{-7}$ s and $t_{A_2} = 10^{-2}$ s. What must the hit ratio H be in order for the access efficiency to be at least 80 percent of its maximum possible value?

5.10. In an n-level memory, the *hit ratio H_i* associated with the memory M_i at level i may be defined as the probability that the information requested by the CPU has been assigned to M_i. Assuming that all information assigned to M_i also appears in M_{i+1}, then $H_1 < H_2 < \cdots < H_n = 1$. Using this definition of H_i, generalize the expression for t_A given in Eq. (5.3) to an n-level memory hierarchy.

5.11. A computer with no multiprogramming capability has a two-level paged virtual

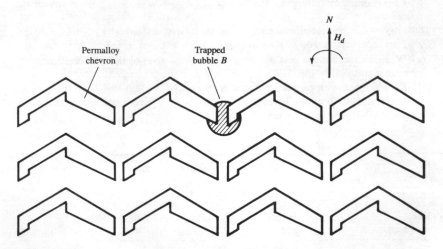

FIGURE 5.67
Chevron tracks for magnetic-bubble propagation.

memory. Main memory has a capacity of 256K 32-bit words and a cycle time of 1 μs. Secondary memory is composed of magnetic-disk units with the following specifications.

Average seek time	25 ms
Average latency	10 ms
Data-transfer rate	50,000 bits/s

It is observed that all disk accesses result from page faults, very few of which require a page from main memory to be copied back to disk. It is determined by measurement that main memory has a hit ratio of 0.99999, and that the average time to access memory as a whole is 2.17 μs. Estimate the page size P, showing all your calculations.

5.12. Consider a three-level memory hierarchy of the form (M_1, M_2, M_3) where M_1 is connected directly to the CPU. Let c_i and S_i denote the cost per bit and total storage capacity of M_i for $i = 1, 2, 3$. Let t_{A_i} be the access time of M_i, i.e., the average time to read one word from M_i to its own output port. Let H_i be the hit ratio of M_i as defined in Prob. 5.10.

  (a) Determine the average cost per bit c and the average access time t_A (with respect to the CPU) for the data given in Fig. 5.68.

  (b) Comment briefly on the performance of this design.

5.13. In the three-level memory hierarchy of Fig. 5.69, p_i denotes the fraction of memory access requests that result in an access to level M_i. When a miss occurs in M_i, a page swap always takes place between M_i and M_{i+1}; the average time for this page swap is t_{B_i}.

  (a) Calculate the average time t_A for the processor to read one word from the memory system.

  (b) It is desired to make $t_A \leq 1.15 \times 10^{-6}$ s, i.e., t_A should not exceed the access time of M_1 by more than 15 percent. This speedup is to be achieved by replacing M_3 by a faster memory technology that reduces t_{B_2} to a new value t'_{B_2}. What should t'_{B_2} be?

  (c) Suggest a more cost-effective way of satisfying the requirement $t_A \leq 1.15 \times 10^{-6}$ s than reducing t_{B_2}. Justify your answer.

5.14. (a) What are the average cost per bit and the access time of the four-level memory system specified in Fig. 5.70?

  (b) Suppose that, as a cost-saving measure, the cache is eliminated from the system. Determine the resulting percentage changes in the system's cost and access time, showing all your calculations.

Level i	Capacity S_i	Cost c_i ($/bit)	Access time t_{A_i} (s)	Hit ratio H_i
M_1 (cache)	1024	0.1000	10^{-8}	0.9000
M_2 (main)	2^{16}	0.0100	10^{-6}	0.9999
M_3 (secondary)	2^{24}	0.0001	10^{-3}	1.0000

FIGURE 5.68
Data for Prob. 5.12.

Level i	Access time t_{A_i} (s)	Access probability P_i	Page transfer time t_{B_i} (s)
M_1	10^{-6}	0.999900	0.001
M_2	10^{-5}	0.000099	0.1
M_3	10^{-3}	0.000001	—

FIGURE 5.69
Data for Prob. 5.13.

5.15. The available space list of a 1K-word memory has the following entries at time t.

Region address	Size (words)
0	200
250	150
450	100
700	185
999	25

The following sequence of allocation and deallocation requests is then received.

Time	$t+1$	$t+2$	$t+3$	$t+4$	$t+5$
Size of block to be allocated	135	25		170	100
Address of block to be deallocated			400		

Determine the available space list after all these requests have been serviced using (*a*) best-fit and (*b*) first-fit allocation. Assume that the memory is searched in ascending address sequence.

5.16. The following page address stream is representative for a particular two-level virtual memory system that uses demand paging and LRU replacement

$$3\ 4\ 2\ 6\ 4\ 7\ 1\ 3\ 2\ 6\ 3\ 5\ 1\ 2\ 3$$

Plot a graph of page hit ratio as a function of main-memory page capacity n for $1 \leq n \leq 8$. Assume that main memory is empty initially.

5.17. Consider the following representative page address trace generated by a two-level virtual memory that uses demand paging and has a main-memory capacity of four pages.

$$1\ 2\ 3\ 4\ 1\ 5\ 2\ 3\ 6\ 5\ 4\ 1\ 6\ 2\ 5\ 4$$

Memory	Capacity (bits)	Cost ($/bit)	Access time(s)	Hit ratio
Cache	2^{10}	10^{-1}	10^{-8}	0.990000
Main	2^{20}	10^{-2}	10^{-6}	0.999900
Secondary	2^{30}	10^{-4}	10^{-2}	0.999999
Tertiary	2^{40}	10^{-6}	10	1.000000

FIGURE 5.70
Data for Prob. 5.14.

Which of the page replacement policies FIFO or LRU is more suitable for use with this system? Show your calculations, and give a short intuitive justification of your answer.

5.18. A variation of the LRU replacement policy, which we call *simplified LRU (SLRU)*, is used in some virtual memory systems. Every page P_i in an SLRU page table has a reference bit R_i associated with it. Whenever P_i is accessed, its reference bit R_i is set to 1. If the access request for P_i causes a page fault, then R_j is reset to 0 for all $j \neq i$, and P_i is brought into main memory M_1. When a page in M_1 must be selected for replacement, the SLRU algorithm scans all the R_i's in a fixed order. The first page encountered with a reference bit of 0 is the one that is replaced. If all the reference bits are 1, then the page with the smallest (logical) address is replaced.

(a) For the page address trace given below, determine the page hit ratio under both SLRU and LRU, assuming that M_1 has a capacity of three pages and is initially empty.

$$2\ 4\ 2\ 3\ 5\ 1\ 3\ 4\ 1\ 2\ 5\ 6$$

(b) Is SLRU a stack replacement policy? Justify your answer.

5.19. Another replacement policy that has been proposed is *least frequently used (LFU)*. Under LFU the block to be replaced from M_1 at any time t is the one that has had the fewest references made to it during the period from $t - T$ to T, where T is some fixed time interval.

(a) Make a brief qualitative comparison between LFU and LRU that identifies two realistic situations where LFU yields a better hit ratio than LRU and vice versa.

(b) Determine whether or not LFU is a stack replacement algorithm.

5.20. Some computers in the PDP/VAX-11 series have caches that use a *random* page-replacement policy, which we will refer to as RAND. The page to be replaced is selected by a fast process that approximates truly random selection, and does not use any data on the page's reference history. Devise a general hardware method for implementing RAND in a cache, explaining clearly how randomness is achieved. Illustrate your answer using the VAX-11/780's cache, which actually employs RAND.

5.21. Assuming page size to be a function of average segment size only, determine the page size 2^k that maximizes memory space utilization when the average segment size is 1100 words and k is required to be an integer.

5.22. Certain microprocessors such as the Intel 80386 allow the programmer to specify any of four different memory organizations: unsegmented and unpaged; segmented and unpaged; unsegmented and paged; segmented and paged. Specify a broad class of system applications or programming environments for which each of these four organizations is best suited.

5.23. (a) Explain why the Intel 80386 microprocessor (Fig. 5.45) employs a two-step rather than a one-step page translation process.

(b) The paging mechanism of the 80386 can be bypassed entirely by setting a certain bit in a control register. The segmentation mechanism cannot be similarly bypassed; however, its effects can be nullified by appropriate programming steps. What are these steps?

5.24. A word-organized RAM is sometimes used to store messages of varying length having the *linked-list* format shown in Fig. 5.71. Each item in the list contains $t + p$ words, where t is the number of words of message text and p is the number of words in the link. The link is the address of the next item in the list. The storage space (shown

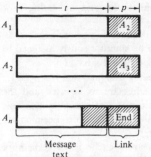

Message text Link

FIGURE 5.71
Linked-list message format for Prob. 5.24.

shaded) not used in the last list item A_n and the space occupied by the links are regarded as overhead, or "waste," space. Assume that the message lengths are randomly distributed with mean value L. Show that wasted space is a minimum when t is chosen to be approximately $\sqrt{2pL}$

5.25. List the main functions performed by a memory management unit. What are the advantages of an on-chip MMU such as that of the Intel 80386 compared with an off-chip MMU such as is needed with the Motorola 68020 microprocessor?

5.26. A computer system is being designed with a fast CPU that requires a main memory M_1 with a word size of 32 bits, a total capacity of 2^{16} words, and a maximum bandwidth of 2×10^7 words/s. Semiconductor RAM is available using two technologies T_1 and T_2. Technology type T_1 has an access time of 50 ns and costs $200 per 1024×8-bit module. Type T_2 has an access time of 200 ns but costs only $100 per 1024×8-bit module. The system is considered suitable for address interleaving, and the access circuitry for m memory modules with m-way interleaving is estimated to cost $5000(m - 1)$. Describe how you would design M_1 to minimize total hardware cost.

5.27. A 32-way interleaved memory is used for program storage. It is found that the branching probability λ of the memory-request queue is 0.25. What is the average number of words accessed per memory cycle?

5.28. A certain supercomputer (a uniprocessor) employs a memory technology with a cycle time of t_M ns. The CPU cycle time is t_{CPU} ns, and the CPU can execute a single three-address instruction in one CPU cycle. If the supercomputer uses m-way interleaving of main-memory addresses, determine a reasonable expression for m as a function of t_M and t_{CPU}, stating all your assumptions.

5.29. In a cache-based memory system using FIFO for cache page replacement, it is found that the cache hit ratio H is unacceptably low. The following proposals are made for increasing H.
(a) Increase the cache page size.
(b) Increase the cache storage capacity.
(c) Increase the main-memory capacity.
(d) Replace the FIFO replacement policy by LRU.
Analyze each proposal to determine its probable impact on H.

5.30. Consider a system containing a 128-byte cache. Suppose that set-associative mapping is used in the cache, and that there are four sets each containing four cache pages (lines). The physical address size is 32 bits, and the smallest addressable unit is the byte.

(a) Draw a diagram showing the organization of the cache and indicating how physical addresses are related to cache addresses.

(b) To what page frames of the cache can the address $000010AF_{16}$ be assigned?

(c) If the addresses $000010AF_{16}$ and $FFFF7Axy_{16}$ can be simultaneously assigned to the same cache set, what values can the address digits x and y have?

5.31. A high-performance high-reliability multiprocessor is being designed that has p CPUs and m-way memory address interleaving. Multiple caches are to be used and the CPUs are to be connected to the memory modules via a very fast shared system bus. Analyze the following design questions and give the answers you deem most appropriate for this application, citing all your reasons.

(a) Where should the caches be placed? The options are a cache in each memory module as in the ECLIPSE, or a cache in each CPU as in the VAX series.

(b) What main-memory updating policy should be used?

5.32. Discuss briefly the advantages and disadvantages of the following cache designs which have been proposed, and in some cases implemented. Identify three nontrivial advantages or disadvantages (one or two of each) for each part of the problem.

(a) An *instruction cache*, which only stores program code but not data.

(b) A *two-level cache*, where the cache system forms a two-level memory hierarchy by itself. Assume that the entire cache subsystem will be built into the CPU.

5.33. It is desired to build a small word-organized associative memory using the 4×4-bit memory circuit of Fig. 5.61 as the basic building block. The memory is to store ten 8-bit words having the format shown in Fig. 5.72. Any one of the fields A, B, and C may be selected as the key. Assume that all stored keys are unique. When a match occurs, the entire matching word is to be fetched (read operation) or replaced (write operation). Draw a logic diagram for the memory including all access circuitry.

5.34. For small values of k, a k-way set-associative cache like that of Fig. 5.56 can be designed efficiently with standard RAMs rather than associative memories implementing the address storage function. The required address comparisons must then be performed outside the storage array; they could clearly be done inside the address store if associative memory cells were used. Carry out the register-level design of the 2-way associative cache of Fig. 5.56 assuming that the memory part is implemented by 512×8-bit RAM ICs, and that standard MSI/LSI components are available for the remainder of the circuit. Briefly compare the cost of your design with one that employs associative memory cells.

5.35. This problem concerns the design of a small *learning memory LM* which has some of the features of an associative cache. Assume that LM must store up to eight 8-bit words. A new data word D presented as input to LM is compared associatively to the current contents of LM. If LM already stores a copy of D, or if the memory is full, then the write request is ignored. Otherwise D is written into LM, which thereby "learns" this new word. The contents of LM can be read out associatively in the usual fashion. Carry out the logic design of LM using the 4×4-bit associative cell C of Fig. 5.61 and standard gate- and register-level components. Use some copies of C to store address tags indicating which locations in LM are occupied. Your answer should

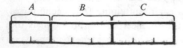

FIGURE 5.72
Associative memory word format for Prob. 5.33.

include a formal language description or a state table defining the behavior of the learning memory, and a register-level block diagram of its structure.

5.36 Consider the associative memory system in Fig. 5.63. Using the instruction set of Fig. 5.64, write a program to compact the memory by transferring all stored character strings to the left end of the cell array, thus eliminating all gaps between records. Assume that an unused cell stores b (blank) in its S register. Suggest some additions to the given instruction set that would simplify compaction.

REFERENCES

1. Batcher, K. E.: "Design of a Massively Parallel Processor," *IEEE Trans. Comput.*, vol. C-29, pp. 836–840, September 1980.
2. Burnett, G. J., and E. G. Coffman, Jr.: "A Study of Interleaved Memory Systems," *AFIPS Conf. Proc.*, vol. 36, pp. 467–474, 1970.
3. Clark, D. W., and J. S. Emer: "Performance of the VAX-11/780 Translation Buffer: Simulation and Measurement," *ACM Trans. Comput. Sys.*, vol. 3, pp. 31–62, February 1985.
4. Cohen, B., and R. McGarity: "The Design and Implementation of the MC68851 Paged Memory Management Unit," *IEEE Micro*, vol. 6, no. 2, pp. 13–28, April 1986.
5. Crane, B. A., and J. A. Githens: "Bulk Processing in Distributed Logic Memory," *IEEE Trans. Electron. Comput.*, vol. EC-14, pp. 186–196, April 1965.
6. Denning, P. J.: "Virtual Memory," *Comput. Surv.*, vol. 2, pp. 153–187, September 1970.
7. El-Ayat, K. A., and R. K. Agarwal: "The Intel 80386—Architecture and Implementation," *IEEE Micro*, vol. 5, no. 6, pp. 4–22, December 1985.
8. Finnila, C. A., and H. H. Love: "The Associative Linear Array Processor," *IEEE Trans. Comput.*, vol. C-26, pp. 112–125, February 1977.
9. Horowitz, E., and S. Sahni: *Fundamentals of Data Structures*, 2d ed., Computer Science Press, Rockville, Md., 1983.
10. Intel Corp.: *Memory Components Handbook*, Santa Clara, Calif., 1984.
11. Knuth, D. E.: *The Art of Computer Programming*, vol. 1, *Fundamental Algorithms*, 2d ed., Addison-Wesley, Reading, Mass., 1973.
12. Kohonen, T.: *Content-Addressable Memories*, 2d ed., Springer-Verlag, Berlin, 1987.
13. Lee, C. Y., and M. C. Paull: "A Content Addressable Distributed Logic Memory with Applications to Information Retrieval," *Proc. IEEE*, vol. 51, pp. 924–932, June 1963.
14. Matick, R. E.: *Computer Storage Systems and Technology*, Wiley, New York, 1977.
15. Mattson, R. L., et al.: "Evaluation Techniques for Storage Hierarchies," *IBM Syst. J.*, vol. 9, pp. 78–117, 1970.
16. Middelhoek, S., P. K. George, and P. Dekker: *Physics of Computer Memory Devices*, Academic, London, 1976.
17. Pohm, A. V., and D. P. Agrawal: *High-Speed Memory Systems*, Reston Publ. Co., Reston, Va., 1983.
18. Roberts, D. C.: "File Organization Techniques," in M. Rubinoff (ed.): *Advances in Computers*, vol. 12, pp. 115–174, Academic, New York, 1972.
19. Shore, J. E.: "On the External Fragmentation Produced by First-Fit and Best-Fit Allocation Strategies," *Commun. ACM*, vol. 18, pp. 433–440, August 1975.
20. Smith, A. J.: "Cache Memories," *Comput. Surveys*, vol. 14, pp. 473–530, September 1982.
21. Strecker, W. D.: "VAX-11/780: A Virtual Address Extension of the DEC PDP-11 Family," *Proc. Nat'l. Comput. Conf.*, pp. 967–980, June 1978. Reprinted in C. G. Bell, J. C. Mudge, and J. E. McNamara (eds.): *Computer Engineering: a DEC View of Hardware Systems Design*, pp. 409–428, Digital Press, Bedford, Mass., 1982.
22. Triebel, W. A., and A. E. Chu: *Handbook of Semiconductor and Bubble Memories*, Prentice-Hall, Englewood Cliffs, N.J., 1982.
23. Watson, R. W.: *Timesharing System Design Concepts*, McGraw-Hill, New York, 1970.

CHAPTER SIX

SYSTEM ORGANIZATION

This chapter is concerned with the way computers and their major components are interconnected and managed at the processor or system level. The methods used for local (bus) and long-distance communication are examined, as well as the design of input-output subsystems. The role of an operating system in providing overall system management functions is also discussed.

6.1 COMMUNICATION

In this section we consider the problems of designing cost-effective local and long-distance communication mechanisms for computer systems.

6.1.1 Introduction

The difficulty in transferring information among the components of a computer is largely dependent on the physical distances separating the components. We distinguish two major cases here: *intrasystem communication*, which occurs within a single computer system and involves information transfer over distances of no more than a meter or so; and *intersystem communication*, which involves communication over longer distances. Intrasystem communication is primarily implemented by means of groups of electrical conductors called buses, which allow parallel (word-by-word) transmission of data. Intersystem communication, on the other hand, is implemented by a variety of physical media, including electrical cables, optical fibers, and radio links. Serial (bit-by-bit) rather than parallel data transmission is used for communicating over longer distances. Serial communication links cost less than parallel, and are also more reliable and simpler to control.

A group of computers, user terminals, and other system components that are linked together over long distances (a kilometer or more) constitute a *computer network*.

Buses. The various processor level components (CPUs, IOPs, main memory, IO or peripheral devices) of a computer system are interconnected by buses. The term bus in this context refers not only to communication paths between the system components but also to mechanisms for controlling access to these paths and supervising the exchange of signals that provide the communication. Many bus organizations are possible. Two very common types are depicted in Fig. 6.1. In Fig. 6.1a a single bus, the system bus, is shared by all components. At any time only two units can communicate via the system bus. Large computer systems with separate IO processors frequently employ the dual bus system of Fig. 6.1b. Here two buses are provided, one for communication between main memory and the processors, and a second for communication between an IOP and the set of IO devices it controls. In most computers, communication with IO devices is a major source of difficulty due to the wide variety of operating characteristics exhibited by these devices. In contrast, communication between processors and main memory is relatively straightforward.

Communication between different processor-level components presents several problems. The distances involved frequently make it impractical to use a common clock for synchronization. For example, if a clock signal with a period

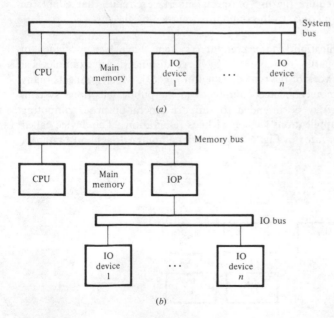

(a)

(b)

FIGURE 6.1
Communication methods within a computer: (a) single shared bus; (b) separate memory and IO buses.

of 100 ns is transmitted to a device 100 m away, that signal will not be received until about 330 ns (3.3 clock periods) later, assuming it travels at the speed of light (300,000 km/s). Furthermore, several signals which are transmitted simultaneously over such distances are likely to arrive slightly out of phase or "skewed" at the destination. For instance, if the 100-m path by which signal A travels has a delay differing by 10 percent from the delay of the path traveled by signal B, the two signals will arrive about 33 ns out of phase. The fact that the various processor-level components process data at widely different rates further suggests that their timing circuits be independent and that communication between them be asynchronous.

A second problem in determining the number and type of signals to be used during intrasystem communication. A system component presents to the outside world a set of data and control lines which are used to connect it to other components. The specifications of these lines or buses and the signals they carry constitute the device's *interface*. The interface of a device depends on its function and its manufacturer. In order to simplify communication within a computer system, various standard bus types have been defined both by computer manufacturers and by standards organizations such as the IEEE in the United States. An example examined later is the bus called Multibus, which was originally developed by Intel Corp. in the mid-1970s as an asynchronous system bus for its 8- and 16-bit microprocessor series, and has been widely adopted by other manufacturers [17]. As indicated in Fig. 6.2, connecting a system component, particularly an IO device, to a bus may require the use of special interface circuits that adapt the component's "natural" interface to the standards imposed by the bus.

Long-distance communication. Many computer systems have been designed in which the component parts are separated by large distances. An example is a simple time-sharing network of the type depicted in Fig. 6.3, which connects many user terminals to a remotely located computer via the public telephone system. Timesharing networks may be intended to support general-purpose computing services or specialized applications such as airlines reservations. The device called a *multiplexer* or *concentrator* in Fig. 6.3 is a small computer designed to connect

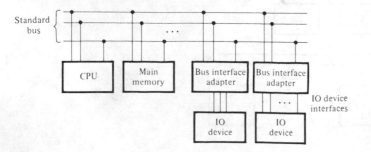

FIGURE 6.2
Typical use of a standard system bus in a computer.

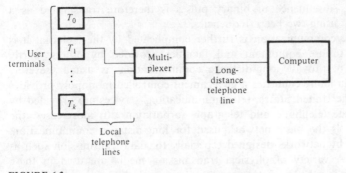

FIGURE 6.3
A remote timesharing network.

the users to the remote computer via a single long-distance path. The multiplexer time-shares the long-distance line among the relatively slow user terminals, giving each user the impression that he is directly connected to the remote computer. This architecture also permits users to gain access to the computer using a local telephone call to the multiplexer rather than a more costly long-distance call directly to the central computer. Many computers and terminals can be linked together in this general way to form a computer network.

Local communication in a computer system is implemented by means of digital (0/1) pulses traveling along lines (wires). This is sometimes referred to as direct current (DC) signaling. As the pulses are transmitted, they become distorted due to line capacitance, external interference (noise), and other phenomena. The amount of distortion increases with the length of the lines and the frequency of the pulses. Beyond a certain point the pulses become unrecognizable and errors in transmission result. Over long distances, therefore, it is more efficient to use alternating current (AC) for data transmission. An appropriate AC signal called the *carrier* is generated and is *modulated* in some manner to produce two distinct types of AC signals that represent the binary values 0 and 1. A device called a *modulator-demodulator*, or *modem*, is required to convert digital pulses to and from the modulated (analog) form used for long-distance communication.

Figure 6.4 illustrates a common modulation technique called *frequency modulation* (FM). The carrier is a sinusoidal signal (sine wave) which can have two frequencies—f_0 representing the bit 0 and f_1 representing 1. If an ordinary "voice-grade" telephone line is being used, f_0 and f_1 might be chosen as 1500 and 2000 Hz, respectively. Sine waves of these frequencies can be heard as pure tones

FIGURE 6.4
Long-distance transmission of binary information using frequency-modulated (FM) signals.

of different pitch. A sequence of binary pulses is therefore transmitted as a sequence of "beeps" using two beep frequencies.

Long-distance communication is further complicated by the fact that it is usually necessary to use equipment and facilities provided by others, partly because the right to provide long-distance communications is usually severely restricted by law. In many countries a government-controlled monopoly provides such services. In the United States, telecommunications services are provided by a number of private telephone and telegraph corporations. In most cases, the telephone network is the basic network used for long-distance communication. This is augmented by networks designed especially for data transmission such as the telex system. A variety of physical transmission media are used in these networks including telephone wires, coaxial cables, optical fibers, radio (microwave) links between ground stations, and radio links via orbiting satellites.

Several other important differences between intra- and intersystem communication methods should be noted. Whereas intrasystem communication is often serial by word, intersystem communication is usually serial by bit. This, of course, is to reduce the cost of the communication equipment. Every long-distance data transfer requires a substantial amount of time to establish the communication path to be used, e.g., the time associated with dialing a telephone number. In order to reduce this overhead, a sequence of many bits called a *message* is usually transmitted at one time.

Interconnection structure. We now consider some of the possible ways the components of a computer system can be interconnected. The *interconnection structure* of a system may be defined as a graph whose nodes represent components of the system such as processors, memories, etc., and whose edges represent physical communication paths such as buses or long-distance transmission lines. A path used to link only two devices is said to be *dedicated*. A path used to transfer information between different devices at different times is said to be *(time-)shared*. Sharing of communication paths is implemented by means of switching units such as the multiplexer of Fig. 6.3. The shared buses of Fig. 6.1 may also be regarded as switching units. Such buses are best represented by explicit nodes of the system graph as is done in Fig. 6.1.

We now consider some common interconnection structures for computer systems. We will refer to the edges of the system graph as (communication) links. The nodes of the graph represent processor-level units such as computers, IO terminals, or switching units. A conceptually simple way of connecting the components of a system is to provide dedicated links between all pairs of components that need to communicate with one another. In the most general case where n units must be connected in all possible ways, $n(n-1)/2$ dedicated paths are needed. The interconnection structure is that of the complete graph of order n [10]. Figure 6.5 shows such a system when $n = 4$.

Dedicated links allow very fast transfer of information through the system. All n devices may send or receive information simultaneously, and there is no delay due to busy connections. Furthermore, systems with dedicated links are

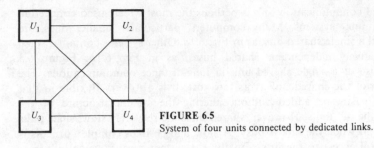

FIGURE 6.5
System of four units connected by dedicated links.

inherently reliable, since the failure of any link affects communication only between the two units connected to that link. Communication between these units may still be possible if they can send information to each other via other units of the system. For example, if the bus linking U_1 and U_4 in Fig. 6.5 fails, U_1 and U_4 may still be able to communicate via U_2 or U_3. The main disadvantage of dedicated paths is their high cost. The number of links needed increases approximately with the square of the number of units. Adding a new unit to the system is difficult, since the new unit must be physically connected to each of the existing units.

At the other end of the spectrum, a single path may be used for all communications among n devices, as illustrated in Fig. 6.6. At any time, only two units can communicate with each other via the shared link; the remaining units are effectively disconnected from one another. A control mechanism is required to supervise sharing of the link among the n devices. This control can be centralized in a special control unit (which may be one of the n units U_i, for example, a CPU), or several units may be capable of controlling the link (decentralized control). In general, connection to the link can be established in two ways.

1. A unit U_i capable of acting as link controller or master initiates the connection of two units to the link, perhaps in response to an instruction in a program being executed by U_i.
2. A unit which is not itself a link controller sends a request to the link controller for access to the common link. The link controller then connects the requesting device to the link if it is not in use. If the link is busy, the requesting unit must wait until it becomes available. If several conflicting requests for access to the link are received simultaneously, the link controller uses some predetermined arbitration scheme to decide which request is granted first.

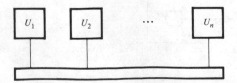

FIGURE 6.6
System connected by a common shared link.

The shared communication link is perhaps the most widely used connection method in computer systems. Many computers, particularly smaller ones, are designed around a single shared bus, as in Fig. 6.1*a*. Other systems contain a small number of relatively independent shared buses, as in Fig. 6.1*b*. Figure 6.3 illustrates the use of a single shared link in long-distance communications. The main attraction of the shared link is its low cost. It is also very flexible in that new units can easily be added without altering the system structure or the connections to the old units. However, shared links are relatively slow, since units are forced to wait when the link is busy. A slow and perhaps complex process is needed to control access to the link. Finally, the system is sensitive to failure of the shared link, which can destroy all communication in the system.

A complete system of dedicated links and a single shared link represent extreme cases. Between these extremes lie various interconnection structures which involve some sharing of data paths but permit more than one data transfer at a time. A *crossbar* connection of the kind shown in Fig. 6.7 is typical. It is used to connect two groups of units $G_1 = \{U_1, U_2, \ldots, U_m\}$ and $G_2 = \{U'_1, U'_2, \ldots, U'_n\}$, so that any unit of G_1 can be connected to any unit of G_2, but two units in the same group need never be connected. This type of dichotomy exists in several places in computer systems. For example, G_1 could be a set of main-memory modules and G_2 a set of processors. Crossbar connections have also been used to connect IO processors to IO devices. As shown in Fig. 6.7, each unit in G_1 (G_2) is connected to a horizontal (vertical) path. The horizontal and vertical paths are in turn connected via a set of $n \times m$ circuits, called *crosspoints,* which can logically connect any horizontal path to any vertical path. At any time, only one crosspoint

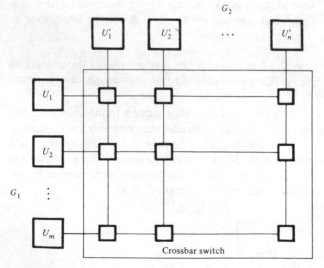

FIGURE 6.7
Crossbar connection of two groups of units.

can be activated in each row and column. If $k = \min \{m, n\}$, then any k distinct units in G_1 can be simultaneously connected to any k distinct units in G_2. Hence this crossbar connection allows up to k data transfers to take place simultaneously. Conflict and delays occur only when two units in G_1 attempt to communicate with the same unit in G_2, or vice versa, at the same time.

Although the crossbar connection allows several simultaneous data transfers, there is only one path connecting each pair of communicating units. This is a common characteristic of local bus organizations; see, for example, Figs. 6.1 and 6.3. Such systems are relatively easy to control, since no decision must be made about the routes used for data transfer. They are, however, vulnerable to failures in communication paths, because alternative paths do not exist. Long-distance communication networks often contain several alternative paths, so the overall reliability of the system is increased.

Figure 6.8 shows a basic organization called a *ring network* that is used in long-distance (and occasionally in local) communication. The main communication path is a closed loop to which units $\{U_i\}$ are connected via special interface switching units. It provides two distinct paths between every pair of users, so that the failure of any link in the main communication loop can be tolerated. Computer networks sometimes take the form of a set of interconnected ring subnetworks.

6.1.2   Bus Control

In this section we will examine the methods that are used to establish and control intrasystem communication via local buses. Two key design issues in this type of communication are the timing of information transfers over the bus, and the selection process by which a device gains access to the bus. For simplicity, we will restrict our attention to the shared bus organization of Fig. 6.6. We will also

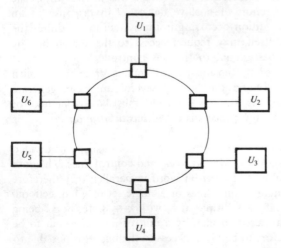

FIGURE 6.8
A ring-structured communication network.

assume that one particular unit acts as the main bus control unit, or *bus master,* and supervises the use of the bus by the other units, the *bus slaves.* In most computers, the CPU is the usual bus master, while the memory and IO interface circuits are the slaves. IOPs and certain other IO controllers can also serve as bus masters. Only a master can initiate data transfers. Bus slaves can only respond to commands issued by a bus master.

Bus systems can be distinguished by the manner in which data transfers over the bus are timed. In *synchronous* buses, each item is transferred during a time slot known in advance to both the source and destination units. This implies that the bus interface circuits of both units are synchronized. Synchronization can be achieved by driving both units from a common clock source, a method that is feasible over short distances. The rising or falling edge of the clock signal, which is one of the bus control signals, determines when other bus signals change value or reach stable (valid) states. Alternatively, each unit may be driven by separate clock signals of approximately the same frequency. Synchronization signals must then be transmitted periodically between the communicating devices in order to keep their clocks in step with each other.

Synchronous communication has the disadvantage that the time slots used for information transfer are largely determined by the slowest units in the system. Thus fast devices may not be able to communicate at their maximum rate. An alternative approach widely used in local bus communications is *asynchronous communication*, in which each item being transferred is accompanied by a separate control signal to indicate its presence to the destination unit. The destination unit may respond with another control signal to acknowledge receipt of the information. Because each device can generate these control signals at its own rate, data-transmission rates can vary with the inherent speed of the communicating devices. This flexibility in transmission rates is achieved at the cost of more complex bus-control circuitry.

A device can be selected for connection to the main bus in two ways. The bus master may initiate the selection of a slave device U in response to an instruction in a program or a condition occurring in the system that requires the services of U. Alternatively, U itself may request access to the shared bus by sending an appropriate bus-request signal to the bus controller. In each case, specific actions must be performed by the bus-control unit in order to establish the logical connection between U and the bus. If several units can generate requests for bus access simultaneously, the bus controller must have a method for selecting one of the units; this selection process is called *bus arbitration.*

Interfacing. The lines that constitute a communication bus can usually be divided into three functional groups: data lines, address lines, and control lines. The data lines are designed to transmit all bits of an n-bit word in parallel; they therefore consist of either two sets of n unidirectional lines or a single set of n bidirectional lines. The data-bus size n is usually a multiple of 8, with $n = 8$, 16, or 32 being common values. Address lines are used to identify a unit or part of a unit to be used in a data transfer and therefore to be given access to the bus. It is possible to use the data lines for transferring addresses as well as data; this is termed data/address multiplexing. This may be done to decrease the cost of the bus; or to decrease the number of external connections (pins) of the units served by the bus. Memory buses usually contain separate address lines, but IO buses usually do not (see Fig. 6.1*b*). This is because every word transfer to main memory must be accompanied by an address, whereas data transfers via an IO bus are usually in long blocks of words, which require only the address of the start of the block. Finally, the bus control lines are used to transfer timing signals and status information about the units in the system. They may also be used to indicate the type of information present on the data lines.

A significant contributor to the cost of a system bus is the number and type of logic circuits required to transfer signals to and from the bus. A bus line represents a logic path with potentially very large fan-in and fan-out. Consequently, interface circuits termed bus *drivers* and *receivers*, which are basically amplifier or buffer circuits, may be needed to transfer signals to the bus and from the bus, respectively.

A special logic circuit technology called *tristate* logic is often used in bus design. It is characterized by the presence of three signal values 0, 1, and Z, where the third value Z is termed the *high-impedance* state. While 0 and 1 typically correspond to two electrical voltage levels, e.g., 0 and 5 V, Z represents the state of a line that is electrically disconnected from all voltage sources, i.e., an open-circuited line. Figures 6.9*a* and *b* define a basic tristate buffer which can serve as a bus-line driver. The inputs x and e are ordinary binary signals that assume only the values 0 and 1; the output z, however, can assume the values 0,

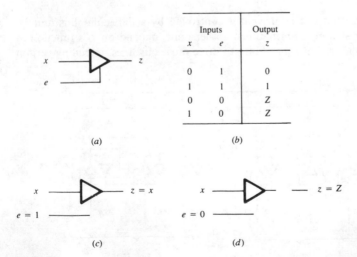

Inputs		Output
x	e	z
0	1	0
1	1	1
0	0	Z
1	0	Z

(a)   (b)

(c)   (d)

FIGURE 6.9
Tristate buffer: (*a*) logic symbol; (*b*) truth table; (*c*) equivalent circuit when enabled; (*d*) equivalent circuit when disabled.

1, and Z. The tristate buffer (and every other tristate device) has a special input line e called *output enable*, which when set to 0 disables the output line z by placing it in the high-impedance state Z. When $e = 1$, the circuit becomes an ordinary noninverting buffer with $z = x$. Figures 6.9b and c show equivalent circuits corresponding to the buffer in the enabled and disabled states.

Tristate logic circuits have two major advantages in the design of shared buses.

1. They greatly reduce fan-in and fan-out constraints on bus lines.
2. They facilitate bidirectional signal transmission over a bus line by allowing the same bus connection to serve as both an input and an output port.

These issues are illustrated by Fig. 6.10, which shows the use of tristate logic for interfacing two units U_1 and U_2 to a set of bidirectional bus lines. If $e_1 = 1$ and $e_2 = 0$, then U_1 drives the bus lines in question, and information is transferred over the bus from U_1 to U_2, in effect making $x_{2,i} = z_{1,i}$ for all i. Conversely, if $e_1 = 0$ and $e_2 = 1$, then U_2 drives the bus, and information is transferred in the opposite direction from U_2 to U_1, making $x_{1,i} = z_{2,i}$ for all i. If $e_1 = e_2 = 0$, then the outputs of both U_1 and U_2 are logically disconnected from the bus, and impose only a minuscule electrical load on the bus. The condition $e_1 = e_2 = 1$ is invalid, since it applies two different signals to each bus line making the resultant bus state indeterminate. Thus proper operation of the bus requires that at most one driver connected to each bus line be enabled at any time. Wired logic circuits of the kind illustrated by Fig. 2.2 and implemented by open-collector bipolar transistor circuits can also be used to drive a common bus line z in a similar manner to a tristate driver.

The bus lines that can be driven or controlled by a particular bus unit U, i.e., used by U for sending information to other units, depend on U's function in the system. Bus masters have the ability to drive most bus lines, including certain

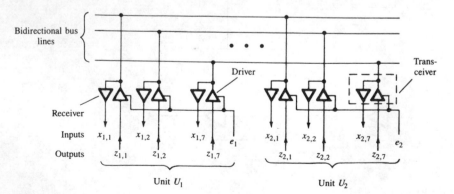

FIGURE 6.10
Use of tristate logic for bus interfacing.

lines that cannot be driven by any slave units. For example, a CPU can drive all data, address, and most control lines of a system bus. A memory unit, on the other hand, can drive the data lines but not the address lines, since it only needs to receive information from the address lines. The memory only drives those lines required for transmitting control signals to bus masters.

Timing. A timing diagram for a typical synchronous system bus appears in Fig. 6.11. The CLOCK signal of period T serves as the timing reference for all bus lines required for transmitting control signals to bus masters.

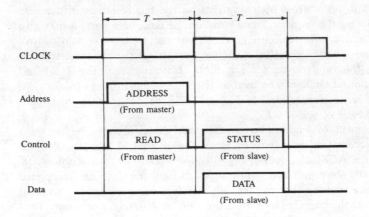

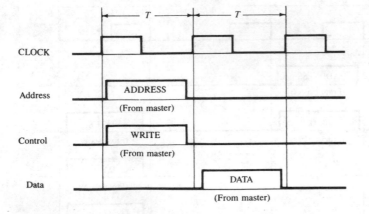

FIGURE 6.11
Synchronous data transfers: (*a*) read; (*b*) write.

when other bus signals change values. Such signal changes are expected to propagate through the bus to their destinations before the next 0-to-1 transition of CLOCK. Figure 6.11 also illustrates some typical signal exchanges between the slave and master units that are currently using the bus; these exchanges follow certain ordering rules called the *bus protocol*. Consider the read operation illustrated by Fig. 6.11a. Communication begins when the bus master places one or more predetermined signals on the control lines specifying the desired bus transaction, e.g., read from memory (load) or read from IO device (input). At the same time it places the address of the desired (part of the) slave unit on the bus's address lines. The potential slaves then examine the control and address signals, and the device with an address matching that on the bus responds in the next clock cycle by placing the requested data word on the bus's data lines; it may also optionally place status information, e.g., (no) error occurred, on certain control lines. A synchronous write operation is similar, except that the bus master rather than the slave is the data source; see Fig. 6.11b. Note that both the 0-to-1 and 1-to-0 transitions of CLOCK can be used as reference points in a bus transaction, and the read or write transactions of Fig. 6.11 can be designed to take place during one clock cycle of period 2T.

The requirement of Fig. 6.11 that the slave device respond in the next available clock cycle can be lifted by providing a control signal called an *acknowledge* signal ACK as shown in Fig. 6.12 for a read bus transaction. ACK is controlled by the slave unit and is not activated until the slave has completed its part of the data transfer. The master unit therefore waits until it has received the ACK signal for the current bus transaction before initiating a new one. Thus using an acknowledge signal allows a delay of one or more bus cycles, sometimes

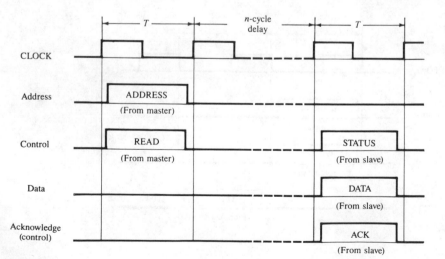

FIGURE 6.12
Synchronous data transfer (read) with wait states.

called *wait states*, to be inserted in a bus transaction to accommodate slower devices. Although ACK may be activated in any clock cycle, its changes must be synchronized with those of CLOCK.

Asynchronous bus timing eliminates the bus's clock signal and replaces it by special timing signals like ACK (Fig. 6.12), which are generated by the communicating units. These units are thus self-timed, and devices with widely different data-transfer rates can communicate asynchronously. Following Ref. 27, we distinguish two cases.

1. *One-way control*, in which timing signals are supplied by one of the two communicating devices
2. *Two-way*, or *interlocked*, *control*, in which both devices generate timing signals

If one-way control is employed, a single control line is used to time each address or data transfer. This control line may be activated by either the source or destination device, either one of which may be the bus master. Figure 6.13a shows a source-initiated data transfer. The source unit places the data word on the data lines. After a brief delay it activates the control line to which we have assigned the generic name DATA READY. The delay is intended to prevent the DATA READY signal from reaching the destination before the data word. Alternatively, the source can activate DATA READY and place data on the data bus at the same time. The destination must then insert a deskewing delay between its receipt of DATA READY and its reading of the data bus. Both the data lines and the DATA READY control line must be held in the active state for a sufficiently long period to allow the destination device to copy the data from the data bus. Figure 6.13b shows a data transfer initiated by the destination device. In this case the destination device initiates the data transfer by activating the control line called DATA REQUEST. The source device responds by placing the required word on the data lines. Again the data must remain active long enough for the destination device to read it.

Often the DATA READY/REQUEST signals are used to gate the data from the source unit to the data bus or from the data bus to the destination unit. Such control signals are called *strobe* signals and are said to strobe the data to or from the bus. For example, the source device, e.g., a keyboard, may generate a data word asynchronously and place it in a latch connected to the bus data lines. A signal on the DATA REQUEST line can be used to activate the clock

FIGURE 6.13
One-way asynchronous data-transfer timing: (*a*) source-initiated; (*b*) destination-initiated.

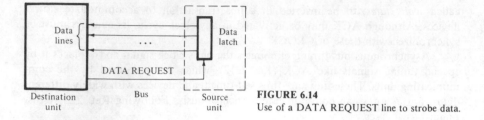

FIGURE 6.14
Use of a DATA REQUEST line to strobe data.

input line of the latch and thereby strobe the data onto the bus. Figure 6.14 illustrates this.

The disadvantage of one-way control is that no verification is provided that the data transfer has been successfully completed. For example, in a source-initiated transfer, the source unit receives no indication that the destination unit has actually received the data transmitted to it. If the destination unit is unexpectedly slow in responding to a DATA READY signal, the data may be lost. This problem can be eliminated by introducing a second control line that allows the destination unit to send a reply signal to the source when it receives a DATA READY signal. This control line is given the generic name DATA AC-KNOWLEDGE or ACK. Figure 6.15*a* shows the exchange of signals often called *handshaking* that accompanies a source-controlled transfer in this case. The source device maintains the data on the bus until it receives the ACK signal. ACK is not activated by the destination device until after it has copied the data from the bus. This scheme allows delays of arbitrary length to occur during the data transfer. A similar technique depicted in Fig. 6.15*b* is used for destination-initiated communication. The source unit activates ACK to indicate that the requested data is

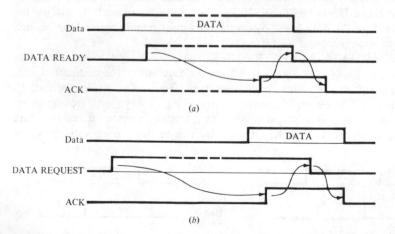

FIGURE 6.15
Asynchronous data transfer using two-way control (handshaking): (*a*) source-initiated; (*b*) destination-initiated.

available on the bus's data lines. The source maintains the data on the bus until the destination unit deactivates DATA REQUEST, an action that serves to verify the successful receipt of the data at its destination. As Fig. 6.15 demonstrates, a pair of control lines can perform the ready, request, and acknowledge functions for all types of asynchronous bus communication.

Figure 6.16 shows a timing diagram for transferring an address and one data word over a widely used asynchronous bus called UNIBUS, which was designed as the system bus for the DEC PDP-11 minicomputer series [4]. This bus contains 56 mostly bidirectional lines, including 16 data lines, 18 address lines, and 22 control lines. At any time two devices, one a bus master and the other a bus slave, can communicate with each other via the UNIBUS. The CPU and certain IO controllers serve as bus masters, while main memory and many IO interface circuits are bus slaves. As Fig. 6.16 indicates, all communication over the UNIBUS is fully interlocked with two handshaking signals named MASTER SYNC and SLAVE SYNC. This example shows the protocol for transferring a data word from a UNIBUS slave to a bus master, e.g., a memory read operation. First the master places the slave's address on the address bus and sets two control lines called CONTROL to indicate that a data transfer from slave to master is to be carried out. All potential slave units connected to the UNIBUS then attempt to decode the contents of the address bus. After a delay of at least 150 ns to allow for worst-case signal propagation delays and address decoding time, the master activates MASTER SYNC to signal that data transfer should begin. On receiving this signal the slave proceeds to fetch the data to be transferred. (If the slave is main memory, a memory read cycle is performed.) The slave then places the data on the data bus and activates SLAVE SYNC. After it receives the SLAVE SYNC signal, the master copies the data from the data bus and deactivates MASTER SYNC. It then waits for at least 75 ns and clears the address and CONTROL

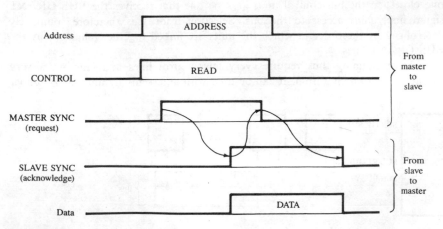

FIGURE 6.16
Asynchronous data transfer from slave to master via the UNIBUS.

lines. The slave responds to the deactivation of MASTER SYNC by clearing the data bus and deactivating SLAVE SYNC. This completes the data transfer and frees the UNIBUS for the next bus transaction.

Arbitration. The possibility exists of several master and/or slave units connected to a shared bus requesting access to it at the same time. A selection mechanism called bus arbitration is therefore required to decide among such competing requests. Following Thurber et al. [27] we distinguish three main arbitration schemes: daisy chaining, polling, and independent requesting. These methods differ in the number of control lines they require and in the speed with which the bus controller can respond to bus-access requests of different priorities. Some bus systems such as the UNIBUS combine several distinct arbitration techniques.

The *daisy-chaining* method is depicted in Fig. 6.17. Three control signals are involved in the arbitration process to which we assign the generic names BUS REQUEST, BUS GRANT, and BUS BUSY. All the bus devices are connected to a common BUS REQUEST line. When activated, it merely serves to indicate that one or more units are requesting use of the bus. The bus control unit responds to a BUS REQUEST signal only if BUS BUSY is inactive. This response takes the form of a signal placed on the BUS GRANT line. On receiving the BUS GRANT signal, a requesting unit enables its physical bus connections and activates BUS BUSY for the duration of its new bus activity.

The main distinguishing feature of the daisy-chaining technique is the manner in which the BUS GRANT signal is distributed. The BUS GRANT line is connected serially from unit to unit as shown in Fig. 6.17. When the first unit that is requesting access to the bus receives the BUS GRANT signal, it blocks further propagation of that signal, activates BUS BUSY, and begins to use the bus. When a nonrequesting unit receives the BUS GRANT signal, it forwards it to the next unit. Thus if two units are simultaneously requesting bus access, the one closest to the bus-control unit, i.e., the one that receives the BUS GRANT signal first, gains access to the bus. Selection priority is therefore completely determined by the order in which the units are linked together (chained) by the BUS GRANT lines.

Daisy-chaining thus requires very few control lines and employs a very simple arbitration algorithm. It can be used with an essentially unlimited number

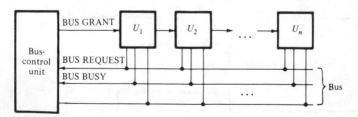

FIGURE 6.17
Bus arbitration using daisy-chaining.

of bus units. Since priority is wired in, the priority of each unit cannot be changed under program control. If it generates bus requests at a sufficiently high rate, a high-priority device like U_1 can lock out a low-priority device like U_n. A further difficulty with daisy-chaining is its susceptibility to failures involving the BUS GRANT line and its associated circuitry. If unit U_i is unable to propagate the BUS GRANT signal, then all $\{U_j\}$ where $j > i$ cannot gain access to the bus.

In a bus-control system that uses *polling*, the BUS GRANT line of the daisy-chain method is replaced by a set of lines called poll count lines which are connected directly to all units on the bus, as depicted in Fig. 6.18. As before, the units request access to the bus via a common BUS REQUEST line. In response to a signal on BUS REQUEST, the bus controller proceeds to generate a sequence of numbers on the poll count lines. These numbers, which may be thought of as unit addresses, are compared by each unit with a unique address assigned to that unit. When a requesting unit U_i finds that its address matches the number on the poll count lines, it activates BUS BUSY. The bus controller responds by terminating the polling process, and U_i connects to the bus.

Clearly, the priority of a bus unit is determined by the position of its address in the polling sequence. This sequence is normally programmable (the poll count lines are connected to a programmable register); hence selection priority can be altered under program control. A further advantage of polling over daisy-chaining is that a failure in one unit need not affect any of the other units. This flexibility is achieved at the cost of more control lines (k poll count lines instead of one BUS GRANT line). Also, the number of units that can share the bus is limited by the addressing capability of the poll count lines.

The third arbitration technique, *independent requesting*, uses separate BUS REQUEST and BUS GRANT lines for each unit sharing the bus. This approach, which is depicted in Fig. 6.19, provides the bus-control unit with immediate identification of all requesting units and enables it to respond very rapidly to requests for bus access. Priority is determined by the bus-control unit and may be programmable. The main drawback of bus control by independent requesting is the fact that $2n$ BUS REQUEST and BUS GRANT lines must be connected

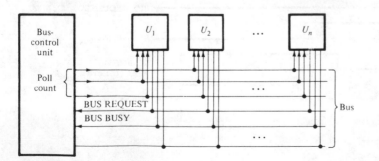

FIGURE 6.18
Bus arbitration using polling.

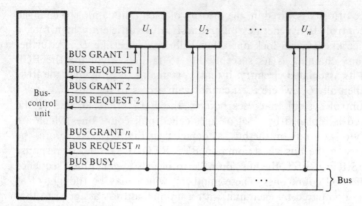

FIGURE 6.19
Bus arbitration using independent requesting.

to the bus-control unit in order to control n devices. In contrast, daisy-chaining requires two such lines, while polling requires approximately $\log_2 n$ lines.

The PDP-11 UNIBUS system introduced earlier combines the independent requesting and daisy-chaining approaches. There are five BUS REQUEST lines in the UNIBUS, each of which is assigned to a fixed priority level. A distinct BUS GRANT line is associated with each BUS REQUEST line. If there are five or fewer units (excluding the CPU, which is the bus controller) connected to the UNIBUS, each may thus use the independent requesting method. If several units are connected to the same BUS REQUEST line, then the corresponding BUS GRANT line is connected in daisy-chain fashion to those units. Thus daisy-chaining determines the priority of devices connected to the same BUS REQUEST line.

Figure 6.20 is a timing diagram for the signals associated with the transfer of control of the UNIBUS from one unit to another. It is assumed that control

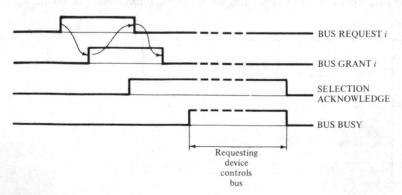

FIGURE 6.20
Timing diagram for transfer of bus control in the UNIBUS.

is to be granted to the device that activates BUS REQUEST line *i*. The CPU acknowledges this request by activating the corresponding BUS GRANT line. When the requesting device receives the BUS GRANT signal, it responds by deactivating BUS REQUEST and activating SELECTION ACKNOWLEDGE. The CPU responds by deactivating BUS GRANT. When any ongoing data transfers are completed, the selected unit takes control of the bus by activating BUS BUSY. The selected unit is now master and can initiate data transfers via the UNIBUS in the manner previously described (Fig. 6.16). It can also initiate an interrupt sequence by activating the INTERRUPT control line, which returns control to the CPU. The device relinquishes control of the UNIBUS after a data transfer by deactivating the BUS BUSY and SELECTION ACKNOWLEDGE lines, as shown in Fig. 6.20. If another unit has been selected as master by the CPU, it may now take control by activating SELECTION ACKNOWLEDGE. In this way control of the UNIBUS can be transferred from unit to unit. Note that only the CPU can activate the BUS GRANT lines. The CPU therefore retains ultimate control of the UNIBUS, since only the CPU can determine which device is master.

Example 6.1   The Multibus (IEEE 796) standard microcomputer system bus [16, 17]. As noted earlier, the Multibus (or Multibus I) was designed by Intel as a standard system bus for microprocessor-based computer products such as single-board microcomputers. Because it ultimately came to be used by many manufacturers, it was also defined in slightly improved form as IEEE Standard 796 (1983). A Multibus system can support a heterogeneous set of 8- and 16-bit microprocessors in multiprocessing configurations; consequently, all bus transactions can use asynchronous timing with handshaking. Figure 6.21 summarizes the 86 lines that make up the basic Multibus. They fall into seven groups:

1. Data lines (16)
2. Address lines (24)
3. Data-transfer commands and handshaking lines (5)
4. Bus-arbitration control lines (6)
5. Interrupt control lines (9)
6. Miscellaneous control lines (6)
7. Power and ground lines (20)

Standard names are specified for these lines, as well as a standardized 86-pin connector and printed-circuit board format for implementing the Multibus. All Multibus signals are considered active or enabled in the zero state, which is variously designated by adding an overbar or the suffix * or / to the signal name in the Multibus literature.

The main data path of the Multibus consists of 16 bidirectional data lines named $\overline{\text{DAT0:15}}$ that can be used for parallel transmission of 1 or 2 data bytes. The 24 address lines $\overline{\text{ADR0:23}}$ allow a memory or IO address space of up to 16M bytes to be addressed. The Multibus has both memory read and write enable lines ($\overline{\text{MRDC}}$ and $\overline{\text{MWTC}}$) and IO read and write enable lines ($\overline{\text{IORC}}$ and $\overline{\text{IOWC}}$);

Signal names		Functions	
$\overline{\text{DAT0:15}}$	16	Data bus	
$\overline{\text{ADR0:23}}$	24	Address bus	
$\overline{\text{MRDC}}$		Memory read enable	Data-transfer commands and handshaking
$\overline{\text{IORC}}$		IO read enable	
$\overline{\text{MWTC}}$		Memory write enable	
$\overline{\text{IOWC}}$		IO write enable	
$\overline{\text{XACK}}$		Acknowledge	
$\overline{\text{BREQ}}$		Bus request	Bus arbitration and timing
$\overline{\text{CBRQ}}$		Common bus request	
$\overline{\text{BUSY}}$		Bus busy	
$\overline{\text{BCLK}}$		Bus clock	
$\overline{\text{BPRN}}$		Bus priority in	
$\overline{\text{BPRO}}$		Bus priority out	
$\overline{\text{INT0:7}}$	8	Interrupt request	Interrupt control
$\overline{\text{INTA}}$		Interrupt acknowledge	
$\overline{\text{CCLK}}$		Master clock	Miscellaneous control
$\overline{\text{INIT}}$		System initialization	
$\overline{\text{BHEN}}$		Byte high enable	
$\overline{\text{INH1:2}}$	2	Inhibit memory	
$\overline{\text{LOCK}}$		Lock bus	
Ground	8		Power and ground
+5 V	8		
+12 V	2		
−12 V	2		

FIGURE 6.21
Structure of the Multibus (IEEE 796) standard bus.

consequently, the $\overline{\text{ADR}}$ lines can be used to address separate memory and IO spaces. The number of the data and address lines actually used is primarily determined by the CPU(s) connected to the Multibus. For example, the Intel 8085, an 8-bit microprocessor, can use only 8 of the 16 data lines. The 8085 has main-memory and IO address spaces of 64K bytes and 256 bytes, respectively; consequently, it needs only 16 of the available address lines. The Intel 80286 16-bit microprocessor, on the other hand, can address 64M bytes of memory, and so can use all the available data and address lines.

Figure 6.22 shows typical asynchronous data transfers over the Multibus with two-way control. The protocol here differs from the examples discussed earlier, e.g., Fig. 6.16, in that the read and write enable signals act both as commands indicating the desired operation and as handshaking timing signals (DATA READY or DATA REQUEST) from the bus master. The corresponding handshaking signal used by the slave unit is called $\overline{\text{XACK}}$ (transfer acknowledge). The figure also shows certain minimum and maximum time delays that must be observed. For example, after the bus

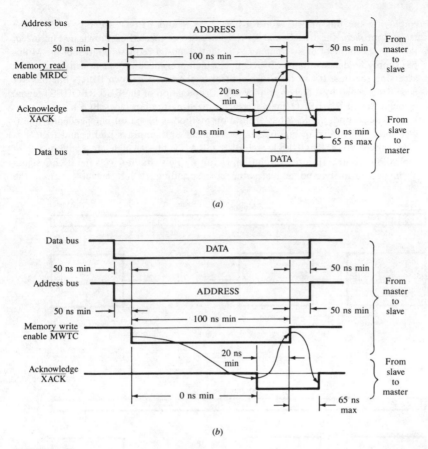

FIGURE 6.22
Asynchronous data transfers via the Multibus: (a) read; (b) write.

master has placed address and data words on the bus in a write operation (Fig. 6.22b), it must wait at least 50 ns for deskewing purposes before activating $\overline{\text{MWTC}}$. (Note that $\overline{\text{MWTC}}$, like all Multibus signals, is active in the 0 state.) $\overline{\text{MWTC}}$ must remain active for at least 100 ns, but there is no upper bound on the $\overline{\text{MWTC}}$ pulse width. $\overline{\text{XACK}}$ can be activated by the slave after an arbitrary delay. $\overline{\text{MWTC}}$ must respond by returning to 1 (inactive) after at least 20 ns. The bus master is required to retain the data and address values unchanged for at least 50 ns after deactivating $\overline{\text{MWTC}}$. Finally, the slave must respond to the deactivation of $\overline{\text{MWTC}}$ by deactivating $\overline{\text{XACK}}$ after at most 65 ns.

Any of a dozen or more units connected to the Multibus can be the bus master, and a set of control lines are provided for transferring control of the bus among the potential masters. The line $\overline{\text{BUSY}}$ is activated by the current bus master, and no other unit can become master while $\overline{\text{BUSY}}$ is active. When the Multibus is not in use ($\overline{\text{BUSY}} = 1$), a unit can gain control of the bus by one of two techniques employing the bus priority control lines $\overline{\text{BPRN}}$ and $\overline{\text{BPRO}}$; see Fig. 6.23. In the *serial* approach, the $\overline{\text{BPRO}}$ and $\overline{\text{BPRN}}$ lines are connected as shown in Fig. 6.23a; this is an example of daisy-chaining. A potential master requests control of the Multibus simply by deactivating its $\overline{\text{BPRO}}$ line, which prevents all lower-priority units from accessing the bus. It can then take control of the bus if its own $\overline{\text{BPRN}}$ line has not been deactivated by a higher-priority unit. Propagation of the BUS REQUEST signal through the $\overline{\text{BPRN}}$-$\overline{\text{BPRO}}$ chain is synchronized by the bus clock $\overline{\text{BCLK}}$.

The second, *parallel*, bus-arbitration method is based on independent requesting, and is illustrated in Fig. 6.23b. Each master unit employs $\overline{\text{BREQ}}$ and $\overline{\text{BPRN}}$ as independent BUS REQUEST and BUS GRANT lines which are connected to a central bus control (priority-resolution) circuit C. This circuit selects the $\overline{\text{BREQ}}$ signal of highest priority and activates the corresponding $\overline{\text{BPRN}}$ signal to grant the

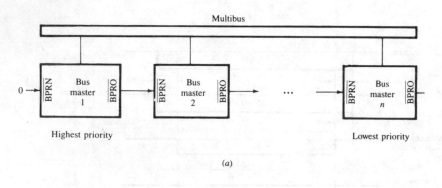

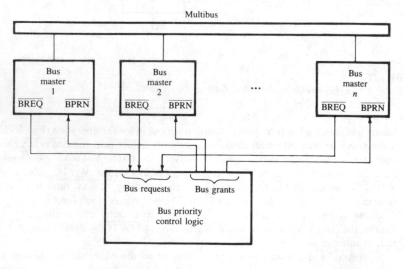

FIGURE 6.23
Multibus arbitration methods: (a) serial (daisy-chaining); (b) parallel (independent requesting).

requesting unit control of the bus. Up to 16 bus masters can be handled by this faster arbitration technique. By making C's priority-resolution circuits programmable, the priority of the requesting units can be varied dynamically, and requests can be resolved by polling.

The remaining control lines of the Multibus perform a variety of useful functions, several of which are discussed further in later sections.

A system bus called Multibus II has been designed by Intel to support 32-bit microprocessors [15]. This bus has a combined set of 32 data-address lines, so that the transmission of 32-bit data words and 32-bit address words over the bus is multiplexed. This allows larger data words and a larger address space to be accommodated with fewer lines than are employed by Multibus I. Multibus II also differs from its predecessor in that it is synchronous, and requires all signals to be sampled at fixed times relative to a system clock signal which is distributed to all units on the bus. The clock typically operates at 10 MHz and, with current interface circuit technologies, achieves operating speeds comparable to those of an asynchronous bus.

6.1.3 Computer Networks

This section presents the basics of intersystem data communication and a brief survey of the main types of computer networks. A computer network is a collection of computers and other system components such as terminals that are linked together over distances ranging from a few meters to thousands of kilometers. The rationale for such networks is to permit sharing of computing resources (hardware, software, or data) that are widely separated. Interactions with the computers take the form of IO operations, implying that the network components are loosely coupled. Many computer networks are *terminal-based* and consist of a single central computer connected to many user terminals. The terminals are often "intelligent" in that they also incorporate microcomputers to perform local data processing tasks. More general *computer-based* networks provide communication links between many independent computers.

Data transmission. A computer network is built around communication links or channels that form the medium for the exchange of information among the network components. Some important data-transmission media are illustrated in Fig. 6.24. For communication over short distances (up to, say, 10 m) at low data-transmission speeds (up to 10^5 bits/s), cables containing sets of insulated wires are used, the flat ribbon cable of Fig. 6.24a being typical. A *twisted-pair* link consists of two insulated wires twisted together as shown in Fig. 6.24b to improve their electrical signal transmission characteristics and minimize electromagnetic interference. Twisted pairs are extensively used for local telephone connections, and for connecting relatively slow digital equipment like user terminals to computers. They have a moderately high bandwidth of about 2^{20} or 1M bits/s. A much higher bandwidth (tens or hundreds of megabits/s) can be attained with

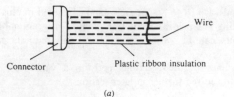

(a)

(b)

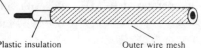

(c)

(d)

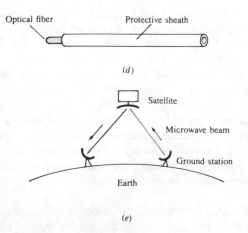

(e)

FIGURE 6.24
Intersystem data transmission media:
(a) ribbon cable; (b) twisted pair; (c) coaxial cable; (d) optical fiber; (e) microwave radio link.

a coaxial cable (Fig. 6.24c), which, however, is bulky and expensive. Still higher bandwidths in the gigabit/s (2^{30} bits/s) range are achieved by optical fiber cables (Fig. 6.24d). Unlike twisted pairs and coaxial cables, which transmit electrical signals, optical fibers use light as the data-transmission medium. They are also smaller and lighter than their electrical counterparts and are immune to electromagnetic interference. However, they require special interface devices to convert data between electrical and optical formats. The final data-transmission method illustrated by Fig. 6.24e involves the transmission of collimated beams of radio (microwave) signals through free space. In the figure, a satellite in geostationary orbit serves to relay an information-carrying microwave beam between two fixed, and possibly very widely separated, stations on the earth's surface. Two microwave ground stations may also communicate directly with each other over distances up to about 50 km.

A physical communication channel can be used to transmit a number of independent signals by various forms of multiplexing which effectively create several logically independent subchannels. The most basic type of multiplexing, termed *time-division* multiplexing in this context, allows the units attached to the channel to take turns in using it. Each pair of communicating units receives undivided use of the channel for a short time period, after which it relinquishes the channel to other units. In *frequency-division* multiplexing, the available data-transmission bandwidth is divided into n subchannels, all of which can transmit data simultaneously. This technique is used extensively for long-distance communication via the telephone system. The use of n physically separate and parallel links to create n independent communication channels is sometimes called *space-division* multiplexing. Depending on the data-transmission technique used, a physical link between two devices may take one of three forms: *simplex*, in which information flow is possible in one direction only; *half-duplex*, which allows information flow in either direction, but in only one direction at a time; and (*full*) *duplex*, where information can flow simultaneously in both directions.

Various standards exist for intersystem communication [9] which are comparable to those for intrasystem buses. For applications such as connecting a terminal or a modem (Fig. 6.4) to a computer, the RS-232 standard promulgated by the U.S. Electronic Industries Association (EIA) is widely used. A similar international standard known as V.24 is sponsored by the Comité Consultatif International de Téléphonie et Télégraphie (CCITT), which is under the aegis of the United Nations. An RS-232/V.24 link allows full-duplex, serial, and asynchronous data transmission via three wires that are attached to each communicating device: transmit (output), receive (input), and common return or signal ground. The standards define a set of control lines indicating such functions as "request to send" and "clear to send." They also give complete electrical and mechanical specifications for the electrical lines and connectors to be used. The maximum physical separation allowed between the communicating devices is 15 m, and data-transmission rates are normally limited to 9600 bits/s. Because of the low bandwidth involved, a flat-ribbon cable may be used. Other standards have been defined for transmission over longer distances and/or at higher speeds. The RS-422/V.11 standard, for example, can be used with a twisted-pair cable for distances up to 100 m and data rates of up to 1M bits/s.

Terminal-based networks. These networks are characterized by the presence of a central computer that communicates with a large number of remote terminals. The terminals can range from general-purpose terminals with keyboard and screen to highly specialized devices such as automatic bank tellers. They perform two main functions: local data processing tasks, which are often fairly simple, e.g., text editing, and the processing needed to communicate with the central computer.

An example of a terminal-based network is found in larger retail stores, where many tens of point-of-sales (POS) terminals are linked to a central computer; see Fig. 1.43. The POS terminals are primarily data-entry devices to process local sales transactions, while the central computer performs such global functions as storewide accounting and inventory control. Terminal-based systems with thousands of terminals can also be found, for example, computer networks used for airline reservations and large computer timesharing systems. One of the earliest computer networks was the American Airlines SABRE (*S*ales *a*nd *B*usiness *R*eservations done *E*lectronically) reservation system built in the 1960s. This prototype of all subsequent reservation systems linked over a thousand terminals scattered throughout the United States to a central computer system maintaining all the airline's flight information. SABRE was required to respond to a reservation inquiry in less than 3 s.

The elements of a typical computer terminal appear in Fig. 6.25. Various IO devices such as keyboards, display screens, and printers form the human interface of the terminal. These are connected via appropriate interface circuits to a microcomputer whose controlling software or firmware determines the "intelligence" of the terminal. Specialized interface circuits for intersystem communication provide the link between the terminal and the remote computer. Particularly useful for this purpose is a general-purpose data communications controller called a *UART* (*u*niversal *a*synchronous *r*eceiver-*t*ransmitter), a VLSI device that can be programmed to accommodate a variety of different data-transmission protocols and operating speeds.

Figure 6.26*a* shows the general structure of a small terminal-based computer network. Terminals close to the central computer can be connected to it directly via an RS-232 or similar interface. Over long distances, a pair of modems are required for each terminal, with an intervening telephone-style link such as a twisted-pair connection; see also Fig. 6.4. Local connections to the modems can follow the RS-232 standard. When the number of terminals is large, one or more special-purpose IO controllers called terminal multiplexers may be employed as depicted in Fig. 6.26*b*. These devices, which are normally transparent both to the terminal users and the central computer, allow the relatively slow terminals to share a high-bandwidth multiplexer-to-multiplexer link, e.g., a telephone line, by

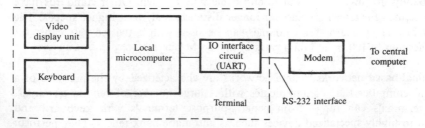

FIGURE 6.25
Architecture of a typical terminal.

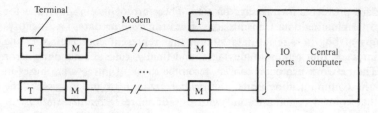

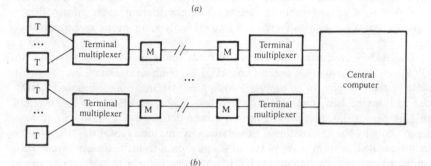

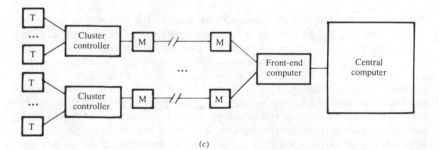

FIGURE 6.26
Examples of terminal-based computer networks.

time-division or, more rarely, frequency-division multiplexing. By this means the cost of the long-distance communication stage is reduced. In more complex networks where rapid response to many terminals is required, the multiplexers are replaced by small computers that form sophisticated communications controllers. Two representative types, a *front-end* computer that handles all communications tasks for the central computer, and *cluster controllers*, each of which manages a group of terminals, are illustrated in Fig. 6.26c. These communications controllers convert all data into multicharacter blocks or messages for more efficient long-distance transmission.

Block-oriented terminal networks of the type illustrated by Fig. 6.26c employ certain standard protocols for message passing. These protocols embody rules for initiating and terminating data transmissions, rules for *framing* data, i.e., identifying the groups of bits in a serial data stream that represent characters and the groups of characters that represent messages, and finally, rules for handling error conditions. The network protocols loosely resemble those of intrasystem buses in that one of the communicating units, the *primary station* or master, issues the commands that control communication with one or more *secondary stations* or slaves. In a terminal-based network, the central computer generally acts as the primary station by, for instance, periodically polling the terminals to request transmission to it of any pending messages. Unlike the bus case, information is transmitted serially over relatively slow and possibly error-prone communication lines.

Two widely used communication protocols for terminal-based networks are BSC (*B*inary *S*ynchronous *C*ontrol) and HDLC (*H*igh-level *D*ata *L*ink *C*ontrol). They have their origins in commercial computer systems, notably those of IBM, whose versions of BSC and HDLC are called Bisync and SDLC (*S*ynchronous *D*ata *L*ink *C*ontrol), respectively. They have been defined as standard communication protocols by the International Standards Organization (ISO). HDLC is more general than BSC in that it supports full-duplex data transmission, whereas BSC is limited to half-duplex operation. HDLC has also come into widespread use in computer-based as well as terminal-based networks.

Example 6.2   The HDLC data communication protocol [9]. The general format of the basic message unit or *frame* in the HDLC format is depicted in Fig. 6.27. The information part is of variable length (from 0 to *n* bits) and is the main data to be communicated, e.g., a line of application-specific code entered by a programmer via a terminal's keyboard. The information field is preceded and followed by 3 bytes of message-control information. The first and last bytes to be transmitted are termed flag fields and serve as delimiters for the frame; they consist of the fixed bit sequence 01111110. The beginning flag is followed by an 8-bit address field which identifies the station to which the frame is being sent. It in turn is followed by an 8-bit control field, whose first two bits place the frame in one of three classes: information (I), supervisory (S), or unnumbered (U).

The I-frame format is the one used for ordinary data transmission. It is characterized by the fact that each frame is transmitted with 3-bit send and receive frame-sequence numbers in its control field; I-frames also have an information field of nonzero length. As a source unit creates a new I-frame, it advances its send

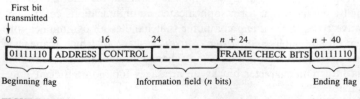

FIGURE 6.27
HDLC frame format.

frame-sequence number by one, so that the destination unit knows which frame to expect next. The destination maintains a receive frame-sequence number; it can therefore detect a missing frame and tell the source which frame to retransmit. The S format is used to initiate and control I-frame transmissions. The control field of an S-frame specifies such network status information as: destination is ready (not ready) to receive data; frame k has been successfully received; frame k has not been successfully received and should be retransmitted. The third (U) format is used to establish and disconnect communication links; its name derives from the fact that no frame-sequence numbers are transmitted. S- and U-frames are the counterparts of command and handshaking signals in bus-control protocols. U-frames require acknowledgment U-frames from the recipient; S-frames do not.

A typical HDLC transaction proceeds via an exchange of frames of various types. It is is set up by the primary station transmitting several U-frames which serve as network commands to the secondary station. The first such frame has a control field containing the command SNRM (*set normal response mode*), which designates the addressed unit as a secondary station. The secondary responds with a U-frame whose control field indicates UA (*unnumbered acknowledgment*) and whose address field contains the secondary's own address, thus allowing the primary to check that the correct secondary is responding. Both the primary and secondary stations also set their respective frame-sequence counters to zero. The primary then transmits a U-frame command such as SARM (*set asynchronous response mode*), which indicates that either station may independently initiate an I-frame transfer. The secondary unit acknowledges SARM with another UA U-frame. The main data transfer then proceeds as a sequence of (duplex) I-frame transmissions. Normal termination of data transmission occurs when the primary transmits the U-frame DISC (disconnect) and the secondary responds with UA. If one device is temporarily unavailable for I-frame transfers, e.g., due to its data buffers being full, it can indicate that to the other device by transmitting an S-frame containing the control-field command RNR (*receive not ready*).

In addition to the error control provided by the checking of frame-sequence numbers and station addresses, every HDLC frame includes a block of 16 parity-check bits which provide error detection for data-transmission errors affecting any part of the frame. The codes used in this application are termed *polynomial* or *CRC* (*cyclic redundancy check*) codes. They are implemented by treating the frame as a number N (a polynomial) and dividing it modulo 2 by a fixed "generator" polynomial G using special hardware. The check bits are computed from the remainder produced by the division process, and are chosen to make the entire frame exactly divisible by G. On receipt of a new frame, the receiving unit repeats the division process and detects an error if the new remainder is nonzero. It can be shown [21] that all single-bit errors and various multiple-bit errors, including *burst* errors, which affect a sequence of consecutive bits (up to 16 in the HDLC case), can be detected. Detection of an error via the check bits causes the receiving unit to request, using an appropriate S-frame message, retransmission of the entire erroneous frame.

Computer-based networks. Next we turn to networks characterized by the presence of multiple distributed computers with decentralized control. This type of network is used extensively for the transmission of files, including electronic mail messages, among users of the different computers on the network. Where communication distances less than a few kilometers are involved, for instance, a computer network within a single building or a university campus, the term *local area network* (LAN) is used. LANs often employ data-transmission links (electrical or optical cables) that are private to the network in question. For computer networks spread over large geographical areas, sometimes termed *wide-area networks* (WANs), the data-transmission facilities are typically supplied by communications companies called *common carriers*, which in many countries are government-owned or -regulated organizations. The various national and international telephone networks are extensively used for both local and long-distance computer communications, but they are increasingly being supplemented by networks designed specifically for digital data transmission. Like the telephone networks, these *public data networks* are composed of a heterogeneous mixture of electrical, optical, and microwave links.

Communication costs are major contributors to the total cost of using a wide-area computer network. There are various techniques for sharing the long-distance communication links to reduce these costs. The establishment of a dedicated data-transmission path from source to destination for each information exchange is called *circuit* or *line switching*. It is the usual mode of communication used in the public telephone network. Circuit switching is initiated by dialing and implemented by telephone exchanges. It has the disadvantage that once a path is established between two locations, it cannot be used by other potential users along the path, even if the utilization of that path is very low.

This problem can be overcome by a technique called *message switching*, whereby intermediate switching centers on a long communication path are used to store data items in a message format like that of Fig. 6.27, and subsequently forward them to the next destination, a process called *store-and-forward*. Messages are collected at each switching center, where they are organized, e.g., grouped into batches, in a manner that makes efficient use of the data paths connected to that center. An analogy can be drawn between message switching and the transmission of mail through the postal system. Compared with circuit switching, message switching can provide a substantial increase in communication-link utilization.

Messages vary greatly in length, so that short messages can be significantly delayed while longer messages are being transmitted. This problem can be minimized in a message-switching system by dividing all messages into short *packets* of fixed length and format and transmitting packets from long messages interspersed with packets from short messages. The store-and-forward switching centers are responsible for sorting the packets from the various messages and transmitting them to their proper next destinations. At the final destination of a message it must be reassembled from its constituent packets. This form of communication, called *packet switching*, is used when very fast communication is required, with small computers acting as the store-and-forward switching centers. We next describe a wide-area packet-switched computer network ARPANET developed by the (Defense) Advanced Research Projects Agency (ARPA, now known as DARPA) around 1970. This influential network served as the prototype for many subsequent packet-switching computer networks.

Example 6.3   The ARPANET computer network [7, 11]. The ARPANET is a large experimental computer network originally designed to link over 50 research institutions in the United States via leased common-carrier lines that have a bandwidth of 50,000 bits/s or more. Figure 6.28 shows the structure of the ARPANET at an early stage in its evolution (1972) when it linked 24 locations ranging from the University of California at Los Angeles (UCLA) to the National Bureau of Standards (NBS) in Washington, D.C. The ARPANET uses packet switching in order to achieve a low average transmission time at reasonable cost. Each node in the network generally contains a small computer called an *interface message processor* (IMP) which performs the store-and-forward functions required for packet switching. An IMP is used to connect one or more computers, called *hosts*, at the same location as the IMP to the ARPANET. Since many different types of computers are used as hosts, the IMP acts as a standard interface device between its hosts and the main long-distance communication network. Each host usually supports a set of interactive IO terminals by which a user gains access to the ARPANET. Facilities also exist to allow IO terminals to be connected directly to the ARPANET without a host computer.

If IMPs are used, a message is transmitted from a source host computer C_1 to a destination host C_2 in the following way. C_1 sends the message to its local IMP, which breaks it into packets of approximately 1000 bits. The IMP then transmits the packets to one or more of the IMPs to which it is directly connected. These IMPs in turn forward the packets toward C_2. The IMPs attempt to choose fast routes through the network based on current traffic conditions, which they continually monitor. Eventually the packets reach the IMP associated with C_2, where the original message is reassembled and sent to C_2.

Some of the original design objectives of the ARPANET are listed below [7].

1. The average packet transmission delay through the network should be less than 0.2 s.
2. The maximum bandwidth for IMP-to-IMP communication should be 85K bits/s.

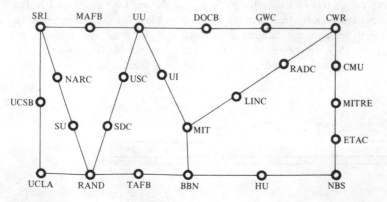

FIGURE 6.28
Structure of the ARPANET, circa 1972.

3. At least two disjoint communication paths should exist between every pair of IMPs.

4. Transmission errors should occur at a rate of 1 bit in 10^{12} or less.

5. The cost of transmitting 1000 packets (about 10^6 bits) should be less than 30 cents.

Figure 6.29 shows the main features of a packet in the ARPANET. The data to be transmitted, which is part of a host-generated message, forms the text field of the packet. The IMP attaches a header field to the text that identifies the packet and specifies its source and destination. Transmission errors are detected by CRC error-detecting codes. Before it forwards a packet, each IMP generates a sequence of check bits, which it attaches to the end of the packet. An IMP retains a copy of each packet it forwards until it receives an acknowledgment signal from the next IMP. If such an acknowledgment is not received, due to detection of a transmission error or because the destination IMP is busy, for example, the source IMP retransmits the packet, perhaps to a different IMP. When an IMP receives a packet from another IMP, it checks the packet for errors. If the packet is found to be error-free, it is stored and an acknowledgment signal is transmitted to the source IMP. The latter may then release the storage area containing its copy of the packet.

Unlike terminal-based networks, the more general computer-based variety frequently contain different types of computers from several manufacturers. Consequently, a standard approach to network design, termed a *network architecture*, is required if the networked computers are to communicate efficiently. This, in turn, requires agreement about hardware and software interfaces and the associated communications protocols at several different levels. Individual computer manufacturers have developed their own network architectures, e.g., IBM's SNA (*System Network Architecture*) and DEC's DECnet. These architectures are generally mutually incompatible in that the corresponding networks cannot be linked together without the use of special network interfaces or *gateways*, which are often expensive and degrade communication speed and flexibility.

Although the goal of a universal or *open system* network to which any manufacturer's computers can be attached remains elusive, ISO developed in the late 1970s a set of guidelines that provide a common basis for computer network design and the development of standard network architectures. These guidelines are known as the *ISO Reference Model for Open Systems Interconnection*. The ISO Reference Model defines a hierarchical set of seven functional levels or *layers*

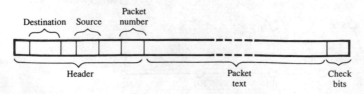

FIGURE 6.29
The ARPANET packet format.

through which users exchange messages in a computer network; these layers are specified in Fig. 6.30. Each layer is associated with certain network services, e.g., error control, and different computers on a network can be thought of as exchanging information between corresponding layers. Consequently, for each layer a separate and possibly standard communication protocol can be defined. The HDLC protocol described earlier (Example 6.2) is an example of a link-layer protocol, while the RS-232/V.24 interface forms the basis of the physical layer in many networks. In general, layers 1 to 3 of the ISO Reference Model involve services associated with data communications functions close to the network hardware, while layers 5 to 7 involve operating systems functions close to the network user. The intermediate transport layer (layer 4) serves to interface the operating system with the network hardware.

LANs. Wide-area networks rely primarily on the public or common-carrier telephone and data networks to provide data-transmission services. The telephone networks are circuit-switched, while both circuit and packet switching are employed by the public data networks. Because of the distances involved and the way the communications facilities are shared, the maximum data-transfer rates over these networks are modest, e.g., 300 to 4800 bits/s through the telephone network. Local area networks, which typically employ short and dedicated connections, can provide much higher data-transmission rates (1M bits/s or more). As low-cost personal computers have proliferated in industrial companies, universities, etc., LANs have become commonplace, and increasingly are linked via gateways to WANs such as the public data networks. A given computer may be directly connected to a LAN that provides rapid access to local resources and, via a network interface processor, slower access to resources on WANs to which the LAN is linked. This effectively creates a "supernetwork" linking vast numbers of computers that can potentially communicate with one another.

In general, we can define a LAN to be a set of independent computers

Layer	Associated services
1. Physical	Electrical and mechanical hardware interfacing to the physical communication medium
2. Link	Message setup, transmission, and error control
3. Network	Establishing message paths in the network (message routing and flow control)
4. Transport	Interfacing network-independent messages with the specific network being used
5. Session	Creation and management of communication channels between the communicating applications programs
6. Presentation	Data-transformation services such as character-code translation or encryption
7. Application	Providing network support functions such as file transfer routines to application programs (network users)

FIGURE 6.30
The protocol layers of the ISO Reference Model.

connected together by short and fast communication links. These links can take several forms, especially serial versions of the bus and ring structures depicted in Figs. 6.6 and 6.8, respectively. The physical data-transmission medium may be a twisted pair, a coaxial cable, or an optical-fiber cable. The electrical media have the advantage of being easy to tap into in order to attach new devices to the network; equivalent connections to an optical link are more difficult to make. The higher-bandwidth transmission media can support frequency-division multiplexing, an operating mode termed *broadband* in this context. A LAN not employing frequency-division multiplexing is termed *baseband*. A CATV (*community antenna television*) or cable TV network is an example of a broadband bus-structured local network that distributes television signals to subscribers via coaxial cable.

A representative bus-oriented baseband LAN technology for computers is *Ethernet*, which was defined as an industrial standard by DEC, Intel, and Xerox Corps. in 1980, and has been widely adopted since then [3]. The Ethernet specification involves only the physical and data-link layers of a LAN. Computer-specific hardware (Ethernet controllers) and software (Ethernet driver routines) are needed to implement the remaining layers of network control. At the physical level, an Ethernet LAN has the structure shown in Fig. 6.31, with a coaxial cable of bandwidth 10 million bits/s forming the backbone of the network. Up to 1024 nodes can be connected to the network and their maximum separation is limited to 2.8 km. Several cable segments may be linked together by repeaters as shown in Fig. 6.31, to form a treelike network of buses. At the data-link level, communication is by messages (also called packets or frames) that contain the usual address, control, and check bits, as well as a variable-length data field. Total message length can range from 64 to 1518 bytes. Physical connections to the coaxial cable are made by a tap unit containing receivers and drivers, as well as the logic for bus arbitration (collision detection) discussed below. This unit is connected via a cable containing several twisted pairs to an Ethernet communications controller in the computer node.

Access to the Ethernet and some other LANs is controlled by an arbitration technique called *CSMA/CD (carrier sense multiple access with collision detection)*. A node (computer) that wishes to transmit a message over the Ethernet first senses (listens to) the coaxial cable via its tap unit, and transmits the message only if it detects no carrier signal, in which case the network is not currently in use. Each message is broadcast throughout the network, and its destination address is examined by all nodes as it reaches them; only the node whose address matches that of the message header actually reads the message. Since all computers on the network have equal access to the coaxial cable, it is possible for two nodes to begin message transmission at the same time. Consequently, as it transmits a message, each node monitors the actual signals on the cable and compares them with the signals that it is transmitting. If the transmitted and detected signals differ, which will be the case if another computer is transmitting a message at the same time, then a *collision* is said to have occurred. On detecting a collision, an Ethernet node ceases transmission and tries to retransmit the same message at a

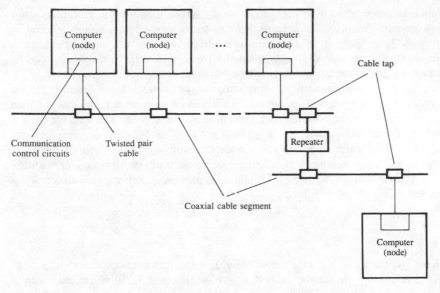

FIGURE 6.31
Structure of a bus-organized LAN (Ethernet).

later time. The time of retransmission is randomly selected by the nodes so that the chances of another collision are slight, although repeated collisions do occur. Measurements of Ethernet performance show that this arbitration scheme is fair, in that if n nodes request continuous access to the network over some period of time T, each node will gain access to the network for a period very close to T/n [23]. The loss of bandwidth due to collisions, even under heavy load conditions, is modest, e.g., less than 10 percent.

Another common technique for controlling access to a LAN is *token passing*, where each node in turn receives and passes on the right to access the network; this right is represented by a special short message called a *token*. The node that possesses the token has exclusive use of the network for transmitting a message, after which it transmits the token to another (fixed) node. Token passing is most commonly used in ring networks, called *token rings*, but is also used for bus-structured LANs (*token buses*). When a token ring is not passing normal messages, the token circulates from node to node around the network. A node having a message to transmit waits until the token reaches it. It then holds the token while it transmits its message. Note that in a ring network, a (nontoken) message is usually passed in one direction from node to node until it reaches the destination node; it may then be forwarded back to the source node to confirm its receipt. After transmitting one message, a node puts the token back into circulation, so that all nodes get roughly equal access to the network.

Network delay. Probably the single most useful measure of communication network performance is the average delay t_D encountered by a message in traveling through the network from its source to its destination. t_D and related parameters can be effectively analyzed using queueing theory [18, 19]. Useful results can be obtained using the single-queue single-server model introduced in Sec. 2.4.4.

First consider a network consisting of a single link or channel L that connects two computers. The computers are viewed as generating messages which request service in the form of data transmission through L. The message arrival rate at L can reasonably be assumed to follow a Poisson distribution with exponential interarrival times. The service (transmission) time depends on many factors, including message length and the bandwidth of the transmission medium. If an exponential service time distribution is assumed, then the network delay is defined by Eq. (2.28) as follows:

$$t_D = \frac{1}{\mu - \lambda}$$

where λ is the mean message arrival rate, μ is the mean service rate, and $\mu > \lambda$. The message length can be treated as an independent random variable with a mean value of m bits. The link L is characterized by its bandwidth or channel capacity c bits per second. The mean service time $1/\mu$ can therefore be taken as m/c. Hence the delay t_D can be rewritten as

$$t_D = \frac{1}{c/m - \lambda} \tag{6.1}$$

The average message delay t_D in a network containing n links $\{L_i\}$ can be modeled by treating each link as a queue with a single server. t_D then has the form

$$t_D = \sum_i \frac{\lambda_i t_i}{\gamma} \tag{6.2}$$

where t_i is the average message waiting time in link L_i, λ_i is its average traffic in messages per second, and γ is the total (Poisson) arrival rate of messages to the network from external sources [18]. Let c_i be the bandwidth of L_i in bits per second and let m be the average length of a message. The mean time taken by L_i to service a message is $m/c_i = 1/\mu$. If we assume that the service time of L_i is exponential, then t_i is defined by (6.1), so that (6.2) can be rewritten as

$$t_D = \sum_i \frac{\lambda_i}{\gamma(c_i/m - \lambda_i)}$$

While Poisson arrival distributions or, equivalently, exponential interarrival time distributions, model the arrival process fairly accurately, the service process is often far from exponential. Consider a single-queue single-server model with Poisson arrivals and an arbitrary service-time distribution characterized by a mean value of $1/\mu$ and a standard deviation of σ. Any queueing discipline that is independent of service time may be used. Under steady-state conditions, the mean queue length l_Q is defined by the *Khinchin-Pollaczek equation* [19]

$$l_Q = \rho + \rho^2 \frac{1 + \sigma^2 \mu^2}{2(1 - \rho)} \qquad (6.3)$$

This is considered to be the fundamental equation for analyzing single-server systems. Note that with exponential service times, $\sigma = 1/\mu$ and (6.3) reduces to (2.26). The mean waiting time or delay t_D follows from (6.3) by Little's equation $t_D = l_Q/\lambda$. No corresponding expressions for l_Q or t_Q are known when the arrival distribution is arbitrary, i.e., non-Poisson. The parameter $\rho = \lambda/\mu$ measures the utilization of the communication links—hence its name "traffic intensity."

Reliability. Let G be a graph with n nodes V and m edges E representing a computer network. The nodes V represent computers or IO terminals, while the edges E represent communication links. For simplicity it will be assumed that these links are bidirectional (half or full duplex) and that G is an undirected graph. Two nodes v_i and v_j are connected if there exists at least one path between v_i and v_j; otherwise they are disconnected. Of prime interest is the possibility of failures that disconnect any two nodes of G. Such failures can be modeled by the removal of nodes or edges from G. We assume that when a node is removed, all edges connected to that node are also removed.

Two basic nonprobabilistic measures of network reliability are the node and edge connectivity of G. The *node connectivity* (or simply the *connectivity*) $c_N(G)$ is defined as the smallest number of nodes whose removal disconnects G, that is, eliminates all paths between at least two nodes, or else reduces G to the trivial 1-node 0-edge graph G_T. Similarly, the *edge connectivity* (or *cohesion*) $c_E(G)$ is the smallest number of edges whose removal disconnects G or reduces it to G_T. The complete graph K_n with n nodes and all $n(n-1)/2$ possible edges, such as that of Fig. 6.5, cannot be disconnected by node removal. It can be reduced to G_T, however, by removing $n-1$ nodes; hence $c_N(K_n) = n - 1$. K_n can be disconnected by removing the $n-1$ edges connected to any one node; hence $c_E(K_n) = n - 1$. It can be shown [10] that for any graph G, edge and node connectivity are related by the inequality $c_N(G) \le c_E(G)$. Unfortunately, it is very difficult to compute the connectivity of an arbitrary large graph.

A frequent assumption made in the analysis of faults in computers is that only single faults, i.e., the failure of just one component, need be considered. This assumes that a fault can be detected and repaired before another occurs. The class of networks that can tolerate a single fault represented by the removal of a node or edge can be characterized by the following result, which is proven in Ref. 10. $c_N(G) \ge 2$ if and only if every pair of nodes in G lie on a common closed loop (cycle). Tolerance of a single failure of this type is a design requirement of the

ARPANET. Clearly the foregoing condition is satisfied by the graph in Fig. 6.28. Thus a single node removal cannot destroy communication in a network if and only if every pair of nodes lie on a closed loop. Since $c_N(G) \le c_E(G)$, this condition is also sufficient (but not necessary) for a network to remain connected after the removal of a single edge. Figure 6.32 shows a graph G with $c_N(G) = 1$ but $c_E(G) = 2$. The single node v_3, whose removal disconnects G, is called a *cutpoint*; it represents the most sensitive node in the graph.

Suppose that in a network containing n links, each link has a probability p of failing. A natural question is: What is the probability $f(p)$ of the network becoming disconnected, so that communication between at least two nodes becomes impossible? The failure probability $f(p)$ may be expressed as

$$f(p) = \sum_{i=0}^{n} C(i)\, p^i\, (1-p)^{n-i} \tag{6.4}$$

where $C(i)$ is the number of sets of i links called *cutsets* whose failure disconnects the original network, and all link failures are assumed to be independent. A measure of the network reliability is $r(p) = 1 - f(p)$. The main difficulty in using $f(p)$ and $r(p)$ is computing $C(i)$. $C(i)$ can be determined by enumeration if n is reasonably small. In the case of very large networks, it may be necessary to use approximate methods such as simulation to compute $C(i)$.

6.2 INPUT-OUTPUT SYSTEMS

The main computing function of a computer involves only two of its components, the CPU and main memory. The CPU fetches instructions and data from main memory, processes them, and stores results in main memory. The other components of the computer may be loosely called the input-output (IO) system, since their purpose is to transfer information between main memory or the CPU and the outside world. The IO system includes IO devices (peripherals), control units for these devices, and the software designed to carry out IO operations.

IO systems may be distinguished by the extent to which the CPU is involved in the execution of IO operations. Unless otherwise stated, IO operation will mean a data transfer between an IO device and main memory, or between an IO device and the CPU. If IO operations are completely controlled by the CPU, i.e., the CPU executes programs that initiate, direct, and terminate the IO operations, the

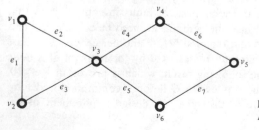

FIGURE 6.32
A graph G with $c_N(G) = 1$ and $c_E(G) = 2$.

computer is said to be using *programmed IO*. Programmed IO is an option in almost all computers. It can be implemented with very little special IO hardware, but can result in the CPU spending a great deal of time performing relatively trivial IO control functions. One such function is testing the status of IO devices to determine if they require servicing by the CPU.

With a fairly modest increase in hardware complexity the IO device can be provided with the ability to transfer a block of information to or from main memory without CPU intervention. This requires that the IO device (or its controller) be capable of generating memory addresses and transferring data to or from the system bus, i.e., it must be a bus master. The CPU is still responsible for initiating each block transfer. The IO device controller can then carry out the transfer without further program execution by the CPU. The CPU and IO controller interact only when the CPU must yield control of the system bus to the IO controller in response to requests from the latter. This type of IO capability is called *direct memory access* (DMA).

The IO device or its controller can also be provided with circuits enabling it to request service from the CPU, i.e., execution of a specific program to service the IO device. This type of request is called an *interrupt*. An interrupt capability frees the CPU from the task of periodically testing IO device status. Unlike a DMA request, an interrupt causes the CPU to switch programs by saving its previous program state and transferring control to a new interrupt-handling program. When the interrupt has been serviced, the CPU can resume execution of the interrupted program. Most computers now have DMA and interrupt facilities, which may require that the system's IO interface contain special DMA and interrupt control units.

A DMA controller has partial control of IO operations. Essentially complete control of IO operations can be relinquished by the CPU if an *IO processor* (IOP) or *channel* is introduced. Like a DMA controller, an IOP has direct access to main memory and can interrupt the CPU; however, it can also execute programs directly. These programs, called IO programs, may employ an instruction set different from that of the CPU—one which is oriented toward IO operations. It is not uncommon for larger systems to use small computers as IOPs. An IOP can perform several independent data transfers between main memory and one or more IO devices, without recourse to the CPU. Usually an IOP is connected to the devices it controls by a separate bus system, called the IO bus or IO interface, as illustrated in Fig. 6.1*b*.

6.2.1 Programmed IO

First we examine programmed IO, a method for controlling IO operations, which is included in most computers. It is particularly useful in small low-speed systems where hardware costs must be minimized. It requires that all IO operations be executed under the direct control of the CPU, i.e., every data-transfer operation involving an IO device requires the execution of an instruction by the CPU. Typically the transfer is between a CPU register, e.g., the accumulator, and a buffer register connected to the IO device. The IO device does not have direct access to main memory. A data transfer from an IO device to main memory requires the execution of several instructions by the CPU, including an input instruction to transfer a word from the IO device to the CPU and a store instruction to transfer the word from the CPU to main memory. One or two additional instructions may be needed for address computation and data word counting.

IO addressing. In systems with programmed IO, IO devices, main memory, and the CPU normally communicate via a common shared bus (the system bus). The address lines of that bus which are used to select main-memory locations can also be used to select IO devices. Each junction between the system bus and the IO device is called an *IO port* and is assigned a unique address. The IO port includes a data buffer register, thus making it little different from a main-memory location with respect to the CPU.

A strategy used in some machines, such as the Motorola 68000 microprocessor series, is to assign part of the main-memory address space to IO ports. This is called *memory-mapped* IO. A memory reference instruction that causes data to be fetched from or stored at address X automatically becomes an IO instruction if X is made the address of an IO port. The usual memory load and store instructions are used to transfer a word of data to or from an IO port; no special IO instructions are needed. Figure 6.33 shows the essential structure of a computer with this kind of IO addressing. The control lines READ and WRITE, which are activated by the CPU on decoding a memory reference instruction, are used to initiate either a memory access cycle or an IO transfer.

In the organization shown in Fig. 6.34, and sometimes called *IO-mapped* IO, the memory and IO address spaces are kept separate. A memory reference instruction activates the READ M or WRITE M control line and does not affect the IO devices. Separate IO instructions are required to activate the READ IO and WRITE IO lines, which cause a word to be transferred between the addressed IO port and the CPU. An IO device and a main-memory location may have the same address. This scheme is used, for example, in the Intel 8085 and 8086

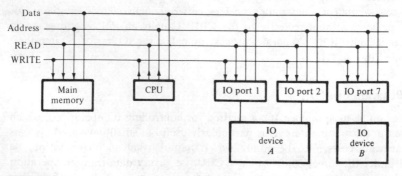

FIGURE 6.33
Programmed IO with shared memory and IO address space (memory-mapped IO).

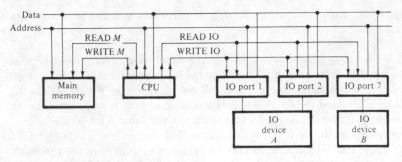

FIGURE 6.34
Programmed IO with separate memory and IO address space (IO-mapped IO).

microprocessor series. A minor modification of the circuit of Fig. 6.34 can combine the memory and IO address spaces if desired. All that is necessary is to disconnect the READ IO and WRITE IO lines from the CPU and reconnect them to the READ M and WRITE M outputs of the CPU.

IO instructions. Programmed IO can be implemented by as few as two IO instructions. For example, the Intel 8085 has two main IO instructions. The instruction IN X causes a word to be transferred from IO port X to the 8085's accumulator register A. The instruction OUT X transfers a word from the accumulator to IO port X. The CPU assigns no meaning to the words transferred to IO devices. The programmer may assign special meanings to them, however. Some words may indicate IO device status and others may be instructions to the IO device.

When an IO instruction such as IN or OUT is encountered by the CPU, the addressed IO port is expected to be ready to respond to the instruction. This generally means that the IO device must transfer data to or from the data bus within a specified period. To prevent loss of information or an indefinitely long IO instruction execution time, it is thus desirable that the CPU know the IO device status, so that a data transfer is carried out when the device is in a known ready state. In programmed IO systems the CPU is usually programmed to test the IO device status before initiating a data transfer. Often the status can be specified by a single bit of information that the IO device can make available on a continuous basis, e.g., by setting a flip-flop connected to the data lines at some IO port.

The determination of IO device status by the CPU requires the following steps.

Step 1. Read the status information.

Step 2. Test the status to determine if the device is ready to begin data transfer.

Step 3. If not ready, return to step 1; otherwise proceed with the data transfer.

Figure 6.35 shows a program written for the Intel 8085 microprocessor that transfers a word of data from an IO device to the CPU accumulator. It is assumed that the device is connected to ports 1 and 2 like device A in Fig. 6.33. The IO device status is assumed to be continuously available at port 1, while the required data is available at port 2 when the status word has the value READY.

If programmed IO is the primary method of controlling IO devices in a computer, additional IO instructions may be provided to augment the simple IN and OUT instructions discussed so far. For example, the DEC PDP-8 has a useful IO instruction TSK which tests the status of the IO device and modifies the CPU program counter based on the test outcome. TSK, which means test IO device status flag and skip the next instruction if the status flag is set, can be implemented by two control lines between the CPU and the IO device, as shown in Fig. 6.36. On decoding TSK, a signal called TEST STATUS is sent by the CPU to the IO device. If the device status flag is set, a return pulse is sent on the SKIP line which is used to increment the program counter, thereby skipping the next instruction. Given an instruction of this type, the IO program of Fig. 6.35 could be simplified as follows:

```
WAIT: TSK   1
      JMP   WAIT
      IN    2
```

A common IO programming task is the transfer of a block of words between an IO device and a contiguous region of main memory. Figure 6.37 shows an input block-transfer program written in Intel 8085 assembly language. (It is assumed that the input device generates data at the rate required by the CPU, so that no status testing is needed.) The Zilog Z80, a microprocessor that is software compatible with the 8085, provides a single instruction INIR (*in*put, *in*dex, and *re*peat) which performs essentially all the functions specified by the last five instructions in Fig. 6.37. Specifically, INIR inputs a word from the IO port addressed by the C register and transfers it to the memory location addressed by the H.L register. It then increments H.L, decrements B (which is used as a word-

Instruction	Comment
WAIT: IN 1	Read IO device status into accumulator
CPI READY	Compare immediate word READY to accumulator; if equal, set flag $Z = 1$, otherwise set $Z = 0$
JNZ WAIT	If $Z \neq 1$ (IO device not ready) jump to WAIT
IN 2	Read data word into accumulator

FIGURE 6.35
Intel 8085 program to read one word from an IO device.

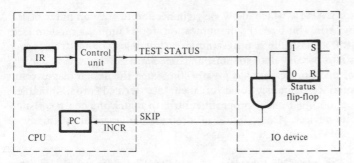

FIGURE 6.36
Implementation of the test status and skip (TSK) IO instruction.

count register), and repeats the transfer, increment, and decrement steps until B = 0. Thus, ignoring differences between 8085 and Z80 instruction names, the 8085/Z80 program of Fig. 6.37 is equivalent to the following Z80 program:

$$
\begin{array}{ll}
\text{LXI} & \text{H, 10} \\
\text{MVI} & \text{B, 100} \\
\text{MVI} & \text{C, 7} \\
\text{INIR} &
\end{array}
$$

It is interesting to compare these instructions to the INPUT and OUTPUT instructions of the IAS computer described in Sec. 1.2.3.

IO interface circuits. The connection of IO devices to a computer system is greatly facilitated by the use of standard circuit packages variously known as IO interface circuits, peripheral interface adapters, etc. These circuits allow devices of widely different characteristics to be connected to a common system bus with a minimum of special-purpose hardware. The simplest interface circuit is a one-word buffer register that acts as an IO port. It is assigned a unique address and is accessed in essentially the same way as a main-memory location. This circuit is particularly useful for parallel (word-by-word) IO communication. Another useful class of

Instruction		Comments
LXI	H, 10	Load memory address register H.L with 10
MVI	B, 100	Load (move immediate) register B with 100
LOOP: IN	7	Read word from input port 7 into accumulator A
MOV	M, A	Store contents of A in memory location M(H.L)
INX	H	Increment memory address register H.L
DCR	B	Decrement register B (used as a byte counter)
JNZ	LOOP	If B ≠ 0, jump to LOOP

FIGURE 6.37
An assembly-language program to input a block of data.

interface circuits are UARTs, which allow easy connection to the computer of IO devices that employ serial (bit-by-bit) communication, for example, a modem (see Fig. 6.25). A UART is basically a programmable shift register that transforms serial data streams into parallel data streams, and vice versa.

The advent of microprocessors has greatly stimulated the design of powerful general-purpose interface circuits. Some of them are termed programmable, because they can be modified under program control to match the characteristics of many different IO devices. A description of a representative circuit of this type follows.

Example 6.4   The Intel 8255 programmable peripheral interface circuit [16]. This circuit, whose general structure is shown in Fig. 6.38, is designed for interfacing IO devices with the Intel 8085 and other 8-bit microprocessors. It is fabricated as a single integrated circuit in a 40-pin DIP: 8 pins serve to connect the 8255 to the 8-bit bidirectional data bus of the CPU; 24 IO pins can be connected to one or more IO devices. These IO pins are programmable in that the functions they perform are determined by a control word issued by a CPU instruction and stored internally in the 8255. This control word can be used to specify a variety of operating modes.

The 24 IO pins of the 8255 are divided into 8-bit groups designated A, B, and C, each of which may be treated as an independent IO port. The C lines are further subdivided into two 4-bit groups C_A and C_B. They are commonly used as control lines, e.g., status or handshaking lines, in conjunction with the A and B IO ports. Two address lines A_0 and A_1 are used to select one of the three ports A, B, and C for use in an IO operation. The fourth address combination is used in conjunction

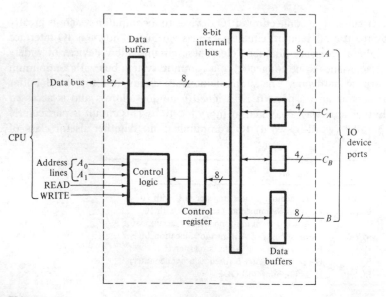

FIGURE 6.38
The Intel 8255 programmable peripheral interface circuit.

with an output instruction OUT CW to store an 8-bit user-specified control word CW in the internal control register of the 8255. This control word has two major functions:

1. It is used to specify whether the A, B, and C ports are to be used as input, output, or (in the case of A and B only) as bidirectional IO ports.
2. It is used to program certain C lines to generate handshaking and interrupt signals automatically in response to actions by an IO device.

Figure 6.39 shows two of the many possible configurations in which the A, B, and C lines are programmed as simple IO ports with no handshaking or interrupt capability. Figure 6.40 shows a configuration in which the A port is programmed to be an input port with timing signals generated by the C lines. The line called DATA READY is used by the IO device to strobe a word into the buffer register at port A. The 8255 then automatically generates a response signal on another C line, which can be sent to the IO device as a DATA ACKNOWLEDGE signal if two-way control is required by the IO device. A third C line generates an interrupt signal which can be sent to the CPU to indicate the presence of data at IO port A.

6.2.2 DMA and Interrupts

The programmed IO method discussed in the preceding section has two main drawbacks.

1. IO transfer rates are limited by the speed with which the CPU can test and service an IO device.
2. The time that the CPU spends testing IO device status and executing IO data transfers can often be better spent on other processing tasks.

The influence of the CPU on IO transfer rates is twofold. First, a delay may occur while an IO device that requires service waits to be tested by the CPU. If there are many IO devices in the system, each device may be tested relatively infrequently. Second, programmed IO transmits data through the CPU rather than allowing it to be passed directly from main memory to the IO device, and vice versa.

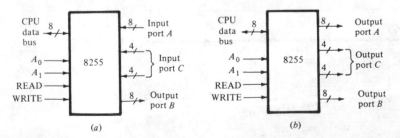

(a) (b)

FIGURE 6.39
Two possible configurations of the Intel 8255 programmable peripheral interface circuit.

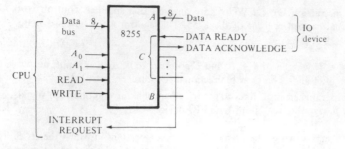

FIGURE 6.40
Configuration of the Intel 8255 to generate handshaking signals and interrupt requests.

DMA and interrupt circuits are used to increase the speed of IO operations and eliminate most of the role played by the CPU in such operations. In each case special control lines to which we assign the generic names DMA REQUEST and INTERRUPT REQUEST go from the IO devices to the CPU. Signals on these lines cause the CPU to suspend its current activities at an appropriate breakpoint and attend to the DMA or interrupt request. Thus the need for the CPU to execute routines that determine IO device status is eliminated. DMA further allows IO data transfers to take place without the execution of IO instructions by the CPU.

A DMA request by an IO device requires the CPU only to yield control of the main-memory (system) bus to the requesting device. The CPU can yield control at the end of any transactions involving the use of this bus. Figure 6.41 shows a typical sequence of CPU actions during an instruction cycle. The instruction cycle is divided into a number of CPU cycles, several of which require use of the system bus. A common technique is to allow the machine to respond to a DMA request at the end of any CPU cycle. Thus during the instruction cycle of Fig. 6.41, there are five points in time (breakpoints) when the CPU can respond to a DMA request. When such a request is received by the CPU, it waits until the

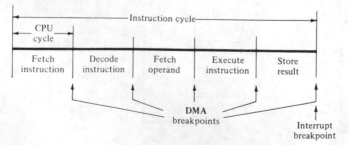

FIGURE 6.41
DMA and interrupt breakpoints during an instruction cycle.

next breakpoint, releases the system bus, and signals the requesting IO device by activating a DMA ACKNOWLEDGE control line.

Interrupts are requested and acknowledged in much the same way as DMA requests. However, an interrupt is not a request for bus control; rather, it asks the CPU to begin executing an interrupt service program. The interrupt program may perform a variety of tasks, such as initiating an IO data transfer, responding to an error encountered by the IO device, etc. The CPU transfers control to this program in essentially the same way it transfers control to a subroutine. The CPU responds to interrupts only between instruction cycles, as indicated in Fig. 6.41.

Direct memory access (DMA). The essential elements of a DMA system are shown in Fig. 6.42. The IO device is connected to the system bus via a special interface circuit, a *DMA controller*, which contains a data buffer register IODR as in the programmed IO case; but in addition there is an address register IOAR and a data count register DC. These registers allow the DMA controller to transfer data to or from a contiguous region of main memory. IOAR is used to store the address of the next word to be transferred. It is automatically incremented after each word transfer. The data count register DC stores the number of words that remain to be transferred. It is automatically decremented after each transfer and tested for zero. When the data count reaches zero, the DMA transfer halts. The controller is normally provided with an interrupt capability, in which case it sends an interrupt to the CPU to signal the end of the data transfer. The logic necessary to control DMA can easily be placed in a single integrated circuit. DMA controllers are available that can supervise DMA transfers involving several IO devices, each with a different priority of access to the system bus.

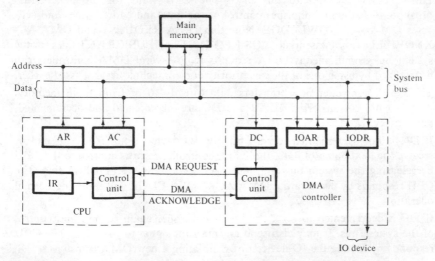

FIGURE 6.42
Circuitry required for direct memory access (DMA).

Data can be transferred in several different ways under DMA control. In a *DMA block transfer* a data-word sequence of arbitrary length is transferred in a single continuous burst while the DMA controller is master of the system bus. This DMA mode is needed by secondary memory devices like magnetic-disk drives where data transmission cannot be stopped or slowed down without loss of data, and block transfers are the norm. Block DMA supports the maximum IO data-transmission rates, but it may require the CPU to remain inactive for relatively long periods. An alternative DMA technique termed *cycle stealing* allows the DMA controller to use the system bus to transfer one, or perhaps several, data words, after which it must return control of the bus to the CPU. This means that long blocks of IO data are transferred by a sequence of DMA bus transactions interspersed with CPU bus transactions. Cycle stealing reduces the maximum IO transfer rate, but it also reduces the interference by the DMA controller in the CPU's activities. It is possible to eliminate this interference completely by designing the DMA interface so that bus cycles are stolen only when the CPU is not actually using the system bus; this is *transparent DMA*. Thus varying degrees of overlap between CPU and DMA operations are possible to accommodate the many different data-transfer characteristics of IO devices.

DMA transfers proceed as follows for the system depicted in Fig. 6.42.

1. The CPU executes two IO instructions, which load the DMA registers IOAR and DC with their initial values. IOAR should contain the base address of the main-memory region to be used in the data transfer. DC should contain the number of words to be transferred to or from that region.

2. When the DMA controller is ready to transmit or receive data, it activates the DMA REQUEST line to the CPU. The CPU waits for the next DMA breakpoint. It then relinquishes control of the data and address lines and activates DMA ACKNOWLEDGE. Note that DMA REQUEST and DMA ACKNOWLEDGE are essentially BUS REQUEST and BUS GRANT lines for the system bus. Simultaneous DMA requests from several DMA controllers can be resolved by using one of the bus priority control techniques discussed earlier.

3. The DMA controller now transfers data directly to or from main memory. After a word is transferred, IOAR and DC are incremented and decremented, respectively.

4. If DC is not decremented to zero but the IO device is not ready to send or receive the next batch of data, the DMA controller returns control to the CPU by releasing the system bus and deactivating the DMA REQUEST line. The CPU responds by deactivating DMA ACKNOWLEDGE and resuming normal operation.

5. If DC is decremented to zero, the DMA controller again relinquishes control of the system bus. It may also send an interrupt signal to the CPU. The CPU responds by halting the IO device or by initiating a new DMA transfer.

As observed earlier, DMA control is often subsumed under a general method for bus arbitration. In Motorola 68000-series computers, for example, the system bus is designed to accommodate various types of bus masters including DMA controllers and certain coprocessors designated DMA coprocessors. Three control lines are provided for bus arbitration: bus request $\overline{BR}$, bus grant $\overline{BG}$, and bus grant acknowledge $\overline{BGACK}$. The $\overline{BR}$ line is an input control line to the CPU and is wire-ORed to all other potential bus masters. It is activated ($\overline{BR} = 0$) when one of those devices U, e.g., a DMA controller, requires control of the system bus. The CPU responds by activating $\overline{BG}$ and relinquishing control of the system bus at the end of its current bus cycle, which it does by driving the data, address, and certain control lines to the high-impedance state. The requesting unit U detects the end of the bus cycle by monitoring these control lines, at which point it activates $\overline{BGACK}$ and deactivates its $\overline{BR}$ signal. The CPU responds to $\overline{BGACK}$ by deactivating $\overline{BG}$. This completes the bus arbitration process. U is now the new bus master and may carry out an arbitrary number of DMA read or write operations. U returns the system bus to the CPU by deactivating $\overline{BGACK}$.

Many CPUs such as those of the 68000 series have no internal mechanisms for resolving multiple DMA requests; this must be done by external logic. Bus access priority is controlled by passing the DMA (bus) grant signal from the CPU through appropriate priority logic to the potential bus masters. External logic may also be needed to implement cycle stealing by forcing the requesting device to deactivate its DMA request signal after some number of bus cycles. In 68000-based machines, these and other DMA control functions are implemented by the Motorola 68450 DMA controller IC, which is designed to support up to four independent and concurrent DMA operations via the 68000 system bus. The 68450 thus contains four copies of the basic DMA controller logic of Fig. 6.42, each constituting a separate *DMA channel*. Additional programmable registers in each DMA channel determine the priority assigned to the channel and the data-transfer modes to be used. A "chaining" mode of operation is supported that allows a channel to reinitialize its address register IOAR and data count register DC automatically at the end of the current block transfer. This enables the 68450 to carry out a sequence of DMA block transfers without reference to the CPU. When its current data count reaches zero, a DMA channel that has been programmed for chained DMA transfers fetches new values of DC and IOAR from a memory region MR that stores a set of DC-IOAR pairs. A special memory address register in every DMA channel holds the base address of MR.

Interrupts. The term interrupt is used in a loose sense for any infrequent or exceptional event that causes a CPU to make a temporary transfer of control from its current program to another program that services the event. Interrupts may be generated by a variety of sources internal and external to the CPU. Interrupts are the primary means by which IO devices obtain the services of the CPU. They greatly increase the performance of the computer by allowing the IO devices direct and rapid access to the CPU and by freeing the CPU from the task of continually testing the status of its IO devices. Interrupts are used primarily to request the CPU to initiate a new IO operation, to signal the completion of an IO operation, and to signal the occurrence of hardware or software errors. Interrupts generated internally by a CPU are called *traps*, and result from such programming errors as an attempt to divide by zero, or attempting to execute a privileged instruction when not in the privileged (operating system) state.

The basic method of interrupting the CPU is by activating a control line (interrupt request) that connects the interrupt source to the CPU. The interrupt signal is then stored in a CPU register which is tested periodically by the CPU, usually at the end of every instruction cycle. On recognizing the presence of the interrupt, the CPU must execute a specific interrupt servicing program. Normally each interrupt source will require execution of a different program; the CPU must therefore determine or be given the address in main memory of the specific interrupt program to be used. A further problem is caused by the presence of two or more interrupt requests at the same time. Priorities must be assigned to the interrupts and the interrupt with the highest priority selected for service.

The CPU responds to an interrupt request by a transfer of control to another program in a manner similar to a subroutine call. The following specific steps are taken.

1. The CPU identifies the source of the interrupt. This may require polling the IO devices.
2. The CPU obtains the memory address of the required interrupt servicing program. This address may be provided by the interrupting device along with its interrupt request.
3. The program counter and other CPU status information are saved as in a subroutine call.
4. The program counter is loaded with the address of the interrupt servicing program. Execution proceeds until a return instruction is encountered, which transfers control back to the interrupted program.

Instructions are usually included in the CPU instruction set for *disabling* or *masking* interrupt requests. Such instructions allow a programmer to effectively disconnect some or all of the interrupt request lines, causing the CPU to ignore certain interrupts. Without such control, an IO device that can generate interrupts rapidly might require too much of the CPU's time and interfere with the CPU's other tasks. When a high-priority interrupt is being serviced, it is desirable that all interrupts of lower priority be disabled. An interrupt enable instruction must subsequently be executed to give the lower-priority interrupts access to the CPU.

Interrupt selection. The problem of selecting one IO device to service from several that have generated interrupts bears a strong resemblance to the arbitration process for bus control discussed in Sec. 6.1.2. Indeed, some interrupt methods require that the interrupting device be given control of the system bus. The various methods used for bus arbitration, daisy-chaining, polling, and independent requesting can all be readily adapted to interrupt processing. These techniques can be implemented by software, hardware, or a combination of both.

The interrupt selection method requiring the least hardware is the *single-line* method illustrated in Fig. 6.43. A single INTERRUPT REQUEST line is shared

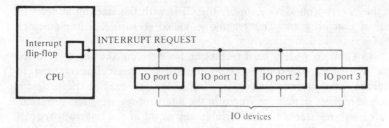

FIGURE 6.43
Single-line interrupt system.

by all IO ports. On responding to an interrupt, the CPU must scan all the IO devices to determine the source of the interrupt. This may be done by activating an INTERRUPT ACKNOWLEDGE line (corresponding to BUS GRANT) connected in daisy-chain fashion to all IO devices. The connection sequence of this line then determines the interrupt priority of each device. Alternatively, the CPU can execute a program that polls each IO device in turn requesting interrupt status information. This approach is often used in single-line interrupt schemes, since it allows interrupt priority to be programmed.

Figure 6.44 depicts another widely used method called *multiple-line* or *multilevel* interrupts, which corresponds to independent requesting of interrupts. Each interrupt request line may be assigned a unique priority. The source of the interrupt is immediately known to the CPU, thus eliminating the need for a hardware or software scan of the IO ports. Unless further measures are taken, the CPU may still have to execute a program that fetches the address of the interrupt-service program to be used. This step can be eliminated by a technique called vectoring of interrupts.

Vectored interrupts. The fastest and most flexible response to interrupts is obtained when an interrupt request from a particular device causes a direct hardware-implemented transition to the correct interrupt-handling program. This

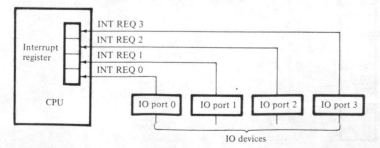

FIGURE 6.44
Multiple-line interrupt system.

requires that the interrupting device supply the CPU with the starting address or *transfer vector* of that program. This technique, called *vectoring*, is implemented in a number of ways.

Figure 6.45 shows a widely used technique for deriving the transfer vector from multiple interrupt request lines. Each interrupt request line is used to generate a unique fixed address, which in turn is used to modify the program counter. Interrupt request signals are stored in the interrupt register. The programmable *interrupt mask* register is used to disable any or all of the interrupt request lines. By setting bit i of this register to 1 (0), interrupt request line i is disabled (enabled). The k masked interrupt signals are fed into a priority encoder that produces a $\lceil \log_2 k \rceil$-bit address which is then inserted into the program counter.

Figure 6.46 illustrates how program control is transferred using this type of vectored interrupt. Suppose that three devices are connected to the four IO ports as shown in Fig. 6.46*a*. Assume that when an interrupt request from IO port i is accepted, the 2-bit address i is generated by the priority encoder and inserted into the program counter PC. For example, if main memory is addressed by byte and main-memory addresses are 4 bytes (32 bits) long, then i can be placed in bits 28 and 29 of PC, and the remaining 30 bits of PC (bits 0:27 and 30:31) can be set

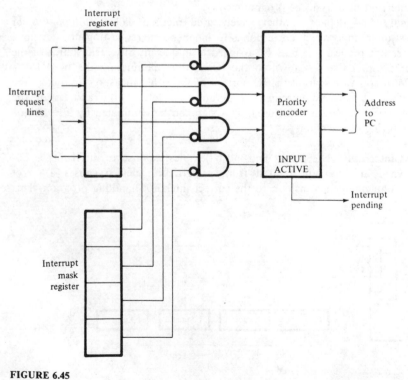

FIGURE 6.45
A vectored interrupt scheme.

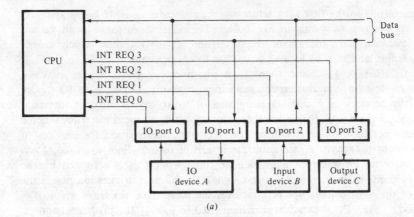

(a)

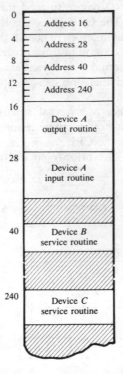

(b)

FIGURE 6.46
(a) A system with vectored IO interrupts. (b) Location of the interrupt servicing programs in main memory.

to 0. This results in the first four address-storage locations of M being assigned to interrupt vectors, as shown in Fig. 6.46b. The contents of these locations are the user-assigned start address of the interrupt service routines, which are of arbitrary length and may be located anywhere in main memory.

In the foregoing scheme there is a one-to-one correspondence between interrupt request lines and interrupt servicing programs. Hence if an IO device requires the services of k distinct programs, it must have k distinct interrupt request lines. Figure 6.47, shows another, more general, vectored interrupt scheme which does not have this restriction. Each IO port may request the services of many different programs. Again multiple interrupt request lines are used. Each IO port also has an interrupt acknowledge line. When this is activated by the CPU in response to an interrupt request signal, the IO port in question places the address of the desired interrupt program on the main data bus from which it is transferred to the CPU. The address is then used to modify the program counter. This approach requires the IO port to be capable of generating at least a partial memory address and of taking temporary control of the data bus.

Another possibility is for an IO device to send the CPU a transfer vector in the form of a CPU instruction. The CPU takes this instruction from the data bus and executes it in the normal manner. Thus if the IO device sends the instruction CALL X to the CPU, execution of this instruction saves essential CPU information such as the program counter, and transfers control to an interrupt-handling routine named X. Vectored interrupts can be implemented in this manner in 8085-based microcomputers.

In order to reduce the number of external connections to the CPU—an important consideration in the case of microprocessors—the interrupt priority selection circuit may be external to the CPU, as in Fig. 6.47. The priority of an interrupt request is determined by the priority circuit input line to which it is

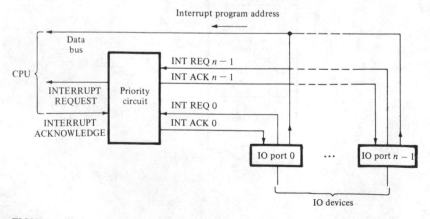

FIGURE 6.47
Another implementation of vectored interrupts.

connected. An interrupt acknowledge signal from the CPU is transmitted to the highest-priority IO port whose interrupt request line is active.

The Multibus standard bus (Fig. 6.21) provides straightforward support for two types of vectored interrupts [17]. Bus lines $\overline{INT0:7}$ serve as independent interrupt request lines of different priority, as in Fig. 6.44. A slave unit requiring interrupt service activates one of these lines and keeps it active until it is serviced by the bus master. In the simpler "non-bus-vectored" mode of operation, the master responds to $\overline{INTi}$ by executing an interrupt program whose start address is stored in one of eight predetermined locations in main memory. This program services the interrupting device and makes it deactivate its request line $\overline{INTi}$. The "bus-vectored" mode of operation is designed to support larger numbers of interrupt sources. Typically, each slave unit is associated with a programmable *interrupt controller*, which is responsible for interfacing the unit's interrupt requests to the Multibus and supplying the Multibus master with interrupt vectors. The Multibus master responds to requests placed on one or more $\overline{INTi}$ lines by briefly activating $\overline{INTA}$ (interrupt acknowledge) and placing the address of the interrupt controller of highest priority on the address lines. This serves to select one of the active interrupt controllers. The bus master then generates a second $\overline{INTA}$ signal causing the selected controller to place an interrupt vector on the Multibus data lines. This vector is read by the bus master and used to service the interrupt. Figure 6.48 shows the signal exchange occurring during a bus-vectored interrupt on the Multibus. The master uses the $\overline{LOCK}$ signal to give it exclusive control of the Multibus for the duration of the interrupt sequence (two bus cycles). No other bus master can use the Multibus as long as $\overline{LOCK}$ is active.

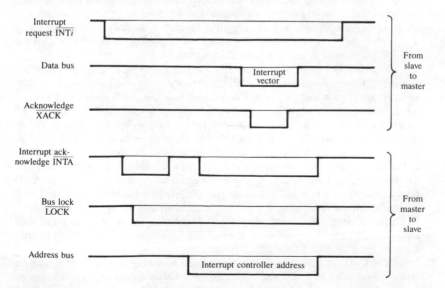

FIGURE 6.48
Bus-vectored interrupt sequence on the Multibus.

Example 6.5   Interrupt control in the Motorola 68000 series [29]. Interrupts in 68000-series computers fall under the heading of *exceptions*, which include program-generated traps and hardware-induced errors as well as external IO interrupts. Each exception has an 8-bit vector number N, which points to a memory location $M(4N)$ that stores the address (the exception vector) of a service program for that exception. Main-memory locations 0:1023 form an exception vector table storing 256 32-bit memory addresses used for exception processing. (Figure 6.46*b* shows a 4-member exception vector table of this type.) Most of the vector table (addresses 256:1023) is reserved for up to 192 user-supplied interrupt vectors; the remaining locations are preassigned by Motorola to specific exception types. For example, on encountering a divide-by-zero instruction, a 68000-series CPU executes a trap sequence that transfers control to the program whose start address is stored in locations $M(20:23)$ corresponding to exception vector number $N = 5$. Two types of vectored interrupts are supported: a general mode in which the interrupting device supplies an 8-bit vector number referring to an entry in the exception vector table; and a simplified "autovector" mode that allows the IO device to request any of seven fixed exception vectors whose addresses (vector numbers) are generated internally by the CPU.

Interrupts in 68000-based computers are processed in the following way. At the end of each instruction cycle the CPU checks to see if any interrupt request is pending and tests its priority as described below. If the CPU accepts the request, it suspends normal instruction processing and enters an interrupt response sequence. The CPU first saves the old contents of the status register SR in a temporary register, and sets the system state to the supervisor mode. It then either reads a vector number N provided by the interrupt source (general interrupt mode) or generates N internally (autovector mode), as specified by control signals provided by the interrupt source. The CPU proceeds to save the contents (return address) of the program counter PC, the old contents of SR, and certain internal information by pushing them into the supervisor stack, one of two stacks maintained by 68000-series CPUs in main memory M. Next, using $4N$ as the address, the CPU executes a memory read cycle causing it to fetch from M the exception vector $M(4N)$ corresponding to N. $M(4N)$ is loaded into PC, and normal instruction processing is resumed.

Figure 6.49 shows a representative hardware interface used for 68000 IO interrupts. Three control lines called $\overline{\text{IPL}}$ (*interrupt priority level*) serve both to make an interrupt request and to indicate its priority level. $\overline{\text{IPL}} = 0$ means that there is no interrupt request, while $\overline{\text{IPL}} = i$, where i ranges from 1 to 7, means that an interrupt of priority level i is being requested. On receiving an interrupt request ($\overline{\text{IPL}} \neq 0$), the CPU compares the number of $\overline{\text{IPL}}$ with three interrupt mask bits I stored in its status register SR. If $\overline{\text{IPL}} \geq I$, the CPU responds to the interrupt request at the end of its current instruction cycle; if $\overline{\text{IPL}} < I$, the interrupt request is ignored. Since SR can be altered by certain (privileged) instructions, whether or not the CPU responds to interrupts is under software control. Setting the interrupt mask I to 0 enables all interrupt requests. If I is set to 7, all interrupts are rejected except those of highest priority ($\overline{\text{IPL}} = 7$), which are nonmaskable. Interrupt sources can thus use up to 192 transfer vectors, each of which can be assigned to any of seven priority levels.

The CPU acknowledges an interrupt request by setting each of its FC (*function code*) output lines to 1 to form a 3-bit signal denoting interrupt acknowledgment. It also places the priority level of the interrupt being acknowledged on address lines A1:3. In the general interrupt mode, the interrupt controller responds by placing an

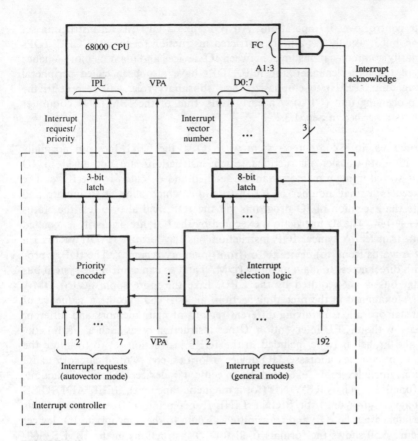

FIGURE 6.49
Interfacing interrupts to the Motorola 68000 CPU.

interrupt vector number N on data lines D0:7. In the circuit of Fig. 6.49 with the 68000 CPU, the FC signals are used directly to strobe the interrupt vector number N onto the data bus. To indicate the autovector mode, the interrupt controller responds to $F = 7$ by activating a special control line ($\overline{\text{VPA}}$ for the 68000 CPU and $\overline{\text{AVEC}}$ for the 68020), causing the CPU to generate N internally using the formula $N = 24 + \text{IPL}$.

6.2.3 IO Processors

The IO processor (IOP) is a logical extension of the IO control methods considered so far. In systems with programmed IO, peripheral devices are controlled directly by the CPU. The DMA concept extends to the IO devices limited control over data transfers to and from main memory. An IOP has the additional ability to execute certain instructions (IO instructions), which give it more complete control over IO operations. An IOP, like a CPU, is an instruction set processor, but it usually has a more restricted instruction set than the CPU. IOPs are primarily communications links between IO devices and main memory—hence the use of the term "channel" for IOP. IOPs have also been called peripheral processing units (PPUs) to emphasize their subsidiary role with respect to the central processing unit (CPU). An early IOP, that of the IBM 7094 computer system, was described in Sec. 1.3.1.

IO instructions. In a computer system with IOPs, the CPU does not normally execute IO data-transfer instructions. Such instructions are contained in IO programs stored in main memory and are fetched and executed by the IOPs. The CPU executes a small number of IO instructions which allow it to initiate and terminate the execution of IO programs via the IOP, and also to test the status of the IO system. The IO instructions executed by the IOP are primarily associated with data transfer. A typical IOP instruction has the form: READ (WRITE) a block of n words from (to) device X to (from) memory region Y. The IOP is provided with direct access to main memory (DMA) and so can control the system bus when that bus is not required by the CPU. Like the more sophisticated DMA controllers examined in the preceding section, an IOP can execute a sequence of data-transfer operations involving different regions of main memory and different IO devices, without CPU intervention. Other instruction types such as arithmetic, logical, and branch may be included in the IOP's instruction set to facilitate the calculation of complex addresses, IO device priorities, etc. A third category of IO instructions includes those executed by specific IO devices. These instructions control functions such as REWIND (for a magnetic-tape unit), SEEK ADDRESS (for a magnetic-disk unit), or PRINT LINE (for a printer). Instructions of this type are fetched by the IOP and transmitted as data to the appropriate IO device.

Figure 6.50 shows the formats used for IO instructions in the IBM S/360-370 series [13]. The CPU supervises IO operations by means of a small set of

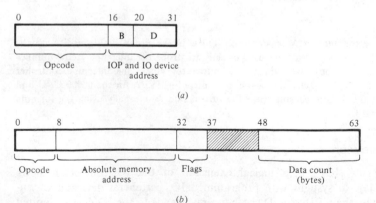

(a)

(b)

FIGURE 6.50
Formats of S/360-370 IO instructions: (a) executed by a CPU; (b) executed by an IOP (channel).

privileged IO instructions with the format of Fig. 6.50a. The address field (bits 16:31) specifies a base register B and a displacement D, which identify both the IO device to be used and the IOP to which it is attached. There are three major instructions of this type: START IO, HALT IO, and TEST IO. START IO is used to initiate an IO operation. It provides the IOP it names with the main-memory address of the IO program to be executed by the IOP. HALT IO causes the IOP to terminate IO program execution. TEST IO allows the CPU to determine the status of the named IO device and IOP. Status conditions of interest include available, busy, not operational, and (masked) interrupt pending.

The IO instructions executed by the IOP are called *channel command words* (CCWs) and have the format shown in Fig. 6.50b. There are three main types.

1. Data-transfer instructions including input (read), output (write), and sense (read status information). These CCWs cause the number of bytes specified in the data count field to be transferred between the specified main-memory area and the previously selected IO device.
2. Branch instructions (called "transfer-in-channel"), which cause the IOP to fetch the next CCW from the specified memory address rather than the next sequential location. This is a simple unconditional jump within an IO program.
3. IO device control instructions. These instructions are transmitted directly to the IO device and are used to specify functions peculiar to that device which do not involve data transfers. For example, a magnetic-tape unit could be instructed to rewind or write a standard tape mark; a printer could be instructed to print a line or eject a page.

Note that the S/360-370 IOP has no significant arithmetic ability.

The opcode of a data-transfer instruction may be transmitted directly to the IO device as the "command" byte during a device selection process. If the IO device requires additional control information, it can be supplied with it via an output data transfer. The flags field of the CCW is used to modify or extend the operation specified by its opcode. For example, a program control flag PCI can be set to instruct the IOP to generate an IO interrupt and make the current IOP status available to the CPU. Another flag specifies "command chaining," which means that the current CCW is followed by another CCW which is to be executed immediately. If this flag is not set, the IOP ceases IO program execution after executing the current CCW.

Figure 6.51 lists an IO program written in S/360-370 assembly language that writes a record on a magnetic tape. The record contains 100 bytes. The tape is assumed to contain two records, the second of which is being replaced. Every CCW contains four fields separated by commas, which correspond to the opcode, memory address, flags, and data count fields of Fig. 6.50b. This program contains only one data-transfer instruction, which transfers 100 bytes to the tape from the memory region called BUFFER1. The other CCWs control operations that are peculiar to magnetic tapes and do not use the memory address or data count

Instruction			Comments
CCW X'07,		, X'40',	Rewind tape
CCW X'37',		X'40,	Skip first record. .
CCW X'01',	BUFFER1	, X'40', 100	Write second record from BUFFER1
CCW X'1F',		, X'40',	Write tape mark
CCW X'07',		, X'00',	Rewind tape and stop

FIGURE 6.51
An S/360-370 IO program to write a record on a magnetic tape.

fields. In all CCWs the opcode and flags have been defined by hexadecimal numbers indicated by the prefix X. The flag field X'40' causes the command chaining flag to be set. In the last CCW no flags are set, so the IOP stops after execution of this CCW.

IOP organization. The structure of a representative system containing an IOP appears in Fig. 6.52. The IOP and CPU share access to a common main memory M via the system bus. M contains separate programs for execution by the CPU and the IOP; it also contains a communication region IOCR used for passing information in the form of messages between the two processors. The CPU can place there the parameters of an IO task, e.g., the address of the IO program(s) to be executed, and the identity of the devices to be used. The CPU and IOP also communicate more directly via special control lines. Standard DMA or bus grant/acknowledge lines are used for arbitration of the system bus between the two processors, as discussed in the preceding section. The CPU can attract the IOP's attention, e.g., when executing an IO instruction like START IO or TEST IO, by activating the ATTENTION line. This typically causes the IOP to begin execution of an IOP program whose specifications have been placed in the IOCR communication area. In an essentially similar fashion, the IOP attracts the CPU's attention by activating one or more INTERRUPT REQUEST lines, causing the CPU to execute an interrupt-service routine that responds to the IOP by, for instance, defining a new IO program for the IOP to execute.

Figure 6.53 shows the behavior of a typical IOP. We now illustrate it for the case of the IBM S/360-370 series. An IO operation begins when the CPU encounters a START IO instruction whose format appears in Fig. 6.50a. This causes the CPU to transmit the IO device address and an attention signal to the specified IOP. The IOP then fetches the channel address word CAW previously placed in a memory location 72, which is a part of the CPU-IOP communication region. The CAW contains the absolute 24-bit starting address of the IO program to be executed by the IOP, as well as a memory protection key. The IOP next initializes the specified IO device for the IO operation by carrying out an IO device selection procedure via a standard communication protocol over the S/360-370 IO bus. This asynchronous IO bus contains over 30 unidirectional lines, including two 8-bit data buses designed for transmitting IO device addresses and status

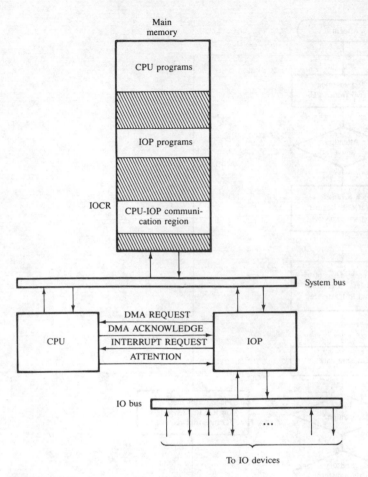

FIGURE 6.52
Representative system containing an IOP.

information, as well as data [14]. The IOP first transmits the address (8 bits) of the required IO device, which responds with its address and a byte of status information. If the status is valid, the IOP outputs a command byte indicating the IO operation to be performed, and data transfer can begin. If the IO device is unavailable for some reason, the IO operation is aborted and an IO interrupt is generated.

The CPU can maintain direct control over the IO operation by periodically executing TEST IO. This causes the IOP to construct a channel status word CSW, which it stores at memory location 64. The CPU can then fetch the CSW and examine it. This type of programmed IO is an inefficient way for the CPU to monitor IO operations, so the IOPs are provided with the ability to send interrupt

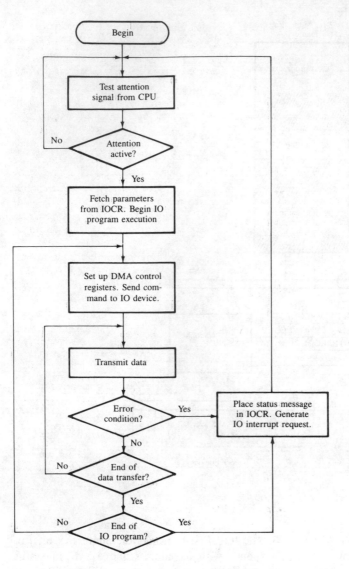

FIGURE 6.53
Behavior of a typical IOP.

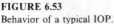

requests to the CPU. The CPU tests for interrupts once during each CPU instruction cycle. Interrupt requests can be masked by an interrupt mask register which forms part of the CPU's program status word register PSW.

When the S/360-370 CPU responds to an IO interrupt, it automatically stores the current PSW as the old PSW at memory location 56 and fetches a new

PSW from location 120. The new PSW contains a program counter field pointing to the interrupt service routine to be used. If it is desired to save the CPU general registers, explicit instructions for this purpose must be included in the interrupt service program. The interrupting IOP updates the channel status word at location 64, which provides the CPU with further information on the source and nature of the interrupt. In general, it may be necessary to execute several instructions and access main memory a number of times in order to complete the transfer of control to the interrupt service program.

Example 6.6   The Intel 8089 IO Processor [6]. The 8089 is a one-chip IOP designed for use in systems based on the Intel 8086 microprocessor and its successors. As shown in Fig. 6.54, it contains a pair of "DMA channels," each of which can control an independent IO operation. In addition to the usual address and data-count registers found in DMA controllers, the 8089's DMA channels have their own program counters and other circuits necessary to execute an instruction set that is specialized toward IO operations. Thus the 8089 can execute two unrelated IO programs concurrently, and logically appears to the CPU like two independent IOPs. The DMA channels share a 20-bit ALU intended mainly for processing memory addresses. They also share the interface circuitry for communication with main memory and IO

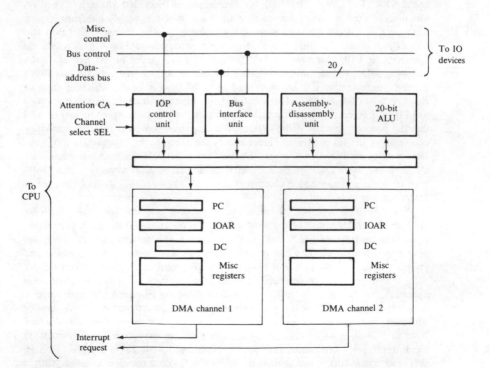

FIGURE 6.54
Structure of the Intel 8089 IOP.

devices. Because of pin constraints—the 8089 is packaged in a 40-pin DIP—the channels also share a 20-bit bidirectional external bus which is used in multiplexed fashion to transmit data or addresses to or from IO devices; the same lines are also used for address and data transmission between the IOP and main memory. Both 8- and 16-bit data words can be transmitted and received by the 8089, which contains the necessary assembly-disassembly circuits for conversion between these two data formats. If desired, external latches and control circuits can be used to create separate system and IO buses. If the 8089 is configured with a local IO bus, then its IO programs can be placed in a local memory attached to that bus, thus reducing the instruction traffic on the shared system bus.

The CPU and 8089 communicate via several message regions in main memory, which are illustrated in Fig. 6.55. Each DMA channel of the IOP has an associated parameter block PB containing a pointer to the channel's current IO program, i.e., a channel address word. PB also contains application-specific input parameters for the IO program, as well as output parameters for variables that the channel is to return to the CPU. These parameters can identify IO buffer regions in main memory, IO device names, data addresses in secondary memory devices, etc. The locations of the two PBs are stored in a channel control block CB which is created by the CPU when the system is powered up or reset. CB is used to store status information and a command from the CPU for each channel. These 1-byte commands fill essentially the same role as the START, TEST, and HALT IO instructions of the S/360-370 series. They are also used by the CPU to enable, disable, or deactivate the channel's interrupt request line. Thus the CPU supervises each IOP channel by writing into its PB region and into its portion of CB. Once it has set up the necessary control information in main memory, the CPU *dispatches* a DMA channel, i.e., initiates an IO operation, by executing a data-transfer instruction such as OUT or MOVE that activates the 8089's channel attention line CA and a second line SEL that indicates which of the two channels is to be dispatched. The selected channel then proceeds to read its command word from CB, e.g., "start IO program execution," which causes the channel to load the IO program pointer from PB into its program counter thereby launching execution of the IO program. The channel then executes the program in much the same way as a CPU. DMA is used by the 8089 to fetch IO instructions from main memory and, of course, for data transfers to and from main memory. Each DMA channel has a programmable channel control (CC) register that defines the type of DMA transfer to be used.

The 8089's instruction set and the corresponding assembly language (which are quite distinct from those of the host CPU) contain about 50 different instruction types. The instructions are broadly similar to those of a general-purpose CPU, but have only a few simple data and address types and very limited data processing and program control capabilities. For example, the arithmetic instructions consist only of add, increment, and decrement with unsigned or twos-complement fixed-point operands. No provision is made for overflow detection in signed arithmetic operations. The major instruction types are data-transfer instructions that move data or address words between the 8089's internal registers and its external memory-IO bus. Note that in addition to IO operations, the 8089 can execute memory-to-memory block transfers very efficiently. The 8089's specialized IO control instructions include: WID (set bus width), which defines the word size for data transfers as either 8 or 16 bits; XFER (transfer), which prepares a channel for a DMA transfer; and SINTR (set interrupt), which activates the channel's interrupt request line, thus enabling an IO program to interrupt the CPU.

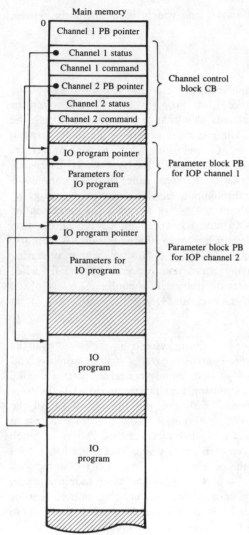

Main memory

FIGURE 6.55
Main-memory organization for the 8089 IOP.

6.3 OPERATING SYSTEMS

Except when they are devoted to a single task, computers are usually managed by a supervisory program called an operating system. The operating system provides a uniform software interface for other system programs and for user-specific applications programs. In multiuser environments, the operating system is responsible for efficient sharing of such resources as CPU time, memory space, IO devices, utility programs, and databases among the users. This section examines some basic issues of operating system design, including concurrency control and IO management, and discusses one widely used operating system, namely UNIX, in some detail.

6.3.1 Introduction

A fundamental characteristic of computer software is that the use made of the resources of the host computer varies from program to program, often in unpredictable ways. Resource requirements also change dynamically during the execution of a single program. For example, most programs alternate between computations which use the CPU, and IO operations which use IO processors and peripheral devices, and do not require the CPU. Clearly, if several independent programs are available for execution at the same time, then the computer's performance as measured by overall throughput, can be improved by assigning one program to the CPU while other programs are assigned for execution by IOPs. The scheduling of concurrent CPU and IO processing is a typical function performed by an operating system. Another important shared resource is memory, both main and secondary, whose efficient utilization is also typically an operating system function. The presence of many concurrent processes, especially when derived from unrelated programs, creates the potential for conflicting usage of the shared resources. The prevention of such conflicts is a basic function of an operating system.

Operating system types. Several types of operating systems have evolved over the years. The earliest and simplest system control programs (batch monitors and spooling systems) developed in the 1950s were mainly concerned with reducing the time required for inputting and outputting user programs (jobs). Jobs were executed sequentially in a single stream, with one job in control of all the computer's resources for the duration of its execution. Consider, for example, a batch monitor for a second-generation computer of the 1950s. A typical batch of jobs then consisted of a stack of punched cards which were placed in a card reader attached as an IO device to the host computer. As each job terminated either normally or abnormally, control was returned to the batch monitor, which performed any additional processing needed, such as printing output files or reporting errors. The monitor then read in the next job in the current batch, whose execution proceeded to termination before the next job was read, and so on.

The concept of *spooling* (from *s*imultaneous *p*eripheral *o*peration *o*n-*l*ine) further reduces input-output time by placing batches of input and output files on secondary memory devices, which can be more rapidly accessed than card readers, printers, etc. In early computers, the spooling medium was often a magnetic tape, and the spooling process was done off-line in a small auxiliary computer. A set of input files were first written to a magnetic tape by the auxiliary computer. The input tape was then transferred to the main computer for processing. The results of processing a batch of jobs were also written onto a magnetic tape, which was then taken off-line for printing. Input-output control of this type fell into disuse with the demise of punched cards and increasing use of interactive terminals by computer users. A limited form of spooling is sometimes found in modern operating systems, with a magnetic-disk unit serving as the spooling medium for output (printer) files created by a single or multiple users.

Modern operating systems may be characterized as efficiently managing a wide range of computer resources, not merely IO. They may also be oriented toward interactive processing (timesharing) with users at on-line terminals, rather than noninteractive batch processing. They provide command languages that allow the user to interact directly with the operating system by specifying the system resources needed for a particular job. Current operating systems have their origins in several influential ones developed in the 1960s. A notable example is IBM's OS/360, which was designed for the original System/360 series. OS/360 is the ancestor of a large number of operating systems which, like the S/360-370 architecture itself, have become de facto commercial standards for larger computers. Early work at Manchester University (Atlas), MIT (Multics), and other research institutions led to the UNIX operating system, which was developed at AT&T Bell Laboratories in the mid-1970s and has since become widely used in smaller machines. Specialized operating systems have also been developed for computers which require extremely short response times (*real-time* systems), and terminal-based wide-area computer networks (*transaction-processing* systems).

Processes. The basic unit of computing managed by an operating system is a *process* or *task*, which is loosely defined as a self-contained program module in the course of execution. The resources needed by a process, including a processor and memory space, are usually allocated to it dynamically during execution. An example of a process is a subroutine being executed by a CPU, or an IO program being executed by an IOP. A process comes into being or is created in response to a user command to the operating system. Processes may also be created by other processes, e.g., in response to exception conditions such as errors or interrupts. When no longer needed, a process (but not the underlying program) can be deleted via the operating system, which means that all record of the process is obliterated and any resources currently allocated to it are released. While in existence, a process has three major states: ready, running, and blocked, as depicted in Fig. 6.56a. In the ready state a process is waiting, perhaps in a queue with other processes, for the resources that it needs to enter the running or active state. A blocked process is waiting for some event to occur, such as completion of another process that provides the first process with necessary data. A transition from one process state to another is triggered by various conditions such as interrupts and user instructions to the operating system.

Figure 6.56b shows the state behavior of a typical user process P in a system with independent IO processing. It is assumed that P runs on the CPU and that running proceeds until an IO instruction is encountered, at which point the operating system is involved and P is changed from running to blocked. The running of P may also be terminated by a timer-generated interrupt, which is used by the operating system to limit the amount of time that any one process is assigned to the IOP. In this case, P is returned to the ready state, where it remains

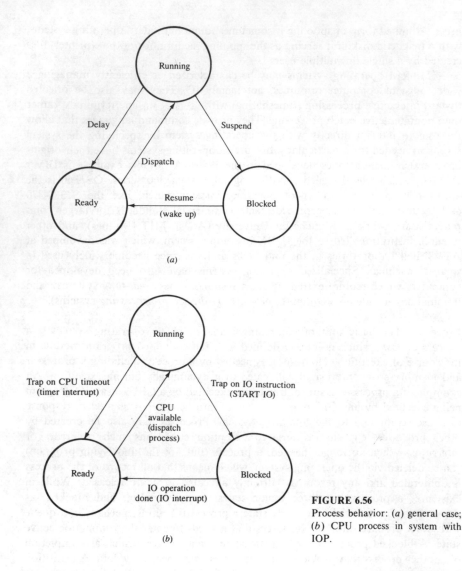

FIGURE 6.56
Process behavior: (a) general case; (b) CPU process in system with IOP.

until rescheduled for execution by the operating system. A new process P' may now be created by the operating system to run on an IOP and carry out the required IO operation. Completion of P' results in an IO interrupt that causes the CPU to transfer P from blocked to ready. At this point P' can be deleted if it is no longer needed by P or other extant processes. As soon as the CPU is available to execute P, i.e., when there are no CPU processes of higher priority ready for execution, P is transferred once more to the running state. It continues running until either it encounters another IO instruction, exceeds its allocated time, or completes execution. In the latter case, a call is made to the operating system, which can then delete *P*.

Execution of a program involves creating and running to completion a set of processes which require varying amounts of CPU, IO, and memory resources. Note that the execution of user processes is interspersed with operating system (supervisor) processes used to control the transitions among user states, and to perform any associated bookkeeping functions. Different processes run at different rates and interact via shared variables or by transmitting messages to one another. Those that involve disjoint resources can be run concurrently or in parallel. The role of the operating system can therefore be regarded as that of managing a set of asynchronous concurrent processes. As processes interact, they are switched between the running, blocked, and ready states.

Kernel. An operating system consists of a large number of computer resource management programs, including processor scheduling routines, virtual memory management routines, and IO device control programs (device drivers). Commonly used utility programs such as programming language translators, text editors, etc., are often considered part of the operating system and are invoked via commands to the operating system. Thus operating systems tend to contain very large amounts of software, far too much to store in main memory in its entirety. The portion of the operating system that remains continuously in main memory is termed the *kernel* or *nucleus*, and consists of the most frequently used part of the operating system. The other less frequently used parts of the operating system, such as file management routines and compilers, reside in secondary (disk) memory, and are only brought into main memory when needed.

The kernel of an operating system is responsible for the creation, deletion, and state-switching of the many processes that define a computer's behavior. This it does by quickly responding to a steady flow of interrupt requests. The interrupts have a variety of sources such as: user-generated requests for operating system services; CPU process suspension and resumption conditions; memory allocation/deallocation requests; memory (page) faults; IO operations; and hardware or software errors. Rapid response is achieved by only briefly disabling other interrupts while responding to the current one, then dispatching or, if necessary, creating an operating system process to execute the appropriate interrupt-handling routine. The performance and reliability of the kernel can be improved by implementing many of its more basic functions in hardware or firmware.

The kernel keeps track of each process by means of a data segment called a *process control block* PCB, which defines the most recent execution state or *context* of the process [28]. The PCB typically contains all the programmable registers of the associated process, including program counter, stack pointers, status register, and general-purpose data and address registers. The PCB normally resides in main memory. When the process is to be executed, its PCB is transferred to the corresponding processor registers. The transfer of control from one process to another, i.e., *context switching*, is therefore implemented by saving the context of the old process in its PCB in memory, and loading the PCB of the new process into the processor in its place. Figure 6.57 shows the PCB used by the VMS operating system for the VAX/11 series. It contains several stack pointers used by the operating system, all the CPU's general registers, the program counter PC, and the program status word PSW. PSW contains the usual CPU status flag bits and the interrupt priority level of the process. The last entries in the PCB specify the base address and length of two page tables, one for the user program and one for the user stack; see Fig. 5.33. As discussed in Example 5.3 in Sec. 5.2.1, these page tables play an essential role in the firmware-implemented address mapping that supports the VAX's virtual memory system. Two VAX instructions SVPCTX (save process context) and LDPCTX (load process context) support context switching by transferring the complete PCB to and from memory, respectively.

6.3.2 Concurrency Control

An operating system supervises a potentially large set of processes that function asynchronously and concurrently. Many of the more subtle problems in designing an operating system are due to occasional attempts by concurrent processes to use shared resources in undesirable or improperly synchronized ways. Two basic problems in concurrency control and their solutions are considered next, namely, mutual exclusion and deadlock.

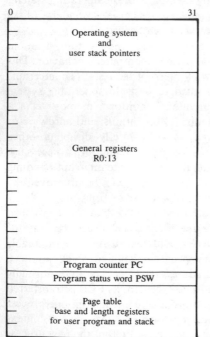

FIGURE 6.57
Process control block PCB for the VAX VMS operating system.

Mutual exclusion. Let two concurrent processes P_1 and P_2 share read and write access to a data region R in main memory. It is generally necessary to prevent one process from writing into R while the other process is reading from it. Thus, unless appropriate precautions are taken, P_2 can modify some variable X of R immediately after P_1 has read its old value, so that P_1's subsequent processing decisions are based on an incorrect value of X. This problem is solved by enforcing certain rules for *mutual exclusion*, so that, in the present instance, P_1 has exclusive access to R for as long as it needs it, without interference from other processes. Shared resources like R that require mutual exclusion are termed *critical*.

A basic software solution to the mutual exclusion problem, is to associate a control variable S termed a *flag* with each critical resource R, which indicates when the resource is being used. (With certain additional restrictions discussed later, S is called a semaphore.) Before attempting to take control of R, a process P first reads its flag S. If $S = 1$ (busy), indicating that some process is already using R, P does not attempt to use R. If, on the other hand, P finds that S is 0, indicating that R is not being used, it immediately sets S to 1 (busy), and then proceeds to use R. When it is finished with R, the process P resets S to 0 so that other processes can use R. For this type of control mechanism to work, it is essential that mutual exclusion be enforced for accessing the semaphore itself during execution of the test-and-set operation (see Prob. 6.28).

Some processors provide a test-and-set instruction for implementing flag (semaphore) control in the kernel of an operating system. To guarantee mutual exclusion, this instruction is designed to be indivisible in the sense that all the steps of its instruction cycle must be completed without interference by other instructions. For example, the 8089 IOP (Example 6.6 in Sec. 6.2.3) has such an instruction called TSL (*t*est and *s*et while *l*ocked). In the following 8089 assembly-language code:

```
            TSL   S, 1, WAIT
     R:     . . .
            . . .                  ; END R                (6.5)
            MOV   S, 0
```

TSL causes the flag variable S to be read from main memory and compared to 0. If $S = 0$, TSL writes the specified 1 value into S, and program control is transferred to the routine R, which uses the resource protected by S. If TSL finds that $S \neq 0$, then it transfers control to the branch address WAIT. To ensure mutual exclusion, TSL activates a special output signal called LOCK on the 8089 chip. This signal is intended to drive the bus lock line of the same name on the Multibus or similar system bus to which the memory storing S is attached; see Fig. 6.21. Activating LOCK prevents any other instruction from using the bus while the TSL instruction cycle is being executed; consequently, TSL has the required exclusive access to S. The final move instruction in the above 8089 code implements $S \leftarrow 0$ to reset the flag. The foregoing R routine is an example of a critical section of an assembly-language program which is protected by the flag S. If the initial TSL statement is replaced by

$$\text{WAIT:} \quad \text{TSL} \quad \text{S, 1, WAIT} \tag{6.6}$$

then the test-and-set operation is executed repeatedly until S becomes available; in effect, the process requesting R waits until S changes from busy to not busy.

The simple flag control mechanism discussed above has several deficiencies. It uses a "busy" form of waiting in which processors spend a great deal of time simply testing the flag S. Moreover, a particular process P may never find $S = 0$ and gain control of R because of competition from other processes. These problems are addressed by a special resource control variable called a semaphore, a concept due to Edsger W. Dijkstra [15]. A *semaphore S* is a nonnegative integer serving as a control flag for a resource R. It has two indivisible procedures WAIT(S) and SIGNAL(S) which can be defined as follows, where P is the process calling WAIT or SIGNAL:

WAIT(S):   **if** $S > 0$ **then** $S \leftarrow S - 1$
                         else suspend P and place in queue Q for R; $\tag{6.7}$
SIGNAL(S):   **if** Q is nonempty **then** dispatch one process from Q
                         else $S \leftarrow S + 1$; $\tag{6.8}$

A semaphore S can be used by encapsulating the code R for a critical resource thus:

$$
\begin{aligned}
&\text{WAIT(S)}\\
&\text{R}\\
&\text{SIGNAL(S)}
\end{aligned}
\tag{6.9}
$$

and initializing S to 1. The first requesting process gains access to R and sets S to 0. Subsequent processes attempting to enter R are queued. Hence only one process can be in the critical region R ensuring that mutual exclusion is preserved. By initializing S to a larger value $k > 1$, the number of processes in the critical region can be limited to k. Although (6.5) and (6.9) are superficially similar, use of the semaphore avoids busy waiting, and the queueing by WAIT and releasing by SIGNAL of requests for R ensure that all requesting processes eventually get to use R in some sequence, e.g., FIFO, determined by the queueing discipline for blocked processes.

The program structures (6.5) and (6.9) represent fairly low-level solutions to the mutual exclusion problem. They may be difficult to use in the design of complex concurrent processes where high-level programming constructs are preferred. One way of introducing concurrency control into high-level languages, also suggested by Dijkstra, is to encapsulate all the procedures and data needed to process a critical resource R in a special program structure $M(R)$ called a *monitor*, which can only be accessed by one process at a time. Hence access to the monitor is subject to mutual exclusion, which can be implemented by the compiler associating test-and-set flags with the monitor's object code. The resource R can only be acquired or released by executing procedures that are contained in $M(R)$. If R is in use, a process calling some monitor procedure PROC that uses R is made to wait until R becomes available. This can be achieved by making

PROC call a WAIT procedure like (6.7) so that the waiting is done outside $M(R)$, thereby preventing the calling process from tying up the monitor with an indefinite wait. The process using R releases it by executing a SIGNAL procedure like (6.8) via the monitor.

Example 6.7 The readers and writers problem. A common situation encountered in an operating system is where several concurrent processes need to read from or write into common files. For example, in a terminal-based computer network such as an airlines reservation system, many terminals need to read the database of flight information concurrently, while a few need to write into it from time to time to update it, e.g., to enter a reservation for a particular flight. In such situations, the reader processes are allowed to access a file simultaneously, but exclusive access must be given to the writer processes.

Figure 6.58 shows a solution to this "readers-and-writers" problem in the form of a monitor named READ_WRITE written in a Pascal-like high-level language [2]. READ_WRITE defines a set of four procedures for controlling access to the database. To read from the database, a reader process calls the monitor procedure BEGIN_READ; after it has finished reading, it calls END_READ. A writer process executes BEGIN_WRITE and END_WRITE in a similar fashion. As long as one reader is active, READ_WRITE permits any number of other readers to access the database at the same time. A writer can access it only when there are no other active users, but it is then given exclusive access. The semaphore writing_allowed provides this exclusive access. The variable reader_count indicates the number of readers that are currently active. Only when reader_count is reset to zero by the last of a group of concurrent reads, is writing enabled via SIGNAL(writing_allowed).

The monitor READ_WRITE gives priority to waiting (queued) read or write requests over newly arriving ones. This prevents waiting processes from being indefinitely delayed by a steady stream of arriving processes. Thus when a writer finishes writing and is executing END_WRITE, it checks to see if there are any waiting readers in the queue associated with the second semaphore reading_allowed. This is specified in Fig. 6.58 by means of the (boolean) function QUEUE(S), which is **false (true)** if the queue associated with the semaphore S is empty (nonempty). The writer process tests QUEUE(reading_allowed) and enables any waiting readers by executing SIGNAL(reading_allowed) before allowing any waiting writers to proceed via SIGNAL(writing_allowed). Similarly, BEGIN_READ allows a reader to proceed only if there are no active or waiting writer processes.

Deadlock. Another well-known synchronization problem in operating systems is *deadlock*, where a process is waiting for an event such as the release of some shared resource, but the event in question never occurs. Suppose, for instance, that processes P_1 and P_2 both require the use of two resources R_1 and R_2 which can only be controlled by one process at a time. Let R_1 be allocated to P_1, which then requests R_2 while still retaining control of R_1. At the same time, let P_2 control R_2 and be requesting control of R_1. If neither process can continue until it obtains control of both processes, then a deadlock results in which each process ends up waiting for the other to release a resource, a circular waiting situation that is characteristic of deadlocks. A single process can also become

```
monitor READ_WRITE;
  var reader_count: integer;
      writer_active: boolean;
      reading_allowed, writing_allowed; semaphore;

  procedure BEGIN_READ;
    begin
      if writer_active or QUEUE(writing_allowed)
        then WAIT(reading_allowed);
      reader_count ← reader_count + 1;
      SIGNAL(reading_allowed);
    end; {Read the file, then execute END_READ}
  procedure END_READ;
    begin
      reader_count ← reader_count − 1;
      if reader_count = 0 then SIGNAL(writing_allowed);
    end;

  procedure BEGIN_WRITE;
    begin
      if reader_count = 0 or writer_active
        then WAIT(writing_allowed);
      writer_active ← true;
    end; {Write to the file, then execute END_WRITE}
  procedure END_WRITE;
    begin
      writer_active ← false;
      if QUEUE(reading_allowed) then SIGNAL(reading_allowed)
        else SIGNAL(writing_allowed);
    end;

begin
  reader_count ← 0;
  writer_active ← false;
end.
```

FIGURE 6.58
Example of a monitor to control access to a database.

deadlocked waiting for an external event such as an acknowledgment signal that fails to appear in an IO bus transaction. Such deadlock conditions can result from hardware failures as well as hardware or software design errors.

The three basic ways of dealing with deadlock problems are prevention, avoidance, and fault tolerance. The prevention approach eliminates all possibility of a deadlock occurring. Less stringent approaches do not completely eliminate the possibility of a deadlock, but attempt to ensure that all potential deadlock situations are avoided. The third approach allows deadlocks to take place, but provides mechanisms for detecting them and recovering from their effects. In practice, all these techniques are used in various parts of a typical operating system, with deadlock prevention techniques playing the major role.

For a deadlock possibility to exist, a number of conditions must be met by the processes and resources involved:

1. *Mutual exclusion.* Each process must have exclusive access to the resources it controls.
2. *Resource waiting.* A process can hold the resources already allocated to it while waiting for access to another.
3. *Nonpreemption.* A process cannot be preempted; it never releases its resources until it has completely finished with them.
4. *Circularity.* A circular chain of processes must exist; each process controls a resource that is being requested by the next process in the chain.

Deadlocks can be prevented by designing the relevant part of an operating system so that one or more of the above conditions cannot occur. Condition 1 usually cannot be eliminated without unacceptably restricting resource sharing; however, each of the other deadlock conditions can be lifted in various ways. For example, no deadlock can occur if a process P is blocked until all the resources it needs become available. This circumvents condition 2 (resource waiting), but it can lead to very inefficient use of available resources. The partial set of resources tied up by P can be freed by requiring P to release them and rerequest them later along with the other resources not yet available. This latter step preempts P's resources, therefore denying condition 3 (nonpreemption). Eliminating conditions 2 or 3 in this fashion can have the undesirable consequence of causing some process requests to be blocked indefinitely. The circularity condition can be removed by assigning a unique number $p(R)$ to each resource R, and enforcing the rule that if P holds R, it can only request additional resources with numbers higher than $p(R)$. This works well if the normal order in which the processes requests the resources closely matches the order in which they are numbered; otherwise P may need to acquire and hold low-numbered resources long before it actually uses them.

Even if all the necessary conditions for deadlock are present, deadlocks can be avoided by deciding dynamically whether satisfying a process's request for resources can lead to deadlock. If a deadlock is determined to be inevitable, then the process in question should obviously not be initiated. A conservative process initiation strategy, which is the basis of some deadlock avoidance algorithms, is to initiate a process only if it can be determined that its resource needs can be fully met even if all the currently active processes make their maximum resource demands. Such strategies require advance knowledge of the current processes' worst-case resource requirements, knowledge that is not always available. In practice, heuristic techniques that do not completely avoid deadlock are often used, especially in noncritical parts of an operating system. An example is a policy of not dispatching a process, e.g., to create a new file, when the availablity of the resources needed, e.g., the amount of free secondary-memory (file) space, drops below some experimentally determined level.

The detection of deadlock situations, either to avoid them or to eliminate them after they occur, implies the ability to check for the circular wait condition defined above. To do this, the operating system must maintain a list of all the resources held by each process and, for each resource, the names of the processes that are waiting to use it. These resource assignments and requests can be represented graphically by means of a *resource allocation graph*, an example of which appears in Fig. 6.59. Here the circles denote processes $\{P_i\}$ and the squares denote resources $\{R_j\}$. An edge or arrow directed from resource R_j to process P_i implies that R_j has been allocated to P_i, while an arrow from P_i to R_j means that P_i is requesting R_j. The existence of a closed loop in which all arrows go in the same direction, in this case, $P_2 \rightarrow R_4 \rightarrow P_5 \rightarrow R_6 \rightarrow P_4 \rightarrow R_1 \rightarrow P_2$, indicates that the given allocation satisfies the circularity condition for a deadlock. Note that the mutual exclusion condition is satisfied by the requirement that only one arrow leave each resource in the resource allocation graph.

Figure 6.60 outlines a recursive procedure CHECK(P,R) to check for circularity conditions leading to deadlock; in effect, it finds closed loops in a resource allocation graph. The procedure is intended to be executed whenever a process P makes a request for resource R; it reports a deadlock if the requested allocation results in a closed loop. Suppose that the procedure is applied to the system of Fig. 6.59 when P_2 makes a new request for control of R_5. Assume that processes and resources are scanned in ascending numerical order determined by the P and R subscripts. On entering CHECK(P_2,R_5), the resources allocated to P_2, namely $\{R_1, R_2, R_3\}$, are scanned. Then the processes waiting for R_1, namely $\{P_4\}$, are identified. Since P_4 does not have R_5 allocated to it, CHECK(P_4,R_5) is now invoked. On reentering the CHECK procedure with $P = P_4$ and $R = R_5$, the

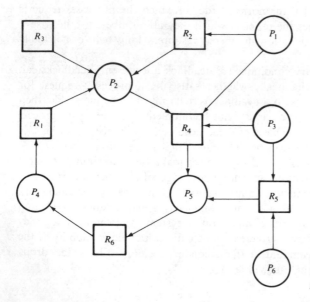

FIGURE 6.59
Example of a resource allocation graph.

```
procedure CHECK(P: process; R: resource);
begin
    for all resources {R_i} allocated to P do
        begin
            for all processes {P_ij} waiting for R_i do
                if P_ij holds R then REPORT(deadlock) else CHECK(P_ij, R);
        end;
end;
```

FIGURE 6.60
Procedure for deadlock detection.

resources $\{R_6\}$ held by P_4 are identified. Then the processes $\{P_5\}$ waiting for R_6 are considered. It is found immediately that P_5 holds R_5 leading to the conclusion that a deadlock exists. This deadlock corresponds to the loop $P_2 \rightarrow R_5 \rightarrow P_5 \rightarrow R_6 \rightarrow P_4 \rightarrow R_1 \rightarrow P_2$.

6.3.3 System Management

The major shared resources supervised by an operating system are memory space and processing time. The memory management function was examined in Sec. 5.2. In this section we consider how an operating system manages CPU and IOP processing time. A multiprogramming environment is assumed in which many jobs are available, and each job alternates between normal processing by a single CPU and IO processing by one or more IOPs or DMA controllers. For example, a job may be executed by the CPU until an IO instruction is encountered, at which point the job is transferred to an IOP; see Fig. 6.56b. If the computer employs paged virtual memory, CPU execution is also suspended when a page fault occurs; again an IO operation is required, this time to perform a page swap.

Processor scheduling. A program can access an IO device and commence IO processing if the device is not busy, i.e., if it is not being used by another program, and if the IOP controlling the device can provide the necessary access channel between the IO device and main memory. Similarly, the CPU must be available before the program can begin CPU processing. Thus each program in a multiprogramming (or multiprocessing) environment can be viewed as being in one of four states:

S_0: Engaged in CPU processing
S_1: Awaiting CPU processing
S_2: Engaged in IO processing
S_3: Awaiting IO processing

When the CPU or an IO device becomes available, a waiting program is selected on some priority basis and assigned to the resource in question.

We now describe a straightforward scheduling technique designed to provide rapid response to requests for IO processing. It is assumed that a single CPU and a set of n IO devices $\{D_i\}$ are available. At any time each IO device can be used by only one program. A batch of m programs $\{Q_i\}$ is available for execution. Each program Q_i is assigned a priority $p(Q_i) \in \{p_0, p_1, p_2, \ldots\}$, where $p_i > p_j$ if $i < j$. Once a program gains access to the CPU, it is not replaced until one of the following events occurs.

1. An IO instruction is encountered by the CPU.
2. An (unmasked) IO interrupt is received by the CPU.
3. The CPU terminates execution of the current program due to encountering a trap instruction or an interrupt.

Figure 6.61 shows the possible state transitions for a program in this system. The CPU can keep track of the states of all the programs by maintaining four tables of the type shown in Fig. 6.62. The tables T_0, T_1, T_2, and T_3 list the programs in states S_0, S_1, S_2, and S_3, respectively. Also listed for each program Q_i is its priority $p(Q_i)$ (in T_1, T_2, and T_3 only) and the IO device $D(Q_i)$ it requires (in T_2 and T_3 only).

Suppose, for example, that the IO operation involving program Q_2 terminates and an IO interrupt is generated. From T_2 in Fig. 6.62 we see that this frees IO device D_1. The CPU responds to the interrupt by transferring control to the operating system, which then searches T_3 to find the highest-priority program, if any, awaiting access to D_1. In this case both Q_0 and Q_8 are waiting. Q_8 has the higher priority; the IO operation it requires is therefore initiated. The Q_8 entry is deleted from T_3 and inserted in T_2. The Q_2 entry is deleted from T_2. If Q_2 requires further processing by the CPU, it is entered into T_1. Figure 6.63 is a flowchart showing the detailed operation of this straightforward scheduling scheme. It can be called *IO driven*, since it can be expected that in most cases a change in state is caused by the initiation or termination of an IO operation.

Performance evaluation. Calculating the performance of a system with overlapped CPU and IO processing is quite difficult. Simulation is often the most practical

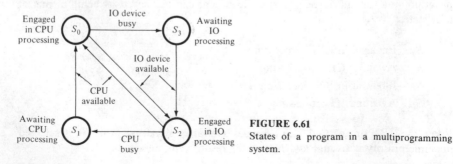

FIGURE 6.61
States of a program in a multiprogramming system.

Q_i		Q_i	$p(Q_i)$		Q_i	$p(Q_i)$	$D(Q_i)$		Q_i	$p(Q_i)$	$D(Q_i)$
Q_5		Q_1	p_0		Q_2	p_1	D_1		Q_0	p_7	D_1
		Q_3	p_5		Q_4	p_3	D_3		Q_8	p_6	D_1
		Q_7	p_0		Q_9	p_2	D_4				
					Q_6	p_9	D_6				
T_0		T_1			T_2				T_3		
Engaged in CPU processing		Awaiting CPU processing			Engaged in IO processing				Awaiting IO processing		

FIGURE 6.62
Tables used by the operating system to record program states.

approach. Analytic performance evaluation is possible if a sufficiently simple model of the system can be constructed. We now describe a queueing system model due to John W. Boyse and David R. Warn [1] that can be solved analytically. The structure of the system is shown in Fig. 6.64. The computer is designed for interactive support of a set of n users at input-output terminals. The operating system supports multiprogramming and a virtual memory system with demand paging. The IO system has m independent logical channels to the secondary memory devices used for paging. The number of programs that can occupy main memory at one time cannot exceed a certain value m, called the *multiprogramming level*.

The system operates as follows. A user enters a request via a terminal for execution of a job involving some program P. If space is available, P is loaded into main memory M, otherwise the request is entered into a queue for main memory. Once loaded, P competes for access to the CPU with the other programs currently available for execution in M. When it gains access to the CPU, P is executed until an IO operation is encountered, e.g., due to a page fault. When this happens, P relinquishes the CPU, which can then begin executing another program. (In this model, P may not perform both CPU and IO operations simultaneously.) After the IO operation terminates, P again seeks access to the CPU. The cycle of CPU and IO operations continues until the job in question has been completed. An appropriate response can then be sent to the user. A delay, the user "think" time, can be expected before the user enters a new request. To simplify the problem further, it is assumed that the only IO operation of interest is paging, that each program is associated with a different IO channel, and that the number of IO channels equals the multiprogramming level m. Hence there is no contention for IO channels.

From the foregoing description, we can conclude that the job in this system may be in any one of four states: waiting for access to M, waiting for access to the CPU, busy with a CPU operation, and busy with an IO operation. These states suggest that a queueing model for the system should include the following

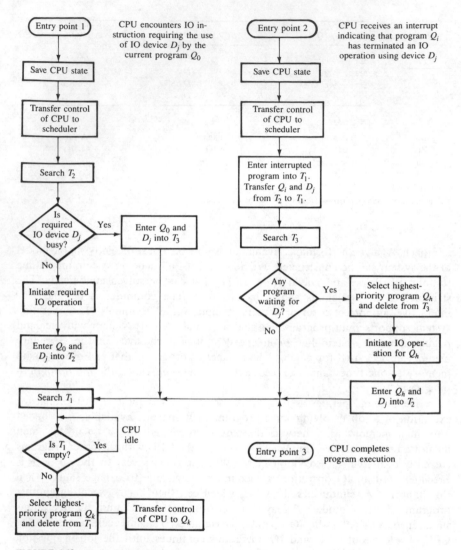

FIGURE 6.63
Flowchart for a multiprogramming scheduler.

components: a queue q_M for access to M; a queue q_{CPU} for access to the CPU; a single server s_{CPU} representing the CPU; and a set of m parallel servers s_1, $s_2, \ldots, s_m$ representing the m IO channels used for paging. Figure 6.65 shows the structure of the queueing model to be used; cf. the somewhat more general central server model of Fig. 2.77.

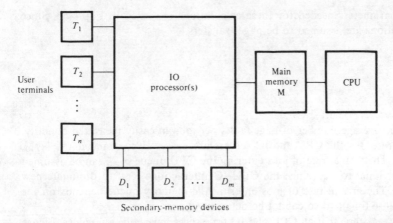

FIGURE 6.64
Structure of an interactive multiprogramming system.

We will now use this model to compute the following important performance measures:

1. The CPU utilization u_{CPU}, defined as the mean fraction of time the CPU is busy
2. The system throughput v, defined as the mean number of jobs completed per unit time
3. The system response time t_R, defined as the mean time between the entry of a job request by a user and his receipt of a response from the computer

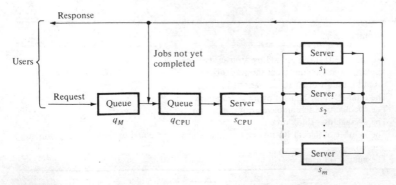

FIGURE 6.65
Queueing model for the multiprogramming system.

The input parameters needed for these calculations are listed in Fig. 6.66. Since all IO operations are assumed to be page transfers,

$$t_{CPU} = \frac{t_C}{f}$$

$$\tag{6.10}$$

$$t_{IO} = \frac{t_I}{f}$$

where f is the average number of page faults per job, an easily measured quantity. The service rates for the CPU and IO servers are $\mu_{CPU} = 1/t_{CPU}$ and $\mu_{IO} = 1/t_{IO}$, respectively. The arrival rate of jobs entering the CPU queue q_{CPU} can be assumed to be proportional to μ_{IO}, since the CPU-IO interactions tend to dominate new job arrivals. The arrival rate of jobs entering the memory queue depends on the system response time and so cannot be determined a priori.

First, we assume that all CPU and IO time slices have constant values. Figure 6.67 shows how the execution of m jobs is overlapped by the CPU in this case. From this diagram we see immediately that

$$u_{CPU} = \frac{m}{t_{CPU} + t_{IO}} = \frac{m}{1 + t_I/t_C}$$

provided that $mt_{CPU} \leq t_{CPU} + t_{IO}$; otherwise $u_{CPU} = 1$ and the system is CPU-bound. The system throughput v in jobs completed per unit time is given by

$$v = \frac{u_{CPU}}{t_C}$$

so that when $mt_{CPU} \leq t_{CPU} + t_{IO}$,

$$v = \frac{m}{t_C + t_I}$$

Parameter	Meaning
t_C	The total CPU time required by an average job
t_{CPU}	The average CPU time from the start or restart of execution of the job by the CPU until the start of an IO operation
t_I	The total IO time required by an average job
t_{IO}	The average time to complete an IO operation
t_Z	The average user think time
m	The number of logical IO channels available (assumed equal to the multiprogramming level)
n	The number of users

FIGURE 6.66
Input parameters for the multiprogramming system model.

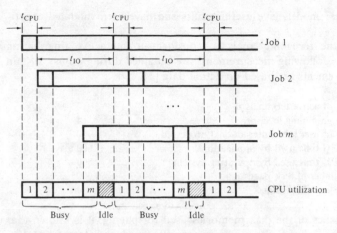

FIGURE 6.67
CPU utilization assuming constant CPU and IO processing time distributions.

To calculate the response time t_R, note that the computer must process an average of n jobs during the period $t_R + t_Z$. The time required to complete n jobs is n/v; hence

$$t_R = \frac{n}{v} - t_Z$$

If $mt_{CPU} \leq t_{CPU} + t_{IO}$, then

$$t_R = \frac{n\, t_C}{u_{CPU}} - t_Z \qquad (6.11)$$

A somewhat more accurate model is obtained if a job's CPU and IO time slices are exponentially distributed with the mean values t_{CPU} and t_{IO}, respectively. The probability that a CPU time slice is less than or equal to t is then defined by an expression of the form

$$p_{CPU}(t) = 1 - e^{-t/t_{CPU}}$$

Similarly,

$$p_{IO}(t) = 1 - e^{-t/t_{IO}}$$

Using these exponential distributions, it can be shown [1] that the CPU utilization is now given by

$$u_{CPU} = 1 - \left[m! \sum_{k=0}^{m} \frac{1}{(m-k)!} \left(\frac{t_{CPU}}{t_{IO}} \right)^k \right]^{-1}$$

Figure 6.68 shows a graph of u_{CPU} as a function of t_{CPU}/t_{IO} for both models when $m = 4$. Although the actual distributions of the CPU and IO times are neither constant nor exponential, these models give useful results and have been validated experimentally.

To illustrate the foregoing analysis, consider an interactive timesharing system for which the following measurements are obtained during a busy 30-min period; these measurements are based on actual data [1].

Number of active terminals n	10
Multiprogramming level m	4
Number of user jobs (interactions) processed	700
Total CPU time used by applications	600 s
Total CPU time used by operating system	800 s
Total number of disk pages read	80,000
Average user think time	4 s

From the characteristics of the disk memories used for paging, it is known that the average IO time associated with a page read is 40 ms, which is therefore taken to be t_{IO}. The average CPU time required by a job is $t_C = (600 + 800)/700 = 2$ s, and the average number f of page faults per job is $80,000/700 = 114.3$. Hence by (6.10), $t_{CPU} = 2000/114.3 = 17.5$ ms, and the ratio t_{CPU}/t_{IO} is $17.5/40 = 0.4375$. Since $m = 4$, the corresponding values of u_{CPU} from Fig. 6.68 are 1.0 for the constant distribution case and 0.80 for the more accurate exponential distribution. The actual CPU utilization from the given data is $(600 + 800)/1800 = 0.78$, indicating good agreement between the measured and predicted figures. The system throughput $v = u_{CPU}/t_C = 0.80/2.0 = 0.40$ jobs/s. From (6.11), the system response time $t_R = 10(2)/u_{CPU} - 4$, which is 16.0 s and 21.6 s for the constant and exponential models of u_{CPU}, respectively. From the measured CPU utilization, we get $t_R = 21.0$ s.

The operating systems of the 1960s such as IBM's OS/360 and Multics (*Mult*iplexed *I*nformation and *C*omputing *S*ervice), an operating system developed jointly by MIT and several industrial organizations, were massive pieces of

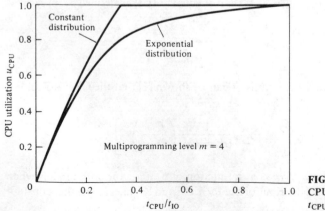

FIGURE 6.68
CPU utilization as a function of t_{CPU}/t_{IO}.

software requiring millions of lines of assembly-language source code in their larger versions. Their complexity was primarily a result of their generality, which aimed at efficiently meeting the needs of all types of computer users. These operating systems and their current successors run on relatively large and expensive computers, and mastering them requires considerable effort on the part of a system or application programmer. UNIX—the name is a play on the word Multics—is a more modest operating system designed at AT&T Bell Laboratories by Dennis M. Ritchie, Ken Thompson, and others to provide a convenient and easily learned software development environment for program developers and users. We now examine this particular operating system in detail.

> **Example 6.8 The UNIX operating system** [22, 26]. The goals of the UNIX designers were to provide a fairly simple interactive operating system oriented toward a general-purpose time-sharing environment. Simplicity was achieved by keeping the operating system proper quite small so that it can readily be implemented on mini- and microcomputers. The kernel of UNIX consists of only about 10,000 lines of source code written mainly in the high-level programming language C, a language developed specifically for implementing UNIX. The use of C as the source language, and the general availability of the source code, gives UNIX a considerable degree of portability between different computer types. The functions provided by UNIX for managing processes, IO, etc., are designed to be quite general, which has the effect of keeping the kernel small and, at the same time, enables UNIX to address an unusually wide number of operating system tasks. In addition, UNIX has associated with it a large set of general-purpose applications programs or *utilities*, such as compilers, debuggers, and text editors. These utilities, most of which are also written in C, have come to be considered an integral part of UNIX and have done much to enhance its popularity. UNIX has a powerful command interpreter called the *shell*, which provides a command language for the process-management facilities of the operating system, as well as access to the UNIX utilities. The operating system can also be accessed via system (supervisor) calls from C programs.
>
> UNIX recognizes two main types of processes, system (supervisor) and user. Each active program or user-created task is treated as a user process. When such a process requires an operating system function due to a trap or interrupt, a system process is invoked which then becomes the running process. System processes execute in the host processor's supervisor or privileged state, while user processes execute in the nonprivileged user state. (Note that these two processor states have hardware support in many computers ranging from the S/360-370 to the 68000 series.) The information associated with a process, termed an *image* in UNIX parlance, consists of the contents of the main memory locations used by the process, along with the processor status and register information constituting a process control block. The process image is constructed from several dynamic segments for instruction, data, and control stack storage. A process's image resides in main memory while it is being executed, but may (except for its process control block) be swapped out of memory when the process is inactive, or its space is needed for another process. UNIX employs a standard FIFO algorithm for allocating both main and secondary memory space.
>
> UNIX makes extensive use of the process concept and has a variety of mechanisms for manipulating processes. The kernel deals with each new task by

creating a process to handle it, so that at any time many different processes may be in concurrent execution. Various UNIX operations invoked by shell commands exist for managing processes. Figure 6.69 lists some representative commands available to the user for process control. Several concurrent processes can be initiated by writing a sequence of commands separated by "&". Processes communicate and synchronize their activities by means of events, which typically are control flags set by the occurrence of some specified condition. A process is suspended by instructing it to wait for an event to occur; it is subsequently dispatched by signaling the occurrence of the event in question.

In a normal uniprocessing UNIX environment only one process can be executed at a time. Processes are executed in timeshared fashion with each process receiving a slice of CPU time of no more than a second or so before it is suspended and a new process dispatched. UNIX assigns a priority number to every process, which determines which one to run next. System processes are given execution priorities based on their expected response needs. For example, processes to control disk transfers receive high priority, while processes that service user terminals receive low priority. User processes have lower priority than the lowest system-process priority. To ensure reasonably rapid user response, user processes that have received relatively little processor time are given higher priority than processes that have received a lot of processor time. Processes with the same priority are run in round-robin fashion. If a suspended process of higher priority wakes up, it preempts a running process of lower priority. To prevent some processes from being indefinitely suspended, UNIX increases the priority of processes that have been ignored for a long time.

A UNIX file is a one-dimensional array of characters (bytes) and is the basic unit for information storage on secondary (disk) memories. Files have no internal structures like the records found in many other file systems. There are essentially no restrictions on the length or contents of a file as seen by the user. Files are stored physically in pages (blocks) of a fixed size, initially 512 bytes, but larger block sizes are used in later versions of UNIX. UNIX maintains a set of internal tables (directories) to keep track of the disk files using a type of indexed-sequential organization to access the stored data.

The logical organization of UNIX files as seen by a user is that of a tree-structured hierarchy. The hierarchical file structure facilitates file management by users, and the protection of individual files and directories from unauthorized access. Special files called *directories* serve to group related files, and a user accesses a file by naming the directory that contains it. A directory can contain other

Command	Function performed
fork	Create a new (child) process
kill	Destroy process
pause	Suspend process until a specified event occurs
ps	Print status information on active processes
sleep	Suspend process execution for a specified time
wait	Wait for a child process to terminate
wake	Resume a suspended process

FIGURE 6.69
Some UNIX commands for process management.

directories leading to the file organization depicted in Fig. 6.70. The directory at the highest level of the tree is known as the *root*, and is denoted by the special name "/". The nondirectory files are at the lowest levels of the tree. The level below the root typically contains major system directories such as *bin*, which contains the UNIX utilities; *dev*, which contains special files including those used to access IO devices; and *usr*, which contains user directories and files. A file or directory is identified by specifying the sequence of directories that contain it, with directory names separated by a slash. For example, the file *mail* in Fig. 6.70 is referred to by */usr/tom/mail*, which is called the file's path name. UNIX provides a large number of operations for manipulating files, e.g., **create, close, copy, open, read,** and **write.**

An unusual feature of UNIX is its extension of the file concept to IO management. IO devices are treated as a special type of file, with device-specific IO driver routines serving to create the file interface to UNIX. Hence all IO operations can be handled by such UNIX file management operations as **open, close, read,** and **write**, which therefore can replace START IO, HALT IO, INPUT, and OUTPUT, respectively. This makes UNIX unusually independent of the characteristics of the IO devices attached to the host system, which enhances this operating system's generality and portability. Note, however, that this generality results in lower IO performance than can be achieved with other IO control methods. File concepts are also used for more general interprocess communication. A process can send **(write)** information to one end of the special queue-like file called a *pipe*, and the information can be received **(read)** from the other end by a second process.

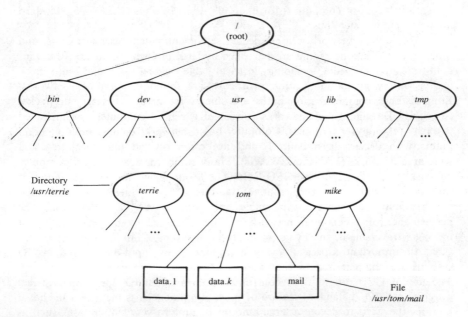

FIGURE 6.70
Logical structure of the UNIX file system.

6.4 SUMMARY

The communication methods used in a computer system depend on the physical distances involved. Intrasystem communication over short distances typically uses parallel buses that transmit binary digital signals. Intersystem communication, on the other hand, is often implemented with serial data transmission and, over long distances, analog rather than digital signals. Many interconnection topologies are possible. They differ in the degree to which the physical communication links are shared, and they offer various tradeoffs between communication bandwidth and cost. The extreme cases are dedicated unit-to-unit links that involve no sharing, and a single link shared by all communicating units.

Intrasystem communication in most computers is handled by a single shared bus; such buses are also found in IO subsystems. Information transfer over the bus may be synchronous or asynchronous, with the latter technique requiring handshaking control signals for timing purposes. At any time only two units, a bus master such as the CPU or a DMA controller, and a bus slave such as a memory unit or an IO port, can be logically connected to the bus. Various bus arbitration techniques such as daisy-chaining, polling, and independent requesting are used to determine which of several requesting units is to be given access to the bus. Buses are characterized by the numbers and types of data, address, and control lines they contain, and the conventions (protocols) used for signal transmission, synchronization, and arbitration. Standard buses have been defined for various types of computers, for example, the Multibus (IEEE 796) standard microcomputer system bus.

A computer network is a connected set of computers, user terminals, and other system components that are separated by large physical distances. Numerous data-transmission media, including electrical cable, optical fiber, and radio links, and a variety of communication protocols, are found in computer networks. Long-distance communication paths are shared by circuit, message, or packet switching. Terminal-based networks consist of a central computer system linked to many remote user terminals. Computer-based networks contain multiple computers with decentralized control, and are often divided into local-area and wide-area networks (LANs and WANs). Many standards also exist for computer networks, with the seven-layer ISO Reference Model providing general guidelines for standardization. A representative standard LAN architecture is Ethernet, which employs a shared coaxial cable link with CSMA/CD arbitration. The performance of a computer network can be measured by the mean delay of messages traversing it, and by its reliability in the event of link failures.

An important aspect of every computer is its input-output system. IO systems are characterized by the extent of CPU involvement in IO operations. The use of CPU programs to control all phases of an IO operation is called programmed IO, a standard feature of most computers. It is inefficient in that it requires the CPU to devote a large amount of time to very simple tasks such as IO data transfers. By providing the IO devices with direct memory access (DMA) controllers, simple data transfers can be implemented independently of the CPU.

The need for the CPU to test an IO device continually to determine its status is eliminated by IO interrupts. An IO interrupt causes the CPU to transfer control from its current program to an interrupt servicing program. Three kinds of interrupts were identified: single-line, multiple-line, and vectored interrupts, which differ in the amount of information transmitted to the CPU by the interrupt request signals.

The maximum independence between CPU and IO operations is achieved by providing IO processors (IOPs). An IOP is capable of executing IO programs that perform complex IO operations. The CPU and IOP communicate via a communication area in main memory, and by channel attention and interrupt request control lines. The CPU initiates an IO operation by placing the address of an IO program and other relevant parameters in the IOP communication area and executing a start IO instruction which activates an attention line. The IOP then proceeds to execute the IO program, which usually involves a sequence of DMA data transfers between main memory and IO devices. An IOP has a limited instruction set oriented toward data transfer and DMA control.

Most computers are controlled by a supervisory program called the operating system, which is responsible for efficient sharing of a computer's central processing, main memory, and IO facilities. The operating system manages a set of concurrent processes which carry out both its own control functions and user tasks defined by applications programs. At any time, one process is running on the host processor (CPU), while the other processes are either ready to be run, or are blocked (suspended) due to the unavailability of some needed resource or information. Processes change state in response to interrupts or supervisor calls (traps), which are handled by the kernel portion of the operating system residing permanently in main memory.

The existence of many processes competing for shared resources can lead to interprocess synchronization problems. One of these is the requirement that a process sometimes have exclusive access to a (critical) shared resource. This mutual exclusion problem can be solved at a low level by control flags or semaphores and, at a higher level, by monitor programs. A related problem is deadlock, which occurs when two or more processes are unable to proceed because each requires resources held by other processes. Deadlock can be prevented or minimized by implementing appropriate resource allocation rules. An efficient system management technique, which is the basis of multiprogramming, is to timeshare processes between CPU and IO processing. One of the more widely used timesharing operating systems designed for smaller computers is UNIX.

PROBLEMS

6.1. Specify the data-transmission media, data formats, and signaling protocols used for each of the following communication tasks: linking the CPU and memory of a microcomputer; linking a detached keyboard to a user terminal; connecting a terminal to a remote computer via the public telephone network. Provide a brief justification for your choices in each case.

6.2. Compare and contrast synchronous and asynchronous buses from the viewpoints of data bandwidth, interface circuit cost, and reliability.

6.3. Define each of the following terms in the context of bus design: handshaking; lock signal; master unit; skew; tristate; wait state.

6.4. Analyze the three bus arbitration methods, daisy-chaining, polling, and independent requesting, with respect to communication reliability in the event of hardware failures.

6.5. Consider the timing diagram for a data transfer via the PDP-11 UNIBUS which appears in Fig. 6.16. Explain why a delay (at least 75 ns) is allowed by the master unit between deactivating MASTER SYNC and clearing the address bus and CONTROL lines.

6.6. Draw timing diagrams for synchronous and asynchronous write operations corresponding to the read operations shown in Figs. 6.12 and 6.16, respectively.

6.7. Explain the function of each of the following signals appearing in the Multibus (IEEE 796) bus: $\overline{\text{BPRN}}$, $\overline{\text{BUSY}}$, $\overline{\text{LOCK}}$, $\overline{\text{MRDC}}$, $\overline{\text{IOWC}}$, $\overline{\text{XACK}}$.

6.8. The Multibus's two inhibit lines $\overline{\text{INH1:2}}$ lines are intended to stop temporarily certain memory locations or IO ports from responding to read or write commands. Thus they make it possible to assign the same addresses to several memory or IO units provided all but one unit is inhibited whenever these addresses are used. In a typical application, a RAM M_1 and a ROM M_2 are attached to the bus and assigned the same set of addresses. M_1 is inhibited by $\overline{\text{INH1}}$, while M_2 is inhibited by $\overline{\text{INH2}}$. Suggest a specific application in computer design where this type of inhibition control might be useful.

6.9. Carry out the logic design of the parallel arbitration unit for the Multibus system of Fig. 6.23b assuming that $n = 8$. Use standard types of SSI/MSI logic components in your design.

6.10. Define each of the following contrasting pairs of terms in the context of computer networks:
(a) Twisted pair vs coaxial cable
(b) Simplex vs duplex
(c) Circuit switching vs packet switching
(d) Local area vs wide area
(e) Baseband vs broadband

6.11. Sketch the system-level design of a terminal multiplexer that is connected to a set of local interactive terminals as shown in Fig. 6.26b. Assume that the multiplexer is microprocessor-based, and that the terminals are connected to it by dedicated twisted pairs. Assume also that HDLC or a similar data-link protocol is used and that the multiplexer employs programmed IO. Give a block diagram showing the multiplexer's internal structure. Also give a one-page flowchart showing the multiplexer's overall operation.

6.12. Compare and contrast the CSMA/CD and token-passing network arbitration techniques from the viewpoints of response time, fairness, and fault tolerance.

6.13. A *private branch exchange* (PBX), which is a small microprocessor-controlled switching unit designed for connecting telephones within a single building to one another and also linking them to outside lines, can form the basis for a low-cost computer LAN. User terminals and computers are connected to the PBX via modems and twisted pair links. Users access the computers via telephone calls routed through the PBX. Write a short essay comparing and contrasting a PBX-based LAN with an Ethernet LAN.

6.14. A single communication line transmits messages from A to B. The line has a capacity (bandwidth) of c bits per second. Messages arrive at A with a Poisson distribution and a mean rate of λ messages per second. The message length measured in bits is an independent random variable with mean value m and second moment s. The mean time to service a message is assumed to be m/c. Derive an expression for the mean message delay t_D in terms of c, λ, m, and s.

6.15. Let G be a graph with n nodes, m edges, and edge connectivity $c_E(G)$. Prove that $c_E(G) \leq \lfloor 2m/n \rfloor$.

6.16. Consider a computer network whose structure is represented by the graph in Fig. 6.32. Let 0.01 be the failure probability of each link in the network. Calculate the probability of the entire network failing, i.e., becoming disconnected.

6.17. Define each of the following IO control methods: programmed IO, DMA controllers, IOPs. List the advantages and disadvantages of each method with respect to program design complexity, IO bandwidth, and interface hardware costs.

6.18. Consider a 32-bit RISC microprocessor with a 32-bit data bus and a 32-bit address bus. The CPU operates at 10 MHz, and a memory load or store instruction cycle takes two CPU clock cycles. Memory-mapped I/O is used and the CPU supports both vectored interrupts and DMA block transfers with arbitrary block length. Typical interrupt response time is ten CPU clock cycles. It is desired to add to the system a disk drive with a data-transfer rate of N bits/s. Estimate the maximum value that N can have for each of the following ways of controlling the disk drive: programmed I/O and DMA. Show all your calculations, and state all your assumptions (both hardware and software).

6.19. (*a*) A typical CPU allows most interrupt requests to be enabled and disabled under software control. In contrast, no CPU provides facilities to disable DMA request signals. Explain why this is so.

(*b*) Suppose that for some reason it is desired to be able occasionally to delay a CPU's response to a DMA request to the end of the current instruction cycle. Design the necessary add-on logic to implement this type of delayed DMA request, assuming that a conventional one-chip CPU is being used whose internal hardware or instruction set cannot be modified. A pair of existing instructions should serve to turn on (enable) and turn off (disable) the DMA delay. State clearly all the assumptions underlying your design.

6.20. Using register-level components, carry out the logic design for the interrupt priority circuit shown in Fig. 6.47. Assume that $n = 8$.

6.21. A computer consists of a CPU and an IO device D connected to main memory M via a one-word shared bus. The CPU can execute a maximum of 10^5 instructions per second. An average instruction requires five machine cycles, three of which use the memory bus. A memory read or write operation uses one machine cycle. Suppose that the CPU is continuously executing "background" programs that require 95 percent of its instruction execution rate but no IO instructions. Now the IO device is to be used to transfer very large blocks of data to and from M.

(*a*) If programmed IO is used and each one-word IO transfer requires the CPU to execute two instructions, estimate the maximum IO data-transfer rate r_{MAX} possible through D.

(*b*) Estimate r_{MAX} if DMA transfer is used.

6.22. Using the data provided by Example 6.5, describe in general terms how each of the following methods can be used to arbitrate among very large numbers of interrupt requests in a conventional computer: daisy-chaining, polling, independent requesting. Assume that a ready-made interrupt priority controller is not available. Illustrate one of your answers with a diagram showing how the relevant signals are interfaced to the CPU.

6.23. In addition to supporting memory-IO communication, some DMA controllers and IOPs also support block transfers from one region of main memory to another, i.e., they perform memory-to-memory communication via DMA block transfers.

    (*a*) Explain how a main memory block transfer can be implemented by an IOP such as the Intel 8089. Describe also the IO instructions needed to set up this type of operation.

    (*b*) What are the advantages and disadvantages of this type of main memory block transfer compared with implementing the same data transfer by means of a BLOCK MOVE instruction, such as is found in many CPU instruction sets.

6.24. An IOP controls data transfers between main memory and a set of IO devices with widely differing data-transfer rates. The IOP can interleave (multiplex) transfers involving several IO devices provided that their combined effect does not exceed the data-transfer capacity of the system. Data transfers are initiated by requests from the IO devices. A request is accepted by the IOP only if it has sufficient spare capacity to service the requesting device. Devise an easily implemented algorithm for use by the IOP to determine whether or not it can accept a service request from an IO device. State all assumptions you make.

6.25. A new computer intended to have very fast and efficient IO processing abilities is being designed. List all the features of the IBM S/360-370 IO system that you would *not* include in the new computer. In each case give your reasons for rejecting the S/360-370 approach and define your alternative approach.

6.26. Define each of the following terms in the context of operating system design: critical code, deadlock, monitor, process, semaphore, spooling.

6.27. What are the advantages of defining two distinct classes of software processes for system management: system (supervisor) processes and user processes? Describe the hardware features typically provided in a CPU to support this process dichotomy.

6.28. The following three-instruction program written in Intel 8086 assembly language is proposed for implementing the wait or test-and-set function for a binary semaphore S. All major actions of the instructions are specified by the comments. The 8086-based CPU is connected via the Multibus to a global memory storing S. The Multibus $\overline{\text{LOCK}}$ signal is not activated unless an instruction to which it is applicable is preceded by the prefix LOCK.

```
WAIT:   TEST S, 0   ; Fetch the variable S and compare to zero. Set the Z flag
                    ;   to 1 if S = 0 (not busy), otherwise set the Z flag to 0.
        JNE WAIT    ; Jump to WAIT if Z = 1, otherwise continue to next
                    ;   instruction.
        MOV S, 1    ; Set S to 1 (busy)
```

    (*a*) Explain clearly why this code fails to meet the mutual exclusion requirement for semaphore access.

    (*b*) Design a replacement program that solves this problem, using comments to explain your instructions. Indicate how exclusive access to S is ensured.

6.29. Write a simple monitor in the style of Fig. 6.58 that provides access to a certain shared resource which can only be used by one process at a time.

6.30. A certain multiprogramming system supports spooling for a low-speed line printer. Lines to be printed are routed in piecemeal fashion from a large number of active jobs to a buffer region on a disk. The lines associated with a job are accumulated on the disk until the job has been completed. At that point all the job's output lines are printed and then deleted from the disk. Explain why deadlocks sometimes occur in this type of spooling system. What actions should the operating system take to recover from a deadlock? How can the operating system be designed to prevent spooling deadlocks?

6.31. Consider the operating system state described by the resource allocation graph G of Figure 6.59. Let resource R_6 and the edges connected to it be removed from G to form a new graph G'.
  (a) Does G' contain a deadlock?
  (b) Suppose that P_3 and P_5 request access to R_3 in G'. Can these new requests lead to deadlock?
  (c) Suppose that P_1 and P_2 request access to a new resource R_7 added to G'. Can this lead to deadlock?

6.32. A hypothetical timesharing system has the following parameters. The system handles up to four concurrent programs, each needing an average of 5 s of CPU time, which is allocated to the job in time slices of average length 0.02 s. CPU processing generally proceeds until an IO operation is required. The average IO operation is a page swap and requires 100 ms. The typical user think time is estimated to be 8 s. Stating your assumptions, estimate the following performance measures:
  (a) The mean system response time when there are four active jobs
  (b) The mean fraction of time the CPU is idle

6.33. (a) Identify and briefly compare the mechanisms available for interprocess communication in the UNIX operating system.
  (b) What are the advantages and disadvantages of treating all IO devices as logical files in the manner of UNIX?

REFERENCES

1. Boyse, J. W., and D. R. Warn: "A Straightforward Model for Computer Performance Prediction," *Comput. Surv.*, vol. 7, pp. 73–93, June 1975.
2. Dietel, H. M.: *Introduction to Operating Systems*, rev. 1st ed., Addison-Wesley, Reading, Mass., 1984.
3. Digital Equipment Corp.: *Introduction to Local Area Networks*, Maynard, Mass., 1984.
4. Digital Equipment Corp.: *PDP-11 Interface Manual*, 2d ed., Maynard, Mass., 1971.
5. Dijkstra, E. W., "Solution to a Problem in Concurrent Programming Control," *Communic. ACM*, vol. 8, p. 569, September 1965.
6. El-Ayat, K. A.: "The Intel 8089: an Integrated IO Processor," *IEEE Computer*, vol. 12, no. 6, pp. 67–78, June 1979.
7. Frank, H., R. E. Kahn, and L. Kleinrock: "Computer Communication Network Design—Experience with Theory and Practice," *AFIPS Conf. Proc.*, vol. 40, pp. 255–270, 1972.
8. Gustavson, D. B.: "Computer Buses—A Tutorial," *IEEE Micro*, vol. 4, no. 4, pp. 7–22, August 1984.
9. Halsall, F.: *Introduction to Data Communications and Computer Networks*, Addison-Wesley, Wokingham, England, 1985.
10. Harary, F.: *Graph Theory*, Addison-Wesley, Reading, Mass., 1969.
11. Heart, F. E., et al.: "The Interface Message Processor for the ARPA Computer Network," *AFIPS Conf. Proc.*, vol. 36, pp. 551–567, 1970.

12. Hoare, C. A. R.: "Monitors: an Operating System Structuring Concept," *Communic. ACM,* vol. 17, pp. 549–557, October 1974. Corrigendum, *Communic. ACM,* vol. 18, p. 95, February 1975.
13. IBM Corp.: *IBM System/370 Principles of Operation,* Publ. GA22-7000-4. White Plains, N.Y., 1974.
14. IBM Corp.: *IBM System/360 and System/370 I/O Interface Channel to Control Unit: Original Equipment Manufacturers' Information,* Publ. GA22-6974-3, Poughkeepsie, N.Y., 1976.
15. Intel Corp.: *Multibus II Bus Architecture Specification Handbook,* Santa Clara, Calif., 1984.
16. Intel Corp.: *Peripheral Design Handbook,* Santa Clara, Calif., 1981.
17. Johnson, J. B., and S. Kassel: *The Multibus Design Guidebook,* McGraw-Hill, New York, 1984.
18. Kleinrock, L.: *Communication Nets: Stochastic Message Flow and Delay,* McGraw-Hill, New York, 1964. (Reprinted by Dover Publications, New York, 1972.)
19. Kleinrock, L.: *Queueing Systems,* vol. I, *Theory,* vol. II, *Computer Applications,* Wiley, New York, 1975 (vol. I) and 1976 (vol. II).
20. Martin, J.: *Telecommunications and the Computer,* 2d ed., Prentice-Hall, Englewood Cliffs, N.J., 1976.
21. Peterson, W. W., and E. J. Weldon: *Error-Correcting Codes,* 2d ed., MIT Press, Cambridge, Mass., 1972.
22. Ritchie, D. M., and K. Thompson: "The UNIX Time-Sharing System," *Bell Sys. Tech. J.,* vol. 57, pp. 1905–1929, July/August 1978.
23. Shoch, J., and J. Hupp: "Measured Performance of an Ethernet Local Network," *Communic. ACM,* vol. 23, pp. 711–721, December 1980.
24. Stone, H. S.: *Microcomputer Interfacing,* Addison-Wesley, Reading, Mass., 1984.
25. Theaker, C. J., and G. R. Brookes: *A Practical Course in Operating Systems,* Springer Verlag, New York, 1983.
26. Thompson, K.: "UNIX Implementation," *Bell Sys. Tech. J.,* vol. 57, pp. 1931–1946, July/August 1978.
27. Thurber, K. J., et al.: "A Systematic Approach to the Design of Digital Bussing Structures," *AFIPS Conf. Proc.,* vol. 41, pp. 719–740, 1972.
28. Toy, W., and B. Zee: *Computer Hardware/Software Architecture,* Prentice-Hall, Englewood Cliffs, N.J., 1986.
29. Triebel, W. A., and A. Singh: *The 68000 Microprocessor,* Prentice-Hall, Englewood Cliffs, N.J., 1986.

Techniques to speed up computers by performing many operations simultaneously or in parallel form the subject of this chapter. Two major types of parallel computers are considered in detail: pipeline (vector) processors and multiprocessors. The endowing of computers with the ability to tolerate faults is also discussed.

7.1 BASIC CONCEPTS

We begin by surveying the different types of parallelism, along with the methods used to classify parallel computers and measure their performance.

7.1.1 Introduction

The term parallel processing refers to a large class of methods that attempt to increase computing speed by performing more than one computation concurrently. A parallel processor is a computer that implements some parallel processing technique. Like any type of computing, parallel processing can be viewed at various levels of complexity. At the gate level, for instance, a distinction is made between serial arithmetic circuits, which process numbers 1 bit at a time, and parallel arithmetic circuits, in which all bits of a number are processed concurrently, i.e., during the same clock cycle. (Compare the serial and parallel adder circuits of Sec. 3.3.1.) At the register level, where the basic unit of information is the word, we distinguish serial and parallel machines based on whether one or more words (instructions or data) can be processed in parallel. Thus a vector computer, which performs computations on all words of a multiword vector simultaneously, is considered to be a type of parallel processor.

All modern computers involve some degree of parallelism. Early electronic computers such as the EDVAC processed data bit by bit and are now classed as *serial computers*. In contrast, later machines like the IAS computer, which carried out their computations word by word, were sometimes termed parallel computers. The introduction of IO processors added a new element of parallelism, allowing both CPU instructions and IO instructions to be executed simultaneously. Because of their almost universal use in modern computers, the foregoing types of parallelism are of limited value for distinguishing computer types. Following current practice, therefore, the term *parallel processor* will be used in this chapter to refer to a computer or a portion thereof that is designed to process more than one basic CPU instruction in parallel. Conventional machines that can only execute one CPU instruction at a time are termed *sequential processors*. (The term *uniprocessor* is also used for such machines, principally to contrast them with a particular class of parallel computers, namely, multiprocessors.)

Motivation. Although sequential computers have increased steadily in performance over the years, primarily as a result of improvements in digital hardware technology, many important computational tasks remain beyond the capabilities of the fastest current machines of this type. Such a task T can sometimes be tackled by breaking it into a set of smaller subtasks that can be solved simultaneously on a parallel computer. Suppose that a parallel processor P_n can be constructed by combining n copies of a sequential processor P_1. If task T can be partitioned into n subtasks $T_1, T_2, \ldots, T_n$ of approximately equal size, and P_n can be programmed so that all its n constituent processors execute their subtasks in parallel, then we would expect P_n to execute T up to n times faster than P_1. This potentially higher performance is the main motivation for the introduction of parallelism into computers.

Another concern of computer designers is that logic and memory devices are approaching ultimate physical limits on their size and speed. While size reductions and speed increases of a few orders of magnitude beyond present levels seem feasible, further improvements in the performance of sequential computers may not be achievable at acceptable cost. On the other hand, a parallel computer with, say, 1024 processors offers a potential speed increase of approximately three orders of magnitude over a comparable sequential computer using the same hardware technology. A further advantage of parallelism is tolerance of hardware and, to a lesser extent, software faults. While failure of its CPU is almost always fatal to a sequential computer, a parallel computer can be designed to continue functioning, perhaps in a degraded mode, in the presence of defective or nonfunctional CPUs.

Some important applications for the highest-performance parallel processors, the so-called *supercomputers*, are listed in Fig. 7.1. These problems are characterized by the fact that they require a vast number of computations, such as floating-point arithmetic operations, on an equally vast number of operands (data points). They can also be fairly easily partitioned into subproblems that can be executed largely independently of one another, thus allowing parallel processing techniques

Expert systems for artificial intelligence
Fluid flow analysis
Geophysical exploration via seismic data analysis
Long-range weather forecasting
Medical diagnosis by computer-assisted tomography
Nuclear reactor modeling
Visual image processing
VLSI circuit design and simulation

FIGURE 7.1
Representative application areas for parallel processors.

to be applied to their solution. For example, many important problems in science and engineering can be formulated mathematically in terms of vectors and matrices, which lend themselves particularly well to parallel processing. The efficient solution of numerical problems of this type has had considerable influence on the architecture of parallel computers.

Parallel processing methods are also important in the solution of many computation-intensive tasks that are nonnumerical and relatively unstructured in nature. For instance, the associative memory architecture discussed in Sec. 5.3.3 has been generalized to a class of highly parallel associative processors that can rapidly perform very complex logical operations like choosing one of a large number of loosely related alternatives. Parallel processors that can mimic aspects of human information processing in this fashion also underlie the so-called fifth-generation computers. At present, however, the parallel algorithms needed by such machines are poorly understood compared with more traditional numerical algorithms.

Illustration. Next we examine some simple examples of parallel processing methods applied to numerical problems. Consider first the task of computing the sum SUM of N numbers (constants) $b_1, b_2, \ldots, b_N$. An obvious algorithm for solving this problem can be expressed as follows in our program-like description language:

$$\text{SUM} \leftarrow 0;$$
$$\textbf{for } i = 1 \textbf{ to } N \textbf{ do } \text{SUM} \leftarrow \text{SUM} + b[i]; \tag{7.1}$$

If this summation algorithm is implemented on a conventional sequential computer, N consecutive add operations, each taking time T_{add}, are required. Certain other bookkeeping operations are also necessary, such as initializing SUM to zero, and the indexing operations implied by the **for-do** loop. These operations depend on implementation details and so are often omitted in gauging the complexity of tasks of this sort. Thus NT_{add} serves as a rough indication of time needed by a sequential computer to execute (7.1). We now consider in detail a simple parallel processing approach to this problem.

Example 7.1 Summation by a one-dimensional array multiprocessor. Consider a hypothetical computer containing n identical processors P_i, each of which is a small sequential computer with its own CPU and local main memory. The n processors are interconnected in the linear (one-dimensional) array configuration depicted in Fig.

7.2. Each P_i is connected via dedicated buses to its left and right neighbors, P_{i-1} and P_{i+1} (where they exist), and communicates with them by means of two special IO operations called **send** and **receive**. The command **send**(NEIGHBOR, MESSAGE) causes P_i to output some data called MESSAGE, e.g., the result of a computational step, either to P_{i-1} (NEIGHBOR = LEFT) or else to P_{i+1} (NEIGHBOR = RIGHT). When P_i executes **receive**(NEIGHBOR, MESSAGE), it waits for MESSAGE to be sent to it from the designated neighbor, and then inputs MESSAGE into its local memory. **send** and **receive** may be programmed by message-handling subroutines or procedures whose implementation details are not of concern here. We assume that the processor array also has unspecified IO facilities connecting it to the outside world via the rightmost processor P_n, as suggested by Fig. 7.2. Clearly, by repeated use of **send** and **receive**, data can be transferred between any processor in the array and the outside world.

The summation problem (7.1) can be solved in parallel on this machine in the following way. Suppose for simplicity that $N = kn$, where k is an integer. The N given numbers are divided into n sets of k numbers and each set is loaded into the local memory of one of the n available processors. Every processor is provided with a copy of a summation program that it executes on its k numbers. Since all processors can operate in parallel, nk additions resulting in n partial sum can be performed in the time required to do k add operations. The partial sums must then be summed to give the final result. We assume that this is done by each processor P_i transmitting its result to its right neighbor P_{i+1}, which then adds the received sum to its own sum and transmits the new result to P_{i+2}. Thus after $n - 1$ sequential summation and data-transfer operations, the final result is stored in P_n.

A program to implement the foregoing parallel summation scheme is given in Fig. 7.3. It is placed in the local memory of each processor P_i and executed using that processor's particular data set (k of the nk numbers to be summed). It is assumed that P_i also stores a variable INDEX, which is its own address i; in other words, each P_i "knows" its location within the array of processors. We also assume that the processor P_n at the end of the array knows that it has only one neighboring processor, and that it interprets the program of Fig. 7.3 accordingly. The communication between the processors is such that each P_i on encountering **receive** waits until P_{i-1} has completed transmission of its result SUM, which P_i then stores internally as LEFTSUM.

The time $T(n)$ needed to execute the parallel summation algorithm on n processors has two main parts. There is a local computation time T_L due primarily to the $k = N/n$ sequential additions performed in parallel by each of the n processors; this may be written $K_1 N/n$, where K_1 is some constant depending on the processor add time, and any associated bookkeeping operations. The second component T_C of $T(n)$ consists of the communication time to send $n - 1$ intermediate results from left to right and to perform the final $n - 1$ additions. T_C may be written as $K_2(n - 1)$, where K_2 is a constant that mainly represents interprocessor communication delays. Thus, ignoring minor constant terms, the n-processor execution time may be approximated by

$$T(n) = T_L + T_C = \frac{K_1 N}{n} + K_2(n - 1) \qquad (7.2)$$

FIGURE 7.2
One-dimensional (linear) array of n processors.

{Each processor P_i computes the sum of its local numbers $b(1:k)$}
    SUM $\leftarrow$ 0;
    for $i = 1$ **to** k **do** SUM $\leftarrow$ SUM $+ b(i)$;
{Processor P_1 sends its local result SUM to P_2}
    if INDEX $= 1$ **then**
    begin
      if $n > 1$ **then** send(RIGHT, SUM);
    end else
{Every remaining P_i waits to receive an external result from P_{i-1}}
    begin
      receive(LEFT, LEFTSUM);
      SUM $\leftarrow$ SUM + LEFTSUM;
      {Each P_i except P_n sends its new value of SUM to P_{i+1}}
      if INDEX $< n$ **then** send(RIGHT, SUM);
    end;

FIGURE 7.3
Parallel summation program for the machine of Fig. 7.2.

Since K_2 measures the time for a relatively slow message-passing IO operation, it is usually much larger than K_1. Thus the reduction in computation time T_L obtained by increasing the number of processors n is offset by the increase in communication time T_C. Tradeoffs of this kind between computation and communication times are common to all parallel processing tasks. The execution time for a comparable sequential computer to solve the summation may be obtained by setting n to 1 in Eq. (7.2), yielding

$$T(1) = T_L = K_1 N \qquad (7.3)$$

As expected, the local processing time T_L increases by a factor of n and the interprocessor communication time T_C reduces to zero.

A problem closely related to the foregoing one is to compute all N partial sums defined by the recurrence relation

$$x_i = x_{i-1} + b_i \qquad \text{for } i = 1, 2, \ldots, N \qquad (7.4)$$

Comparing this to (7.1), we see that the latter is designed to compute only one number SUM $= x_N$ as the final result. However, with a relatively trivial modification, (7.1) and the program of Fig. 7.3 can be made to compute and store the ordered set or *vector* of N values denoted $(x_1, x_2, \ldots, x_N)$, in place of the single or *scalar* value x_N. The relation (7.4) may be rewritten as a set of N equations thus:

$$
\begin{aligned}
x_1 \qquad\qquad\qquad &= b_1 \\
-x_1 + x_2 \qquad\qquad &= b_2 \\
-x_2 + x_3 \qquad &= b_3 \\
\cdots\cdots\cdots\cdots\cdots\cdots\cdots\cdots&\cdots \\
-x_{N-1} + x_N &= b_N
\end{aligned}
\qquad (7.5)
$$

The solution of these equations is the required vector of N partial sums.

Now (7.5) is a special case of a set of linear equations which have the following general form:

$$a_{1,1}x_1 + a_{1,2}x_2 + \cdots + a_{1,m}x_m = b_1$$
$$a_{2,1}x_1 + a_{2,2}x_2 + \cdots + a_{2,m}x_m = b_2$$
$$\cdots\cdots\cdots\cdots\cdots\cdots\cdots\cdots\cdots\cdots$$
$$a_{n,1}x_1 + a_{n,2}x_2 + \cdots + a_{n,m}x_m = b_n$$

(7.6)

Here the $a_{i,j}$'s and b_i's can represent either integer (fixed-point) or real (floating-point) numbers, and the x_i's are integer or real variables whose values are to be determined. Equations (7.6) can be expressed more concisely as

$$A \times X = B$$

where A denotes the two-dimensional array or matrix

$$\begin{bmatrix} a_{1,1} & a_{1,2} & \cdots & a_{1,m} \\ a_{2,1} & a_{2,2} & \cdots & a_{2,m} \\ \cdots & \cdots & \cdots & \cdots \\ a_{n,1} & a_{n,2} & \cdots & a_{n,m} \end{bmatrix}$$

the operator $\times$ denotes matrix multiplication, and X and B denote the (column) vectors

$$X = \begin{bmatrix} x_1 \\ x_2 \\ \cdot \\ \cdot \\ \cdot \\ x_m \end{bmatrix} \quad B = \begin{bmatrix} b_1 \\ b_2 \\ \cdot \\ \cdot \\ \cdot \\ b_n \end{bmatrix}$$

The matrix A can be decomposed into a set of n row vectors or m column vectors, so that the solution of sets of equations like (7.5) and (7.6) is essentially a *vector processing* task. Problems of the foregoing type occur frequently in scientific computation; for example, they underlie most of the supercomputer applications listed in Fig. 7.1. The regular structure of vector problems makes them well suited to solution by parallel processing methods.

Consider, for instance, evaluation of the expression

$$a_{1,1}x_1 + a_{1,2}x_2 + \cdots + a_{1,m}x_m = b_1$$

(7.7)

which forms row 1 of (7.6). In vector notation this can be written as

$$A_1 \cdot X = b_1$$

where $\cdot$ denotes a vector operation called *dot product*. Evaluation of (7.7) clearly requires m pairs of scalars to be multiplied. These (scalar) multiplications can all be done simultaneously if appropriate parallel multiplier circuits are available. Each multiplier independently multiplies two scalar components of A_1 and X yielding a product $y_j = a_{1,j}x_j$. The summation of the m products $y_1, y_2, \ldots, y_m$, which was discussed earlier for the system of Fig. 7.3, can also take advantage of parallel processing. Note that $y_1, y_2, \ldots, y_m$ may be regarded as a vector. Suppose that

$m = 2k$ and that at least k independent adders are available. We can simultaneously perform the k required additions thus:

$$z_1 \leftarrow y_1 + y_2, \quad z_2 \leftarrow y_3 + y_4, \quad \ldots, \quad z_k \leftarrow y_{m-1} + y_m$$

Now the final sum b_1 can be expressed as the sum of the k numbers $z_1, z_2, \ldots, z_k$. By performing $k/2$ additions in parallel on the z_j's, we can further halve the number of operands. Continuing in this manner we obtain b_1 after performing a total of $m - 1$ additions in $\log_2 m$ addition time steps. Thus with sufficient parallelism available, and ignoring any communication overhead, the entire evaluation of the dot product of two vectors of length m need take no more than one multiplication time and $\log_2 m$ addition times.

Implementation. As illustrated above, the primary advantage of parallel processing is the achievement of higher computational speed. A price is paid for this speed in the need for a significant amount of extra hardware. Consequently, parallel processors did not come into widespread use until technological improvements, such as the development of VLSI circuits, greatly lowered the cost and size of computer hardware.

Roughly speaking, by increasing the effective number of processors by a factor of n, an n-fold increase in computing performance becomes possible. In practice, this maximum performance speedup is rarely achieved, because it is difficult to keep all members of a set of parallel processors continually working at their maximum rates. Interdependencies among subtasks may require a processor to wait until other processors supply certain results that it needs. In the parallel summation algorithm discussed for the one-dimensional processor array (Fig. 7.3), for instance, the processors on the right are kept waiting for data to be sent from their left neighbors. In addition, the processors in a parallel computer usually share common resources such as main-memory modules, IO devices, or operating system subroutines, that can only be used by one processor at a time. Thus if some processor requests immediate access to a memory module that is being used by another processor, the requesting processor must wait until the required module is released by the first processor. A major issue, therefore, in designing and programming parallel systems is to avoid conflicts in the use of shared resources. The extent to which all processors can be kept busy depends on the computer architecture, the tasks being performed, and the manner in which the tasks have been programmed.

In general, parallel computers are much more difficult to program than sequential ones. As illustrated by Fig. 7.3, parallel computers may require special programming languages that allow processors to communicate with one another, and can specify complex actions like vector and matrix operations. Many issues in parallel programming are still only partially understood, so that the achievement of an acceptable level of performance may require a large and costly software development effort. This is especially true when programming for tasks which, unlike the examples discussed above, display little overt parallelism. Although there is evidence [24] that most programs for sequential computers contain significant amounts of potential parallelism that could be exploited by a parallel computer, this parallelism is often difficult to recognize. Ordinary programs also contain significant numbers of inherently sequential operations which cannot be processed in parallel. As discussed in Sec. 7.1.3 below, even a small percentage of sequential operations can have a large detrimental effect on the performance of a parallel computer. Removal of these sequential features is a major challenge in the design of algorithms, programming languages, and compilers for parallel processing.

7.1.2 Types of Parallel Processors

There are many ways of classifying parallel processors based on their structure or behavior. The major classification methods consider the number of instructions and/or operand sets that can be processed simultaneously, the internal organization of the processors, the interprocessor connection structure, or the methods used to control the flow of instructions and data through the system.

Flynn's classification. A typical central processing unit (CPU) operates by fetching instructions and operands from main memory, executing the instructions, and placing the results in main memory. The steps associated with the processing of an instruction form an instruction cycle; see Fig. 7.4. The instructions can be viewed as forming an *instruction stream* flowing from main memory to the processor, while the operands form another stream, the *data stream*, flowing to and from the processor, as depicted in Fig. 7.5.

Michael J. Flynn has made an informal and widely used classification of processor parallelism based on the number of simultaneous instruction and data streams seen by the processor during program execution [13]. Suppose that a processor P is operating at its maximum capacity, so that its full degree of parallelism is being exhibited. Let m_I and m_D denote the minimum number of instruction and data streams, respectively, that are being actively processed in any of the seven steps listed in Fig. 7.4. m_I and m_D are termed the instruction- and data-stream *multiplicities* of P, and measure its degree of parallelism. Note that m_I and m_D are defined by the minimum instead of the maximum number of streams flowing at any point, since the most limiting components of the system (its bottlenecks) determine the overall parallel processing capabilities.

Computers can be roughly divided into four major groups based on the values of m_I and m_D associated with their CPUs.

---

1. Generate the next instruction address.
2. Fetch the instruction.
3. Decode the instruction.
4. Generate the operand addresses.
5. Fetch the operands.
6. Execute the instruction.
7. Store the results.

FIGURE 7.4
Major steps in processing an instruction.

FIGURE 7.5
Instruction and data streams in a simple computer.

1. *Single instruction stream single data stream (SISD):* $m_I = m_D = 1$. Most conventional machines with one CPU containing a single arithmetic-logic unit capable only of scalar arithmetic fall into this category. SISD computers and sequential computers are thus synonymous.

2. *Single instruction stream multiple data stream (SIMD):* $m_I = 1$, $m_D > 1$. This category includes machines such as ILLIAC IV that have a single program control unit and multiple execution units. It also includes associative processors like the Goodyear Aerospace MPP [3] mentioned in Sec. 5.3.3, and the DAP (*D*istributed *A*rray *P*rocessor) computer designed by International Computers Ltd. [16].

3. *Multiple instruction stream single data stream (MISD):* $m_I > 1$, $m_D = 1$. Not many parallel processors fit well into this category. Computers like the Cray-1 [29] and Control Data Corp.'s CYBER 205 [7], which rely heavily on pipeline processing, may be considered as MISD machines if the viewpoint is taken that a single data stream passes through a pipeline, and is processed by different (micro-) instruction streams in different segments of the pipeline. Fault-tolerant computers where several CPUs process the same data using different programs belong to the MISD class. The results of such apparently redundant computations can be compared and voted upon to detect and eliminate faulty results.

4. *Multiple instruction stream multiple data stream (MIMD):* $m_I > 1$, $m_D > 1$. This covers multiprocessors, which are computers with more than one CPU and the ability to execute several programs simultaneously. Examples of multiprocessors which are examined further in this chapter are Carnegie-Mellon University's Cm* [21] and the NCUBE/ten [14]. Pipeline processors like the Cray-1 are also sometimes included in this category, under the assumption that each segment of a pipeline has its own distinct data stream as well as a distinct (micro-) instruction stream.

It should be noted that the foregoing classification depends on a somewhat subjective distinction between control (instructions) and data. (See the discussion of these concepts in Sec. 2.1.1.) The term stream is equally vague and subject to varying interpretations. Hence it may not always be clear to which of the four Flynn classes a particular machine belongs. For example, whether to classify pipeline processors as MISD or MIMD hinges on the definition of data and instruction streams; a case can also be made for calling these machines SIMD [22]. Perhaps to avoid this issue, these machines are often simply termed pipeline computers or, reflecting one of their major applications, vector processors. The Flynn classification scheme is essentially behavioral and says nothing about a computer's structure. We turn now to some other ways of classifying parallel computers based on their overall structure or interconnection topology.

Structural classification. A computer system can be viewed as a set of $n \geq 1$ processors (CPUs) $P_1, P_2, \ldots, P_n$ and $m \geq 0$ shared (main) memory units or modules $M_1, M_2, \ldots, M_m$ communicating via an interconnection network N, as illustrated in Fig. 7.6. (Again for simplicity, we do not consider IO processors or peripheral devices in the classification process.) In a typical sequential computer $n = m = 1$, and N is a single shared bus (the system bus) over which all processor-memory communication takes place. In general, the memory units constitute a global main memory that provides a convenient message depository for processor-processor communication. A system with this organization is called a *shared-memory computer*. A global memory can, however, be a major system bottleneck, particularly when the processors must share large amounts of information, since normally only one processor can access a given memory module at a time. If the processors are provided with their own local memories, then the global memory can be reduced in size, or even eliminated completely. To separate the functions of processing (computation) and memory, we will refer to a processor with no associated main memory (but with registers or other temporary storage units such as caches) as a *processing element* or *PE*. CPUs and IOPs are examples of PEs. A *processor* is thus the combination of a PE and a local main memory; it may also include some external communications (IO) facilities forming, in effect, a small self-contained computer. In a system with little or no global memory, processing elements communicate via messages transmitted between their local memories, as in the system of Fig. 7.2. In this case the main memory is the sum of the local memories, and the system may be referred to as a *distributed-memory computer*. The term *message-passing computer* is also used for these machines. Figure 7.7 illustrates the main structural differences between shared-memory and distributed-memory systems.

The internal structure of the interconnection network N is also used to classify parallel computers. A representative selection of interconnection topologies appears in Fig. 7.8. Because of the ease with which it can be designed and controlled, the *single shared bus* (Fig. 7.8a) is widely used in parallel as well as sequential systems. When n, the number of PEs, and m, the number of main memory units, are large, extremely fast buses are required, and special design precautions

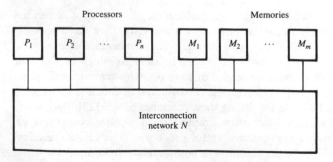

FIGURE 7.6
General structure of a system with $n \geq 1$ processors and $m \geq 0$ memory units.

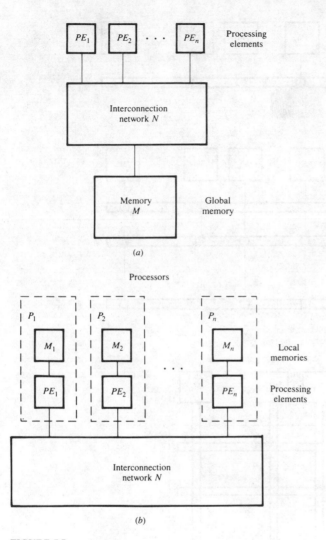

FIGURE 7.7
(*a*) Shared-memory and (*b*) distributed-memory systems.

must be taken to minimize contention for access to the bus. Bus contention can be relieved (but not necessarily eliminated completely) by providing several independent buses, forming the *multiple-bus* network depicted in Fig. 7.8*b*. Each processor and memory is connected to one or more of the available buses, each of which has all the attributes of an independent system bus. Besides reducing the communication load per bus, a degree of fault tolerance is provided, since the system can be designed to continue operation, possibly with reduced performance, if an individual bus fails. The *crossbar* interconnection network of Fig. 7.8*c* is a special kind of

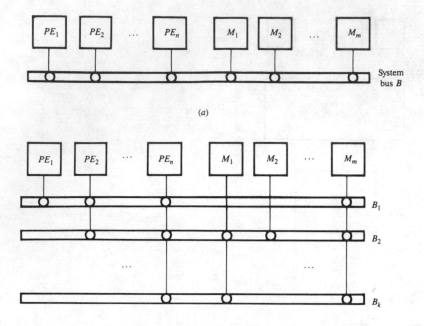

(a)

(b)

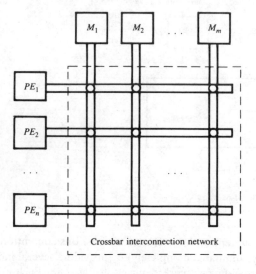

Crossbar interconnection network

(c)

FIGURE 7.8
Interconnection network structures: (a) single bus; (b) multiple buses; (c) crossbar; (d) tree; (e) hyper-cube (n-cube).

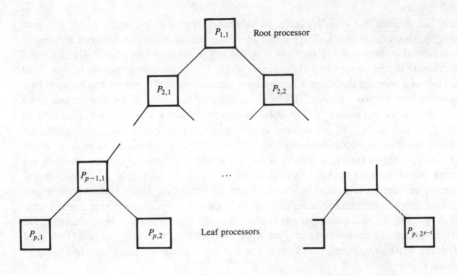

(d)

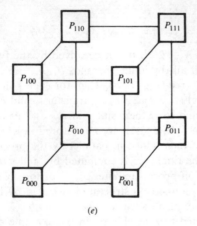

(e)

multiple-bus system in which each PE has a (horizontal) bus linking it to all memories or, equivalently, each memory has a (vertical) bus linking it to all PEs. An $n \times m$ crossbar allows up to MAX$\{n, m\}$ bus transactions to take place simultaneously. However, in the worst case where all the processors attempt to access the same memory unit M_i simultaneously, the number of bus transactions drops to one. Although crossbar networks have been employed by a few computer systems (see Fig. 1.26, for example), their hardware (wiring) complexity quickly becomes prohibitive as m and n increase.

Figures 7.8d–7.8e illustrate various network topologies in which high-speed dedicated connections (uni- or bidirectional buses) are provided between each system component, which is typically an independent processor, and a small group of neighboring components. They differ from the communication network structures considered in Sec. 6.1.3 in that the neighboring processors are physically close and cooperate in the processing of common tasks. The computer structure of Fig. 7.8d is that of a *tree*, in this case a binary tree, because each PE not in the bottom row is connected to two PEs (its "children") in the row below it. The name derives from the fanciful resemblance of Fig. 7.8d to an upside-down tree, with $P_{1,1}$ serving as the "root," and $P_{p,1}$: $P_{p,2^{p-1}}$ serving as the "leaves." The total number of processors in this binary tree computer is $n = 2^p - 1$, so that the number p of rows or levels of the tree is approximately $\log_2 n$. Processors communicate with one another via **send** and **receive** IO operations of the type presented in Example 7.1. While neighboring processors (a parent and a child) can communicate fairly rapidly, communication between nonneighboring processors is slower, requiring intermediate processors to act as store-and-forward message transfer stations. For example, to transmit data D from $P_{2,1}$ to $P_{2,2}$ requires the following two-step process: first send D from $P_{2,1}$ to the root processor $P_{1,1}$ and store it there temporarily; then send D from $P_{1,1}$ to $P_{2,2}$.

Like all multiprocessors with specialized interconnection structures, tree machines are well suited to certain kinds of parallel processing. Consider again the summation problem

$$\text{SUM} = b_1 + b_2 + \cdots + b_N$$

discussed earlier, where $N = 2^{p-1}$. It can be solved by the following tree-oriented parallel algorithm. Load all the input operands $b_1, b_2, \cdots, b_N$ into the 2^{p-1} leaf processors of the binary tree (Fig. 7.8d). Then for each pair b_j and b_{j+1} stored in the children of some level-$(p - 1)$ PE $P_{p-1,i}$, transfer b_j and b_{j+1} to $P_{p-1,i}$, compute the sum $y_j = b_i + b_{i+1}$, and store the result y_j in $P_{p-1,i}$. This reduces the number of operands to be added in half, and all are now stored in level-$(p - 1)$ processors. These $N/2$ operands are then added in parallel by the processors in level $p - 2$, and so on. Eventually the final sum is computed by, and stored in, the root node $P_{1,1}$. The entire summation process requires $p - 1$ or $\log_2 N$ addition times.

The computer interconnection structure illustrated by Fig. 7.8e is that of an n-dimensional *hypercube*, also called a (*binary*) *n-cube*. 2^n processors are used, each of which is connected to n neighbors. In the example of Fig. 7.8e, $n = 3$ so eight processors are used, and the cubelike structure can be clearly seen. If each processor is indexed by an n-bit binary address as shown in the figure, then P_i is a neighbor of P_j if and only if their addresses i and j differ by 1 bit. The hypercube structure has been shown to be suitable for a fairly wide range of programming tasks. Although originally proposed in the early 1960s, hypercube architectures did not reach the commercial development stage until around 1985. Many other interconnection structures have been proposed for parallel computers besides those of Fig. 7.8, but relatively few of them have actually been implemented.

We can further distinguish computers on the basis of the unit-to-unit connection paths provided by their interconnection networks. These paths may be *static*, i.e., fixed and unchangeable, or *dynamic*, i.e., reconfigurable under system control.

The single-bus, multiple-bus, and crossbar interconnections of Figs. 7.8a to 7.8c are all examples of dynamic interconnection structures, whereas the tree and hypercube (Figs. 7.8d and 7.8e) are static. The conventional single system bus of Fig. 7.8a is designed to allow any of the n processors to connect to any of the m memories for one or more bus cycles, e.g., to fetch an instruction. In a subsequent cycle some other processor-memory pair may use the bus to communicate. Thus the units communicating over the bus vary dynamically. In contrast, each processor in the binary tree configuration (Fig. 7.8d) has dedicated buses to its nearest neighbors, and can only communicate with other processors indirectly.

A very general class of dynamic interconnection networks can be constructed from 2-state switching elements of the kind depicted in Fig. 7.9. Each switch S has a pair of input buses X_1, X_2, a pair of output buses Z_1, Z_2, and some control logic not shown in the figure. All four buses are identical and can function as processor-processor or processor-memory links. S has two states determined by a control line c: a *through* or *direct* state illustrated in Fig. 7.9b where $Z_1 = X_1$ (i.e., Z_1 is connected to X_1) and $Z_2 = X_2$; and a *cross* state where $Z_1 = X_2$ and $Z_2 = X_1$ (Fig. 7.9c). Using S as a building block, *multistage switching networks* of the type shown in Fig. 7.10 can be constructed for use as interconnection networks in parallel computers. The particular network of Fig. 7.10 contains 12 switching elements arranged into three stages (columns), and is intended to provide dynamic connections between eight processors P_0:P_7. By setting the control signals of the switching elements in various ways, a large number of different interconnection patterns are possible. These possibilities are, in general, determined by the number of stages, the fixed connections linking the stages, and the dynamic states of the switching elements.

Figure 7.11 shows three of the many possible switch settings or states of the multistage switching network N of Fig. 7.10. In the case of Fig. 7.11b, for instance,

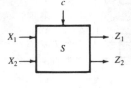

(a)

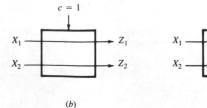

(b)

(c)

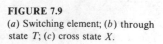

FIGURE 7.9
(a) Switching element; (b) through state T; (c) cross state X.

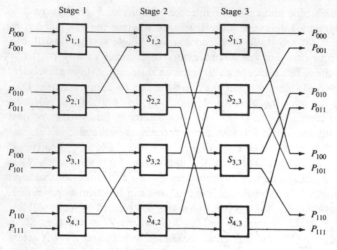

FIGURE 7.10
Three-stage switching network.

the four switching elements $S_{1,2}$, $S_{2,2}$, $S_{3,2}$, $S_{4,2}$ forming stage 2 are set to the cross state, while the eight remaining switches are set to the through state. It can be seen that the output of P_{000} is connected to the input of P_{010} and vice versa, P_{001} is connected to P_{011}, and so on. In general, the switch settings of Fig. 7.11b simultaneously connect the output of P_{ijk} to the input of $P_{i\bar{j}k}$. On comparing these con-

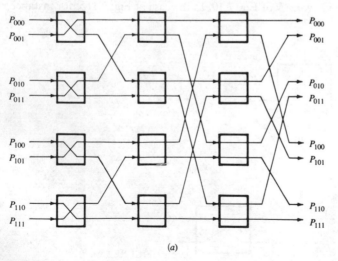

(a)

FIGURE 7.11
Some states of the three-stage switching network.

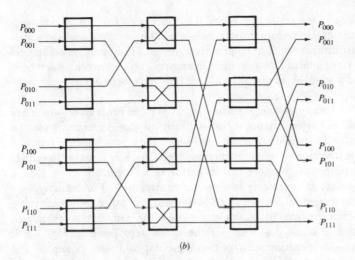

(b)

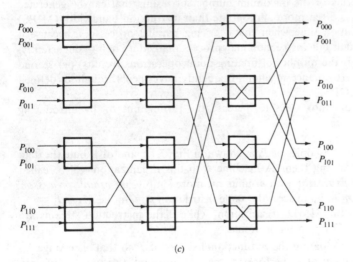

(c)

nection patterns with the static hypercube structure of Fig. 7.8e, we see that, in the state of Fig. 7.11c, N provides all the connections linking the top four processors of the hypercube to the bottom four. Thus the parallel top-to-bottom communication allowed by the hypercube can be obtained indirectly in an 8-processor system that uses N as its interconnection network. The same type of parallel communication along the other two dimensions of the hypercube can be simulated by setting N to the states shown in Figs. 7.11a and 7.11c. Since N provides all the interconnections of a static hypercube in this manner, it has been called the *indirect hypercube* interconnection network. N can also provide some other useful interconnection patterns not possible in the static hypercube. The price paid for this interconnection flexibility is the communication delay caused by the switches, and the sometimes complex algorithms needed to control their states. Many parallel computers designed around large multistage switching interconnection networks have been proposed [30], and a number of machines of this type have been built.

Overlap modes. Another important classification of parallel processors, which has both structural and behavioral implications, is based on the mechanisms used to overlap the execution of individual operations, where the operations are typically considered at the instruction or microinstruction level. Consider a sequential SISD processor P. For simplicity, suppose that P performs a single operation I on a single input data stream D, producing an output data stream D'. Furthermore, let I be executed in m sequential steps (which may also be called phases, cycles, microoperations, etc.). I could, for example, represent the complete processing of any instruction from P's instruction set via the seven steps listed in Fig. 7.4; it could also be a single operation such as floating-point addition. A simple and convenient measure of the performance of P is its *throughput* or *data bandwidth* b_D, measured in terms of the maximum number of results that can be generated per unit time. This is often more appropriate than instruction bandwidth (MIPS) or instruction execution time when characterizing parallel processors, because it allows for the fact that one instruction may process many data items concurrently. An example of b_D is the number of floating-point operations (results) per second or *FLOPS*. High-performance machines frequently have their throughput defined in megaflops (MFLOPS).

There are two major ways to increase the throughput b_D by introducing parallelism.

1. We can use m distinct copies of P, as shown in Fig. 7.12, and distribute the data to be processed among them. A machine with this organization will be called here a *multiunit processor* with m units or, more simply, an *m-unit processor*. Note that if the m units process the same instruction stream, i.e., $I_1 = I_2 = \cdots = I_m$, we obtain the SIMD organization, while if the instruction streams are distinct, the MIMD organization results.

2. We can physically separate the m functional stages of P so that each stage S_i, now called a *segment* of P, performs some operation on a distinct set of data operands. When S_i has computed its results, it passes them (along with unprocessed input operands, if necessary) to S_{i+1} for further processing, and receives a

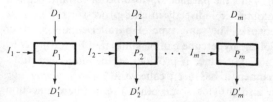

FIGURE 7.12
An m-unit processor with multiple data streams.

new set of inputs from S_{i-1}. Thus the processor can contain up to m independent data items, all in different stages of their processing. Buffer registers and other control logic must be placed between the segments, so that the segment operations do not interfere with one another. The result is the *m-segment pipeline processor* depicted in Fig. 7.13.

The parallelism of a pipeline processor derives from the fact that m independent operations can be performed simultaneously in the m segments. Unlike the m-unit case where the same operation is done in parallel on m different data sets $d_1, d_2, \ldots, d_m$, a pipeline performs a different operation on each d_i. A pipeline therefore resembles an assembly line where each d_i is in a different stage (segment) of assembly at any point in time, and d_i must pass through all segments to complete its processing. Program control units (instruction processors) are frequently pipelined with segments corresponding to some or all of the operations listed in Fig. 7.4.

If an m-unit processor and an m-segment pipeline perform the same overall functions, and are designed using the same circuit technologies, their throughput b_D will be approximately equal, and provide an m-fold improvement in speed over a comparable sequential processor. For example, a four-segment pipeline processor P_4 for floating-point addition (see Fig. 1.27) can be expected to equal the performance of four copies of a nonpipelined floating-point adder P under suitable operating conditions. P_4 is more complex and costly than P because of the extra hardware needed to define and buffer the segments; however, P_4 is likely to be less costly than the four copies of P (plus control logic) needed to build a four-unit floating-point adder. Not all operations have the multistep structure required for pipelining, and the degree of parallelism attainable is limited by the number of steps defining the segments. Nevertheless, it has been found cost-effective to make pipelining the major technique for achieving parallelism for many computers in the supercomputer range; these machines are therefore referred to as pipeline computers. Nonpipeline computers are called multiunit computers here, although they are

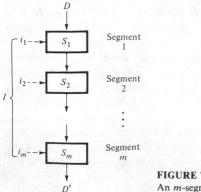

FIGURE 7.13
An m-segment pipeline processor.

often referred to simply as parallel computers in the literature. Note that in many m-unit computers, the parallelism is due to the presence of m independent CPUs, so these machines can also be classified as multiprocessors. Note too that the multiunit and pipeline concepts are easily combined in a single machine. For example, some large pipeline computers have k independent m-segment pipelines for floating-point addition, which collectively form a k-unit processor offering a performance speedup factor of km.

It is clear from the foregoing discussion that the same computer can be classified in several different ways, depending on the aspects of its parallelism that are singled out for attention. The NCUBE/ten, for example, can be called a (distributed-memory) multiprocessor, an MIMD computer, a hypercube computer, or just a parallel computer. The Cray X-MP computer, on the other hand, which is composed of several Cray-1 pipeline processors, is variously called a pipeline computer, a (pipelined) multiprocessor, and a vector processor. In our detailed analysis of the design of parallel processors, we consider them under the two main headings, pipeline processors (Sec. 7.2) and multiprocessors (Sec. 7.3).

7.1.3 Performance Considerations

The performance of a parallel processor depends in complex and hard-to-define ways on the system's architecture and the degree of parallelism in programs it executes. There are several simple performance measures such as speedup and processor utilization (efficiency) which provide rough performance estimates. The system's interconnection structure and main-memory architecture also have a significant impact on performance.

Basic measures. The usual performance measures discussed for sequential computers in Chap. 2 are of limited value in characterizing parallel computers. Individual or average instruction execution times are not very useful, since they do not measure the impact of what might be loosely called the system's *parallelism degree n*, e.g., the number of processors or the number of pipeline segments available. Sometimes, especially in theoretical studies, the time $T(n, N)$ needed to execute more complex operations such as sorting a list of N numbers, or inverting an $N \times N$ matrix, is given as a performance measure for a machine of parallelism n. Such measures may be expressed in approximate form using the *O-notation* $O(f(n, N))$, where stating that $T(n, N) = O(f(n, N))$ means that there exist constants k and $N_0 > 0$, whose exact values are not usually specified, such that $T(n, N) \leq kf(n, N)$ for all $N > N_0$. As N, the problem size or dimension, increases beyond some lower limit N_0, the execution time $T(N)$ grows at a rate that is less, within a constant factor k, than that of the function $f(n, N)$. For example, from (7.2) we can state that the summation of N numbers on the n-processor one-dimensional array of Fig. 7.3 takes time $T(N, n) = O(N/n + n)$. Note that this figure is not the actual time to execute the task in question; rather it is a rough indication of the growth rate of the execution time.

   The performance of an individual processor or processing element in high-performance machines may be measured by the instruction execution rate or instruction bandwidth b_I, using units such as MIPS. The corresponding measure of data bandwidth or throughput b_D is typically MFLOPS; other multiples such as GFLOPS (a gigaflops is 10^3 MFLOPS) are also used. In parallel computers the interprocessor communication mechanisms, and the extent to which they are used, strongly influence overall system performance. For example, if a parallel processor is composed of n processors, each with performance p (MIPS, MFLOPS, etc.), it may be stated that the system has a (potential or maximum) performance of np. Performance figures of this sort, which are frequently cited by computer manufacturers, are achievable only for certain classes of highly parallel programs or algorithms where the maximum possible parallelism in computation is attained, and communication delays are minimized. Under more typical operating conditions, when a mixture of tasks with varying degrees of parallelism are encountered, significantly lower performance levels can be expected.

   There are some general measures of performance for parallel computers that attempt to capture the effect of the degree of parallelism n on overall system performance. One such measure is the *speedup* $S(n)$, which is defined as the ratio of the total execution time $T(1)$ on a sequential computer to the corresponding execution time $T(n)$ on the parallel computer for some class of tasks of interest, i.e.,

$$S(n) = \frac{T(1)}{T(n)}$$

It is usually reasonable to assume that $T(1) \leq nT(n)$, in which case $S(n) \leq n$. In Example 7.1, where N numbers are being summed on a one-dimensional n-processor array, $T(n)$ and $T(1)$ are defined by Eqs. (7.2) and (7.3), respectively, yielding the speedup formula

$$S(n) = \frac{K_1 N}{K_1 N/n + K_2(n - 1)}$$

$$\approx \frac{n}{1 + Kn/k}$$

where $K = K_2/K_1$ is a system constant, and $k = N/n$. If the interprocessor communication delays are ignored by setting K_2 to zero, then $S(n)$ becomes n, which is obviously the best possible speedup achievable with n processors. On the other hand, if K_2 is large enough relative to n, it is possible for $S(n)$ to become less than one, in which case a single sequential processor with no interprocessor communication requirements is faster than an n-processor system!

   A closely related performance measure, which can be expressed as a single number (a fraction or a percentage), is the *efficiency* E_n, which is the speedup per degree of parallelism, and is defined as follows:

$$E(n) = \frac{S(n)}{n}$$

$E(n)$ is also an indication of processor *utilization*, and may be so named. In general, speedup and efficiency provide rough estimates of the performance changes that can be expected in a parallel processing system by increasing the parallelism degree n, e.g., by adding more processors. These measures should be used with caution, however, since they depend on the programs being run, and can change dramatically from program to program, or from one part of a program to another.

A program or algorithm Q may sometimes be characterized by its degree of parallelism n_i, which is the minimum value of n for which the efficiency and the speedup reach their maximum values at time i during the execution of Q. Thus n_i represents the maximum level of parallelism that can be exploited by Q at time i. Figure 7.14 shows how n_i might vary with i for a specific program that exhibits a modest degree of parallelism. $S(n)$ and $E(n)$ are plotted against n in Fig. 7.15 using the data provided by Fig. 7.14 and Eqs. (7.8) and (7.9). Note that n_i can change precipitously from time to time in fairly unpredictable ways. It is also difficult to measure the n_i in designs where program or processor functions overlap in subtle ways, as is often the case.

Some indication of the influence of program parallelism on the performance of a parallel computer may be seen from the following analysis. Suppose that all computations of interest on a parallel processor can be divided into two simple groups involving floating-point arithmetic only: vector operations employing vector operands of some fixed length N, and scalar operations where all operands are scalars ($N = 1$). Let f be the fraction of all floating-point operations that are executed as scalar operations, and let $1 - f$ be the fraction executed as vector operations. $1 - f$ is thus a measure of the degree of parallelism in the programs being executed, and varies from 1, corresponding to maximum parallelism (all vector operations), to 0 (all scalar operations). Suppose that vector and scalar operations are performed at throughput rates of b_v and b_s MFLOPS, respectively. Let the average system throughput be b. Then b, b_v, and b_s are related by the following useful formula:

$$\frac{1}{b} = \frac{f}{b_s} + \frac{1-f}{b_v} \tag{7.8}$$

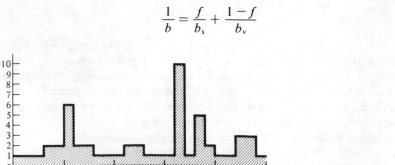

FIGURE 7.14
Plot of the maximum inherent parallelism of a program Q.

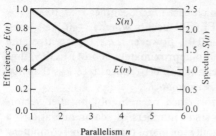

FIGURE 7.15

Efficiency and speedup for the program of Fig. 7.14.

The execution time for a single N-component vector operation is $T_v = N/b_v$, while that of a single scalar operation is $T_s = 1/b_s$. These parameters are related by

$$T_v = T_0 + \frac{NT_s}{n}$$

where T_0 is some fixed *setup* or *startup time* that is independent of vector length, and n is the processor parallelism degree. When N is large, T_0 can be ignored, so that this equation reduces to $T_v = NT_s/n$. Substitution into (7.8) yields

$$b = \frac{nb_s}{1 + (n - 1)f} \text{ MFLOPS} \tag{7.9}$$

Since b_s, the scalar throughput, and n, the processor parallelism, can be assumed to be constants, Eq. (7.9) defines a hyperbola. Figure 7.16 is a plot of b against f

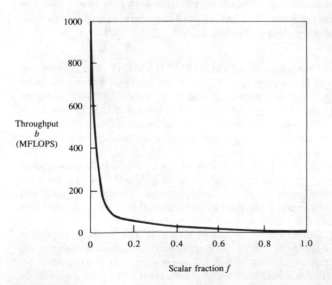

FIGURE 7.16

Effect of scalar operations on supercomputer performance.

for $b_s = 10$ MFLOPS and $n = 100$, in which case (7.9) becomes $b = 1000/(1 + 99f)$. The maximum performance of 1 GFLOPS occurs when $f = 0$, i.e., when there are no scalar operations. When $f = 0.01$, however, i.e., 1 percent of the computations are scalar, b drops from 1000 to approximately 500 MFLOPS, thus cutting the system throughput in half. Increasing f to 0.1 reduces b to less than 100 MFLOPS, an order of magnitude drop in performance.

This analysis suggests that the performance of a highly parallel vector-oriented machine is very sensitive even to small numbers of scalar operations, a conclusion that has been verified experimentally for many types of supercomputers. Hence it is often worthwhile to devote considerable effort to "vectorize" or "parallelize" programs for such machines to eliminate scalar operations. If we take the speedup $S(n)$ to be b/b_s, then (7.9) can be rewritten as

$$S(n) = \frac{n}{1 + (n - 1)f} \tag{7.10}$$

With f interpreted broadly as the fraction of nonparallelizable operations or instructions, then (7.10) is often referred to as *Amdahl's law*, after Gene M. Amdahl, one of the architect's of the IBM System/360. Clearly, $S(n)$ varies with f in the manner illustrated by Fig. 7.16.

Interconnection issues. A parallel computer's interconnection network plays a major role in determining its performance. As noted earlier, static interconnection structures such as trees are best suited to the execution of algorithms that require infrequent interprocessor communication (to share operands or intermediate results, etc.) and confine most communication to neighboring processors. We now examine an important real computer, ILLIAC IV, and show how its interconnections facilitate certain types of numerical problem solving.

> **Example 7.2 Parallel processing in ILLIAC IV** [33]. ILLIAC IV is an experimental computer developed at The University of Illinois in the late 1960s and manufactured by Burroughs Corp. Its architecture is derived from the SOLOMON computer designed at Westinghouse Electric Corp. in the early 1960s. ILLIAC IV, which operated from 1970 to 1981, was one of the first supercomputers to employ parallel processing on a large scale. As such, it provided valuable insights into the problems of designing and programming such machines.
>
> The general structure of ILLIAC IV is shown in Fig. 7.17. It contains a set of 64 identical processors (referred to as processing units or PUs in ILLIAC IV literature) with a common external control unit CU. Each processor P_i comprises a processing element PE_i and a local memory M_i. PE_i includes a general-purpose ALU capable of executing a conventional instruction set that contains 64-bit floating-point operations, while M_i is a RAM with a capacity of 2048 64-bit words. The CU plays the role of program control unit for the system, It can directly access information stored in any of the processor memories, whereas each P_i has access only to its local memory M_i. The CU decodes instructions and, when an instruction for the PEs is encountered, the CU broadcasts it to all PEs simultaneously via special control lines. Thus a common instruction stream is executed by all PEs; however, each PE uses operands stored in

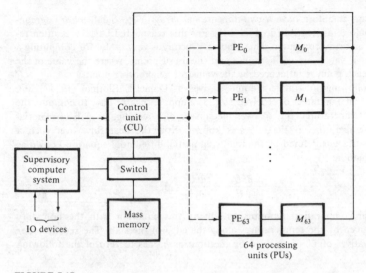

FIGURE 7.17
Structure of ILLIAC IV.

its local memory. ILLIAC IV is therefore a distributed-memory SIMD machine, capable of processing up to 64 separate data streams simultaneously under the control of a single instruction stream. A supervisory computer system (a single Burroughs B6500 in the original design, but subsequently several computers) performs housekeeping functions such as program compilation and input-output management.

Suppose for example, that it is desired to add two 64-component vectors $X = (x_0, x_1, \ldots, x_{63})$ and $Y = (y_0, y_1, \ldots, y_{63})$ to form the result $Z = (z_0, z_1, \ldots, z_{63})$. The CU first stores the ith components x_i and y_i of X and Y in memory locations x and y, respectively, of processor memory M_i for $i = 1, 2, \ldots, 63$. It then broadcasts the fixed-point or floating-point add instruction

$$z \leftarrow x + y;$$

to all PEs, causing 64 scalar additions to take place simultaneously. This produces the desired vector result Z in just one scalar addition time. Again the ith component z_i is stored in a fixed location z in the local memory of processor P_i. If vectors of greater length than 64 must be processed, they are divided into 64-word chunks by the CU and the chunks are processed sequentially. Shorter vectors of length $k < 64$ are handled by selectively setting a flag F to 1 in, say, the first k processors $P_0, P_1, \ldots, P_k$ only, and then broadcasting the conditional instruction

$$\textbf{if } F = 1 \textbf{ then } z \leftarrow x + y;$$

to all processors. Note that careful advance placement of the data in the processor memories is essential to correct operation.

In addition to the common data and control buses that link the processors to the CU, ILLIAC IV has direct paths linking each P_i to four neighboring processors. Specifically, P_i is connected to P_j if $j = i \pm 1$ (modulo 64) or $j = i \pm 8$ (modulo 64).

The processors therefore have a two-dimensional *array* or (toroidal) *mesh* interconnection structure, as depicted in Fig. 7.18. For this reason ILLIAC IV is often referred to as an array computer. This kind of structure is very useful for computing a function whose values are defined on a grid (mesh) of points, where the value of the function at each point is influenced by the values of neighboring points.

The following illustrative example is given by Daniel L. Slotnick (1924–1986), who was the chief architect of ILLIAC IV [33]. Suppose that we have to compute the steady-state temperature $U(x, y)$ over the surface of a rectangular slab of material where the temperature at the edges is known. Now the heat flow over such a continuous surface is defined by the following partial differential equation known as Laplace's equation:

$$\frac{\partial^2 U}{\partial x^2} + \frac{\partial^2 U}{\partial y^2} = 0 \tag{7.11}$$

The required computation amounts to solving this equation with the boundary conditions given by the temperatures along the edge of the slab. The second-order partial derivatives of U are defined by the limit as h goes to zero of the following expressions:

$$\frac{\partial^2 U}{\partial x^2} = \frac{U(x + h, y) - 2U(x, y) + U(x - h, y)}{h^2}$$

$$\frac{\partial^2 U}{\partial y^2} = \frac{U(x, y + h) - 2U(x, y) + U(x, y - h)}{h^2} \tag{7.12}$$

For small values of h, these expressions can be used to approximate the partial derivatives. Therefore, if we substitute (7.12) into (7.11), we obtain the following discrete approximation to Laplace's equation:

$$\frac{U(x + h, y) + U(x - h, y) + U(x, y + h) + U(x, y - h) - 4U(x, y)}{h^2} = 0$$

which yields

$$U(x, y) = \frac{U(x + h, y) + U(x - h, y) + U(x, y + h) + U(x, y - h)}{4} \tag{7.13}$$

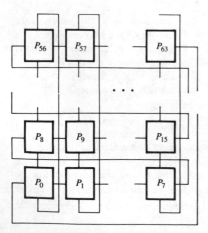

FIGURE 7.18
Data paths between processors in ILLIAC IV.

This equation has the simple intuitive interpretation that the temperature at position (x, y) is the average of the temperature at the four neighboring points at distance h from (x, y) along the x and y axes.

To solve the original heat flow problem, assume that the slab is covered by an 8×8 rectangular grid with 64 vertices $(x, y) = (ih, jh)$, where i and j assume the values 0:7. Thus the grid points are labeled $(0, 0), (0, h), \ldots, (0, 7h), (h, 0), (h, h), \ldots, (7h, 6h), (7h, 7h)$. We can now define a one-to-one mapping of the 64 temperature values $U(x, y)$ into the 64 processors of ILLIAC IV as follows: $U(x, y)$ where $(x, y) = (ih, jh)$ is stored in the local memory of processor P_k if and only if $k = 8i + j$ (modulo 64). This results in the assignment shown in Fig. 7.19. Clearly each $U(x, y)$ is in a processor that is adjacent to, i.e., directly connected to, the four processors storing the values $U(x + h, y)$, $U(x - h, y)$, $U(x, y + h)$, and $U(x, y - h)$ needed to compute $U(x, y)$ according to (7.13). The values associated with the grid points on the slab boundary are assumed to be constant throughout the calculation, so the corresponding processors only need to communicate with some of their neighbors. These processors therefore execute their programs in a somewhat different manner from the internal processors; the differences in question are easily handled by conditional instructions of the form

if processor address = boundary address **then** skip action;   (7.14)

The steady-state temperature values at all 36 internal grid points of the slab are computed as follows using a standard computation technique called *relaxation*. The known values of the $U(x, y)$ at the slab boundary points are stored in the corresponding 28 processors at the boundary of the processor array; the 36 internal $U(x, y)$ variables are set to some fixed initial value such as zero. Every processor is supplied with a copy of a program that implements Eq. (7.13). As noted above, conditional instructions like (7.14) allow the internal and boundary processors to be distinguished. Each processor then independently computes a value for $U(x, y)$ and sends it to its immediate neighbors. (Note that only the interprocessor connections shown by heavy lines in Fig. 7.19 are needed to transmit U values in this particular problem.) The data

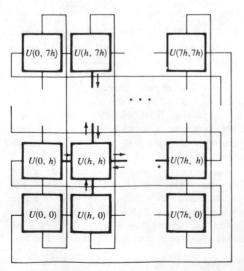

FIGURE 7.19
Data storage and communication for the heat-flow problem.

received from the neighboring processors are used to compute a new value of $U(x, y)$ according to (7.13). This process is repeated until the difference between two successive values of $U(x, y)$ computed in all internal processors is very small. It can readily be seen that the 36 internal $U(x, y)$ values change gradually until a final equilibrium value, which is the average of the values stored in the neighboring processors, is reached. Since ILLIAC IV computes the 36 internal values of $U(x, y)$ in parallel, it exhibits a speedup of approximately 36 over a comparable sequential processor executing the same program. A maximum speedup of 64 is possible in applications where all processors can be utilized in parallel. Little time is lost in communicating intermediate results, since the interconnection structure of the processor array precisely matches the communication requirements of the relaxation algorithm employed to solve (7.13).

Memory issues. A basic problem in all parallel computers with a shared main memory is that of moving data and instructions between the processors and main memory at sufficiently high rates to maintain the system performance close to its maximum level. One common solution is to partition the memory into multiple modules or memory banks with address interleaving, as discussed in Sec. 5.3.1. The individual memory modules can be accessed in parallel, thereby increasing the system's effective memory bandwidth. The data and instruction addresses must be distributed in a balanced fashion among the available memory modules by the system software, and special hardware is needed to control access to the memory modules.

We now consider how these problems were tackled in the case of the Control Data STAR-100, a commercial supercomputer designed in the late 1960s. Although only a few copies of the STAR-100 were produced, it served as a prototype for the later and more successful Cyber 200 series manufactured by CDC (and subsequently by its ETA subsidiary) in the 1980s. These machines are all examples of vector processors in which pipelines are the major means of achieving parallel processing.

> **Example 7.3 Information flow in the STAR-100** [15]. The STAR-100 is designed around a CPU containing two multifunction pipelines that can process 64-bit fixed-point and floating-point operands. Pipeline processor 1 performs addition and multiplication. The second pipeline processor performs addition, multiplication, division, and square-root extraction; it also contains a floating-point division unit which is not pipelined. Each 64-bit pipeline can be partitioned into two 32-bit pipelines capable of processing two sets of 32-bit operands in parallel. Hence there are, in effect, four independent 32-bit pipelines. The CPU cycle time is 40 ns, and each of the four pipelines can produce a new 32-bit (floating-point) result every 40 ns, in its fastest or *streaming* mode of operation. The main memory of the STAR-100 has a capacity of 4M bytes (2^{22} bytes), and was constructed from ferrite cores with a cycle time of 1.28 μs, i.e., it requires 1.28 μs to read or write a single word in main memory. The performance goal of the STAR-100 can be stated succinctly as follows: the throughput b_D should be 100 MFLOPS. In other words, the system should be capable of producing 10^8 32-bit floating-point results per second. We now briefly retrace the designers' steps in determining a memory configuration to achieve this level of performance [15].

In the streaming mode of operation, results are generated by the pipeline processors at a rate of $4 \times 32 = 128$ bits every 40 ns, i.e., 4096 bits per memory cycle (1.28 μs), and must be stored at that rate in main memory. (Unlike other vector processors such as the Cray-1, the STAR-100 and its Cyber-series successors contain essentially no temporary storage registers in the CPU.) Most results require two 32-bit input operands; hence up to 2×4096 data bits must be fetched every memory cycle. Allowance must also be made for fetching instructions, say one 32-bit instruction per result, which amounts to 4096 instruction bits per memory cycle. We conclude that it is necessary to fetch 3×4096 bits and store 4096 bits every 1.28 μs; this corresponds to a memory bandwidth of $3 \times 4096 + 4096 = 16,384$ bits per memory cycle, or 1.28 $\times 10^{10}$ bits/s. Now $16,384 = 32 \times 512$, so it was decided to partition main memory into 32 interleaved modules and use a memory word size of 512 bits. Each memory module therefore has a capacity of 2048 words.

Figure 7.20 shows the overall organization and main data paths of the STAR-100. The CPU and main memory are linked by four high-speed buses: two for fetching input data, one for storing result data, and one for fetching instructions and communicating with the IO system. Special read and write control units distribute the memory access requests to the designated modules and buffer the incoming and outgoing streams of information. Each of the four memory buses consists of 128 lines, and can transmit 128 bits every 40 ns. During streaming operation, therefore, 128×4

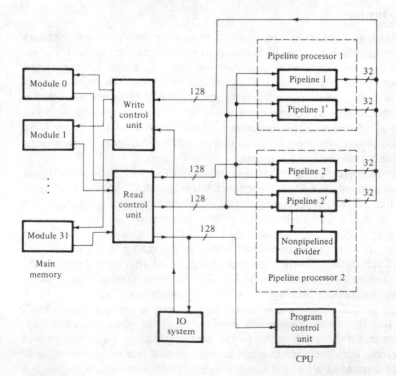

FIGURE 7.20
Information flow in the CDC STAR-100.

$\times 32 = 16,384$ bits can be transferred over the four buses each memory cycle; this exactly matches the memory bandwidth needed to achieve the 100 MFLOPS performance objective.

High-speed pipeline processors of the type found in the STAR-100 have come to be widely used in commercial supercomputers. They are used in such machines as the Cray-1, the CDC Cyber 205, the Fujitsu VP-200, and the NEC SX-1, all of which were introduced in the decade 1976–1985. They are also the basis of add-on vector (co-)processors, such as the vector processing extension to the System/370 architecture defined by IBM in the mid-1980s [19]. The architecture of pipeline processors is examined in depth in the following section.

7.2 PIPELINE PROCESSORS

The design and control of pipeline processors is examined in this section. The two principal pipeline types, instruction and arithmetic, are discussed, as well as the structure and programming requirements of high-performance vector processors.

7.2.1 Introduction

A pipeline processor consists of a sequence of processing circuits, called segments or stages, through which a stream of operands can be passed; see Fig. 7.13. Partial processing of the operands takes place in each segment, and a final fully processed result is obtained only after an operand set has passed through the entire pipeline. In some cases it may be necessary to make several complete passes through the pipeline in order to process a particular data set; in other cases, the data need not pass through all segments so the unnecessary segments are selectively skipped. As noted earlier, an m-segment pipeline has approximately the same peak throughput as a similar multiunit processor with m units.

In the most basic pipeline structure illustrated in Fig. 7.21, the operands pass through all m segments in a fixed sequence. Each segment S_i consists of an input register or latch R_i, and a processing circuit C_i which may be combinational or sequential. The R_i's act as intersegment buffers, and compensate for any differences in the propagation delays through the C_i's. Typically, a common clock signal causes all the R_i's to change state synchronously at the start of a clock period of the pipeline. Each R_i then receives a new set of input data D_{i-1} from the preceding segment S_{i-1}, except R_1 whose data is supplied from an external source. D_{i-1} represents the results computed by C_{i-1} during the preceding clock period. Once D_{i-1} has been loaded, R_i is logically disconnected from its input source, and C_i proceeds to use D_{i-1} to compute a new data set D_i. Thus in each clock period, every segment transfers its old results to the next segment, and also computes a new set of results. Any operation that can be decomposed into a sequence of well-defined suboperations of about the same complexity can, in principle, be realized by a pipeline processor of this sort.

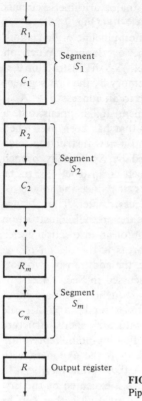

FIGURE 7.21
Pipeline processor structure.

Pipeline types. There are two areas of computer design where pipelining seems to be particularly appropriate:

1. The transfer of instructions through various stages of the CPU instruction cycle, including fetch opcode, decode opcode, compute operand addresses, fetch operands, execute instruction, and store results. This amounts to realizing most or all of the CPU in the form of a multifunction pipeline called an *instruction pipeline*. Various CPU registers and functional circuits for program control and data processing then effectively form the buffer registers and processing circuits of the pipeline. A simple form of this type of pipelining is also used at the microinstruction level.
2. The implementation of arithmetic operations, especially the more complex ones such as multiplication, floating-point operations, and vector operations. A pipeline processor for this purpose is called an *arithmetic pipeline*.

Some simple forms of pipelining can be found in almost every computer in the partial overlapping of certain (micro) instruction processing steps. A computer is not usually referred to as pipelined, however, unless its major arithmetic circuits are implemented by pipelines as, for instance, in the STAR-100 (Fig. 7.20).

Figure 7.22 shows the simplest two-segment instruction pipeline organization, which allows instruction fetching and execution to be overlapped. When an instruction I_i with address A_i is being executed by segment S_2, the instruction I_{i+1} with the next consecutive address A_{i+1} is fetched from memory by the first segment S_1. Except when I_i is a branch instruction causing a jump to an address $A_j \neq A_{i+1}$, I_{i+1} is the next instruction required by the execution segment. If I_i happens to be a branch to a nonconsecutive address, the instruction I_{i+1} that has been prefetched during the execution of I_i may have to be discarded, and a new instruction fetch cycle must be initiated by S_1 after I_i has been executed by S_2. Usually branch instructions form a small fraction of the total number of instructions to be executed, typically 20 percent or less. Several techniques to reduce the impact of branch instructions on pipeline performance will be discussed later. Thus 2-stage pipelining allows most instructions to be prefetched while the preceding instruction is being executed, thereby decreasing the average duration of an instruction cycle.

One of the most successful pipeline application areas is the design of the more complex arithmetic circuits. Consider, for example, the addition of two normalized floating-point numbers x and y, which was discussed in Sec. 3.4.2. This operation can be implemented by the following four-step sequence: compare exponents, align mantissas (equalize exponents), add mantissas, and normalize the result. This yields the four-segment pipeline processor with the general structure shown in Fig. 7.23. Suppose that x has the normalized floating-point representation (x_M, x_E), where x_M is the mantissa (fraction), and x_E is the exponent with respect to some base $B = 2^k$. Note that both x_M and x_E are fixed-point numbers. In the first step of adding $x = (x_M, x_E)$ to $y = (y_M, y_E)$, which is executed by the first segment S_1 of the pipeline, x_E and y_E are compared, an operation that can be performed by subtraction of the exponents. This operation, which requires a fixed-point adder, identifies the smaller of the exponents, say x_E, whose mantissa x_M can then be modified by shifting in the second segment S_2 of the pipeline to form a new mantissa x'_M that makes $(x'_M, y_E) = (x_M, x_E)$. In the third step, the mantissas x'_M and y_M, which are now properly aligned, are added. This fixed-point addition

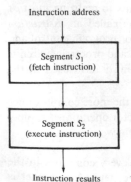

Instruction address

Segment S_1
(fetch instruction)

Segment S_2
(execute instruction)

Instruction results

FIGURE 7.22
Simple two-segment instruction pipeline.

$x = (x_M, x_E)$ $y = (y_M, y_E)$

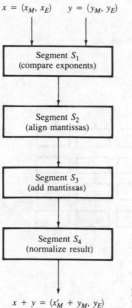

Segment S_1
(compare exponents)

Segment S_2
(align mantissas)

Segment S_3
(add mantissas)

Segment S_4
(normalize result)

$x + y = (x'_M + y_M, y_E)$

FIGURE 7.23
Four-segment floating-point adder pipeline.

may produce an unnormalized result; hence a fourth step is needed to normalize the result. Normalization can be implemented by counting the number k of leading zeros of the mantissa (or leading ones in the case of negative mantissas), shifting the mantissa k digit positions to normalize it, and making a corresponding adjustment in the exponent.

The behavior of the foregoing adder pipeline when performing a sequence of n additions of the form $x_i + y_i$ is illustrated by Fig. 7.24 for the case $n = 6$; this problem is encountered when adding two n-component real (floating-point) vectors. At any time, each of the four segments can contain a pair of partially processed scalar operands denoted (x_i, y_i). The buffering in the segments ensures that segment S_i only receives as inputs the results computed by segment S_{i-1} during the preceding clock period. If T seconds is the pipeline clock period, i.e., the execution time of each segment, then it takes a total time of $4T$ to compute the single sum $x_i + y_i$. This is approximately the time required to do one floating-point addition using a nonpipelined processor, plus the delay due to the buffer registers. Once all four segments of the pipeline have been filled with data, a new sum emerges from the fourth segment every T seconds. Consequently, N consecutive additions can be done in time $(N + 3)T$, implying that the pipeline's speedup is

$$S(4) = \frac{4N}{N + 3}$$

For large N, $S(4) \approx 4$ and results are generated at a rate about four times that of a comparable nonpipelined adder.

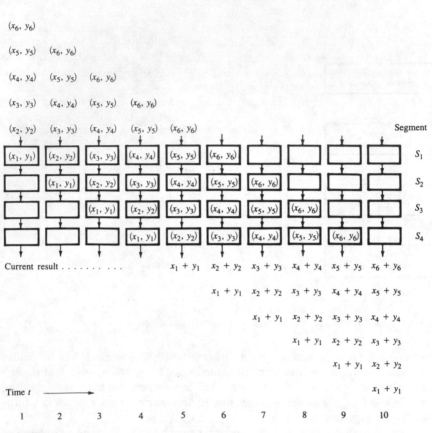

FIGURE 7.24
Operation of the floating-point adder pipeline.

The basic pipeline structure illustrated in Figs. 7.23 and 7.24 can be characterized as a single-function processor organized as a one-dimensional or linear array of processing circuits (segments). The capabilities of pipeline processors can be increased by segments that can perform several alternative operations, or by allowing data to be routed between segments in more than one way. The result is a *multifunction* pipeline which can be reconfigured under instruction or microinstruction control to perform a variety of different functions. Pipeline processors can also be organized as multidimensional arrays of segments, where data flows from segment to segment in several different directions at once. Processors of this type composed of identical segments have been termed *systolic arrays*, to reflect the fact that data flows between segments in a regular and rhythmic fashion. Two-dimensional systolic structures have some potential advantages for VLSI design, and provide highly parallel and fast implementations of such complex numerical functions as convolution and matrix multiplication [26].

Pipeline design. Designing a pipeline processor to implement a given function involves first finding an appropriate multistage sequential algorithm for computing the target function. The algorithm stages, which are implemented by the processing circuits of the segments, must be balanced in the sense that they all have roughly the same execution time. High-speed buffer registers are placed between the stages to allow all necessary data items (partial or complete results) to be transferred between the segments without interfering with one another. The buffers are normally designed to be clocked at the maximum possible rate that allows data to be transferred reliably between segments.

Figure 7.25 shows the register-level design of a floating-point adder pipeline based on the nonpipelined design of Fig. 3.69, and employing the four-segment

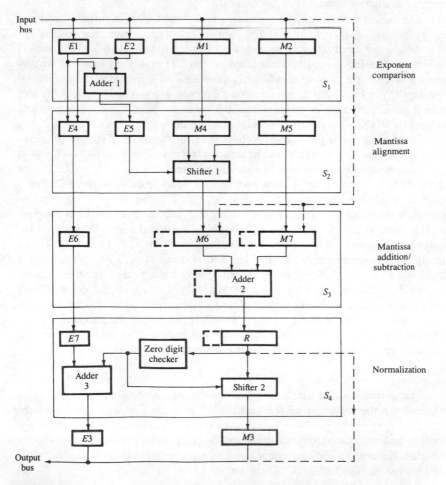

FIGURE 7.25
Pipelined version of the floating-point adder of Fig. 3.69.

organization of Fig. 7.23. The most significant change from the nonpipelined case is the inclusion of buffer registers to define and isolate the four segments. A further modification has been made to permit fixed-point as well as floating-point addition. The circuits that perform the mantissa addition in segment S_3, and the corresponding buffers, are enlarged, as shown by broken lines in Fig. 7.25, to accommodate full-word fixed-point operands. To perform a fixed-point addition, the input operands are routed through S_3 only, bypassing the other three segments. Thus the circuit of Fig. 7.25 is a simple example of a multifunction pipeline that can be configured either as a four-segment floating-point adder or else as a one-segment fixed-point adder. Of course, fixed-point and floating-point subtraction can also be performed by this circuit; subtraction and addition are not usually regarded as distinct functions in this context.

The same function may be segmented in different ways in different computers, depending on such factors as the data representation used, the style of the logic design, the need to share segments with other functions in a multifunction pipeline. A floating-point adder may have as few as two and as many as six segments. For example, five-segment adders have been built in which the normalization stage (S_4 in Fig. 7.25) is split into two segments, one to count the number k of leading zeros (or ones) in an unnormalized mantissa, and a second segment to perform the k shifts necessary to normalize the mantissa.

Whether or not a particular function or set of functions F should be implemented by a pipeline or nonpipeline processor can be analyzed as follows. Suppose that F can be broken down into m independent steps $F_1, F_2, \ldots, F_m$. Let F_i be realizable by a logic circuit C_i with propagation delay (execution time) T_i. For a pipelined implementation of F to be feasible, the T_i's should all be of approximately the same duration; otherwise, the longest T_i's create bottlenecks in the pipeline that force the faster segments to wait, doing no useful computation, until the slower segments become available. Assume, therefore, that $T_i = T_C$ for all i. Thus a nonpipelined implementation P_1 of F has a total delay of mT_C or, equivalently, a bandwidth of $1/(mT_C)$. Suppose that F can be also implemented by an m-segment pipeline P_m with the structure shown in Fig. 7.21. Let T_R be the delay of each segment attributable to buffer register R_i and its associated control logic. The total delay of one segment of P_m is therefore $T = T_C + T_R$; hence the bandwidth of P_m is $1/(T_C + T_R)$. We conclude that P_m has greater bandwidth than P_1, i.e., pipelining increases performance, if the following condition is satisfied:

$$mT_C > T_C + T_R$$

The usefulness of a single-function pipeline can sometimes be considerably enhanced by the inclusion of feedback paths from the segment outputs to the primary inputs of the pipeline. This enables the results computed by certain segments to be used in subsequent calculations by the pipeline. We next illustrate this important concept by adding feedback to a four-segment floating-point adder pipeline like that of Fig. 7.25.

Example 7.4 Summation by a pipeline processor. Consider again the problem of computing the sum of N floating-point numbers $b_1, b_2, \ldots, b_N$ discussed earlier (Sec.

7.1). Clearly it can be solved by adding successive pairs of numbers using a basic adder pipeline and storing the partial sums temporarily in external registers. The summation can be done much more efficiently by modifying the adder as shown in Fig. 7.26. Here a feedback path has been added to the output of the final segment S_4 allowing its results to be fed back directly to the first segment S_1. A register R has also been connected to the output of S_4, where its results can be stored for an indefinite period before being fed back to S_1. The input operands of the modified pipeline are derived from four separate sources: a variable X that is typically obtained from a CPU register or a main-memory location; a constant source K, which can apply such operands as the all-0 and all-1 words; the output of segment S_4, representing the result computed by S_4 in the preceding clock period; and, finally, an earlier result computed by the pipeline and stored in the output register R.

The N-number summation problem is solved by the pipeline of Fig. 7.26 in the following way. The external operands $b_1, b_2, \ldots, b_N$ are entered into the pipeline in a continuous stream via input X. This requires a sequence of register or memory fetch operations, which are easily implemented if the operands are stored in contiguous register/memory locations. While the first four numbers b_1, b_2, b_3, b_4 are being entered, the all-0 word denoting the floating-point number zero is applied to the pipeline input K, as illustrated in Fig. 7.27 for times $t = 1{:}4$. After four clock periods, i.e., at time $t = 5$, the first sum $0 + b_1 = b_1$ emerges from S_4 and is fed back to the primary inputs of the pipeline. At this point, the constant input $K = 0$ is replaced by the current result $S_4 = b_1$. The pipeline now begins to compute $b_1 + b_5$. At $t = 6$, it begins to compute $b_2 + b_6$; at $t = 7$, computation of $b_3 + b_7$ begins, and so on. When $b_1 + b_5$ emerges from the pipeline at $t = 8$, it is fed back to S_1 to be added to the latest incoming number b_9, to initiate computation of $b_1 + b_5 + b_9$. (This case does not apply to Fig. 7.27, where $b_8 = b_N$ is the last item to be summed.) In the next time period, the sum $b_2 + b_6$ emerges from the pipeline and is fed back to be added to the

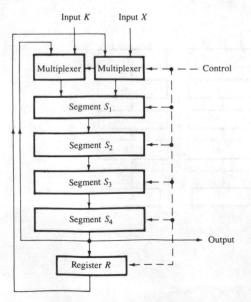

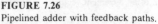

FIGURE 7.26
Pipelined adder with feedback paths.

incoming number b_{10}. Thus at any time, the pipeline is engaged in computing in its four segments, four partial sums of the form

$$
\begin{aligned}
b_1 + b_5 + b_9 + b_{13} + \cdots \\
b_2 + b_6 + b_{10} + b_{14} + \cdots \\
b_3 + b_7 + b_{11} + b_{15} + \cdots \\
b_4 + b_8 + b_{12} + b_{16} + \cdots
\end{aligned}
\tag{7.15}
$$

Once the last input operand b_N has been entered into the pipeline, the feedback structure is again altered to allow the four partial sums in (7.15) to be added together

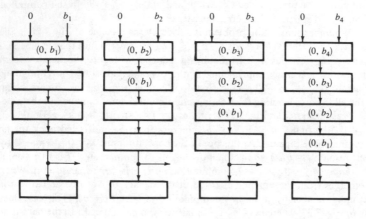

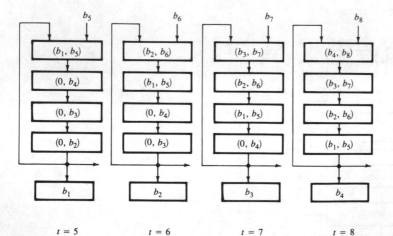

FIGURE 7.27
Summation of an 8-element vector.

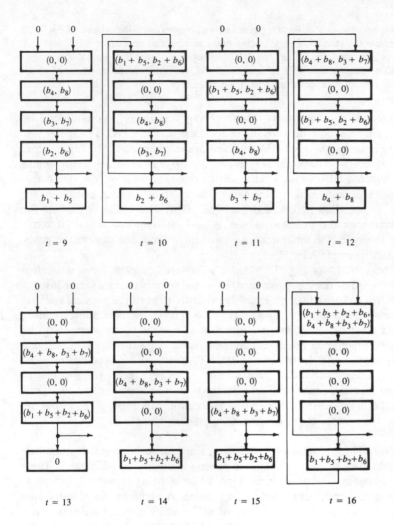

to produce the desired result $\text{SUM} = b_1 + b_2 + \cdots + b_N$. The necessary modification to the feedback structure is shown in Fig. 7.27 for the case where $N = 8$. At $t = 9$, the external inputs to the pipeline are disabled by setting them to zero, and the first of the four partial sums $b_1 + b_5$ at the output of segment S_4 is stored in register R. Then at $t = 10$, the new result $b_2 + b_6$ from S_4 is fed back to the pipeline inputs, along with the previous result $b_1 + b_5$ obtained from R. Thus computation of $b_1 + b_5 + b_2 + b_6$, which is the sum of half of the input operands, begins at this point. After a further delay of one time period, computation of the other half-sum $b_3 + b_7 + b_4 + b_8$ begins. When $b_1 + b_5 + b_2 + b_6$ emerges from S_4 at $t = 14$, it is stored in R until $b_4 + b_8 + b_3 + b_7$ emerges from S_4 at $t = 16$. At this point the outputs of the S_4 and R are fed back to S_1, and computation of SUM begins. The final result is produced four time periods later, at $t = 20$ in the case of $N = 8$.

It is easily seen that for the general case of N operands, the scheme of Fig. 7.27 can compute the sum of $N \geq 4$ floating-point numbers in time $(N + 11)T$, where T is the pipeline clock period, i.e., the delay per segment. Since a comparable nonpipelined adder requires time $4NT$ to compute SUM, we obtain a speedup here of about $4N/(N + 11)$, which approaches 4 as N increases.

In many pipelined computers, the foregoing summation operation can be invoked by a single vector instruction. In the case of the CDC STAR-100, for instance, there is an instruction SUM which computes the sum of the components of a specified floating-point vector $B = (b_1, b_2, \ldots, b_N)$ of arbitrary length N and places the result in a CPU register. The starting (base) address of B, which corresponds to a block of main memory, the name C of the result register, and the vector length N are all specified by operand fields of SUM. The use of a pipeline for summation simplifies the problem of storing and communicating partial sums; compare, for example, the multiprocessor solution to the same summation problem discussed in Example 7.1.

It can be seen from Fig. 7.27 that a relatively complex pipeline control sequence (hardwired or microprogrammed) is needed to implement a vector instruction. This control complexity contributes significantly to both the physical size and cost of pipeline supercomputers. Furthermore, to achieve the maximum speedup, the input data must be stored in a manner that allows the vector elements to be entered into the pipeline at the maximum rate required by the pipeline, viz., one number every clock cycle. In the case of the STAR-100, these operands must be stored in contiguous locations in main memory. If they happen to be stored in noncontiguous locations, then additional instructions must be executed to reposition the data before execution of the SUM instruction can begin. This, of course, contributes to the complexity of programming pipeline computers.

Pipeline control. The major goal in controlling a pipeline processor is to maximize the speedup obtained or, equivalently, the processor utilization (efficiency). These performance parameters depend on the types of tasks being processed, as well as the order in which they are presented to the pipeline. A useful means of visualizing pipeline behavior is a *space-time diagram*, which indicates segment utilization as a function of time. It takes the form of an $n \times T(N)$ rectangle or grid, where n is the number of pipeline segments, and $T(N)$ is the number of clock periods required to execute a given set of N tasks. Figure 7.28 shows the space-time diagram for a sequence of N additions executed by a four-segment adder pipeline; cf. Fig. 7.24. The unshaded areas denote busy segments, and the numbers they contain denote the particular set of operands or instructions being processed. All the segments are fully utilized except at the beginning and end of the addition sequence. The ratio of the unshaded (busy) area to the total (shaded and unshaded) area of the space-time diagram is the efficiency $E(n)$; in the case of Fig. 7.28, this ratio is $E(4) = N/(N + 3)$. The speedup may also be obtained from the space-time diagram via the relation $S(n) = nE(n)$. It is obvious that a new operation can be initiated as soon as the first segment S_1 becomes available, so maximum efficiency and speedup are

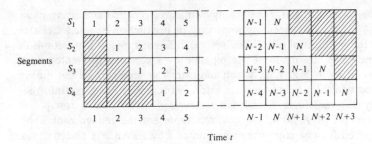

FIGURE 7.28
Space-time diagram for a sequence of N additions by a four-segment pipeline adder.

achieved by the simple strategy of initiating a new add operation every clock period, or as soon as new data become available.

Pipeline operations involving feedback, which allows a segment to be used more than once while processing the same data, require a more complicated mechanism to control the initiation of new tasks efficiently. Figure 7.29 is the space-time diagram for the vector summation operation illustrated in Fig. 7.27, where $n = 4$, $N = 8$, and $T(N) = 19$. Because of the presence of feedback, each segment is used several times, and each segment is unused at certain times in the course of a single summation. Clearly a new summation operation of the same kind cannot begin until time $t = 17$, after the current operation uses segment S_1 for the last time. If a second summation is initiated at the wrong time, e.g., at $t = 9$, then both the first and second summations will attempt to use segment S_1 at $t = 10$, a situation termed a *collision*. However, simple add operations of the kind depicted in Fig. 7.28 could be initiated at $t = 9, 11, 13, 14, 15$, without colliding with the summation operation. Thus, up to five add instructions, if available for execution at the appropriate times, could be interleaved with the eight-element summation operation, thereby increasing the pipeline efficiency.

In general, pipeline collisions are avoided by inserting carefully chosen delays between the start of consecutive operations. Following the work of Edward S. Davidson [9, 23], we now consider a pipeline control strategy to avoid collisions

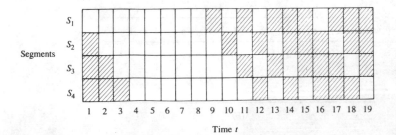

FIGURE 7.29
Space-time diagram for the summation of Fig. 7.27.

and maximize performance. Let P be a single-function pipeline consisting of m segments $S_1, S_2, \ldots, S_m$ and executing some task or instruction denoted I. (Later we will consider the problem of scheduling several different types of instructions in the same pipeline.) The use made of the pipeline by I can be represented by a space-time diagram, as in Fig. 7.29, which indicates the segments in use during every clock period while I is being executed. Here we represent the same information in a slightly different form R called a *reservation table*. The m rows of R represent the segments of P, while the columns represent the sequence of $T(N)$ time periods required for one complete execution of I by P. An x is placed at the intersection of row S_i and column C_j if segment S_i is required by I at time $t = j$. Figure 7.30*a* shows the reservation table corresponding to the eight-element summation using the pipeline of Fig. 7.26; cf. the corresponding space-time diagram in Fig. 7.29. If the algorithm of Fig. 7.27 is used to add the pairs of numbers b_1, b_2 (which would be very inefficient), then the smaller reservation table of Fig. 7.30*b* results.

Two operations of type I that are initiated k time units apart will collide at segment S_i of P, if row i of the corresponding reservation table R contains two x's that are separated by a horizontal distance of k. In the case of Fig. 7.30*b*, for instance, a collision will occur at every segment S_i if $k = 1$, 4, or 5. Let F be a set of numbers, called the *forbidden list* of R, whose entries are the distances between

	Time t																		
Segment	**1**	**2**	**3**	**4**	**5**	**6**	**7**	**8**	**9**	**10**	**11**	**12**	**13**	**14**	**15**	**16**	**17**	**18**	**19**
S_1	x	x	x	x	x	x	x	x		x		x				x			
S_2		x	x	x	x	x	x	x	x		x		x				x		
S_3			x	x	x	x	x	x	x	x		x		x				x	
S_4				x	x	x	x	x	x	x	x		x		x				x

(*a*)

	Time t								
Segment	**1**	**2**	**3**	**4**	**5**	**6**	**7**	**8**	**9**
S_1	x	x				x			
S_2		x	x				x		
S_3			x	x				x	
S_4				x	x				x

(*b*)

FIGURE 7.30
Pipeline reservation tables for N-component vector summation: (*a*) $N = 8$ corresponding to Fig. 7.29; (*b*) $N = 2$.

all distinct pairs of x's in every row of R. The collision conditions for R are characterized by the following easily proven result. Two operations initiated k clock periods apart collide if and only if k is in the forbidden list F of R. Thus the most basic pipeline operating requirement of avoiding collisions is easily met by delaying new tasks by time periods not appearing in the forbidden list. Much less obvious is how to select intertask delays to maximize the pipeline's performance.

The maximum number of collision-free operations that can be initiated per unit time under steady-state conditions corresponds to the pipeline's instruction bandwidth b_I. The delay occurring between the start of two successive pipeline operations is termed *latency*. Thus maximizing the (average) bandwidth b_I is equivalent to minimizing the average latency. We denote the *minimum average latency* by L_{min}; hence $L_{min} = 1/b_I$. A complicated control strategy, which is described below, may be required to minimize the average latency. A simpler design goal is the *minimum constant latency*, defined as the smallest number L such that any number of operations can be initiated L clock periods apart without causing collisions. L can be derived from the forbidden list F using the fact that L is the smallest integer such that hL is not in F for some integer $h \geq 1$.

The forbidden lists for the reservation tables of Figs. 7.30a and 7.30b are {1, 2, 3, 4, 5, 6, 7, 8, 9, 10, 11, 12, 13, 14, 15} and {1, 4, 5}, respectively. Thus, as observed earlier, successive eight-element vector summations with the reservation table of Fig. 7.30a must be initiated at least 16 clock cycles apart, since the latencies L and L_{min} are both 16. In the case of Fig. 7.30b, new operations can be initiated as few as 2 cycles apart. However, the minimum constant latency $L \neq 2$, since $2 \times 2 = 4$ is in F; in this case $L = 3$. If operations are scheduled at $t = 1$ and 3, a third operation cannot be initiated until $t = 9$, as demonstrated by the space-time diagram of Fig. 7.31a. The average latency for the pipeline scheduling scheme defined by Fig. 7.31b is 4, since two new tasks are initiated every 8 clock cycles. The minimum average latency is achieved for this example, when new operations are initiated $L_{min} = 3$ clock cycles apart, as shown in Fig. 7.31b. Observe that in the latter case, the steady-state efficiency or processor utilization of the pipeline is 100 percent.

An efficient way to record the control state of a pipeline is by using collision vectors [9]. A *collision vector* CV for a given reservation table R at time t is a binary vector $c_1 c_2 \cdots c_{M-1} c_M$, where the ith bit c_i is 1 if initiating a new pipeline operation at time $t + i$ will result in a collision; c_i is 0 otherwise. An *initial collision vector* CV_0 is obtained from the forbidden list F of R as follows. Element c_i of CV_0 is set to 1 if i is in F, and c_i is set to 0 otherwise, for $i = 1, 2, \ldots, M$, where M is the maximum element in F. A convenient way to store CV is in a shift register $CR = CR_1 : CR_M$, which we term the *collision register*. By inspecting CR_1 at time t, we can determine whether starting a new pipeline operation in the next clock cycle $t + 1$ will result in a collision. A simple left shift of CR, with the rightmost position CR_M being set to 0, prepares CR_1 for inspection in the next clock period. If it is decided to initiate a new operation at $t + 1$, then CR is left-shifted and its contents are replaced by $CR \vee CV_0$, where CV_0 is the initial collision vector obtained from F as specified above, and $\vee$ denotes the bitwise OR operation. This ensures that

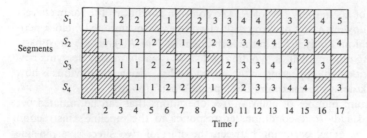

FIGURE 7.31
Pipeline scheduling strategies for the reservation table of Fig. 7.30b: (a) nonoptimal; (b) optimal.

CR defines all the collision possibilities due either to ongoing pipeline operations or the newly initiated operation.

To illustrate the foregoing concepts, consider again the reservation table in Fig. 7.30b. Since $F = \{1, 4, 5\}$, $M = 5$ and the corresponding initial collision vector CV_0 is 10011. The collision register CR is initially set to 00000. When it is decided, say at $t = 0$, to start the first pipeline task at $t = 1$, CR is left-shifted and ORed with CV_0, resulting in CR $= 00000 \vee 10011 = 10011 = CV_0$. At $t = 1$, the new pipeline task is initiated, and CR is again inspected. Since $CR_1 = 1$, it is concluded that a new operation cannot be initiated, and CR is merely shifted during this cycle, changing its contents to 00110. At $t = 2$, CR is found to contain 00110 with $CR_1 = 0$, allowing a new operation to be initiated at $t = 3$. If a second pipeline operation is initiated in the next cycle, CR is shifted and ORed with CV_0, therefore becoming 01100 $\vee$ 10011 = 11111 at $t = 3$. Five subsequent shifts are needed before CR_1 again becomes 0 at $t = 8$. A third operation cannot therefore begin until $t = 9$, as shown by Fig. 7.31a. If no new task is started at $t = 3$, CR is found to be 01100, indicating that a new operation can start at $t = 4$. If a new pipeline operation is then initiated at $t = 4$, CR becomes successively 11000 and 11000 $\vee$ 10011 $= 11011$, implying that a third operation can begin at $t = 7$; this is the situation illustrated by Fig. 7.31b. Note that at $t = 6$, CR becomes 01100, repeating the pattern encountered at $t = 3$.

An optimal schedule for initiating new operations can be derived from the state behavior of the collision register CR. For this purpose we construct a type of condensed state diagram for CR, which we will refer to as a *task initiation diagram* (TID). The states of the TID are all the collision vectors $\{CV_i\}$ formed by the OR operation CR $\vee$ CV_0, when new pipeline tasks can be initiated. (The other states of CR are formed by shifting these vectors and, for simplicity, are excluded from the TID.) An arrow is drawn from CV_i to CV_j if there is a sequence of state transitions of CR changing its state from CV_i to CV_j; the arrow is labeled with the minimum number of state transitions n_{ij} required. Thus n_{ij} denotes the minimum latency between the task initiations represented by the TID states CV_i and CV_j. A closed path or loop in the TID corresponds to the task initiation schedule for the pipeline that can be sustained indefinitely without collisions. Let s be the sum of the n_{ij} labels along the arrows forming the loop, divided by the number of arrows in the loop. Clearly s is the average latency of the corresponding schedule of pipeline task initiations. It can be shown [23], and is intuitively reasonable, that the average latency of the pipeline is minimized by choosing a task initiation sequence corresponding to a loop of the TID with a minimum value of s; that value of s is then the minimum average latency L_{min}.

Figure 7.32 shows the TID derived from the reservation table of Fig. 7.30b, where the initial collision vector $CV_0 = 10011$. It is derived in straightforward fashion by examining all the possible states and state transitions of the corresponding CR in the manner described earlier. The states included in the TID are all those loaded into SR when new tasks can be initiated, namely, the three states $CV_0 = 10011$, $CV_1 = 11011$, and $CV_2 = 11111$ identified above. For example, the self-loop labeled 3 on state CV_1 is a consequence of the following sequence of state transitions involving CR.

Time (clock cycle)	Initial state of CR	Actions taken
t	$11011 = CV_1$	Initiate new task. Shift CR.
$t + 1$	10110	Shift CR.
$t + 2$	01100	Select new task for initiation. Shift CR. Replace CR by CR $\vee$ $CV_0 = 11000 \vee 10011$.
$t + 3$	$11011 = CV_1$	Initiate new task. Shift CR.

The TID of Fig. 7.32 contains several loops corresponding to different pipeline control strategies with various average latencies. For example, the loop formed by the two arrows linking CV_0 and CV_2 has an average latency $s = (2 + 6)/2 = 4$, and corresponds to the space-time diagram of Fig. 7.31a. The self-loop of state CV_1 has the minimum average latency $s = L_{min} = 3$, and therefore maximizes pipeline

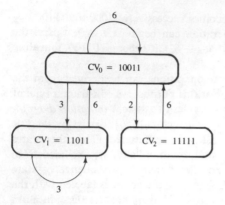

FIGURE 7.32
Task initiation diagram (TID) for Fig. 7.30b.

performance; using this loop for pipeline control yields the space-time diagram of Fig. 7.31b. The analysis confirms our previous observation that the optimum scheduling strategy for this example is to initiate a new operation 3 cycles after the previous operation. Hence a simple logic circuit based on a modulo-3 counter suffices to control this particular pipeline.

7.2.2   Pipeline Structures

As discussed in the preceding section, there are two major pipeline categories, instruction and arithmetic. Instruction pipelines are multifunction reconfigurable pipelines designed to speed up a computer's program-control functions by overlapping the processing of several different instructions. They are found in many types of computers, including conventional SISD machines, and are normally invisible to the programmer. Arithmetic pipelines, on the other hand, are single- or multifunction processors designed to execute a special class of numerical (and occasionally nonnumerical) operations very fast. They are the major device for achieving parallelism in supercomputers of the vector processing variety.

Instruction pipelines. A basic instruction pipeline can be formed by partitioning the instruction cycle into a fetch segment and an execute segment as illustrated in Fig. 7.22. This increases the system throughput by overlapping instruction fetching and execution. While instruction I_i with address A_i is being executed by segment S_2, the instruction I_{i+1} with the next consecutive address A_{i+1} is fetched from memory by segment S_1. If on executing I_i it is determined that a jump must be made to a nonconsecutive instruction address $A_j \neq A_{i+1}$, then the prefetched instruction I_i in S_1 is discarded. Thus the pipeline cycle used to fetch I_{i+1} has been wasted. This problem can be expected to occur fairly infrequently, however, because few instructions produce branching, for example, only 17 percent of the instructions forming the Gibson Mix (Fig. 2.58). Moreover, not all executions of branch instructions actually cause program jumps. A conditional branch of the form **if** $C = $ **true then go to** A_j causes a branch to A_j only when condition C holds. C can often be selected so that it is true no more than half the time.

Figure 7.33 shows a simple implementation of a two-stage instruction pipeline (actually a microinstruction pipeline) used in many microprogrammed control units. This is essentially the generic controller of Fig. 4.39 repackaged into two sequential segments. The fetch segment S_1 is composed of the microprogram counter μPC, which is the address source for microinstructions, and the control memory CM which stores the microinstructions. Note that μPC is appropriately positioned to serve as the buffer register for segment S_1, and is therefore used for this purpose in Fig. 7.33. It is only necessary to increment μPC to generate the next consecutive microinstruction address, which is fetched while the current microinstruction is in the execution phase. The execution segment S_2 contains the microinstruction register μIR, the microinstruction decoders, and the logic for selecting microinstruction branch addresses. Again a preexisting register μIR can be adapted for use as the segment buffer register for S_2. Microinstruction execution is fairly simple compared with the corresponding operation at the instruction level. It primarily involves decoding the control and condition select fields of the current microinstruction μI, as well as distributing the resulting control signals. If μI specifies branching, a branch address, which is typically obtained directly from μI itself, is fed back to S_1. This branch address is loaded into μPC, replacing its previous contents, and causing any ongoing fetch operation in S_1 to be aborted.

A typical pipelined CPU has the overall organization shown in Fig. 7.34. Its

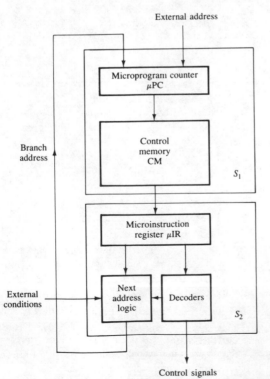

External address

Branch
address

External
conditions

Control signals

FIGURE 7.33
Pipelined microprogram control unit.

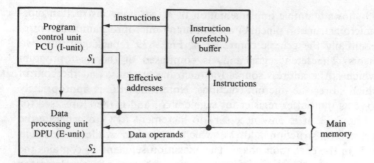

FIGURE 7.34
Organization of a pipelined CPU.

two major segments are the program-control unit (I-unit) PCU and the data processing unit (E-unit) DPU. Each of these segments may be further partitioned into subsegments, yielding an instruction pipeline with upward of a dozen segments. A possible pipeline structure containing five segments is outlined in Fig. 7.35. Each segment typically makes use of certain common facilities which may be external to the instruction pipeline proper, including the general registers and the arithmetic-logic circuits of the CPU, and the main-memory access circuitry. The PCU part of

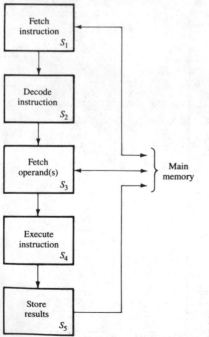

FIGURE 7.35
Five-segment instruction pipeline.

the pipeline (approximately the first three segments shown in the figure) has primary responsibility for generating instruction and operand addresses, fetching instructions and operands, and decoding opcodes; while the DPU is responsible for processing the operands and storing the results. Because they determine the instruction execution sequence, branch instructions may be partly or wholly processed in the PCU. The outcome of a conditional branch depends on results computed in the DPU, which therefore must be returned to the instruction addressing logic in the PCU. The PCU may also use part of the DPU for such functions as effective address computation. Consequently, considerable interaction occurs between the two units, requiring fairly complex intersegment feedback. The pipeline control logic is further complicated by the need to ensure that the different parts of instructions concurrently in various segments of the pipeline do not get out of step, for example, by allowing one instruction to read a CPU register R before new data has been written into R by an earlier instruction.

Instruction pipeline structure is also complicated by the need of various segments to transfer information to and from main memory. In order for the CPU to have available a sufficient supply of instructions to fill the instruction pipeline, the CPU may contain a mechanism for prefetching several instructions, and a small high-speed memory called an *instruction buffer* for storing them in the CPU; see Fig. 7.34. The instruction buffer stores a queue of instructions, usually prefetched from consecutive addresses in main memory, and is accessed by the PCU in a first-in first-out (FIFO) basis. Instruction prefetching from main memory can be done on a cycle-stealing basis, to minimize its impact on system bus efficiency. An alternative or supplement to an instruction buffer is a cache memory, which is positioned between the CPU and M; see Sec. 5.3.2. Although a cache requires more complex control logic than an instruction buffer, it allows both instructions and data to be prefetched from M. It also can store nonconsecutive instructions to which it provides direct (random) access. The IBM 3033 computer, for example, a System/370-compatible mainframe introduced in 1978, has a pipelined CPU employing both an instruction buffer and a large high-speed cache [6].

Figure 7.36 describes the segments of the instruction pipeline employed in the Amdahl 470V/7, another 1978-vintage System/370-compatible computer [1]. The CPU is partitioned into a total of 12 segments with the listed functions. Two segments named start buffer and read buffer are designed to communicate with a memory control unit called the S-unit (storage unit), which is directly responsible for all main memory accesses, and manages a 32K-byte cache (termed the high-speed buffer in Amdahl literature) rather than an instruction-only queue. These segments effectively transfer instructions or data operands between the pipeline and the cache. All instruction results are checked for errors in segment S_{11}, using parity-check codes in most cases. If an error is detected, the instruction in question is automatically reexecuted, an error-recovery technique called *instruction retry*.

The influence of branch instructions on the performance of an instruction pipeline may be roughly estimated as follows. Suppose that the pipeline has m segments, and that each instruction cycle contains m pipeline clock cycles, corresponding to one complete pass through the pipeline. If there are no branch instruc-

Segment	Name	Actions performed
S_1	Compute instruction address	Requests instruction at next sequential address from storage control unit (S-unit)
S_2	Start buffer	Initiates cache (high-speed buffer) to read instruction
S_3	Read buffer	Reads instruction from cache into I-unit
S_4	Decode instruction	Decodes instruction opcode
S_5	Read GPRs	Reads general-purpose registers (GPRs) used as address (base and index) registers
S_6	Compute operand address	Computes address of current memory operand
S_7	Start buffer	Initiates cache to read memory operand
S_8	Read buffer	Reads operand from cache into I-unit; also reads register operands
S_9	Execute 1	Passes data to E-unit and begins instruction execution
S_{10}	Execute 2	Completes instruction execution
S_{11}	Check result	Performs code-based error check on result
S_{12}	Write result	Stores result in CPU register

FIGURE 7.36
Segments of the Amdahl 470V/7 instruction pipeline.

tions in the instruction streams being processed, then one instruction is processed every clock cycle making 1 instruction/cycle the pipeline instruction execution rate or throughput. Let p be the probability of encountering a conditional or unconditional branch instruction. Let q be the probability that execution of a branch instruction I causes a jump to a nonconsecutive address. Assume that each such jump requires the pipeline to be cleared, destroying all ongoing instruction processing, when I emerges from the last segment (this is a pessimistic assumption). Branch instructions of this sort effectively decrease the execution rate of the pipeline by a factor of m.

Consider an instruction sequence of length r that is streaming through the pipeline. The number of instructions causing branches to take place is pqr, and these instructions are executed at a rate of $1/m$ instructions/cycle. The remaining $(1 - pq)r$ nonbranching instructions are processed at the maximum rate of 1 instruction/cycle. Hence the total number of clock cycles n_c needed to process all r instructions is

$$n_c = pqrm + (1 - pq)r$$

implying that the average instruction execution rate (bandwidth) b_I of the pipeline, measured in instructions executed per clock cycle, is given by

$$b_I = \frac{r}{n_c} = \frac{r}{pqrm + (1 - pq)r}$$

Hence,
$$b_I = \frac{1}{1 + pq(m - 1)} \text{ instructions/cycle} \qquad (7.16)$$

with the maximum value $b_I = 1$ occurring when $q = 0$, i.e., when no branching occurs during program execution. Note that a comparable nonpipelined instruction processor has $b_I = 1/m$. If $p = 0.2$, $q = 0.5$ and $m = 5$ (as in Fig. 7.35), which are typical values for instruction pipelines, then Eq. (7.16) implies that $b_I = 0.76$. Hence, in this representative case, pipelining increases the instruction bandwidth from $1/m = 0.20$ to 0.76, an improvement by a factor of almost 4. The improvement in b_I is less for longer pipelines, since each branch to a nonconsecutive instruction address causes more partially processed instructions to be discarded. A compiler or a programmer can increase instruction pipeline throughput somewhat by employing fewer branch instructions (to reduce p), and by constructing conditional branch instructions so that the more probable results of the condition tests cause no branching (to reduce q).

Pipelined computers employ various hardware techniques to minimize the performance degradation due to instruction branching. The Amdahl 470V/7, for example, uses special branch-resolution logic that sends the result of a branch condition test from the E-unit to the I-unit before the conditional branch instruction has been completely processed. This allows the I-unit to initiate processing of the correct next instruction with a loss of data in only 3 of its 12 pipeline segments. A different approach is taken by the IBM 3033. Its instruction buffer is divided into three separate buffers: one holds a normal sequence of consecutive instructions prefetched under the assumption that no branches will occur; the other two buffers hold prefetched instruction sequences starting at up to two branch addresses specified by previously decoded branch instructions. Thus when the 3033 CPU decodes an unconditional branch instruction of the form **go to** A_j, and has an instruction buffer with available space, it proceeds to prefetch and process instructions starting at location A_j. In the case of a two-way conditional branch instruction with two target branch addresses A_j and A_k, the CPU selects one branch address for prefetching. If, when the conditional branch instruction is subsequently executed, it turns out that the wrong selection was made by the CPU, then time is lost while the correct instruction is fetched. If the CPU has anticipated the outcome of the condition test correctly, then the required next instruction is either already in the instruction pipeline or is stored in an instruction buffer.

RISC machines also rely on instruction pipelines that overlap instruction fetch and execute to achieve single-cycle execution for most instructions. A technique called *delayed jump* or *branch with execute* is used in some RISCs to reduce the penalty due to pipeline flushes on program branching. In general, a delayed branch instruction I_1 causes the instruction I_2 immediately following I_1 to be executed while the instruction I' at the target address specified by I_1 is being fetched. The execution of I' then follows that of I_2 rather than I_1 as would normally be the case. For example, in the IBM 801 RISC, there is an alternative branch with execute form of every normal branch instruction [28]. Thus the instruction sequence

$$\begin{array}{lll} \text{LOAD} & \text{R1, A} \\ \text{BNZ} & \text{L} & \quad (7.17) \end{array}$$

for the 801 containing the normal conditional branch instruction BNZ (*b*ranch if *n*onzero) idles the CPU while the instruction at the branch address L is being fetched. Suppose that BNZ is replaced by the corresponding branch-and-execute instruction BNZX and the instruction order is reversed as follows:

$$\begin{array}{lll} \text{BNZX} & \text{L} \\ \text{LOAD} & \text{R1, A} \end{array} \qquad (7.18)$$

The modified program segment (7.18) has precisely the same meaning as (7.17), but now the LOAD instruction is executed while the instruction specified by BNZX is being fetched. The compiler of the 801 is able to translate about 60 percent of program branches into the branch-with-execute form.

Arithmetic pipelines. Most of the more complex arithmetic functions encountered in computer instruction sets can, in principle, be implemented by pipelining. Arithmetic pipelines have been constructed for performing a single arithmetic function such as floating-point addition (see Fig. 7.25), or for performing all basic operations on fixed-point and floating-point numbers. Fixed-point addition and subtraction are too simple to be efficiently partitioned into suboperations suitable for pipelining. However, as we shall see, fixed-point adders are useful components in pipelines implementing more complex operations. Among the basic fixed-point functions, multiplication is most suitable for pipelining, while division can be implemented by modifying a multiplier pipeline to execute the repeated multiplication algorithm for division discussed in Sec. 3.3.2. Pipelined arithmetic processors are usually found as functional units in the data processing part of a CPU. As such they can either be a permanent part of an instruction pipeline or, as is more often the case, can be dynamically linked to the instruction pipeline when required by some instruction in process. Arithmetic pipelines can also have the role of special-purpose auxiliary processors designed to execute some small class of instructions.

Consider the task of multiplying two n-bit binary numbers $X = x_0 x_1 \cdots x_{n-1}$ and $Y = y_0 y_1 \cdots y_{n-1}$. Combinational array multipliers of the kind described in Sec. 3.3.2 are easily converted to pipelines by the addition of buffer registers. Figure 7.37 shows a pipelined array multiplier which employs the 1-bit multiply-and-add cell M of Fig. 3.36, and has $n = 3$. Each cell M computes a 1-bit product of the form $x_i y_j$, and adds it to a product bit obtained from the preceding segment, and to the carry-bit generated by the cell on its right. Thus the n cells in each segment S_i, for $i = 0, 1, 2, \ldots, n - 1$, compute a partial product of the form

$$P_i = P_{i-1} + x_{n-i-1} 2^i Y \qquad (7.19)$$

with the final product $P_{n-1} = XY$ being computed by the last segment. In addition to storing the partial products in temporary buffer registers, the multiplicand Y and all unused multiplier bits must also be buffered. Clearly an n-segment multiplier pipeline of this type can overlap the computation of n separate products, as required, for example, when multiplying fixed-point vectors, and can generate a new result every clock cycle. Its main disadvantage is the relatively slow speed of the segment logic, which employs ripple-carry propagation. The number of M cells

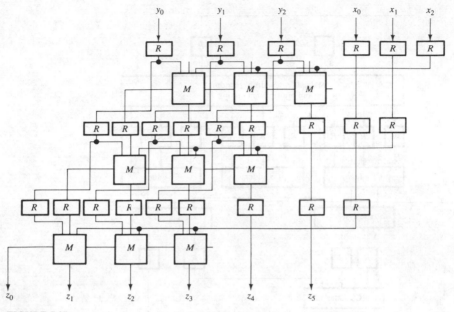

FIGURE 7.37
Multiplier pipeline using ripple-carry propagation.

needed is n^2, and the number of 1-bit buffer registers R is approximately $3n^2$ (see Prob. 7.14); hence this type of multiplier is also fairly costly in hardware. For these reasons, it is rarely used.

Multiplier pipelines are often based on the faster carry-save (Wallace tree) approach, also described in Chap. 3. Figure 7.38 shows a pipelined version of the carry-save multiplier appearing in Fig. 3.50, which is similar to the multiplication pipelines found in the STAR-100 [15] and other computers. Four segments are employed here. The first segment decodes the multiplier and gates appropriately shifted copies of the multiplicand into the carry-save adder circuit. Multiplier recoding may be done in this segment to reduce the number of additions required. The output of the first segment is a set of numbers (partial products) which are then summed by a treelike carry-save adder. The carry-save adder tree has been divided into two segments by the insertion of buffer registers, is shown in the figure. The fourth and final segment contains a parallel adder to perform carry assimilation. This multiplier can easily be modified to handle floating-point numbers. The input mantissas are processed using the basic fixed-point multiplier pipeline. The exponents are combined using a separate fixed point-adder, and a normalization circuit is added.

Complex multifunction arithmetic pipelines are found in most highly pipelined computers, for example, the STAR-100 (see Example 7.3). We now consider a typical arithmetic pipeline, which is used in the Texas Instruments ASC (*A*dvanced *S*cientific *C*omputer), another early supercomputer.

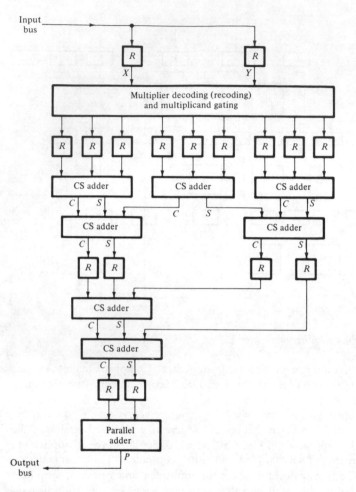

FIGURE 7.38
A pipelined carry-save multiplier.

Example 7.5   Arithmetic Pipeline of the TI ASC [34, 36]. This machine contains a reconfigurable eight-segment pipeline capable of performing all basic arithmetic (both fixed-point and floating-point) and logical functions on 64-bit (double-word) operands, and is designed to support a full range of scalar and vector instructions. The eight segments of this pipeline and their interconnections are shown in Fig. 7.39. The data flow between the segments is reconfigured dynamically to match each instruction being executed, and contains both segment bypass and feedback paths. The functions of the various segments of the ASC arithmetic pipeline are summarized in Fig. 7.40. A memory buffer holds two 8-word queues of X and Y input operands, which it supplies to the input segment S_1, while an 8-word output queue holds results sent from the output segment S_8. The ASC pipeline is designed to process 64-bit operands at a maximum rate of one result per clock period (60 ns), corresponding to a throughput of about 16 MFLOPS.

Figure 7.41 shows the specific segments and data paths used for three representative pipelined instructions. Floating-point addition (Fig. 7.41a) is done by the four-segment group S_2:S_5 in the manner described in detail earlier. Fixed-point multiplication is carried out in the two segments S_6 and S_7, as shown in Fig. 7.41b. A technique similar to that of Fig. 7.37 is used, with the multiply segment S_6 producing a product in the form of a carry-sum pair C, S, similar to that obtained from the second-last segment of the multiplier of Fig. 7.37. The carry assimilation needed to convert C, S to the final product $X \times Y$ is performed by an adder in the accumulate segment S_7.

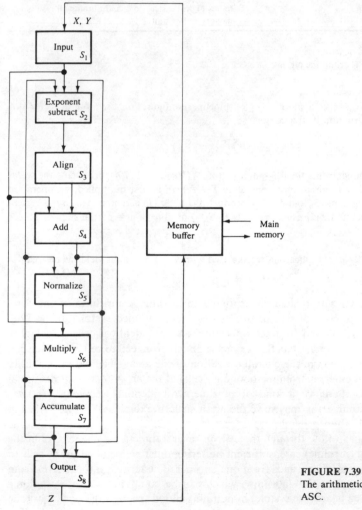

FIGURE 7.39
The arithmetic pipeline of the TI ASC.

Segment	Name	Actions performed
S_1	Input	Reads all input operands from memory buffer unit
S_2	Exponent subtract	Compares exponents during floating-point addition and subtraction
S_3	Align	Performs variable-length shifts for mantissa alignment and shift instructions
S_4	Add	Performs 64-bit fixed-point addition
S_5	Normalize	Normalizes results of floating-point operations
S_6	Multiply	Performs 32-bit fixed-point or floating-point multiplication producing product in carry-save form
S_7	Accumulate	Accumulates results of repeated operations, and performs carry assimilation during multiplication
S_8	Output	Executes logical instructions and outputs all results to memory buffer unit

FIGURE 7.40
Segments of the ASC arithmetic pipeline.

Figure 7.41c shows a more complex pipeline configuration used for a vector dot product instruction that computes

$$Z_n = \sum_{I=1}^{n} X(I) \times Y(I)$$

for two n-dimensional floating-point vectors $X(1:n)$ and $Y(1:n)$, producing the scalar result Z_n. Each pair of input operands $X(I)$, $Y(I)$ is first multiplied, an operation requiring segments S_6 and S_7. The product $X(I) \times Y(I)$ is then added to the current accumulated sum Z_{I-1} using segments S_2:S_5 to produce a new partial sum

$$Z_I = Z_{I-1} + X(I) \times Y(I) \tag{7.20}$$

Consequently n multiplications interspersed with $n-1$ additions yield the desired dot product z_n.

Systolic arrays. Closely related conceptually to arithmetic pipelines of the foregoing kind are the class of regular processing circuits termed systolic arrays [26]. They are typically formed by interconnecting a set of identical cells in a highly regular array-like manner. Data flows synchronously from cell to cell, with each cell performing a small step in the overall operation of the array. The data is not fully processed until it emerges from the boundary cells of the array. A one-dimensional systolic array is therefore a kind of pipeline with identical segments. A two-dimensional systolic array may have the mesh structure depicted in Fig. 7.18, but has simpler cells than general-purpose processors (CPUs). In general, a systolic array allows data to flow through the cells in several directions at once. As in the one-dimensional (pipeline) case, sufficient buffering must be included in the cells to isolate different sets of operands from one another. The term *systolic* derives from the rhythmic nature of the data flow, which can be compared with the rhythmic contraction of the heart (the systole) in pumping blood through the body. Systolic processors have been designed to implement a number of complex arithmetic operations such as convolution (see Prob. 7.15), matrix multiplication, and various solution techniques for linear equations. We illustrate the basic concepts by a two-dimensional systolic array designed to perform matrix multiplication.

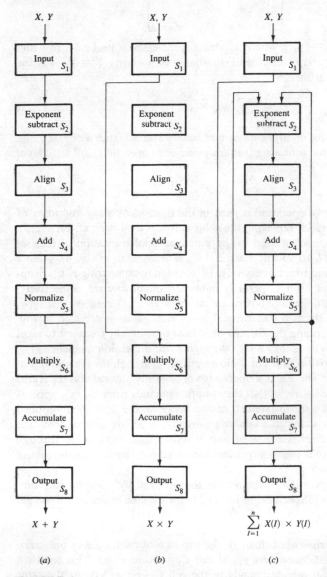

$$X + Y$$

$$X \times Y$$

$$\sum_{I=1}^{n} X(I) \times Y(I)$$

(a)

(b)

(c)

FIGURE 7.41

ASC pipeline configuration for (a) floating-point addition; (b) fixed-point multiplication; (c) floating-point vector dot product.

Let X be an $n \times n$ matrix of fixed-point or floating-point numbers defined as follows:

$$X = \begin{bmatrix} x_{1,1} & x_{1,2} & \cdots & x_{1,n} \\ x_{2,1} & x_{2,2} & \cdots & x_{2,n} \\ \cdots\cdots\cdots\cdots\cdots\cdots\cdots \\ x_{n,1} & x_{n,2} & \cdots & x_{n,n} \end{bmatrix}$$

For brevity, we write $X = [x_{i,j}]$, where $x_{i,j}$ denotes the element in the ith row and jth column of X. The product of X and another $n \times n$ matrix $Y = [y_{i,j}]$ is the $n \times n$ matrix $Z = [z_{i,j}]$ defined by

$$z_{i,j} = \sum_{k=1}^{n} x_{i,k} \times y_{k,j} \tag{7.21}$$

A systolic array for matrix multiplication may be constructed from a cell (see Fig. 7.42a) that executes the following multiply-and-add operation on individual numbers (scalars)

$$z \leftarrow z' + x \times y \tag{7.22}$$

Note that the same type of operation is used in the fixed-point array multiplier of Fig. 7.36, with 1-bit operands replacing the n-bit numbers used here; cf. Eq. (7.19). This is also the basic operation used in the pipelined implementation of the dot product operation [Eq. (7.20) above]. Each cell $C_{i,j}$ is designed to receive its x and y operands from the left and top, respectively. In addition to computing z, $C_{i,j}$ propagates its preceding x and y input operands rightward and downward, respectively. The systolic matrix multiplier is constructed from $n(2n - 1)$ cells of this type, which are connected in the two-dimensional mesh configuration depicted in Fig. 7.42b. The n operands forming the ith row of X flow horizontally from left to right through the ith row of cells as they might through a one-dimensional pipeline. The n operands forming the jth column of Y flow vertically through the jth column of cells in a similar fashion. The x and y operands are carefully ordered and separated by zeros as shown in the figure, so that the specific operands pairs $x_{i,k}, y_{k,j}$ appearing in (7.21) meet at an appropriate cell of the array, where they are multiplied according to (7.22), and added to a running sum z'. The z's are emitted from the left side of $C_{i,j}$, so that there is a flow of partial results from right to left through the array. Each row of cells eventually issues the corresponding row of the matrix product Z from its left side.

To illustrate the operation of the matrix multiplier array, consider the computation of $z_{1,1}$ in Fig. 7.42. Specializing Eq. (7.21) for the case where $n = 3$, we get

$$z_{1,1} = x_{1,1}y_{1,1} + x_{1,2}y_{2,1} + x_{1,3}y_{3,1}$$

The operand $x_{1,1}$ flows rightward through the top row of cells meeting only zero values of y and z, until it encounters $y_{1,1}$ at cell $C_{1,3}$ at time $t = 3$. This cell then computes $z = x_{1,1}y_{1,1} + 0$, which it sends to the cell $C_{1,2}$ on its left. At the same time, $C_{1,3}$ forwards $y_{1,1}$ to the second row of cells for use in computing the second row of the result matrix Z; it also forwards $x_{1,1}$ to its right neighbor $C_{1,4}$. In the

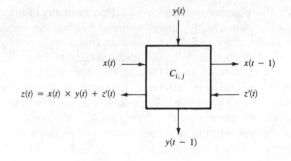

(a)

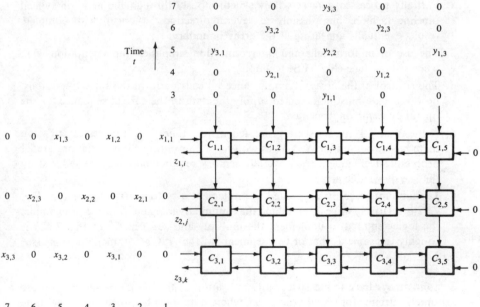

FIGURE 7.42
Systolic array for matrix multiplication: (a) basic cell; (b) 3×5 matrix multiplier structure.

next clock cycle ($t = 4$), $x_{1,2}$ and $y_{2,1}$ are applied to cell $C_{1,2}$. This cell therefore computes $z = x_{1,2}y_{2,1} + z'$, where $z' = x_{1,1}y_{1,1}$. Finally, at $t = 5$, the last pair of operands $x_{1,3}$ and $y_{3,1}$ converge at the boundary cell $C_{1,1}$, which computes $z = x_{1,3}y_{3,1} + z'$, using the value $z' = x_{1,1}y_{1,1} + x_{1,2}y_{2,1}$ supplied by $C_{1,2}$; z is then the desired result $z_{1,1}$. At time $t = 6$, $C_{1,1}$ emits a zero, and at $t = 7$, it emits the next element $z_{1,2}$ of Z. This process continues until all the elements of the first row of Z have been generated. Concurrently, and in a similar fashion, the remaining rows of cells compute the other rows of Z. Note, however, that $x_{i+1,j}$ is produced two time units later than $x_{i,j}$. It follows that the last element ($z_{n,n}$) to be computed emerges from the array at time $t = 4n - 3$. Thus using $O(n^2)$ cells, this systolic array performs matrix multiplication in $O(n)$ time (linear time). Roughly speaking, this systolic array generates n elements of the product matrix Z in one step (actually two time units in the present example).

The major characteristics of a systolic array can be deduced from the foregoing example.

1. It provides a high-degree of parallelism by processing many sets of operands concurrently.
2. Partially processed data sets flow synchronously through the array in typical pipeline fashion (but possibly in several directions at once), with complete results eventually appearing at the array boundary.
3. The use of uniform cells and interconnection simplifies implementation, e.g., when using single-chip VLSI technology.
4. The control of the array is simple, since all cells perform the same operations; however, care must be taken to supply the data in the correct sequence for the operation being implemented.
5. If the X and Y matrices are generated in real time, it is unnecessary to store them before computing $X \times Y$, as with most conventional sequential or parallel processing techniques. Thus overall memory requirements may be reduced by the use of systolic arrays.
6. The amount of hardware needed to implement a systolic array like that of Fig. 7.42 is relatively large, even taking maximum advantage of VLSI. For example, the logic required to implement the multiply-and-add cell $C_{i,j}$ of Fig. 7.42b is roughly the same as that of two segments of the ASC's arithmetic pipeline (see Fig. 7.41b).

Systolic arrays have found successful application in the design of special-purpose arithmetic circuits for signal processing, where data must be processed in real-time at very high speeds using operations like matrix multiplication.

7.2.3   Vector Supercomputers

As discussed in Sec. 7.1, many important scientific problems can be efficiently formulated in terms of vectors. Commercial supercomputers have the ability to process vectors, and related data structures such as matrices and multidimensional arrays, much faster than conventional computers. Many of the most successful of these machines rely on arithmetic pipelines designed for very high-speed vector operations; consequently such machines are often referred to as *vector processors*. [Nonpipelined parallel computers like ILLIAC IV (see Example 7.2) can also handle vectors very efficiently, and therefore may be called vector processors; however, such machines have been less widely used.] In this section, the structure and programming requirements of pipelined vector processors are considered in detail.

Pipeline processing was first employed on a large scale in the CDC STAR-100 and the TI ASC, which were designed in the mid-1960s, but only a few of these early supercomputers were manufactured. One of the first commercially successful pipelined supercomputers was the Cray-1, introduced by Cray Research Inc. in 1976. This is the forerunner of a family of compatible machines, including the Cray X-MP series introduced in 1982. In 1981, Control Data introduced the Cyber/ETA 205, another successful pipelined supercomputer, that was strongly influenced by previous CDC machines like the STAR-100 and the 6600/7600 series. (It is interesting to note that the chief architect of these early CDC machines and the Cray series is the same person, namely, Seymour Cray.) In the mid-1980s, pipelined supercomputers began to be produced by several Japanese manufacturers, e.g., Fujitsu's VP-200 and NEC Corporation's SX-2. The Fujitsu machine was notable in having a fair degree of compatibility with the IBM System/370 architecture, which, more than 20 years after its introduction, remains a de facto standard for conventional mainframe computer systems. The introduction by IBM itself of the vector extension to the System/370 in 1986 is an indication that the distinction between mainframe computers and vector processors has become blurred.

A common characteristic of the foregoing computers is their extremely high (supercomputing) speeds, varying from a peak performance of 160 MFLOPS for the Cray-1, to 1300 MFLOPS (1.3 GFLOPS) in the case of the SX-2. These performance levels are achieved by multiple pipeline processors, supported by very large and fast memory and I/O systems. For example, the SX-2 has a basic pipeline clock period of 8 ns, 80K bytes of CPU registers for vector storage, and 256M bytes of main memory. All these computers are oriented toward scientific programming using the FORTRAN programming language, with language extensions and special support software to enhance their vector processing performance.

Vector operations. A vector V is an ordered set or one-dimensional array of n data items such as fixed-point numbers, floating-point numbers, or logical entities, all of which are called scalars. The vector V may be written in row form as $[V_1, V_2, \ldots, V_n]$ or, omitting commas, as $[V_1 \, V_2 \cdots V_n]$; alternatively, it may be represented in column form thus:

$$V = \begin{bmatrix} V_1 \\ V_2 \\ \cdot \\ \cdot \\ \cdot \\ V_n \end{bmatrix}$$

In programming languages, where subscripts (and sometimes lowercase letters) are avoided, the Ith element or component V_I of V is written as $V(I)$ or $V[I]$, and the index I is equated to a register or main-memory address in the target computer. The number n of scalars forming V is the vector's *length* or *size*. A d-dimensional array, which is composed of scalars with d indices of the form $V(I_1, I_2, \ldots, I_d)$ can be decomposed into vectors (one-dimensional arrays) in various ways. For example, the rows and columns of an $n \times n$ matrix, which is a two-dimensional array, are vectors of length n, while the diagonals of the matrix constitute vectors whose length ranges from one to n.

A conventional sequential computer is designed to process scalar operands one at a time. Consequently, operations on vectors of length n must be broken down into n scalar steps. Consider, for example, the vector addition

$$Z \leftarrow X + Y \tag{7.23}$$

involving vectors of length $n = 1000$. This complex operation could be specified by 1000 add statements as follows, using FORTRAN as a representative programming language:

$$
\begin{aligned}
&Z(1) = X(1) + Y(1) \\
&Z(2) = X(2) + Y(2) \\
&\cdots\cdots\cdots\cdots\cdots\cdots\cdots\cdots \\
&Z(1000) = X(1000) + Y(1000)
\end{aligned}
\tag{7.24}
$$

A much more succinct representation of these 1000 scalar add instructions is given by the two-statement FORTRAN DO loop:

$$
\begin{aligned}
&\text{DO } 10 \text{ I} = 1, 1000 \\
10 \quad &Z(I) = X(I) + Y(I)
\end{aligned}
\tag{7.25}
$$

which reads: for index I ranging from 1 to 1000, execute (do) all statements up to and including the statement labeled 10. Execution of (7.25) on a sequential computer still requires the 1000 separate scalar add operations listed in (7.24). A vector processor, on the other hand, has a set of vector instructions (as well as the usual scalar instructions) that allow operations like (7.23) to be specified by a single vector instruction, and treat the vectors like single operands. Each vector operation may be decomposed internally into scalar suboperations, but these suboperations are executed in a highly parallel fashion, resulting in much faster execution times than can be achieved with sequential computers. Suppose, for instance, that an m-segment pipelined adder is available to perform the vector addition defined by (7.25). If the components X(I) and Y(I) are supplied to the pipeline at the maximum (streaming) rate of one pair of input operands every clock cycle, then a scalar result Z(I) is produced every clock cycle, so that the overall vector result Z is computed approximately m times faster than it could be on a comparable sequential computer. Vector operations also normally require some auxiliary bookkeeping instructions to define the vector length n, and to compute the indices (addresses) I = 1:1000, as specified by the DO part of (7.25).

Vector processors are designed to deal with vectors of varying length n in a consistent and uniform manner. Large values of n lead to problems of storing the vectors efficiently, so that they can be moved rapidly to and from the pipelines where they are processed. Two approaches are possible.

1. The currently required vectors (or major portions of them) can be stored in CPU registers while being processed. This *register-to-register* approach is used by the Cray-1 computer, whose CPU contains a set of eight vector registers, each capable of storing a 64-element vector, where each element contains 64 bits (8 bytes), the word size of the machine.
2. The CPU pipelines can access their vector operands directly in main memory; this is done in the STAR-100 and its successors. This approach, called *memory-to-memory* architecture, reduces CPU complexity at the expense of higher memory bandwidth requirements.

In all cases, pipelined supercomputers require a very short effective memory cycle time. This is usually achieved by employing very fast RAM circuits, multiple memory modules with address interleaving, and data and/or instruction buffers such as caches. The addresses of vector components must also be easily and rapidly computable by the memory control units. For this reason, the Cray-1 requires vector elements to be stored in memory locations that are separated by a constant number s of memory locations before they can be processed by a vector instruction; s is termed the vector's *stride*. The Cyber 205 has the more restrictive requirement that all elements of a vector be stored in contiguous memory locations, i.e., the stride must be one. If the vector components are not properly positioned in memory for a particular vector instruction, they must first be repositioned, a data-transfer operation called *gather*, before the instruction can be issued. Gather operations (and the corresponding *scatter* operations that return the gathered results to their original locations) introduce appreciable overhead in vector computations.

The instruction sets of pipelined computers contain the standard (scalar) data-transfer, data processing, and program-control instructions of conventional computers, augmented by instructions that process vectors, or various combinations of scalars and vectors. Figure 7.43 lists a representative set of the vector instructions taken from the ASC [34], which employs memory-to-memory architecture. The characteristics of the vectors being processed are stored in a vector parameter file of the ASC's CPU. These include the addresses of the first elements of up to three vector operands X, Y, and Z, that is, the addresses of X(1), Y(1), and Z(1), and the vector length n, which is stored in a length register L. A typical vector instruction of the form $Z \leftarrow f(X, Y)$ is implemented as follows. The index address I is initialized to 1, and the input operands X(I) and Y(I) are fetched from main memory via the memory buffer. The X(I) and Y(I) scalar operands are then entered into one of the ASC's four multifunction pipelines, which is set to compute the required function f; see Figs. 7.39 and 7.41. During each clock cycle, I is incremented, L is decremented, and another pair of vector elements are loaded into the pipeline; this process continues until L = 0. As each result $f(X(I), Y(I))$ emerges

Instruction	Description
Vector add (VA)	$Z(I) \leftarrow X(I) + Y(I)$ for $I = 1, 2, \ldots, n$
Vector add magnitude (VAM)	$Z(I) \leftarrow X(I) + |Y(I)|$ for $I = 1, 2, \ldots, n$, where $|Y(I)|$ denotes the absolute value of $Y(I)$
Vector subtract (VS)	$Z(I) \leftarrow X(I) - Y(I)$ for $I = 1, 2, \ldots, n$
Vector multiply (VM)	$Z(I) \leftarrow X(I) \times Y(I)$ for $I = 1, 2, \ldots, n$
Vector divide (VD)	$Z(I) \leftarrow X(I) \div Y(I)$ for $I = 1, 2, \ldots, n$
Vector dot product (VDP)	$Z(1) \leftarrow \sum_{I=1}^{n} X(I) \times Y(I)$
Vector and (VAND)	$Z(I) \leftarrow X(I) \wedge Y(I)$ for $I = 1, 2, \ldots, n$
Vector logical shift (VSL)	$Z(I) \leftarrow \mathrm{SHIFT}(X(I))$ for $I = 1, 2, \ldots, n$, where $X(I)$ is shifted by an amount and direction specified by $Y(I)$
Vector arithmetic compare (VC)	Compare $X(I)$ to $Y(I)$ for $I = 1, 2, \ldots, n$; set $Z(I)$ to indicate greater than, less than, or equal
Vector maximum (VMAX)	$Z(I) \leftarrow \mathrm{MAX}\{X(I),Y(I)\}$ for $I = 1, 2, \ldots, n$
Vector merge (VMG)	$Z \leftarrow [X(1),Y(1),X(2),Y(2), \ldots, X(n),Y(n)]$
Vector replace (VREP)	$Z(I+1) \leftarrow Y(J)$ if $X(J) = I$ for $J = 1, 2, \ldots, m$
Vector search for largest element (VL)	The elements of X are scanned, and the index I of the largest element is determined and stored at a specified address

FIGURE 7.43
Representative vector instructions from the TI ASC.

from the pipeline, it is stored in memory location $Z(I)$. In the ASC, the indices of X, Y, and Z may be incremented by different amounts by setting certain parameters in the vector parameter file. The vector instructions listed in Fig. 7.43 have different versions for different data formats including fixed-point, floating-point, single-precision (32 bits), and double-precision (64 bits). Where applicable, the given mnemonics refer only to the single-precision fixed-point (32-bit integer) case.

Example 7.6 The Cray-1 computer [22, 29]. The Cray-1's overall system structure is indicated in Fig. 7.44. At its heart is a CPU containing some 12 pipeline processors (termed functional units in Cray literature) that implement a comprehensive set of scalar and vector instructions. These processors communicate directly with a large set of high-speed registers, giving the Cray-1 a register-to-register architecture, in contrast with the memory-to-memory architecture of such machines as the STAR-100 and the ASC. The CPU clock period is 12.5 ns, allowing single pipeline throughput of up to 80 MFLOPS; higher throughput is achieved by operating several pipelines in parallel. The 160 MFLOPS peak performance figure usually cited for the Cray-1 is achieved by operating two of its floating-point pipeline processors in parallel at their maximum speeds. The basic word size of the machine is 64 bits, and is used for fixed-point (twos-complement integer) and floating-point numbers. 24-bit integers are also used to represent memory and IO channel addresses. The main memory of the Cray-1 has a capacity of 2^{20} 64-bit words. Each word is stored with 8 check bits, enabling the memory to correct single-bit errors and detect double-bit errors. The memory cycle time is 50 ns, or four times the CPU clock period. Main memory is partitioned into 16

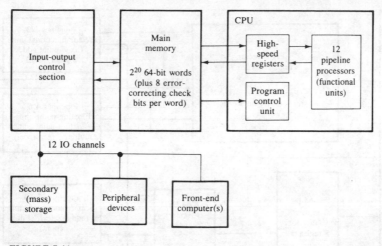

FIGURE 7.44
System organization of the Cray-1.

modules with 16-way address interleaving, so that a maximum memory bandwidth of 4 words per CPU clock cycle, or 320×10^9 words/s, can be achieved. The input-output section of the Cray-1 controls the transfer of data between the main memory and a secondary (disk) storage system of extremely high capacity and speed. Various other I/O devices can be attached to the Cray-1, including one or more small "front-end" computers that communicate with a large number of low-speed peripheral devices. A front-end computer also serves as the system host or manager.

The internal organization of the Cray-1 CPU is outlined in Fig. 7.45. The main data processing circuits are 12 functional units, all of which employ pipelining to some extent. They fall into four groups, known as the vector, floating-point, scalar, and address units. The principal pipeline processors, which give the Cray-1 much of its massive computing power, are the vector (fixed-point) and floating-point units (pipelines 1:6 in Fig. 7.45). These processors transfer their operands directly to and from a set of eight vector (V) registers, each capable of storing a 64-element (64-word) vector; the V registers therefore have a collective capacity of $2^{15} = 32K$ bits. The scalar functional units execute various arithmetic-logic operations on single-word (64-bit) data, and communicate with eight 64-bit scalar (S) registers. Finally, the two address units (pipelines 11 and 12) process 24-bit addresses using the eight 24-bit address (A) registers. Note that pipelining is incorporated into all functional units, even those performing relatively simple operations like fixed-point addition, to ensure that all units can produce a new result every 12.5 ns, and also to allow some of the pipelines to be linked or *chained* together to form larger pipelines for certain combinations of instructions. This important pipeline chaining feature is discussed later.

A key design issue for all vector supercomputers is how to transfer data and instructions between the main memory and the CPU sufficiently fast to keep the CPU operating at its maximum speed. As noted above, the Cray-1 employs 16-way memory address interleaving and a set of fast V, S, and A registers in its CPU. In addition, the CPU contains several sets of registers that amount to a third level in the

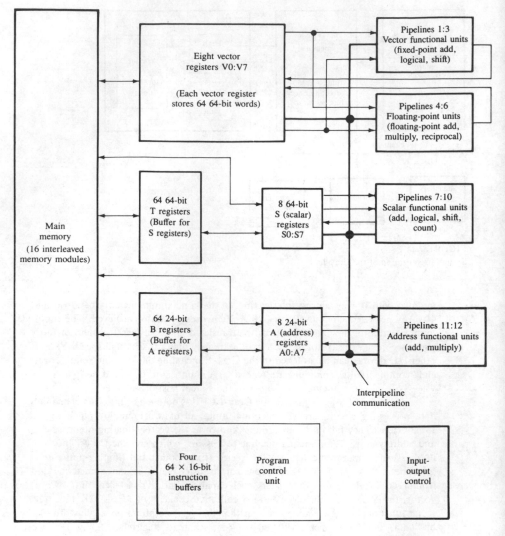

FIGURE 7.45
Major components and data paths of the Cray-1 CPU.

memory hierarchy, and can be loosely compared to a cache system. The A and S registers are linked to main memory via two larger register sets called the B and T registers, respectively. These "back-up" register sets are useful for holding small sets of operands that are needed repeatedly by the A or S registers; they require only one clock cycle to transfer a word to or from the corresponding main register set. Moreover, the A and S registers (and also the V registers) can communicate with main memory via relatively fast block-transfer operations that move from 1 to 64 words under control of a single instruction. The effective rate at which instructions are transferred to the CPU is also increased by the presence of four instruction buffers, each of which can hold a 128-byte portion of a program. The CPU can execute program loops directly from any one of these buffers, thereby greatly reducing the number of instruction fetches from main memory.

The Cray-1 has a powerful set of vector instructions that include most of the operations discussed earlier (Fig. 7.43). A single vector instruction allows several operand sets, corresponding to different vector elements, to be processed in parallel. In addition, the Cray-1 allows several different vector (or scalar) instructions to be executed concurrently under certain conditions. Suppose that a vector instruction I_1 requires as its input an n-element vector computed by another vector instruction I_2. It may be possible to overlap these instructions in such a way that I_2 can begin execution as soon as I_1 produces the first element of its result, instead of waiting until I_1 produces its entire n-element result. This technique which is called *chaining* is implemented automatically in the Cray-1 by connecting the output of the pipeline associated with I_1 to the input of the pipeline associated with I_2. Pipeline chaining is possible only when the chained instructions have no conflicts in their use of CPU registers or functional units. Consider, for example, the following sequence of three Cray-1 vector instructions involving 64-element floating-point vector operands [22]:

I_1:   Read vector X from main memory into vector register V0
I_2:   V2 ← S1 × V0, where S1 is a scalar register
I_3:   V3 ← V1 + V2

Let execution of the memory read instruction I_1 begin at time $t = 0$. After some initial setup time, in this case 9 clock cycles, the first element $X(0)$ of X is available for loading into V0; each remaining element $V(i)$ is available in the CPU at $t = i$. At $t = 9$, while $X(0)$ is being loaded into V0, a copy of it is sent to the input of the multiply unit (pipeline 5) for use by the multiply instruction. I_2 therefore begins execution at $t = 9$ using pipeline 5, and produces its first result element after another 9 clock cycles; this result is sent both to V2 and to the add unit, pipeline 4. At $t = 18$, the vector add instruction I_3 begins execution, obtaining its operands from vector register V1 and the output of the multiply pipeline. I_3 completes the 64-element vector addition in 72 clock cycles, including a fixed overhead of 8 clock cycles. Thus execution of the entire sequence of instructions involving 64 one-word memory reads, 64 multiplications, and 64 additions, takes only 90 clock cycles. The chaining effectively reconfigures the CPU as shown in Fig. 7.46, creating a composite pipeline consisting of a multiply pipeline followed by an add pipeline. (The memory read function can also be included in this composite pipeline.) 128 floating-point results, namely, the new contents of vector registers V2 and V3, are generated, in 90×12.5 ns, which is equivalent to a throughput of 114 MFLOPS.

All vector operations using pipeline processors have a certain setup time or overhead T_0 associated with them. In the case of a register-to-register machine like the Cray-1, this includes the time required to load the vector length register VL and other control registers, and to load at least one of the vector operand (V) registers. For most instructions, this setup time is constant for vector lengths up to some maximum size N_{max}; the Cray-1 has $N_{max} = 64$, the number of V registers. The influence of T_0 and N_{max} on system performance may be estimated as follows.

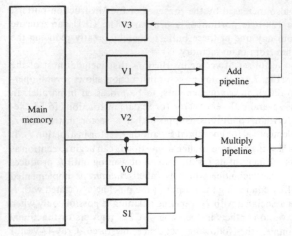

FIGURE 7.46
Data flow when chaining multiply and add instructions.

The average time required to process a vector of length $N \leq N_{\max}$ is

$$T_V = T_0 + NT_{\text{clock}}$$

where $T_{\text{clock}} = T_s/n$ is the clock period of an n-segment pipeline or set of pipelines. All vector operands must be partitioned into subvectors of length $N_{\max}$ or less for processing, and each such segment requires a setup time of T_0. Suppose that a given set of vector operands is chopped into v segments of average length $N \leq N_{\max}$ during processing. The total setup time required by these operands is vT_0, and the corresponding total computation time is vNT_{clock}. The system throughput in scalar results per unit time, e.g., MFLOPS, is

$$b = \frac{vN}{vT_0 + vNT_{\text{clock}}}$$

Hence,
$$b = \frac{1}{T_0/N + T_{\text{clock}}} \tag{7.26}$$

Clearly when there is no setup time, the theoretical maximum throughput of $1/T_{\text{clock}}$ is reached. When $T_0 \neq 0$, the throughput b given by (7.26) increases as N is increased; the maximum value of b occurs when $N = N_{\max}$, while the minimum occurs when $N = 1$, i.e., when all operations are effectively scalar. Thus the Cray-1 can be expected to operate most efficiently with vectors of length 64; however, a speedup greater than unity can be achieved in some cases for vectors containing as few as three or four elements. Memory-to-memory vector processors tend to have larger values of T_0 and consequently are less efficient when processing short vectors.

Programming issues. To make efficient use of pipelined computers like the Cray-1, application programs must be structured to take advantage of the available vector processing features. Scalar programs designed for conventional SISD machines generally need to be *vectorized* so that maximum use is made of the system's pipelines (and the corresponding vector instructions), vector registers, pipeline chaining facilities, and the like. The vectorization process can be accomplished either manually by the programmer, or automatically by a *vectorizing compiler preprocessor* that attempts to reorganize the original code into a form containing the maximum degree of parallelism for the host computer and compiler being used. For the scientific applications where vector processors are most frequently employed, FORTRAN, often with machine-specific vector extensions, is the principal programming language. Manual or automatic vectorization then basically involves organizing a FORTRAN program so that during compilation the FORTRAN statements can be mapped directly into long vector instructions in the host computer. Consider for example, the FORTRAN DO loop

$$\begin{array}{ll} & \text{DO } 10 \text{ I} = 1, \text{ N}, 2 \\ 10 & \text{Z(I)} = \text{X(I)} * \text{Y(I)} \end{array} \qquad (7.27)$$

This states that the scalar multiplication operation $Z(I) = X(I) \times Y(I)$ is to be done with the index I covering the range from 1 to N in increments of 2, i.e., $I = 1, 3, 5, \ldots, N - 1$. This clearly corresponds to a vector multiplication of the form $Z \leftarrow X \times Y$. If an appropriate vector multiply is in the instruction repertoire of the host computer, then (7.27) can be replaced by (compiled into) a single vector multiply instruction. DO loops of this kind provide the major means of specifying vector operations via the FORTRAN language.

Closer examination of (7.27) reveals some possible complications. For example, if I denotes the address in main memory of corresponding components of the vectors X, Y, and Z, then the vector is being stored with stride 2. This causes no problems in machines which, like the Cray-1, can fetch and store vectors of any constant stride. A vector processor like the Cyber 205, however, which requires the vector stride to be one, must precede (7.27) by a gather operation and follow it by a scatter operation as follows (here N is assumed to be 99):

$$\begin{array}{ll} & \text{DO } 5 \text{ I} = 1, 50, 1 \\ & \text{J} = \text{I} * 2 - 1 \\ & \text{X(I)} = \text{X(J)} \\ 5 & \text{Y(I)} = \text{Y(J)} \\ & \text{DO } 10 \text{ I} = 1, 49, 2 \\ 10 & \text{Z(I)} = \text{X(I)} * \text{Y(I)} \\ & \text{DO } 15 \text{ I} = 1, 50, 1 \\ & \text{J} = \text{I} * 2 - 1 \\ 15 & \text{Z(J)} = \text{Z(I)} \end{array} \qquad (7.28)$$

The overhead of the gather-scatter operations must be weighed against the speed advantage resulting from the now-vectorized multiplication DO loop. Note that the vectorized code (7.28) will run more slowly on a scalar machine than the original code (7.27) due to the extra memory references. Another problem arises if the vector length parameter N is small. The setup time T_0 of short vectors can outweigh the speed advantage of vectorization; see Eq. (7.26). In such cases, say with N = 5, it may be more efficient to "unroll" the DO loop of (7.27) into a simple sequence of scalar multiplications as follows:

$$Z(1) = X(1) * Y(1)$$
$$Z(3) = X(3) * Y(3)$$
$$Z(5) = X(5) * Y(5)$$

A number of software tools capable of automatically vectorizing a given (scalar) program have been developed, for example, the Cray FORTRAN (CFT) compiler, and the PARAFRASE compiler preprocessor developed at the University of Illinois [25]. While such tools can significantly improve the execution speed of a FORTRAN program that was originally written for a scalar computer, they are far from being able to produce optimal code for every application. Such optimization may require a difficult process of program "tuning," to make the fullest use of the pipeline structure, vector registers, addressing modes, etc., of the target computer, as well as to take into account the abilities and limitations of any vectorization software to be used. For example, the CFT compiler will not automatically attempt to vectorize a DO loop like

$$\text{DO } 10 \text{ I} = 1, 100, 1$$
$$10 \qquad X(I) = X(I + J) + Y \tag{7.29}$$

because of the appearance of the X vector with different, and possibly interdependent, index values on the left and right sides of the (recursive) statement 10 in (7.29). The compiler cannot tell if the $X(I + J)$ values needed to compute $X(I)$ will always be available at the right times in the course of a vector add operation. If the programmer knows that the specific I and J values being used will permit vectorization, e.g., if J will always be greater than 100, he can explicitly direct the CFT compiler to vectorize (7.29) in the following way:

```
          CDIR$ IVDEP
          DO 10 I = 1, 100, 1
10        X(I) = X(I + J) + Y
```

The keyword CDIR$ introduces a Cray compiler directive, in this case IVDEP (*ignore vector dependencies*), which causes the compiler to vectorize the DO loop by compiling it into a vector add instruction. Another Cray-specific compiler directive is SHORT LOOP, which declares that the number of iterations in the next DO loop is at most 64, the length of a Cray-1 vector register.

In general, the vectorization problem is tackled by attempting to identify the time-consuming portions of a program, and replacing them with different, but functionally equivalent, code that is tailored to the vector processing features of the computer under consideration. Figure 7.47 lists a few representative program construction rules intended to enhance the performance of vector processors. Several of these rules have been illustrated already; we now give a few more examples. Consider the following code segment.

$$\text{DO } 10 \text{ I} = 1, N, 1$$
$$10 \qquad Z(IZ(I)) = X(IX(I)) * Y(I) + P/Q \tag{7.30}$$

1. Combine consecutive short (DO) loops of equal length into a single long loop.
2. Replace very short loops by equivalent loop-free code.
3. Relocate invariant code outside a loop.
4. Eliminate repeated occurrence of common subexpressions within a loop.
5. Avoid complicated indexing within loops, e.g., by employing separate gather and scatter loops.
6. Avoid placing function or subroutine calls within a loop.
7. Avoid using decision (IF) statements within a loop.
8. Use compiler directives, when appropriate, to vectorize recursive loops.

FIGURE 7.47
Program design guidelines to enhance vectorization.

Here the subexpression P/Q implies that a time-consuming division operation is to be performed in each of the N iterations through the loop. Since the same value of P/Q is recomputed every time, it is much more efficient to compute it once outside the loop by a statement like

$$TEMP = P/Q$$

and replace P/Q in (7.30) by TEMP, as recommended by rule 3 of Fig. 7.47. The code (7.30) also illustrates indirect addressing, where, for instance, two fetches are required by $X(IX(I))$, one to fetch its index $J = IX(I)$ using the loop variable I, and a second to fetch $X(J)$ itself. These fetches cannot always be vectorized since they may involve nonconstant strides. A possible solution, suggested by rule 5, is to perform the first set of fetches to obtain the $IX(I)$ and $IZ(I)$ index values in separate DO loops as shown below.

```
        TEMP = P/Q
        DO 5 I = 1, N, 1
5       TEMPX(I) = X(IX(I))
        DO 10 I = 1, N, 1
10      TEMPZ(I) = TEMPX(I) * Y(I) + TEMP
        DO 15 I = 1, N, 1
15      Z(IX(I)) = TEMPZ(I)
```

7.3 MULTIPROCESSORS

This section considers the architecture of computers with multiple CPUs. Systems with various types of static and dynamic interconnection structures, including shared buses, hypercubes, and multistage interconnection networks are examined. The basic principles of fault-tolerant computing are also discussed.

7.3.1 Introduction

A multiprocessor is an MIMD computer system characterized by the presence of several CPUs or, more generally, processing elements (PEs), which cooperate on common or shared computational tasks. Multiprocessors are distinguished from multicomputer systems and computer networks, which are systems with multiple PEs operating independently on separate tasks. The various PEs making up a multiprocessor typically share such resources as communication facilities, IO devices, program libraries, databases, etc., and are controlled by a common operating system.

The two main reasons for including multiple PEs in a single computer system are to improve performance and to increase reliability. Performance (throughput) improvement is obtained either by allowing many PEs to share the computation load associated with a single large task, or else by allowing many smaller tasks to be performed in parallel in separate PEs. A multiprocessor composed of n identical processors is an example of an n-unit processor that can, in principle, provide n times the performance of a comparable single-unit (SISD) system or uniprocessor. A major goal in designing n-processor systems is to achieve a speedup $S(n)$ that is as close to n as possible. System reliability is improved by the fact that the failure of one CPU need not cause the entire system to fail. The functions of the faulty processor (and its local resources) can be taken over by the other processors; consequently, multiprocessors allow fault tolerance to be incorporated into the system. Of particular interest is the ability of fault-tolerant multiprocessors to operate correctly at a reduced or degraded performance level in the presence of hardware or software failures, a property called *graceful degradation*. By enabling such facilities as secondary memory units and system software to be shared efficiently, a multiprocessor architecture can lead to a significant reduction in overall system cost.

Multiprocessor types. As discussed in Sec. 7.1.1, multiprocessors can be classified by the organization of their main-memory systems; see Fig. 7.7. If main memory, or a major portion thereof, can be directly accessed by all the PEs of a multiprocessor, then the system is termed a shared-memory computer, and the shared portion of main memory is called global memory. Information can therefore be shared among the processors simply by placing it in the global memory. Distributed-memory computers, on the other hand, have no global memory. Instead each processing element PE_i has its own private or local main memory M_i. Following the usage of Sec. 7.1, we will refer to the combination of PE_i and M_i as the processor P_i. In shared-memory systems in which all of main memory is global, the terms processing element and processor coincide. Distributed-memory systems share information by transmitting it in the form of messages between the local memories of different processors; such message passing requires a series of relatively slow IO operations. Shared-memory and distributed-memory multiprocessors are also called *tightly coupled* and *loosely coupled*, respectively, reflecting the speed and ease with which they can interact on common tasks. Multiprocessors are sometimes classified by the interconnection structures employed to support processor-processor and processor-memory communication. A sampling of the possible communication structures appears in Fig. 7.8, including shared buses, crossbar switches, and hypercube connections. Figure 7.10 illustrates another important class of interconnection structure, namely, multistage switching networks. These interconnection methods provide various tradeoffs between hardware cost, communication speed, and programming complexity, tradeoffs which are explored further in this section.

Multiprocessors involving a small number (fewer than 10) of cooperating CPUs have existed since the 1960s. Figure 7.48 shows an early scheme for loosely coupling two IBM System/360-370 series computers, each with its own main memory and operating system, by means of a special IO device called a *channel-to-channel* adapter CTC [5]. The CTC allows each computer to regard the other as one of its IO devices so that data can be transmitted from computer to computer as follows:

1. CPU_1 initiates execution of an output (write) IO program addressed to the CTC.
2. In response to the first write command, the CTC sends an interrupt signal to CPU_2 via IOP_2.
3. CPU_2 responds to the interrupt by initiating execution of an input (read) IO program addressed to the CTC.
4. Data transfer now proceeds asynchronously from M_1 to M_2 via the CTC. When the data transfer is completed, both CPUs are interrupted.

This type of communication via messages transmitted through the IO subsystem is typical of distributed-memory multiprocessors.

An example of an early shared-memory or tightly coupled commercial multiprocessor, the CDC Cyber-70 Model 74, appears in Fig. 7.49. This machine, which was introduced in 1972, contains two CPUs that are essentially the same as that of the CDC 6600 uniprocessor. The CPUs share a single main-memory unit, and are supervised by a common operating system called SCOPE (*S*upervisory *C*ontrol of *P*rogram *E*xecution). The system also accommodates up to 20 peripheral processing units (PPUs), most of which are used as IO processors. One

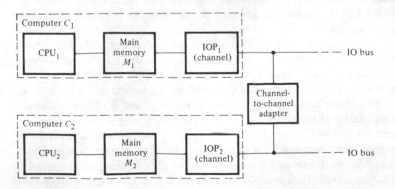

FIGURE 7.48
Loosely coupled system of two S/360-370 computers.

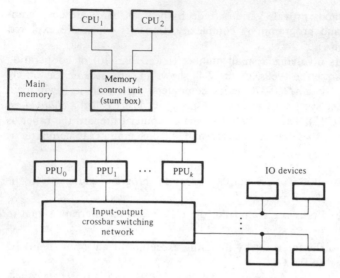

FIGURE 7.49
Control Data Cyber-70 Model 74 multiprocessor.

PPU, however, is devoted to executing operating system routines, and thus functions as a system monitor or host processor. The PPUs communicate with main memory via a shared bus, while a special high-speed memory controller (the "stunt box") handles CPU-memory communication. Address interleaving is used to minimize memory access conflicts among the CPUs and PPUs. The peripheral processors communicate with a set of 12 independent IO buses via a crossbar switch that allows many IO devices to engage in data transmission simultaneously. The SCOPE operating system distributes tasks on a priority basis to the various CPUs and PPUs as they become available. A variable number of independent programs may be executed in timeshared mode (multiprogramming), while the presence of two CPUs enables two different programs to be executed simultaneously (multiprocessing).

A more recent example of a tightly-coupled multiprocessor, the Cray X-MP, is shown in Fig. 7.50 [17]. It can contain one, two, or more CPUs that are very similar to that of the Cray-1 (Fig. 7.45), with various enhancements to improve performance and support multiprocessing. (X-MP stands for *extension multiprocessor*.) The CPUs share access to common main memory and IO systems that are both larger and faster than the Cray-1's. For example, a four-processor Cray X-MP may have up to 8M (2^{23}) words of main memory with 64-way address interleaving. An even larger secondary memory unit called a solid-state storage device (SSD) is available which can perform the functions of a magnetic-disk memory, but at much higher speeds. The SSD is useful for supercomputing tasks that require extremely fast IO data-transfer rates in addition to fast data processing by the CPU. The individual CPUs incorporate several improvements over the Cray-1,

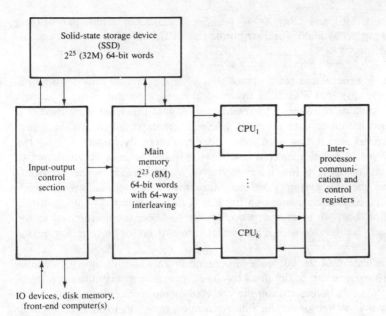

FIGURE 7.50
System organization of the Cray X-MP.

including a shorter clock cycle (9.5 ns versus 12.5 ns for the Cray-1), more memory and IO ports, and new hardware support for vector gather-scatter and chaining operations. In addition to having shared access to main memory, the Cray X-MP CPUs can communicate via several sets of shared high-speed registers found in the interprocessor communication and control region of Fig. 7.50. Each register set contains eight 64-bit shared scalar ST registers, eight 24-bit shared SB address registers, and additional registers for synchronization purposes. The ST and SB registers supplement the nonshared T and B buffer registers found in each CPU; see Fig. 7.45. The shared registers may be allocated dynamically to any group of CPUs by the operating system.

As developments in VLSI technology in the 1980s ushered in powerful 1-chip microprocessors, and memory (RAM) chips with capacities in the 10^5- to 10^7-bit range, it has become economically feasible to build *massively parallel* multiprocessors, with hundreds or even thousands of processors. For example, the NCUBE hypercube multiprocessor introduced in 1986 can have up to 1024 processors, each of which contains a powerful 32-bit CPU, a 128K- or 512K-byte local memory, and their associated communication logic, all packaged in only seven IC chips. (This machine is discussed further later.) While such computers have the potential of providing extremely high performance, they also pose problems in algorithm and program design which are far from being fully solved. Thus although reasonably efficient vectorizing compilers exist for pipelined supercomputers like the Cray-1 and Cray X-MP (see Sec. 7.2.3), comparable parallelizing compilers are not yet available for distributing tasks efficiently in a massively parallel multiprocessor.

Performance. In general, the performance goal of an n-processor multiprocessor is to provide a speedup that is as close to the ideal (linear) speedup, $S(n) = n$, as is possible at reasonable software or hardware cost. A multiprocessor composed of n CPUs with instruction or data bandwidth b might be expected to achieve a performance level of nb. It has been observed experimentally, however, that the speedup achieved in practice is often much less than n. This may be attributed to various causes, including a low inherent degree of parallelism in the programs being executed, inefficiencies in task distribution (load balancing) among the available processors, as well as contention for access to the shared system resources, e.g., a common host or front-end processor. It has been conjectured that the speedup typically achievable with n processors ranges from $\log_2 n$ to $n/\log_e n$ (see Prob. 7.21).

Some indication of the influence of contention for shared memory on multiprocessor performance can be obtained by considering a system containing n processors $P_1, P_2, \ldots, P_n$ connected to m interleaved memory modules $M_1, M_2, \ldots, M_m$ via a crossbar switch or similar interconnection network, as in Fig. 7.8c. All programs and data needed by the processors are stored in the m-module main memory, and thus must be accessed via the crossbar switch. It is reasonable to assume that the instruction or data bandwidth b of a processor P_j is roughly proportional to the rate at which P_j performs memory access operations. The latter is in turn proportional to the average number of busy memory modules B. Suppose the probability that any processor P_j generates a request for access to memory module M_i to perform a read or write operation is $1/m$, i.e., the memory requests are distributed uniformly. Hence the probability that M_i is idle, and therefore free to respond to memory requests, is $(1 - 1/m)^n$. This implies that the probability p_i that M_i is busy is $1 - (1 - 1/m)^n$. If M_i is busy when a new request for access to it is received, the new request is not serviced until M_i becomes free again. The average number of busy memory modules B is therefore given by

$$B = \sum_{i=1}^{m} p_i = m \left[1 - \left(1 - \frac{1}{m} \right)^n \right] \tag{7.31}$$

As might be expected, if m is fixed and $n \to \infty$, then $B \to m$. Similarly, if n is fixed and $m \to \infty$, then (7.31) yields $B = n$, that is, all processors are kept busy. Figure 7.51 shows a plot of B against m for several small values of n. From the above analysis it can be concluded that the performance of a multiprocessor can be improved by placing information that is frequently accessed by P_j, e.g., its main programs, in a local memory assigned to P_j, while limiting the use of global memory to the storage of infrequently shared program code and data.

Operating system. Multiprocessors impose special requirements both on the operating systems needed to control them and the programming techniques needed to

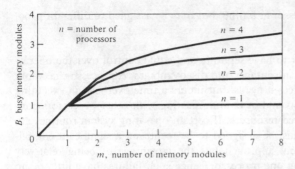

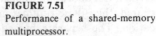

FIGURE 7.51
Performance of a shared-memory multiprocessor.

make effective use of their parallelism. The operating system for a multiprocessor resembles that of a uniprocessor with multiprogramming capability since it must allow multiple users to timeshare the system resources, which now include multiple CPUs, in a nonconflicting manner. The fact that the jobs or processes being executed concurrently in a multiprocessor may use the same system or application programs, or process the same data, leads to some special problems in maintaining the consistency of the shared programs and data as seen by the various processors. Ordinary programming languages are inadequate to take advantage of the parallel processing capabilities of multiprocessors; either they must be augmented by special features like the **send** and **receive** commands used in Example 7.1 (see Fig. 7.3), or else special languages designed for parallel programming, e.g., Occam, must be used.

To prevent conflicting use of each shared resource by several processes, the operating system function associated with allocating that resource should be exercised by only one CPU at a time. Three general ways of organizing the operating system of a multiprocessor to meet this objective have been defined.

1. *Separate operating system.* Each processor can independently execute all the operating system routines it needs. In very loosely coupled multiprocessors like that of Fig. 7.48, every processor may have its own copy of the entire operating system. In many cases it is too wasteful of memory space to provide all processors with a complete copy of the operating system. Consequently, only a copy of the kernel of the operating system is assigned to each processor; the remaining routines are placed in a shared part of primary or secondary memory.

2. *Master-slave operating system.* A single processor designated the master, front end, or host has permanent responsibility for the execution of all operating system routines. The remaining processors, which may be termed slaves, do not perform operating system functions (except perhaps minor ones), and can only obtain them on request from the master processor. This type of multiprocessor operating system is also be termed *centralized.*

3. *Distributed operating system.* The operating system routines are distributed among the available processors, so that each operating system function is

assigned to only one processor at a time, but may be assigned to different processors at different times.

Allowing each processor to have separate and equal control over the operating system functions has both advantages and disadvantages. A processor has more direct control over the resources it needs, but incurs a time overhead in executing the operating system functions and in communicating with other processors concerning the allocation of shared resources. If certain operating system routines are shared, then these routines must be designed to be reentrant, a significant complication. The separate but equal approach has the advantage of being relatively insensitive to failures affecting one processor, since such failures have little or no impact on the other processors. This type of operating system can therefore incorporate graceful degradation of the system performance in the event of localized failures. The relation between the slaves and the master in a master-slave operating system is similar to that between the IOPs and the CPU in a uniprocessor. This method is used in the CDC Cyber-70 series (see Fig. 7.49), where one of the PPUs serves as the master processor. The slave processors communicate with the master either via an interrupt or supervisor call instruction. Master-slave operating systems are easy to design since their code need not be reentrant, and all resource conflict resolution is centralized in the master processor. They are, however, vulnerable to failures of the master processor, which can result in a catastrophic system failure. The third, distributed, method of operating system design is the most complex, but is also the most flexible. Again the operating system routines must be reentrant, but they can be distributed among the available processors to optimize load balancing and maximize utilization of the resources of the multiprocessor. An example of an operating system of this type is found in the dual-processor IBM 3081.

Parallel programming. A programmer can exploit the parallelism of a pipelined vector processor such as the Cray-1 by optimizing the use of a small number of vector operations that correspond to the available pipelined functions; see Sec. 7.2.3. A multiprocessor's parallelism is of a more general kind since the parallel units (which are effectively general-purpose computers) can act on many unrelated data streams simultaneously, and perform unrelated operations on them. The parallelism is thus between multiple subprograms, rather than between the suboperations of a few vector instructions. This type of parallelism can be fairly easily exploited by the operating system in a multiuser environment where many independent jobs are available for execution. There is then no need to synchronize the execution of the different tasks, and conflicts for shared facilities can be expected to occur infrequently and in a predictably random pattern. Multiprocessor parallelism can also be exploited directly by applications programmers when coding highly structured parallel algorithms, including many involving vector and matrix calculations, in an efficient manner. It is much harder to exploit the parallelism in ordinary sequential programs, although there is evidence that such programs contain a great deal of implicit parallelism [24]. In this case, the programmer or a parallelizing compiler or compiler preprocessor must somehow identify the subtasks or instructions that can be executed in parallel. At present little is known about this problem, and the design of general-purpose parallelizing software remains a formidable research problem.

As an example of a simple and well-structured parallel programming task, consider the following FORTRAN DO loop:

$$SUM = 0$$
$$DO\ 10\ I = 1,\ 1000,\ 1$$
$$10 \quad SUM = SUM + B(I)$$

representing the summation problem introduced in Sec. 7.1.1. We can achieve a speedup factor of about 4, corresponding to execution by a four-segment pipeline (see Example 7.4 for a description of the pipeline solution), by distributing the vector addition to four parallel processors P_1, P_2, P_3, and P_4 in a multiprocessor. Each processor P_J can be assigned to execute code of the general form

$$SUMJ = 0$$
$$DO\ 10\ I = J,\ 1000,\ 4 \qquad\qquad (7.32)$$
$$10 \quad SUMJ = SUMJ + B(I)$$

causing it to compute the sum of one-fourth of the components of the vector $B = ((B(1),B(2), \ldots , B(1000))$. Processor P_2, for instance, computes the partial sum $SUM2 = B(2) + B(6) + \cdots + B(998)$. The final result is obtained by having one of the processors execute the FORTRAN statement

$$SUM = SUM1 + SUM2 + SUM3 + SUM4 \qquad\qquad (7.33)$$

This example raises several basic issues concerning synchronization among the processors and resource contention. Suppose that the vector B is stored in a global memory M with m-way address interleaving, and each element B(I) of B occupies one word of memory. If $m = 4$, then each processor will address all its memory read requests for B(I) to a separate module of M, and no contention for memory access will result. If, however, $m \neq 4$, or address interleaving is not used, then the processors will contend for access to the B vector, resulting in a loss of performance of the type illustrated by Fig. 7.51. Memory contention on instruction fetches can also be expected if each processor's program is stored in M.

Although the four processors are executing essentially the same code, they do so asynchronously and cannot be expected to start or finish at the same time, or even at predictable times. Before (7.33) can be executed by, say, P_1, the processor must be able to ascertain that the partial sums SUM2, SUM3, and SUM4 have been fully computed by the other three processors. For this purpose, each processor P_J may be required to set a flag ENDJ that is 0 while P_J is executing (7.32), and becomes 1 when the final result SUMJ is available. Thus process synchronization can be accomplished by modifying (7.32) as follows:

$$ENDJ = 0$$
$$SUMJ = 0$$
$$DO\ 10\ I = J,\ 1000,\ 4$$
$$10 \quad SUMJ = SUMJ + B(I)$$
$$ENDJ = 1$$

To ensure that P_1 waits until all SUMJs are available, we modify (7.33) to

$$15 \quad END = END1 + END3 + END3 + END4$$
$$IF \; (END \; .LT. \; 4.0) \; GO \; TO \; 15 \qquad\qquad (7.34)$$
$$SUM = SUM1 + SUM2 + SUM3 + SUM4$$

The first two statements of (7.34) form a busy wait loop during which P_1 continually tests the ENDJ flags until the desired termination condition is present. In a shared-memory multiprocessor these flags should be stored in global memory. In a distributed-memory system the flags may be dispensed with; each processor can communicate its result SUMJ to P_1 by sending it a message containing the data in question. In a FORTRAN environment, this message transfer can be implemented by special FORTRAN I/O subroutines of the form SEND(destination, message) and RECEIVE(source, message). (No standard format for this type of statement presently exists.) In the current example, the statement

$$CALL \; SEND \; (P1, \; ENDJ)$$

would be appended to (7.32) and three statements of the form

$$CALL \; RECEIVE \; (PJ, \; ENDJ)$$

for $J = 2, 3, 4$ would precede (7.33).

Various high-level language features have been proposed that allow a programmer to indicate potentially parallelizable parts of a program without specifying such machine-dependent details as the type or degree of parallelism available in the host computer, the memory organization used, or the like. For example, the **begin-end** delimiters of block-structured languages such as Pascal can be augmented by the block delimiters **cobegin-coend**. While a **begin-end** block encloses statements that must be executed in a fixed specified sequence, a **cobegin-coend** block encloses statements that may be executed in parallel in any order. For example, in the code fragment

$$\textbf{begin}$$
$$S_0;$$
$$\textbf{cobegin}$$
$$S_1, S_2, \ldots, S_k \qquad\qquad (7.35)$$
$$\textbf{coend}$$
$$S_{k+1}$$
$$\textbf{end}$$

the k statements $S_1, S_2, \ldots, S_k$ can be executed in parallel on independent processors after S_0 has been executed. They can also be executed sequentially if only a uniprocessor is available, in which case the order of execution of the statements in $S_1, S_2, \ldots, S_k$ does not matter. Only after the statements in the **cobegin-coend** block have been completely executed can the next sequential operation S_{k+1} be processed. Equivalent delimiters to **cobegin** and **coend** proposed for some parallel programming languages are **fork** (begin execution of a set of parallel processes) and **join** (wait for termination of a set of parallel processes). In the Occam language, the special keywords **seq** and **par** replace **begin** and **cobegin**, respectively, while **end** and **coend** are indicated implicitly by indentation conventions. The Occam equivalent of (7.34) is therefore

$$
\begin{aligned}
&\textbf{seq} \\
&\quad S_0 \\
&\qquad \textbf{par} \\
&\qquad\quad S_1 \\
&\qquad\quad S_2 \\
&\qquad\qquad . \\
&\qquad\qquad . \\
&\qquad\qquad . \\
&\qquad\quad S_k \\
&\qquad S_{k+1}
\end{aligned}
$$

Whether or not a given set of (sequential) operations or processes can be executed in parallel depends on such architectural features of the host computer as the numbers and types of processors available, the memory organization used, etc. It also depends on the absence of conflict among the operations themselves in the use of common operands. Such data dependencies can readily be analyzed to obtain conditions that are sufficient (but not necessary) to ensure that a given set of operations can be executed in parallel. Following the work of A. J. Bernstein [4], we now derive some general and easily checked conditions which identify parts of a program that can be executed in parallel. (See also the discussion of data dependencies among microinstructions in Sec. 4.3.2.) Suppose that $S = S_1,\ S_2,\ S_3$ denotes three consecutive portions (statements, procedures, etc.) of a given sequential program. The execution of S_3 is required to begin only after both S_1 and S_2 have been completely executed. We wish to determine the extent to which S_1 and S_2 can be executed in parallel, assuming that two or more general-purpose processors with a shared main memory are available for the execution of S. The state of the computation being carried out by S_1 and S_2 may be specified by the current values of main memory locations $M(S_1,\ S_2)$ or, equivalently, the set of program variables, that are modified during the execution of S_1 and S_2. We formally define S_1 and S_2 to be *parallelizable* if the state of $M(S_1,\ S_2)$ immediately before the execution of S_3 begins, is independent of the starting times and execution rates of S_1 and S_2. In other words, S_1 and S_2 can be processed independently and asynchronously but the final results as measured by $M(S_1,\ S_2)$ will always be the same.

Let the memory locations (program variables) that are accessed, either for reading or writing, by each S_i in $S_1,\ S_2,\ S_3$ be divided into two groups: the *input set* I_i consisting of all memory locations that are read at least once by S_i; and the *output set* O_i consisting of all memory locations that are written into at least once by S_i. I_i and O_i are not disjoint since each includes all locations that are both read from and written into by S_i. S_1 and S_2 are parallelizable if the following three *parallelization conditions* are met:

1. S_1 does not read from any memory locations that are written into by S_2, i.e., I_1 and O_2 are disjoint.

2. S_2 does not read from any memory locations that are written into by S_1, i.e., I_2 and O_1 are disjoint.

3. S_3 does not read from any locations that are written into by both S_1 and S_2, i.e., I_3 and the intersection of O_1 and O_2 are disjoint.

Denoting set intersection by $\cap$ and the empty set by ϕ, we write the foregoing conditions concisely as follows. S_1 and S_2 in the sequence S_1, S_2, S_3 are parallelizable if the following three equations are satisfied:

$$I_1 \cap O_2 = \phi \tag{7.36}$$

$$I_2 \cap O_1 = \phi \tag{7.37}$$

$$I_3 \cap O_1 \cap O_2 = \phi \tag{7.38}$$

As an example, consider the segment of sequential code listed in Fig. 7.52a. Applying the foregoing analysis to statements L_1, L_2, L_3 we obtain $I_1 = \{A, B, C, D\}$, $O_1 = \{P\}$, $I_2 = \{D, E, F\}$, $O_2 = \{Q\}$, $I_3 = \{A, F, P\}$ and $O_3 = \{R\}$. It is easily seen that the required conditions (7.36) to (7.38) for L_1 and L_2 to be parallelizable are satisfied. L_3 cannot be executed in parallel with L_1, since $I_3 \cap O_1 = \{P\} \neq \phi$, thus violating (7.37). In a similar fashion, we can show that L_3, L_4, L_5 satisfy the parallelization conditions, implying that L_3 and L_4 are parallelizable. If we execute L_1 and L_2 in parallel, however, we must ensure that the three groups $L_1, L_2, \{L_3, L_4\}$, with $\{L_3, L_4\}$ corresponding to S_3, also satisfy condition (7.38). Letting I_{34} denote the input set of $\{L_3, L_4\}$, we obtain $I_{34} = \{A, F, P, Q\}$. Hence $I_{34} \cap O_1 \cap O_2 = \{A, F, P, Q\} \cap \{P\} \cap \{Q\} = \phi$, as required. We conclude, therefore, that the foregoing code segment can be parallelized as indicated in Fig. 7.52b.

7.3.2 Multiprocessor Architectures

In this section we examine in detail a representative group of multiprocessors of both the shared-memory and distributed-memory varieties, many of which were

```
begin                              begin
  L₁: P ← A + B + C * D              cobegin
  L₂: Q ← (D + E)*F                    L₁: P ← A + B + C * D,
  L₃: R ← sqrt(P)/(A + F)              L₂: Q ← (D + E)*F
  L₄: S ← P * Q                      coend
  L₅: T ← 7.0 * log(S + A)           cobegin
end                                    L₃: R ← sqrt(P)/(A + F),
                                       L₄: S ← P * Q
                                     coend
                                       L₅: T ← 7.0 * log(S + A)
                                   end

              (a)                              (b)
```

FIGURE 7.52
Program segment (a) before and (b) after parallelization.

briefly introduced earlier. We classify these architectures primarily by their interconnection structures, and consider three main types of interconnections: shared buses, dedicated (static) buses, and multistage switching networks.

Shared-bus systems. Because of its simplicity and low cost (see Sec. 6.1.2), small multiprocessors are most frequently built around a single shared bus B. All system processing elements (CPUs and IO processors), main-memory modules, and IO devices are attached directly to B, and can timeshare its communication facilities. Thus only one pair of units on the bus can use B at a time, either for CPU-memory or IO-memory communication. The memory and IO devices on B are global to all the processing elements; hence single-bus multiprocessors are basically of the shared-memory variety. The bus B is clearly a potential communication bottleneck, leading to contention and delay whenever two or more units request access to main memory. This severely limits the number of processors that can be included in such a system without an unacceptable degradation in performance.

The performance of a single-bus multiprocessor can be greatly improved by supplying each processing element with either a cache or a local memory. This allows much of the routine memory traffic to be taken off the global bus, so that the latter can be reserved primarily for interprocessor communication. If a local memory is used, then the CPU's address space is partitioned between local and global memory, and a local bus is needed for communication between the CPU and the local memory. This bus may also be used to support a local IO subsystem as illustrated in Fig. 7.53. Many commercial CPUs, including the more powerful microprocessors, can be configured as multiprocessors in this way. The Intel 8086 family of microprocessors [20], for example, was designed to support shared-bus multiprocessor architectures, with the Multibus (IEEE 796) standard bus serving as the global bus, and a somewhat simpler bus serving as the optional local bus.

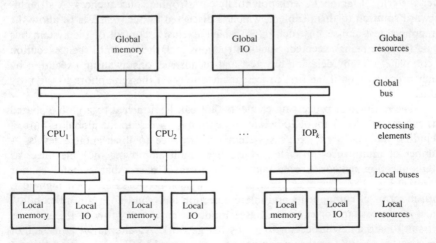

FIGURE 7.53
Shared-bus multiprocessor with global and local resources.

Despite its relative simplicity, the shared-bus architecture of Fig. 7.53 exhibits some of the basic contention and synchronization problems common to all multiprocessors. Consider the situation where two CPUs share a region R of global memory where mutual exclusion (see Sec. 6.3.2) applies, i.e., only one processor should have access to the shared region at a time. Access to R is conveniently controlled by means of a semaphore F, which indicates whether R is currently being used by some other process ($F = 1$), or is available for use by a new process ($F = 0$). Before it attempts to access R a processor first reads F, which must be stored in global memory. If it finds $F = 0$, it then changes F to 1 and proceeds to use R. If it finds that F is already 1, then it does not attempt to use R. The mutual exclusion requirement can be violated if it is possible for two processors to independently access the flag at the same time and find $F = 0$. This violation can occur if a second processor CPU_2 can read the semaphore after the first processor CPU_1 has read it, but before CPU_1 has changed the semaphore to 1. The problem lies in the fact that the semaphore test-and-set instructions issued by the CPUs may be broken down into interleaved bus cycles as follows:

Global bus cycle t	Action
i	CPU_1 fetches semaphore $F = 0$.
$i + 1$	CPU_2 fetches semaphore $F = 0$.
$i + 2$	CPU_1 sets F to 1.
$i + 3$	CPU_2 sets F to 1.

At time $t = i + 4$, both CPU_1 and CPU_2 assume that they have exclusive control over the critical region R, with potentially catastrophic consequences. A straightforward solution to this problem, which is discussed in Sec. 6.3.2, is to allow the semaphore test-and-set instruction(s) to have exclusive control of the system bus while they are being executed. Such instructions lock the bus until their execution is complete, thereby delaying any test-and-set instructions awaiting execution by other processors until the first processor has safely set the semaphore to the busy value.

The number of processing elements that can be attached to a global shared bus can rarely exceed about 20 before contention for access to the global resources, including the bus itself, reduces system performance to unacceptable levels. A number of multiprocessor systems have been built employing multiple buses as interconnection networks, especially in the form of a crossbar switch; see, for example, Fig. 7.8c. The main disadvantages of such networks are their high cost, both in terms of components and interconnection lines, and a certain inflexibility. An $n \times n$ crossbar, for example, has component costs that grow as n^2, and it is difficult to add a new processor to a crossbar network. An alternative approach of lower cost is to link together a number of single-shared bus systems via additional buses, as illustrated by the following example.

Example 7.7 The Carnegie-Mellon Cm* multiprocessor [21]. The Cm* (pronounced see-em-star) is an experimental multiprocessor built at Carnegie-Mellon University in the late 1970s. Its processors are organized into *clusters*, each of which is a small shared-bus multiprocessor containing up to 14 processors and their associated local memory and IO units, as indicated in Fig. 7.54. Thus a typical Cm* configuration might contain five 10-processor clusters. A commercial microprocessor, the DEC LSI-

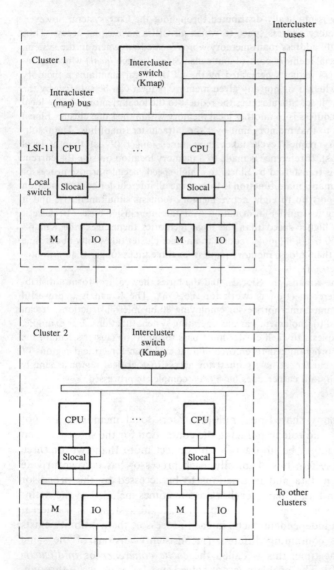

FIGURE 7.54
System organization of the Cm*.

11, a relative of the PDP-11 family, serves as the processing element (CPU), and the standard bus defined for the LSI-11 is used as the local bus to the CPU's own memory and IO devices. The processors within a cluster are linked to one another via an intracluster or "map" bus. The intracluster buses are, in turn, connected via pairs of intercluster buses. Serial IO links connect the clusters to a host computer (a PDP-11/10) that provides most of the usual user support and resource-management facilities.

Main memory is physically distributed throughout the Cm* system; however, there is a single memory address space to which all CPUs have equal access. Thus each CPU can directly address main-memory words located anywhere in the system. Each CPU has a special memory control unit called Slocal (switch *local*) which examines all memory access requests generated by the CPU. Slocal maintains a memory map that indicates whether or not any given memory request can be satisfied by the CPU's local memory; if so, Slocal routes the request to the local memory via the local (LSI-11) bus. If the address is to another local memory within the same cluster, Slocal transfers the request to that memory unit over the intracluster (map) bus. The resulting nonlocal memory request cycle takes three times longer (9 μs) than a local memory request (3 μs). If reference is made to a memory location outside the current cluster, that request is transferred by Slocal to a high-speed special-purpose processor called a Kmap. A Kmap's main function is to manage all intercluster communication requests. It can support up to eight active memory requests simultaneously, and it uses packet switching to transfer information over the intercluster buses. Because it operates at a much higher speed than the local memories themselves (the Kmap's CPU cycle time is 150 ns), a memory request to another cluster takes only about nine times longer (27 μs) than a local memory request, or three times longer than a nonlocal intracluster request.

Collectively the Kmaps, the Slocals, and the buses they control form a distributed shared-bus interconnection network for the Cm*. The Kmap is a powerful horizontally programmed microprocessor employing 80-bit microinstructions. It can be microprogrammed to implement various operating system functions. For example, since all memory requests to each cluster must pass through the cluster's Kmap, the Kmap can be microprogrammed to enforce mutual exclusion for critical regions of memories within its cluster. A new request for access to a critical region is simply delayed by the Kmap until earlier ones have been completely processed.

Cache coherence. In many shared-bus multiprocessors local memories are not used, and caches play a vital role in reducing the contention for the shared system bus. Without caches it might be impractical to connect more than two or three processors to the same system bus. Typically, each processor has its own private cache which allows both data and instructions to be accessed by the processor without using the system bus. (Shared caches are sometimes included in the main-memory modules, but such caches do not help to reduce the system bus traffic.) If a multiprocessor has an independent cache in each processor, the possibility exists of two or more caches containing different (inconsistent) versions of the same information at the same time; this is called the *cache coherence* or *multicache consistency* problem [10]. The problem is not solved just by using write-through, which, as discussed in Sec. 5.3.2, causes both the cache and main (global) memory to be updated whenever a memory write operation is performed. For example, one processor may update variable X in both its cache and global memory. If another processor then changes X, the new value of X will be written into global memory, but the two caches will contain different values for X. Subsequent reads from the caches may lead to inconsistent results. Thus a mechanism that allows each cache to be informed about changes to shared information stored in any other cache is needed to ensure cache coherence.

The cache coherence problem can be solved by hardware and/or software means. Hardware-only solutions have the advantage of higher speed and program transparency, but are quite expensive. Software-based methods of ensuring cache consistency require the ability to tag information during program compilation as either cacheable or noncacheable. In the software approach, all writeable shared items are tagged as noncacheable, meaning they can only be accessed directly from main memory. Cache coherence can then be implemented by a write-through policy that requires a processor to mark a shared cache item X as invalid, or to be deallocated, whenever the processor writes into X. When the processor references X again, it is forced to bypass the cache and access main memory thereby always acquiring the most recent version of X. This approach can significantly degrade system performance. Invalidation may, for example, force the removal of needed data from the cache, thus reducing its hit ratio, which, in turn, tends to increase the main-memory traffic.

A possible hardware-based solution to cache coherence is for a processor to broadcast its write operations to all caches in the system (and to main memory) via the shared bus. Every cache then examines its assigned addresses to see if the broadcast item is presently allocated to it. If it is, the cache page (line) in question is either updated or invalidated. The disadvantage of this technique is that every cache write forces all caches to check the broadcast data, making the caches unavailable for normal processing. This scheme with cache invalidation has been used in several IBM S/360-370 series computers, e.g., the model 3033. A related method is to have each cache continuously monitor all bus activity on the system bus in order to detect references to its stored data by other processors. When such a reference occurs, each cache then directly updates the status of its own contents.

Static interconnection networks. Many interconnection structures have been proposed for multiprocessors which employ nonshared buses to link the processors; such buses are also termed static or dedicated. Each bus forms a direct physical link between a fixed pair of processors called neighbors, and, in general, allows communication between neighboring processors to proceed at the maximum possible rate without interference from other processors. Using more links allows greater interprocessor communication speeds to be achieved, but increases hardware costs both in terms of the links themselves and the interfaces that must be provided between the processors and the links. The extreme case of providing dedicated links for all pairs of processors in an n-processor system requires a total of $n(n-1)/2$ k-line links with $k(n-1)$ lines attached to each processor; such an interconnection structure is impractical except for very small values of n and k. In practice, direct connections are only provided between a small subset of the possible processor pairs; for example, a mesh connection links each processor directly to only four other processors. Nonneighboring processors communicate indirectly via intermediate processors which relay a message from neighbor to neighbor in store-and-forward fashion until the destination is reached. Indirect communication of this type is relatively slow, and, if used extensively, can have a very negative impact on system performance. The amount of such communication that occurs depends both on the multiprocessor's interconnection structure and the communication requirements of the programs being executed. The interprocessor connections are therefore selected to balance hardware cost against communication delay for some broad class of applications.

The topology or graph structure defined by the processors and their interconnections provides a useful way to characterize a multiprocessor, and has a major influence on its cost and performance. Figure 7.55 shows graphs representing various important static interconnection structures [12], most of which were encountered earlier in this chapter. Here the nodes denote processors, each including a CPU, a local memory, and, possibly, IO connections, while the edges denote static nonshared interprocessor links, which are typically composed of pairs of unidirectional (full duplex) lines. The linear or one-dimensional array structure of Fig. 7.55a is used in Example 7.1 (Fig. 7.2), while the mesh or two-dimensional array structure of Fig. 7.55b occurs in the systolic multiplier of Fig. 7.42. (The interprocessor connections of ILLIAC IV depicted in Fig. 7.19 constitute a *toroidal mesh*, because the meshlike interconnections can be drawn without crossovers on the surface of a torus.) The ring structure of Fig. 7.55c adds an extra link to the linear structure (Fig. 7.55a), thereby cutting in half the length of the longest path linking any two processors. It also introduces some tolerance of bus failures by providing two rather than one communication path between each processor pair. The graph of Fig. 7.55d is a type of tree called a *star* for obvious reasons, and has a central or root node connected to all $n - 1$ other nodes. The three-dimensional hypercube structure is depicted in Fig. 7.55e, while the complete graph for $n = 6$ nodes appears in Fig. 7.55f. The ring, hypercube, and complete graphs are considered to be *homogeneous*, because each node has precisely the same types of connections to the remainder of the system as all the other nodes, thereby making the nodes interchangeable. For instance, each node x has the same number $d(x)$ of neighbors; $d(x)$ is called the *degree* of x and is a measure of its bus interface complexity. The other three examples in Fig. 7.55 are *inhomogeneous* since not all nodes have the same degree.

Figure 7.56 summarizes some pertinent properties of the foregoing interconnection networks. The number of connections or edges and the maximum node degree are an indication of the hardware cost of the interconnection structure. The *distance* between two processors is defined to be the number of edges along a shortest path in the interconnection network from one processor to the other. The maximum of the interprocessor distances is an indication of the worst-case communication delays that the network can introduce. In the examples of Fig. 7.55, the total number of connecting edges ranges from $n(n - 1)/2$ or approximately $n^2/2$

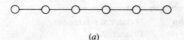

(a)

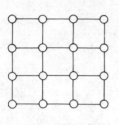

(b)

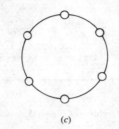

(c)

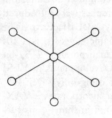

(d)

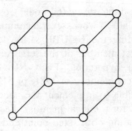

(e)

(f)

FIGURE 7.55
Static interconnection structures:
(a) linear; (b) mesh; (c) ring;
(d) star; (e) hypercube; (f) complete.

for large n in the complete-graph case, to the minimum possible value of $n - 1$ in the case of the linear and star graphs. The complete graph and the star share the largest node degrees, while the linear structure has the largest internode distance. The other networks exhibit various compromises between hardware cost and delay. Of particular interest is the hypercube structure, which achieves a reasonable balance between all three parameters. Because of this, it has been the network of choice for a number of commercial massively parallel computers. We now consider one such machine in detail.

Example 7.8   The NCUBE/ten hypercube [14]. Although hypercube multiprocessors were proposed as early as 1962, the first working machine was not demonstrated until

Interconnection structure	Number of connections	Maximum node degree	Maximum internode distance
Linear	$n - 1$	2	$n - 1$
Ring	n	2	$n/2$
Mesh $(n^{1/2} \times n^{1/2})$	$2(n - n^{1/2})$	4	$2(n^{1/2} - 1)$
Star	$n - 1$	$n - 1$	2
Hypercube $(n = 2^k)$	$n \log_2 n$	$\log_2 n$	$\log_2 n$
Complete	$n(n - 1)/2$	$n - 1$	1

FIGURE 7.56
Comparison of the interconnection structures of Fig. 7.55, assuming each connects n nodes.

the completion of the six-dimensional (64-node) Cosmic Cube computer at Caltech in 1983. Influenced by the Caltech work, several commercial hypercubes were introduced in the mid-1980s, including the NCUBE series developed by NCUBE Corp. The NCUBE/ten is the largest member of the series and, as its name suggests, is a 10-dimensional (1024-node) hypercube. Each NCUBE node incorporates a 32-bit microprocessor and a local memory of 128K or 512K bytes. Developments in VLSI technology make it possible to implement the node processor using only seven ICs, one for the CPU and six for the local memory. Each processor incorporates a VAX-like instruction set, including both fixed-point and floating-point arithmetic instructions, and all the necessary logic for memory management and IO control. The peak performance goal of each processor is 2 MIPS or 0.5 MFLOPS; hence the full 1024-node system has a potential throughput of 500 MFLOPS. Since this exceeds the maximum throughput of the Cray-1 (Example 7.6) by a factor of 3, the NCUBE/ten can be classed as a massively parallel supercomputer. The system organization of the NCUBE/ten is illustrated in Fig. 7.57. The main hypercube H is packaged into 16 printed-circuit boards each of which contains a 64-node hypercube that forms a *subcube* of H. Communication with the outside world uses up to eight IO boards, at least one of which contains a host computer (based on an Intel 80286 processor) which is responsible for executing the operating system (a version of UNIX named AXIS). Host IO boards, and other IO boards that are specialized for such tasks as graphics control, provide the NCUBE/ten with a peak IO throughput of about 720M bytes/s to support its high data processing rates.

The node processing element of the NCUBE/ten is equipped with 11 high-speed IO channels, each consisting of a serial input line and a serial output line. Ten of these channels connect the processing element to neighboring nodes, as required in a 10-dimensional hypercube; the eleventh channel connects to a host IO board. As suggested by Fig.7.57, the connections between the processor boards and the IO boards are distributed evenly, so that each IO board has direct connections to 128 processor nodes in eight different processor boards; these nodes constitute a seven-dimensional subcube. This allows the NCUBE/ten to sustain its very high IO throughput for such IO-intensive applications as real-time image processing. Processor-processor communication is implemented by transmitting messages between buffer areas in the local memories of adjacent nodes. Each interprocessor IO channel has associated with it an address register pointing to its buffer area, and a count register indicating the number of bytes to be sent or received. Once a message transfer has been initiated by a proces-

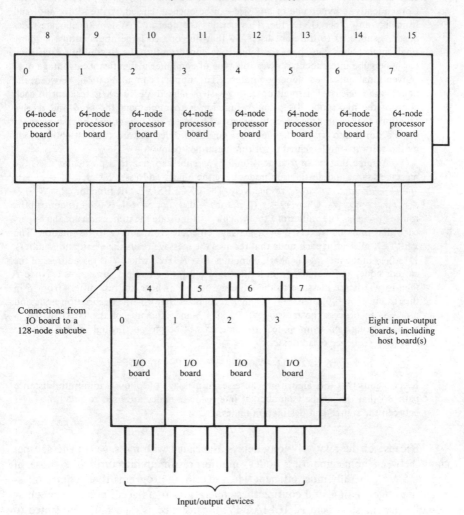

FIGURE 7.57
System organization of the NCUBE/ten.

sor, the processor can continue with other tasks, while the interprocessor message transfer proceeds as an independent DMA operation between the memories of the communicating nodes. A broadcasting instruction is also supported, which allows the same data to be transmitted to all processors in the hypercube (see Prob. 7.27 for further details).

The operating system of the NCUBE/ten provides all the usual UNIX system management and programmer support functions (see Example 6.8). It treats a hypercube of processors as a device, which in the UNIX philosophy is a special type of file. Consequently, a hypercube of any size can be opened, closed, written into, and read from like any other UNIX file. This permits the operating system to allocate independent subcodes to different users, so that one or two large applications or many small applications can share the hypercube concurrently. The flexibility to partition the hypercube into subcubes gives this type of computer a significant advantage over conventional pipelined supercomputers. To support communication between the nodes, the nucleus of a small operating system named VERTEX is resident in each node of the hypercube. Its primary function is to implement the **send** and **receive** functions that permit messages to be passed between any two nodes. Each message is broken down into fixed-length packets, and forwarded toward the destination node by the software-implemented algorithm described below.

Assume that in an n-dimensional hypercube assigned to a particular user, the message source and destination nodes have the binary addresses $S = s_{n-1}s_{n-2} \cdots s_1 s_0$ and $D = d_{n-1}d_{n-2} \cdots d_1 d_0$, respectively. The EXCLUSIVE-OR function $R = S \oplus D = r_{n-1}r_{n-2} \cdots r_1 r_0$, where $r_i = s_i \oplus d_i$ for $i = 0, 1, \ldots, n-1$, is used to control the routing process. The values of i for which $r_i = 1$ indicate the dimensions of the hypercube that must be traversed by a message en route from source to destination. The VERTEX nucleus in each node that receives the message reads the destination address D (a field in the message header), computes $R = P \oplus D$, where P is the address of the current node, and scans R from left to right until it encounters some $r_j = 1$. Node P then forwards the message to the adjacent node P' whose address differs from P in the jth bit. If $R = 0$, then $P = D$ and P recognizes that it is the destination node and proceeds to process the message. Thus in a 6-node subcube of the NCUBE/ten, a message being sent from node 7 to node 45 will be passed through nodes with the following sequence of addresses:

$$S = 000111 \rightarrow 100111 \rightarrow 101111 \rightarrow 101101 = D$$

It is obvious that this algorithm causes each message to follow a minimum-distance path, so that the smallest number of intermediate nodes are used to relay messages between the source and destination nodes.

Because of the relatively long delays associated with message transfers, especially between nonneighboring nodes, multiprocessor architectures like those of Fig. 7.55 are generally most efficient when executing programs that require infrequent message passing, and confine these operations to adjacent nodes as much as possible. The mesh-structured ILLIAC IV, for instance, is especially well suited to the computation of functions defined over a two-dimensional space represented by a grid of points, where the value of a function f at some grid point (x, y) can be expressed in terms of values of f at the four neighboring grid points. In such cases, the processor at each grid point need only communicate data to its four immediate neighbors in the course of the parallel computation of f. The computation in this manner of the temperature on a two-dimensional surface is discussed in Example 7.2. Thus the interconnection network of the computer and the data flow pattern of the algorithm being executed have the same abstract form, namely, that of a mesh graph. Optimum performance can be expected when the algorithm and computer structures match in this manner. We now formalize this concept in terms of graphs.

Let $G(A)$ be a graph representing the structure of an algorithm or program A. Let the nodes of $G(A)$ be the points $\{P_i\}$ at which some function f is evaluated by executing A. Two points P_1 and P_2 of $G(A)$ are connected by an edge if and only if data is transferred between P_1 and P_2 during the execution of A. As before, a graph $G(N)$ whose nodes are processors and whose edges are interprocessor communication links represents the interconnection structure N of a multiprocessor. Algorithm A is said to be *embeddable* in N if and only if every node in $G(A)$ can be mapped into a distinct node in $G(N)$ such that all nodes that are adjacent in $G(A)$ are also adjacent in $G(N)$. In graph-theoretical terms, A is embeddable in N if $G(A)$ is isomorphic to a subgraph of $G(N)$. It is easily seen from Fig. 7.55 that a p-node algorithm with the structure of a linear array or path is embeddable in an n-node ring or mesh network provided $n \geq p$. Clearly a multiprocessor is, to a first approximation, best suited to the execution of algorithms that are embeddable in it.

We can also use the embeddability concept to compare different interconnection structures. Let C_1 with (static) interconnection network N_1 and C_2 with interconnection network N_2 be multiprocessing computers employing similar processors. If N_1 is embeddable in a sufficiently large version of N_2, then C_2 will be said to be able to *simulate* C_1. This means that any algorithm embeddable in C_1 is also embeddable in C_2, so that C_2 is at least as powerful as C_1 from a static structural viewpoint. Thus referring to Fig. 7.55 again, it is obvious that a system for which $G(N)$ is a complete graph (Fig. 7.55f) is a universal simulator, since every n-processor computer C can be simulated by an n-processor computer C' for which $G(C')$ is complete. A mesh-structured system (Fig. 7.55b) can simulate a path (Fig. 7.55a) or a ring (Fig. 7.55c). It cannot, however, simulate a hypercube (Fig. 7.55c), since for $n > 4$, every node of an n-dimensional hypercube has greater degree than every node of the mesh. A mesh also cannot simulate a star containing more than five nodes, since the central node of the star has degree greater than 4. If the requirement that adjacent nodes only be mapped into adjacent nodes is lifted, then, of course, any general-purpose multiprocessor can simulate any other computer but the interprocessor communication delays may no longer be comparable.

A motivation for using the hypercube as the interconnection structure for massively parallel computers is its ability to simulate a wide variety of other structures. For example, it can obviously simulate the path and star structures of Fig. 7.55. Less obvious is the fact that a mesh of any size can be simulated by a hypercube. To see this, note again that the nodes of an n-dimensional hypercube can be labeled by n-bit binary addresses such that each node address differs in the ith a bit from the address of the neighbor with which it shares dimension i; such a labeling is illustrated in Fig. 7.8e for the case $n = 3$. To show that an arbitrary $n_1 \times n_2$ mesh embeds in an n-dimensional hypercube for some n, we attach binary addresses to the nodes of the mesh in which adjacent addresses differ by exactly 1 bit as in the hypercube labeling. The basic idea is to construct the address $A(x, y)$ for each mesh node (x, y) in two parts $A(x)$ and $A(y)$ such that neighboring nodes in the x dimension have the same $A(y)$, but their $A(x)$'s differ in 1 bit; similarly, neighboring nodes in the y dimension have the same $A(x)$, but their $A(y)$'s differ in 1 bit. Figure 7.58a shows this type of labeling for the 12-node 3×4 mesh, where the first

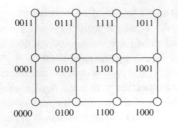

(a)

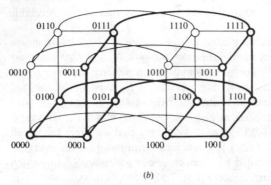

(b)

FIGURE 7.58
(a) A 3×4 mesh; (b) embedding the mesh in a four-dimensional hypercube.

2 bits of each node address are $A(x)$ and the second two are $A(y)$. An embedding of this mesh into the 16-node four-dimensional hypercube appears in Fig. 7.58b, where $A(x, y)$ is mapped into the hypercube node with the same 4-bit address. The nodes and edges of the hypercube that correspond to those of the mesh are shown by heavy lines.

The sequence of addresses along any row or column of the mesh of Fig. 7.58a forms part of a k-bit 2^k-member *Gray code sequence* G_k, which may be defined recursively as follows.

1. $G_1 = 0, 1$.
2. Let $G_k = g_0, g_1, \ldots, g_{2^k-2}, g_{2^k-1}$. G_{k+1} is formed by first preceding all members of the sequence G_k by 0, then repeating G_k with the order reversed and all members preceded by 1. In other words,

$$G_{k+1} = 0g_0, 0g_1, \ldots, 0g_{2^k-2}, 0g_{2^k-1}, 1g_{2^k-1}, 1g_{2^k-2}, \ldots, 1g_1, 1g_0$$

For example, $G_2 = 00, 01, 11, 10$ and $G_3 = 000, 001, 011, 010, 110, 111, 101, 100$. Clearly the foregoing construction ensures that consecutive members of a Gray code sequence differ in exactly 1 bit. To embed it in a hypercube, an $n_1 \times n_2$ mesh is labeled by making $A(x)$ be the xth member of G_{m_1} and $A(y)$ be the yth member of G_{m_2}, where x and y assume the values 0, 1, 2, . . . , $\lceil \log_2 n_2 \rceil$ and 0, 1, 2, . . . , $\lceil \log_2 n_1 \rceil$, respectively. In the case of the mesh in Fig. 7.58a, for instance, $n_1 = 3$, $n_2 = 4$, and $\lceil \log_2 n_1 \rceil = \lceil \log_2 n_2 \rceil = 2$. Adjacent nodes of the mesh that are labeled in this fashion have addresses differing in exactly 1 bit. Each node of the mesh is mapped to the hypercube node with the same address; consequently, adjacent nodes in the mesh are mapped into adjacent nodes in the hypercube. We conclude that every $n_1 \times n_2$ mesh can be simulated by an n-dimensional hypercube with $n \geq \lceil \log_2 n_1 \rceil + \lceil \log_2 n_2 \rceil$.

Multistage switching networks. Another important class of dynamic interconnection structures for massively parallel multiprocessors are constructed from one or more stages of small interconnection networks called switching elements. A network designed to connect k_1 inputs to k_2 outputs is called a $k_1 \times k_2$ switching network, and the maximum number of switching elements lying along any input-output path is the number of stages. Each link to a switching element or processor port is a uni- or bidirectional bus containing k wires. To reduce hardware costs and meet pin limitations, k is often 1, i.e., communication through the switching network is serial or bit by bit. Figure 7.10 shows an example of a three-stage 8×8 switching network composed of twelve 2×2 switching elements. An example of a three-stage 8×8 network appears in Fig. 7.59. (This type of network is termed an omega network and is defined later.) Many different topologies have been proposed for multistage switching networks, primarily to control processor-memory or processor-processor communication in shared-memory or distributed-memory multiprocessors, respectively. We now examine the major characteristics of some typical multistage switching networks, concentrating on those designed for processor-to-processor communication.

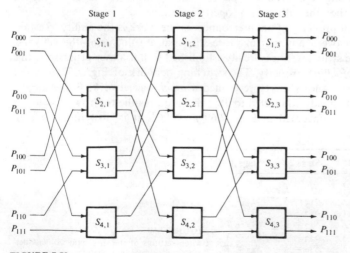

FIGURE 7.59
Three-stage 8×8 omega switching network.

The purpose of a multistage switching network SN is to provide a flexible and cost-effective set of communication links between N processors. We assume that these processors form the sources and destinations of SN, so that the network dimensions are $N \times N$. Since processors are usually identified by n-bit binary addresses, it is convenient to make $N = 2^n$. In multiprocessor applications, SN is configured to allow a message or, more often, a fixed-length package, to be transferred simultaneously between from one to $N/2$ pairs of processors. The processor pairs that are connected to each other at any time are determined by the states of the switching elements, each of which can be in either the through (T) or cross (X) state (see Fig. 7.9). Control logic associated with the interconnection network sets the switch states dynamically to meet the interconnection requests from the processors. The controller maintains a particular network state for sufficiently long to allow one or more messages to be transferred. It then changes the network state to match the source-destination requirements of the next set of messages, and so on. It is assumed here that a processor can buffer or queue each of its outgoing messages until the switching network is ready to transfer it. Incoming messages are accepted by the processors as soon as they are available.

A fundamental requirement of a multistage switching network is that it be possible to connect every processor P_i to every other processor P_j by at least one configuration or state of the network; this is termed the *full-access* property. It is easy to show that the omega network of Fig. 7.59 is a full-access network. Figure 7.60 shows the seven unique switch configurations needed to connect P_{000} to each of the other processors; here $S_{i,j} = T(X)$ indicates that switch i of stage j is set to the through (cross) state. A complete network configuration in which P_{000} is connected to P_{001} is illustrated in Fig. 7.61. In this state, the network also connects P_{010}, P_{100}, and P_{110} to P_{011}, P_{101}, and P_{111} respectively, thus providing simultaneous communication among four processor pairs. If the number of stages is reduced from three to two, then the full-access property is lost.

Another useful property of an interconnection network is the ability to establish a connection between any pair of processors that are not using the network, without altering the switch settings already established to link other processors; this is termed the *nonblocking* property. The switching network of Fig. 7.59 does not possess this property, and is therefore termed a *blocking* network. For example, suppose that P_{000} is already connected to P_{001}; this requires the top row of switches to be set to TTX, as specified in Figs. 7.60 and 7.61. It is now impossible to

Destination	Stage 1	Stage 2	Stage 3
P_{001}	$S_{1,1} = T$	$S_{1,2} = T$	$S_{1,3} = X$
P_{010}	$S_{1,1} = T$	$S_{1,2} = X$	$S_{2,3} = T$
P_{011}	$S_{1,1} = T$	$S_{1,2} = X$	$S_{2,3} = X$
P_{100}	$S_{1,1} = X$	$S_{2,2} = T$	$S_{3,3} = T$
P_{101}	$S_{1,1} = X$	$S_{2,2} = T$	$S_{3,3} = X$
P_{110}	$S_{1,1} = X$	$S_{2,2} = X$	$S_{4,3} = T$
P_{111}	$S_{1,1} = X$	$S_{2,2} = X$	$S_{4,3} = X$

FIGURE 7.60
Switch settings of the three-stage omega network to connect P_{000} to each of the other processors.

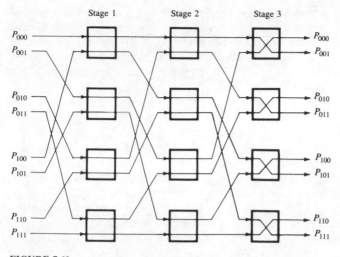

FIGURE 7.61
One state of the omega network.

connect P_{100} either to P_{010} or P_{011}. The preexisting setting of $S_{1,1}$ creates a path from P_{100} through stage 1 to $S_{2,2}$. No links exist from $S_{2,2}$ to $S_{2,3}$, the third-stage switching element connected to P_{010} and P_{011}; hence $S_{2,2}$ cannot be set to forward data to P_{010} or P_{011}. This type of blocking can result in communication delays, and is similar to that occurring in a single-bus system when several processors attempt to use the system bus simultaneously. Nonblocking interconnection networks require an excessive number of switches for most computer applications. An $N \times N$ cross-bar switch is an example of a nonblocking network because it allows any idle row to be connected to any idle column. However, it contains N^2 complex crosspoint switches, whereas an $N \times N$ omega network contains only $(N/2) \log_2 N$ simpler 2×2 switches.

A few basic interstage wiring patterns serve to characterize the multistage switching networks most widely used in multiprocessor designs. Each such pattern may be considered as a mapping ψ from a set of sources $\{S_i\}$ to a set of destinations $\{D_{\psi(i)}\}$, for $i = 0, 1, \ldots, N - 1$. S_i is the address or label of an output port of a processor or switching element, and $D_{\Psi(i)}$ is the address of an input port of a processor or switching element to which S_i is wired. The *shuffle connection*, for example, is defined by the following mapping function:

$$\sigma(i) = 2i + \lfloor 2i/N \rfloor \qquad \text{(modulo } N\text{)} \qquad (7.40)$$

Here σ is referred to as the *shuffle function*, and is illustrated by Fig. 7.62*a* for $N = 8$. The name shuffle comes from the fact that the destination addresses 0, 1, 2, 3, 4, 5, 6, 7 can be mapped into (connected to) the source addresses 0, 4, 1, 5, 2, 6, 3, 7 by interleaving the first half 0, 1, 2, 3 of the port address sequence with the second half 4, 5, 6, 7 in the manner of a perfectly shuffled deck of cards. Let each address i

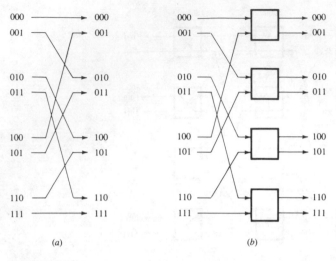

(a)   (b)

FIGURE 7.62
(a) Shuffle connection for $N = 8$; (b) single-stage shuffle-exchange network.

be represented by the corresponding n-bit binary number $b_{n-1}b_{n-2} \cdots b_0$. An equivalent definition to (7.40) is

$$\sigma(i) = b_{n-2}b_{n-3} \cdots b_0 b_{n-1} \tag{7.41}$$

indicating that the shuffle function corresponds to using a 1-bit left rotation of the source address bits to determine the destination address. By following a shuffle connection with $N/2$ switching elements, each of which can exchange (cross) a pair of buses, we obtain the single-stage *shuffle-exchange network*, which is illustrated in Fig. 7.62b for the case $N = 8$. A network constructed from $n = \log_2 N$ cascaded shuffle-exchange stages is called an *omega network*. Thus the multistage switching network of Fig. 7.59 is an 8×8 omega network. Large omega networks have been designed for a number of computers, e.g., the processor-to-memory interconnection network in the Ultracomputer, a shared-memory multiprocessor developed at New York University in the early 1980s.

The indirect hypercube switching network of Fig. 7.10 is based on the *butterfly connection* depicted in Fig. 7.63a, which is so called because of the resemblance of the figure to a butterfly with its body in a horizontal position at the center and its wings spread out above and below. The 4×4 single-stage *butterfly network* is illustrated in Fig. 7.63b; here the butterfly connection is placed before rather than after the set of $N/2$ switching elements. Consider an $N \times N$ multistage network with n stages $1, 2, \ldots, n$ and port addresses $i = 0, 1, \ldots, N - 1$, where, as before, $i = b_{n-1}b_{n-2} \cdots b_0$. The kth *butterfly function* β_k is defined as follows for $k = 1, \ldots, n - 1$:

$$\beta_k(b_{n-1} \cdots b_{k+1}b_k b_{k-1} \cdots b_1 b_0) = b_{n-1} \cdots b_{k+1}b_0 b_{k-1} \cdots b_1 b_k$$

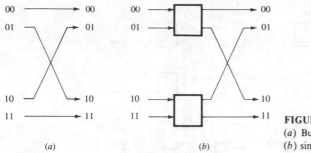

FIGURE 7.63
(a) Butterfly connection for $N = 4$;
(b) single-stage butterfly network.

Thus β_k interchanges bits 0 and k of the source address to obtain the destination address. For example, when $k = 1$ and $N = 4$, we obtain

$$\beta_1(00) = 00$$
$$\beta_1(01) = 10$$
$$\beta_1(10) = 01$$
$$\beta_1(11) = 11$$

corresponding to the interconnection pattern on Fig. 7.63a. It is easily seen that in the indirect hypercube network of Fig. 7.10, the wiring patterns following stages 1 and 2 are defined by β_1 and β_2, respectively, with $N = 8$. The final connection pattern following stage 3 in Fig. 7.10 employs another type of connection, called the *inverse shuffle*, which is defined by the following *inverse shuffle function* σ^{-1}:

$$\sigma^{-1}(i) = b_0 b_{n-1} b_{n-2} b_{n-3} \cdots b_1 \qquad (7.42)$$

Note that (7.42) is the same as definition (7.41) of the shuffle function σ with the direction of the address bit rotation reversed. Note also that the wiring pattern following stage 3 in Fig. 7.10 is identical to the wiring pattern preceding any stage of the shuffle exchange network of Fig. 7.62, with all the arrows reversed. Figure 7.64 shows a 16×16 version of the indirect hypercube network. In general, an $N \times N$ indirect hypercube network consists of $\log_2 N$ stages of $N/2$ switching elements, where the wiring pattern following the stages are defined by $\beta_1, \beta_2, \ldots, \beta_{n-1}, \sigma^{-1}$.

Indirect hypercube and shuffle-exchange networks have very similar properties. Suppose that the directions of all the arrows in an $N \times N$ shuffle-exchange network are reversed, implying that the shuffle connection σ in each stage is replaced by σ^{-1}. The resulting $N \times N$ *inverse omega network* and the $N \times N$ indirect hypercube network are essentially the same multistage switching network drawn in different ways. Consequently, for each state of the indirect hypercube network, there is a state of the inverse omega network that connects the N processors in exactly the same way, and vice versa. This equivalence is not obvious (a clear proof can be found in Ref. 27), and accounts for the many names under which this class of multistage switching networks appears in the literature (inverse omega, indirect binary n-cube, butterfly, SW banyan, etc.). Consider the 8×8

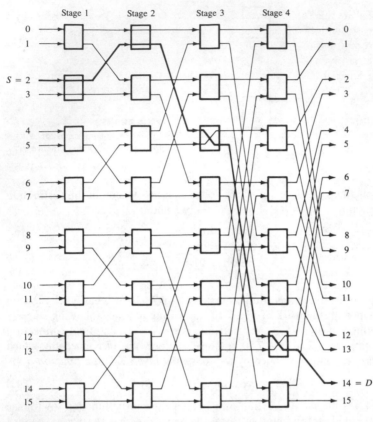

FIGURE 7.64
16 × 16 indirect hypercube network.

inverse omega network configuration obtained by reversing all the arrows of Fig. 7.61. In the given state, this inverse omega network provides exactly the same processor-to-processor connections as the 8 × 8 indirect hypercube configuration appearing in Fig. 7.11a. The equivalence of the inverse omega and indirect hypercube networks implies that the omega network is equivalent to the inverse indirect hypercube network; the latter is known as the *generalized cube network* [30].

The switching elements in each stage of the foregoing interconnection networks effectively control one bit of the destination address to which a message is sent. Since an address contains $n = \log_2 N$ bits, at least $\log_2 N$ stages must be present for an $N \times N$ switching network to have the full access property. Consequently, all the foregoing examples (the omega network, the indirect hypercube network, and their inverses) contain exactly $\log_2 N$ stages. With this number of stages it is also easy to determine the switch settings needed to connect an arbitrary pair of processors, since each stage controls one bit (dimension) of the address space. We illustrate this for the omega and indirect hypercube cases. Suppose that a source processor with binary address $S = s_{n-1}s_{n-2} \cdots s_1 s_0$ is to be connected to a destination processor with address $D = d_{n-1}d_{n-2} \cdots d_1 d_0$. As in the static hypercube routing algorithm (Example 7.8), we compute $R = S \oplus D = r_{n-1}r_{n-2} \cdots r_1 r_0$, and use R to control the switch settings of the network. If $r_i = 0$ then all the switches in stage $i + 1$ (assuming again that the stages are numbered $1, 2, \ldots, n$) are set to the through (T) state; these switches are set to the cross (X) state if $r_i = 1$. For example, Fig. 7.64 shows the switch settings to connect source $S = 2$ to destination $D = 14$. In this case, $R = 0010 \oplus 1110 = 1100$, requiring two through and two cross switch settings as indicated. The heavy lines in Fig. 7.64 show the path along which messages travel from S to D. The correctness of the above routing strategy follows from the fact that stage $i + 1$ of the various networks corresponds to dimension i of the static hypercube connection, as illustrated by Fig. 7.11. If all switches are set to T, then $S = D$, i.e., each processor is connected to itself via a path through $\log_2 N$ switches. Changing the state of the switch in stage $i + 1$ along this path from T to X has the effect of connecting the source processor to the destination processor that differs from it in the ith address bit, i.e., in the ith dimension. It follows directly from this discussion that there is only one path through each of the foregoing ($\log_2 N$)-stage networks linking every source-destination pair.

The routing of messages through a multistage switching network can be implemented by a centralized controller attached to the network that examines all source-destination address pairs S, D generated by processors, and sets the appropriate switching elements to the states specified $R = S \oplus D$. An alternative approach is to attach R as a *routing tag* to each message to be transmitted from S to D, and use R to set the switching element states as the message passes through the network. When the message enters a switch $S_{j,i+1}$ in stage $i + 1$, $S_{j,i+1}$ examines the routing tag R, using control logic added to the switch for this purpose. $S_{j,i+1}$ then sets its own state to T if the $r_i = 0$, and to X if $r_i = 1$. Thus the centralized network controller can be replaced by decentralized control logic distributed throughout the switching elements. Each message determines its own path through the interconnection network and so can be viewed as self-routing. For example, to transmit a message from $S = 2$ to $D = 14$, in the four-stage switching network of Fig. 7.64, the routing tag $R = r_3 r_2 r_1 r_0 = 1100$ is appended to the message generated by the source processor P_2. The switch $S_{2,1}$ attached to P_2 in stage 1 inspects bit r_0 of R. Since $r_0 = 0$, $S_{2,1}$ sets itself to the through state T. This causes the message to be sent to the topmost switch $S_{1,1}$ in stage 2, which also sets its state to T since $r_1 = 0$. The message proceeds to the final two stages, which set themselves to the cross state X since $r_2 = r_3 = 1$.

The BBN Butterfly computer developed in the late 1970s is an example of a commercial multiprocessor based on a multistage switching network [8]. It is a shared-memory MIMD computer in which the switching network connects N processors to N memory modules that form a large global memory. The number of processors N can range from 1 to 256; the structure of a typical 16-processor Butterfly is illustrated in Fig. 1.45 (Sec. 1.4.3). The processors are based on the

Motorola 68000 CPU, and each is housed with one memory module on a single printed-circuit board. This allows the processor to have fast access to that "local" memory module by effectively bypassing the interconnection network. (Note, however, that this memory module is included in the address space of every processor in the system.) Every processor also contains a microprogrammed coprocessor, the Processor Node Controller, based on the AMD 2901, which handles virtual memory management, message transfer to and from the multistage switching network, and related functions.

The Butterfly's switching network employs single-chip 4×4 switching elements, each of which is obtained by cascading two copies of the basic butterfly network of Fig. 7.63b. Consequently, the processor-memory interconnection network is a general $N \times N$ butterfly network composed of $\log_2 N$ stages of 2×2 switches; this is the source of the computer's name. Data transmission through the network is by bit-serial messages which can be transmitted at a rate of 32M bits/s along any processor-memory path. Each message contains its destination address and is made self-routing in the manner described above by using 2 bits of the destination address to determine the setting of each 4×4 switch through the message passes. Should two messages attempt to use the same link in the switching network simultaneously, one is allowed to proceed and the other is retransmitted after a short delay. This type of contention is application-dependent, but has been found to increase the execution time of a typical program by only a few percent.

7.3.3 Fault-Tolerant Computers

Fault tolerance has been defined as "the ability of a system to execute specified algorithms correctly regardless of hardware failures and program errors" [2]. It is of concern in most computer systems, while in some applications, e.g., spacecraft control and telephone switching, fault tolerance is a major design goal. Most hardware failures have physical causes such as component wear or electromagnetic interference. The nature and frequency of hardware failures can often be determined experimentally, which makes it possible to study the faults and their consequences using analytic or simulation models. Software faults, on the other hand, are primarily due to design mistakes and are much more difficult to deal with.

Fault tolerance is intimately associated with the concept of redundancy. When a component fails, its duties must be taken over by other, fault-free, components of the system. If those components are intended to improve only the reliability of the system and do not significantly affect its computing performance, they are termed *redundant*. Redundancy may be introduced:

1. By having multiple copies of critical hardware components or subsystems (hardware redundancy)
2. By including several alternative programs for critical operations (software redundancy)

3. By using error-correcting or error-detecting codes for information representation (information redundancy)

4. By repeating critical operations several times (time redundancy)

The goal of these redundant design features is to prevent the physical causes of failure, which are termed *faults* here, from producing information values or operating modes called *errors* that can lead to system failure. In this section, we will be mainly concerned with the use of hardware redundancy to achieve fault tolerance. Information redundancy was briefly discussed in Sec. 3.1.2.

Design techniques. Two major approaches termed static and dynamic redundancy have been identified for designing fault-tolerant systems. *Static* redundancy refers to the use of redundant components which form a permanent part of the system, and serve to mask the error signals generated by faults. An example of static information redundancy is found in the use of error-correcting codes. A general form of static redundancy is implemented by replacing a critical component that generates a signal X by $n \geq 3$ copies of that component which are configured to generate n independent copies of X in parallel. (If the component in question is a processor, then the resulting system is a type of multiprocessor.) The n versions of X are then applied to a circuit called a *voter* or *decision element*, which is designed to output the value of X appearing on the majority of its n inputs. Thus error signals produced by any of the replicated units are masked by the voter, provided more than half of the units produce the correct X value at all times. A system of this type with n identical units and a voter is said to employ *n-modular redundancy* (nMR). A frequently implemented version called *triple modular redundancy* (TMR), in which $n = 3$, is shown in Fig. 7.65. In this case the behavior of the voter is defined by the logic equation

$$X = X_1 X_2 + X_1 X_3 + X_2 X_3$$

where $+$ denotes the (word) OR operation; this is the well-known majority function. The voter output X always has the correct value if no more than one of the signals X_1, X_2, X_3 is incorrect. Thus a TMR system is capable of tolerating faulty behavior by any one of the triplicated units. Although static redundancy can be implemented at any complexity level, it is normally implemented at the processor

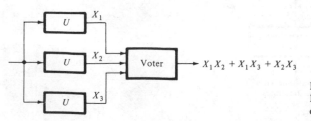

FIGURE 7.65
Example of triple modular redundancy (TMR).

level where the replicated units are CPUs, memory modules, switching networks, or entire computers.

A system with *dynamic redundancy* tolerates faults by actively reorganizing the system so that the functions of the faulty unit are transferred to one or more fault-free units. This is usually achieved in three major steps, as illustrated in Fig. 7.66.

Step 1 (fault diagnosis). Test or diagnostic procedures are carried out to detect the fault, and to isolate it to a replaceable or repairable unit.

Step 2 (fault elimination). The fault is effectively removed from the system either by repairing the faulty unit, replacing it by a spare unit, or logically reconfiguring the system around the fault.

Step 3 (recovery). Procedures are executed to restore the system to a state that existed before the fault occurred. Normal operation is resumed from that point.

Although more complex than static redundancy, dynamic redundancy has the advantage that faulty units can be more rapidly located and eliminated. In the static case, faults can accumulate undetected until a total system failure occurs.

Figure 7.67 shows an example of a fault-tolerant system employing dynamic redundancy. This is termed a *duplex* system because it contains two identical (duplicated) copies of the basic nonredundant or *simplex* unit. The two units operate in tandem, performing the same operations on the same or duplicated data at the same time. A circuit called a *match detector* or *equality checker* does a

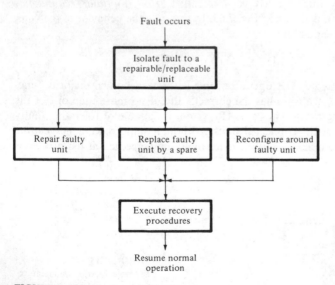

FIGURE 7.66
Fault tolerance using dynamic redundancy.

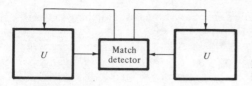

FIGURE 7.67
Fault-tolerant duplex system.

continuous comparison of the results generated by the duplicated units. When a mismatch is detected, indicating the occurrence of a fault, normal operation is temporarily suspended, and a testing or diagnosis procedure is initiated to identify the faulty unit. Once identified, the faulty unit is disconnected from the system, logically if not physically. The system can then be restarted as a simplex system using only the fault-free unit. The failed unit may be repaired off-line and eventually restored to the system.

Example 7.9   Bell No. 1 ESS [11, 35]. The No. 1 ESS (*Electronic Switching System*) is a computer-controlled telephone exchange introduced in 1964 to replace the electromechanical (relay) switching networks long used in this application. It is the prototype of a series of electronic switching systems designed by AT&T Bell Laboratories and other telephone companies. A primary design goal of No. 1 ESS is that the total *downtime*, i.e., time when the system is unable to process telephone calls, should not exceed 2 hours over the system's projected 40-year life. Furthermore, the system is required to function unattended for long periods. These very stringent reliability goals are achieved by a number of design techniques. Components with extremely high intrinsic reliability are used. The system is organized as a duplex system that can detect faults and reconfigure around them automatically. All critical subsystems are duplicated, including the CPUs, memory units, and intrasystem buses. Special circuits, including match detectors for duplicated units, are included to detect faults as soon as possible after they occur. The checking circuits are augmented by an extensive set of diagnostic programs designed to locate faulty units to the smallest replaceable units (plug-in circuit packages).

Figure 7.68 indicates the overall organization of No. 1 ESS. It consists of a duplicated programmable computer of fairly conventional design that controls a large multistage switching network. This network serves to connect telephone lines, and resembles the computer interconnection networks discussed in the preceding section. In the No. 1 ESS, however, it is seen merely as an IO device by the central computer. Telephone calls arriving at the switching network are processed by programs stored in a read-only memory called the program store. A read-write memory named the call store is used to hold temporary information, e.g., the digits dialed, associated with processing a telephone call. The program and call stores together form the main memory of the No. 1 ESS. To achieve the desired fault tolerance, the CPU, program store, call store, and main buses are duplicated as depicted in Fig. 7.68. The telephone switching network is not duplicated, since it has redundant input-output paths that make it inherently fault-tolerant.

In normal operation, the No. 1 ESS is configured as two identical computers, each with its own CPU, buses, and memory units. Only one of the computers, referred to as the active one, actually controls the telephone network at any time. The other computer, called the standby system, operates in parallel with the active

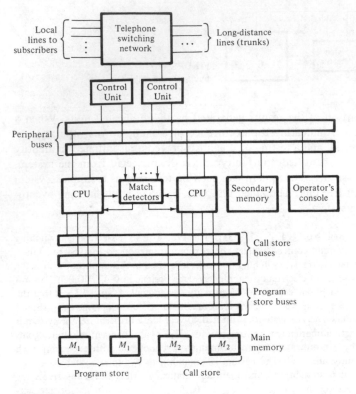

Local lines to subscribers — Telephone switching network — Long-distance lines (trunks)

Control Unit   Control Unit

Peripheral buses

CPU   Match detectors   CPU   Secondary memory   Operator's console

Call store buses

Program store buses

M_1 M_1 M_2 M_2 Main memory

Program store   Call store

FIGURE 7.68
System organization of the No. 1 ESS.

computer and their results are continually compared via match detectors. When a disagreement between the two computers is detected, an interrupt is generated, causing both machines to begin executing a "fault-recognition" program. This self-testing program exercises the hardware where the mismatch occurred with the aim of rapidly identifying the faulty computer. Note that execution of the fault-recognition program is interleaved with telephone call processing, so that the testing process does not halt the system. If the active computer determines that it is at fault, it deactivates itself and passes control of the telephone network to the standby computer, which then becomes the active computer. Special emergency circuits are present to forcibly disconnect the active computer if the fault prevents it from doing it itself. If the standby machine is identified as the faulty one, it is logically detached from the system by the active computer. In either case, the faulty computer is taken off-line and required to execute (with some help from the other computer, if necessary) a series of diagnostic programs that attempt to isolate the faulty circuit. In the meantime, the fault-free computer continues to process telephone calls. Once the fault has been located, a message is sent to a maintenance console, and the circuit packages specified by the system are replaced manually by spare circuits. The repaired system is then restarted manually and normal duplex operation is resumed.

While a computer system can be made very reliable by fault-tolerant design techniques, it is impossible to guarantee tolerance of *all* conceivable failure modes. For example, if two of the triplicated units in a TMR system produce identical erroneous outputs, the system output will be incorrect. Similarly, if certain faults occur simultaneously in both parts of a duplex system they may escape detection by the match detectors and the system may fail. The No. 1 ESS systems have been carefully monitored in the field to determine their actual fault tolerance and the causes of nontolerated system failures. By 1978, with more than a thousand No. 1 ESS's in operation, steady improvements in the system hardware, software, and operating procedures had reduced the annual downtime from 70 min per year in 1965 to about 5 min per year, which is close to the original design goal. Data reported in 1978 [35] indicate that only about 20 percent of system downtime was then due to hardware failures, most of which were failures of a single unit. Software design errors (program bugs) accounted for an additional 15 percent of the downtime. The complex fault isolation and recovery processes, which involve both hardware and software, were determined to contribute about 35 percent of the downtime, e.g., due to failure of the system to transfer control automatically to the standby computer when necessary. The remaining 30 percent of the downtime was attributed to human error, such as replacement of the wrong circuit package by the maintenance personnel.

Complete replication of a unit that is subject to failure is not always necessary in the design of fault-tolerant systems. Consider again multistage switching networks of the kind discussed in Sec. 7.3.2; the telephone switching network of Fig. 7.68 is also of this type. A ($\log_2 N$)-stage $N \times N$ switching network such as an omega network provides only one communication path between each source-destination pair. Consequently, the failure of any switch along the path can destroy communication between certain sets of nodes, which may amount to a system failure. Such communication failures can be tolerated by introducing an extra stage of switches into the interconnection network, instead of duplicating the entire network. This follows from the fact that an extra stage of the appropriate type can double the number of paths between each source-destination pair in such a way that a single switch fault can only block one of these paths. Adding several extra stages can further increase the network's fault tolerance.

A specific example of a fault-tolerant switching network with redundant IO paths is the *extra-stage cube network* [30], which adds another stage to the input side of a generalized cube network. The extra stage is composed of $N/2$ switching elements that are modified as shown in Fig. 7.69a. A pair of multiplexers M and demultiplexers D are added to the basic 2×2 switching element S of Fig. 7.9, and can be set either to disable (bypass) S, as shown in Fig. 7.69b, or else to enable S, as in Fig. 7.69c. The modified switching elements are also used to replace the output stage of the original network, and additional control logic is introduced to set the states of all the multiplexers and demultiplexers. We assume that the latter are very reliable, so that in the event of a fault affecting a switching element, we can use the multiplexers and demultiplexer circuits to reconfigure around the faulty element.

Figure 7.70a shows an 8×8 generalized cube network (this is the inverse of

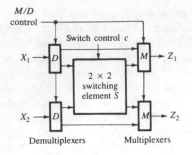

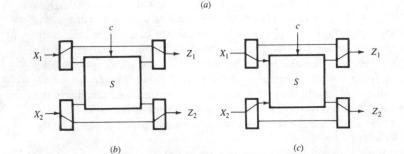

FIGURE 7.69
(a) Modified switching element for the extra-stage cube network: (b) disabled state; (c) enabled state.

the indirect hypercube network of Fig. 7.10), while the corresponding 8×8 extra-stage cube network appears in Fig. 7.70b. During normal (fault-free) operation, the modified switches in the extra input stage (stage 0) are disabled, while those of the output stage 3 are enabled. In this operating mode, the network behaves exactly like the basic indirect hypercube network, and stages 1:3 are controlled in the same manner to route information through the network. Suppose that a fault F occurs in some stage m and is detected by an appropriate fault-diagnosis procedure. If m is input stage 0, then no action is taken; the stage-0 switching elements simply are kept in the disabled state. If the fault is in the output stage $n = \log_2 N$, then stage m is disabled while stage 0 is enabled. For a fault in any intermediate stage, stages 0 and n containing the modified switching elements are both enabled. It is not hard to demonstrate that in all cases communication is possible between any processor pair without going through the faulty switching element. The heavy line in Fig. 7.70a, for instance, shows the normal communication path between processors 2 and 6. If the switching element in stage 1 of this path becomes faulty, then in the extra-stage implementation, communication is rerouted along the alternative path indicated in Fig. 7.70b.

Reliability. The ability of a system to tolerate faults can be measured in various ways. One useful fault-tolerance measure is *availability*, defined as the fraction or

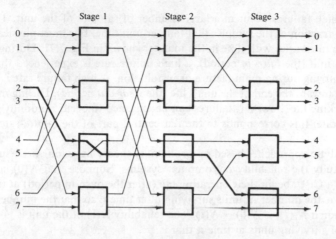

(a)

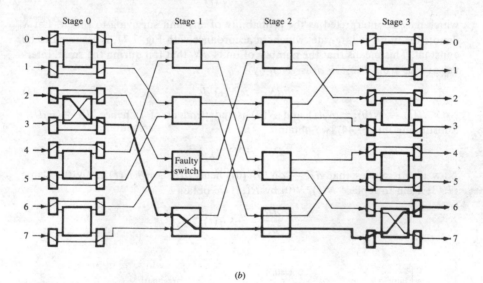

(b)

FIGURE 7.70
(a) 8 × 8 generalized cube network; (b) the corresponding extra-stage cube network.

percentage of its operating lifetime during which the system is not disabled by faults. Thus the target availability of the No. 1 ESS (2 hours of downtime in 40 years) is 99.9994 percent. A more widely used performance measure is the *reliability* $R(t)$, which is defined as the probability of a unit or system surviving (functioning correctly) for a period of length t. The reliability of a unit is determined by the extent to which failures occur in a large number of samples of the unit. The *failure rate* is the fraction of the samples that fail per unit time. For most physical devices, the failure rate varies with time in the manner shown in Fig. 7.71. During the early life of the unit (the *burn-in* period), a high failure rate is experienced that reflects faults occurring during manufacture or installation. A high failure rate is again encountered toward the end of the unit's life (the *wear-out* period). During most of the unit's working life, however, failures can be expected to occur randomly at a fairly constant rate; this corresponds to the flat central part of the failure-rate graph of Fig. 7.71.

Analytic approaches based on probability theory have long been successfully used to study the reliability of computer systems. Suppose that $N(0)$ copies of a unit, e.g., a CPU, begin their operating life (after the burn-in period) at time $t = 0$. Let $N(t)$ be the number of units surviving after time t, so that the number of failed units, denoted $N_f(t)$, is $N(0) - N(t)$. The reliability $R(t)$ of the unit is given by the fraction of surviving units at time t, that is,

$$R(t) = \frac{N(t)}{N_0(t)} \tag{7.43}$$

which may be interpreted as the probability of any unit surviving to time t. Let λ denote the unit's failure rate, which, in accordance with Fig. 7.71, is assumed to be constant. This means that the number of units dN_f that fail during the small interval of time from t to $t + dt$ is given by

$$dN_f = \lambda N(t)\, dt \tag{7.44}$$

Now $N(t) = N(0) - N_f(t)$ and $N(0)$ is independent of t; hence $dN = -dN_f$. Substituting into (7.44), we obtain

$$dN = -\lambda N(t)\, dt$$

Now (7.43) implies that $dR = dN/dN(0)$; hence $dR = -\lambda N(t)\, dt/N(0)$. Using (7.43) again to replace $N(t)/N(0)$ by $R(t)$, we obtain

$$\frac{dR}{dt} = -\lambda R(t)$$

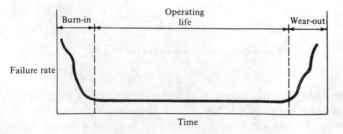

FIGURE 7.71
Typical variation of failure rate with time.

Integration with the boundary value $R(0) = 1$ yields

$$R(t) = e^{-\lambda t} \qquad (7.45)$$

This is the classical *exponential law* of failure, which is very frequently used to model the reliability of the components in a computer system.

From the reliability $R(t)$ we can obtain a single number MTTF called the *mean time to failure*, which is a useful measure of the expected working life of a unit. Letting $F(t)$ denote the *unreliability* $1 - R(t)$, MTTF can be defined as follows:

$$\text{MTTF} = \int_0^\infty t f(t) \, dt \quad \text{where } f(t) = \frac{dF(t)}{d(t)} \qquad (7.46)$$

The MTTF corresponding to the exponential reliability function (7.45) is

$$\text{MTTF} = \int_0^\infty t \lambda e^{-\lambda t} \, dt = \frac{1}{\lambda}$$

Hence the expected working life of a unit with an exponentially distributed reliability is the reciprocal of its failure rate.

Once the failure rates of the individual components of a system are known or can be estimated, it becomes possible to calculate the reliability of the entire system. Two basic circuit structures from a reliability point of view are the series and parallel configurations appearing in Fig. 7.72. In a series system (Fig. 7.72a), it is assumed that if any component fails, the entire system fails. Hence the system reliability which, for brevity, we denote by R instead of $R(t)$, is a product of the component reliabilities, i.e.,

$$R = \prod_{i=1}^n R_i$$

In a parallel system (Fig. 7.72b), on the other hand, all components must fail in order for the system to fail. Hence the system's unreliability $F = 1 - R$ is the product of the component unreliabilities $1 - R_i$, from which it follows that

$$R = 1 - \prod_{i=1}^n (1 - R_i) \qquad (7.47)$$

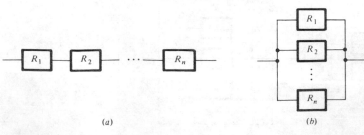

(a)   (b)

FIGURE 7.72
Two basic reliability structures: (a) series and (b) parallel.

As these equations show, adding units in series decreases reliability, while adding parallel units increases reliability. Thus a parallel connection of n units is a basic fault-tolerant structure as, for example, in the case of duplex and TMR systems, where $n = 2$ and 3, respectively. Many systems can be decomposed into a sequence of series and parallel subsystems, and their reliability can be calculated from the above equations. For example, the series-parallel system S in Fig. 7.73 consists of two subsystems S_1 and S_2 which are connected in series; S_1 and S_2 are themselves purely parallel systems. Assuming that each individual unit has reliability R, the system reliability $R(S)$ is given by

$$R(S) = [1 - (1 - R)^3][1 - (1 - R)^2]$$
$$= 6R^2 - 9R^3 + 5R^4 - R^5$$

Let us now apply the foregoing analytic tools to the TMR system of Fig. 7.65. Assume that each of the triplicated units has reliability $R(t) = e^{-\lambda t}$ and that the voter has reliability $R_v(t) = e^{-\lambda_v t}$. Let $P_i(t)$ denote the probability of any of the triplicated units surviving to time t. The system reliability $R_3(t)$ is given by

$$R_3(t) = [P_2(t) + P_3(t)]R_v$$

Now $P_2(t) = \binom{3}{2}(e^{-\lambda t})(1 - e^{-\lambda t})$, while $P_3(t) = (e^{-\lambda t})^3$; hence

$$R_3(t) = (3e^{-2\lambda t} - 2e^{-3\lambda t})e^{-\lambda_v t} \qquad (7.48)$$

The voter is usually much simpler than the functional units; consequently, its reliability is very high. If we assume $R_v(t) = 1$, that is, if we ignore the possibility of voter failure, then (7.48) reduces to

$$R_3(t) = 3e^{-2\lambda t} - 2e^{-3\lambda t} \qquad (7.49)$$

Figure 7.74 shows a plot of this equation for $\lambda = 0.01$. The reliability of a single unit $R_1(t) = e^{-\lambda t}$ is shown for comparison. It can be seen that for values of R less than about $0.7/\lambda$, the reliability of the TMR system is greater than that of the simplex system; however, beyond this point the reliability is less. In practice, the reliability of a TMR system can be better than the foregoing analysis suggests, since the system may continue to function correctly even if two units fail. For

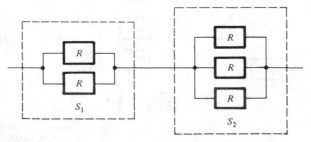

FIGURE 7.73
Example of a series-parallel system.

example, if the two failed units never generate incorrect output signals at the same time, then the voter still produces the correct output.

The unreliability density function $f(t)$ corresponding to (7.49) is

$$f(t) = \frac{d}{dt}[1 - R_3(t)] = 6e^{-2\lambda t} - 6e^{-3\lambda t}$$

Substituting into (7.46) yields the TMR mean time to failure MTTF_3.

$$\text{MTTF}_3 = \int_0^\infty t(6e^{-2\lambda t} - 6e^{-3\lambda t}) \, dt \qquad (7.50)$$

Integrating (7.50) by parts, we obtain

$$\text{MTTF}_3 = [t(-3e^{-2\lambda t} + 2e^{-3\lambda t})]_0^\infty - \int_0^\infty (-3e^{-2\lambda t} + 2e^{-3\lambda t}) \, dt$$
$$= \tfrac{5}{6}\lambda$$

Since the MTTF of the corresponding simplex system is $1/\lambda$, the MTTF of the TMR system is the smaller of the two. This is consistent with Fig. 7.74 which shows that while the TMR system's initial reliability is high, it falls off more rapidly than the simplex reliability as the two systems age.

Repair. The foregoing reliability analysis considered only static systems in which there are no maintenance or repair activities. No matter how fault-tolerant such a system is made, it can be expected that its reliability $R(t) \to 0$ as $t \to \infty$. With repair, however, it is possible to increase the system's probability of functioning correctly at time t beyond $R(t)$ to a value termed the (*instantaneous*) *availability* $A(t)$. In general, $A(t)$ is the sum of $R(t)$, the probability that no faults occurred up to time t, and the probability that the system failed before t, but was repaired and continues to survive. With regular repair, it is possible to make $A(t)$ approach a nonzero steady-state value as t increases. In a dynamic system that is always repaired after a failure occurs, its working life consists of an alternating sequence of

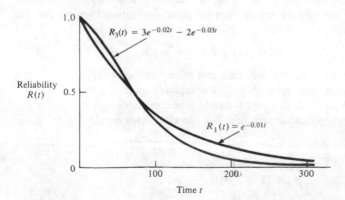

FIGURE 7.74
Reliability comparison between a TMR system and the corresponding simplex system.

periods of fault-free normal operation, and periods during which the system is down for repairs. The system's actual availability, therefore over its entire lifetime L is the ratio of its total fault-free working life to L. If the system is made "as good as new" by the repair process, then the expected (average) duration between the completion of a repair and the occurrence of the next fault is the system's MTTF. Similarly, we may characterize the duration of the repair process by the *mean time to repair* MTTR, which is the expected time between system failure and the completion of repair. The expected availability A of the system, which is usually what is meant by the term availability, is therefore given by the following useful formula:

$$A = \frac{\text{MTTF}}{\text{MTTF} + \text{MTTR}} \tag{7.51}$$

The denominator MTTF + MTTR is referred to as the *mean time between failures* MTBF and is approximately the same as MTTF when MTTR is very small. Equation (7.51) indicates that availability can be increased either by increasing the system's inherent reliability as indicated by MTTF, or else by reducing the time needed for repair after a fault occurs.

We now consider a queueing-theoretic model that is appropriate for a multiprocessor or multicomputer system where faulty units are continually being repaired or replaced. The system contains a total of n units, such that under steady-state conditions, i units are being repaired, while the remaining $n - i$ units are working normally. The repair facility is modeled by a queue of faulty units waiting for repair at a server that represents the repair process. The mean arrival rate at the repair facility is denoted by λ_i and is assumed to be the same as the failure rate. The mean service rate is denoted by μ_i. Note that λ_i and μ_i are functions of i, the number of failed units. Let p_i denote the steady-state probability that i units are not working. Our first goal is to derive an expression for p_i in terms of λ_i, μ_i, and n. Let h denote a short time interval. The probability of one unit failing during the period h is $\lambda_i h$. Similarly, the probability of the repair of a failed unit being completed in time h is $\mu_i h$. If h is sufficiently small that the probability of more than one unit failing or completing repair in time h is negligible, then p_i can be expressed as follows:

$$p_i = p_{i-1} p_A + p_i(p_B + p_C) + p_{i+1} p_D \tag{7.52}$$

where p_A = probability that one unit fails and none completes repair
      p_B = probability that no units fail or complete repair
      p_C = probability that one unit fails and one completes repair
      p_D = probability that no unit fails but one completes repair

The expressions below for p_A, p_B, p_C, and p_D follow directly from these definitions:

$$p_A = \lambda_{i-1} h (1 - \mu_{i-1} h)$$
$$p_B = (1 - \lambda_i h)(1 - \mu_i h)$$
$$p_C = \lambda_i h \mu_i h$$
$$p_D = (1 - \lambda_{i+1} h) \mu_{i+1} h$$

Substituting into (7.52) and neglecting terms in h^2, we obtain

$$p_i = p_{i-1}\lambda_{i-1}h + p_i(1 - \lambda_i h - \mu_i h) + p_{i+1}\mu_{i+1}h$$

This immediately simplifies to

$$p_{i+1} = \frac{p_i(\lambda_i + \mu_i) - p_{i-1}\lambda_{i-1}}{\mu_{i+1}} \tag{7.53}$$

Now when $i = 0$, no units are waiting for repair; hence $\mu_0 = 0$. Substituting 0 for i in (7.52), and noting that $p_{-1} = 0$, we obtain

$$p_1 = p_0 \frac{\lambda_0}{\mu_1} \tag{7.54}$$

Setting $i = 1$ in (7.53) and substituting for p_1 using (7.54) yields

$$p_2 = p_0 \frac{\lambda_0 \lambda_1}{\mu_1 \mu_2}$$

Continuing in this way we can deduce the following expression for p_i in terms of p_0:

$$p_i = p_0 \prod_{j=0}^{i-1} \left(\frac{\lambda_j}{\mu_{j+1}} \right) \tag{7.55}$$

In order to simplify the problem further, we assume that λ_i and μ_i are constants, that is, $\lambda_i = \lambda$ and $\mu_i = \mu$. Equation (7.55) then becomes $p_i = p_0\rho^i$, where, as in Sec. 2.3.4, $\rho = \lambda/\mu$. Now $\Sigma_{i=0}^n p_i = 1$; therefore,

$$p_0 = 1 - \sum_{i=0}^{n} p_i = 1 - p_0 \sum_{i=1}^{n} p_i$$

Hence

$$p_0 = \left[\sum_{i=0}^{n} \rho^i \right]^{-1}$$

Replacing the geometric progression $\Sigma_{i=0}^n \rho^i$ by $(1 - \rho^{n+1})/(1 - \rho)$, and noting that $p_n = p_0 \rho^n$, we obtain

$$p_n = \frac{\rho^n(1 - \rho)}{1 - \rho^{n+1}} \tag{7.56}$$

The (steady-state) availability of the system, defined as the probability that at least one unit is working under steady-state conditions, is given by

$$A = 1 - p_n$$

Substituting from (7.56), we obtain the following expression for the availability of an n-unit system:

$$A = \frac{1 - \rho^n}{1 - \rho^{n+1}} \tag{7.57}$$

When $n = 1$, $A = 1 - p_1 = p_0$, and Eq. (7.57) reduces to

$$A = \frac{1}{1 + \rho} = \frac{1/\lambda}{1/\lambda + 1/\mu}$$

which is equivalent to (7.51) with MTTF = $1/\lambda$ and MTTR = $1/\mu$.

7.4 SUMMARY

Computers capable of executing several instructions or processing several data items simultaneously are referred to as parallel. Parallelism can be achieved by using multiple copies of a processor such as an ALU or CPU, or by designing the system in the form of a multistage pipeline, or by a combination of these approaches. The motivations for parallel processing are to increase throughput beyond what is possible with sequential computers and also, in some instances, to enhance flexibility and reliability. Many methods for classifying a computer system's parallelism have been proposed. A widely used example is Flynn's classification in terms of instruction and data stream multiplicities; most parallel computers fall into either the SIMD or the MIMD category. Also useful are the distinctions made between shared-memory and distributed-memory (message-passing) architectures, and classifications based on interconnection structures. Typical examples of static interconnection structures are meshes, trees, and hypercubes, while dynamic interconnections are provided by shared buses, crossbar switches, and multistage switching networks.

The performance of a parallel processor is difficult to analyze since it depends, often in complex ways, on system architecture and program organization. A simple numerical measure of performance is the speedup $S(n)$, defined as the ratio of the execution time of a particular task on a system whose degree of parallelism is one, i.e., a sequential computer, to the execution time of the same task on a version of the computer whose parallelism is n. A related measure is efficiency $E(n)$ defined as $S(n)/n$. The actual speedup achieved in a particular case is usually less than the maximum possible value n (linear speedup) due to such effects as contention for memory access, the setup time associated with parallel operations, and the presence of inherently sequential or nonparallelizable code.

A pipeline processor is composed of cascaded segments through which a data stream can flow. Each segment contributes a part of the data processing required, and all segments operate in parallel on different data items. An m-segment pipeline represents a less costly alternative to an m-unit (parallel) processor with comparable throughput. Pipelining is used primarily for instruction cycle control and for certain arithmetic operations. An instruction pipeline is a program control unit that partitions the instruction cycle into a sequence of steps such as opcode fetch, opcode decode, operand fetch, execute, and operand store. A second type of pipeline is the arithmetic pipeline, which is suitable for implementing the more complex arithmetic operations like multiplication and floating-point addition. By adding feedback paths and segment bypasses, a single pipeline processor can be used for multiple functions. The control of pipeline processors can be quite complex. They are usually designed to minimize the delay or latency between successive operations. Systolic arrays represent a generalization of the pipeline concept to allow operand streams to flow in several directions and along several dimensions simultaneously. Pipelining has been very successfully applied to vector and matrix operations, and so is the basis of many commercial vector processors (supercomputers) such as the Cray-1 and its successors. Programs written in languages such as FORTRAN must usually be carefully structured (vectorized) to run efficiently on vector processors, a task that can be partially automated by a vectorizing compiler preprocessor.

A single computer system containing more than one CPU is called a multiprocessor. A multiprocessor has higher potential throughput and reliability than the corresponding uniprocessor. Multiprocessors are distinguished by the way the processors communicate with one another. This communication may be tightly coupled via shared memory, or loosely coupled via messages transmitted between the processors' IO subsystems. Multiprocessors also have special programming requirements to permit a programmer to indicate groups of instructions that can be executed in parallel (**cobegin-coend** blocks), and to specify communication between loosely coupled processors (**send** and **receive** instructions). It is generally quite difficult to redesign (parallelize) sequential code to run efficiently on a multiprocessor.

Multiprocessors have been designed around a variety of interconnection networks, of which the (multiple) shared bus is perhaps the easiest to implement, and therefore the most common for smaller multiprocessors. Recent advances in VLSI technology have made it feasible to construct massively parallel distributed-memory machines based on such interconnection structures as (static) meshes, trees, and hypercubes. These machines exhibit various tradeoffs between processor throughput, communication delays, and programming complexity. They can also be characterized by their ability to simulate other interconnection structures efficiently. Another class of massively parallel multiprocessors with either shared or distributed memory rely on multistage switching networks for processor-memory or processor-processor communication. These networks employ 2×2 switches connected to form ($\log_2 N$)-stage $N \times N$ switching networks, such as the essentially equivalent omega and indirect hypercube switching networks.

Multiple processors are often included in a system with the primary goal of increasing its fault tolerance. This goal is achieved by some form of redundancy such as the presence of multiple copies of (critical) hardware components like the CPU. An example of this is n-modular redundancy (nMR) in which n copies of a component are present, along with voter circuits to determine the correct signals in the presence of faults. Fault tolerance may also be obtained by providing facilities (1) to detect and diagnose faults, (2) to eliminate them from the system by reconfiguration or repair, and (3) to institute recovery by restoring the system to normal fault-free operation. This dynamic approach requires that the components subject to failure be at least duplicated as, for instance, in the No. 1 ESS, a duplex system. A computer's degree of fault tolerance can be measured by its reliability R, its availability A, and its mean times to failure (MTTF) and repair (MTTR).

PROBLEMS

7.1. (a) Suppose that each processor P_i in the linear array of Fig. 7.2 stores a positive number b_i. It is desired to determine the largest value b_{max} stored in the array, where $b_{max} \geq b_i$ for all i. Write a parallel program in the style of Fig. 7.3 which performs this computation and outputs b_{max} from the rightmost processor P_n.

(b) Modify your program for part (a) of this problem so that it also determines the location (index) j of the processor P_j storing b_{max}. If several processors store b_{max}, then the smallest index of these processors is required. Again give your answer in the style of Fig. 7.3.

7.2. Redesign the parallel summation program of Fig. 7.2 for execution by the binary tree computer whose structure appears in Fig. 7.8d. Assume that $N = 2^{p-1}$ and that the N numbers to be added are stored in the leaf nodes initially. The final sum is to be stored in the topmost (root) node.

7.3. Classify under each of the three headings:

> Shared or distributed memory
> Pipelined or parallel (multiunit)
> SIMD/MIMD/MISD

the following computers mentioned in this chapter: ASC, Cm*, Cray X-MP, ILLIAC IV, NCUBE/ten, STAR-100. Briefly give your reasons for placing each computer in a particular class.

7.4. Write an essay comparing and contrasting shared-memory and distributed-memory parallel processors from the viewpoints of hardware organization, programming ease, operating system complexity, and fault tolerance.

7.5. Parallel processors are sometimes classified on the basis of the *granularity* of their parallelism, which refers to the smallest units of information that can be processed in parallel. Fine-grain parallel processors can simultaneously execute several independent instructions, which could be in the same or different programs. Coarse-grain processors can execute large independent tasks simultaneously; however, individual instructions or parts of a task cannot be parallelized. The intermediate medium-grain class is represented by machines that can execute short instruction sequences like DO loops in parallel. Classify the granularity (fine, medium, or coarse) of the following computers: ASC, Cm*, Cray-1, Intel 8086, ILLIAC IV, NCUBE/ten.

7.6. A certain computer system that contains n parallel processors can complete a given task Q in $30n^{0.6} + 10 \log_2 n$ time units.

(a) What is the system's speedup and efficiency when executing Q?

(b) For what numbers of processors does the efficiency exceed 70 percent?

7.7. Let 10 be the degree of parallelism of a vector processing computer C. Let f be the fraction of the operations performed by C that are strictly scalar, i.e., cannot be processed in parallel. Assume that all other operations are processed at the maximum possible (vector) rate. Let 6.5 be the speedup achieved by C for the tasks under consideration.

(a) What is f?

(b) By how much must f be reduced to increase the speedup to 9.0?

7.8. Consider the heat-flow problem for ILLIAC IV discussed in Example 7.2. Assume that neighboring processors communicate via **send** and **receive** commands. Write an

				Time			
Segment	1	2	3	4	5	6	7
S_1	x			x			
S_2		x					x
S_3			x				
S_4					x		
S_5						x	

FIGURE 7.75
Pipeline reservation table for Prob. 7.10.

informal program in the style of Fig. 7.3 that implements the relaxation algorithm to solve the heat-flow problem defined on an 8×8 grid. Your program should be designed to execute correctly on any of the available 64 processors, and should be fully documented with comments. Outline how you would revise your program to accommodate the heat-flow problem defined on a 16×16 grid, assuming that the number of processors remains at 64.

7.9. (a) List the advantages and disadvantages of designing a floating-point processor in the form of a k-segment pipeline rather than a k-unit parallel processor.

(b) A floating-point pipeline has four segments S_1, S_2, S_3, and S_4 whose delays are 100, 90, 100, and 110 ns, respectively. What is the pipeline's maximum throughput in MFLOPS?

7.10. For the pipeline reservation table appearing in Fig. 7.75, calculate the forbidden set F, the minimum constant latency L, and the minimum average latency L_{min}. Also construct a task initiation diagram (TID) for this pipeline.

7.11. Calculate the minimum constant latency L and the minimum average latency L_{min} for the pipeline reservation table of Fig. 7.76.

7.12. Explain the following paradoxical statement: The throughput of a pipeline processor can sometimes be maximized by judiciously inserting delays in the pipeline's input data stream.

7.13. In digital signal processing it is sometimes necessary to multiply a high-speed stream of n-bit numbers Y_1, Y_2, Y_3 ... by a single number X. The output should be a stream

					Time					
Segment	1	2	3	4	5	6	7	8	9	10
S_1	x					x				
S_2		x					x			
S_3			x					x		
S_4				x				x		
S_5	x				x				x	
S_6						x				
S_7		x					x			
S_8										x

FIGURE 7.76
Pipeline reservation table for Prob. 7.11.

of n-bit results Y_1X, Y_2X, Y_3X, ... moving at the same rate as the input stream. Assuming that X and Y_i are positive n-bit binary fractions, design a pipeline processor to carry out this type of multiplication efficiently. If the pipeline is constructed from gates of average delay d, estimate its data bandwidth.

7.14. Consider the logic diagram for a pipelined 3×3 multiplier appearing in Fig. 7.37.

(a) The six unconnected line stubs attached to some of the M cells are redundant in that they always carry the logic value 0. Certain connected lines are also redundant in this sense, and are only included to make the segments uniform. Identify all such redundant connections.

(b) Consider a general $n \times n$ version of this multiplier pipeline. Assuming that the segments are identical and are labeled S_0, S_1, ..., S_{n-1}, show that the total number of 1-bit buffer registers of type R needed is $3n^2 - n$.

7.15. Let $X = x_0, x_1, \ldots, x_{n-1}$ and $Y = y_0, y_1, \ldots, y_{n-1}$ be two fixed-point vectors of length n. The double-length vector $Z = z_0, z_1, \ldots, z_{2n-2}, z_{2n-1}$ defined by

$$z_i = \sum_{j=0}^{n-i} x_j \times y_{i-j}$$

where $x_j = y_j = 0$ if $j < 0$, is called the *convolution* of X and Y, and is useful in such applications as signal processing. Design a one-dimensional systolic array to implement convolution. The array should have the general structure shown in Fig. 7.2 with the X, Y, and Z vectors flowing horizontally. Describe the functions of the processing cell, and draw a diagram illustrating the operation of the systolic array in the style of Fig. 7.42*b*.

7.16. (a) Compare and contrast the memory-to-memory architecture used in the Cyber 205 with the register-to-register organization of the Cray-1.

(b) Explain what is meant by chaining as defined for the Cray-1. Briefly discuss its advantages and disadvantages.

7.17. Consider a vector supercomputer that processes vectors whose average length is N. The average setup time for vector operations is T_0, and the CPU (and pipeline) clock period is T_{clock}. Derive an expression for the efficiency E of the computer in terms of N, T_0, and T_{clock}.

7.18. Explain why it is usually desirable to avoid both very long and very short DO loops in FORTRAN code intended for a vector processor. What factors determine if a particular DO loop is of appropriate length for a particular processor?

7.19. Consider the following segments of FORTRAN code. Analyze each one and restructure (vectorize) it to improve its performance when executed on a vector processor like the Cray-1. Justify all the changes you introduce. [The operators LT, GT, and EQ denote less than, greater than, and equals, respectively. The statement IF (I .LT. J) X means: if I is less than J then execute X; otherwise continue to the next statement.]

(a)
```
        DO 10 I = 1, N, 1
        A(I) = B(I) * C(I) + 3.1415926
        Z(I) = B(I) * C(I) * D(I)
     10 CONTINUE
```
(b)
```
        DO 10 I = 1, N, 1
        A(I) = B(I) + C(I)
        IF (I .LT. 10) A(I) = A(I) * K1
        IF (I .GT. 90) A(I) = A(I) * K2
        IF (I .EQ. J1) A(I) = -A(I)
     10 CONTINUE
```

7.20. It is frequently argued that the single large (super) computer is approaching its performance limits, and that future advances in computation will depend on the interconnection of very large numbers of slow but inexpensive microprocessors. List the arguments for and against this viewpoint.

7.21. It has also been conjectured based on the observed performance of real multiprocessors, that because of memory and bus conflicts, algorithm inefficiencies, etc., the actual speedup $S(n)$ obtained when n identical processors are used to execute a single large program Q lies between $\log_2 n$ and $n/\log_e n$. Show that assuming the probability of being able to assign Q to i processors is $1/i$, for $i = 1, 2, \ldots, n$ leads to the upper bound $n/\log_e n$ on $S(n)$. What does this result imply about the issue discussed in Prob. 7.20?

7.22. Write an essay on the new features needed in standard (sequential) programming languages and operating systems to support computation on loosely coupled massively parallel multiprocessors.

7.23. (a) Prove by means of a counterexample that the parallelization conditions (7.36) to (7.38) are not necessary for two code segments to be parallelizable. (They are sufficient conditions only.)

(b) Let $S_1, S_2, \ldots, S_k$ denote a sequence of k operations in a program. Suppose that execution of these operations on a uniprocessor produces the same results regardless of the order of execution of the k S_i's. Show that this does not imply that the S_i's are parallelizable on a multiprocessor.

7.24. Prove that the general problem of determining whether two program segments are parallelizable is undecidable by showing that a solution to this problem implies a solution to the halting problem for Turing machines defined in Sec. 1.1.3. (*Hint:* Assume an algorithm A to determine parallelizability exists, and consider applying A to a program containing the statement: **if** Turing machine T halts after at most n steps **then** S_1 **else** S_2.)

7.25. A useful measure of communication delay in static multiprocessor interconnection structures is the average distance d_{av} between all pairs of nodes (processors). Calculate d_{av} as a function of n for any three of the six structures listed in Fig. 7.56.

7.26. Consider a complete p-level binary tree structure of the kind illustrated by Fig. 7.8d. Prove that any such tree can be simulated by a hypercube. (*Hint:* Use induction on p.)

7.27. A multiprocessor node must sometimes send a message to more than one other processor, a task referred to as *broadcasting*. Suppose that a node P_0 in an n-dimensional hypercube system has to broadcast a message to all $2^n - 1$ other processors. The broadcasting is subject to the constraints that the message can be forwarded (retransmitted) by a node only to a neighboring node, and each node can transmit only one message at a time. Assume that each message transmission between adjacent nodes requires one time unit. In a two-dimensional system, for example, P_0 could broadcast a message MESS as follows. At time $t = 0$, P_0 sends MESS to P_1. At $t = 1$, P_0 sends MESS to P_2 and P_1 sends MESS to P_3, thus completing the broadcast in 2 time units. Construct a general broadcasting algorithm for the n-dimensional case that allows a message to reach all nodes in n time units. Specify clearly the algorithm used by each node to determine the neighboring nodes to which it should forward an incoming message.

7.28. Repeat Prob. 7.8, this time designing the 8×8 heat-flow program to run on a 64-processor hypercube computer that simulates a mesh computer. Specify completely the function you use to map the problem's gridpoints onto the nodes of the hypercube.

7.29. Construct a diagram for a 16×16 omega network similar to that for the 16×16

indirect hypercube network of Fig. 7.64. Show the switch settings required to connect input port 3 to output port 12.

7.30. The through (T) and cross (X) states of the switching element S of Fig. 7.9 can be augmented by the two additional states defined in Fig. 7.77. These are termed the upper (U) and lower (L) broadcast states, because they allow an incoming message to be sent to both output ports simultaneously; cf. Prob. 7.27. Show that if the two-state switch S of Fig. 7.9 is replaced by the four-state switch S', then an $N \times N$ omega network has a state that allows data on any of its input ports to be broadcast directly to any subset of its output ports.

7.31. Determine whether or not the 4×4 switching element used in the BBN Butterfly computer has the full access and nonblocking properties.

7.32. (*a*) Identify the types of faults that interrupt telephone-call processing by the No. 1 ESS, i.e., the failures that are not tolerated by the system.

   (*b*) The on-board computers of unmanned spacecraft are required to be very fault-tolerant. Discuss the suitability of the design philosophy of the No. 1 ESS for this application. Where some feature of the No. 1 ESS is unsuitable for space-craft use, suggest an alternative way of achieving the desired fault tolerance.

7.33. (*a*) A system is constructed from n copies of a unit U connected in parallel. If the reliability of U is 0.9, how many copies of U are needed in order for the system reliability to be (*i*) at least 0.99, and (*ii*) at least 0.9999?

   (*b*) A certain computer installation crashes regularly once a week. It takes an average of 2 hours for maintenance personnel to restore normal operation. What are the system's availability and MTTF?

7.34. A variant of TMR called *TMR/Simplex* has triplicated units and a match circuit to identify the failed unit when the first failure occurs. The system begins operation as a TMR configuration. When the first failure is detected, the system structure is changed from TMR to simplex using one of the two correctly working units. Normal operation then continues until the simplex configuration fails. If the reliability of each unit is $e^{-\lambda t}$ and the voter and match circuit are perfectly reliable, calculate the reliability and MTTF of the TMR/Simplex system.

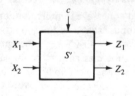

(*a*)

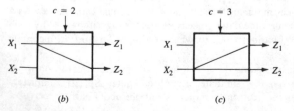

(*b*)   (*c*)

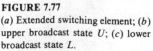

FIGURE 7.77
(*a*) Extended switching element; (*b*) upper broadcast state U; (*c*) lower broadcast state L.

7.35. The fault detection and recovery mechanisms of real fault-tolerant computers are not perfect, for example, a typical diagnostic procedure for a complex system detects no more than 90 percent of the faults. This imperfection is quantified in the notion of *coverage c*, which is defined as the probability that a system recovers given that a fault has occurred. For example, the reliability $R(S)$ of a parallel system of two units with individual reliability R (a duplex system) is given by

$$R(S) = R + cR(1 - R) \tag{7.58}$$

which is equivalent to (7.47) with $R_1 = R_2 = R$ and $c = 1$. The first term of (7.58) is the probability that the one unit survives; the second term is the probability that one unit fails, the second unit survives, and the fault detection and recovery process is successful. Generalize (7.58) to the case where there are n parallel units of reliability R.

REFERENCES

1. Amdahl Corp.: *Amdahl 470V/7 Machine Reference Manual*, publ. G1003 0-01/A, Sunnyvale, Calif., 1978.
2. Avizienis, A.: "Fault Tolerant Computing—An Overview," *IEEE Computer*, vol. 4, no. 1, pp. 5–8, January/February 1971.
3. Batcher, K. E.: "Design of a Massively Parallel Processor," *IEEE Trans. Comput.*, vol. C-29, pp. 836–840, September 1980. (Reprinted in Ref. 17, pp. 104–108.)
4. Bernstein, A. J.: "Analysis of Programs for Parallel Processing," *IEEE Trans. Electronic Computers*, vol. EC-15, pp. 757–763, October 1966.
5. Blaauw, G. A.: "The Structure of System/360: Part V—Multisystem Organization," *IBM System J.*, vol. 3, pp. 181–195, 1964.
6. Connors, W. D., J. H. Florkowski, and S. K. Patton: "The IBM 3033: An Inside Look," *Datamation*, vol. 25, no. 5, pp. 198–218, May 1979.
7. Control Data Corp.: *CDC Cyber 200 Model 205 Technical Description*, Minneapolis, November 1980.
8. Crowther, W., et al.: "The Butterfly Parallel Processor," *IEEE Computer Arch. Tech. Comm. Newsletter*, pp. 18–45, September/December 1985.
9. Davidson, E. S.: "The Design and Control of Pipelined Function Generators," *Proc. IEEE Conf. Systems, Networks and Computers*, Oaxtepec, Mexico, pp. 19–21, January 1971.
10. Dubois, M., and F. A. Briggs: "The Effect of Cache Coherency in Multiprocessors," *IEEE Trans. Comput.*, vol. C-31, pp. 1083–1099, November 1982. (Reprinted in Ref. 17, pp. 312–328.)
11. Downing, R. W., J. S. Novak, and L. S. Tuomenoksa: "No. 1 ESS Maintenance Plan," *Bell System Tech. J.*, vol. 43, pp. 1961–2109, September 1964.
12. Feng, T. Y.: "A Survey of Interconnection Networks," *IEEE Computer*, vol. 14, pp. 12–27, December 1981. (Reprinted in Ref. 17, pp. 109–124.)
13. Flynn, M. J.: "Very High-Speed Computing Systems," *Proc. IEEE*, vol. 54, pp. 1901–1909, December 1966.
14. Hayes, J. P., et al.: "A Microprocessor-Based Hypercube Supercomputer," *IEEE Micro*, vol. 6, no. 5, pp. 6–17, October 1986.
15. Hintz, R. G., and D. P. Tate: "Control Data STAR-100 Processor Design," *Proc. 6th IEEE Computer Soc. Conf. (Compcon 72)*, San Francisco, Calif., pp. 1–4, September 1972.
16. Hockney, R. W., and C. R. Jesshope: *Parallel Computers*, Adam Hilger Ltd., Bristol, England, 1981.
17. Hwang, K.: *Tutorial: Supercomputers—Design and Applications*, IEEE Computer Soc. Press, Silver Spring, Md., 1985.
18. Hwang, K., and F. A. Briggs: *Computer Architecture and Parallel Processing*, McGraw-Hill, New York, 1984.

19. IBM Corp.: *IBM System/370 Vector Operations*, publ. SA22-7125-0, Poughkeepsie, N.Y., January 1986.

20. Intel Corp.: *iAPX 86,88 User's Manual*, Santa Clara, Calif., July 1981.

21. Jones, A. K., and E. F. Gehringer (eds.): *The Cm* Multiprocessor Project: A Research Review*, Carnegie-Mellon Univ., Dept. of Computer Sci., rept. CMU-CS-80-131, July 1980.

22. Jordan, T. L.: "A Guide to Parallel Computation and Some Cray-1 Experiences," in G. Rodrigue (ed.): *Parallel Computations*, Academic Press, New York, pp. 1–50, 1982.

23. Kogge, P. M.: *The Architecture of Pipelined Computers*, McGraw-Hill, New York, 1981.

24. Kuck, D. J., et al.: "Measurement of Parallelism in Ordinary FORTRAN Programs," *IEEE Computer*, vol. 1, no. 1, pp. 37–46, January 1974.

25. Kuck, D. J., et al.: "The Structure of an Advanced Vectorizer for Pipelined Processors," *Proc. COMPSAC 80*, pp. 709–715, 1980. (Reprinted with revisions in Ref. 17, pp. 163–178.)

26. Mead, C., and L. Conway: *Introduction to VLSI Design*, Addison-Wesley, Reading, Mass., 1980.

27. Parker, D. S., Jr.: "Notes on Shuffle/Exchange-Type Switching Networks," *IEEE Trans. Comput.*, vol. C-29, pp. 213–222, March 1980.

28. Radin, G.: "The 801 Minicomputer," *IBM J. Res. and Dev.*, vol. 27, pp. 237–246, May 1983.

29. Russell, R. M., "The Cray-1 Computer System," *Commun. ACM*, vol. 21, pp. 63–72, 1978. (Reprinted in Ref. 31, pp. 743–752.)

30. Siegel, H. J.: *Interconnection Networks for Large-Scale Parallel Processing*, Lexington Books, Lexington, Mass., 1985.

31. Siewiorek, D. P., C. G. Bell, and A. Newell: *Computer Structures: Principles and Examples*, McGraw-Hill, New York, 1982.

32. Siewiorek, D. P., and R. S. Swarz: *The Theory and Practice of Reliable System Design*, Digital Press, Bedford, Mass., 1982.

33. Slotnick, D. L.: "The Fastest Computer," *Sci. Amer.*, vol. 224, pp. 76–88, February 1971.

34. Texas Instruments Inc.: *The ASC System Central Processor*, publ. H 1005P, Austin, Tex., 1975.

35. Toy, W. N.: "Fault-Tolerant Design of Local ESS Processors," *Proc. IEEE*, vol. 66, pp. 1126–1145, October 1978. (Reprinted in Ref. 32, pp. 461–496.)

36. Watson, W. J.: "The TI ASC—A Highly Modular and Flexible Super Computer Architecture," *AFIPS Conf. Proc.*, vol. 41, pp. 221–228, 1972. (Reprinted in Ref. 31, pp. 753–762.)

INDEX